BARNET & STUBBS'S

Practical Guide to Writing

with Additional Readings

Sixth Edition

BARNET & STUBBS'S

Practical Guide to Writing

with Additional Readings

Sixth Edition

Sylvan Barnet
TUFTS UNIVERSITY

Marcia Stubbs
WELLESLEY COLLEGE

HarperCollins*Publishers*

Credit lines for the photos, cartoons, illustrations, and copyrighted materials appearing in this work appear in the Acknowledgments section beginning on page 771. This section is to be considered an extension of the copyright page.

Library of Congress Cataloging-in-Publication Data.

Barnet, Sylvan.
    [Practical guide to writing]
    Barnet & Stubbs's practical guide to writing / Sylvan Barnet,
Marcia Stubbs.—6th ed., with additional readings.
      p. cm.
    Includes bibliographical references.
    ISBN 0–673–39878–1 (soft) :
    1. English language—Rhetoric. I. Stubbs, Marcia. II. Title.
III. Title: Barnet and Stubbs's practical guide to writing.
IV. Title: Practical guide to writing.
PE1408.B4314   1990
808'.042—dc20   89–10880
                                 CIP

6-RRC-95 94

Preface

Where there is too much,
something is missing.

We have tried to keep this proverb in mind; we hope we
have written a compact book rather than an undiscriminating one.

The book is designed for college courses in which students
write essays, instructors read them, and students and instructors
together discuss them. We hope we offer a practical guide to all
three activities. The student, looking for information about choosing a topic, writing an analysis, constructing a paragraph, using a
semicolon, can use the text as a guide to the week's writing assignment. The instructor can suggest chapters or passages the student should consult in revising a draft or in starting the next assignment. Students and instructors together can discuss the exercises,
the techniques used in the reprinted essays, the assumptions we
make, and the suggestions we offer.

Although we include discussions and examples of description
and narration, we emphasize analysis, exposition, and argument
because those are the chief activities, usually rolled into one, that
we all engage in, both in school and later. When students write
papers, or professors write reports, or psychiatric social workers
write case studies, most of what they write is exposition, a statement of what's what that they have arrived at by analyzing or
dividing the subject into parts, and because they want to be believed, they construct as persuasive an argument as possible.

In addition to including many examples from the writing of
our students, we have included more than fifty short essays, as
well as numerous paragraphs from books and essays, the work for
the most part of first-rate contemporary writers. These essays appear in the chapters on Analysis, Definition, Exposition, Persuasion, Description, Narration, Acquiring Style, and in Part Four,
which consists of twenty selections. There are also a sample book

review, a sample record review, a summary, an explication, two essays based on interviews, and two research papers. We include all these readings both to illustrate ways of writing and to provide students with something to write about. The suggested exercises often require the students to write about something outside of themselves. The Polonian advice, offered to Laertes—"This above all, to thine own self be true"—seems to us as useless to most people of college age as it is to Laertes. As Erik Erikson has helped us to see, most young people are engaged in a "search for something and somebody to be true to." They experiment with roles in a search for "the rock-bottom of some truth."[1] Asked to write about how they spent last summer, they may feel a profound uneasiness; however necessary last summer was, they are not sure what it added up to, and they are not yet distant enough from their experience to be articulate about it. Some exercises do present opportunities for introspection, and all of them in fact require it, but we think that much of a student's writing should be directed outward, not solely a look into the heart but a look around—at people, at places, and especially at ideas.

We have tried therefore to balance the advice "Trust your feelings," "Ask yourself questions," with prescriptions: "Avoid clichés," "Keep your reader in mind." We have tried to increase the student's awareness that writing is both an exploration of self ("Choose a topic you can write about honestly") and a communication with others ("Revise for clarity").

Chapter 1 includes three essays by students, a brief article by Philip Roth, and some informal exercises. Instructors may find these passages useful for the first few class meetings. During the first week of the semester, we commonly suggest that students browse through the book from beginning to end, reading what interests them, skimming the rest, and generally familiarizing themselves with the book's contents and organization. But because each chapter can stand by itself, the instructor can assign chapters for study in whatever seems a suitable order, probably interweaving chapters on writing, revising, and editing. Similarly, the student can consult whatever passages seem most relevant to writing, revising,

---

[1] *Identity: Youth and Crisis* (New York: W. W. Norton, 1968), pp. 235–36.

or correcting a particular essay. After all, it has never been established that in a college course in English certain topics must be taught before others. Listen to Boswell describing a conversation, more than two hunderd years ago, with Dr. Johnson:

> We talked of the education of children; and I asked him what he thought was best to teach them first. JOHNSON: "Sir, it is no matter what you teach them first, any more than what leg you shall put into your breeches first. Sir, you may stand disputing which is best to put in first, but in the meantime your breech is bare. Sir, while you are considering which of two things you should teach your child first, another boy [or girl] has learnt them both."

A Note to the Sixth Edition

Users of earlier editions will find throughout the text many revisions, new exercises, new essays, and new topics. Most extensive are the changes in Chapters 1 and 2. Chapter 1 concentrates on getting started: finding something to write about; distinguishing between subject, topic, and thesis; preliminary thoughts about audience and purpose. It recommends several invention techniques and provides guidelines for keeping a journal (formerly in a later chapter). Chapter 2, largely new to this edition, focuses on revising drafts; it includes a discussion of peer review, and a case history of a student paper, from assignment through several revisions. It concludes with an overview of the writing process, from subject to essay. ("Analysis," formerly Chapter 2, is now Chapter 3.)

In making these changes we have responded to requests from many loyal users of our book and are indebted to many colleagues, students, editors, and other friends. These include Lois Avery, Houston Community College; Don Richard Cox, University of Tennessee; Cinthia Gannett, University of New Hampshire; Brenda Gotthelf, Houston Community College; Viki Hull, Southern Methodist University; Hope Rajala, Scott, Foresman; Alice Robertson, Arizona State University; Judith Stanford, Rivier College; John Swan, Bennington College; Barbara Weaver, Ball State University; Lance Wilcox, University of Minnesota.

We also remain indebted to: John Ambrose, Jeannine Atkins, Richard Audet, Barbara Balfour, Hannah Barrett, Tim Barretto,

James Beaton, Pat Bellanca, Kay Berenson, Helle Bering-Fensen, Barbara Jane Berk, Morton Berman, Phyllis Braumlich, Gary Brienzo, Daniel V. Brislane, Lillian Broderick, James Brothers, Pearl L. Brown, Peter Brunette, Carroll Burcham, Pat Burnes, William Burto, A. Butrym, Terry P. Caesar, Joan Carberg, Susan Carlisle, Thomas Carnicelli, Sally Carson, Cynthia Chapin, Charles H. Christensen, Sandra Christianson, Sarah Clark, Michael Cleary, John M. Clum, James Cobb, Phyllis Cole, William F. Coles, S. Cooney, Shirley Corvo, John Covell, Claire Crabtree, Leslie Crabtree, Mary Ann Creadon, Mary Bryan H. Curd, Leopold Damrosch, Marlene Baldwin Davis, Robert Dees, Tom De Palma, Imogene De Smet, Aviva Diamond, T. Di Paolo, Pat Dorazio, Nicholas Durso, James Early, Nathaniel Elliott, Doris Eyges, Marina Femmer, Denise Ferguson, Cathy Fiore, Nancy E. Fischer, Terry Flaherty, Thomas F. Flynn, Jan Fontein, C. Dennyy Freese, John Fugate, Krin Gabbard, Cynthia Galivan, Thomas J. Gasque, Walker Gibson, David Giele, James Gifford, Walker Gilmer, David Goldfaden, Margaret Gooch, John Grass, Jack Guillon, Steve Hamelman, Nigel Hampton, James Hauser, Owen Hawley, Mark Heidmann, Thomas W. Herzing, Gervase Hittle, Robert Hosmer, Susan Jamison, Owen Jenkins, Peter M. Johnson, Ronna C. Johnson, Mary D. Jones, George Kearns, Joseph Keefe, Robert Keefe, Kathryn Keller, Dr. Frank Kelly, Nancy Kneeland, Judith Kohl, Molly Moore Kohler, Roberta Kramer, George Kugler, Richard L. Lane, Andrea La Sane, Jonathan Lawson, Elsie Leach, Helen M. Lewis, Peter Lindblom, E. Darlene Lister, Marget Livesay, Jane Lump, Kathryn Lynch, Ian C. Mackenzie, Teruko Maki, D'Ann Madewell, Victoria McCabe, Leo McCauley, Joan McCoy, Patricia McGowan, Ken McLaurin, George Marcopoulos, Sr. Lynda Martin-Boyle, H.O.O.M., Celeste A. Meister, Michael Meyer, George Miller, Eva Mills, Melodie Monahan, Joan Moon, Betty Morgan, Denise Muller, Margaret A. Murphy, Richard Muth, Robert A. Myers, Barbara Nelson, Thomas Newkirk, J. Stephan Newmann, Donald Nontelle, Jo Anna Norris, Richard D. Olson, John O'Neill, Mary O'Sullivan, Joan Patrie, Donald Pattow, Mary Mocsary Pauli, Douglas Peterson, Russell O. Peterson, Bill Pierce, Elaine Plasberg, Carolyn Potts, Charles Quagliata, S. Quiroz, John Rath, Martha Reid and her colleagues at William and Mary, Stephen Reid, Gerald Richman, Leo Rockas, Judith Root, Zelda Rouillard, Melissa

Ruchhoeft, Scott Ruescher, Richard Sandler, Stephen Sapious, Frances W. Sauers, Carl Schaffr, Gerald Schiffhorst, Sybil Schlesinger, Carmen Schmersahl, William Scott, Patrick W. Shaw, James M. Siddens, Earl Sigmund, Joyce Monroe Simmons, Martha Simonsen, Edward Sims, Mark Slater, James Slattery, Audrey Smith, John Smolens, James Sodon, Jay Soldner, David Solheim, Dr. Harold Spicer, Robert Stein, Ann Steinmetz, Frances M. Stowe, Kay Sturdivant, Elaine Supowitz, Ann M. Tarbell, Luther T. Tyler, Larry Uffelman, Kathy Valdespino, Renita Weems, Adrienne Weiss, Melinda Westbrook, Dorothy Widmayer, Lisa Wien, Anita C. Wilson, Howard Winn, Donald Winters, Elizabeth Wood, Arthur P. Wooley, Hae Yong Yi, Mallory Young, and all our students, from whose mistakes we hope to profit.

Sylvan Barnet
Marcia Stubbs

Contents

3 *Analysis* 52

4   *Paragraphs*   105

5   *Definition*   143

8   *Description*   276

11 *Special Assignments, Special Forms*   *430*

PART TWO

Revising   *473*

12 *Revising for Conciseness*   *475*

PART FIVE

Editing   697

17 *Manuscript Form*   699

18 *Punctuation*   708

19 *Spelling* *742*

20 *Usage* *748*

PART ONE

Writing

The Balloon of the Mind

Hands, do what you're bid:
Bring the balloon of the mind
That bellies and drags in the wind
Into its narrow shed.
        —WILLIAM BUTLER YEATS

1

Discovering
Ideas

STARTING

How to Write: Writing as a Physical Act

"One takes a piece of paper," William Carlos Williams wrote, "anything, the flat of a shingle, slate, cardboard and with anything handy to the purpose begins to put down the words after the desired expression in mind." Good advice, from a writer who produced novels, plays, articles, book reviews, an autobiography, a voluminous correspondence, and more than twenty-five books of poetry, while raising a family, enjoying a wide circle of friends, and practicing medicine in Rutherford, New Jersey. Not the last word on writing (we have approximately 85,000 of our own to add), but where we would like to begin: "One takes a piece of paper . . . and . . . begins to put down the words. . . ."

Writing is a physical act, like swimming, and like most physical acts, to be performed skillfully, to bring pleasure to both performer and audience, it requires practice. Talent helps. But few of us are born to become great writers, just as few of us are born to become great swimmers. Nevertheless, we can learn to write, as we can learn to swim, for all practical purposes, including pleasure.

3

In this book we offer some suggestions, definitions, rules, and examples to help you learn not simply to write, but to write well. We hope they will help you avoid some of the trials and errors—and the fear of drowning—that sometimes accompanies uninstructed practice.

Why Write: Writing as a Mental Activity

Born writers often describe their need to write as a compulsion, an inner drive to put their feelings and ideas into words; they also regularly complain that writing is hard work. ("Hard labor for life" was Joseph Conrad's summary of his own career.) For the rest of us, writing may be easier, because it is *not* our vocation and perhaps we may demand less than perfection from ourselves. But it's still hard work, and we usually need something to motivate us to take it on. In real life (as opposed to school) people are regularly motivated by their jobs and other interests to put their ideas in writing. Scientists and social scientists write proposals for research, and then report, again in writing, the results of their work to their sponsors and colleagues. Parents and other citizens write their petitions and grievances to school boards and lawmakers; through prepared talks and newsletters, volunteers reach the communities they serve. In short, anyone who is engaged with ideas or who wants to influence the course of events finds it necessary to put what Williams called "the desired expression in mind" into words on paper.

As a student, you may not always see a connection between the assignment you are given today and the need you will have several years from now to put your ideas in writing. The rewards of seeing your proposal accepted or of serving your community are probably a bit distant to motivate you to write five hundred words on an assigned topic this week. There is, though, a closer reward. "To be learning something new," said Aristotle, "is ever the chief pleasure of humankind." We believe that. We also believe that writing is not simply a way to express ideas, but a way to acquire them. Whenever you put your thoughts into words on a page, whether you scribble a few words on a scrap of paper while you eat lunch, or type your final draft of an essay on a computer keyboard, you are not simply recording what you already know. You are discovering ideas and storing them on paper or disk and also in your own memory. To quote Aristotle again, "What is expressed is impressed."

We emphasize ideas because we are making some assumptions about you: that you are an adult, that you're acquiring an education, either in school or on your own, and that the writing skill you need most help with is the expression of ideas in clear expository essays. Most of our book will concentrate on that skill. We begin, then, with some ideas about ideas.

Some Ideas about Ideas: Invention

Would-be writers have one of two complaints: either "I have the ideas but I don't know how to express them," or "I have nothing to say." When we are faced with a blank page, words and even ideas may seem to elude us. We must actively seek them out. Since classical times the term "invention" has been used to describe the process of finding something to say. Invention includes activities with which you may already be familiar, such as free writing, brainstorming, listing, and clustering. A related activity is the practice of keeping a journal. In the following pages we'll briefly describe several invention strategies and provide guidelines for keeping a journal. All of these activities have one step in common: starting to write by writing.

Starting to Write by Writing

Suppose your assignment is to respond to a recent editorial. You have chosen an editorial, read it several times, underlined a few key sentences, made a few notes. You have some ideas, but they don't seem connected; you don't know how to start. Here are five suggestions for getting started.

1. *Sit down and start writing.* Don't be surprised if you must actively resist the temptation to do something else, to procrastinate. (It is a universal law that given two tasks, one of which is writing, a person will prefer the other task.) Watch yourself think of other things to do, but take control. Resist the temptation to sharpen a pencil, to make a cup of soup, to call your mother. Now

is *not* the time to do your laundry or to make your bed. Sit down and start. Following the next suggestion may help you to start.

2. *Give yourself a time limit.* If procrastination is a chronic problem (as it is for many writers), try limiting the amount of time you will spend in your first session. Tell yourself that you'll work without interruption for half an hour (or twenty minutes or fifteen minutes—you may need to experiment). We all want to delay starting tasks we're anxious about. If at the start you limit each writing session to fifteen or twenty minutes, you accomplish two things. You reduce or even eliminate anxiety—the thought of working at your desk for fifteen minutes is not nearly as daunting as the thought of writing four or five pages. And after fifteen or twenty minutes you will have *something* down on paper, something you can start with and can even look forward to working on during your next session. Then in your next session, if you find that after fifteen or twenty minutes you want to continue, you can allow yourself to add another fifteen minutes or so, but take a break after that. You will have accomplished your immediate goal: to get started. Gradually you can build up to working on your essay for an hour at a time, or whatever is reasonable, given the assignment and your schedule. Of course, you can follow this advice only if you have started to work on an assignment reasonably soon after you have received it. Setting a time limit for the initial stages of writing will help you to get an early start. So will the next suggestion.

3. *Start with something easy.* Start anywhere. Start with what comes to mind first. You might, for example, start by summarizing the article you are responding to or by sketching any one of your ideas about it. *Don't think you must start with an introductory paragraph;* you can write an introduction later, once your ideas have become better defined. The point is, it doesn't matter where you begin, only that you do begin. Simply start putting one word after another, and keep going.

4. *Write freely.* Deliberately put out of your mind any rules about writing you may have learned. Forget about the five paragraph essay, along with the opening paragraph. Don't worry about grammar or spelling or punctuation. No one but you is going to read what you write. If you can't think of the right word, write something close to it, or leave a blank space for the word, and

move on. If you find yourself going in the "wrong" direction, that is, a direction you hadn't anticipated, keep writing anyway. Maybe there's something down the road worth thinking about; you won't know until you get there. If, for example, you are writing about why you disagree with one argument in the editorial, a point on which you agree with the author may occur to you. Fine. Write it down now, while you're thinking of it. You can organize your points of agreement and disagreement later. If, however, you reach what appears to be a dead end, simply move on, or start again someplace else. You are writing to discover what you think, and it's a good idea to work at the quickest pace you can. (Take Satchel Paige's advice: Don't look back; something might be gaining on you.)

5. *Plan to revise later.* Don't worry about making false starts. After a few false starts (and probably more than one session), your ideas will begin to take visible form on the page. But don't expect them to appear at this early stage in final form, beautifully organized and in polished sentences. Ideas rarely exist that way in one's mind. In fact, until we put them in words, ideas are usually only rough ideas or images, not clear thoughts at all. But if you start to write by writing, quickly and without looking back, you will have the satisfaction of seeing your ideas begin to take form on paper, and it's much easier to improve ideas once you see them in front of you than it is to do the job in your head. You can always delete or discard, add or improve. In fact, as we will suggest many times in this book, the secret of good writing is *rewriting*. Once you learn to control your urge to procrastinate, to wait until you're better prepared, or are more inspired, or have thought of the perfect way to begin, you will find that in starting to write by writing, you have mined some ideas on your topic and have come close to expressing them. (As E. M. Forster wrote, "How do I know what I think until I see what I say?") You may even have come close to producing a first draft. You can determine if you are near a first draft by looking back over what you've written and saved. Whether or not you like what you read (your response probably depends more on your temperament than on your actual accomplishment) take a rest from it. Do something else while your subconscious works over the material you've unearthed (invented). Now you can make your bed, or if you like, just climb into it.

Listing

Listing is another way to discover ideas or to pin them down by writing. The process is something like making a shopping list. You write down "soap" and are immediately reminded that you also must pick up some laundry. Similarly, for example, if in response to an assignment you have chosen to write on "the third world," you might begin by listing reasons for including courses on third world countries in the curriculum. If one reason comes to mind and you write it down—

practical for students in the 90s

and it leads to another—

understand other cultures

and another—

promote understanding of 3rd world

"   "   of minority cultures

better understanding U.S. history

you find more ideas than you knew you had.

One reason generates others for following a course of action. Similarly, a list of reasons for or against a position or action is often the backbone of an essay that makes an argument. Listing is also often a good way to make a decision. You list (perhaps in a journal, which we discuss later in this chapter) the reasons for dropping a course or for taking a job, and then the reasons against. Listing is often useful too when you are making a comparison (of two figures in a photograph, for example, or two characters in a story, or two positions on an issue). Start writing by listing the similarities, and then list the differences. Or, start writing both lists at once, making brief entries, as they occur to you, in parallel columns.

In the above examples, listing was used to develop a topic. Listing can also help you to find a topic to write about. Suppose, for example, you have been assigned to write an essay on a form of popular culture that interests you. You can begin simply by listing some of the possibilities that occur to you as you think about the subject:

<u>Popular Culture</u>
Movies, sci-fi, sci-fi movies?
TV movies, detective serials
Cosby?
Soap operas (Why are they called operas?)
The blues
Music videos
Mysteries—Murder She Wrote
Male/Female Detectives

But having written "the blues" above, you begin to think of the words:

When a woman takes the blues
She tucks her head and cries
But when a man catches the blues
He catches a freight and rides

By the time you have written these lyrics out from memory, you have pretty much decided that you'll write on the blues. You're interested in the blues and already know something about them; you have some records and tapes at hand; and an idea for an essay is beginning to form:

"He catches a freight and rides . . ."

Why all this talk of traveling? (Take heed: An unanswered question is an essay topic in disguise.) You begin to search your memory, perhaps you play some tapes, look at some record covers, maybe take some notes. The blues are full of travel, you find, but of different kinds. You begin, once again, to make a list, to jot down words or phrases:

disappointed lover   back to the South
travel to a job   life is a trip
from the South   jail
fantasy travel

Your new list provides more than a topic; you are now several steps closer to a draft of an essay that you think maybe you can write, on the reason for (or meaning of?) travel in the blues.

Clustering

Clustering (or *mapping*) is similar to listing, though it takes
a different visual form. Sometimes ideas don't seem to line up vertically, one after another. Instead, they seem to form a cluster,
with one idea or word related to a group of several others. It may
be useful then to start by putting a key word or phrase (let's stay
with TRAVEL IN THE BLUES) in a circle in the center of a page,
and then to jot down other words as they occur, encircling them
and connecting them appropriately. A map or cluster might look
like this:

If you start writing by putting down words that occur to you in a
schematic way—in a map or cluster—it may help you to visualize
the relationship between ideas. The visualization may also prompt
still other ideas and the connections between them.

Asking Questions (and Answering Them)

Almost the first thing a journalist learns to do in getting a
story is to ask six questions:

Who? What? When? Where? Why? How?

If you borrow this approach, asking yourself questions and answering them, you will often find that you can get a start on a writing project. The questions that journalists ask are appropriate to their task: to report what happened, who made it happen, how it happened, and so on. Learning to write academic essays is largely learning to ask—and to answer—questions appropriate to academic disciplines. In analyzing a painting or a sculpture an art historian answers such basic questions as:

> When, where, and by whom was the work made?
> Where would the work originally have been seen?
> What purpose did the work serve?
> In what condition has the work survived?

and then, depending on the work, more detailed questions. If, for example, the work is a landscape painting, the following questions might be appropriate.

> What is the relation between human beings and nature?
>
> What does the medium (oil paint or water color, for instance) contribute?
>
> What is the effect of light in the picture?
>
> What is the focus of the composition?
> How does the artist convey depth?

and so on.

Similarly, a social scientist writing a review of research on a topic might ask about each study under review:

> What major question is posed in this study?
> What is its chief method of investigation?
> What mode of observation was employed?
> How is the sample of observations defined?

Students in art history courses and social science courses learn what the useful questions are by listening to lectures, participating in class discussions, and reading assigned books and articles. But the learning is passive and largely subconscious. When writing an art history or sociology paper, however, students must actively learn and practice the forms of critical inquiry at the heart of each discipline.

In a writing course, the subject is writing—not art history, sociology, or anything else. Commonly, however, writing assignments are designed to give students practice in critical reading and in such other essential skills as summarizing, analyzing, and evaluating written texts. We explain these skills, therefore, in some detail in many places in this text. Here by way of introduction, we take you through a brief exercise in invention: discovering ideas by *asking questions and answering* them.

First read the following article from *The New York Times*. (We have numbered the paragraphs to facilitate reference to them.)

The Newark Public Library
Philip Roth [1]

1   What will the readers of Newark do if the City Council goes ahead with its money-saving plan to shut down the public library system on April 1? Will they loot the stacks as Newarkers looted furniture and appliance stores in the riot of 1967? Will police be called in to Mace down thieves racing off with the *Encyclopaedia Britannica?* Will scholars take up sniping positions at reference room windows and school children "seize" the main Washington Street building in order to complete their term papers? If the City Council locks up the books, will library card holders band together to "liberate" them?

2   I suppose one should hope not. Apparently there must be respect for Law and Order, even where there is none for aspiration

---

[1] In February 1969, after riots had already destroyed much of Newark's black slum neighborhoods, the Newark City Council voted to strike from the city budget the $2.8 million required to finance the Newark Museum and the Newark Public Library. Hundreds of Newark residents vehemently opposed this move, which would have shut down two exceptional civic institutions. In the face of the protest, the Council eventually rescinded their decision. This article appeared on the editorial page of *The New York Times*, March 1, 1969, about two weeks after the Council had announced the budget cutback [Roth's note].

and curiosity and quiet pleasure, for language, learning, scholarship, intelligence, reason, wit, beauty, and knowledge.

3   When I was growing up in Newark in the forties we assumed that the books in the public library belonged to the public. Since my family did not own many books, or have much money for a child to buy them, it was good to know that solely by virtue of my municipal citizenship I had access to any book I wanted from that grandly austere building downtown on Washington Street, or from the branch library I could walk to in my neighborhood. No less satisfying was the idea of communal ownership, property held in common for the common good. Why I had to care for the books I borrowed, return them unscarred and on time, was because they weren't mine alone, they were everybody's. That idea had as much to do with civilizing me as any I was ever to come upon in the books themselves.

4   If the idea of a *public* library was civilizing so was the place, with its comforting quiet, its tidy shelves, its knowledgeable, dutiful employees who weren't teachers. The library wasn't simply where one had to go to get the books, it was a kind of exacting haven to which a city youngster willingly went for his lesson in restraint and his training in self-control. And then there was the lesson in order, the enormous institution itself serving as instructor. What trust it inspired—in both oneself and in systems—first to decode the catalogue card, then to make it through the corridors and stairwells into the open stacks, and there to discover, exactly where it was supposed to be, the desired book. For a ten-year-old to find he actually can steer himself through tens of thousands of volumes to the very one he wants is not without its satisfactions. Nor did it count for nothing to carry a library card in one's pocket; to pay a fine if need be; to sit in a strange place, beyond the reach of parent and school, and read whatever one chose, in anonymity and peace; finally, to carry home across the city and even into bed at night a book with a local lineage of its own, a family-tree of Newark readers to which one's name had now been added.

5   In the forties, when Newark was mostly white and I was being raised there, it was simply an unassailable fact of life that the books were "ours" and that the public library had much to teach us about the rules of civilized life, as well as civilized pleasures to offer. It is strange, to put it politely, that now when Newark is mostly black, the City Council (for fiscal reasons, we are told) has reached a decision that suggests that the books don't really belong to the public after all, and that the lessons and pleasures a library provides for

the young are no longer essential to an education. In a city seething with social grievances there is, in fact, probably little that could be *more* essential to the development and sanity of the thoughtful and ambitious young than access to those libraries and books. For the moment the Newark City Council may, to be sure, have solved a fiscal problem; it is too bad, however, that they are unable to calculate the frustration, cynicism, and rage that such an insult must inevitably generate, or to imagine what shutting down the libraries may cost the community in the end.

Questions

Now answer the following questions.

1. a. What was the occasion for this article?
   b. What was Roth's response?
2. a. How does Roth support his position in paragraph 3? Why does he mention his childhood?
   b. What are the two main reasons he gives in paragraph 3 in support of his position?
3. What does Roth mean by "civilizing" in paragraphs 3 and 4?
4. In paragraph 5, what new reasons does he state or imply in support of his position?
5. How does he engage our interest in his first two paragraphs? How does he enlist our support for his point of view?
6. How successful is he?

If you were now to take your answers and revise them a bit you would have an essay something like the student's essay that follows. (Numbers in parentheses refer to the questions.)

On Philip Roth's "The Newark Public Library"

The City Council of Newark introduced a plan to shut down the public library system in order to save money. (1a) Philip Roth in his article (<u>The New York Times</u>, March 1,

1969), argues that the closing of the libraries will be a costly mistake, and that the action will be an insult to the citizens of Newark. (1b)

He supports his position by telling how the library helped him when he was young. (2a) He says that the public library gave him a chance to use books that his family couldn't afford, but more important, the very idea of a public library, of the communal ownership of books, played a part in civilizing him. (2b) By civilizing Roth means socializing. The quiet and orderly fashion in which the library was arranged and run taught him restraint, and taught him to value solitude, privacy, and self-control. Looking for books was itself a lesson in order: he learned, for example, that he could find, through the card catalog, one book among the many thousands there. (3)

Roth suggests that since Newark has become predominantly black, the City Council's attitude toward the library's functions and importance has changed. He implies that the Council's plan is irresponsible and discriminatory. He points out that in a city with as many social problems as Newark's, the lessons and pleasures given to the young by the library are more, not less, essential to their education. He says that although the Council's move may solve an immediate fiscal problem, it will in the end create greater social problems because of the frustration and rage it will generate. (4)

Keeping a Journal

Writing in a journal is for many professional writers a way to both stimulate ideas and to keep a record of those ideas for future use. A journal is an ideal place to store some of the thoughts that you may have scribbled on little scraps of paper during the day, especially those that are not yet usable for a current writing project. Rereading journal entries is often a good way to get started on a new project. Writing daily in a journal, also helps writers to remain fluent. As we said at the start, writing is a physical act, and to keep in trim, one should practice daily. (Or, to be honest, as close to daily as you can manage.) Keeping a journal, then, is practical; for many writers it is, from the start, enjoyable.

Because they have so many uses, journals are often assigned in writing courses. If keeping a journal is required of you, you may be asked to write in a loose-leaf notebook—so that pages may be turned in occasionally, and your instructor won't have to stagger home with twenty or thirty notebooks. If you keep a journal strictly for your own use, write with whatever materials feel comfortable: pen, pencil, typewriter; loose sheets, bound notebook, or whatever. (Dr. William Carlos Williams often wrote poems on prescription blanks.) A word processor is useful for all phases of journal keeping: writing, storing, retrieving, rereading, and printing entries.

Guidelines

1. *When to write?* Any time; ten to fifteen minutes a day if possible. Some people find it helpful to establish a regular time of day for writing, just before they go to sleep, for example. Habits can be helpful; but not all of us can or should lead well-regulated lives. Writing for a minute or two several times a day may work best for you.

2. *How long is an entry?* An entry may be a few words, a line or two, a few pages. There's no special length, but keep writing for the length of time it takes to complete a useful entry.

3. *Form.* Date each entry but then write freely. Don't correct or revise. Don't worry about spelling, vocabulary, punctuation. Use whatever language, idiom, voice you wish. It's a good way to keep in touch with yourself, and the friends and family you've temporarily left. You *can* go home again; you can, that is, if you don't leave college an educated zombie.

4. *As for content,* write about anything that comes to mind. But don't confuse a journal with a diary. A diary mentions things

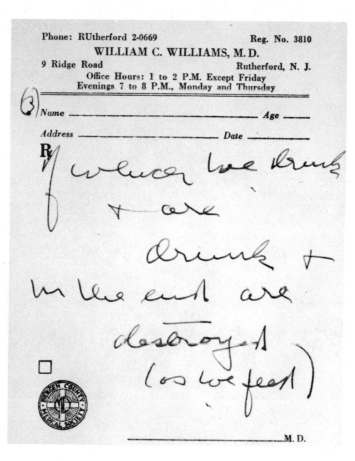

Phone: RUtherford 2-0669   Reg. No. 3810
WILLIAM C. WILLIAMS, M. D.
9 Ridge Road   Rutherford, N. J.
Office Hours: 1 to 2 P.M. Except Friday
Evenings 7 to 8 P.M., Monday and Thursday

Name _____ *Age* _____

Address _____ *Date* _____

℞

℞ / when we drink
+ are

drunk +
in the end are
destroyed
(as we feel)

_____ M. D.

that have happened ("Concert at 8, with J. and R."); a journal reflects on the happenings. A diary lists appointments; a journal records events, but gives some sense of why they were meaningful. Think of your journal as a record of your life now, which you might read with pleasure some years from now when many of the rich details of your daily experience would otherwise be buried in your memory. Still, it's probably better to write "Had a peanut butter sandwich for lunch" than to write nothing.

Write down your thoughts, feelings, impressions, responses, dreams, memories. May Sarton once said, "The senses are the keys to the past." If you have a strong sensory memory of something—the mixed smell of saltwater, sand, and machinery oil, for example—try to describe it in words, and then to track it down. You may find a buried scene from your childhood that you can rescue from your memory by a train of associations. If you keep tracking, and writing, you may discover why that scene is important.

Here, to prime the pump, are some examples of journal entries.

Examples

1. It is difficult to believe that not understanding a physics problem isn't the worst problem in the world.

2. Old people have been following me all my life. . . . And at times scaring me out of my wits. When I was a very young child, one of my mother's best friends was an old crone named Bettina. . . . A witch-like figure dressed (always) in black with a pointed nose and chin. She had startling blue eyes that pierced one's being and a voice that cackled and shrieked in Italian. She filled the air with ethnic gossip and snide attacks on the marital behavior of her daughter, deriding her treatment of her son-in-law of whom she was extremely fond. My mother would smile and nod, all the while cooking, a major occupation of her life.

Subject—Echoes from My Childhood
Topic—Kitchen Memories

3. "Teruko-san! How come you don't understand what I am saying to you!! How come you are repeating these errors so many times!! One! Two! Three! Go!!" My arms, hands, fingers and even my brain are frozen. Tears are running down my cheek. My both hands are sitting on the keyboard frighteningly. Silence. I hear my heart, beating thump thump thump. With a deep sigh, Mrs. Ikebuchi closes the page of a score which is blackened with fingering numbers, circles and crosses. Without saying any words, she leaves the room, and goes to the kitchen. The lesson is over. I sigh and wipe off my tears with the back of my hands, pick up the scores, go to the living room and sit on the tatami-floor stiffly. "By the

way Teruko-san, did you see my gardenia? It is so beautiful! Come! come and see it!" She comes out from the kitchen with a big round black lacquer tray with tea and cookies on it. She puts the tray on the table and walks out to the garden to the gardenia bush. "Isn't this pretty?" "Yes." "Isn't this a nice smell?" "Yes." Mrs Ikebuchi walks back to the living room and I follow her three steps behind and sit on the tatami-floor stiffly again. Mrs. Ikebuchi pours tea and asks me merrily, "How much sugar do you want? how much cream do you want? which cookie do you want? rabbit? elephant? or duck?" I answer politely, "two sugars, please? (it is cube sugar), that's enough, thank you (for cream). May I have a rabbit?" "Oh you like the rabbit! Good! By the way do you know the story about the rabbit? Ah—what was it? Ah, Peter Rabbit!" Her story is going on and on and on. Meanwhile I finish my tea and cookie. "Well, Teruko-san, see you next Monday." I stand up, my legs are numb from sitting on the tatami-floor, and start to walk slowly, my toes are tickling. I pick up my scores and bow and say "Thank you very much." Walk out the sliding door. Release! I skip home.

4. 9/20 Lab was a trip today. Right before my eyes, I observed an egg cell being invaded by an army of sperm cells. Think of it. That's how I began. I used to be a nothing, and now I'm something, an "I." (I was only looking at a sea urchin's egg, but that sure beats not looking at a sea urchin's egg.)

5. A belief I had when I was small: For some reason I thought every person was allowed only a certain number of words per life time. Of course, at that time in my life I was quiet, except when I was mad and all reason left me.

6. Political scientists are masters of Instant Prose who like to stuff sentences as full of multisyllabic words as possible so that it takes 10 minutes to decipher a paragraph. For example:

> "Mann's survey leads us to believe that alongside consensual processes of voluntary deference, nationalism, and rational support of the government (the mobilization of bias, deference to political symbols, or indoctrination in hegemonoic ideology—according to various viewpoints) there also exists a vast reservoir of dissensus."

7. Anticipating something is like falling off a cliff and never reaching the bottom.

8. Intro to Women's Studies upset me today. We talked about the role of women in religion. We discussed how feminist theologians (the*a*logians?) believe that God is not necessarily a man but could be a woman. Their argument is that the Bible was translated and interpreted by men for their own purposes. They wanted to utilize the Bible to give women a subordinate role to men. I do believe that, or at least I think all this is worth questioning. But it's hard for me—no, sad—to think of God as a woman when I have grown to love him as a man, a father.

FOCUSING

What to Write About: Subject, Topic, Thesis

If you're taking a course in composition, you will probably receive assignments to write on something you are reading or on something out of your personal experience, which may include your experience of books. In other courses, it's usually up to you to choose a *subject* from those covered in the course, to focus on a *topic* within the subject, and to narrow the topic by formulating a *thesis.* Any assignment requires you to narrow the subject so that you can treat it thoroughly in the allotted space and time. Therefore you write not on *Time* magazine, but on the political bias of *Time,* or on a comparison of *Time* and *Newsweek,* based on one or two issues of each, arguing for the superiority of one over the other; not on political primaries (a subject), but on a specific proposal to abolish them (a topic); not on penguins (a subject), but on the male penguin's role in hatching (a topic). A good general rule in finding a topic is to follow your inclinations: focus on something about the subject that interests you.

Suppose your assignment is to read the Book of Ruth in the Hebrew Bible and to write an essay of 500–1000 words on it. If you start with a topic like "The Book of Ruth, A Charming Idyll" you're in trouble. The topic is much too vague. In writing about it you'll find yourself hopping around from one place in the book to another, and in desperation saying insincere things like "The Book of Ruth is probably one of the most charming idylls in all literature," when you haven't read all literature, have precious little idea of what *idyll* means, and couldn't define *charm* precisely if your life depended on it.

What to do? Focus on something that interested you about the book. (If you read the book with pencil in hand, taking some notes, underlining some passages, putting question marks at others, you'll have some good clues to start with.) The book is named after Ruth, but perhaps you find Naomi the more interesting character. If so, you might jot down: "Although the Book of Ruth is named after Ruth, I find the character of Naomi more interesting."

Stuck again? Ask yourself some questions. *Why* do you find her more interesting? To answer that question, reread the book, focusing your attention on all the passages in which Naomi acts or speaks or is spoken of by others. Ruth's actions, you may find, are always clearly motivated by her love for Naomi. But Naomi's actions are more complex, more puzzling. If you're puzzled, trust your feeling—*there is something puzzling there. What* motivated Naomi? Convert your question to "Naomi's Motivation" and you have a *topic.*

With this topic in mind, if you explore Naomi's actions one by one you may conclude that "Although Naomi shows in many of her actions her concern for her daughter-in-law, her actions also reveal self-interest." Now you have a *thesis,* that is, a brief statement of your main point. It's a bit awkwardly worded but you can work on a smoother, more natural expression later.

"Naomi's Motivation" is a topic in literary criticism, but if your special interest is, for example, economics, or sociology, or law, your topic might be one of these:

Economic Motivation in the Book of Ruth
Attitudes toward Intermarriage in the Book of Ruth
The Status of Women in the Book of Ruth

Any one of these topics can be managed in 500–1000 words. But remember, you were assigned to write on the Book of Ruth. Formulate a thesis with evidence from that book. Suppress the impulse to put everything you know about economics or intermarriage or the-status-of-women-through-the-ages in between two thin slices, an opening sentence and a concluding sentence, on the Book of Ruth.

Let's take another example. Suppose that in a course on Modern Revolutionary Movements you're assigned a term paper on any subject covered by the readings or lectures. A term paper is usually about three thousand words and requires research. You're interested in Mexican history, and after a preliminary search you decide to focus on the Revolution of 1910 or some events leading up to it. Depending on what is available in your library, you might narrow your topic to one of these:

Mexican Bandits—The First Twentieth Century Revolutionists

The Exploits of Joaquin Murieta and Tiburcio Vasquez—Romantic Legend and Fact

(See pages 345–46, on narrowing a topic in research.)

In short, it is not enough to have a subject (the Book of Ruth, revolutions); you must concentrate your vision on a topic, a significant part of the field, just as a landscape painter or photographer selects a portion of the landscape and then focuses on it. Your interests are your most trustworthy guides to the portion of the landscape on which to focus.

Once you think you know what your topic is, try to formulate a thesis sentence. This sentence may or may not appear in your final paper—think of it as a working hypothesis, a proposition to be proved:

Naomi's character is more interesting than Ruth's.

Murieta and Vasquez were in the vanguard of a revolution.

Closing the Newark Public Library will incur enormous social costs.

Your "working thesis" will help you to maintain your focus, to keep in mind the points that you must support with evidence, such as quotations, facts, statistics, reasons, descriptions, and illustrative anecdotes. But be prepared to modify your working thesis, perhaps more than once, and perhaps substantially. Once you begin amassing evidence and arguments, you may find that they support a different thesis. Your best ideas on your topic may turn out to be radically different from the ideas with which you began. As we pointed out earlier, writing is not simply a way to express ideas you already have, it's also a way to acquire them.

Although essays based on substantial research almost always include an explicit thesis sentence in the finished essay, short essays based on personal experience often do not. An essay recounting a writer's experience of racism, for example, or conveying the particular atmosphere of a neighborhood, is likely to have a central idea or focus, a *thesis idea*, rather than a *thesis sentence*. But whether stated or implied, the thesis idea must be developed (explained, supported, or proved) by evidence presented in the body of the essay. The kind of evidence will vary, of course, not only with your topic, but also with your audience and purpose.

DEVELOPING IDEAS

Materials that writers use to develop ideas, to explain and support a thesis, are largely byproducts of the writer's thinking about a topic and formulating a thesis. The materials, for the most part, are already at hand from the reading, notetaking, freewriting, questioning, and remembering that are part of the writing process from beginning to end. Materials for developing an essay on Naomi's motivation will be primarily brief quotations from The Book of Ruth, quotations that the essay writer introduces and explains. Similarly, materials for an essay on the blues will be quotations from a thoughtful selection of lyrics. An essay on a memorable experience, one that led to an interesting idea, will rely on the writer's memory of that experience, examined with a reader in mind. In all of these instances, in fact, imagining a reader is an important means of developing ideas.

Thinking About Audience and Purpose

Thinking about the audience for whom a piece of writing is intended and thinking about what the writer wants that audience to understand and to believe are always important at the final stages of writing. You read over a draft you have written to see if it will be clear and interesting to someone else, to someone who is not you, who does not know what you know, and does not necessarily share your beliefs. Will your reader understand that technical term? Should you define the term, or can you substitute a more familiar word? Have you identified the source of a quotation? And is it clear why you are using the quotation at this point in your essay? Are paragraphs arranged in a clear sequence? Have you provided transitions? And so on. Reading your draft (preferably aloud), imagining an audience, you can often spot unclear patches, and then revise them. Reading your draft to an actual audience, a friend or classmate, is even better.

But thinking about audience and purpose can be helpful at earlier stages of writing too, when you are trying to develop an idea and to work up evidence to support it. If you are uncertain how to begin, or if, on the other hand, you are overwhelmed by the materials you have unearthed and don't know how to sort them out, try asking yourself these questions:

> Who are my readers?
> What do they need to know?
> What do I want them to believe?

When you ask, "Who is my reader?" the obvious answer might seem to be the teacher who assigned the essay. But that answer, when you think about it, is likely to be the least helpful. Why bother to write for someone who presumably knows all the answers? Moreover "writing for the teacher" has been known to inspire inappropriate responses, ranging from stilted or inflated writing to half-hearted attempts to guess "the right answer." Such responses are unsurprising, especially from students who have written little in high school except answers on tests. Their experience has hardly prepared them for the kinds of writing they are expected to do in college or later in their professions.

If, when trying to develop a topic, you feel lost, that you "have nothing to say," perhaps your experience as a writer so far has also been limited by your role as a student mostly to performing on tests or "writing for the teacher." If this has been your experience, we suggest that you try to remember writing that you have felt comfortable about and enjoyed. Think of letters that you have written to friends, or an article you wrote for the school paper, or a business brochure you prepared. In those (or similar) instances, you knew both who your readers were and what you wanted them to know and to believe. In writing an essay, try to put yourself in a similar frame of mind. The writing assignment may have included instructions about the audience your essay should address. If not, imagine a reader who is in many ways your counterpart—that is someone intelligent and reasonably well informed—but who does not happen to be you and who therefore can't know your thoughts unless you explain them clearly and thoroughly.

In other words, we suggest that you begin thinking of yourself not as a student but as a writer. Like writers out in the real world, *when you write you are the teacher.* If you have a topic but are uncertain how to develop it, ask yourself what a reader who knows less than you do about your topic needs to know and what you want that reader to believe. Write for that reader.

Writing from Experience: Two Examples

Let's look at two essays, each written by a student during the first week of the semester in a composition course. The students were invited as an introductory exercise to write about an idea provided by their own experience, something they knew or understood well that they could describe or explain to others who were unfamiliar with it. Perhaps you are familiar with such an assignment. You try to think of something interesting you've done, but you've led a most unremarkable life. Your classmates, all strangers, seem to know more than you do about almost everything. They've all been to Europe—well, some of them. All you did last summer was file cards and run errands in an office full of boring people. Here is the first student's essays, on, as it happens, a boring job.

Example 1A
A Lesson

```
      As I look back at it, my first thought is that my job

was a waste of time.  It consisted of compiling information

from the files of the Water and Assessor's Department in a

form suitable for putting on the city's computer.  Supposedly
```

```
this would bring the water billing and property taxing to an
efficient level.  If the job sounds interesting, don't be de-
ceived.  After the first week of work, I seriously doubted
that I would survive through the summer.

     But I was able to salvage a lesson in the self-disci-
pline of coping with people.  Of course we all know how to
succeed with friends, family, acquaintances, and employers.
But try it in a situation where you have a distinct disadvan-
tage, where you are the seller and they are the customers.
And remember, the customer is always right.

     By observing the situation, though I was not a partici-
pant, I learned that patience, kindness, and understanding
can remove the difficulties you cross at the time.
```

Not a bad topic, really. One can learn something valuable from a boring, menial, frustrating job. Or if not, one can examine boredom (what exactly is it? is it the same as impatience? how does it come about? how does it feel?) and write about it without boring the reader. But this essay doesn't teach us anything about boredom. It doesn't allow us through concrete, specific details to feel with the writer that we too would have doubted we could survive the summer. Instead, it offers generalizations such as "compiling information from our files" and "a form suitable for putting on the city's computer." These words give us no sense of the tedium of daily transferring numbers from five hundred manila index cards to five hundred gray index cards. In fact, the essay gives us almost no sense of the job. The second paragraph ends with the words "the customer is always right," but nothing in the essay suggests that the writer (whose work "consisted of compiling information from the files") had any contact with customers. We really don't know what she did. Nor does the essay present any evidence that the experience was redeemed by a lesson in "patience, kindness, and understanding."

As it turns out, there was no such lesson. In class discussion, the student frankly admitted that the job was a waste of time. She had, out of habit, tried to come up with some pious thought to please the instructor. The habit had short-circuited the connection between the student's feelings and the words she was writing. The class discussion led to some genuinely interesting questions. Why, for example, are we reluctant to admit that something we've done was a waste of time? "The job was a waste of time" would have been, for most of us, a more productive thesis than "I was able to salvage a lesson." What experiences lead to the conclusions: I must write what the instructor expects; the instructor expects a pious thought? (We'd like to hear from a student willing to explore that topic in 500–1000 words.)

The class discussion, as we said, revealed the student's real attitude toward her job. The questions that, as readers, the class asked also provided a focus for the writer which helped her to formulate a more productive thesis. It's helpful to imagine such a discussion with real readers in the early stages of writing as you grope for what you have to say. For although it would be tidy if writers could simply, and in the following order, (1) choose a subject, (2) focus on a topic, (3) formulate a thesis, (4) support the thesis in the body of the essay, things don't often work out that way. More commonly, writers discover their topic, formulate their thesis and develop support for their thesis in the act of writing and revising, in asking questions and in answering them, in discarding the answers, or even the questions, and starting again.

Example 2

Now look at the second essay, again on a common experience. Ask yourself as you read it, or reread it, what makes it uncommonly interesting.

Dedication Doth Not a Good Teacher Make

```
    The worst teacher I ever had was a brilliant and charm-

ing man.  Fergy (it was short for Mr. Ferguson) had written

the textbook we used for Chemistry.  He had designed his

house and built it himself, getting professional help only
```

for the electricity and plumbing. He could remember the
scores of all the football games he'd seen, and the names of
the players on each team. He never kept lists--"Lists rot
the memory," he said--so he memorized which type of lab implement he kept in which of fifty drawers, and he could tell
you instantly, without pause. Sometimes we would ask him
where a certain type of obscure bottle could be found just to
test him, but he never failed. "Middle left-hand drawer in
Lab Station Six," would say old Fergy, and in that middle
left-hand drawer it would be. I never knew him to forget a
name, a face, or a formula, either.

   That, I think, was his failing as a teacher. Because he
had no trouble grasping or recalling a concept, he had trouble in understanding how we could. The one thing his extraordinary mind seemed unable to comprehend was that it was extraordinary, that not everyone could think as completely and
as easily as he. If the class had questions he would try to
answer them, but he tended to complicate and expand on ideas,
rather than to simplify them. He could not believe that we
needed not expansion but explanation, with the result that we
soon learned not to ask too many questions for fear of extra
material to learn. And it did become a fear of learning, because, try as we would, we somehow never managed to pin down
concepts like electron shells and the wave theory of gravita-
tion, but we would still have to answer for them on tests--
and, ultimately, at home. (I never decided which was worse,
knowing that once again I had made a complete fool of myself
by taking a chem test, or having to listen to my parents sigh
and claim that I could have done better if I'd tried.)

   Fergy would have been horrified to know that he had this
discouraging effect on us. He loved us and he loved teaching

and he loved chemistry. He was always available for outside
help, not only for chemistry, but for any problem, whether in
English or your social life. He tried to make class interesting by telling little anecdotes and playing with the chemicals. Actually, he was funny, and interesting, and charming, and he kept us hoping that we'd understand chem so that
he would approve of us and so we could relax and enjoy him.
But although he is one of the best people it has been my good
fortune to have known, he never did manage to teach me a lick
of chemistry.

As you study this book, you'll frequently find questions following examples of writing. Skills in reading and writing are closely
intertwined. If you practice asking and answering questions as you
read, as well as when you write, the skills you develop will reinforce each other. Try answering the following questions on "Dedication Doth Not a Good Teacher Make":

What is the writer's thesis?
How does she support the thesis?
If you found the essay interesting, what makes it interesting?
If you found it convincing, what makes it convincing?

The Groucho Marx Complex

Clearly—examining these essays should make it clear—there
is no such thing as an uninteresting life, or moment in life. There
are only uninteresting ways to talk about them. It's also clear that
some people are more interested in introspection and in talking
and writing about their personal experiences than others. The others may be suffering from the Groucho Marx Complex: as Groucho
put it, "I don't want to belong to any club that would have me as
a member." Students who freeze at the notion of writing about
themselves often feel that everything they have done is so ordi-

nary, no one else could possibly be interested in it; anything they know is so obvious, everyone else must know it already. If this is your problem, remember that no one else knows exactly what you know; no one else can know what it feels like to live inside your skin. If you work at summoning up from your memory concrete and specific details, you can turn the most ordinary experience into a first-rate essay.

Remember too that writing from your own experience does not necessarily mean writing about private experience. We all have areas of experience we'd rather keep private, and we have a right to remain private about them. The important thing in writing about experience is, as Marianne Moore said, that "we must be as clear as our natural reticence allows us to be." Think, then, of experiences that you are willing to share and to be clear about. If, for example, you have just learned in a psychology course what "operant conditioning" means, define it for someone unfamiliar with the term. You might find yourself narrating an experience of your own to exemplify it; to be clear, you will have to provide an example. Or if an object in a local museum or craft exhibit or store interests you, ask yourself a question—why do I like it?—and you'll probably be able to turn an object into an experience. You'll also be turning an experience into an object—an essay—that will interest your readers.

Writing academic papers frequently requires examining and evaluating texts and other evidence beyond your personal experience or previous knowledge. Nevertheless, you still must trust your own ideas. Trusting your own ideas does not, of course, mean being satisfied with the first thought that pops into your head. Rather, it means respecting your ideas enough to examine them thoughtfully; it means testing, refining, and sometimes changing them. But it is always your reading of a text, your conduct of an experiment, your understanding of an issue that your essay attempts to communicate.

Starting to write by writing will help you to discover ideas interesting enough to develop. Along the way, trying out various means to engage a reader's interest as well, you will clarify your ideas and understand them more deeply than you could have imagined had you not put them into words on paper.

EXERCISES

1. Make two lists of reasons, one for taking an action, and the other against. Examples: dropping a course, changing jobs, making an expensive purchase, calling someone you don't know but would like to know, majoring in . . . (whatever you're now thinking of), becoming a vegetarian.

2. Quickly scan several editorials or Op-ed pieces in *The New York Times* (or another newspaper or news magazine) until you find one that you really want to *read*. Read it. Then for each paragraph, or group of paragraphs, write one or two questions that call for a summary of the paragraph's content or an explanation of the paragraph's purpose. Overall, your questions should explore why the editorial is particularly interesting or effective.

3. Write a piece somewhat like Roth's (page 12–14) in which you respond to a current proposal in your community. (Suggested length: 500 words.) Or, respond to Roth's article. (Perhaps something he says reminds you of something you have read or experienced; or maybe you agree or disagree strongly with some point he makes.)

4. Write journal entries on two or three assignments (of writing, reading, lab work, or problem sets) made in your courses in the first two weeks of classes.

5. Write a journal entry recalling, in as much detail as you can, your earliest memory.

6. Narrow the following subjects to a topic. Then for each find a more specific focus for a 500–word essay.

> Example:
> Mental Retardation
>> Housing for the mentally retarded
>>> A controversial proposal to house mentally retarded adults in my neighborhood

a. Homelessness	e. Gun control
b. Athletic scholarships	f. Animal rights
c. Welfare reform	g. AIDS
d. The Olympics	h. The writing requirement

7. Formulate a thesis sentence for two topics derived from exercise 6.

8. Explain something clearly—a process, a concept, a place, an experience—that you know well but that others in your class may not know about or may understand less well than you. Suggested length: 500 words.

9. Think about how you usually respond to a writing assignment. Try to trace, step by step, your thoughts, actions, and feelings from the moment that you receive an assignment to the moment that you turn in a finished essay. How does your experience compare with the process of writing that we describe and recommend in these chapters? If you find great differences between our account and your experience how do you account for them?

   Looking back, what experiences have you had as a writer, in class or out, that have lead to your current practice and attitude toward writing? Do you find writing under some circumstances (writing letters, for example, or writing for a school newspaper) easier than others?

   Turn your reflections into an essay of about 500 words.

2

*R*evising Drafts

I have never thought of myself as a good writer.
Anyone who wants reassurance of that should read
one of my first drafts. But I'm one of the world's
great revisers.

— JAMES MICHENER

READING DRAFTS

In Chapter 1, we focused on how to have ideas and how to
get them down on paper. We suggested that from the start of a
project the writer is almost simultaneously both inventing ideas
and refining them. But we also advised that, particularly at the
start, it's often best to suspend critical judgment, if you can, until
you have begun to capture your thoughts, however roughly expressed, on paper. In this chapter, we will focus on ways to improve and refine rough drafts. And, first, we want to make what
may seem like an obvious point: *to improve the draft you have
written, you must first read it.* Moreover, you must try to read it
objectively.

Asking Questions

To read your draft objectively, to make sure that you have
said what you intended to say, first put it aside for a day, or at
least for a couple of hours. Then read it through thoughtfully, as
if you were not the writer, but someone reading it for the first
time. As you read, try to imagine the questions such a reader might

want or need to ask you to understand what you meant. Then, read your draft again, asking yourself the following questions:

1. Does the draft present an idea? Does it have a focus or make a unified point?
2. Is the idea (or are the ideas) clearly supported? Is there convincing evidence? Are there sufficient specific details?
3. Is the material effectively organized?

There are, of course, many other questions you might ask, and we'll suggest some before we're done. But let's start with these.

1. *Does the draft present an idea? Does it have a focus or make a unified point?* If, on reading your draft objectively, you find that it doesn't have an idea, a point to develop, then there's probably no reason to tinker with it (or to hand it in). It may be best to start again, using the invention techniques we discussed earlier. (Rereading the assignment is probably a good idea too.)

Let's suppose, however, that you do find some interesting material in your draft but that you're not yet sure what it adds up to. The chances are that some extraneous material is getting in your way—some false starts, needless repetition, or interesting but irrelevant information. Some pruning is probably in order.

Picasso said that in painting a picture he advanced by a series of destructions. A story about a sculptor makes a similar point. When asked how he had made such a lifelike image of an elephant from a block of wood, the sculptor answered, "Well, I just knocked off everything that didn't look like elephant." Often, revising a draft begins with similar "destruction." Having identified the main point that you want to pursue, don't be afraid to hack away competing material until you can see that point clearly in its bold outline. Of course you must have a lot of stuff on paper to begin with (at the start, nothing succeeds like excess). But often you must remove some of it before you can see that you have in fact roughly formulated the main point you want to make, and even produced some evidence to support it.

2. *Is the idea (or the ideas) supported? Have I introduced convincing evidence?* Writers are always reluctant to delete. Students with an assignment to write 500 or 1000 words by a deadline are, understandably, among the most reluctant. But, almost certainly, once you have settled on the focus of your essay, you

will be adding material as well as deleting it. It isn't enough simply to state a point; you must also prove or demonstrate it.

If you argue, for example, that smoking should be banned in all public places, including professors' offices, you must offer reasons for your position and also meet possible objections with counterarguments; perhaps you will cite some statistics. If you are arguing that in the *Apology* Socrates' definition of truth goes beyond mere correspondence to fact, you will need to summarize relevant passages of the *Apology* and introduce quotations illuminating Socrates' definition. Almost always a draft needs the addition of specific details and examples to support and clarify its generalizations.

3. *Is the material effectively organized?* As you hack off the irrelevancies and add the specific details and examples that will clarify and strengthen your point, as your draft begins more and more to "look like elephant," ask yourself if the parts of your draft are arranged in the best order. If you have given two examples, or stated three reasons, with which one is it best to begin? Ask yourself if paragraphs are in a reasonable sequence. Will the relationship of one point to the next be clear to your reader? Does the evidence in each paragraph support the point of that paragraph? (The same evidence may be more appropriate to a different paragraph.) Does your opening paragraph provide the reader with a focus? Or, if it performs some other important function, such as getting the reader's attention, does the essay provide the reader with a focus soon enough?

In general, in working on the organization of drafts, follow two rules:

(a) Put together what belongs together.

(b) Put yourself in the position of your reader. Make it as easy as possible for the reader to follow you.

Peer Review

Occasionally a writing assignment will specify the reader you should address. For example: "Write a letter to the editor of your hometown newspaper arguing that. . . ." More often, your reader must be imagined. We usually suggest imagining someone in your class who has not thought about your topic or considered the specific evidence you intend to examine.

In many writing classes students routinely break up into small groups to read and discuss each other's work. Peer review (as this practice is commonly called) is useful in several ways.

First, peer review gives the writer a real audience, readers who can point to what puzzles or pleases them, who ask questions and make suggestions, who may often disagree (with the writer or with each other) and who frequently, though not willfully, *misread*. Though writers don't necessarily like everything they hear (they seldom hear, "This is perfect. Don't change a word!"), reading and discussing their work with others almost always gives them a fresh perspective on their work, and a fresh perspective may stimulate thoughtful revision. (Having your intentions *misread*, because your writing isn't clear enough, can be particularly stimulating.)

Moreover, when students write drafts that will be commented on, they are doing what writers in "the real world" do. Like journalists, scholars, engineers, lawyers—anyone whose work is ordinarily reviewed many times, by friends and spouses, by colleagues, and by editors, before the work is published—students who write drafts for peer review know they will have a chance to discuss their writing with their colleagues (other students) before submitting a final version for evaluation. Writers accustomed to writing for a real audience are able, to some extent, to internalize the demands of a real audience. Even as they work on early drafts, they are sensitive to what needs to be added, or deleted, or clarified. Students who discuss their work with other students derive similar benefits. They are likely to write and revise with more confidence, and more energy.

The writer whose work is being reviewed is not the sole beneficiary. When students regularly serve as readers for each other, they become better readers of their own work, and consequently better revisers. Learning to write is in large measure learning to read.

Peer review in the classroom takes many forms; we'll look in a moment at an example as we trace a student's essay that is revised largely as a result of peer review. But even if peer review is not part of your writing class, you may want to work with a friend or another student in the class, reading each other's drafts. (One caution: be sure to acknowledge in a footnote or an endnote any substantial contribution, in idea or wording, a reader has made to your essay. Peer review is not intended to be collaborative writing.)

From Assignment to Essay: A Case History

On September 12, Suki Hudson was given the following assignment: Write an essay (roughly 500 words) defining racism or narrating an experience in which you were either the victim or the perpetrator of a racist incident. Bring a first draft with two copies to class on September 16th for peer review. Revised essay due September 26.

Suki kept no record of her first thoughts and jottings on the topic, but what follows is an early attempt to get something down on paper. Because it was far from the finished essay she would write, not yet even a first draft, we label it Zero Draft:

```
Zero Draft, Sept. 13:
It was a warm sunny day in the playground.  My three-year-old
brother and other children were playing gaily until one of
the boys' mothers interrupted.  She called her son, whispered
something, and when he went back to the playground he ex-
cluded my brother from playing together.  I didn't know what
to call the incident, but my heart ached as I watched my lit-
tle brother enviously looked at the other kids.  I immedi-
ately left the playground with him, and the playground has
never been the same since that day.
```

At that point, having reached the end of the anecdote, Suki stopped. What she had written was not yet an essay, and it was far short of the suggested 500 words, but it was a start, which is all she had hoped to accomplish on this first try.

Later she read what she had written, and asked a friend to read it and see if he had any suggestions. It was a frustrating conversation. The friend didn't understand why Suki thought this was a "racist incident." Why did Suki leave the playground? Why hadn't she just asked the boy's mother for an explanation? The questions took her by surprise; she felt annoyed, then miserable. So she changed the subject.

But "the subject" didn't go away. Still later, she wrote the following account of the conversation in her journal:

Sept. 13:

    I asked J to read my paper and he thought I was being paranoid. Why didn't I just ask the boy's mother what was the matter? But I could not have even thought of going up to the woman to question her motives. It was beyond my control if she wanted to be ignorant and cruel to a different race. (Or was it really my ignorance to walk away from a simple ex-planation?)

The following day, looking over what she had written, it occurred to her to try using both the anecdote and the journal entry. Maybe in a concluding paragraph she could explain why what happened in the playground was obviously a racist incident. Here is the conclusion:

Sept. 14

    Most people in modern society don't recognize the more subtle cases of racism. People feel if they are not assault-ing physically they are not violating the law, and as long as they are living according to the law, racism is not commit-ted. However, the law or the constitution does not protect the human heart from getting hurt, and without a doubt the most critical racist action could be committed by close friends or their loved ones.

But having written that last line Suki was struck by some-thing odd about it. The woman in the playground was not a loved one, nor was she a close friend. Still, it was true that racist acts can be committed by friends, and even if the acts are undramatic, they should be recognized as racist acts. At this point, she thought that she had a thesis for her essay, but she also realized that she had begun to recall a different experience. Starting again, she wrote the following account:

> In Korea, I had a very close friend whose father was Chinese. Although her mother was a Korean woman, they were treated as foreign people in town, and they were singled out on many occasions. Her father died when she was little, but everyone in town knew she was a half Chinese. Her mother ran a Chinese restaurant, and they lived very quietly. My family knew her mother well and I was close friends with the girl, and for many years I was the only friend she ever had. However, as I entered junior high school my new group of friends didn't approve of her background, and I drifted away from her. She was a very quiet, shy person, and although I stopped calling or visiting her, she always remembered me on holidays to send presents. After graduating from junior high school, she went to Taiwan to live with her grandparents, whom she had never met. I gathered she could not stand the isolation any longer at her age. Many years later, I realized how cruel I had been to her, and I tried to locate her without success.

The following day Suki combined the two drafts (hoping to come closer to the 500 words), added a new concluding paragraph, and (rather disgusted with the whole assignment), typed up her first draft to hand in the next day. She photocopied it, as instructed, for peer review in class.

As we said earlier, peer review in the classroom takes many forms. Ordinarily, the instructor distributes some questions to be answered by both the writer and the readers. Typically the writer is asked to speak first, explaining how far along he or she is in

Questions for
Peer Review   Writing 125R   September 16, 1989

Read each draft once, quickly. Then read it again, with the
following questions in mind:

1. What is the essay's topic? Is it one of the assigned topics,
or a variation from it? Does the draft show promise of
fulfilling the assignment?

2. Looking at the essay as a whole, what thesis (main idea) is
stated or implied? If stated, where is it stated? If implied,
try to state it in your own words.

3. Looking at each paragraph separately:
What is the basic point (the topic sentence or idea)?
How does the paragraph relate to the essay's main idea or to the
previous paragraph?
Is each sentence clearly related to the previous sentence?
Is the paragraph adequately developed? Are there sufficient
specific details or examples?
Is the transition from one paragraph to the next clear?

4. Look again at the introductory paragraph. Does it focus your
attention on the main point of the essay? If not, does it
effectively serve some other purpose? Does the opening sentence
interest you in the essay? Do you want to keep reading?

5. Is the conclusion clear? Is the last sentence satisfying?

6. Does the essay have a title? Is it interesting? informative?

writing the essay, and what help readers might give. The writer might also be asked "What are you most pleased with in your writing so far?"

Readers are then asked to respond. Instructions may vary, depending upon the particular assignment, but the questions distributed in Suki's class are fairly typical (page 40). (You will see that some questions resemble the questions we suggest you ask yourself—not surprising, when you consider that the example comes from one of our classes.)

First Draft

What follows is first the draft Suki gave the two members of her group, and then a summary of the group's discussion. Before reading her draft aloud (the procedure the instructor recommended for this session) Suki explained how she had happened to narrate two experiences and asked which narrative she should keep, or if she could keep both.

First Draft   S. Hudson

                                                              Sept. 16

It was a warm sunny day in the playground. My three—
year-old brother and other children were playing gaily until
one of the boys' mothers interrupted. She called her son to
whisper something, and when he went back to the playground he
excluded my brother from playing together. I didn't know
what to call the incident, but my heart ached as I watched my
little brother enviously looked at other kids. I immediately
left the playground with him, and the playground has never
been the same since that day.

A friend of mine said I was being paranoid. It would
have been appropriate to ask the boy's mother what was the
matter, or if she had anything to do with the kids excluding
my brother from playing. But I could not have even thought
of going up to the woman to question her motives. It was be-

yond my control if she wanted to be ignorant and cruel to a different race, or perhaps my ignorance to walk away from a simple explanation.

Most people in modern society recognize only the dramatic instances of racism, and on a daily basis people don't recognize the more subtle cases of racism. People feel if they are not assaulting physically they are not violating the law, and as long as they are living according to the law, the racism is not commited. However, the law or the constitution does not protect the human heart from getting hurt, and without a doubt the most critical racist action could be committed by close friends or their loved ones.

In Korea, I had a very close friend whose father was Chinese. Although her mother was a Korean woman they were treated as foreign people in town, and they were singled out on many occasions. Her father died when she was little, but everyone in town knew she was a half Chinese. Her mother ran a Chinese restaurant, and they lived very quietly. My family knew her mother well and I was close friends with the girl, and for many years I was the only friend she ever had. However, as I entered junior high school my new group of friends didn't approve of her background and I drifted away from her. She was a very quiet, shy person, and although I stopped calling or visiting her, she always remembered me on holidays to send presents. After graduating from junior high school, she went to Taiwan to live with her grandparents, whom she had never met. I gathered she could not stand the isolation any longer at her age. Many years later, I realized how cruel I have been to her, and I tried to locate her without success.

She was a victim in a homogeneous society, and had to

experience the pain she did not deserve. It is part of human
nature to resent the unknown, and sometimes people become
racist to cover their fears or ignorance.

Summary of Peer Group Discussion

1. The group immediately understood why the friend (in the second paragraph) had difficulty understanding that the first incident was racist. It might well have been racist, but, they pointed out, Suki had said nothing about the racial mix at the playground. It does become clear by the fourth paragraph that the writer and her brother are Korean, but we don't get this information early enough, and we know nothing of the race of the woman who whispers to her son. Suki had neglected to say—because it was so perfectly obvious to her—that she and her brother were Korean; the mother, the other child, in fact all others in the playground, were white.

2. Suki's readers confirmed her uneasiness about the third paragraph. They found it confusing. (a) Suki had written "people don't recognize the more subtle cases of racism." Did she mean that the mother didn't recognize her action as racist, or that Suki didn't? (b) In the first paragraph Suki had written "I didn't know what to call the incident." But then the second paragraph is contradictory. There she seems to accuse the mother of being "cruel to a different race." (c) And the last sentence of the third paragraph, they agreed, in which Suki writes of racist acts "committed by close friends," did not tie in at all with the first part of the essay, although it did serve to introduce the second anecdote.

3. Her group was enthusiastic, though, about Suki's telling of the two stories and advised her to keep both. Both were accounts of more or less subtle acts of racism. One student thought that they should appear in chronological order: first the Korean story and then the more recent story, set in the playground. But both readers were sure that she could find some way to put them together.

4. They were less sure what the essay's thesis was, or whether it even had one. One student proposed:

Subtle racist acts can be as destructive as dramatic instances (implied in paragraph 3).

The other proposed combining:

It is part of human nature to resent the unknown

and

. . . sometimes people become racist to cover their fears of ignorance (from the final paragraph).

All three members of Suki's group (Suki included) thought that the ideas in the essay were supported by the narratives. But the draft didn't yet hang together; Suki would have to work on the way the separate parts connnected.

5. One member of the group then pointed out that the second paragraph could be deleted. The friend mentioned in it (who called Suki "paranoid") had been important to Suki's thinking about her first draft, but served no useful purpose in the draft they were looking at, and other details in that paragraph were murky.

6. On the other hand, the first paragraph probably needed additional details about the setting, the people involved, what each did. How does a three-year-old know he's been excluded from a play group? What happened? What did the other children do? What did he do? And, as the group had seen at once, some details were needed to establish the racist nature of the incident. They also reminded Suki that her essay needed a title.

7. Finally, some small details of grammar. Suki's English is excellent, although English is her second language (her third actually). But the other two in her group, being native speakers of English, were able to catch the slightly odd diction in

"she always remembered me on holidays to send presents"

and in

"my heart ached as I watched my little brother enviously looked at other kids."

Suki asked if the past tense was right in

"I realized how cruel I have been to her"

and the others supplied:

"I realized how cruel I had been to her"

(though they could not explain the difference).

Several days later Suki consulted her notes and resumed work on her draft, and by September 25th, the night before it was due, she was able to type the final version.

Suki Hudson

Writing 125R

September 26, 1989

Two Sides of a Story

It was a warm sunny day in the playground. My three-year-old brother and two other small boys were playing to-gether in the sandbox. My brother was very happy, digging in the sand with a shovel one of the other boys had brought, when one of the mothers sitting on a bench across from me called to her son. She bent over and whispered something to him, and he went right over to my brother and pulled the shovel out of his hand. He pushed my brother aside and moved to the other side of the sandbox. The other boy followed him, and they continued to play. My heart ached as I watched my little brother enviously looking at the other kids. I didn't fully understand what had happened. I looked across at the mother, but she turned her head away. Then I picked up my brother and immediately left the playground with him.

I thought the woman was extremely rude and cruel, but I didn't think then that she was behaving in a racist way. We had only recently come here from Korea, and although I had

been told that there was much racism in America, I thought
that meant that it was hard for some people, like blacks, to
find jobs or go to good schools. In some places there were
street gangs and violence. But I didn't understand that
there could be subtle acts of racism too. I was aware in the
playground that my brother and I were the only Koreans, the
only nonwhites. When the woman turned her face away from me
it felt like a sharp slap, but I was ignorant about her motives. I only guessed that she told her child not to play
with my brother, and I knew that the playground was never the
same since that day.

That incident was several months ago. When I started to
think about it again recently, I thought also of another time
when I was ignorant of racism.

In Korea, I had a very close friend whose father was
Chinese. Although her mother was a Korean woman they were
treated as foreign people in town, and they were singled out
on many occasions. Her father died when she was little, but
everyone in town knew she was half Chinese. Her mother ran a
Chinese restaurant, and they lived very quietly. My family
knew her mother well and I was close friends with the girl,
and for many years I was the only friend she ever had. However, as I entered junior high school my new group of friends
didn't approve of her background and I drifted away from her.
She was a very quiet, shy person, and although I stopped
calling or visiting her, she always remembered to send me
presents on holidays. After graduating from junior high
school, she went to Taiwan to live with her grandparents,
whom she had never met. I gathered she could not stand the
isolation any longer at her age. Many years later, I realized how cruel I had been to her, and I tried to locate her
without success.

She was a victim in a homogeneous society, and had to experience pain she did not deserve. There was no law to protect her from that, just as there was no law to protect my little brother. Perhaps the woman in the playground did not realize how cruel she was being. She probably didn't think of herself as a racist, and maybe she acted the way I did in Korea, without thinking why. It isn't only the dramatic acts that are racist, and maybe it isn't only cruel people who commit racist acts. It is part of human nature to fear the unknown, and sometimes people become racist to cover their fears, or ignorance.

AN OVERVIEW: FROM SUBJECT TO ESSAY

We each must work out our own procedures and rituals (John C. Calhoun liked to plough his farm before writing); but the following suggestions may help. The rest of the book will give you more detailed advice.

1. *If a topic is assigned, write on it;* if a topic is not assigned, turn a subject into a topic. Get an early start. The day the assignment is given, try to settle on a topic that interests you. Do this by employing any and all of the strategies—free-writing, listing, clustering, asking questions, keeping a journal—that we have discussed. When you look over your jottings, take note of what especially interests you, and try to decide what topic you can sensibly discuss in the assigned length. Unfortunately, almost none of us can in a few pages write anything of interest on a large subject. We simply cannot in five hundred words say anything readable (that is, true and interesting to others) on subjects as broad as music, sports, ourselves. Given such subjects, we have nothing to say, probably because we are desperately trying to remember what we have heard other people say. Trying to remember blocks our efforts to look hard and to think. To get going, we must narrow

such subjects down to specific topics: from music to country music, from sports to commercialization of athletics, from ourselves to a term with a roommate.

2. *Get a focus.* Once you have turned a subject into a topic, you need to shape the topic by seeing it in a particular focus, by having a thesis, an attitude, a point: Country music is popular because . . . ; College athletes are exploited . . . ; Problems between roommates can be avoided if. . . . Probably you won't find your exact focus or thesis immediately, but you will be able to jot down a few things, including some questions to yourself that come to mind on the topic you have carved out of the broad subject. For example: Why is country music popular? What kind of people like it? Why are some performers more successful than others?

If you ask yourself questions now, you'll probably be able to answer them a day or two later. It doesn't matter whether you make each jotting on a separate card or group them on a sheet of paper as a list or in a few roughly sketched paragraphs; the important thing is to write something, perhaps a few generalizations, perhaps a few striking details, perhaps some of each. If you compose on a word processor, make a print-out after a page or two. You'll probably find that reading what you have jotted down leads to something else—something you probably would not have thought of if you hadn't jotted down the first thing. Few of us have good ideas about anything at the start, but as we put our ideas into words we find better ideas coming to mind.

Remember, too, that keeping your audience and your purpose in mind will help you to produce ideas. If, for example, you assume that you are writing about country music to interest a reader who is unfamiliar with it, you will begin to find things that you must say.

3. *Turn your reveries into notes.* Put your jottings aside for a day or two (assuming you have a week to do the essay), but be prepared to add to them at any moment. Useful thoughts—not only ideas, but details—may come to you while you are at lunch, while you read a newspaper or magazine, while your mind wanders in class. Write down these thoughts. Do not assume that you will remember them when you come to draft your essay.

4. *Sort things out.* About two days before the essay is due, look over your jottings and see if you can discover a workable

thesis in them. This might be a good moment to practice free writing on your topic, or to arrange your notes into what looks like a reasonable sequence.

Perhaps now is the time to give your essay a provisional title. A title will help you to keep your thesis in focus. Don't be afraid to be obvious. If you look back at some of the titles of sections in this book, you will see such things as "Why Write?" "Starting to Write by Writing," and "Developing Ideas." Such titles help the writer to keep to the point, while letting readers know what the topic will be. (Leave uninformative titles to the Marx Brothers: "Duck Soup," "Horse Feathers.") Sometimes word-play produces an attractive but still informative title, for example a student's "If You Have *Time,* read *Newsweek.*"

In any case, whether or not you choose a title at this point, you should now have a focus. Next, look again at your jottings and add what comes to mind. Keep asking yourself questions, and try to jot down the answers. Draw arrows to indicate the sequence you think the phrases should be in.

5. *Write.* Even if you are not sure that you have a thesis and an organization, start writing. Don't delay; you have some jottings, and you have a mind that, however casually, has already been thinking. Don't worry about writing an effective opening paragraph (your opening paragraph will almost surely have to be revised later anyway); just try to state and develop your point, based on the phrases or sentences you have accumulated, adding all of the new details that flow to mind as you write. If you are stuck, ask yourself questions. Have I supported my assertions with examples? Will a comparison help to clarify the point? Which quotation best illustrates this point? If you are not using a word processor, leave lots of space between the lines, leave wide margins, and write on one side of the page only. Later you'll fill the spaces with additional details, additional generalizations, and revisions of sentences. Keep going until you have nothing left to say.

6. *Save what you can.* Immediately after writing the draft, or a few hours later, look it over to see how much you can salvage. Don't worry about getting the exact word here or there; just see whether or not you have a thesis, whether or not you keep the thesis in view, and whether or not the points flow reasonably. Delete irrelevant paragraphs, however interesting; shift para-

graphs that are relevant but that should be somewhere else. You can do this best by scissoring the sheets and gluing the pieces onto another paper in the right order. (If you use a word processor, you can move paragraphs just by hitting some keys on the keyboard.) Don't assume that tomorrow you will be able to remember that the paragraph near the bottom of page 3 will go into the middle of page 2. Scissor and glue it, or move the block, now, so that when you next read the essay you will easily be able to tell whether in fact the paragraph does belong in the middle of page 2. Finally, settle on a title. Probably you can't do much more with your manuscript at this moment. Put it aside until tomorrow.

7. *Revise.* Reread your draft, first with an eye toward large matters. Revise your opening paragraph or write one to provide the reader with a focus; make sure each paragraph grows out of the previous one, and make sure you keep the thesis in view. Remember, *when you write, you are the teacher.* As you revise, make sure that assertions are supported by evidence; try to imagine that you are the reader, and let this imagined reader tell you where you get off the point, where you are illogical, where you need an example—in short, where you are in any way confusing.

Next, after making the necessary large revisions, read the draft with an eye toward smaller matters: make sure that each sentence is clear and readable. (You can do this only by reading slowly—preferably aloud, unless you have developed the ability to hear each sentence, each word, in the mind's ear.) Let's say that in telling a reader how to handle disks for a word processor, you have written, "When you write the label for the disk, use a felt pen." You notice, in revising, that the reader may wonder *why* a pencil or a ballpoint pen should not be used, and so you'll alter the sentence to "Because the pressure of a pencil or a ballpoint pen can damage the surface of the disk, label the disk with a felt pen."

Cross out extra words; recast unclear sentences. Keep pushing the words, the sentences, the paragraphs into shape until they say what you want them to say from the title onward. (This contest between writers and their words is part of what Muhammad Ali had in mind when he said, referring to his work on his autobiography, "Writing is fighting.") Correct anything that disturbs you—for instance, awkward repetitions that grate.

8. *Edit.* When your draft is as good as you can make it, take care of the mechanical matters: if you have any doubt about the spelling of a word, check it in a dictionary; if you are unsure about a matter of punctuation, check it in this book. You will also find instructions about manuscript form (for example, where to put the title, what margins to leave) in this book. And be sure to acknowledge the source not only of quotations but also of any ideas that you borrowed, even though you summarized or paraphrased them in your own words. (On plagiarism, see pages 362–364.)

9. *Prepare the final copy.* Now write or type the final copy; if you are on the schedule, you will be doing this a day before the essay is due. (If you take our advice and use a word processor, you already have a final copy on a disk and now need only to instruct the machine to print it.) After writing, typing, or printing it, you will probably want to proofread it; there is no harm in doing so, but even if you do it now, you will have to proofread again later because at the moment you are too close to your essay. If you put the essay aside for a few hours and then reread it, again aloud, you will be more likely to catch omitted words, transposed letters, inconsistent spelling of names, and so forth. Change these neatly (see pages 670–672.)

10. *Hand the essay in on time.*

In short, the whole business of moving from a subject to a finished essay on a focused topic adds up to Mrs. Beeton's famous recipe: "First catch your hare, then cook it."

3

Analysis

All there is to writing is having ideas. To learn to write is to learn to have ideas.

— ROBERT FROST

Look at this drawing by Pieter Brueghel the Elder, entitled "The Painter and the Connoisseur" (about 1565), and then jot down your responses to the questions that follow.

Questions

1. One figure is given considerably more space than the other. What is probably implied by this fact?
2. What is the painter doing (beside painting)?
3. What is the connoisseur doing?
4. What does the face of each figure tell you about the character of each figure? The figures are physically close; are they mentally close? How do you know?

Now consider this brief discussion of the picture.

> The painter, standing in front of the connoisseur and given more than two-thirds of the space, dominates this picture. His hand holds the brush with which he creates, while the connoisseur's hand awkwardly fumbles for money in his purse. The connoisseur apparently is pleased with the picture he is looking at, for he is buying it, but his parted lips give him a stupid expression and his eyeglasses imply defective vision. In contrast, the painter looks away from the picture and fixes his eyes on the model (reality) or, more likely, on empty space, his determined expression suggesting that he possesses an imaginative vision beyond his painting and perhaps even beyond earthly reality.

This paragraph is a concise piece of analysis. It doesn't simply tell us that the picture shows two people close together; it separates the parts of the picture, pointing out that the two figures form a contrast. It explains why one figure gets much more space than the other, and it explains what the contrasting gestures and facial expressions imply. The writer of the caption has "read" the picture by seeing how the parts function, that is, how they relate to the whole.

Most of the material that you read in courses, except in literature courses, is chiefly analytic: you read of the various causes of a revolution, of the effects of inflation, or of the relative importance of heredity and environment. Similarly, most of your writing in college will be chiefly analytic: you will analyze and explain to your reader the characters in a play, the causes and effects of poverty, the strengths and weaknesses of some proposed legislative action.

CLASSIFYING AND THINKING

Analysis (literally a separating into parts) is not only the source of much writing that seeks to explain, it is a way of thinking, a way of arriving at conclusions (generalizations), or of discovering how conclusions were arrived at. It is, at its simplest, an adult version of sorting out cards with pictures of baseball players on them. Now, if you have identical items—for instance, one hundred bricks to unload from a truck—you can't sort them; you can only divide them for easier handling into groups of, say, ten, or into armloads. But if the items vary in some way you can sort them out. You can, for example, put socks into one drawer, underwear into another, trousers or dresses in a closet—all in an effort to make life a little more manageable. Similarly, you can sort books by size or by color or by topic or by author; you do this, again, in order to make them manageable, to make easier the job of finding the right one later, and so, ultimately, to learn about what is in the book.

When you think seriously or when you talk about almost anything, you also sort or classify. When you think about choosing courses at school, you classify the courses by subject matter, or by degree of difficulty ("Since I'm taking two hard courses, I ought to look for an easy one"), or by the hour at which they are offered, or by their merit as determined through the grapevine, or by the degree to which they interest you. When you classify, you establish categories by breaking down the curriculum into parts, and by then putting into each category courses that significantly resemble each other but that are not identical. We need categories or classifications; we simply cannot get through life treating every object as unique. Almost everything has an almost infinite number of characteristics and can therefore be placed in any number of categories, but for certain purposes (and we must know our purposes) certain characteristics are significant. It is on these significant characteristics that we fasten.

In classifying, the categories must be established on a single basis of division: you cannot classify dogs into purebreds and small dogs, for some dogs belong in both categories. You must classify them into consistent, coordinate categories, let us say either by breeding or by size. Of course you can first classify or sort dogs into purebreds and mutts and *then* sort each of these groups into two subordinate categories, dogs under twelve inches at the shoulder and dogs twelve inches or more at the shoulder. The categories, as we shall see in a few minutes, will depend on your purpose. That the categories into which things are sorted should be coordinate is, alas, a principle unknown to the American Kennel Club, which divides dogs into six groups. The first four seem reasonable enough: (1) sporting dogs (for example, retrievers, pointers, spaniels), (2) hounds (bassets, beagles, whippets), (3) working dogs (sheepdogs, St. Bernards, collies), (4) terriers (airedales, Irish terriers, Scottish terriers). Trouble begins with the fifth classification, toy dogs (Maltese, Chihuahuas, toy poodles), for size has not been a criterion up to now. The sixth category is desperate: nonsporting dogs (chow chow, poodle, dalmatian). Nonsporting! What a category. Why not nonworking or nonhound? And is a poodle really more like a chow chow than like a toy poodle?[1] Still, the classifications are by now established. Every purebred must fit into one and only one, and thus every purebred can be measured against all of the dogs that in significant ways are thought to resemble it.

EXAMPLES OF ANALYTIC THINKING

Thinking, if broadly defined, must include intuitions and even idle reveries, but most of what we normally mean by serious thinking is analysis, classifying into categories and seeing how the

---

[1] The American Kennel Club's categories, though, are better than those given in an old Chinese encyclopedia, whose fourteen classifications of dogs (according to Jorge Luis Borges) include "those belonging to the Emperor," "stuffed dogs," "free-running dogs," "those getting madly excited," "those that look like flies from the distance," and "others." Equally zany were the labels on the five cells in the jail at Beaufort, Texas, a few decades ago: White Male, White Female, Colored Male, Colored Female, and U.S. Marines.

categories relate to each other. For example, if we turn our minds to thinking about punishment for killers, we will distinguish (probably after a good deal of listing and fiddling with the lists) at least between those killers whose actions are premeditated, and those killers whose actions are not. And in the first category we might distinguish between

1. professional killers who carefully contrive a death
2. killers who are irrational except in their ability to contrive a death, and
3. robbers who contrive a property crime and who kill only when they believe that killing is necessary in order to commit that crime.

One can hardly talk usefully about capital punishment or imprisonment without making some such analysis of killers. You have, then, taken killers and sorted or separated or classified them, not for the fun of inventing complications but for the sake of educating yourself and those persons with whom you discuss the topic. Unless your attitude is the mad Queen of Hearts's "Off with their heads," you will be satisfied with your conclusion only after you have tested it by dividing your topic into parts, each clearly distinguished from the others, and then showed how they are related.

A second example: if you think about examinations—especially if you think about them with the aid of pencil and paper—you may find that they can serve several purposes. Examinations may test knowledge, intelligence, or skill in taking examinations; or they may stimulate learning. Therefore, if you wish to discuss what constitutes a good examination, you must decide first what purpose an examination *should* serve. Possibly you will decide that in a particular course an examination should chiefly stimulate learning, but that it should also test the ability to reason. To arrive at a reasonable conclusion, a conclusion worth sharing, and if need be, defending, you must first recognize and sort out the several possibilities.

A third example of analytical thinking: In 1966, Congress, turning its attention to automobile safety, accused the automobile industry of lacking concern. In fact, the automobile industry had had a good record in three areas:

1. it had worked for safer highway engineering;
2. it had stimulated and supported interest in driver-education;
3. it had developed good procedures for detecting defects in cars on the assembly line.

The success of its efforts in these areas had been demonstrated by substantial reductions in the number of accidents on new or improved highways, and in the number of accidents caused by trained drivers.

Yet a problem remained: although the number of accidents per thousand miles driven had decreased, accidents of course still occurred, and in fact (since more people were driving more miles) the total number of accidents was increasing. It was plain that if the number of accidents was to be reduced, it would *not* be enough to

1. improve road conditions
2. educate drivers
3. eliminate defective automobiles.

Gradually—or, rather, suddenly in 1966—a new solution to reducing the number of accidents was conceived. Analytic thinking recognized a fourth reason why people were injured in automobiles: sound cars—cars without defects—were not adequate to withstand shocks when *im*properly driven. Given this perception, it was easy to propose a fourth method of reducing accidents:

4. build cars that withstand shocks even when improperly driven.

This all seems pretty obvious today, but it was a bold new idea, a conceptual leap, in the late 1960s. It represented, so to speak, a new way of looking at the problem.

Often the keenest analytic thinking considers not only what parts are in the whole, but what is *not* there—what is missing in relation to a larger context that we can imagine. The new solution to reducing the number of automobile accidents represented something of this sort of imaginative leap, but here is a neater example. If we analyze the women in the best-known fairy tales, we will find that most are either sleeping beauties or wicked step-mothers. These categories are general: "sleeping beauties" includes all passive women valued only for their appearance, and "wicked step-mothers" includes Cinderella's cruel older sisters. (Fairy godmothers form another category, but they are not human beings.) Analysis helps us to discover the almost total absence of resourceful, productive women. ("Almost total," rather than "total," because there are a few resourceful women in fairy tales, such as Gretel.) A thoughtful essay might begin with a general statement to this effect and then support the statement with an analysis of "Cinderella," "Little Red Riding Hood," and "Snow White."

ASKING QUESTIONS AS AN AID TO ANALYTIC THINKING

When we begin to think analytically about a topic, whether it is the appropriate treatment of killers, or ways of reducing automobile accidents, or the roles of women in fairy tales, we don't instantly see what the parts are and how we can separate and discuss them. Only when we get into the topic, perhaps by freewriting or by listing or mapping, do we begin to see the need for subtle distinctions. Remember, though, you can stimulate your ability to see distinctions (and thus to have ideas) by asking yourself questions:

1. To what group does it belong?
2. How do the parts work together?
3. To what may it usefully be compared or contrasted?
4. What are its uses, purposes, functions?
5. What are its causes—immediate causes and remote causes?
6. What are its consequences—immediate and ultimate?

An essay chiefly devoted to answering such questions is an analytic essay, though of course you may think analytically in preparation for some other kind of writing too. For example, a finished essay may be primarily narrative—a story, true or false. The process of analytic thinking will help you, as you move from rough notes and lists or outlines to drafts and further outlines, to decide what episodes to include, whether to give the episodes consecutively or to begin at the end and then use a flashback, whether to quote dialogue or to report it indirectly.

In this chapter, however, we are concerned chiefly with a process of analytic thinking that finally manifests itself in an analytic essay—that is, in an essay chiefly devoted to showing the reader how the parts of a topic are related or explaining how one part functions in relation to the whole.

ANALYSIS AND SUMMARY

Analysis should be clearly distinguished from summary. The word "summary" is related to "sum," the total something adds up to. (We say "adds *up* to" because the Greeks and Romans counted upward, and wrote the total at the top.)

A summary is a condensation or abridgement; it briefly gives the reader the gist of a longer work. Or, to change the figure, it boils down the longer work, resembling the longer work as a bouillion cube resembles a bowl of soup. A summary of Philip Roth's "On the Newark Public Library" (page 12) will reduce the essay; perhaps to a paragraph or two, perhaps even to a sentence. It will not call attention to Roth's various strategies, and it will not evaluate his argument; it will merely present the gist of what he says.

If, then, you are asked to write an analysis of something you have read, you should not hand in a summary. On the other hand, however, a very brief summary may appropriately appear within an analytic essay. Usually, in fact, the reader needs some information, and the writer of the essay will summarize this infomation briefly. For example, the student who wrote about Roth's essay is *summarizing* when she writes,

> Roth, in his article . . . argues that the closing of the libraries will be a costly mistake, and that the action will be an insult to the citizens of Newark,

She is summarizing because she is briefly reporting, without personal comment, what Roth said.

On the other hand, she is *analyzing* when she writes:

> By overdramatizing the possible reactions, Roth gains the interest of the reader.

In this sentence, the writer is not reporting *what* Roth said but is explaining *how* he achieved an effect.

Most of your writing about other writing will be chiefly analytical, but it will probably include (for the benefit of the reader) an occasional sentence or even a paragraph summarizing some of your reading. And part of your preparation for writing your essay may involve writing summaries as you take notes on the reading you are going to analyze. But if the assignment calls for an analysis, do not hand in a summary.

COMPARING

We have already said that writers often use comparison as an analytic tool. (Strictly speaking, if one emphasizes the differences rather than the similarities, one is contrasting rather than comparing, but it is common to call both processes "comparing.") Writers come to understand X (and then help their readers to understand it) by seeing how X resembles or differs from Y.

The point of a comparison is not to list similarities or differences but to illuminate. Notice in the following paragraph, written during World War II, how George Orwell clarifies our understanding of one kind of military march, the goose-step, by calling attention to how it differs from the march used by English soldiers. (Orwell might have contrasted the goose-step with the march used by American soldiers, but he was an Englishman writing for Englishmen. One of Orwell's allusions perhaps needs explanation today. The Vichy government was a puppet government installed in France by the Germans.)

> One rapid but fairly sure guide to the social atmosphere of a country is the parade-step of its army. A military parade is really a kind of ritual dance, something like a ballet, expressing a certain philosophy of life. The goose-step, for instance, is one of the most horrible sights in the world, far more terrifying than a dive-bomber. It is simply an affirmation of naked power; contained in it, quite consciously and intentionally, is the vision of a boot crashing down on a face. Its ugliness is part of its essence, for what it is saying is "Yes, I *am* ugly, and you daren't laugh at me," like the bully who makes faces at his victim. Why is the goose-step not used in En-

gland? There are, heaven knows, plenty of army officers who would be only too glad to introduce some such thing. It is not used because the people in the street would laugh. Beyond a certain point, military display is only possible in countries where the common people dare not laugh at the army. The Italians adopted the goose-step at about the time when Italy passed definitely under German control, and, as one would expect, they do it less well than the Germans. The Vichy government, if it survives, is bound to introduce a stiffer parade-ground discipline into what is left of the French army. In the British army the drill is rigid and complicated, full of memories of the eighteenth century, but without definite swagger; the march is merely a formalised walk. It belongs to a society which is ruled by the sword, no doubt, but a sword which must never be taken out of the scabbard.

> — George Orwell,
> "England, Your England"

An essay may be devoted entirely to a comparison, say of two kinds of tribal organization, but even an essay that is not devoted entirely to a comparison may include a paragraph or two of comparison, for example to explain something unfamiliar by comparing it to something familiar. Let's spend a moment discussing how to organize a paragraph that makes a comparison—though the same principles can be applied to entire essays.

The first part may announce the topic, the next part may discuss one of the two items being compared, and the last part may discuss the other. We can call this method *lumping,* because it presents one item in a lump, and then the other in another lump. Or the discussion of the two items may run throughout the paragraph, the writer perhaps devoting alternate sentences to each. We can call this method *splitting,* for obvious reasons. Because almost all writing is designed to help the reader to see what the writer has in mind, it may be especially useful here to illustrate this second structure, splitting, with a discussion of visible distinctions. The following comparison of a Japanese statue of a Buddha with a Chinese statue of a bodhisattva (a slightly lower spiritual being, dedicated to saving humankind) shows how a comparison can run throughout a paragraph.

The Buddha sits erect and austere, in the lotus position (legs crossed, each foot with the sole upward on the opposite thigh), in full con-

*Sakyamuni Buddha (wood, 33½"; Japanese, late tenth
century).*

trol of his body. The carved folds of his garment, equally severe,
form a highly disciplined pattern. The more earthly bodhisattva wears
naturalistically carved flowing garments, and sits in a languid, sensuous posture known as "royal ease," the head pensively tilted
downward, one knee elevated, one leg hanging down. Both figures
are spiritual but the Buddha is remote, constrained, and austere;
the bodhisattva is accessible, relaxed, and compassionate.

Notice, by the way, that although this paragraph on two
images is chiefly devoted to offering an analysis, it also offers a

Bodhisattva Kuan Yin (wood, 56½"; Chinese, twelfth century).

synthesis (literally, a combining of separate elements to form a coherent whole). That is, the analytic discussion of the Buddha calls attention to its posture and its garments, but it also brings these elements together, seeing the figure as "remote, constrained, austere." Similarly, the discussion of the bodhisattva calls attention to the posture and garments, and synthesizes these, or brings them together, by characterizing the image as "accessible, relaxed, compassionate." And notice, finally, that the paragraph brings the two images together, characterizing both as "spiritual."

Ways of Organizing Short Comparisons

Comparisons, we have said, are usually organized either by lumping or by splitting. Writers *lump* when they discuss all, or almost all, of one item at once—in a lump, so to speak—and then go on to discuss all, or almost all, of the second in another lump. On the other hand, writers *split* when they keep moving back and forth between the two things compared, so that the paragraph resembles a seven-layer cake. The paragraph comparing the two Buddhist sculptures illustrates splitting. An outline of that paragraph might look like this:

The Buddha
   cranial bump
   robe and unadorned head
The bodhisattva
   rich garment
   crown
The Buddha
   color
The bodhisattva
   color
The Buddha
   pose
   carving of garment
The bodhisattva
   pose
   carving of garment
Summary of the two figures

Since the paragraph is fairly short, and it makes only a few points, and none of the points is especially hard to grasp, you probably had little or no difficulty keeping all of the material in mind. But there is a danger; a writer who splits rather than lumps, and who goes on for a long time, may fail to convey an overall view and therefore may confuse rather than clarify. It's impossible to say exactly how long "a long time" is, but let's think about a paragraph somewhat longer than the one on the two sculptures.

An orange grown in Florida usually has a thin and tightly fitting skin, and it is also heavy with juice. Californians say that if you want to eat a Florida orange you have to get into a bathtub first. California oranges are light in weight and have thick skins that break easily and come off in hunks. The flesh inside is marvelously sweet, and the segments almost separate themselves. In Florida, it is said that you can run over a California orange with a ten-ton truck and not even wet the pavement. The differences from which these hyperboles arise will prevail in the two states even if the type of orange is the same. In arid climates, like California's, oranges develop a thick albedo, which is the white part of the skin. Florida is one of the two or three most rained-upon states in the United States. California uses the Colorado River and similarly impressive sources to irrigate its oranges, but of course irrigation can only do so much. The annual difference in rainfall between the Florida and California orange-growing areas is one million one hundred and forty thousand gallons per acre. For years, California was the leading orange state, but Florida surpassed California in 1942, and grows three times as many oranges now. California oranges, for their part, can safely be called three times as beautiful.

— John McPhee,
Oranges

The passage is interesting, but so much information is given, and in so zig-zagging a way, that a reader may find it difficult to absorb and keep straight all of these facts about two kinds of oranges. Without looking back, do you recall which orange has the thicker skin? And which orange has segments that almost separate themselves? If you are from California or Florida you probably know the answers, but it's our guess that most readers of McPhee's paragraph do not emerge with a complete idea about either kind of orange. In short, one may ask if perhaps lumping would not have been better than splitting.

An outline of McPhee's paragraph, in its present form, might look like this:

Florida orange: thin skin; heavy juice

California orange: light weight, thick skin, sweet flesh, not especially juicy

California: arid, hence thick albedo (white)

Florida: lots of rain

California: irrigation, but limited effect

Florida and California: amount of rainfall

Florida and California: number of oranges

California and Florida: beauty of oranges

Somewhat surprisingly, in making a point about, say, California oranges, McPhee does not always comment on the comparable point in Florida oranges. For instance, he tells us that the segments of a California orange "almost separate themselves," but he does not say anything about the segments of Florida oranges, and so the point is not present in our outline.

If you *really* wanted to know about these two kinds of oranges—say you were going to buy a crate of one kind or the other—would you want to read an account that kept splitting? Might you not prefer to be told first about one kind, as fully as possible, so you could get it firmly in mind, and then to be told about how the second kind differs?

Further, although admittedly we have given only an extract from McPhee's book, one might well ask, What is the *point* of his comparison? Perhaps if we grasped his point, his thesis, all of the details would fall into place. But is his point that one kind of orange is better for eating whereas the other kind is better for drinking? Or that even though most people prefer Florida oranges, *he* likes California oranges because of their physical appearance? This second guess perhaps is right, since he ends the paragraph by saying that California oranges are "three times as beautiful" as Florida oranges. Obviously if McPhee had adopted and kept in view a thesis such as either of these, he would have written a somewhat different paragraph. But putting aside the issue of whether the paragraph needs a more evident thesis, let's rewrite the paragraph, lumping instead of splitting, in order to see if lumping makes it clearer. We'll try to stay as close to McPhee's points as possible, so the two paragraphs can easily be compared, though we will give the thesis (California oranges are preferable) a little more weight than McPhee gives it. An outline of the alternate version might look like this:

Two kinds of oranges
Florida: more numerous oranges; rainy climate;
        juicy, thin-skinned oranges
California: arid climate;
        thick albedo, less juicy;
        sweet, beautiful

Now for the lumped version of McPhee's paragraph:

Florida and California both produce oranges, but since 1942 Florida has outproduced California, and today grows three times as many oranges as California does. Florida oranges are not only more numerous but, because Florida is one of the two or three most-rained upon states in the United States, they are far juicier than California oranges, even if the type of orange is the same as that grown in California. A Florida orange, heavy with juice, usually has a thin and tightly fitting skin. A California orange, even though irrigated by the Colorado River, will weigh less, be less juicy, and will have a thick albedo (the white part of the skin) that breaks easily and comes off in hunks. Can nothing be said in behalf of the California orange? The flesh of the California orange, though less juicy, is marvelously sweet, and the segments almost separate themselves. Florida may grow three times as many oranges, but California oranges can safely be called three times as beautiful.

As we mentioned, in this rewriting we have tried to stay pretty close to McPhee, touching on almost all of his points. (The remarks about getting into a bathtub and about running over an orange with a ten-ton truck are deliberately omitted. Is the omission a loss?) You may want to try your hand at rewriting the paragraph more freely, lumping rather than splitting, adopting whatever thesis you wish, and adding whatever details you wish.

    Whether in any given piece of writing you should compare by lumping or by splitting will depend largely on your purpose and on the complexity of the material. We can't even offer the rule that splitting is good for brief, relatively obvious comparisons, lumping for longer, more complex ones, though such a rule usually works. We can, however, give some advice:

1. If you split, in re-reading your draft
   (a) *imagine your reader,* and ask yourself if it is likely that this reader can keep up with the back-and-forth movement. Make sure (perhaps by a summary sentence at the end) that the larger picture is not obscured by the zig-zagging;
   (b) *don't leave any loose ends.* Make sure, as we mentioned earlier, that if you call attention to points 1, 2, and 3 in X, you mention all of them (not just 1 and 2) in Y.
2. If you lump, do not simply comment first on X and then on Y.
   (a) *Let your reader know where you are going,* probably by means of an introductory sentence;
   (b) *Don't be afraid in the second half to remind the reader of the first half.* It is legitimate, and even desirable, to relate the second half of the comparison to the first half. A comparison organized by lumping will not break into two separate halves if the second half develops by reminding the reader how it differs from the first half.

Longer Comparisons

Now let's think about a comparison that extends through two or three paragraphs. If one is comparing the indoor play and the sports of girls with those of boys, one can, for example, devote a paragraph to girls, and then a separate paragraph to boys. The paragraphs will probably be connected by beginning the second one with "Boys, on the other hand," or some such transitional expression. But one can also devote a paragraph to indoor play (girls and boys), and a separate paragraph to sports (again girls and boys). There is no rule, except that the organization and the point of the comparison be clear.

Consider these paragraphs from an essay by Sheila Tobias on the fear of mathematics. The writer's thesis in the essay is that although this fear is more commonly found in females than in males, biology seems not to be the cause. After discussing some findings (for example, that girls compute better than boys in elementary school, and that many girls tend to lose interest in mathematics in junior high school) the writer turns her attention away from the schoolhouse. Notice that whether a paragraph is chiefly about boys or chiefly about girls, the writer keeps us in mind of the overall point: reasons why more females than males fear math.

> Not all the skills that are necessary for learning mathematics are learned in school. Measuring, computing, and manipulating objects that have dimensions and dynamic properties of their own are part of the everyday life of children. Children who miss out on these experiences may not be well primed for math in school.
>
> Feminists have complained for a long time that playing with dolls is one way of convincing impressionable little girls that they may only be mothers or housewives—or, as in the case of the Barbie doll, "pinup girls"—when they grow up. But doll-playing may have even more serious consequences for little girls than that. Do girls find out about gravity and distance and shapes and sizes playing with dolls? Probably not.
>
> A curious boy, if his parents are tolerant, will have taken apart a number of household and play objects by the time he is ten, and, if his parents are lucky, he may even have put them back together again. In all of this he is learning things that will be useful in physics and math. Taking parts out that have to go back in requires some examination of form. Building something that stays up or at least stays put for some time involves working with structure.
>
> Sports is another source of math-related concepts for children which tends to favor boys. Getting to first base on a not very well hit grounder is a lesson in time, speed, and distance. Intercepting a football thrown through the air requires some rapid intuitive eye calculations based on the ball's direction, speed, and trajectory. Since physics is partly concerned with velocities, trajectories, and collisions of objects, much of the math taught to prepare a student for physics deals with relationships and formulas that can be used to express motion and acceleration.

The first paragraph offers a generalization about "children," that is, about boys and girls. The second paragraph discusses the play of girls with dolls, but discusses it in a context of its relevance, really irrelevance, to mathematics. The third paragraph discusses the household play of boys, again in the context of mathematics. The fourth paragraph discusses the outdoor sports of boys, but notice that girls are not forgotten, for its first sentence is "Sports is another source of math-related concepts for children which tends to favor boys." In short, even when there is a sort of seesaw structure, boys on one end and girls on the other, we never lose sight of the thesis that comprises both halves of the comparison.

Ways of Organizing an Essay Devoted to a Comparison

Let's now talk about organizing a comparison or contrast that runs through an entire essay, say a comparison between two political campaigns, or between the characters in two novels. Remember, first of all, one writes such a comparison not as an exercise, but in order to make a point, let's say to demonstrate the superiority of X to Y.

Probably your first thoughts, after making some jottings, will be to lump rather than to split, that is, to discuss one half of the comparison and then to go on to the second half. We'll discuss this useful method of organization in a moment, but here we want to point out that many instructors and textbooks disapprove of such an organization, arguing that the essay too often breaks into two parts and that the second part involves a good deal of repetition of categories set up in the first part. They prefer splitting. Let's say you are comparing the narrator of *Huckleberry Finn* with the narrator of *The Catcher in the Rye,* in order to show that despite superficial similarities, they are very different, and that the difference is partly the difference between the nineteenth century and the twentieth. An organization often recommended is something like this:

1. first similarity (the narrator and his quest)
   a. Huck
   b. Holden
2. second similarity (the corrupt world surrounding the narrator)
   a. society in *Huckleberry Finn*
   b. society in *The Catcher in the Rye*
3. first difference (degree to which the narrator fulfills his quest and escapes from society)
   a. Huck's plan to "light out" to the frontier
   b. Holden's breakdown

And so on, for as many additional differences as seem relevant. Here is another way of splitting and organizing a comparison:

1. first point: the narrator and his quest
    a. similarities between Huck and Holden
    b. differences between Huck and Holden
2. second point: the corrupt world
    a. similarities between the worlds in *Huck* and *The Catcher*
    b. differences between the worlds in *Huck* and *The Catcher*
3. third point: degree of success
    a. similarities between Huck and Holden
    b. differences between Huck and Holden

But a comparison need not employ either of these methods of splitting. There is even the danger that an essay employing either of them may not come into focus until the essayist stands back from the seven-layer cake and announces, in the concluding paragraph, that the odd layers taste better. In one's preparatory thinking one may want to make comparisons in pairs, but one must come to some conclusions about what these add up to before writing the final version. The final version should not duplicate the thought processes; rather, it should be organized so as to make the point (formulated in a thesis sentence) clearly and effectively. The point of the essay is not to list pairs of similarities or differences, but to illuminate a topic by making thoughtful comparisons. Although in a long essay one cannot postpone until page 30 a discussion of the second half of the comparison, in an essay of, say, fewer than ten pages, nothing is wrong with setting forth half of the comparison and then, in the light of what you've already said, discussing the second half. True, an essay that uses lumping will break into two unrelated parts if the second half makes no use of the first or fails to modify it; but the essay will hang together if the second half looks back to the first half and calls attention to differences that the new material reveals.

The danger of organizing the essay into two unrelated lumps can be avoided if in formulating your thesis you remember that the point of a comparison is to call attention to the unique features of something by holding it up against something similar but significantly different. If the differences are great and apparent, a comparison is a waste of effort. ("Blueberries are different from elephants. Blueberries do not have trunks. And elephants do not grow on bushes.") Indeed, a comparison between essentially and evidently unlike things can only obscure, for by making the comparison the writer implies there are significant similarities, and readers can only wonder why they do not see them. The essays that do break into two halves are essays that make uninstructive comparisons: the first half tells the reader five things about baseball, the second half tells the reader five unrelated things about football.

A NOTE ON ANALOGY

An analogy explains something by calling attention to its resemblances, point by point, to something *fundamentally different.* Here is a brief example:

> The atom is like a miniature solar system: electrons revolve around a nucleus the way planets orbit the sun.

Or consider the old analogy comparing a government in time of stress to a ship in a storm: the captain corresponds to the monarch, the officers correspond to aristocrats with political power; the crew corresponds to the general public, which must do as it is told. If the ship is to get through stormy weather (wartime, or a famine), the crew must obey the captain. (We are not here concerned with the value of this analogy as a strong argument; we are concerned only with explaining what an analogy is.)

Two additional points:

1. McPhee's comparison of a Florida orange with a California orange (page 65) is *not* an analogy, because the things compared are fundamentally of the same nature.
2. Strictly, an analogy calls attention to several points of resemblance, but the word is often loosely used for any comparison between things that are fundamentally unlike. Thus, the saying that "You don't change horses in midstream" may be called an analogy, even though the speaker does not offer explicit equivalents for the stream and the horses and the rider.

The point of an analogy, like the point of most other comparisons, is to clarify; the unfamiliar is explained in the light of the familiar. Thus, as we saw a moment ago, a writer may compare the atom to a solar system, on the assumption that the reader who has no knowledge about the atom may have at least a little knowledge about the solar system.

But an analogy may serve a second purpose, adding a pleasant homely note, a reassuring touch of the ordinary world in writing that otherwise might seem remote. For instance, an insurance company which deals with disasters and their statistical probability seeks to make itself agreeable by saying that it offers "an umbrella for a rainy day."

And now for a third point, which will seem to contradict much that we have already said about analogy making things easy: an analogy may go the other way, adding an interesting complication, making the familiar seem a bit unfamiliar.

Consider this passage:

> Tracking the career of Woody Allen is exhausting but exhilarating, like mountain climbing. Just when you reach the top, another peak appears. At the same time, the terrain below—through which you've passed and which you think you know—seems to change, taking on unexpected contours and colors that can only be seen from the new plateau. Some earlier peaks look small. Others cast surprisingly long shadows. The only constant is that you're in a land not quite like any other.
>
> — Vincent Canby

Canby might simply have said that with each new work, Woody Allen makes us re-examine his entire career. His analogy between keeping an eye on Woody Allen and climbing mountains, however, clarifies for us his sense that Woody Allen's work is vast, something to be explored, a unique, changing territory, and so forth. Still, it must be admitted that Canby's analogy (which was the opening paragraph of a newspaper review of a film) serves more to arouse interest than to explain the unfamiliar by comparing it to the familiar. After all, most readers of his review probably were more familiar with Woody Allen's films than they were with mountain climbing.

A CHECKLIST FOR
REVISING COMPARISONS:

1. Is the point of the comparison—your reason for making it—clear?
2. Do you cover all significant similarities and differences?
3. Is the passage readable, that is, is it clear and yet not tediously

mechanical? ("*A* is, *B* is. Moreover *A* is, whereas *B* is," is clear, but numbing.)
4. Is lumping or is splitting (see page 61) the best way to make this comparison?
5. If you are offering a value judgment, is it fair? Have you over-looked weaknesses in your preferred subject, and strengths in your less preferred subject?

EXPLAINING AN ANALYSIS

As we have suggested, the writer of an analytical essay arrives at a thesis by asking questions and answering them, by separating the topic into parts and by seeing—often through the use of lists and scratch outlines—how those parts relate. Or, we might say, analytic writing presupposes detective work: the writer looks over the evidence, finds some clues, pursues the trail from one place to the next, and makes the arrest. Elementary? Perhaps. Let's observe a famous detective at work.

The Science of Deduction
Arthur Conan Doyle

"I wonder what that fellow is looking for?" I asked, pointing to a stalwart, plainly dressed individual who was walking slowly down the other side of the street, looking anxiously at the numbers. He had a large blue envelope in his hand, and was evidently the bearer of a message.

"You mean the retired sergeant of Marines," said Sherlock Holmes.

"Brag and bounce!" thought I to myself. "He knows that I cannot verify his guess."

The thought had hardly passed through my mind when the man whom we were watching caught sight of the number on our door, and ran rapidly across the roadway. We heard a loud knock, a deep voice below, and heavy steps ascending the stair.

"For Mr. Sherlock Holmes," he said, stepping into the room and handing my friend the letter.

Here was an opportunity of taking the conceit out of him. He little thought of this when he made that random shot. "May I ask, my lad," I said, in the blandest voice, "what your trade may be?"

"Commissionaire, sir," he said, gruffly. "Uniform away for repairs."

"And you were?" I asked; with a slightly malicious glance at my companion.

"A sergeant, sir, Royal Marine Light Infantry, sir. No answer? Right, sir."

He clicked his heels together, raised his hand in salute, and was gone.

I confess that I was considerably startled by this fresh proof of the practical nature of my companion's theories. My respect for his powers of analysis increased wondrously. There still remained some lurking suspicion in my mind, however, that the whole thing was a prearranged episode, intended to dazzle me, though what earthly object he could have in taking me in was past my comprehension. When I looked at him, he had finished reading the note, and his eyes has assumed the vacant, lack-lustre expression which showed mental abstraction.

"How in the world did you deduce that?" I asked.

"Deduce what?" said he, petulantly.

"Why, that he was a retired sergeant of Marines."

"I have no time for trifles," he answered, brusquely; then with a smile, "Excuse my rudeness. You broke the thread of my thoughts; but perhaps it is as well. So you actually were not able to see that that man was a sergeant of Marines?"

"No, indeed."

"It was easier to know it than to explain why I know it. If you were asked to prove that two and two made four, you might find some difficulty, and yet you are quite sure of the fact. Even across the street I could see a great blue anchor tattooed on the back of the fellow's hand. That smacked of the sea. He had a military carriage, however, and regulation side whiskers. There we have the marine. He was a man with some amount of self-importance and a certain air of command. You must have observed the way in which he held his head and swung his cane. A steady, respectable, middle-aged man, too, on he face of him—all facts which led me to believe that he had been a sergeant."

"Wonderful!" I ejaculated.

"Commonplace," said Holmes, though I thought from his expression that he was pleased at my evident surprise and admiration.

— From *A Study in Scarlet*

Even when, as a writer, after preliminary thinking you have solved a problem, that is, focused on a topic and formulated a thesis, you are, as we have said before, not yet done. It is, alas, not enough simply to present the results of your analytical thinking to a reader who, like Dr. Watson, will surely want to know "How in the world did you deduce that?" And like Holmes, writers are often impatient; we long to say with him "I have no time for trifles." But the real reason for our impatience is, as Holmes is quick to acknowledge, that "It was easier to know it than to explain why I know it." But explaining to readers why or how, presenting both the reasoning that led to a thesis and the evidence that supports the reasoning, is the writer's job.

In your preliminary detective work (that is, in reading, taking notes, musing, jotting down some thoughts, and writing rough drafts) some insights (perhaps including your thesis) may come swiftly, apparently spontaneously, and in random order. You may be unaware that you have been thinking analytically at all. In preparing your essay for your reader, however, you become aware, in part because you must become aware. You must persuade *your* Dr. Watson that what you say is not "brag and bounce," to replace your reader's natural suspicion with respect for your analysis (and for yourself), you must, we repeat, explain your reasoning in an orderly and interesting fashion and you must present your evidence.

In the hypothetical example on pages 9–10, we showed a writer of an essay musing over the frequency of the motif of travel in the blues. Perhaps, we imagined, those musings were triggered by a few lines he happened to remember, or to hear. The writer then began to ask himself questions, to listen to some records, to jot down some notes. His thesis (which turned out to be that themes of travel are a metaphor for the trip through life) might have been formulated only in a late draft. But it might easily have occurred to the writer much earlier. Perhaps the thesis came almost simultaneously with the writer's first musings. But no matter when or how he arrived at a conclusion interesting enough to offer as the thesis of an essay, he still had the job of explaining to his reader (and perhaps to himself) how he had arrived at it. He probably had to examine his own thought processes carefully—replaying them in slow motion to see each part separately. He would certainly have had to marshal some evidence from available books and records. And he would have had to arrange the parts of his analysis and the supporting evidence clearly and interestingly to demonstrate the accuracy of his conclusion to a reader who knew less about the blues than he did.

To turn to another example, notice how Jeff Greenfield, on pages 88–91, solves and presents his case, one involving another famous detective. We will never know in what order the thoughts leading to his thesis came to him. But we can observe how Greenfield organized and supported his analysis. How can we do this? Elementary. By asking questions and answering them.

EXERCISES

1. Analyze the seating patterns in a cafeteria or other public room. Are groups, including groups of empty chairs, perceptible? If you perceive groups (classifications), specify them, and if possible draw inferences about the people who form these groups.
2. Look over the birthday cards in a store. What images of girls and women are presented? Are they stereotyped images of passivity and domesticity? If such images predominate, what exceptions are there? Do the exceptions fall into categories? What images of boys and men are presented? Are they stereotyped images of vigor and authority? Again, if there are exceptions, do they form a pattern? Are certain kinds of images conspicuous by their absence? (After you have studied the rack for a while, and jotted down some notes, you may

find it useful to buy two or three cards, so that when you
write your essay—of 500–1000 words—you will have some
evidence at hand.)

3. With the general reader in mind, write an essay of 500 words
analyzing why people have pets.

4. Write an essay of not more than three paragraphs analyzing
the functions of one of the following:
credit-noncredit grading
a minor character in a TV series
the death penalty
the preface to this book
the Twenty-fifth Amendment to the Constitution

5. It is often said that television has had a bad effect on sports.
If you believe this, write an essay of 500–1000 words setting
forth these effects.

6. In a paragraph analyze the appeals of an advertisement. An
advertisement for a book club may, for example, appeal both
to snobbism and to frugality; an advertisement for a cigarette
may appeal to vanity, and perhaps also to reason, by giving
statistics about the relatively low amount of tar. If possible,
include a copy of the advertisement with your paper.

7. An aunt has offered to buy you a subscription to *Time* or
Newsweek. Compare in about 500 words the contents of the
current issues and explain which magazine you prefer. (If neither magazine is of interest, try comparing *Sport* and *Sports
Illustrated* or *Cosmopolitan* and *Ms.*)

8. Compare baseball with hockey or soccer as a sport suitable
for television. Consider the visual appeals of the sports, the
pace—including the degree to which the camera operator can
predict the action and thus follow it with the camera, the
opportunity for replays and for close-ups—and anything else
you think relevant.

9. Compare the function of the setting in *The Tonight Show*
with *Saturday Night Live*.

10. Write a paragraph comparing a magazine advertisement of
the 1990s with a counterpart of the 1950s. (You can easily
find ads for cars and cigarettes in old copies of *Time* and
Newsweek in your library.) How are the appeals similar and

Sitting Bull and Buffalo Bill, 1885.

how are they different? Include copies of the advertisements with your paper.

11. The photograph above of Sitting Bull and Buffalo Bill was taken in 1885 by William McFarlane Notman. Reread the discussion of Brueghel's drawing on page 53, and then write two or three paragraphs describing and analyzing this photograph, paying special attention to the contrasting poses, expressions, and costumes. (Reading brief biographical accounts of Buffalo Bill [William Frederick Cody] and Sitting Bull will help you to understand the photograph. Append a

Photographer unknown. Picasso's Son Paul on a Donkey, *c. 1923. S.P.A.D.E.M., Paris/V.A.G.A., New York, 1985.*

list of "Works Cited" to your paper, and document where appropriate. See pages 382–96.)

12. Reread the discussion of Brueghel's drawing on page 53, and of the comparison on pages 61–62, and then write a paragraph comparing the photograph of Picasso's son Paul with the painting that Picasso made from it in 1923. Imagine your audience as visitors to a Picasso exhibition at a museum, reading a label on the wall next to the two works.

13. Study the two drawings (pp. 82–83) by Francisco Goya (1746–1828), entitled "El amor y la muerte" (Love and

Pablo Picasso. Paul, Son of the Artist. 1923. Gouache, 40 × 52 inches. S.P.A.D.E.M., Paris/V.A.G.A., New York, 1985.

Death). They show a woman holding a dying lover, who has fought a duel for her. The first version, at left, is a watercolor; the revision is in chalk. Write a brief essay of one to three paragraphs comparing them.

Woman Holding Up Her Dying Lover. Francisco de
Goya y Lucientes. Spanish, 1746–1828. Brush and gray
wash, touched with brown wash. 9¼ × 5¹¹⁄₁₆ in.
(234 × 145 mm). Gift of Frederick J. Kennedy Memorial
Foundation. 1973. 700b. Courtesy, Museum of Fine
Arts, Boston.

Francisco de Goya y Lucientes, *El amor y la muerte*.
Courtesy, Museo del Prado, Madrid.

Robert Frank. Covered Car—Long Beach, California, 1956.

Walker Evans. Westchester, New York, Farm House, 1931.

14. Assume that photographs say something. Compare what the two photographs on page 84 say.

15. Read the New Testament parable below (Luke 10:29–36), and then answer the questions that follow. In answering the questions, you may wish to consult the following sources: Luke 10:25–28; *The Interpreter's Bible;* a dictionary; an historical atlas.

But [a certain lawyer], willing to justify himself, said unto Jesus, "And who is my neighbor?"

And Jesus answering said, "A certain man went down from Jerusalem to Jericho, and fell among thieves, which stripped him of his raiment, and wounded him, and departed, leaving him half dead. And by chance there came down a certain priest that way: and when he saw him, he passed by on the other side. And likewise a Levite, when he was at the place, came and looked on him, and passed by on the other side. But a certain Samaritan, as he journeyed, came where he was: and when he saw him, he had compassion on him, and went to him, and bound up his wounds, pouring in oil and wine, and set him on his own beast, and brought him to an inn, and took care of him. And on the morrow when he departed, he took out two pence, and gave them to the host, and said unto him, 'Take care of him; and whatsoever thou spendest more, when I come again, I will repay thee.' Which now of these three, thinkest thou, was neighbor unto him that fell among the thieves?"

And he said, "He that showed mercy on him."

Then said Jesus unto him, "Go, and do thou likewise."

  a. Explain the context of the parable: To whom does Jesus tell it, and under what circumstances? (See Luke 10:25–28.)
  b. What is the distance between Jerusalem and Jericho? In a sentence or two, describe what you imagine to be conditions of travel in that place at the time of the parable.
  c. What position did a priest hold among the Jews? A Levite?
  d. What was the relationship between Samaritans and Jews?
  e. A parable instructs us in our behavior through a comparison (the word "parable" derives from a Greek word meaning to stand beside, to persuade). To whom are we to compare ourselves? Which characters suggest our habitual behavior? Which character suggests the ideal toward which we should strive.? Which character suggests the ideal toward which we should strive?
  f. Jesus says, "Go, and do thou likewise." Explain in your own words what we are to do.

16. Analyze the following two accounts of Sitting Bull's life from the *Encyclopaedia Britannica*. The first is from the 11th edition, published in 1911; the second from the 15th edition, published in 1974. Write an essay of approximately 750 words comparing the two entries. Your essay should have a thesis formulating for your reader the chief differences between the entries. How might the contrast between the two entries be explained or accounted for?

SITTING BULL (*c.* 1837–1890), a chief and medicine man of the Dakota Sioux, was born on Willow Creek in what is now North Dakota about 1837, son of a chief named Jumping Bull. He gained great influence among the reckless and unruly young Indians, and during the Civil War led attacks on white settlements in Iowa and Minnesota. Though he had pretended to make peace in 1866, from 1869 to 1876 he frequently attacked whites or Indians friendly to whites. His refusal to return to the reservation in 1876, led to the campaign in which General George A. Custer and his command were massacred. Fearing punishment for his participation in the massacre, Sitting Bull with a large band moved over into Canada. He returned to the United States in 1881, and after 1883 made his home at the Standing Rock Agency. Rumours of a coming Indian Messiah who should sweep away the whites, and Indian dissatisfaction at the sale of their lands, created such great unrest in Dakota in 1889–1890 that it was determined to arrest Sitting Bull as a precaution. He was surprised and captured by Indian police and soldiers on Grand river on the 15th of December 1890, and was killed while his companions were attempting to rescue him.

— *Encyclopaedia Brittannica*
11th Edition, 1911

Sitting Bull, Indian name TATANKA IYOTAKE (b. *c.* 1831 near Grand River, Dakota Territory, U.S.—d. Dec. 15, 1890, on the Grand River in South Dakota), Teton Dakota Indian chief under whom the Sioux tribes united in their struggle for survival on the North American Great Plains. Proud and haughty, he is remembered for his lifelong distrust of white men and his stubborn determination to resist alien domination.

Born into the Hunkpapa Sioux—a nomadic and warlike tribe— Sitting Bull early in life became a leader of the powerful Strong Heart warrior society and, later, a participant in the Silent Eaters, a select group concerned with tribal welfare. His first skirmish with white soldiers occurred in June 1863 during the U.S. Army's retaliation against the Santee Sioux after the "Minnesota Massacre," in which the Teton Sioux had no part. For the next five years he was in frequent hostile contact with the Army, which was invading the Sioux hunting grounds and bringing ruin to the Indian economy. Respected for his courage and wisdom, he was made principal chief of the entire Sioux nation in about 1867.

When gold was discovered in the Black Hills in the mid-1870s, a rush of prospectors invaded lands guaranteed to the Indians by the Second Treaty of Ft. Laramie (1868). Late in 1875 all Sioux were ordered to settle on reservations by Jan. 31, 1876, or be considered hostile to the United States. Even had Sitting Bull been willing to comply, he could not possibly have moved his village 240 miles (390 kilometres) in the bitter cold by the specified time.

In March Gen. George Crook took the field against the hostiles, and Sitting Bull responded by summoning the Sioux, Cheyenne, and certain Arapaho to his camp in Montana Territory. There on June 17 Crook's troops were forced to retreat in the Battle of the Rosebud. The Indian chiefs then moved their encampment into the valley of the Little Bighorn River. At this point Sitting Bull performed the Sun Dance, and when he emerged from a trance induced by self-torture, he reported that he had seen soldiers falling into his camp like grasshoppers from the sky. His prophecy was fulfilled on June 25, when Lt. Col. George Armstrong Custer rode into the valley and he and all the men under his immediate command were annihilated.

Strong public reaction among whites to the Battle of the Little Bighorn resulted in stepped-up military action. The Sioux emerged the victors in their battles with U.S. troops, but though they might win battle after battle, they could never win the war. They depended on the buffalo for their livelihood, and the buffalo, under the steady encroachment of whites, were rapidly becoming extinct. Hunger led more and more Sioux to surrender, and in May 1877 Sitting Bull led his remaining followers across the border into Canada. But the Canadian government could not acknowledge responsibility for feeding a people whose reservation was south of the border, and after four years, during which his following dwindled steadily, famine forced Sitting Bull to surrender. After 1883 he lived at the Standing Rock Agency, where he vainly opposed the sale of tribal lands. In 1885, partly to get rid of him, the Indian agent allowed him to join Buffalo Bill's Wild West show, in which he gained international fame.

Beginning about 1889, the spread of the Ghost Dance religious movement prophesying the advent of an Indian messiah who would sweep away the whites and restore former traditions augmented the unrest already stirred among the Sioux by hunger and disease. As a precaution, Indian police and soldiers were sent to arrest the chief. Seized on Grand River, Dec. 15, 1890, Sitting Bull was killed while his warriors were trying to rescue him. He was buried at Ft. Yates, but his remains were moved in 1953 to Mobridge, S.D., where a granite shaft marks his resting place.

Sitting Bull appears to have had qualities of leadership that were not common among Plains Indians. Among the Sioux he was admired as a loving father of his people, a singer of songs, a man always affable and pleasant in manner and devoutly religious, and a prophet whose prayers were strong.

Two biographies include Stanley Vestal's *Sitting Bull, Champion of the Sioux* (1932) and F. B. Fiske's *Life and Death of Sitting Bull* (1932).

— *Encyclopaedia Brittanica*
15th Edition, 1974

ANALYSIS AT WORK

Columbo Knows the Butler Didn't Do It
Jeff Greenfield

1   The popularity of *Columbo* is as intense as it is puzzling. Dinner parties are adjourned, trips to movies postponed, and telephone calls hastily concluded ("It's starting now, I gotta go." "Migod, it's 8:40, what did I miss?"), all for a detective show that tells us whodunit, howhedunit, and whyhedunit all before the first commercial.

2   Why? Peter Falk's characterization is part of the answer of course; he plays Lieutenant Columbo with sleepy-eyed, slow-footed, crazy-like-a-fox charm. But shtick—even first-class shtick—goes only so far. Nor is it especially fascinating to watch Columbo piece together clues that are often telegraphed far in advance. No, there is

something else which gives *Columbo* a special appeal—something almost never seen on commercial television. That something is a strong, healthy dose of class antagonism. The one constant in *Columbo* is that, with every episode, a working-class hero brings to justice a member of America's social and economic elite.

3   The homicide files in Columbo's office must contain the highest per-capita income group of any criminals outside of antitrust law. We never see a robber shooting a grocery store owner out of panic or savagery; there are no barroom quarrels settled with a Saturday Night Special; no murderous shoot-outs between drug dealers or numbers runners. The killers in Columbo's world are art collectors, surgeons, high-priced lawyers, sports executives, a symphony conductor of Bernsteinian charisma—even a world chess champion. They are rich and white (if Columbo ever does track down a black killer, it will surely be a famous writer or singer or athlete or politician).

4   *Columbo's* villains are not simply rich; they are privileged. They live the lives that are for most of us hopeless daydreams: houses on top of mountains, with pools, servants, and sliding doors; parties with women in slinky dresses, and endless food and drink; plush, enclosed box seats at professional sports events; the envy and admiration of the Crowd. While we choose between Johnny Carson and *Invasion of the Body-Snatchers,* they are at screenings of movies the rest of us wait in line for on Third Avenue three months later.

5   Into the lives of these privileged rich stumbles Lieutenant Columbo—a dweller in another world. His suspects are Los Angeles paradigms: sleek, shiny, impeccably dressed, tanned by the omnipresent sun. Columbo, on the other hand, appears to have been plucked from Queens Boulevard by helicopter, and set down an instant later in Topanga Canyon. His hair is tousled, not styled and sprayed. His chin is pale and stubbled. He has even forgotten to take off his raincoat, a garment thoroughly out of place in Los Angeles eight months of the year. Columbo is also unabashedly stunned by and envious of the life style of his quarry.

6   "Geez, that is some car," he tells the symphony conductor. "Ya know, I'll bet that car costs more than I make in a year."

7   "Say, can I ask you something personal?" he says to a suspect wearing $50 shoes. "Ya know where I can buy a pair of shoes like that for $8.95?"

8   "Boy, I bet this house musta cost—I dunno, hundred, what, hundred fifty thousand?"

9   His aristocratic adversaries tolerate Columbo at first because they misjudge him. They are amused by him, scornful of his manners, certain that while he possesses the legal authority to demand their cooperation, he had neither the grace nor wit to discover their misdeeds. Only at the end, in a last look of consternation before the final fadeout, do they comprehend that intelligence may indeed find a home in the Robert Hall set. All of them are done in, in some measure, by their contempt for Columbo's background, breeding, and income. Anyone who has worked the wrong side of the counter at Bergdorf's, or who has waited on tables in high-priced restaurants, must feel a wave of satisfaction. ("Yeah, baby, *that's* how dumb we working stiffs are!")

10   Further, Columbo knows about these people what the rest of us suspect: that they are on top not because they are smarter or work harder than we do, but because they are more amoral and devious. Time after time, the motive for murder in *Columbo* stems from the shakiness of the villain's own status in high society. The chess champion knows his challenger is his better; murder is his only chance to stay king. The surgeon fears that a cooperative research project will endanger his status; he must do in his chief to retain sole credit. The conductor owes his position to the status of his mother-in-law; he must silence his mistress lest she spill the beans and strip him of his wealth and position.

11   This is, perhaps, the most thorough-going satisfaction *Columbo* offers us: the assurance that those who dwell in marble and satin, those whose clothes, food, cars, and mates are the very best, *do not deserve it.* They are, instead, driven by fear and compulsion to murder. And they are done in by a man of street wit, who is afraid to fly, who can't stand the sight of blood, and who never uses force to take his prey. They are done in by Mosholu Parkway and P. S. 106, by Fordham U. and a balcony seat at Madison Square Garden, by a man who pulls down $11,800 a year and never ate an anchovy in his life.

12   It is delicious. I wait only for the ultimate episode: Columbo knocks on the door of 1600 Pennsylvania Avenue one day. "Gee, Mr. President, I really hate to bother you again, but there's *just one thing. . . ."*

Questions

1. What is Greenfield's thesis? Where does he state it?
2. Describe what Greenfield is doing in his first paragraph; in his second paragraph.

3. Beginning with the third paragraph, Greenfield looks first at the characterization of the hero and villains, then at the underlying conflict, and finally at the implicit meaning of the conflict. Why does he present the parts of his analysis in this order?

---

*T*oward an Education for Women

Mary Field Belenky, Blythe McVicker Clinchy, Nancy Rule Goldberger, and Jill Mattuck Tarule

1   We begin with the reminiscences of two ordinary women, each recalling an hour during her first year at college. One of them, now middle aged, remembered the first meeting of an introductory science course. The professor marched into the lecture hall, placed upon his desk a large jar filled with dried beans, and invited the students to guess how many beans the jar contained. After listening to an enthusiastic chorus of wildly inaccurate estimates the professor smiled a thin, dry smile, revealed the correct answer, and announced, "You have just learned an important lesson about science. Never trust the evidence of your own senses."

2   Thirty years later, the woman could guess what the professor had in mind. He saw himself, perhaps, as inviting his students to embark upon an exciting voyage into a mysterious underworld invisible to the naked eye, accessible only through scientific method and scientific instruments. But the seventeen-year-old girl could not accept or even hear the invitation. Her sense of herself as a knower was shaky, and it was based on the belief that she could use her own firsthand experience as a source of truth. This man was saying that this belief was fallacious. He was taking away her only tool for knowing and providing her with no substitute. "I remember feeling small and scared," the woman says, "and I did the only thing I could do. I dropped the course that afternoon, and I haven't gone near science since."

3   The second woman, in her first year at college, told a superficially similar but profoundly different story about a philosophy class she had attended just a month or two before the interview. The teacher came into class carrying a large cardboard cube. She placed it on the desk in front of her and asked the class what it was. They said it was a cube. She asked what a cube was, and they said a cube

contained six equal square sides. She asked how they knew that this object contained six equal square sides. By looking at it, they said. "But how do you know?" the teacher asked again. She pointed to the side facing her and, therefore, invisible to the students; then she lifted the cube and pointed to the side that had been face down on the desk, and, therefore, also invisible. "We can't look at all six sides of a cube at once, can we? So we can't exactly *see* a cube. And yet, you're right. You know it's a cube. But you know it not just because you have eyes but because you have intelligence. You invent the sides you cannot see. You use your intelligence to create the 'truth' about cubes."

4   The student said to the interviewer,

It blew my mind. You'll think I'm nuts, but I ran back to the dorm and I called my boyfriend and I said, "Listen, this is just incredible," and I told him all about it. I'm not sure he could see why I was so excited. I'm not sure I understand it myself. But I really felt, for the first time, like I was really in college, like I was—I don't know—sort of *grown up*.

5   Both stories are about the limitations of firsthand experience as a source of knowledge—we cannot simply see the truth about either the jar of beans or the cube—but there is a difference. We can know the truth about cubes. Indeed, the students did know it. As the science professor pointed out, the students were wrong about the beans; their senses had deceived them. But, as the philosophy teacher pointed out, the students were right about the cube; their minds had served them well.

6   The science professor was the only person in the room who knew how many beans were in that jar. Theoretically, the knowledge was available to the students; they could have counted the beans. But faced with that tedious prospect, most would doubtless take the professor's word for it. He is authority. They had to rely upon his knowledge rather than their own. On the other hand, every member of the philosophy class knew that the cube had six sides. They were all colleagues.

7   The science professor exercised his authority in a benign fashion, promising the students that he would provide them with the tools they needed to excavate invisible truths. Similarly, the philosophy teacher planned to teach her students the skills of philosophical analysis, but she was at pains to assure them that they already possessed the tools to construct some powerful truths. They had built cubes on their own, using only their own powers of inference, without the aid of elaborate procedures or fancy apparatus or even

a teacher. Although a teacher might have told them once that a cube contained six equal square sides, they did not have to take the teacher's word for it; they could have easily verified it for themselves.

8   The lesson the science professor wanted to teach is that experience is a source of error. Taught in isolation, this lesson diminished the student, rendering her dumb and dependent. The philosophy teacher's lesson was that although raw experience is insufficient, by reflecting upon it the student could arrive at truth. It was a lesson that made the student feel more powerful ("sort of grown up").

9   No doubt it is true that, as the professor in May Sarton's novel *The Small Room* says, the "art" of being a student requires humility. But the woman we interviewed did not find the science lesson humbling; she found it humiliating. Arrogance was not then and is not now her natural habitat. Like most of the women in our sample she lacked confidence in herself as a thinker; and the kind of learning the science teacher demanded was not only painful but crippling.

10   In thinking about the education of women, Adrienne Rich writes, "Suppose we were to ask ourselves, simply: What does a woman need to know?" A woman, like any other human being, does need to know that the mind makes mistakes; but our interviews have convinced us that every woman, regardless of age, social class, ethnicity, and academic achievement, needs to know that she is capable of intelligent thought, and she needs to know it right away. Perhaps men learn this lesson before going to college, or perhaps they can wait until they have proved themselves to hear it; we do not know. We do know that many of the women we interviewed had not yet learned it.

Questions

1. How is the professor in the first anecdote characterized? Look particularly at the words used in paragraphs 1 and 2 to describe him. How is the student characterized? Look back at the first sentence: Why do the writers use the word "ordinary" to describe both students? Why did they not simply say, "We begin with the reminiscences of two women"?
2. In paragraph 5 the writers say, "Both stories are about the limitations of firsthand experience as a source of knowledge." What

else do the stories have in common? What are the important differences? What particular difference is most relevant to the main point of the essay?

3. Look again at paragraph 6. The science teacher is described as being "authority." The students "had to rely upon his knowledge rather than their own." Is this relationship between teacher and students more likely in science courses than in philosophy or literature courses? Is it inevitable in sciences courses? If so, why?

4. What is the main point of the concluding paragraph? Do the two anecdotes support this point? To what extent does your own experience confirm it, or not confirm it?

---

*N*onviolent Resistance
Martin Luther King, Jr.

1   Oppressed people deal with their oppression in three characteristic ways. One way is acquiescence: the oppressed resign themselves to their doom. They tacitly adjust themselves to oppression, and thereby become conditioned to it. In every movement toward freedom some of the oppressed prefer to remain oppressed. Almost 2800 years ago Moses set out to lead the children of Israel from the slavery of Egypt to the freedom of the promised land. He soon discovered that slaves do not always welcome their deliverers. They become accustomed to being slaves. They would rather bear those ills they have, as Shakespeare pointed out, than flee to others that they know not of. They prefer the "fleshpots of Egypt" to the ordeals of emancipation.

2   There is such a thing as the freedom of exhaustion. Some people are so worn down by the yoke of oppression that they give up. A few years ago in the slum areas of Atlanta, a Negro guitarist used to sing almost daily: "Ben down so long that down don't bother me." This is the type of negative freedom and resignation that often engulfs the life of the oppressed.

3   But this is not the way out. To accept passively an unjust system is to cooperate with that system; thereby the oppressed become

as evil as the oppressor. Noncooperation with evil is as much a moral obligation as is cooperation with good. The oppressed must never allow the conscience of the oppressor to slumber. Religion reminds every man that he is his brother's keeper. To accept injustice or segregation passively is to say to the oppressor that his actions are morally right. It is a way of allowing his conscience to fall asleep. At this moment the oppressed fails to be his brother's keeper. So acquiescence—while often the easier way—is not the moral way. It is the way of the coward. The Negro cannot win the respect of his oppressor by acquiescing; he merely increases the oppressor's arrogance and contempt. Acquiescence is interpreted as proof of the Negro's inferiority. The Negro cannot win the respect of the white people of the South or the peoples of the world if he is willing to sell the future of his children for his personal and immediate comfort and safety.

4   A second way that oppressed people sometimes deal with oppression is to resort to physical violence and corroding hatred. Violence often brings about momentary results. Nations have frequently won their independence in battle. But in spite of temporary victories, violence never brings permanent peace. It solves no social problem; it merely creates new and more complicated ones.

5   Violence as a way of achieving racial justice is both impractical and immoral. It is impractical because it is a descending spiral ending in destruction for all. The old law of an eye for an eye leaves everybody blind. It is immoral because it seeks to humiliate the opponent rather than win his understanding; it seeks to annihilate rather than to convert. Violence is immoral because it thrives on hatred rather than love. It destroys community and makes brotherhood impossible. It leaves society in monologue rather than dialogue. Violence ends by defeating itself. It creates bitterness in the survivors and brutality in the destroyers. A voice echoes through time saying to every potential Peter, "Put up your sword." History is cluttered with the wreckage of nations that failed to follow this command.

6   If the American Negro and other victims of oppression succumb to the temptation of using violence in the struggle for freedom, future generations will be the recipients of a desolate night of bitterness, and our chief legacy to them will be an endless reign of meaningless chaos. Violence is not the way.

7   The third way open to oppressed people in their quest for freedom is the way of nonviolent resistance. Like the synthesis in Hegelian philosophy, the principle of nonviolent resistance seeks to

reconcile the truths of two opposites—acquiescence and violence—while avoiding the extremes and immoralities of both. The nonviolent resister agrees with the person who acquiesces that one should not be physically aggressive toward his opponent; but he balances the equation by agreeing with the person of violence that evil must be resisted. He avoids the nonresistance of the former and the violent resistance of the latter. With nonviolent resistance, no individual or group need submit to any wrong, nor need anyone resort to violence in order to right a wrong.

8   It seems to me that this is the method that must guide the actions of the Negro in the present crisis in race relations. Through nonviolent resistance the Negro will be able to rise to the noble height of opposing the unjust system while loving the perpetrators of the system. The Negro must work passionately and unrelentingly for full stature as a citizen, but he must not use inferior methods to gain it. He must never come to terms with falsehood, malice, hate, or destruction.

9   Nonviolent resistance makes it possible for the Negro to remain in the South and struggle for his rights. The Negro's problem will not be solved by running away. He cannot listen to the glib suggestion of those who would urge him to migrate en masse to other sections of the country. By grasping his great opportunity in the South he can make a lasting contribution to the moral strength of the nation and set a sublime example of courage for generations yet unborn.

10   By nonviolent resistance, the Negro can also enlist all men of good will in his struggle for equality. The problem is not a purely racial one, with Negroes set against whites. In the end, it is not a struggle between people at all, but a tension between justice and injustice. Nonviolent resistance is not aimed against oppressors but against oppression. Under its banner consciences, not racial groups, are enlisted.

11   If the Negro is to achieve the goal of integration, he must organize himself into a militant and nonviolent mass movement. All three elements are indispensable. The movement for equality and justice can only be a success if it has both a mass and militant character; the barriers to be overcome require both. Nonviolence is an imperative in order to bring about ultimate community.

12   A mass movement of militant quality that is not at the same time committed to nonviolence tends to generate conflict, which in turn breeds anarchy. The support of the participants and the sympathy of the uncommitted are both inhibited by the threat that bloodshed will engulf the community. This reaction in turn encour-

ages the opposition to threaten and resort to force. When, however, the mass movement repudiates violence while moving resolutely toward its goal, its opponents are revealed as the instigators and practitioners of violence if it occurs. Then public support is magnetically attracted to the advocates of nonviolence, while those who employ violence are literally disarmed by overwhelming sentiment against their stand.

Questions

1. Analysis is a term from science, and to some people it suggests coldness, a dispassionate clinical examination. Point to passages in this essay where King communicates his warmth, or sympathy, or passion.
2. In the first paragraph the passage about Moses and the children of Israel is not strictly necessary; the essential idea of the paragraph is stated in the previous sentence. Why, then, does King add this material? And why the quotation from Shakespeare?
3. Pick out two or three sentences that seem to you to be especially effective, and analyze the sources of their power. You can choose either isolated sentences or (because King often effectively links sentences with repetition of words or of constructions) consecutive ones.
4. In a paragraph, set forth your understanding of what nonviolent resistance is. Use whatever examples from your own experience or reading you find useful. In a second paragraph, explain how Maya Angelou's "Graduation" (page 321) offers an example of nonviolent resistance.

The Statue of Liberty: Transcending the Trivial
Paul Goldberger

---

1   If there was anything off-putting about the wild and extravagant praise for the Statue of Liberty over the Fourth of July weekend, it was the ubiquitousness of the image of the statue. That face,

that long, flowing gown of copper, and most particularly that seven-pointed crown, seemed to be everywhere. There were pictures of the statue from every angle, taken at every time of day and night, on television, in newspapers and magazines. There were logotypes made from the statue's face on all kinds of commercial products, and a stage designed to echo its crown as a backdrop for the televised celebratory events. There were posters of the statue in store windows. And as the hysteria reached its peak, there were those souvenir green foam-rubber hats that allowed each and every tourist to turn his head into liberty's crown.

2   The miracle of it all is how well the Statue of Liberty survived all of this. Through it all—through the overblown, overproduced extravaganzas, the souvenirs, everything—the dignity of the statue itself seemed never to be compromised. The events of Liberty Weekend focused more attention on a single object than almost any single object can possibly bear, and that object came through it with every bit of its dignity intact.

3   What is it about the Statue of Liberty that has made it transcend the trivial so remarkably? Almost any other object would have crumbled into cliché because of the intensity of the spotlight that has been shined on the Statue of Liberty, but the statue now, after all of this attention, seems as strong and as fresh as ever. It stood above all attempts to reduce it to a kind of visual slogan.

4   Part of the reason, of course, is not the statue itself, but what it symbolizes—the idea of freedom, though it has been trivialized by many, in and of itself transcends all slogans and easy, glib symbolism. But that does not really explain why the Statue of Liberty could hold such power over us as we saw it again and again, for hour after hour, day after day.

5   Neither is it explained by Frédéric Auguste Bartholdi's talent as a sculptor, which was considerable, though hardly of a scale to command the highest position in European art. One does not look at a Bartholdi and forget Rodin.* And though the architect Richard Morris Hunt, who designed the statue's splendid classical base, was a greater figure in his profession than Bartholdi was in his, Hunt would hardly have been remembered as one of the great figures in 19th-century American architecture if he had only designed this base.

6   Is it the simple idea of monumental sculpture, then—the very notion of an immense statue, so much bigger than life, that is unusual enough that it continues to seem fresh to the eye, even after a hundred years? It is true that there is not much sculpture at such

Fridmar Damm/Leo de Wys, Inc.

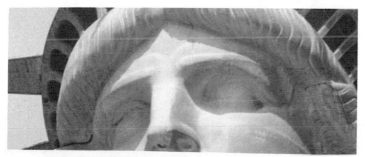

Richard Laird/Leo de Wys, Inc.

vast scale produced in our culture, and there never has been. Monumentality is something we have always been of two minds about—once we have it we honor it, but we commit to building it with the greatest of reluctance.

7   It is really not any one of these things, but all of them, in exquisite balance, that contributed to the success of the Statue of Liberty as a work of art. The statue *is* a powerful symbol of an essential value in our society; it is not the only such symbol, but it is the most intensely personal one, and the only one of its kind. But it is also a fine piece of sculpture, gracefully proportioned, and existing in tandem with a perhaps even finer piece of architecture. And its scale makes it a very special kind of monumental work.

8   In the end, though, there is another factor, perhaps the most important of all. The Statue of Liberty was not placed where it stands by accident. It is not in the middle of Nebraska, or even in the middle of Brooklyn. It is out in the harbor, on an island, where it faces out to the sea, and it performs a gesture of welcoming.

9   By so doing, it enters into an essential relationship with the city, and this is the real key to its brilliance as a symbol. The Statue of Liberty actually turns the harbor into a door; it makes the place where the sea becomes New York Bay an entry, not just a body of water, and it makes the city itself, not to mention the nation that lies to its west, seem more tangible, more understandable, more coherent as a place.

10   To the visitor seeing the statue from the water, this great figure standing at the edge pulls New York together, giving the city an anchor more powerful, in its way, than the Empire State Building. The city that is too large and too busy to stop for anyone seems, through this statue, to stop for everyone. Suddenly its intense activity becomes background, and the statue itself becomes foreground: we cannot ask of a monument that it do anything more.

Questions

1. Re-read the opening paragraph. Why do you suppose Goldberger uses repetition ("That face, that . . . gown"; "there was . . . there was") so insistently? And why, in the light of his

---

Bartholdi . . . Rodin the sculptor of the Statue of Liberty was Auguste Bartholdi (1834–1904); Auguste Rodin (1840–1917) is far more famous and is usually regarded as the greatest sculptor of the period.

second paragraph, do you suppose he chose to make the point he did in the first paragraph?

2. Where does Goldberger first announce his thesis? Where does he most fully clarify it? Do you find this structure satisfactory? Why, or why not?

3. Your city or town or campus probably has some "monumental" structure—perhaps a statue in a public space, or a fountain, or a house of worship or a city or state hall. ("Monument," by the way, comes from the Latin *monere*, "to remind"; a monument commemorates a person, thing, or event by reminding the viewer.) In 500–750 words, describe the monument to someone unfamiliar with the work and with the community in which it stands, and then analyze the reasons for its appeal, or lack of appeal.

Introducing Children *to Death*
Lawrence Kutner

1   A child must accomplish four tasks when a friend or family member dies: understand the nature of death and why this one occurred; grieve for the dead person; commemorate that person, and go on with his life. His success at coping with these tasks will be based, in part, on how his parents introduce him to death. By understanding how children at different ages comprehend and deal with the death of someone they love, parents can help ease their fears and reduce their confusion.

2   Child psychologists recommend that parents begin talking to their children about death while they are preschoolers. "Quite young children have a greater understanding of death than we give them credit for," said Dr. Sandra S. Fox, the director of the Good Grief Program at the Judge Baker Children's Center in Boston. The program helps children, their parents, and their teachers cope with death. Although child-development experts once assumed that children could not comprehend death until they were three years old, many parents of toddlers say their children appear to have some understanding of what it means.

3   The cue for the first discussion may be your child's question about someone who died or a question that comes up when you

pass by a cemetery or funeral procession. If no such natural oppor-tunity appears, you should raise the issue, rather than assume that your child has all the information he needs. As with discussions with preschoolers about sex, you need not go into great detail. The implied message that you are open to talking about the subject may be as important as any facts you give your child.

4   Dr. Fox prefers to describe death to children as what happens when the body stops working. "It's honest for kids, and you can add religious or spiritual layers to it if you want," she said. She also encourages parents to use the word "death." Euphemisms like "expire" and "lost" may confuse and frighten children.

5   By the time a child enters first or second grade, he often envi-sions death as a spirit who comes to get him, especially if he can't run fast enough to escape. The image is similar to a game of tag in which death is "it" and chases everyone who plays. By picturing death this way, the child can imagine himself immortal if only he can stay out of that fearsome grasp.

6   While this image makes sense when he hears about the death of someone who is old or very sick, he is much more confused when someone who is young and healthy dies. To resolve that con-fusion, he may call the dead person names or denigrate him in some other way. By doing so he creates a distance between him and death. Had he been the one, he could have run fast enough.

7   Because he once wished his father was dead, a young child may also believe that he caused his father's fatal car accident months later. He may be afraid and ashamed to mention this to anyone and may carry that undeserved guilt, consciously or subconsciously, for years. This type of magical thinking can be seen even in adoles-cents.

8   "You can't expect two children of the same age to respond the same way to a death," said Dr. J. William Worden, an assistant professor of psychology at the Harvard Medical School and a prin-cipal investigator in a child bereavement study at Harvard. Grief in a child may appear as anger instead of sadness. A preschooler has difficulty distinguishing between bad information and "badness" in the message-bearer. He may physically or verbally attack the person who tells him that someone he loves has died, an act that can be very upsetting to parents or teachers who are dealing with their own grief.

9   Adolescents often feel more comfortable grieving with their peers than with adults. They may view the death of someone in their family as embarrassing and may try to hide it from outsiders.

10   The task of commemorating is especially important if the person who died was your child's classmate. When a child dies, his teachers often clean out his desk while none of the other students are around. This adds to the mystery surrounding death and the feeling that it's something the children shouldn't talk about. Dr. Fox recommends that teachers or parents ask the children what they would like to do with the dead child's desk. Many children will want the desk put in a special place for a few months while they sort out their feelings.

11   Some high schools hold memorial services for students who die from illness or accidents but ignore those who commit suicide. They are concerned that calling attention to a teen-age suicide may glamorize it and may lead to more suicides. "This is a serious mistake because it tells children that we value some lives, but not others," Dr. Fox said.

12   Even preschoolers may need to participate in a ritual that acknowledges the death of someone close. For some children, that may be a ceremony at home; for others, it may mean viewing the body or attending the funeral. Psychologists recommend giving your child a choice, never forcing him to go. Ask your child what he expects to happen at the funeral, so that you can correct his misconceptions. If you take a young child to a funeral home, do it before or after regular viewing hours so that neither you nor your child is distracted by other visitors.

13   Finally, a child must learn to go on with his life. Many children need help understanding how this is different from forgetting the person who died, Dr. Fox said.

Questions

1. Kutner's advice is addressed to parents of young children. As a piece of writing, why might his article interest readers who are not parents? Are there readers who might be interested in the topic but feel excluded by Kutner's article?

2. Kutner lists four tasks children need to accomplish when they are confronted with death. What are they? From your own experience, would you agree that Kutner's classification is useful? Are there other "tasks" you would add?

3. In paragraph 7, Kutner makes an assumption about children's thoughts on death. What is the assumption? Do you believe it is warranted?

4. Kutner quotes two authorities in his analysis. If you were (or are) a parent, would you be inclined to consult with these authorities? In your own community, how might you determine what resources are available or find an authority to interview on children and grief?

5. What does Kutner appear to recommend in dealing with the suicide of high school students? He does not touch on deaths from violent crime or drug abuse. How do you think high schools should treat such deaths? If you have had personal experience of such deaths, how did your high school treat them?

6. In his concluding paragraph, Kutner addresses the last task he lists in his first paragraph: "A child must learn to get on with his life." If you find this last paragraph less helpful than it might be, what can you add to it from your own experience or understanding?

7. If you have read Baker's autobiographical essay "Coming to Grips with Death" (pages 338–42), in an essay of 500–1000 words compare Baker's account (of his father's death) with Kutner's analysis. Or, compare Kutner's analysis with your own experience of "coming to grips with death."

4

Paragraphs

Paragraph Form and Substance

It is commonly said that a good paragraph has *unity* (it makes one point, or it indicates where one unit of a topic begins and ends); it has *organization* (the point or unit is developed according to some pattern); and it has *coherence* (the pattern of development, sentence by sentence, is clear to the reader). We will say these things too. Moreover, we will attempt to demonstrate that, generally speaking, they are true. Along the way we also hope to show you how to shape your ideas into effective paragraphs. But first we feel obliged to issue this warning: you can learn to write a unified, organized, coherent paragraph that no one in his or her right mind would choose to read. Here is an example, which we ask you to force yourself to read through. (It may remind you of many paragraphs you wrote in order to graduate from high school.)

```
    Charles Darwin's great accomplishments in the field of

natural science resulted from many factors.  While innate

qualities and characteristics played a large part in leading

him to his discoveries, various environmental circumstances
```

```
and events were decisive factors as well.  Darwin, himself,

considered his voyage on the Beagle the most decisive event

of his life, precisely because this was to him an educational

experience similar to if not more valuable than that of col-

lege, in that it determined his whole career and taught him

of the world as well.
```

Notice that the paragraph is unified, organized, and coherent. It has a topic sentence (the first sentence). It uses transitional devices ("while," "as well," "Darwin," "himself") and, as is often helpful, it repeats key words. But notice also that it is wordy, vague, and inflated ("in the field of," "many factors," "qualities and characteristics," "circumstances and events," "precisely because," "educational experience," "similar to if not more valuable than"). It is, in short, thin and boring. Who but a hired sympathy (John Ciardi's definition of an English teacher) would read it? To whom does it teach what?

Consider, by contrast, these two paragraphs from the beginning of another essay on Darwin:

> Charles Darwin's youth was unmarked by signs of genius. Born in 1809 into the well-to-do Darwin and Wedgwood clans (his mother was a Wedgwood, and Darwin himself was to marry another), he led a secure and carefree childhood, happy with his family, indifferent to books, responsive to nature. The son and grandson of impressively successful physicians, he eventually tried medical training himself, but found the studies dull and surgery (before anesthesia) too ghastly even to watch. So, for want of anything better, he followed the advice of his awesome father (6'2", 336 pounds, domineering in temperament) and studied for the ministry, taking his B.A. at Christ's College, Cambridge, in 1831.
>
> Then a remarkable turn of events saved Darwin from a country parsonage. His science teacher at Cambridge, John Stevens Henslow, arranged for Darwin the invitation to be naturalist on H.M.S. *Beagle* during a long voyage of exploration. Despite his father's initial reluctance, Darwin got the position, and at the end of 1831 left England for a five-year voyage around the globe that turned out to be not only a crucial experience for Darwin himself, but a passage of consequence for the whole world.
>
> — Philip Appleman

Notice how full of life these paragraphs are, compared to the paragraph that begins by asserting that "Charles Darwin's great accomplishments in the field of natural science resulted from many factors." These far more interesting paragraphs are filled with specific details, facts and names that combine to convey ideas. We finish reading them with a sense of having learned something worth knowing, from someone fully engaged not only with the topic, but also with conveying it to someone else.

The one indispensable quality of a good paragraph, the quality that the first paragraph on Darwin lacks, is *substance*. A paragraph may define a term, describe a person or a place, make a comparison, tell an anecdote, summarize an opinion, draw a conclusion; it may do almost anything provided that it holds the readers' attention by telling them something they want or need to know, or are reminded of with pleasure.

But even a substantial paragraph, as we shall soon see, does not guarantee the reader's attention, because readers (like writers) are often lazy and impatient. The important difference is that readers can afford to be. If they find that they must work too hard to understand you, if they are puzzled or confused by what you write, if the effort they must expend is greater than their reward, they can—and will—stop reading you. The art of writing is in large part the art of keeping your readers' goodwill while you teach them what you want them to learn. Now, experienced writers can usually tell—not so much while they are writing as while they are revising—what does or does not make a satisfactory unit, and their paragraphs do not always exactly follow the principles we are going to suggest. But we think that by following these principles, more or less as you might practice finger exercises in learning how to play the piano, you will develop a sense of paragraphing. Or, to put it another way, you will improve your sense of how to develop an idea.

PARAGRAPH UNITY: TOPIC SENTENCES, TOPIC IDEAS

The idea developed in each paragraph often appears, briefly stated, as a topic sentence. Topic sentences are most useful, and are therefore especially common, in paragraphs that offer arguments; they are much less common, because they are less useful, in narrative and descriptive paragraphs.

A topic sentence often comes at the beginning of a paragraph, but it may come later, even at the end; it may even be dispensed with if the topic idea—the idea that unifies the sentence of the paragraph—is clear without an explicit statement. (You have just read the topic sentence of this paragraph. The rest of the paragraph will develop the threefold point that a topic sentence often begins a paragraph, often ends a paragraph, and often is omitted.) The topic sentence usually is the first sentence in the paragraph— or the second, following a transitional sentence—because writers usually want their readers to know from the start where the paragraph is going. And, because writers want to keep their readers' attention, an opening topic sentence should be as precise and as interesting as possible (*not* "People oppose school busing for several reasons," but "People offer many good reasons for opposing school busing, but seldom offer their real reasons"). Sometimes, though, you may not wish to forecast what is to come; you may prefer to put your topic sentence at the end of the paragraph, summarizing the points that earlier sentences have made, or drawing a generalization based on the earlier details. Even if you do not include a topic sentence anywhere in the paragraph, the paragraph should have a topic idea—an idea that holds the sentences together.

Examples of Topic Sentences at Beginning and at End, and of Topic Ideas

1. The following paragraph begins with a topic sentence.

The Marx Brothers' three best films at Paramount—*Monkey Business* (1931), *Horse Feathers* (1932), and *Duck Soup* (1933)— all hurl comic mud at the gleaming marble pillars of the American temple. The target of *Monkey Business* is money and high society, the rich society snobs merely happen to be gangsters who made their money from bootlegging. The target of *Horse Feathers* is the university; knowledge and the pursuit of it are reduced to thievery, bribery, lechery, and foolishness. The target of *Duck Soup* is democracy and government itself; grandiose political ceremonies, governmental bodies, international diplomacy, the law courts, and war are reduced to the absurd. All three films also parody popular "serious" genres—gangster films, college films, and romantic European-kingdom films. The implication of this spoofing is that the sanctified institution is as hollow and dead as the cinematic cliché; the breezy, chaotic, revolutionary activities of the comic anarchists give society's respectable calcifications a much-deserved comeuppance.

— Gerald Mast

The first sentence announces the topic. Everything that follows this topic sentence develops or amplifies it, first by commenting one by one on the three films named at the outset, then by speaking of the three films as a group, and then by offering a closely related generalization (the films spoof serious films) and a comment on the implications of this generalization. In short, the writer begins by stating or summarizing his idea, then offers specific evidence to support it, and then offers a related idea. The development is from the general to the particular and then again to the general.

2. Next, a paragraph with the topic sentence at the end.

If we try to recall Boris Karloff's face as the monster in the film of *Frankenstein* (1931), most of us probably think of the seams holding the pieces together, and if we cannot recall other details we assume that the face evokes horror. But when we actually look at a picture of the face rather than recall a memory of it, we are perhaps chiefly impressed by the high, steep forehead (a feature often associated with intelligence), by the darkness surrounding the eyes (often associated with physical or spiritual weariness), and by the gaunt cheeks and the thin lips slightly turned down at the corners (associated with deprivation or restraint). The monster's face is of course in some ways shocking, but probably our chief impression as we look at it is that this is not the face of one who causes suffering but of one who himself is heroically undergoing suffering.

What is the difference between putting the topic sentence at the beginning and putting it at the end? A paragraph that begins with the topic sentence offers readers the satisfaction of receiving, as they move through the paragraph, what was promised at the outset. On the other hand a paragraph with the topic sentence at the end, such as this one on the monster, usually offers readers the pleasure of mild suspense during most of the paragraph and finally, in the topic sentence, offers the clarification that they had half anticipated.

When the topic sentence is at the end, the paragraph usually develops from the particular to the general, the topic sentence serving to generalize or summarize the information that precedes it. Such a topic sentence can be especially effective in presenting an argument: the reader hears, considers, and accepts the evidence before the argument is explicitly stated, and if the evidence has been effectively presented the reader willingly accepts the conclusion.

3. Next, a paragraph without a topic sentence:

> A few years ago when you mentioned Walt Disney at a respectable party—or anyway this is how it was in California, where I was then—the standard response was a headshake and a groan. Intellectuals spoke of how he butchered the classics—from *Pinocchio* to *Winnie the Pooh,* how his wildlife pictures were sadistic and coy, how the World's Fair sculptures of hippopotamuses were a national if not international disgrace. A few crazies disagreed, and since crazies are always the people to watch, it began to be admitted that the early Pluto movies had a considerable measure of *je ne sais quoi,* that the background animation in *Snow White* was "quite extraordinary," that *Fantasia* did indeed have *one* great sequence (then it became two; now everyone says three, though there's fierce disagreement on exactly which three).
>
> — John Gardner

The topic here is, roughly, "Intellectuals used to scorn Disney, but recently they have been praising him." Such a sentence could easily begin the paragraph, but it is not necessary because even without it the reader has no difficulty following the discussion. The first two sentences talk about Disney's earlier reputation; then the sentence about the "crazies" introduces the contrary view and the rest of the paragraph illustrates the growing popularity of this contrary view. The paragraph develops its point so clearly and consistently (it is essentially a narrative, in chronological order) that the reader, unlike the reader of a complex analytic paragraph, does not need the help of a topic sentence either at the beginning, to prepare for what follows, or at the end, to pull the whole together.

UNIFYING IDEAS INTO PARAGRAPHS

Although we emphasize unity in paragraphs, don't assume that every development or refinement or alteration of your thought requires a new paragraph. Such an assumption would lead to an essay consisting entirely of one-sentence paragraphs. A good paragraph may, for instance, both ask a question and answer it, or describe an effect and then explain the cause, or set forth details and then offer a generalization. Indeed, if the question or the effect or the details can be set forth in a sentence or two, and the answer or the cause or the generalization can be set forth in a sentence or two, the two halves of the topic should be pulled together into a single paragraph. Only if the question (for example) is long and complex and the answer equally long or longer, will you need two or more paragraphs—or, to put it more precisely, will your reader need two or more paragraphs.

Let's consider three paragraphs from an essay on ballooning. In the essay from which the following paragraphs are taken, the writer has already explained that ballooning was born in late eighteenth-century France and that almost from its start there were two types of balloons, gas and hot air. Notice that in the paragraphs printed below the first is on gas, the second is chiefly on hot air (but it helpfully makes comparisons with gas), and the third is on the length of flights of both gas and hot-air balloons. In other words, each paragraph is about one thing—gas balloons, hot-air balloons, length of flight—but each paragraph also builds on what the reader has learned in the previous paragraphs. That the third paragraph is about the flights of gas *and* of hot-air balloons does not mean that it lacks unity; it is a unified discussion of flight lengths.

> Gas balloons swim around in air like a sleeping fish in water, because they weigh about the same as the fluid they're in. A good, big, trans-Atlantic balloon will have 2,000 pounds of vehicle, in-

cluding gas bag and pilot, taking up about 30 cubic feet (as big as a refrigerator), plus 300 pounds of a "nothing" stuff called helium, which fills 30,000 cubic feet (as big as three houses). Air to fill this 30,000 cubic feet would also weigh 2,300 pounds, so the balloon system averages the same as air, floating in it as part of the wind.

Hot-air balloons use the same size bag filled with hot air instead of helium, kept hot by a boot-sized blowtorch riding just over the pilot's head. Hot air is light, but not as light as helium, so you can't carry as much equipment in a hot-air balloon. You also can't fly as long or as far. Helium will carry a balloon for days (three and a half days is the record), until a lot of gas has leaked out. But a hot-air balloon cools down in minutes, like a house as soon as its heat source runs out of fuel; and today's best fuel (heat-for-weight), propane, lasts only several hours.

A good hot-air flight goes a hundred miles, yet the gas record is 1,897 miles, set by a German in 1914 with the junk (by today's standards) they had then. Unmanned scientific gas balloons have flown half a million miles, staying up more than a year. Japan bombed Oregon in World War II with balloons. Two hot-air balloonists, Tracy Barnes and Malcolm Forbes, have made what they called transcontinental flights, but each was the sum of dozens of end-to-end hops, trailed by pick-up trucks, like throwing a frisbee from Hollywood to Atlantic City.

— David Royce

Now contrast the unity of any of the previous three paragraphs on ballooning with the lack of focus in this paragraph from a book on athletic coaching.

Leadership qualities are a prerequisite for achievement in coaching. A leader is one who is respected for what he says and does, and who is admired by his team. The coach gains respect by giving respect, and by possessing knowledge and skills associated with the sport. There are many "successful" coaches who are domineering, forceful leaders, gaining power more through fear and even hate than through respect. These military-type men are primarily from the old school of thought, and many younger coaches are achieving their goals through more humanistic approaches.

Something is wrong here. The first half of the paragraph tells us that "a leader is one who is respected for what he says and does," but the second half of the paragraph contradicts that assertion, telling us that "many" leaders hold their position "more through fear and even hate than through respect." The trouble is *not* that the writer is talking about two kinds of leaders; a moment ago we saw that a writer can in one paragraph talk about two kinds of balloons. The trouble here is that we need a unifying idea if these two points are to be given in one paragraph. The idea might be: There are two kinds of leaders, those who are respected and those who are feared. This idea might be developed along these lines:

> Leadership qualities are a prerequisite for achievement in coaching, but these qualities can be of two radically different kinds. One kind of leader is respected and admired by his team for what he says and does. The coach gains respect by giving respect, and by possessing knowledge and skills associated with the sport. The other kind of coach is a domineering, forceful leader, gaining power more through fear than through respect. These military-type men are primarily from the old school of thought, whereas most of the younger coaches achieve their goals through the more humane approaches of the first type.

ORGANIZATION IN PARAGRAPHS

A paragraph needs more than a unified point; it needs a reasonable organization or sequence. After all, a box containing all of the materials for a model airplane has unity (all the parts of the plane are there), but not until the parts are joined in the proper relationship do we get a plane. In the following paragraph, a sentence is out of place.

> Leonardo da Vinci's *Mona Lisa* has attracted and puzzled viewers for almost five hundred years, and I don't suffer from the delusion that I can fully account for the spell the picture casts. Still, I think it is easy enough to account for at least part of the mystery. The most expressive features of a face are the mouth and the eyes, and we notice that Leonardo slightly blurred or shaded the corners of the mouth so that its exact expression cannot be characterized, or, if we characterize it, we change our mind when we look again. Lisa herself is something of a mystery, for history tells us nothing

Leonardo da Vinci: Mona Lisa.

about her personality or about her relationship to Leonardo. The corners of her eyes, like the corners of her mouth, are slightly obscured, contributing to her elusive expression.

Which sentence is out of place in the paragraph you have just read? How might you work it into its proper place?

Exactly how the parts of a paragraph will fit together depends, of course, on what the paragraph is doing.

1. If it is *describing* a place, it may move from (for example) a general view to the significant details—or from immediately striking details to some less obvious but perhaps more important ones. It may move from near to far, or from far to near, or from the past to the present.
2. If it is *explaining,* it may move from (for example) cause to effect, or from effect to cause, or from past to present; or it may offer an example.
3. If it is *arguing,* it may move (for example) from evidence to conclusion, or from a conclusion to supporting evidence; or it may offer one piece of evidence, for instance an anecdote (a short narrative), that illustrates the argument.

In the following paragraph, written by a student, we move *chronologically*—from waking at 7:00 A.M., to washing and combing, to readiness for the day's work, and then to a glance at the rest of the day that will undo the 7:00 A.M. cleanup.

I can remember waking at seven to Ma's call. I'd bound out of bed because Ma just didn't allow people to be lazy. She'd grab me and we'd rush to the bathroom for the morning ritual. Bathing, toothbrushing, lotioning, all overseen by her watchful eyes. She didn't let anything go by. No missing behind the ears, no splashing around and pretending to bathe. I bathed and scrubbed and put that lotion on till my whole body was like butter on a warm pan. After inspection it was back to my room and the day's clothes were selected. A bit of tugging and I was dressed. Then she'd sit me down and pull out the big black comb. That comb would glide through my hair and then the braiding would begin. My head would jerk but I never yelled, never even whimpered. Finally I was ready. Ready to start the day and get dirty and spoil all of Ma's work. But she didn't care. She knew you couldn't keep a child from getting dirty but you could teach it to be respectable.

If a paragraph is classifying (dividing a subject into its parts) it may begin by enumerating the parts and go on to study each, perhaps in climactic order. Here is an example.

> The chief reasons people wear masks are these: to have fun, to protect themselves, to disguise themselves, and to achieve a new identity. At Halloween, children wear masks for fun; they may, of course, also think they are disguising themselves, but chiefly their motive is to experience the joy of saying "boo" to someone. Soldiers wore masks for protection, in ancient times against swords and battle-axes, in more recent times against poison gas. Bank robbers wear masks to disguise themselves, and though of course this disguise is a sort of protection, a robber's reason for wearing a mask is fairly distinct from a soldier's. All of these reasons so far are easily understood, but we may have more trouble grasping the reason that primitive people use masks in religious rituals. Some ritual masks seem merely to be attempts to frighten away evil spirits, and some seem merely to be disguises so that the evil spirits will not know who the wearer is. But most religious masks are worn with the idea that the wearer achieves a new identity, a union with supernatural powers, and thus in effect the wearer becomes—really becomes, not merely pretends to be—a new person.

Notice that the first sentence offers four reasons for wearing masks. The rest of the paragraph amplifies these reasons, one by one, and in the order indicated in the first sentence. Since the writer regards the last reason as the most interesting and the most difficult to grasp, he discusses it at the greatest length, giving it about as much space as he gives to the first three reasons altogether.

The way in which a paragraph is organized, then, will depend on what the writer is trying to do—what the writer's purpose is. Almost always one of the writer's purposes is to make something clear to a reader. Among the common methods of organizing a paragraph, and keeping things clear, are:

1. general to particular (topic sentence usually at the beginning)
2. particular to general (topic sentence usually at the end)
3. enumeration of parts or details or reasons (probably in climactic order)
4. question and answer

5. cause and effect
6. comparison and contrast
7. analogy
8. chronology
9. spatial order (e.g. near to far, or right to left)

The only rule that can cover all paragraphs is this: readers must never feel that they are stumbling as they try to follow the writer to the end of the paragraph. They should not have to go back and read the paragraph again to figure out what the writer had in mind. It is the writer's job, not the reader's, to give the paragraph its unity and organization. A paragraph is not a maze; it should be organized so that the reader can glide through it in seconds, not minutes.

Vladimir Koziakin: Spaghetti.

Coherence in Paragraphs

In addition to having a unified point and a reasonable organization, a good paragraph is coherent: A reader can unhesitatingly follow its train of thought. Coherence can often be achieved, in revising a paragraph, by inserting the right transitional words or by taking care to repeat key words.

Transitions

Richard Wagner, commenting on his work as a composer of operas, once said "The art of composition is the art of transition," for his art moved from note to note, measure to measure, scene to scene. Because transitions establish connections between points, they contribute to coherence. Here are some of the most common transitional words and phrases. In effect, they are cues that alert the reader to what will follow.

1. *amplification* or *likeness:*
similarly, likewise, and, also, again, second, third, in addition, furthermore, moreover, finally

2. *emphasis:*
chiefly, equally, indeed, even more important

3. *contrast or concession:*
but, on the contrary, on the other hand, by contrast, of course, however, still, doubtless, no doubt, nevertheless, granted that, conversely, although, admittedly

4. *example:*
for example, for instance, as an example, specifically, consider as an illustration, that is, such as, like

5. *consequence* or *cause and effect:*
thus, so, then, it follows, as a result, therefore, hence

6. *restatement:*
in short, that is, in effect, in other words

7. *place:*
in the foreground, further back, in the distance

8. *time:*
afterward, next, then, as soon as, later, until, when, finally, last, at last

9. *conclusion:*
finally, therefore, thus, to sum up

Consider the following paragraph:

> Folklorists are just beginning to look at Africa. A great quantity of folklore materials has been gathered from African countries in the past century and published by missionaries, travelers, administrators, linguists, and anthropologists incidentally to their main pursuits. No fieldworker has devoted himself exclusively or even largely to the recording and analysis of folklore materials, according to a committee of the African Studies Association reporting in 1966 on the state of research in the African arts. Yet Africa is the continent supreme for traditional cultures that nurture folklore. Why this neglect?
>
> — Richard M. Dorson

The reader gets the point, but the second sentence seems to contradict the first: the first sentence tells us that folklorists are just beginning to look at Africa, but the next tells us that lots of folklore has been collected. An "although" between these sentences would clarify the author's point, especially if the third sentence were hooked on to the second, thus:

> Folklorists are just beginning to look at Africa. Although a great quantity of folklore materials has been gathered from African countries in the past century by missionaries, travelers, administrators, linguists, and anthropologists incidentally to their main pursuits, no fieldworker has devoted himself . . .

But this revision gives us an uncomfortably long second sentence. Further revision would help. The real point of the original passage, though it is smothered, is that although many people have incidentally collected folklore materials in Africa, professional folklorists have not been active there. The contrast ought to be sharpened:

> Folklorists are just beginning to look at Africa. True, missionaries, travelers, administrators, linguists, and anthropologists have collected a quantity of folklore materials incidentally to their main pursuits, but folklorists have lagged behind. No fieldworker . . .

In this revision the words that clarify are, of course, the small but important words "true" and "but." The original paragraph is a jigsaw puzzle, missing some tiny but necessary pieces.

When you are writing a first draft, of course, you need not stop and worry about whether or not the transitions in your thoughts will be clear to a reader. For most writers, saying something and saying it clearly are two different processes, and if you are like most writers it is best to attend to one thing at a time. The first thing is to get something down on paper. But after you have a rough draft, reread it with a reader in mind. Check each paragraph, sentence by sentence, to see if each sentence is clearly related to the preceding one. Ask yourself if a transitional word or phrase ("first," "in addition," "nevertheless," "by contrast") would make the relationship clearer to your reader. If you find that the relationship is unclear, you may have to do more than provide a transition; you may have to rethink the point or extensively revise the sentence. In any case, your goal is to allow your imagined reader, furnished with proper clues, to move effortlessly through your essay.

Repetition

Coherence is achieved not only by means of transitional words and phrases but also through the repetition of key words. When you repeat words or phrases, or when you provide clear substitutes (such as pronouns and demonstrative adjectives), you are helping the reader to keep step with your developing thoughts. Grammatical constructions too can be repeated, the repetitions or parallels linking the sentences or ideas.

In the following example, notice how the repetitions provide continuity.

> Sir Kenneth Clark's *The Nude* is an important book; and, luckily, it is also most readable; but it is not a bedside book. Each sentence needs attention because each sentence is relevant to the whole, and the incorrigible skipper will sometimes find himself obliged to turn back several pages, chapters even, in order to pick up the thread of the argument. Does this sound stiff? The book is not stiff because it is delightfully written. Let the student have no fears; he is not going to be bored for a moment while he reads these 400 pages; he is going to be excited, amused, instructed, provoked, charmed, irritated and surprised.

Notice not only the exact repetitions ("each sentence," "stiff") but also the slight variations, such as "an important book," "not a bedside book"; "he is not going," "he is going"; and the emphatic list of participles ("excited, amused, instructed," and so on) at the conclusion.

Here is another example of a paragraph that unobtrusively uses repetition.

> The main skill is to keep from getting lost. Since the roads are used only by local people who know them by sight nobody complains if the junctions aren't posted. And often they aren't. When they are it's usually a small sign hiding unobtrusively in the weeds and that's all. County-road-sign makers seldom tell you twice. If you miss that sign in the weeds that's *your* problem, not theirs. Moreover, you discover that the highway maps are often inaccurate about county roads. And from time to time you find your "county road" takes you onto a two-rutter and then a single rutter and then into a pasture and stops, or else it takes you into some farmer's backyard.
>
> — Robert M. Pirsig

What repetitions do you note? (For additional comments on repetition and variation as transitions, see pages 525–527.)

Transitions between Paragraphs

As you move from one paragraph to the next—from one step in the development of your thesis to the next—you probably can keep the reader with you if you make the first sentence of each new paragraph a transition, or perhaps a transition and a topic sentence. The first sentence of a paragraph that could follow the paragraph quoted a moment ago on Kenneth Clark's *The Nude* might run thus:

> Among the chief delights of these 400 pages are the illustrations.

Clearly "Among the chief delights of these 400 pages" is a transition, picking up the reference to "400 pages" near the end of the previous paragraph, and the rest of the sentence introduces the topic—the illustrations—of the new paragraph. Only if your two paragraphs are extremely complex, and you believe the reader needs lots of help, will you need to devote an entire paragraph to a transition between two other paragraphs. Often a single transitional word or phrase (such as those listed on pages 118–119) will suffice.

GROUPS OF PARAGRAPHS

Since a paragraph is, normally, a developed idea, and each developed idea has its place in explaining your thesis, as one paragraph follows the next readers feel they are getting somewhere. Consider the neat ordering of ideas in the following four consecutive paragraphs. The paragraph preceding the first of these was chiefly concerned with describing several strategies whereby the Marx Brothers succeeded in making full-length talking films, in contrast to the short silent films of a decade earlier. In the first of the following paragraphs, "also" provides the requisite transition.

The Marx Brothers also overcame the problem of the talkies by revealing individual relationships to talk. Groucho talks so much, so rapidly, and so belligerently that talk becomes a kind of weapon. He shoots word bullets at his listeners, rendering them (and the audience) helpless, gasping for breath, trying to grab hold of some argument long enough to make sense of it. But before anyone can grab a verbal handle, Groucho has already moved on to some other topic and implication that seems to follow from his previous one—but doesn't. Groucho's ceaseless talk leads the listener in intellectual circles, swallowing us in a verbal maze, eventually depositing us back at the starting point without knowing where we have been or how we got there. Groucho's "logic" is really the manipulation of pun, homonym, and equivocation. He substitutes the quantity of sound and the illusion of rational connection for the theoretical purpose of talk—logical communication.

Chico's relationship to talk also substitutes sound for sense and the appearance of meaning for meaning. To Chico, "viaduct" sounds like "why a duck," "wire fence" like "why a fence," "short-cut" like "short cake," "sanity clause" like "Santa Claus," "dollars" like "Dallas," "taxes" like "Texas." He alone can puncture Groucho's verbal spirals by stopping the speeding train of words and forcing Groucho to respond to his own erroneous intrusions. Groucho cannot get away with his coy substitution of sound for sense when Chico makes different (but similar) sounds out of the key terms in Groucho's verbal web. Chico's absurd accent (this Italian burlesque would be considered very impolite by later standards) makes him hear Groucho's words as if he, the Italian who speaks pidgin English, were speaking them.

The substitution of sound for sense reaches its perfection in Harpo, who makes only sounds. Harpo substitutes whistling and beeps on his horn for talk. Ironically, he communicates in the films as well as anybody. He communicates especially well with Chico, who understands Harpo better than Groucho does. Chico continually interprets Harpo's noises for Groucho. The irony that a bumbling foreign speaker renders a mute clown's honks, beeps, and whistles into English so it can be understood by the supreme verbal gymnast plays a role in every Marx Brothers film.

Harpo also substitutes the language of the body for speech. In this system of communication, Harpo uses two powerful allies—props and mime. He gives the password ("swordfish") that admits him to a speakeasy by pulling a swordfish out of his pocket. He impersonates Maurice Chevalier by miming a Chevalier song to a phonograph record, produced out of his coat especially for the occasion. Or he orders a shot of Scotch in the speakeasy by snapping into a Highland fling. In these early talkies, talk became one of the comic subjects of the films as well as one of the primary comic devices. As in the early Chaplin sound films, the Marx Brothers made talk an ally simply by treating it so specially.

— Gerald Mast

A few observations on these paragraphs may be useful. Notice that the first sentence of the first paragraph is, in effect, an introduction to all four paragraphs; because it is too thin to stand by itself, this transition is acceptably attached as a preface to the first paragraph of what is really a unit of four paragraphs. Second, notice that the first paragraph is devoted to Groucho, the second to Chico, and the third and fourth to Harpo. We might think that symmetry requires that Harpo get only one paragraph, like his brothers, but the writer, feeling that each of Harpo's two languages—noises and gestures—is a major point and therefore worth a separate paragraph, rightly allows significance to overrule symmetry. Third, note the simple but adequate transitions at the beginnings of the paragraphs: "Chico's relationship to talk also," "The substitution of sound for sense reaches its perfection in Harpo," and "Harpo also substitutes the language of the body for speech." Although the repetition of "also" is a trifle mechanical, it serves to let the readers know where they will be going. Finally, notice that this unit discussing the three brothers is arranged climactically; it ends with Harpo, who is said to achieve "perfection" in the matter under discussion. And in this discussion of distorted language, the two paragraphs on Harpo similarly are arranged to form a climax: the second, not the first, gives us the ultimate distortion, language that is not even sound.

PARAGRAPH LENGTH

Of course hard-and-fast rules cannot be made about the lengths of paragraphs, but more often than not a good paragraph is between one hundred and two hundred words, consisting of more than one or two but fewer than eight or ten sentences. It is not a matter, however, of counting words or sentences; paragraphs are coherent blocks, substantial units of your essay, and the spaces between them are brief resting places allowing the reader to take in what you have said. One page of typing (approximately 250 words) is about as much as the reader can take before requiring a slight break. On the other hand, one page of typing with half a dozen paragraphs is probably faulty because the reader is too often interrupted with needless pauses and because the page has too few *developed* ideas: an assertion is made, and then another, and another. They are unconvincing because they are not supported with detail. To put it another way, a paragraph is a room in the house you are building. If your essay is some five hundred words long (about two double-spaced typewritten pages) you probably will not break it down into more than four or five rooms or paragraphs; if you break it down into a dozen paragraphs, readers will feel they are touring a rabbit warren rather than a house.

The Use and Abuse of Short Paragraphs

A short paragraph can be effective when it summarizes a highly detailed previous paragraph or group of paragraphs, or when it serves as a transition between two complicated paragraphs, but unless you are sure that the reader needs a break, avoid thin paragraphs. A paragraph that is nothing but a transition can usually be altered into a transitional phrase or clause or sentence that starts the next paragraph. But of course there are times when a short paragraph is exactly right. Notice the effect of the two-sentence paragraph between two longer paragraphs:

After I returned to prison, I took a long look at myself and, for the first time in my life, admitted that I was wrong, that I had gone astray—astray not so much from the white man's law as from being human, civilized—for I could not approve the act of rape. Even though I had some insight into my own motivations, I did not feel justified. I lost my self-respect. My pride as a man dissolved and my whole fragile moral structure seemed to collapse, completely shattered.

That is why I started to write. To save myself.

I realized that no one could save me but myself. The prison authorities were both uninterested and unable to help me. I had to seek out the truth and unravel the snarled web of my motivations. I had to find out who I am and what I want to be, what type of man I should be, and what I could do to become the best of which I was capable. I understood that what had happened to me had also happened to countless other blacks and it would happen to many, many more.

— Eldridge Cleaver

If the content of the second paragraph were less momentous, it would hardly merit a paragraph. Here the brevity helps to contribute to the enormous impact; those two simple sentences, set off by themselves, are meant to be equal in weight, so to speak, to the longer paragraphs that precede and follow. They are the hinge on which the door turns.

Now read the following horrible example, a newspaper account—chiefly in paragraphs of one sentence each—of an unfortunate happening.

Fish Eat Brazilian Fisherman
Reuters

MANAUS, BRAZIL—Man-eating piranha fish devoured fisherman Zeca Vicente when he tumbled into the water during a battle with 300 farmers for possession of an Amazon jungle lake.

Vicente, a leader of a group of 30 fishermen, was eaten alive in minutes by shoals of the ferocious fish lurking in Lake Januaca.

He died when the farmers—packed in an armada of small

boats—attacked the fishermen with hunting rifles, knives, and bows and arrows after they refused to leave.

The farmers, who claimed the fishermen were depleting the lake's fish stocks, one of their main sources of food, boarded the fishing vessels and destroyed cold storage installations.

Last to give way was Vicente, who tried to cut down the farmers' leader with a knife. But farmers shot him and he fell wounded into the water, and into the jaws of the piranhas.

Fifteen persons have been charged with the attack which caused Vicente's death and the injury of several other fishermen.

Lake Januaca, about four hours from this Amazon River town by launch, is famous for its pirarucu and tucunare fish which are regarded as table delicacies.

Most marvelously wrong is the final paragraph, with its cool guidebook voice uttering as inappropriate a fact as is imaginable, but what concerns us at the moment is the journalist's common practice of writing one-sentence paragraphs. Probably all six paragraphs (the seventh, final paragraph is irrelevant) can be effectively combined into one paragraph. Better, perhaps, the material can be divided into two paragraphs, one describing the event and another describing the cause or background. At the most, there is the stuff of three paragraphs, one on the background, one on the event itself, and one on the consequences (fifteen people are charged with the attack). Imagine how it could be reorganized into one paragraph, into two paragraphs, and into three. Which do you think would be most effective? Even the present final paragraph can be worked in. How?

If you spend a few minutes revising the newspaper account of the Brazilian fisherman's death, you will notice that sometimes you can make at least a small improvement merely by joining one paragraph to the next, such as the second to the third. But unsatisfactory short paragraphs usually cannot be repaired so simply; most are unsatisfactory not because sentences have been needlessly separated from each other, but because sentences with generalizations have not been supported by details. Consider these two consecutive paragraphs from a student's essay on Leonardo's *Mona Lisa*.

Leonardo's ''Mona Lisa,'' painted about 1502, has caused many people to wonder about the lady's expression. Different viewers see different things.

The explanation of the puzzle is chiefly in the mysterious expression that Leonardo conveys. The mouth and the eyes are especially important.

If you have read pages 113–114 you know that we have already made some use of Mona Lisa's mysterious expression, but here is another version, strengthening the two feeble paragraphs we have just quoted.

Leonardo's ''Mona Lisa,'' painted about 1502, has caused many people to wonder about the lady's expression. Doubtless she is remarkably life-like, but exactly what experience of life, what mood, does she reveal? Is she sad, or gently mocking, or uncertain or self-satisfied, or lost in day-dreams? Why are we never satisfied when we try to name her emotion?

Part of the uncertainty may of course be due to the subject as a whole: What can we make out of the combination of this smiling lady and that utterly unpopulated landscape? But surely a large part of the explanation lies in the way that Leonardo painted the face's two most expressive features, the eyes and the mouth. He slightly obscured the corners of these, so that we cannot precisely characterize them; and although on one viewing we may see them one way, on another viewing we may see them slightly differently. If today we think she looks detached, tomorrow we may think she looks slightly threatening.

This revision is not simply a padded version of the student's earlier paragraphs; it is a necessary clarification of them, for without the details the generalizations mean almost nothing to a reader.

INTRODUCTORY PARAGRAPHS

As the poet Byron said, at the beginning of a long part of a long poem, "Nothing so difficult as a beginning." Woody Allen thinks so too. In an interview he said that the toughest part of writing is "to go from nothing to the first draft."

We can give two pieces of advice. Unfortunately, they are apparently contradictory.

1. *The opening paragraph is unimportant.* It's great if you can write a paragraph that will engage your readers and let them know where the essay will be taking them, but if you can't come up with such a paragraph, just put down anything in order to prime the pump.

2. *The opening paragraph is extremely important.* It must engage your readers, and, probably by means of a thesis sentence it should let the readers know where the essay will be taking them.

The contradiction is, as we said, only apparent, not real. The first point is relevant to the opening paragraph of a *draft;* the second point is relevant to the opening paragraph of the *final version.* Almost all writers—professionals as well as amateurs—find that the first paragraphs in their drafts are false starts. Don't worry too much about the opening paragraphs of your draft; you'll almost surely want to revise your opening later anyway. (Surprisingly often your first paragraph may simply be deleted; your second, you may find, is where your essay truly begins.)

When writing a first draft you merely need something—almost anything may do—to break the ice. But in your finished paper the opening cannot be mere throat-clearing. The opening should be interesting. Among the commonest *un*interesting openings are:

1. a dictionary definition ("Webster says. . . .")
2. a restatement of your title. The title is (let's assume) "Anarchism and the Marx Brothers," and the first sentence says, "This essay will study the anarchic acts of the Marx Brothers." True, there is a thesis statement here, but there is no information about the topic beyond what has already been given in the title, and there is no information about you either, that is, no sense of your response to the topic, such as might be present in, say, "The Marx Brothers are funny, but one often has the feeling that under the fun the violence has serious implications."

3. a platitude, such as "Ever since the beginning of time, human beings have been violent." Again, such a sentence may be fine if it helps you to start drafting, but because it sounds canned and because it is insufficiently interesting it should not remain in your final version.

What is left? What *is* a good way for a final version to begin? Your introductory paragraph will be at least moderately interesting if it gives information, and it will be pleasing if the information provides focus: that is, if it lets the reader know exactly what your topic is, and where you will be going. Remember, when you write, *you* are the teacher; it won't do to begin,

```
George Orwell says he shot the elephant because . . .
```

We need at least,

```
George Orwell, in ''Shooting an Elephant,'' says he shot
the elephant because . . .
```

Even better is,

```
In ''Shooting an Elephant,'' George Orwell sets forth
his reflections on his service as a policeman in Burma.  He
suggests that he once shot an elephant because . . . but his
final paragraph suggests that we must look for additional
reasons.
```

Compare, for example, the opening sentences from three essays written by students on Anne Moody's *Coming of Age in Mississippi.* The book is the autobiography of a black woman, covering her early years with her sharecropper parents, her schooling, and finally her work in the civil rights movement.

```
The environment that surrounds a person from an early age
tends to be a major factor in determining their character.
```

This is what we call a *zonker* (see page 476), an all-purpose sentence that serves no specific purpose well. Notice also the faulty reference of the pronoun (the plural "their" refers to the singular "a person"), the weaseling of "tends to be a major factor," and the vagueness of "early age" and "environment" and "character." These all warn us that the writer will waste our time.

    It is unfortunate but true that racial or color prejudice
    shows itself early in the life of a child.

Less pretentious than the first example, but a tedious laboring of the obvious, and annoyingly preachy:

    Anne Moody's autobiography, Coming of Age in Mississippi,
    vividly illustrates how she discovered her black identity.

Surely this is the best of the three openings. Informative and focused, it identifies the book's theme and method, and it offers an evaluation. The essayist has been considerate of her readers: if we are interested in women's autobiographies, life in the South, or black identity we will read on. If we aren't, we are grateful to her for letting us off the bus at the first stop.

    Let's look now not simply at an opening sentence but at an entire opening paragraph. Here is an example from a relatively personal essay, an essay entitled "Interviewing for Oral History." As a reader can guess from the title, and from the paragraph, the student's focus is on how to conduct an interview. She begins by briefly telling the reader how she acquired her experience, but she also provides a focus; by the end of the paragraph the reader knows that the essay will give information about how to conduct an interview.

    Waltham will celebrate its 250th birthday this year with
    a six hundred page hardcover book containing more than four
    hundred photographs. This document, which took over two
    years to complete, details Waltham's ethnic history with
    taped, personal interviews of first and second generation
    residents. As a volunteer for the Interviewing Project, I
    not only had the pleasure of hearing about historical events

```
firsthand from the people who experienced them, but I also
learned something else: I learned how to interview for oral
histories.
```

Here is a second example, this one from a less personal and more analytic essay. Notice how the student provides the reader with the necessary information about the book he is discussing (the diary of a man whose son is brain-damaged) and also focuses the reader's attention on the topic that he will discuss (the quality that distinguishes this diary from others).

```
Josh Greenfeld's diary, A Place for Noah, records the at-
tempts of a smart, thoughtful man to reconcile himself to his
son's autism, a severe mental and physical disorder.  Most
diaries function as havens for secret thoughts.  And Green-
feld's diary does frequently supply a voice to Greenfeld's
darkest fears about who will ultimately care for Noah.  It
provides, too, an intimate glimpse of a family striving to
remain a coherent unit despite their tragedy.  But beyond af-
fording such urgent and personal revelations, A Place for
Noah, in chronicling the isolation of the Greenfelds, reveals
how inadequate and ineffectual our medical and educational
systems are in responding to families victimized by cata-
strophic illness.
```

Again, these two examples are not from drafts but are from final versions. They are both fairly direct, but of course you can provide interest and focus by other, more indirect means. Among them are:

1. a quotation
2. an anecdote or other short narrative
3. an interesting fact (a statistic, for instance, showing the reader that you know something about your topic)
4. a definition of an important term—but not merely one derived from a desk dictionary

5. an assertion (in an essay offering a proposal) that a problem exists
6. a glance at the opposition (disposing of it)
7. a question—but an interesting one, such as "Why do we call some words obscene?"

Many excellent opening paragraphs do not use any of these devices, and you need not use any of them if they seem unnatural to you. But observe in your reading how widely and successfully these devices are used. Here is an example of the second device, an anecdote that makes an effective, indeed an unnerving, introduction to an essay on aging.

> There is an old American folk take about a wooden bowl. It seems that Grandmother, with her trembling hands, was guilty of occasionally breaking a dish. Her daughter angrily gave her a wooden bowl, and told her that she must eat out of it from now on. The young granddaughter, observing this, asked her mother why Grandmother must eat from a wooden bowl when the rest of the family was given china plates. "Because she is old!" answered her mother. The child thought for a moment and then told her mother, "You must save the wooden bowl when Grandma dies." Her mother asked why, and the child replied, "For when you are old."
>
> — Sharon R. Curtin

The following paragraph—the first in a student's essay comparing two portraits by the American painter John Singleton Copley—also begins with a story, this one a bit of autobiography.

> Several Sundays ago while I was wandering through the Museum of Fine Arts, a professorial bellow shook me.   Around the corner strode a well-dressed mustachioed member of the art historical elite, a gaggle of note-taking students following in his wake. "And here," he said, "we have John Singleton Copley."   He marshalled his group about the rotunda, explaining that, "as one can easily see from these paintings, Copley never really learned to paint until he went to England."

The third strategy, an interesting detail, shows the reader that you know something about your topic and that you are worth reading. We have already seen (page 106) a rather quiet example of this device, in a paragraph about Charles Darwin, which began

"Charles Darwin's youth was unmarked by signs of genius." Here is a more obvious example, from an essay on blue jeans:

> That blue jeans or denims are not found only in Texas is not surprising if we recall that jeans are named for Genoa (Gene), where the cloth was first made, and that denim is cloth *de Nimes*, that is, from Nimes, a city in France.

(These scraps of learning are to be had by spending thirty seconds with a dictionary.)

The fourth strategy, a definition, is fairly common in analytic essays; the essayist first clears the ground by specifying what the topic really is. Here is the beginning of an essay on primitive art.

> The term "primitive art" has come to be used with at least three distinct meanings. First and most legitimate is its use with reference to the early stages in the development of a particular art, as when one speaks of the Italian primitives. Second is its use to designate works of art executed by persons who have not had formal training in our own art techniques and aesthetic canons. Third is its application to the art works of all but a small group of societies which we have chosen to call civilized. The present discussion will deal only with the last.
>
> — Ralph Linton

The author reviews three meanings of the term, and focuses our attention on the relevant one by putting it last.

The fifth strategy, the assertion that a problem exists, is common in essays that make proposals. The following example is the first paragraph of an essay that offers suggestions to employers on how to deal with discontented employees. Notice that the paragraph does not in fact offer the author's proposal; it simply points out that there really is an unsolved problem, and the reader infers that the essay will provide the solution.

> For over four decades, management has been jumping on and off a succession of behavioral-science bandwagons searching for *the* answer to harmonious and productive industrial relations:
> —Human relations in the 1930's and 1940's
> —Participative management in the 1950's
> —T-groups in the 1960's
> —Job enrichment in the 1970's

Despite considerable enthusiasm and a few well-publicized successes, these and other potentially effective behavioral-science tools have had a discouragingly high failure rate in the corporate sector. Moreover, in the current climate of employee alienation and mounting grievances about nonfinancial matters, management is increasingly turning to the behavioral theorists for help—with similarly disappointing results.

— David Sirota and Alan D. Wolfson

The sixth strategy, a glance at the opposition, is especially effective if the opposing view is well-established, but while you state it, you should manage to convey your distrust of it. We have already seen one example, in the paragraph about Copley's paintings. How does the writer convey her distrust of the opinion quoted in the paragraph? She tells us that she heard a "bellow" and she saw "a well-dressed mustachioed member of the art historical elite" leading "a gaggle of note-taking students." She then quotes the man's condescending remark about Copley: "One can easily see from these paintings, Copley never really learned to paint until he went to England." Surely it's not hard to sense that the essay will argue against this smug evaluation. Her next paragraph explicitly states her thesis.

Here is another example of a paragraph that glances at the opposition:

One often hears, correctly, that there is a world food crisis, and one almost as often hears that not enough food is produced to feed the world's entire population. The wealthier countries, it is said, jeopardize their own chances for survival when they attempt to subsidize all of the poorer countries in which the masses are starving. Often the life-boat analogy is offered: There is room in the boat for only X people, and to take in $X + 1$ is to overload the boat and to invite the destruction of all. But is it true that the world cannot and does not produce enough food to save the whole population from starving?

— V. Nagarajan

The seventh strategy, a question, is briefly but adequately illustrated by a paragraph from an essay in which a student discussed the connection between Frankenstein and the ancient Greek myth of Prometheus:

Mary Shelley did not simply call her book *Frankenstein;* she called it *Frankenstein or, The Modern Prometheus.* But who was Prometheus, and why did Mary Shelley include him in the title?

Obviously the writer will go on to summarize the myths of Prometheus (there are more than one), and will demonstrate the correspondence of the relevant myth.

Here is another opening paragraph (this one from an essay on writing business letters) that uses a question:

> In large corporations all over the country, people are playing a game of paddleball—with drafts of letters instead of balls. Volley after volley goes back and forth between those who sign the letters and those who write them. It's a game nobody likes, but it continues, and we pay for it. The workday has no time for such unproductiveness. What causes this round robin of revision?
>
> — John S. Fielden

Lest a reader assume, however, that an opening must be of one of these seven kinds, we quote an opening that doesn't fit our list:

> Time and again I wanted to reach out and shake Peter Fonda and Dennis Hopper, the two motorcyclist heroes of *Easy Rider,* until they stopped their damned-fool pompous poeticizing on the subject of doing your own thing and being your own man. I dislike Fonda as an actor; he lacks humor, affects insufferable sensitivity and always seems to be fulfilling a solemn mission instead of playing a part. I didn't believe in these Honda hoboes as intuitive balladeers of the interstate highways, and I had no intention of accepting them as protagonists in a modern myth about the destruction of innocence. To my astonishment, then, the movie reached out and profoundly shook me.
>
> — Joseph Morgenstern

Here Morgenstern deliberately misleads us in his first three sentences. When he reverses direction in the final sentence, he emphasizes the chief point he wants to make.

Such an opening paragraph is a variation of the surefire method we suggested at the outset: you cannot go wrong in suggesting your thesis in your opening paragraph. Ofen such a paragraph moves from a rather broad view to a narrower one. This kind of introductory paragraph can be conceived as a funnel, wide at the top and narrowing into what will be the body of the essay. A common version of this kind of paragraph offers some background and concludes with the subject at hand.

> In *Frankenstein,* Mary Shelley frames the novel with narratives of two similar characters who meet markedly different fates. Frankenstein, the medical researcher, and Walton, the explorer, are both passionately determined to push forward the boundaries of human knowledge. But while Walton's ambition to explore unknown regions of the earth is directed by reason and purpose, Frankenstein's ambition to create life is unfocussed and misguided. This difference in the nature of their ambitions determines their fates. Walton's controlled ambition leads him to abandon his goal in order to save the lives of his crew members. When we last see him, he is heading toward home and safety. Frankenstein's unchecked ambition leads to his own death and the self-destruction of his creature.

But bear in mind that although the first sentence of an introductory paragraph may be broader, more general than the last, it must nevertheless have substance. "Charles Darwin's great accomplishments in the field of natural science resulted from many factors" (look back at page 105) is so broad, so general, so lacking in substance, that it teaches us nothing either about Darwin or about the writer of the essay. If your opening sentence lacks substance, it will not matter what you say next. No one will bother to read more.

CONCLUDING PARAGRAPHS

Concluding paragraphs, like opening paragraphs, are especially difficult if only because they are so conspicuous. Fortunately, you are not always obliged to write one. Descriptive essays, for example, may end merely with a final paragraph, not with a paragraph that draws a conclusion. In an expository essay explaining a process or mechanism you may simply stop when you have finished. Just check to see that the last sentence is a good one, clear and vigorous, and stop. In such essays there is usually no need for a crescendo signaling your farewell to the reader. Persuasive essays are more likely to need concluding paragraphs, not merely final paragraphs. But even persuasive essays, if they are short enough, may end without a formal conclusion; if the last paragraph sets forth the last step of the argument, that may be conclusion enough.

Let's assume, however, that you do feel the need to write a concluding paragraph. With conclusions, as with introductions, try to say something interesting. It is not of the slightest interest to say "Thus we see . . ." and then echo your title and first paragraph. There is some justification for a summary at the end of a long paper because the reader may have half forgotten some of the ideas presented thirty pages earlier, but a paper that can easily be held in the mind needs something different. A good concluding paragraph does more than provide an echo of what the writer has already said. It rounds out the previous discussion, normally with a few sentences that summarize (without the obviousness of "We may now summarize"), but it also may draw an inference that has not previously been expressed. To draw such an inference is not to introduce a new idea—a concluding paragraph is hardly the place for a new idea—but is to see the previous material in a fresh perspective. A good concluding paragraph closes the issue while enriching it. For example, an essay on being assaulted and robbed ends with these two paragraphs:

> What do they take when they rob you? Maybe a thousand dollars' worth of stuff. A car. A jar of pennies and small change— the jar, which they would proably end up breaking, worth more than the change inside. A portable radio bought years before at an Army PX. Little things that it takes days to discover are missing.
>
> And what else? The ability to easily enter a darkened apartment or to freely open the door after going out. The worst loss is the sense of private space, whether it's in your head or your home, and you can never be certain it will not be invaded again.
>
> — Charles T. Powers

Powers moves from the theft of material objects to the psychological implications of the theft, that is, to a more profound kind of robbery. This is not a new topic because the idea is implicit throughout a discussion of assault and robbery and so it enlarges rather than abandons the topic. It is just that Powers is explicitly stating the idea for the first time.

In the first two chapters of this book we tried to make the point that what you write depends partly on your audience. It depends also, of course, on you—on your purpose in writing and on your attitude toward your subject and toward your audience.

And what you write in your concluding paragraph will depend on everything that precedes it. For instance, if you have been writing an argument and have been bombarding your reader with statistics, you may feel that now is the time to ease up, to end in a more conversational, relaxed manner. Or, conversely, if you have been making your point rather genially, you may feel that in your last paragraph you want to hammer the point home, unforgettably.

Because all writers have to find out what they think about any given topic, and have to find the strategies appropriate for presenting these thoughts to a particular audience, we hesitate to offer a do-it-yourself kit for final paragraphs, but the following simple devices often work:

1. End with a quotation, especially a quotation that amplifies or varies a quotation used in the opening paragraph.
2. End with some idea or detail from the beginning of the essay and thus bring it full circle.
3. End with an allusion, say to a historical or mythological figure or event, putting your topic in a larger framework.
4. End with a glance at the readers—not with a demand that they mount the barricades, but with a suggestion that the next move is theirs.

If you adopt any of these devices, do so quietly; the aim is not to write a grand finale, but to complete or round out a discussion.

Here are two concluding paragraphs; notice how they wrap things up and at the same time open out by suggesting a larger frame of reference. The first example, from a student's essay on Anthony Burgess's *A Clockwork Orange*, includes quotations from the book and an allusion to a common expression.

> Both worlds, youthful anarchy and repressive government, are undesirable. For while ''you can't run a country with every chelloveck comporting himself in Alex's manner of the night,'' there should never be a government with the power to ''turn you into something other than a human being . . . with no power of choice any longer.'' What is frightening is that there is no apparent solution to this futuristic society's dilemma. In fact, with the friendly alliance of Alex and the

```
Minister of the Interior at the end of the book come hints

that society may soon enjoy the worst of both worlds.
```

The second is a concluding paragraph from a student's essay on
Black Elk Speaks, the life story of an Oglala Sioux holy man. The
paragraph includes quotations, and then goes on to suggest that
the rest is up to the reader.

```
    ''Truth comes into this world with two faces.  One is

sad with suffering and the other laughs; but it is the same

face.''  The terrible tragedy of the Indian people can never

fully be undone.  Their ''hoop is broken, and there is no

center anymore.''  But perhaps the rising circulation of

Black Elk's story will inspire people to look more closely

into person-to-person and person-to-nature relationships.

Black Elk's message ''was given to him for all men and it is

true and it is beautiful,'' but it must be listened to,

understood, and acted on.
```

All essayists will have to find their own ways of ending each
essay; the four strategies we have suggested are common but they
are not for you if you don't find them comfortable. And so, rather
than ending this section with rules about how to end essays, we
suggest how not to end them: don't merely summarize, don't say
"in conclusion," don't introduce a totally new point, and don't
apologize.

A CHECKLIST FOR REVISING PARAGRAPHS

1. Does the paragraph *say* anything? Does it have substance?
2. Does the paragraph have a topic sentence? If so, is it in the best
   place? If the paragraph doesn't have a topic sentence, might one
   improve the paragraph? Or does it have a clear topic idea?
3. If the paragraph is an opening paragraph, is it interesting enough
   to attract and to hold a reader's attention? If it is a later para-

graph, does it easily evolve out of the previous paragraph, and
lead into the next paragraph?

4. Does the paragraph contain some principle of development, for
instance from cause to effect, or from general to particular?

5. Does each sentence clearly follow from the preceding sentence?
Have you provided transitional words or cues to guide your
reader? Would it be useful to repeat certain key words, for clarity?

6. What is the purpose of the paragraph? Do you want to summarize, or tell a story, or give an illustration, or concede a point,
or what? Is your purpose clear to you, and does the paragraph
fulfill your purpose?

7. Is the closing paragraph effective, and not an unnecessary restatement of the obvious?

EXERCISES

1. Reread the paragraph on page 122, in which a topic sentence
(about three films by the Marx Brothers) begins the paragraph. Then write a paragraph with a similar construction,
clarifying the topic sentence with details. You might, for example, begin thus: "When facing a right-handed batter, a left-
handed pitcher has a distinct advantage over a right-handed
pitcher." Another possible beginning: "All three major television networks offer pretty much the same kinds of entertainment during prime time."

2. Reread the paragraph on page 109, discussing the face of
Frankenstein's monster, and then write a paragraph on some
other widely known face (Boy George? Madonna?), ending your
paragraph with a topic sentence. The cover of a recent issue
of *Time* or *Newsweek* may provide you with the face you need.

3. The following paragraph is unified, but incoherent. How could
it be reorganized?

Abortion, the expulsion of a fetus which could not develop and
function alone successfully, is an issue which has caused much discussion in the past decade. There exist mainly two opposing groups
concerning this subject, but many people's opinions lie somewhere
in the middle. Some believe that abortions should be legalized un-
conditionally throughout the United States, while others believe that
abortions should be illegal in all cases.

4. The following paragraph is both unified and fairly well organized, but it is still lacking in coherence. What would you do to improve it?

> The cyclist must also master prerace tactics. Not only what to wear and what food to bring are important, but how to strip the bike of unnecessary weight. Cycling shoes are specially designed for bike racing. They have a metal sole that puts the energy directly to the pedal, thus efficiently using one's power. The food that one brings is important in a long-distance race. It must not only be useful in refueling the body, but it must be easily eaten while pedaling. Candy bars and fruit, such as bananas, satisfy both requirements. The bike must be stripped of all unnecessary weight, including saddlebags and reflectors. Some cyclists drill holes in parts of the frame, saddle post, and handlebars to lessen the weight of the bike.

5. On page 112 we printed a paragraph on athletic coaches and we also printed a more unified revision of the paragraph. But the revision is still weak, for it lacks supporting details. Revise the revision, giving it life.

6. Here is the opening paragraph of an essay (about 750 words) on the manufacture of paper in the fifteenth century, the days of the earliest printed books. On the whole it is very good, but the unity and the organization can be improved. Revise the paragraph.

> We take paper for granted, but old as it is it did not always exist. In fact, it was invented long after writing was invented, for the earliest writing is painted or scratched on cave walls, shells, rocks, and other natural objects. Paper was not even the first manufactured surface for writing; sheets made from papyrus, a reed-like plant, were produced about 2500 B.C., long before the invention of paper. Although the Chinese may have invented paper as early as the time of Christ, the oldest surviving paper is from early fifth-century China. The Arabs learned the secret of paper-making from the Chinese in the eighth century, but the knowledge traveled slowly to Europe. The oldest European paper, made by the Moors in Spain, is of the twelfth century. Early European paper is of poor quality and so not until the quality improved, around the fourteenth century, did paper become widely used. Most writing was done on parchment, which is the skin of a sheep or goat, and vellum, which is the finer skin of a lamb, kid, or calf. Whatever the animal, the skin was washed, limed, unhaired, scraped, washed again, stretched, and rubbed with pumice until a surface suitable for writing was achieved. Until it was

displaced by paper, in the fourteenth century, parchment was the chief writing surface in Europe.

7. Here is the concluding paragraph of a book review. Analyze and evaluate its effectiveness.

> Mr. Flexner's book is more than a political argument. He has written so vividly and involved us so deeply that there are moments when we yearn to lean over into the pages, pull Hamilton aside, and beg him to reconsider, to pity, to trust, to wait, or merely to shut up. Yet the book's effect is not melodramatic. It is tragic—a tragedy not of fate but of character, the spectacle of an immensely gifted man who tried to rule a nation and could not rule himself.
>
> — Naomi Bliven

8. Read the following paragraph. Observe its organization. Then read the instructions below.

> Q. *My house is centrally air-conditioned and I am thinking of installing either a ceiling fan in my living room or an attic exhaust fan in the hallway leading to the three rear bedrooms. Which would be the best and most energy-efficient?*
> A. This is like comparing apples and oranges. A ceiling fan is used to circulate air inside the house and stir up a breeze; a whole-house attic exhaust fan is used to draw cool air in from outside through several open windows (usually through bedroom windows at night after the outside air has cooled off). The ceiling fan can be used when the air-conditioning system is running, to help create a slight breeze that will enable you to turn the air-conditioner's thermostat to a higher setting. But you would use the attic fan only when the air-conditioner is off, or if you wanted to cool the house before turning the system on in the morning. On a marginal day the ceiling fan might keep you comfortable without air-conditioning; an attic fan at night might eliminate the need for air-conditioning.

Write one paragraph following the organization of the paragraph above as closely as you can. Your paragraph should compare two things that seem to you as unlike as "apples and oranges." Example: running and dieting (to lose weight); golf and tennis (as spectator sports); attending a small college and a large university; alpine and cross country skiing. . . .

5
Definition

Many things are not what they sound like: there is no lead in a lead pencil; a two-by-four is one and five-eighths inches in thickness and three and three-eighths inches in width; peanuts are not nuts (they are vegetables, related to peas and beans); coffee beans are not beans (they are the pits of a fruit). And "bad" can mean "good."

Asked to define a word, we may sound like Polonius talking about Hamlet (II.ii.92–94):

> Your noble son is mad.
> Mad call I it, for, to define true madness,
> What is't but to be nothing else but mad?

A dictionary can be a great help, of course; but don't begin an essay by saying "Webster says. . . ." Because the name Webster is no longer copyrighted, it appears on all sorts of dictionaries, bad as well as good.[1] Moreover, there is no staler opening.

---

[1] Of the five desk dictionaries that we recommend, two have "Webster" in the title: *Webster's New Collegiate Dictionary* and *Webster's New World Dictionary*. The other three recommended desk dictionaries are *The American College Dictionary*, *The American Heritage Dictionary of the English Language*, and *The Random House Dictionary of the English Language: College Edition*. If you didn't receive one of these five as a graduation present, you should buy one. "Pocket"

ING

A course in writing is partly, even largely, a course in thinking. And "thinking" implies getting straight in one's own mind the meanings of the words one is using, and clearly conveying those meanings to readers. Notice how the following passage, the opening paragraph of an essay on the Scholastic Aptitude Test, neatly points out that "ability" can mean two different things. Only when the ground is cleared, by definition of crucial terms, can the writer go on to discuss whether or not the SAT is a useful device. In short, writers often find that they must define their terms at the outset.

> The idea that colleges should choose among applicants on the basis of their "academic ability" appeals to both educators and the public. But "ability" has two distinct meanings, which imply different admissions policies. In one usage academic ability means an *existing* capacity to do academic work. In the other usage academic ability means a *potential* capacity to do such work. To say that an applicant "has the ability to do differential calculus," for example, can mean either that the applicant can already do differential calculus or that the applicant could learn differential calculus given opportunity and motivation. To avoid this ambiguity, psychometricians usually call the ability to learn something an "aptitude" while calling current mastery of a skill or body of knowledge "achievement."
>
> — Christopher Jencks and James Crouse

---

dictionaries and "concise" dictionaries, which contain about 55,000 entries, are not adequate substitutes for any of these five, which contain 130,000–170,000 entries. You should also become acquainted, in the library, with the great *New English Dictionary (NED)*, issued in ten volumes, 1888–1928; reissued in twelve volumes in 1933 as the *Oxford English Dictionary (OED)*, and in subsequent years equipped with four supplementary volumes, the most recent of which was issued in 1986. In 1989, however, a twenty-volume edition was issued, collating into a single alphabetical order not only the original volumes and the supplementary volumes, but also about 5,000 recent words, such as *acid rain, badmouth, brain-dead, crack,* and the *pits.* The *OED* is unrivalled in its citations of illustrative quotations indicating the meanings of a word over the centuries. Far less exhaustive, but useful, are three American unabridged dictionaries: *Webster's Third New International Dictionary, Funk and Wagnall's New Standard Dictionary of the English Language,* and *The Random House Dictionary of the English Language,* second edition.

BRIEF DEFINITIONS

Because they keep their audience in mind, and have a sense of their audience's needs, experienced writers, when writing for the general reader, define specialized terms. The definitions may be very brief, as in this example from an essay entitled "The Race for Supercomputers":

> Venture capitalists, the specialized firms that raise money for new technological inventions, are extremely reluctant to invest in an expensive long-term development prospect in an industry where machines are born and become largely obsolete in just two years.
>
> — Peter H. Lewis

The writer, suspecting that the reader might not know what "venture capitalists" are, quietly informed the reader that they are firms that raise money for new technological inventions. Because the definition is offered without a fanfare, those readers who already know the meaning of the term will not feel that the author is talking down.

Here's another example of a brief but helpful definition:

> A Muslim, or follower of Islam, is *muslim,* "faithful" or "devoted" to God.

The student who wrote this sentence rightly believed that his readers would be interested in learning that "Muslim" comes from the adjective *muslim,* "faithful" or "devoted." More important, suspecting that some of his readers would not know that a Muslim is a follower of Islam, he offered this brief definition. As you can guess, he soon went on to define Islam.

Here is a third inconspicuous but helpful definition, this one from the first paragraph of a newspaper essay on how to prevent a car from skidding:

> Your car rolls along on its tires. That's its normal way of getting around in this world. When the tires slide instead of roll, then you have a skid.
>
> — Diane McCluggage

Notice, by the way, that the definition of a skid ("the tires slide") is clarified by a comparison ("instead of roll"). Definitions often use comparisons as a means of clarifying. Consider the following passage:

The advanced economies are moving into the postindustrial era, one in which the movement and production of information are becoming as important as the movement and production of goods. Already, more than half the workers in advanced economies like the United States and Japan spend most of their time gathering, manipulating, analyzing and distributing information, rather than producing goods or services.

— John Pollack

Pollack could have defined the postindustrial era simply by saying that it is an age characterized by the movement and production of information, but he clarifies his point by comparing the postindustrial era with the industrial era (an age characterized by the movement and production of goods, or of goods and services).

Almost any essay on a moderately specialized topic will include brief definitions of the sort just given. In revising a draft, keep two points in mind:

1 Your sense of your *audience* will largely determine which words must be defined, and at what length;
2 if you conclude that a brief definition probably will be helpful, offer it clearly but unobtrusively, so that those readers who already know (or think they know) the meaning of the term will not feel that you are speaking condescendingly.

Some of your assignments, however, will require you to write definitions that run a sentence, a paragraph, or even several pages. We'll see some examples in a moment.

DEFINING BY SYNONYM

Usually when we are trying to define a word we can come up with at least a single word as a synonym. We define *helix* by saying "spiral," or *to civilize* by saying "to socialize." Defining by synonym, however, doesn't go very far; it merely equates one word with another. And often no close synonym exists. In any case, defining by synonym is only a beginning.

Often, too, words are used carelessly as synonyms. To clear the ground, an essayist may find it necessary to explain why two words are *not* synonyms. George Kane argues, for example, that to use the words *terrorist* and *guerrilla* interchangeably blurs a valuable distinction:

> There has been a good deal of discussion of late about the precise difference between a terrorist and a guerrilla. It is not yet generally realized that there has been a major shift of meaning such as often occurs in the development of language. In earlier times the distinction between the two arose from the difference in the choice of objectives and the methods employed. Both used violence, which was illegal, i.e., not exercised by regular armed forces or police. Guerrillas, however, used it against such regular military and police forces or their installations. They did not normally attack ordinary civilians, still less third parties. Terrorists, on the other hand, usually took care to avoid the armed forces and police of the adversary and instead made war on civilians. They preferred identifiable public figures, with a special liking for elderly cabinet ministers, but were willing to settle for supermarkets, bus stations, kindergartens, and similar unmilitary objectives. They preferred, again, to attack the civilians of the adversary, but if, for any reason, this was not feasible they were willing to indulge in the casual murder of travelers or bystanders of other countries. The guerrilla would delay an operation against an enemy force if there was a danger of injuring civilians; the terrorist was willing to blow up a planeload of randomly selected passengers in order to kill one of them or even to get a prime-time spot on television. This was the distinction between guerrillas and terrorists. It is no longer. As these terms are used today in the media and elsewhere, the distinction no longer relates to strategy or tactics or even objectives, but to ideology and sentiment. To put it simply, a terrorist is one who attacks me or my friends; a guerrilla is one who attacks those to whom I am hostile or indifferent.

DEFINING BY ORIGIN

Sometimes we know the origin of the word, and the origin may be worth recounting for the light it sheds on the present meaning.

Low Rider. A Los Angeles nickname for ghetto youth. Originally the term was coined to describe the youth who had lowered the bodies of their cars so that they rode low, close to the ground; also implied was the style of driving that these youngsters perfected. Sitting behind the steering wheel and slumped low down in the seat, all that could be seen of them was from their eyes up, which used to be the cool way of driving. When these youthful hipsters alighted from their vehicles, the term *low rider* stuck with them, evolving to the point where all black ghetto youth—but *never* the soft offspring of the black bourgeoisie—are referred to as low riders.

— Eldridge Cleaver

Or we may know the foreign origins of an English word; *pornography,* for example, come from Greek words meaning "writing about prostitutes." That's interesting enough and relevant enough to be useful. Or take *yoga.* If you are writing an essay on yoga, you may want to say something like this:

The word "yoga" comes from a Sanskrit root meaning "to join," "to yoke," and indeed our words "join" and "yoke" both come from this same root. Yoga seeks to join or to yoke the individual's consciousness to its spiritual source.

A student began an expository essay on karate thus:

```
Karate, which comes from two Japanese words meaning ''empty
hand,'' is an art of self-defense that uses no weapons. It
relies only on kicks delivered with the sole of the foot or
the blade of the foot or the kneecap; strokes, delivered with
the fist, blade of the hand, palm, or arm; and thrusts, de-
livered with the fist, palm, elbow, or crown of the head.
```

You don't have to know Greek or Sanskrit or Japanese to be able to say such things; to learn a word's origins, or etymology (from the Greek, meaning "true word"), you need only to look in a good dictionary. (You might want to check up on jujitsu and judo.) The etymology may be interesting and relevant and therefore worth mentioning. But of course a word's present meaning may be far from its original meaning, or those of its origins. *Doctor,* for instance, is from a medieval Latin word meaning "teacher." Although this etymology is relevant if you are talking about the classroom skills of Ph.D.'s, it is probably of no use to you or to your reader if you are talking about the word in its commonest sense today, "physician."

Stipulating a Definition

You may stipulate (contract for) a particular meaning of a word. For instance, you may stipulate that by vegetarians you mean people who eat only vegetables, fruit, and nuts, or you mean people who eat these and also fish, eggs, and milk products. Or if for instance you are writing about Catholics, you may stipulate that in your essay the word refers to all who have been baptized into the Catholic faith. Or you may stipulate that it refers only to those who consider themselves practicing Catholics. As another example, take the expression "third world people." This term has at least three related but separate meanings:

1. a group of nations, especially in Africa and Asia, that are not aligned with either the Communist or the non-Communist blocs.
2. the aggregate of underdeveloped nations of the world.
3. the aggregate of minority groups within a larger predominant culture

In fact, a fourth meaning, a variation of the third, seems to be most common in recent American writing: the aggregate of minority groups *other than blacks and Asians* within the United States. Many discussions of third world people limit themselves to American Indians and to Spanish-speaking people, apparently considering American blacks and Asians as part of the larger predominant culture. Thus, in an essay you may announce what you mean by "third world": "In this essay, 'third world' refers not to A or B but to C."

Stipulative definitions are often necessary. Although technical words have relatively stable meanings, many of the words that you will be defining—words such as *education* and *society*—have so many meanings that the reader won't know what you mean until you explain which definition you are using.

Formal Definition

A formal definition is a kind of analysis. It normally takes a term (for instance, *professor*) and places it within a class or family ("a teacher") and then goes on to differentiate it from other members of the class ("in a college or university"). Such a definition is sometimes called *inclusive/exclusive* because it includes the word in a relevant category and then excludes other members of that category. Plato is said to have defined *man* as "a featherless biped," but a companion pointed out that this definition is not sufficiently exclusive: a plucked chicken fits the definition. Plato therefore amended it satisfactorily by adding "with flat toenails." Another example: in Hitchcock's *Stage Fright,* Marlene Dietrich suggests that "Detectives are merely policemen with smaller feet." If this definition is inaccurate, it is not because of its structure.

Notice, by the way, that a definition demands a parallel form—for example, a noun for a noun: "A *professor* is a *teacher* in a college or university"; "*terrorism* is *violence* deliberately directed against civilians." Avoid saying "A professor is when you teach. . . ."

What use can be made of formal definition? Suppose you are writing about organic food. You may want to clear the ground by saying something like this:

> All food contain chemicals (milk contains about a hundred, potatoes about a hundred fifty), and from a chemical point of view, all foods are organic, for they are compounds containing carbon. So-called organic foods do not differ from other foods in their chemical makeup. They have, however, been grown with the help of fertilizers or pesticides of only animal or vegetable origin rather than with the help of manufactured chemicals.

Or suppose you want to discuss sharks. A desk dictionary will give you something like this: "a cartilaginous (as opposed to bony) fish with a body tapering toward each end." Such a definition puts sharks within the family of a type of fish and then goes on to exclude other members of this family (which happens also to include rays) by calling attention to the distinctive shape of the shark's body. But if you are not writing a strictly formal definition you may want to talk not only about sharks as remote objects but about your sense of them, your response to them:

> Although the shark and the ray are closely related, being cartilaginous rather than bony fish, the two could scarcely be more different in appearance. The ray, a floppy pancake-like creature, is grotesque but not terrifying; the shark, its tapering body gliding through the water, is perhaps the most beautiful and at the same time the most terrifying sight the sea can offer.

In short, a formal definition can structure your definition even if you go beyond it.

LONGER DEFINITIONS

Most of the terms we try to define in college courses require lengthy definitions. If you are going to say anything of interest about capitalism or obscenity or freedom or poverty you will have to go far beyond a formal definition. If you are writing on a subject you care about, you may find that you will have to write at least several paragraphs until you get to the limits of the word. *Definition,* by the way, is from the Latin *de* "off" and *finis* "end, limit."

One way of getting toward the limits of the word is to spend some sentences, perhaps a paragraph, on a comparison or contrast. In the paragraph on sharks, half of one sentence compares sharks to rays, which are closely related to sharks but different. In a more extended definition of a less easily defined topic, more space might be devoted to establishing distinctions. For example, the writer of an essay on gallows humor (briefly defined as humor that domesticates a terrifying situation by making fun of it) might wish to compare it with black humor (not the humor of black people, but a brutal or sadistic humor). The superficial similarity of gallows humor to black humor might require the essayist to discuss black humor in order to make clear the special quality of gallows humor; but of course the discussion of black humor should be clearly subordinated to the main topic lest the essay lose focus.

The point of such a strategy is to help the reader see something clearly by holding it against something similar but significantly different. The following extended definition of a proverb follows such a strategy.

> A proverb is a concise didactic statement that is widely used in an unchanging form. Among the examples that come to mind are "Look before you leap," "A rolling stone gathers no moss," and "Red sky at night, sailors' delight." These, and almost all other proverbs that one can think of, concisely and memorably summarize everyday experience. This everyday experience is usually a matter of conduct; even "Red sky at night, sailors' delight"—which seems purely descriptive—is followed by "Red sky at morning, sail-

ors take warning." Most commonly, proverbs advise the hearer to avoid excess.

We should distinguish proverbs from other concise utterances. Clichés such as "cool as a cucumber," "last but not least," and "a sight for sore eyes," though they may be called proverbial phrases, often do not offer advice implicitly or explicitly. More important, clichés are not complete sentences. He or she or they can be or are or were "cool as a cucumber"; but a proverb has an independent and unvarying form. Proverbs should be distinguished, too, from such conventional utterances as "Good morning," "Thank you," and "Please pass the salt." These are unvarying, but unlike proverbs they are not didactic.

Closer to proverbs, superficially at least, are epigrams, such as Oscar Wilde's "A cynic is a man who knows the price of everything and the value of nothing." Most epigrams are obviously literary; they usually employ a clever contrast (antithesis) that is rare in proverbs. And most epigrams, unlike proverbs, are not really communal property: their authorship is known, and they are not used by ordinary people in ordinary speech. When used by someone other than the author, they are used by educated speakers or writers as conscious quotations. In contrast, the speaker of a proverb, though he knows that he did not invent it, rightly feels that it is part of his own wisdom.

Notice that this extended definition of proverbs begins by including the proverb within a class ("concise didactic statement") and then proceeds to exclude other members of the class by specifying that a proverb is "widely used in an unchanging form." The definition, then, is inclusive and exclusive; it includes the term to be defined within a class, and it excludes other members of the class.

Notice too that *examples* are given throughout. If the examples were omitted, the paragraphs would be less lively and less clear. How many examples should be given? There is no rule, and we can only suggest that when you are revising a draft you give enough to inform and satisfy your imagined readers, and not so many examples that you begin to bore them.

The definition of a proverb was just that; it was not a focused essay on proverbs. And it was not an attempt to woo the reader to be interested in proverbs or an attempt to persuade the reader that proverbs really have no wisdom to offer because they are often contradictory ("Look before you leap" contradicts "He who hesitates is lost," and "Birds of a feather flock together" contradicts "Opposites attract"). Rather, it was an attempt to make clear the meaning of a word. If more space had been available, especially if the word were a more elusive one, such as *equality* or *personality* or *feminism,* the essay might have had the following structure:

1. statement of the need for a definition
2. survey of the usual definitions (calling attention to their inadequacy)
3. the writer's definition, set forth with illustrative examples, comparisons, and contrasts

Clearly the heart of such an essay is the third part.

Though some essays seek to do nothing more than to define a term, essays with other purposes often include paragraphs defining a word. Here, from a long essay on the recent fad for country music, are some paragraphs defining country music. Notice how this selection moves from a moderately jocose and obviously imprecise definition ("anything that Grandma can hum, whistle, or sing is country") to a list of the subjects of country music and then to a hypothetical example.

> What is the fuss all about? Glen George, manager of Kansas City's country radio KCKN, says: "Anything that Grandma can hum, whistle or sing is country." Its traditional message is one of despair, hope, loss, death, the land and, often with cloying sentimentality, love. Country lyrics have always been the cry of the common man. They can, and do give comfort to everyone from sharecroppers and truck-stop waitresses to University of Texas Football Coach Darrell Royal, former Energy Czar John Love, Novelist Kurt Vonnegut, Jr. and Operatic Tenor Richard Tucker. Says Moon Mullins, program director of the all-country WINN in Louisville: "If you listen to our station long enough, one of our songs will tell your story."
>
> Cynics like to say that whomever the story belongs to, it will probably deal with trucks, trains, prison, drinking (or moonshine), women misbehaving ("slippin' around" in the country vernacular) or death. The ideal country song might be about a guy who finally gets out of prison, hops a truck home, finds that his wife is slippin'

around, gets drunk, and staggers to his doom in front of a high-balling freight.

The music itself, at least as purveyed by many of the superstars of Nashville and Bakersfield, has a vanilla sameness to it that often does not reflect the pain and sorrow of the words. The voices of the singers are often less charged with emotion than their blues and rock counterparts. Most male country stars have deep bass baritones that seem to say: this man sits tall in the saddle. Women stars tend to have bright, unstrained sopranos—or a Lynn Anderson kind of nasal chirpiness—that rule out not only women's lib but any other kind of defiance. In the past, country lyrics have been astonishingly repressive. Blind loyalty to husband, parents, even political leaders has been a common theme. When men have sung about women, the subject (always excepting long-suffering Mother) has often been the pain, not the pleasure.

Today, however, country is taking on a new sound, a new diversity and message as well. Partly that is due to the influence of rock, partly to the visible softening of the once strong accents of American regionalization. Says Kris Kristofferson, 37, the former Rhodes scholar who is now a leader of country's progressive wing: "There's really more honesty and less bullshit in today's music than ever before."

— *Time*

A CHECKLIST FOR REVISING DEFINITIONS

1. Are brief definitions made fairly unobtrusively, so that readers will not feel they are needlessly being lectured?
2. If the definition is lengthy, is the need for a definition adequately explained?
3. Is the etymology or origin of the word sufficiently helpful so that it ought to be mentioned?
4. Are adequate examples given to clarify the definition?
5. Is the term distinguished from a near synonym—for instance communism from socialism, terrorism from guerilla warfare? Will a comparison help to define the term? (For instance, a definition of Marxism might distinguish Marxism from Leninism, or from the communism practiced in China.)
6. If the term is complex, have you adequately divided the material into comprehensible parts?

7. If you are stipulating a definition, are you fairly confident that your proposed definition will be acceptable to a reasonable reader?

EXERCISES

1. Define, for an audience unfamiliar with the term, blues or heavy metal or soul or folk music in 250–500 words.
2. Write one paragraph defining one of the following terms: security blanket, twilight zone, holding pattern. Your paragraph should disclose the origin of the term (if you can't find it, make a reasonable guess) and some examples of current use distinct from its original meaning.
3. On July 14, 1789, Louis XVI asked a courtier, "Is it a revolt?" "No, sire," the courtier replied. "It's a revolution." In a paragraph, explain the courtier's reply.
4. Write an opening paragraph for an essay in which you stipulate a meaning for *death,* or *vegetarianism,* excluding one or two other meanings. Don't write the essay, just the opening paragraph.
5. In a paragraph explain the difference between "a reason" (for some action) and "an excuse." Provide a specific example, real or invented. Your audience is someone who expects you to offer an excuse.
6. If you are fluent in a language other than English, or in a dialect other than Standard American, write a paragraph defining for native speakers of Standard American a word that stands for some concept. Examples: Spanish *machismo* or *commoción,* Yiddish *haimish* or *chutzpa,* Japanese *shibui* or *amae,* German *Gemütlichkeit,* black English *bad* or *the dozens.*
7. Write an essay of approximately 500 words on the word *natural* as it is used to advertise products such as cereals, yogurt, cosmetics, and cigarettes. Your essay should stipulate a definition of natural, and should have a thesis. An example of a thesis: "Yogurt may be a wholesome food, but most commercial yogurts are not as 'natural' as we are led to believe."

8. Write an essay (about 500 words) explaining one of the following terms: horror film, situation comedy, soap opera, junk food, nostalgia, ethnic joke, yuppie. Your essay will probably include a definition, reference to several examples, and perhaps an extended discussion of one example, explaining the reasons for its popularity, or arguing its merits or lack of merits. Your essay, then, will probably blend exposition with narration, description, and argument.

DEFINITION AT WORK

Mechanic's Feel
Robert M. Pirsig[2]

1   The mechanic's feel comes from a deep inner kinesthetic feeling for the elasticity of materials. Some materials, like ceramics, have very little, so that when you thread a porcelain fitting you're very careful not to apply great pressures. Other materials, like steel, have tremendous elasticity, more than rubber, but in a range in which, unless you're working with large mechanical forces, the elasticity isn't apparent.

2   With nuts and bolts you're in the range of large mechanical forces and you should understand that within these ranges metals are elastic. When you take up a nut there's a point called "finger-tight" where there's contact but no takeup of elasticity. Then there's "snug," in which the easy surface elasticity is taken up. Then there's a range called "tight," in which all the elasticity is taken up. The force required to reach these three points is different for each size of nut and bolt, and different for lubricated bolts and for locknuts. The forces are different for steel and cast iron and brass and aluminum and plastics and ceramics. But a person with mechanic's feel knows when something's tight and stops. A person without it goes right on past and strips the threads or breaks the assembly.

3   A "mechanic's feel" implies not only an understanding for the elasticity of metal but for its softness. The insides of a motorcycle contain surfaces that are precise in some cases to as little as one ten-thousandth of an inch. If you drop them or get dirt on them or scratch them or bang them with a hammer they'll lose that precision. It's important to understand that the metal *behind* the surfaces can normally take great shock and stress but that the surfaces themselves cannot. When handling precision parts that are stuck or difficult to manipulate, a person with mechanic's feel will avoid

---

[2]Editors' note: This passage is not an independent essay. It is taken from Pirsig's *Zen and the Art of Motorcycle Maintenance* (New York: Bantam, 1975), pp. 317–18. In the previous paragraph Pirsig has mentioned kinesthesia, sensitive muscular response to things.

damaging the surfaces and work with his tools on the nonprecision surfaces of the same part whenever possible. If he must work on the surfaces themselves, he'll always use softer surfaces to work them with. Brass hammers, plastic hammers, wood hammers, rubber hammers and lead hammers are all available for this work. Use them. Vise jaws can be fitted with plastic and copper and lead faces. Use these too. Handle precision parts gently. You'll never be sorry. If you have a tendency to bang things around, take more time and try to develop a little more respect for the accomplishment that a precision part represents.

Questions

1. Is Pirsig sufficiently specific?
2. What is the function of the first sentence in the third paragraph?

Television Addiction
Marie Winn

1   The word "addiction" is often used loosely and wryly in conversation. People will refer to themselves as "mystery book addicts" or "cookie addicts." E. B. White writes of his annual surge of interest in gardening: "We are hooked and are making an attempt to kick the habit." Yet nobody really believes that reading mysteries or ordering seeds by catalogue is serious enough to be compared with addictions to heroin or alcohol. The word "addiction" is here used jokingly to denote a tendency to overindulge in some pleasurable activity.

2   People often refer to being "hooked on TV." Does this, too, fall into the lighthearted category of cookie eating and other pleasures that people pursue with unusual intensity, or is there a kind of television viewing that falls into the more serious category of destructive addiction?

3   When we think about addiction to drugs or alcohol, we frequently focus on negative aspects, ignoring the pleasures that accompany drinking or drug-taking. And yet the essence of any seri-

ous addiction is a pursuit of pleasure, a search for a "high" that normal life does not supply. It is only the inability to function without the addictive substance that is dismaying, the dependence of the organism upon a certain experience and an increasing inability to function normally without it. Thus a person will take two or three drinks at the end of the day not merely for the pleasure drinking provides, but also because he "doesn't feel normal" without them.

4   An addict does not merely pursue a pleasurable experience and need to experience it in order to function normally. He needs to *repeat* it again and again. Something about that particular experience makes life without it less than complete. Other potentially pleasurable experiences are no longer possible, for under the spell of the addictive experience, his life is peculiarly distorted. The addict craves an experience and yet he is never really satisifed. The organism may be temporarily sated, but soon it begins to crave again.

5   Finally a serious addiction is distinguished from a harmless pursuit of pleasure by its distinctly destructive elements. A heroin addict, for instance, leads a damaged life: his increasing need for heroin in increasing doses prevents him for working, from maintaining relationships, from developing in human ways. Similarly an alcoholic's life is narrowed and dehumanized by his dependence on alcohol.

6   Let us consider television viewing in the light of the conditions that define serious addictions.

7   Not unlike drugs or alcohol, the television experience allows the participant to blot out the real world and enter into a pleasurable and passive mental state. The worries and anxieties of reality are as effectively deferred by becoming absorbed in a television program as by going on a "trip" induced by drugs or alcohol. And just as alcoholics are only inchoately aware of their addiction, feeling that they control their drinking more than they really do ("I can cut it out any time I want—I just like to have three or four drinks before dinner"), people similarly overestimate their control over television watching. Even as they put off other activities to spend hour after hour watching television, they feel they could easily resume living in a different, less passive style. But somehow or other while the television set is present in their homes, the click doesn't sound. With television pleasures available, those other experiences seem less attractive, more difficult somehow.

8   A heavy viewer (a college English instructor) observes:

9   "I find television almost irresistible. When the set is on, I cannot ignore it. I can't turn it off. I feel sapped, will-less, enervated.

As I reach out to turn off the set, the strength goes out of my arms. So I sit there for hours and hours."

10   The self-confessed television addict often feels he "ought" to do other things—but the fact that he doesn't read and doesn't plant his garden or sew or crochet or play games or have conversations means that those activities are no longer as desirable as television viewing. In a way a heavy viewer's life is as imbalanced by his television "habit" as a drug addict's or an alcoholic's. He is living in a holding pattern, as it were, passing up the activities that lead to growth or development or a sense of accomplishment. This is one reason people talk about their television viewing so ruefully, so apologetically. They are aware that it is an unproductive experience, that almost any other endeavor is more worthwhile by any human measure.

11   Finally it is the adverse effect of television viewing on the lives of so many people that defines it as a serious addiction. The television habit distorts the sense of time. It renders other experiences vague and curiously unreal while taking on a greater reality for itself. It weakens relationships by reducing and sometimes eliminating normal opportunities for talking, for communicating.

12   And yet television does not satisfy, else why would the viewer continue to watch hour after hour, day after day? "The measure of health," writes Lawrence Kubie, "is flexibility . . . and especially the freedom to cease when sated."[1] But the television viewer can never be sated with his television experiences—they do not provide the true nourishment that satiation requires—and thus he finds that he cannot stop watching.

Questions

1. So far as developing a definition goes, what is Winn doing in her first two paragraphs? That is, what function do the paragraphs serve? Might these paragraphs appear with equal effectiveness at the end?

2. In which paragraphs does Winn most explicitly define addiction? How many characteristics of addiction does she find? How many paragraphs does she devote to these characteristics? Do you think that the number of paragraphs is appropriate?

3. In paragraph 12 Winn writes, "And yet television does not satisfy, else why would the viewer continue to watch hour after

[1] Lawrence Kubie, *Neurotic Distortion and the Creative Process* (Lawrence: University of Kansas Press, 1958).

hour?" Drawing on your knowledge of someone—perhaps
yourself—who watches television "hour after hour," would you
say that such prolonged viewing is proof that television does not
satisfy?

---

*S*ophistication
Bergen Evans

1   Words are living, protean things. They grow, take roots, adapt
to environmental changes like any plant or animal. Take *sophisticated,* for example. Originally it meant "wise." Then, through its
association with the Sophists, it came to mean "over subtle," "marked
by specious but fallacious reasoning," "able to make the worse appear the better reason."

2   While retaining this meaning, it acquired the additional, derivative sense of "adulterated." A tobacconist in Ben Jonson's "The
Alchemist" is said to sell good tobacco: "he doesn't sophisticate it,"
they say, with other materials. Montaigne had the idea of adulteration in mind when he said that philosophy was nothing but "sophisticated poetry." And so did the eleventh edition of *The Encyclopaedia Britannica* when it said (1913) that ground rice was "one
of the chief sophistications" of ginger powder.

3   From adulteration to corruption is a short step and the meaning of corruption ran side by side with that of adulteration. Coryat
(1611) called dyed hair "sophisticated." Lear, going mad in the
storm, starts to strip off his clothes because they are trappings of
civilization and civilized man is "sophisticated." Judge Walter J.
LaBuy of the Federal District Court in Chicago, in sentencing an
enterprising young woman who was married to twelve sailors and
drawing a dependent's allotment from each of them, told her, with
stern disapproval, that she was "thoroughly sophisticated" (Chicago *Tribune*). Judge LaBuy may have been blending both meanings.

4   Up until about thirty years ago, the most common meaning
conveyed by the word was of a particular kind of corruption, the
corruption of idealism by worldly experience. And this is still given
as its principal meaning in most dictionaries.

5   Then suddenly the attitude implicit in the word was reversed; it ceased to mean unpleasantly worldly-wise and came to mean admirably world-wise. Something—possibly depression-begotten cynicism, urbanization, army experience, the perfume ads, or the glamorous pornography of the picture magazines—had led the populace to revise its estimate of worldly wisdom. For the past fifteen years *sophistication* has been definitely a term of praise.

6   And even more. "Sophistication," writes Earl Wilson, "means the ability to do almost anything without feeling guilty." Blum's, the celebrated San Francisco candy manufacturers, on opening a branch store in New York, wooed their new clientele by advising them that their "old-fashioned, home-made-type candies" had been "sophisticated" by their master candy maker. Lloyd Shearer informs the readers of *Parade* that a famous movie actress' husband "seemed sophisticatedly impervious to jealousy," losing his wife "graciously, understandingly and philosophically . . . to another man." It is no wonder that—gog-eyed with awe and envy—a sophomore English class at New Trier High School, in Winnetka, Ill., defined sophistication as "a grace acquired with maturity."

7   The beginnings of this reversal can be seen in the words of Duke Ellington's "Sophisticated Lady" (1933). The lady of the title has "grown wise." Disillusion is "deep in her eyes." She is "nonchalant . . . smoking, drinking . . . dining with some man in a restaurant." She misses "the love of long ago" but, plainly, has no intention of returning to its meager ecstasies. She has lost innocence but has acquired polish, and when she dines some man picks up the tab. In the minds of many rustic maidens this—one gathers from the change in *sophisticated*'s meaning—was to be preferred to dewy freshness that dined alone at home on leftovers or carried lunch in a paper bag. And by 1958 in John O'Hara's *From the Terrace*, *sophistication* had come to signify not corruption but almost the irreducible minimum of good manners.

8   Not content wich such audacious change, about three years ago *sophisticated* went hog wild and started to mean "delicately responsive to electronic stimuli," "highly complex mechanically," "requiring skilled control," "extraordinarily sensitive in receiving, interpreting and transmitting signals." Or at least that is what one must guess it means in such statements as "Modern radar is vastly more sophisticated than quaint, old-fashioned radar" *(Time);* later "The IL–18 is aeronautically more sophisticated than the giant TU–114." "Pioneer V is exceedingly sophisticated" (Chicago *Sun-Times*) and "The Antikythera mechanism is far more sophisticated than any described in classical scientific texts" *(Scientific American).*

9   The connections between these and any previously established meanings of the word are not clear, but since they are definitely favorable, they must spring some way from the post-Ellington uses. My own guess would be this: the sophisticated are not unperceiving, insensitive clods; on the contrary, they are particularly aware of nuances, act on the merest hints, are moved by suasion and respond to subtle stimuli. They don't have to be shoved. They know their way around and move with ease in their allotted orbits.

Questions

1. At the end of his fifth paragraph, Evans (writing in 1961) says "For the past fifteen years sophistication has been definitely a term of praise." Where did he find his evidence?
2. Thirty years later, is *sophistication* still a term of praise? What is your evidence? What words currently might be considered antonyms for *sophisticated*?

On Friendship
Margaret Mead and Rhoda Metraux

1   Few Americans stay put for a lifetime. We move from town to city to suburb, from high school to college in a different state, from a job in one region to a better job elsewhere, from the home where we raise our children to the home where we plan to live in retirement. With each move we are forever making new friends, who become part of our new life at that time.

2   For many of us the summer is a special time for forming new friendships. Today millions of Americans vacation abroad, and they go not only to see new sights but also—in those places where they do not feel too strange—with the hope of meeting new people. No one really expects a vacation trip to produce a close friend. But surely the beginning of a friendship is possible? Surely in every country people value friendship?

3   They do. The difficulty when strangers from two countries meet is not a lack of appreciation of friendship, but different expectations about what constitutes friendship and how it comes into being.

In those European countries that Americans are most likely to visit, friendship is quite sharply distinguished from other, more casual relations, and is differently related to family life. For a Frenchman, a German or an Englishman friendship is usually more particularized and carries a heavier burden of commitment.

4   But as we use the word, "friend" can be applied to a wide range of friendships—to someone one has known for a few weeks in a new place, to a close business associate, to a childhood playmate, to a man or woman, to a trusted confidant. There are real differences among these relations for Americans—a friendship may be superficial, casual, situational or deep and enduring. But to a European, who sees only our surface behavior, the differences are not clear.

5   As they see it, people known and accepted temporarily, casually, flow in and out of Americans' homes with little ceremony and often with little personal commitment. They may be parents of the children's friends, house guests of neighbors, members of a committee, business associates from another town or even another country. Coming as a guest into an American home, the European visitor finds no visible landmarks. The atmosphere is relaxed. Most people, old and young, are called by first names.

6   Who, then, is a friend?

7   Even simple translation from one language to another is difficult. "You see," a Frenchman explains, "if I were to say to you in France, 'This is my good friend,' that person would not be as close to me as someone about whom I said only, 'This is my friend.' Anyone about whom I have to say *more* is really less."

8   In France, as in many European countries, friends generally are of the same sex, and friendship is seen as basically a relationship between men. Frenchwomen laugh at the idea that "women can't be friends," but they also admit sometimes that for women "it's a different thing." And many French people doubt the possibility of a friendship between a man and a woman. There is also the kind of relationship within a group—men and women who have worked together for a long time, who may be very close, sharing great loyalty and warmth of feeling. They may call one another *copains*—a word that in English becomes "friends" but has more the feeling of "pals" or "buddies." In French eyes this is not friendship, although two members of such a group may well be friends.

9   For the French, friendship is a one-to-one relationship that demands a keen awareness of the other person's intellect, temperament and particular interests. A friend is someone who draws out your own best qualities, with whom you sparkle and become more

of whatever the friendship draws upon. Your political philosophy assumes more depth, appreciation of a play becomes sharper, taste in food or wine is accentuated, enjoyment of a sport is intensified.

10   And French friendships are compartmentalized. A man may play chess with a friend for thirty years without knowing his political opinions, or he may talk politics with him for as long a time without knowing about his personal life. Different friends fill different niches in each person's life. These friendships are not made part of family life. A friend is not expected to spend evenings being nice to children or courteous to a deaf grandmother. These duties, also serious and enjoined, are primarily for relatives. Men who are friends may meet in a café. Intellectual friends may meet in larger groups for evenings of conversation. Working people may meet at the little *bistro* where they drink and talk, far from the family. Marriage does not affect such friendships; wives do not have to be taken into account.

11   In the past in France, friendships of this kind seldom were open to any but intellectual women. Since most women's lives centered on their homes, their warmest relations with other women often went back to their girlhood. The special relationship of friendship is based on what the French value most—on the mind, on compatibility of outlook, on vivid awareness of some chosen area of life.

12   Friendship heightens the sense of each person's individuality. Other relationships commanding as great loyalty and devotion have a different meaning. In World War II the first resistance groups formed in Paris were built on the foundation of *les copains*. But significantly, as time went on these little groups, whose lives rested in one another's hands, called themselves "families." Where each had a total responsibility for all, it was kinship ties that provided the model. And even today such ties, crossing every line of class and personal interest, remain binding on the survivors of these small, secret bands.

13   In Germany, in contrast with France, friendship is much more articulately a matter of feeling. Adolescents, boys and girls, form deeply sentimental attachments, walk and talk together not so much to polish their wits as to share their hopes and fears and dreams, to form a common front against the world of school and family and to join in a kind of mutual discovery of each other's and their own inner life. Within the family, the closest relationship over a lifetime is between brothers and sisters. Outside the family, men and women find in their closest friends of the same sex the devotion of a sister, the loyalty of a brother. Appropriately, in Germany friends usually are brought into the family. Children call their father's and

their mother's friends "uncle" and "aunt." Between French friends, who have chosen each other for the congeniality of their point of view, lively disagreement and sharpness of argument are the breath of life. But for Germans, whose friendships are based on mutuality of feeling, deep disagreement on any subject that matters to both is regarded as a tragedy. Like ties of kinship, ties of friendship are meant to be irrevocably binding. Young Germans who come to the United States have great difficulty in establishing such friendships with Americans. We view friendship more tentatively, subject to changes in intensity as people move, change their jobs, marry, or discover new interests.

14   English friendships follow still a different pattern. Their basis is shared activity. Activities at different stages of life may be of very different kinds—discovering a common interest in school, serving together in the armed forces, taking part in a foreign mission, staying in the same country house during a crisis. In the midst of the activity, whatever it may be, people fall into step—sometimes two men or two women, sometimes two couples, sometimes three people—and find that they walk or play a game or tell stories or serve on a tiresome and exacting committee with the same easy anticipation of what each will do day by day or in some critical situation. Americans who have made English friends comment that, even years later, "you can take up just where you left off." Meeting after a long interval, friends are like a couple who begin to dance again when the orchestra strikes up after a pause. English friendships are formed outside the family circle, but they are not, as in Germany, contrapuntal to the family nor are they, as in France, separated from the family. And a break in an English friendship comes not necessarily as a result of some irreconcilable difference of viewpoint or feeling but instead as a result of misjudgment, where one friend seriously misjudges how the other will think or feel or act, so that suddenly they are out of step.

15   What, then, is friendship? Looking at these different styles, including our own, each of which is related to a whole way of life, are there common elements? There is the recognition that friendship, in contrast with kinship, invokes freedom of choice. A friend is someone who chooses and is chosen. Related to this is the sense each friend gives the other of being a special individual, on whatever grounds this recognition is based. And between friends there is inevitably a kind of equality of give-and-take. These similarities make the bridge between societies possible, and the American's characteristic openness to different styles of relationship makes it possible for him to find new friends abroad with whom he feels at home.

Questions

1. In your experience, are there differences between what women and men mean by and expect from friendship? Explain in a short essay of one or two paragraphs.
2. How have your requirements for friendship changed since you were a child? Explain, in an essay of 500 words, in which you define what a friend meant to you at a specific time in your childhood, and what the term has come to mean.

---

*T*he Androgynous Man
Noel Perrin

1   The summer I was sixteen, I took a train from New York to Steamboat Springs, Colo., where I was going to be assistant horse wrangler at a camp. The trip took three days, and since I was much too shy to talk to strangers, I had quite a lot of time for reading. I read all of *Gone With the Wind*. I read all the interesting articles in a couple of magazines I had, and then I went back and read all the dull stuff. I also took all the quizzes, a thing of which magazines were even fuller then than now.

2   The one that held my undivided attention was called "How Masculine/Feminine Are You?" It consisted of a large number of inkblots. The reader was supposed to decide which of four objects each blot most resembled. The choices might be a cloud, a steam engine, a caterpillar and a sofa.

3   When I finished the test, I was shocked to find that I was barely masculine at all. On a scale of 1 to 10, I was about 1.2. Me, the horse wrangler? (And not just wrangler, either. That summer, I had to skin a couple of horses that died—the camp owner wanted the hides.)

4   The results of that test were so terrifying to me that for the first time in my life I did a piece of original analysis. Having unlimited time on the train, I looked at the "masculine" answers over and over, trying to find what it was that distinguished real men from people like me—and eventually I discovered two very simple patterns. It was "masculine" to think the blots looked like man-

made objects, and "feminine" to think they looked like natural objects. It was masculine to think they looked like things capable of causing harm, and feminine to think of innocent things.

5   Even at sixteen, I had the sense to see that the compilers of the test were using rather limited criteria—maleness and femaleness are both more complicated than *that*—and I breathed a huge sigh of relief. I wasn't necessarily a wimp, after all.

6   That the test did reveal something other than the superficiality of its makers I realized only many years later. What it revealed was that there is a large class of men and women both, to which I belong, who are essentially androgynous. That doesn't mean we're gay, or low in the appropriate hormones, or uncomfortable performing the jobs traditionally assigned our sexes. (A few years after that summer, I was leading troops in combat and, unfashionable as it now is to admit this, having a very good time. War is exciting. What a pity the 20th century went and spoiled it with high-tech weapons.)

7   What it does mean to be spiritually androgynous is a kind of freedom. Men who are all-male, or he-men, or 100 percent red-blooded Americans, have a little biological set that causes them to be attracted to physical power, and probably also to dominance. Maybe even to watching football. I don't say this to criticize them. Completely masculine men are quite often wonderful people: good husbands, good (though sometimes overwhelming) fathers, good members of society. Furthermore, they are often so unself-consciously at ease in the world that other men seek to imitate them. They just aren't as free as us androgynes. They pretty nearly have to be what they are; we have a range of choices open.

8   The sad part is that many of us never discover that. Men who are not 100 percent red-blooded Americans—say, those who are only 75 percent red-blooded—often fail to notice their freedom. They are too busy trying to copy the he-men ever to realize that men, like women, come in a wide variety of acceptable types. Why this frantic imitation? My answer is mere speculation, but not casual. I have speculated on this for a long time.

9   Partly they're just envious of the he-man's unconscious ease. Mostly they're terrified of finding that there may be something wrong with them deep down, some weakness at the heart. To avoid discovering that, they spend their lives acting out the role that the he-man naturally lives. Sad.

10   One thing that men owe to the women's movement is that this kind of failure is less common than it used to be. In releasing themselves from the single ideal of the dependent woman, women have

more or less incidentally released a lot of men from the single ideal of the dominant male. The one mistake the feminists have made, I think, is in supposing that *all* men need this release, or that the world would be a better place if all men achieved it. It wouldn't. It would just be duller.

11   So far I have been pretty vague about just what the freedom of the androgynous man is. Obviously it varies with the case. In the case I know best, my own, I can be quite specific. It has freed me most as a parent. I am, among other things, a fairly good natural mother. I like the nurturing role. It makes me feel good to see a child eat—and it turns me to mush to see a 4-year-old holding a glass with both small hands, in order to drink. I even enjoyed sewing patches on the knees of my daughter Amy's Dr. Dentons when she was at the crawling stage. All that pleasure I would have lost if I had made myself stick to the notion of the paternal role that I started with.

12   Or take a smaller and rather ridiculous example. I feel free to kiss cats. Until recently it never occurred to me that I would want to, though my daughters have been doing it all their lives. But my elder daughter is now 22, and in London. Of course, I get to look after her cat while she is gone. He's a big, handsome farm cat named Petrushka, very unsentimental, though used from kittenhood to being kissed on the top of the head by Elizabeth. I've gotten very fond of him (he's the adventurous kind of cat who likes to climb hills with you), and one night I simply felt like kissing him on the top of the head, and did. Why did no one tell me sooner how silky cat fur is?

13   Then there's my relation to cars. I am completely unembarrassed by my inability to diagnose even minor problems in whatever object I happen to be driving, and don't have to make some insider's remark to mechanics to try to establish that I, too, am a "Man With His Machine."

14   The same ease extends to household maintenance. I do it, of course. Service people are expensive. But for the last decade my house has functioned better than it used to because I've had the aid of a volume called "Home Repairs Any Woman Can Do," which is pitched just right for people at my technical level. As a youth, I'd as soon have touched such a book as I would have become a transvestite. Even though common sense says there is really nothing sexual whatsoever about fixing sinks.

15   Or take public emotion. All my life I have easily been moved by certain kinds of voices. The actress Siobhan McKenna's, to take a notable case. Give her an emotional scene in a play, and within 10 words my eyes are full of tears. In boyhood, my great dread was

that someone might notice. I struggled manfully, you might say, to suppress this weakness. Now, of course, I don't see it as a weakness at all, but as a kind of fulfillment. I even suspect that the true he-men feel the same way, or one kind of them does, at least, and it's only the poor imitators who have to struggle to repress themselves.

16   Let me come back to the inkblots, with their assumption that masculine equates with machinery and science, and feminine with art and nature. I have no idea whether the right pronoun for God is He, She or It. But this I'm pretty sure of. If God could somehow be induced to take that test, God would not come out macho, and not feminismo, either, but right in the middle. Fellow androgynes, it's a nice thought.

Questions

1. Drawing on Perrin, in a sentence or two offer a definition of androgyny.
2. Perrin is concerned with defining androgyny, but is his central purpose to offer a definition? What is his thesis?
3. Drawing on Perrin, in a sentence or two define either masculinity or femininity.
4. Write a one-paragraph summary (perhaps five or six sentences) of Perrin's essay.
5. In two or three paragraphs, totaling perhaps 150 words, comment on Perrin's skill as a writer. You may, for example, want to call attention to his tone, his use of narrative, or his analytic power. In any case, call attention to those qualities that you think make the essay readable or unreadable.

---

*T*he Male Myth
Paul Theroux

1   There is a pathetic sentence in the chapter "Fetishism" in Dr. Norman Cameron's book *Personality Development and Psychopathology*. It goes: "Fetishists are nearly always men; and their commonest fetish is a woman's shoe." I cannot read that sentence

without thinking that it is just one more awful thing about being a man—and perhaps it is the most important thing to know about us.

2   I have always disliked being a man. The whole idea of manhood in America is pitiful, a little like having to wear an ill-fitting coat for one's entire life. (By contrast, I imagine femininity to be an oppressive sense of nakedness.) Even the expression "Be a man!" strikes me as insulting and abusive. It means: Be stupid, be unfeeling, obedient and soldierly, and stop thinking. Man means "manly"—how can one think "about men" without considering the terrible ambition of manliness? And yet it is part of every man's life. It is a hideous and crippling lie; it not only insists on difference and connives at superiority, it is also by its very nature destructive—emotionally damaging and socially harmful.

3   The youth who is subverted, as most are, into believing in the masculine ideal is effectively separated from women—it is the most savage tribal logic—and he spends the rest of his life finding women a riddle and a nuisance. Of course, there is a female version of this male affliction. It begins with mothers encouraging little girls to say (to other adults), "Do you like my new dress?" In a sense, girls are traditionally urged to please adults with a kind of coquettishness, while boys are enjoined to behave like monkeys toward each other. The 9-year-old coquette proceeds to become womanish in a subtle power game in which she learns to be sexually indispensable, socially decorative and always alert to a man's sense of inadequacy.

4   Femininity—being ladylike—implies needing a man as witness and seducer; but masculinity celebrates the exclusive company of men. That is why it is so grotesque; and that is also why there is no manliness without inadequacy—because it denies men the natural friendship of women.

5   It is very hard to imagine any concept of manliness that does not belittle women, and it begins very early. At an age when I wanted to meet girls—let's say the treacherous years of 13 to 16—I was told to take up a sport, get more fresh air, join the Boy Scouts, and I was urged not to read so much. It was the 1950's and, if you asked too many questions about sex, you were sent to camp—boy's camp, of course: the nightmare. Nothing is more unnatural or prisonlike than a boys' camp, but if it were not for them, we would have no Elks' Lodges, no poolrooms, no boxing matches, no marines.

6   And perhaps no sports as we know them. Everyone is aware of how few in number are the athletes who behave like gentlemen. Just as high-school basketball teaches you how to be a poor loser,

the manly attitude toward sports seems to be little more than a recipe for creating bad marriages, social misfits, moral degenerates, sadists, latent rapists and just plain louts. I regard high-school sports as a drug far worse than marijuana, and it is the reason that the average tennis champion, say, is a pathetic oaf.

7   Any objective study would find the quest for manliness essentially right wing, puritanical, cowardly, neurotic and fueled largely by a fear of women. It is also certainly philistine. There is no book hater like a Little League coach. But, indeed, all the creative arts are obnoxious to the manly ideal, because at their best the arts are pursued by uncompetitive and essentially solitary people. It makes it very hard for a creative youngster, for any boy who expresses the desire to be alone seems to be saying that there is something wrong with him.

8   It ought to be clear by now that I have an objection to the way we turn boys into men. It does not surprise me that when the President of the United States has his customary weekend off, he dresses like a cowboy—it is both a measure of his insecurity and his willingness to please. In many ways, American culture does little more for a man than prepare him for modeling clothes in the L. L. Bean catalogue. I take this as a personal insult because for many years I found it impossible to admit to myself that I wanted to be a writer. It was my guilty secret, because being a writer was incompatible with being a man.

9   There are people who might deny this, but that is because the American writer, typically, has been so at pains to prove his manliness. But first there was a fear that writing was not a manly profession—indeed, not a profession at all. (The paradox in American letters is that it has always been easier for a woman to write and for a man to be published.) Growing up, I had thought of sports as wasteful and humiliating, and the idea of manliness as a bore. My wanting to become a writer was not a flight from that oppressive role playing, but I quickly saw that it was at odds with it. Everything in stereotyped manliness goes against the life of the mind. The Hemingway personality is too tedious to go into here, but certainly it was not until this aberrant behavior was examined by feminists in the 1960's that any male writer dared question the pugnacity in Hemingway's fiction. All that bullfighting and arm-wrestling and elephant shooting diminished Hemingway as a writer: One cannot be a male writer without first proving that one is a man.

10   It is normal in America for a man to be dismissive or even somewhat apologetic about being a writer. Various factors make it

easier. There is a heartiness about journalism that makes it accept-able—journalism is the manliest form of American writing and, therefore, the profession the most independent-minded women seek (yes, it is an illusion, but that is my point). Fiction writing is equated with a kind of dispirited failure and is only manly when it produces wealth. Money is masculinity. So is drinking. Being a drunkard is another assertion, if misplaced, of manliness. The American male writer is traditionally proud of his heavy drinking. But we are also very literal-minded people. A man proves his manhood in America in old-fashioned ways. He kills lions, like Hemingway; or he hunts ducks, like Nathanael West; or he makes pronouncements, like "A man should carry enough knife to defend himself with," as James Jones is said to have once told an interviewer. And we are familiar with the lengths to which Norman Mailer is prepared, in his en-dearing way, to prove that he is just as much a monster as the next man.

11   When the novelist John Irving was revealed as a wrestler, peo-ple took him to be a very serious writer. But what interests me is that it is inconceivable that any woman writer would be shown in such a posture. How surprised we would be if Joyce Carol Oates were revealed as a sumo wrestler or Joan Didion enjoyed pumping iron. "Lives in New York City with her three children" is the typ-ical woman-writer's biographical note, for just as the male writer must prove he has achieved a sort of muscular manhood, the woman writer—or rather her publicists—must prove her motherhood.

12   There would be no point in saying any of this if it were not generally accepted that to be a man is somehow—even now in fem-inist-influenced America—a privilege. It is on the contrary an un-merciful and punishing burden. Being a man is bad enough; being manly is appalling. It is the sinister silliness of men's fashions that inspires the so-called dress code of the Ritz-Carlton Hotel in Bos-ton. It is the institutionalized cheating in college sports. It is a pa-thetic and primitive insecurity.

13   And this is also why men often object to feminism, but are afraid to explain why: Of course women have a justified grievance, but most men believe—and with reason—that their lives are much worse.

Questions

1. Taking Theroux's point of view, write a brief definition of "manliness." Then, in a sentence, say something to the effect

that this is the gist of Theroux's definition of manliness in the article, and go on to write a paragraph which could be used as the first paragraph of an essay either affirming or rejecting Theroux's view.

2. In paragraph 6 Theroux says that "high school basketball teaches you how to be a poor loser." Think about this, and then write a paragraph that in effect offers a definition of a "poor loser" but that also shows how a high school sport teaches one to be a poor loser.

3. Theroux speaks of "the Hemingway personality" and of "the pugnacity in Hemingway's fiction." If you have read a work by Hemingway, write a paragraph in which you explain (to someone unfamiliar with Hemingway) what Theroux is talking about.

4. Let's assume that a reader says he or she doesn't quite understand Theroux's final paragraph. Write a paragraph explaining it.

5. Theroux makes some deliberately provocative statements, for example:

> Nothing is more unnatural or prisonlike than a boys' camp.

> Everyone is aware of how few in number are the athletes who behave like gentlemen.

> The quest for manliness . . . [is] fueled largely by a fear of women.

Choose one such statement from the essay and consider what you would need to do to argue effectively against it. You needn't produce the argument, but simply consider how such an argument might be constructed.

6. If you have read Russell Baker's "The Flag" (page 591) and Noel Perrin's "The Androgynous Man" (page 167), list the areas of agreement you find in these essays and Theroux's.

6

Exposition

In our discussion of analytic writing (page 53), we said that most of the essays a student reads and writes are chiefly analytic; that is, by separating something into its parts the essayist draws conclusions and explains those conclusions.

But most writing can also be classified as exposition, persuasion (or argument), description, or narration. This does not mean, of course, that any given essay must belong exclusively to one of these four kinds of writing. More often than not a single essay combines at least two. For example, an expository essay on Zen Buddhism—an essay chiefly concerned with explaining what Zen is—may include a description of a Zen monastery, a narrative of the writer's visit to the monastery, and an argument (that is, a reasoned statement) for the relevance of Zen to us. If the essay is primarily exposition, the descriptive and narrative and argumentative parts will chiefly function to enliven and clarify the explanation of Zen. Similarly, an essay that is primarily an argument for the relevance of Zen to American life may have to sketch the tenets of the creed (exposition) and may tell an anecdote or recount the history of Zen (narration) in order to strengthen the argument.

In a college catalog, the information telling students how to apply or how to register or how to complete the requirements for a degree is exposition (from the Latin *exponere,* "to put forth"), a setting forth of information. It doesn't assume a disagreement, so it doesn't seek to persuade. But notice that those paragraphs in the catalog describing the lovely campus are not exposition but description—or, more exactly, description and persuasion combined, because they seek to persuade the reader to come to the campus. Exposition, too, may be permeated by persuasion, because writing that explains something usually at the same time seeks to persuade us that the topic is worth our attention. But exposition in its purest form seeks only to explain—to expose, we might say—what's what.

Admittedly, then, these four kinds or modes of writing—exposition, persuasion, description, and narration—are often blended in varying degrees, but at this stage it is useful to consider them separately, partly because each of them can help you to produce and to clarify ideas. If, for instance, you remember that one of your roles as a writer is to explain material to an audience—that is, to write exposition—you will find yourself asking yourself a question we have already raised, What do my readers need to know?

For the sake of clarity, then, we will talk about relatively pure examples of these four kinds of writing as we take them up one by one in this and the next three chapters. To talk about them all at once would require the skill of Stephen Leacock's knight, who leaped on his horse and rode madly off in all directions.

Here is a short piece, primarily expository. If typed, double-spaced, it would probably be a little more than one page.

In Search of the Elusive Pingo

Canadian scientists are preparing an expedition to the Beaufort Sea to study underwater ice formations that are blocking use of the Northwest Passage as a long-sought commercial route.* The formations, called pingoes, are cones of antediluvian ice, coated with frozen muck, that stick up like fingers from the bottom of the sea

*This piece was written in 1974.

to within 45 feet of the surface. They could rip the bottom of ships, such as supertankers, that ride deep in the water.

The pingoes are an obstacle to exploitation of oil resources and expansion of trade in the Arctic region that were expected to follow the successful pioneer voyage of the S.S. *Manhattan* through the ice-clogged Northwest Passage five years ago. One tanker ripped open could disrupt the ecological balance of much of the region.

The existence of the pingoes was not known until 1970 when scientists aboard the Canadian scientific ship *Hudson,* using special sonar equipment to plot the shape of the Beaufort Sea's basin, detected batches of them that the *Manhattan* was lucky to miss. Since then, oceanographers have charted about 200 pingoes, and there is no telling how many more there are.

Scientists at the United States Geological Survey and the Bedford Institute of Oceanography in Nova Scotia, where the *Hudson*'s expedition originated, have been exploring the origin of the pingoes and seeking in vain ways to neutralize them. Dynamiting has proved ineffective. So scientists from Bedford are going back this summer for another look.

You may not want to learn much more about pingoes, but we hope you found this brief account clear and interesting. You might ask yourself how the writer sustains your interest:

1. Is the title attractive?
2. What expression in the first paragraph is especially effective? Why?
3. Are the paragraphs given in a coherent order?
4. Is the final paragraph a satisfactory ending?

By asking such questions and then answering them, you will discover some of the principles of good expository writing.

EXPLAINING A PROCESS

Exposition need not, of course, explain only the remote or the unfamiliar. Often an expository essay presents in an authoritative way information of interest to a special audience. A good deal of the reading you will study and of the writing you will do consists of examining

1. how something came about, for example how a presidential candidate developed a winning strategy, or how a laboratory experiment was performed *(an informative process analysis)*, or
2. it may explain how to do something, for example how to deal with a person who is crying, or how to play tennis *(a directive process analysis)*.

These two kinds of analysis usually employ a chronological organization. Often, though, they begin with some sort of overview, for instance with an assertion of the importance of the topic, or a description of the finished product (say, the president taking office). The rest of the essay then explains the stages leading up to it.

Here, from a popular book by a physician, is a directive process analysis.

7

*H*ow to Deal with the Crying
Leonard Cammer

    If you are a soft, sentimental person you probably cannot stand to see your sick relative cry. It breaks you up. However, where tears serve as a necessary emotional outlet they can be encouraged. In a grief reaction especially, when the person has suffered a loss, crying comes easily and produces a healthy release for pent-up emotion. Momentarily, the tears wash away the depressed feelings.

    However, when an exhausting bout of tearfulness continues on and on with extreme agitation, breast beating, and self-abuse, it is time for you to call a halt. Let me show you how to terminate almost any flood of tears by the correct use of a psychologic device.

    First, sit directly in front of your relative and say, "Go on crying if you want to, but face me. Look into my eyes." It is a simple fact that no one can sustain crying while gazing straight into another's eyes. If the person does what you ask, his tears will stop. Not right away; he may continue to cry and avert his gaze. Take his hands in yours and again coax him to look at you. You may have to repeat the request several times, but at last he will turn and fix his eyes on you, almost hypnotically. The flow of tears then trickles to an end, and the person may begin to talk about the things that give him mental pain.

Every time you shorten such a spell of crying you stem the waste of energy and give the person a chance to preserve his or her stamina in fighting the depression.

Questions

1. In addition to describing a process, the essay begins by explaining the value of crying and ends by explaining the value of bringing crying to an end. Would the essay be equally good if the first paragraph came last? Why?
2. Although the essay is fairly impersonal, we do get some sense of a human being in the words. Try, in a sentence or two, to characterize the author.
3. Cammer is explaining a process, not offering an argument, yet (like every other writer) he must somehow persuade his readers that he knows what he is talking about. How does he persuade us?

Let's look now at an essay by a student, Susan Pope. The assignment was to write an essay on a process that the student knew well and that yet would probably be unfamiliar to the general reader. Here is the finished essay on giving elementary instruction in tennis.

Susan Pope

Tennis Tips to a Beginning Player

The beginning player needs tennis tips on the two basic skills of tennis: footwork, the way in which you move to prepare to hit the ball, and form, the way in which you hit the ball. The most important coaching command relevant to both skills is ''Concentrate and keep your eye on the ball.'' As soon as you see the opposing player hit the ball, determine

where it will land and move quickly to that spot, never taking your eyes from the ball.

Moving requires footwork, the most subtle and often
overlooked aspect of tennis. In order to hit the ball well,
you must first reach it in plenty of time. When receiving a
serve you should stand behind the point where you expect to
receive the ball; you may then run smoothly forward to receive it rather than tripping backwards. Stand, facing the
net, with your feet shoulder width apart, knees flexed, and
holding the neck of your racket lightly in your free hand.
This is called the ready position. Bounce up and down on the
balls of your feet and prepare to move. The instant the
server makes contact with the ball, jump; this enables you to
move quickly in any direction. Move laterally by jumping and
sliding with your feet parallel; never cross your feet.
After completing your swing, return immediately to the center
of the back court line, assume the ready position, bounce on
the balls of your feet, and prepare to move again. If you
can predict where your opponent will return the ball, move to
this area instead and assume your ready stance. The objective of footwork is to reach the ball quickly so you can prepare to hit it with good form.

Form involves the position and use of the parts of your
body as you hit the ball. By the time you have reached the
place where you intend to hit the ball, you should have completed you backswing, cocking your racket back until it
points behind you. A short backswing resulting from not
bringing your racket back soon enough will almost always result in a mistake. On the other hand, by having your racket
back, you still may be able to successfully return a ball hit
beyond the physical range you can usually reach.

As you wait for the ball with your racket held back,
plant your feet firmly, shoulder width apart. If you are using forehand, your left shoulder should be pointing approximately in the direction you wish to hit the ball. Concentrate on firmly gripping the racket handle because a loose
grip can result in a wobbly shot. As the ball comes toward
you, bend your knees and step with your lead foot toward the
ball, the left foot when using forehand. The ball often goes
in the net if you hit it standing stiffly. Keep your wrist
and elbow rigid as you swing at the ball; using either of
these joints for the force of your swing will cause inconsis-
tency in your ground strokes and promote tennis elbow. Use
your arm and shoulder as a unit and twist your torso, throwing the weight of your body onto your lead foot and into your
swing. Make your swing quick, snappy, and parallel to the
ground. If your stroke is not level, the ball will either be
scooped up into the air by a rising swing or be hit directly
into the net by a swing directed toward the ground. Stroke
through the ball as if it were not there and then follow
through with your swing bringing the racket up over your
shoulder close to your ear. You will have good control over
the ball if you hit it in the middle of your racket, the
sweet spot, when it is slightly in front of you. Deviations
from these basic coaching instructions may cause problems
with your form and weaken your ground strokes. Try to concentrate on them while you practice until you develop an unconscious, smooth, consistent swing.

It requires conscious effort to pinpoint the flaws in
your tennis game but often your repeated errors will indicate
what you are doing incorrectly. Footwork and form, the ba-
sics of the game of tennis may be constantly improved with

```
attention to a few coaching tips.  Most important, however,
remember to ''keep your eye on the ball.''
```

Questions

1. The essay addresses itself to a beginning player. How successful, for a beginner, would you expect these tips to be?
2. An earlier draft of the essay began with the following paragraph:

```
Playing tennis requires determined practice and hard work.
There are many well-known coaching suggestions which can
help improve the consistency of your ground strokes and
thereby increase your confidence in your game.  With prac-
tice, you can integrate these coaching prompts until you
execute them automatically.  Your concentration may then
be focused on game strategy, such as how to capitalize on
your opponent's weaknesses, and on more difficult strokes,
such as the top spin.
```

Do you agree with the writer's decision to drop the paragraph from her revised essay? Why, or why not?

A CHECKLIST FOR REVISING PROCESS ESSAYS

1. Do I know the process well enough to write about it? (If your knowledge of some parts is sketchy, talk with some experts, or do some research in the library.)
2. Is the organization clear? Are the stages in the process adequately specified?
3. Have I consistently kept in mind a specific audience, and ex-

plained everything that the reader needs to know? Are technical words adequately defined?

4. Have I made clear, early in the essay, the interest or value of the process?

WRITING A SUMMARY

What a Summary Is

One extremely common sort of exposition or "putting forth" is the summary. The ability to write an accurate summary (abridgment, condensation) is central to much academic work: for taking notes on reading, and for writing essay examinations, laboratory reports, book reviews, and other informative and analytical essays.

The need to write summaries continues in professional life. Scientists usually begin a scientific paper with an abstract, lawyers write briefs (which are, as the name implies, documents that briefly set forth all the facts and points of law pertinent to a case), and business executives must constantly reduce long memoranda and reports to their essential points. In short, the ability to write summaries is an essential skill to acquire and to practice.

Here are a few principles that govern summaries:

1. A summary is much briefer than the original. It is not a paraphrase—a word-by-word translation of someone's words into your own. A paraphrase is usually at least as long as the original, whereas a summary is rarely longer than one-fourth the original, and usually is much briefer. An entire essay may be summarized in a sentence or two.

2. A summary usually achieves its brevity by omitting almost all the concrete details of the original, presenting only the sum that the details add up to.

3. A summary is accurate; it has no value if it misrepresents the point of the original.

4. The writer of a summary need not make the points in the same order as that of the original. If the writer of an essay has delayed revealing the main point until the end of the essay, the

summary rearranges the order, stating the main point first. Occasionally, when the original author has presented an argument in a
disorderly or confusing sequence, one writes a summary in order
to disengage the author's argument from its confusing structure.

5. A summary normally is written in the present tense because although the author wrote the piece last year or a hundred
years ago, we assume in writing a summary that the piece speaks
to us today.

6. Because a summary is openly based on someone else's
views, it is usually not necessary to use quotation marks around
key words or phrases from the original. Nor is it necessary to
repeat "he says" or "she goes on to prove." From the opening
sentence of a summary it should be clear that what follows is what
the original author says.

Here is a summary of Barnet and Stubbs on "summary":

> A summary is a condensation or abridgment. Its chief charac-
> teristics are: 1) it is rarely more than one-fourth as long as the
> original; 2) its brevity is usually achieved by leaving out most of
> the concrete details of the original; 3) it is accurate; 4) it may rear-
> range the organization of the original, especially if a rearrangement
> will make things clearer; 5) it normally is in the present tense; 6)
> quoted words need not be enclosed in quotation marks.

How to Write a Summary

Although one may want to write a summary of, say, each
act of *Macbeth*, students usually summarize nonliterary material,
especially such material as essays or chapters in textbooks on business, history, philosophy, and sociology. Our own method is to
scan the entire essay or chapter first, to get the gist of it and to
see if perhaps the material includes its own summaries, either at
the end of the whole or (if it consists of several parts) at the end
of each part. If it does, you're in luck.

If it doesn't, we suggest that on rereading you jot down, after
reading each paragraph, a sentence summarizing the gist of the
paragraph. (A very long or a poorly unified paragraph may require two sentences, but make every effort to boil the paragraph
down to a dozen or so words.) Of course if a paragraph consists

merely of a transitional sentence or two ("We will now turn to another example") you will lump it with the next paragraph. Similarly, if for some reason you encounter a series of very short paragraphs—for instance three examples, each briefly stated, and all illustrating the same point—you probably will find that you can cover them with a single sentence. But if a paragraph runs to half a page or more of print, it's probably worth its own sentence of summary. In fact, your author may summarize the paragraph, in the paragraph's opening sentence, or in its final sentence.

Here is a student's paragraph-by-paragraph summary of Philip Roth's "The Newark Public Library" (page 12):

1. If the City Council shuts down the Newark public library will there be looting, sniping, etc.?
2. I hope not; I hope there is respect for Law and Order, even if there is none for thoughtfulness and pleasure.
3. When I was a child in Newark, the knowledge that the books belonged to the public was comforting to me, and it also civilized me by developing in me a sense of my responsibility as a citizen.
4. The library, quiet and tidy, provided a lesson in order, fostering self-restraint and also self-confidence.
5. The City Council thinks it is solving a fiscal problem, but its solution—an insult to the community—may be very costly in frustration, cynicism, and rage.

When you have written your sentence summarizing the last paragraph, you may have done enough if the summary was intended simply as an aid for your own private use, for example if it is to help you review material for an examination. But if you are going to use it as the basis of a summary within an essay you are writing, of course you will want to reshape it. In an essay of your own, you probably won't want to include a summary longer than three or four sentences, so your job will be to reduce and combine the sentences you have jotted down. Indeed, you may even want to reduce the summary to a single sentence. One student summarized Roth's essay thus:

> Roth, in his article, "The Newark Public Library," argues that the closing of the libraries will be a costly mistake, and that the action will be an insult to the citizens of Newark.

Of course different writers will produce different summaries of Roth's essay. A writer who feels he or she wants to devote a little more space to summarizing Roth's essay might come up with this summary:

> Roth, in his article, "The Newark Public Library," explains in some detail how, when he was a child, the public library gave him confidence and a sense of responsibility. In its orderliness, and in its demand for quiet, it exerted a civilizing effect. The City Council may think that by shutting down the library it is solving a fiscal problem, but it is unaware of the rage that this insult will generate in the citizens (now, mostly black) in Newark.

If you think that your reader needs a summary, you'll also have to think about how long—that is, how detailed—the summary should be. Your awareness of your reader's needs will then guide you as you draw upon your summaries of the paragraphs.

EXERCISES

(Reminder: A good expository essay anticipates questions a reader may have about *how, who, what, why, when,* and *where.*)

1. Addressing an audience pretty much like yourself—say, your classmates—in 300–500 words explain a process with which you are familiar but which is likely to be new to them. Examples: how to perform a card trick, win an argument, repair an oriental rug, judge the show potentials of a thoroughbred puppy, refinish a table, prepare for a marathon, develop a photograph. (A reminder: readable process essays not only let the reader understand something; they also let the reader hear a human voice, and they usually contain passages implying that the process has its rewards. If you choose a topic you are strongly interested in, you will probably find that an interesting voice emerges, and that the process will engage the reader.)

2. Reread the essay on pingoes (page 176), and then write an expository essay of similar length (about 250 words) on

something that is likely to be unfamiliar to your classmates. Examples: a little-known group of musicians; a little-known kind of cooking; a natural phenomenon you have closely observed.

3a. Summarize the following paragraph in one or two sentences:

> No society, whether human or animal, can exist without communication. Thoughts, desires, appetites, orders—these have to be conveyed from one brain to another, and they can rarely be conveyed directly. Only with telepathy do we find mind speaking straight to mind, without the intermediacy of signs, and this technique is still strange enough to seem a music-hall trick or a property of science fiction. The vast majority of sentient beings—men, women, cats, dogs, bees, horses—have to rely on signals, symbols of what we think and feel and want, and these signals can assume a vast variety of forms. There is, indeed, hardly any limit to the material devices we can use to express what is in our minds: we can wave our hands, screw up our faces, shrug our shoulders, write poems, write on walls, carve signs out of stone or wood, mould signs with clay or butter, scrawl sky-signs with an aircraft, semaphore, heliograph, telephone, run a pirate radio transmitter, stick pins in dolls. A dog will scratch at a door if it wants to be let in; a cat will mew for milk; a hostess will ring a bell for the course to be changed; a pub-customer will rap with a coin for service; a wolf will whistle; the people in the flat upstairs will bang with a stick if our party is too noisy. One can fill pages with such examples, bringing in the language of flowers and the signaling devices of honey-bees, but one will always end up with human speech as the most subtle, comprehensive, and exact system of communication we possess.
>
> — Anthony Burgess

b. Summarize the following three paragraphs (introducing an essay on soap operas) in one or two sentences:

> What does the powerful teaching tool of television have to say to its viewers about desirable attitudes toward life and its problems? And what does the Media Establishment assume that *we* assume about the way this world functions? With these questions, I approached soap operas and evening series—programs that claimed to present ordinary existence, though heightened for drama and catering to everyone's curiosity about how the other half lives.
>
> In between commercial breaks, I noted a deeply disturbing factor in so many of the dramas: the lack of any sense of process, of

the eternal truth that events have consequences, and that people can and do influence what happens to them and to others. What I saw instead was a consistent, insistent demonstration of *randomness*, a statement that life is unpredictable and out of control. With rare exceptions what happens on-screen suggests that no one can trust her or his own judgment and (other side of the same coin) that no one, friend, kin, or lover, is really trustworthy.

We may identify with the actors because we all face unpredictable events, but we get no clues to coping with them. No one seems talented at solving the puzzles of life: even J.R. Ewing was shot. Nobody shows us how to decide on the fidelity of kin or associates, no love is certain. Let a wedding date be set and you can be pretty sure the ceremony won't come off. Report a death and expect the corpse to show up in a future segment fleeing a crime, amnesiac, or as survivor of a "fatal" plane crash. Says one of a pair of embracing lovers, "I don't know anything about you." Par for the course. Later in the same segment (of "Another World") a young woman tells a young man she doesn't love him. But wait a minute! She has been hypnotized, it seems, in a program I missed, and here she is on tape declaring she *does* love him to the hypnotist. Not only don't we/they know anything about the others in their lives, they/we don't understand ourselves either. The Guiding Lights we seek are shrouded in fog.

— Elizabeth Janeway

4. Choose a current editorial and summarize it in about one-fourth its number of words. Include a copy of the editorial with your summary.
5. Using the outline of "Columbo Knows the Butler Didn't Do It" (pages 433–34) and the essay itself (pages 89–91), write a summary of the essay, in about 250 words.
6. Read "It's the Portly Penguin That Gets the Girl" (pages 190–92) and then attend a lecture in your community on a topic that interests you. Go prepared to take notes and, if possible, meet the speaker. Then write a two- to three-page summary of the lecture, including some of your sense of the speaker and perhaps of the occasion.
7. Write an expository essay objectively setting forth someone else's views on a topic or limited range of topics. Suggested length: 500 words. Your source for these views should be a published interview. If possible, submit a copy of the inter-

view with your essay. Suggested sources: *Black Women Writers at Work,* ed. Claudia Tate (New York: Continuum, 1983); Dick Cavett and Christopher Porterfield, *Cavett* (New York: Harcourt Brace Jovanovich, 1974); *Rolling Stone Interviews* (New York: Paper-back Library, 1971); *The Playboy Interviews with John Lennon and Yoko Ono,* ed. G. Barry Golson (New York: Playboy Press, 1981); Charles Thomas Samuels, *Encountering Directors* (New York: G. P. Putnam's Sons, 1972); *Particular Passions: Intimate Talks with Women Who Have Shaped Our Times,* ed. Lynn Gilbert and Gaylen Moore (New York: Clarkson N. Potter, 1981); *Writers at Work: The Paris Review Interviews,* ed. Malcolm Cowley (New York: Viking Press, 1958–1968); and the *Paris Review,* a quarterly publication, which usually includes an interview with an author. If you found Philip Roth's essay (pages 12–14) interesting, you may want to summarize an interview with Roth. He prints several of them in his *Reading Myself and Others* (New York: Farrar, Straus & Giroux, 1975).

EXPOSITION AT WORK

It's the Portly Penguin That Gets the Girl, French Biologist Claims

Anne Hebald Mandelbaum

---

1   The penguin is a feathered and flippered bird who looks as if he's on his way to a formal banquet. With his stiff, kneeless strut and natural dinner jacket, he moves like Charlie Chaplin in his heyday dressed like Cary Grant in his.

2   But beneath the surface of his tuxedo is a gallant bird indeed. Not only does he fast for 65 days at a time, sleep standing up, and forsake all others in a lifetime of monogamy, but the male penguin also guards, watches over, and even hatches the egg.

3   We owe much of our current knowledge of the life and loves of the king and emperor penguins to—*bien sûr*—a Frenchman. Twenty-eight-year-old Yvon Le Maho is a biophysiologist from Lyons who visited the University last week to discuss his discoveries and to praise the penguin. He had just returned from 14 months in Antarctica, where he went to measure, to photograph, to weigh, to take blood and urine samples of, to perform autopsies on—in short, to study the penguin.

4   Although his original intent had been to investigate the penguin's long fasts, Monsieur Le Maho was soon fascinated by the amatory aspect of the penguin. Copulating in April, the female produces the egg in May and then heads out to sea, leaving her mate behind to incubate the egg. The males huddle together, standing upright and protecting the 500-gram (or 1.1-pound) egg with their feet for 65 days. During this time, they neither eat nor stray: each steadfastly stands guard over his egg, protecting it from the temperatures which dip as low as −40 degrees and from the winds which whip the Antarctic wilds with gusts of 200 miles an hour.

5   For 65 days and 65 nights, the males patiently huddle over the eggs, never lying down, never letting up. Then, every year on July 14th—Bastille Day, the national holiday of France—the eggs hatch and thousands of penguin chicks are born, M. Le Maho told his amused and enthusiastic audience at the Biological Laboratories.

6   The very day the chicks are born—or, at the latest, the following day—the female penguins return to land from their two-and-a-half month fishing expedition. They clamber out of the water and toboggan along the snow-covered beaches toward the rookery and their mates. At this moment, the males begin to emit the penguin equivalent of wild, welcoming cheers—*"comme le cri de trompette,"* M. Le Maho later told the *Gazette* in an interview—"like the clarion call of the trumpet."

7   And, amid the clamorous thundering of 12,000 penguins, the female recognizes the individual cry of her mate. When she does, she begins to cry to him. The male then recognizes *her* song, lifts the newborn chick into his feathered arms, and makes a beeline for the female. Each singing, each crying, the males and females rush toward each other, slipping and sliding on the ice as they go, guided all the while by the single voice each instinctively knows.

8   The excitement soon wears thin for the male, however, who hasn't had a bite to eat in more than two months. He has done his duty and done it unflaggingly, but even penguins cannot live by duty alone. He must have food, and quickly.

9   Having presented his mate with their newborn, the male abruptly departs, heading out to sea in search of fish. The female, who has just returned from her sea-going sabbatical, has swallowed vast quantities of fish for herself and her chick. Much of what she has eaten she has not digested. Instead, this undigested food becomes penguin baby food. She regurgitates it, all soft and paplike, from her storage throat right into her chick's mouth. The chicks feed in this manner until December, when they first learn to find food on their own.

10   The penguins' reproductive life begins at age five, and the birds live about 25 years. Their fasting interests M. Le Maho because of its close similarities with fasting in human beings. And although many migratory birds also fast, their small size and indeed their flight make it almost impossible to study them closely. With the less-mobile and non-flying penguin, however, the scientist has a relatively accessible population to study. With no damage to the health of the penguin, M. Le Maho told the *Gazette,* a physiobiologist can extract blood from the flipper and sample the urine.

11   "All fasting problems are the same between man and the penguin," M. Le Maho said. "The penguin uses glucose in the brain, experiences ketosis as does man, and accomplishes gluconeogenesis, too." Ketosis is the build-up of partially burned fatty acids in the blood, usually as a result of starvation; gluconeogenesis is the making of sugar from non-sugar chemicals, such as amino acids. "The

penguin can tell us a great deal about how our own bodies react to fasting conditions," M. Le Maho said.

12   He will return to Antarctica, M. Le Maho said, with the French government-sponsored *Expéditions Polaires Françaises* next December. There he will study the growth of the penguin chick, both inside the egg and after birth; will continue to study their mating, and to examine the penguin's blood sugar during fasting.

13   During the question-and-answer period following his talk, M. Le Maho was asked what the female penguin looks for in a mate. Responding, M. Le Maho drew himself up to his full five-foot-nine and said, *"La grandeur."*

Questions

1. Outline the essay, and then describe the organization.
2. Pick out three or four sentences that strike you as especially interesting, not just because they contain odd facts but because of the ways the sentences are written.

But Can You Say It in 1's and 0's?

Peter H. Lewis

1   In the nightmare I'm back at the University of Mars and the final exam in computer science starts in 20 seconds. But there must be some mistake! I'm a poetry major and I've never been in this class before. Suddenly the professor appears: It's Art Fleming, and I'm in Jeopardy.

"The answer is," Mr. Fleming begins, "they changed the architecture to get EMC as a square of the clock frequency for 80386 processors at 16-plus megahertz, and to get switchless setup and faster I/O data transfer with burst capability. What is the question?"

Panic strikes as the clock ticks away. "I . . . be . . . um. . . ."

"That's right, I.B.M.!" Mr. Fleming says. "And now for the bonus round. The answer is, SDLC, LAN, LU 6.2, X.25, Asynch, Netbios, Token Ring, VT100."

5   "How do you expect me to communicate with you crazy people?" I scream.

"That's right!" shouts Mr. Fleming. "Don Pardo, tell him what he's won."

"Congratulations," Mr. Pardo says. "You win a license for OS/2EE1.1 with Presentation Manager and a lifetime supply of all the jargon we use in the computer industry."

Ah, jargon. Sometimes we forget that not everyone who uses a computer knows, or even wants to know, the odd terms used by computer professionals.

We drive a car, for instance, and somehow manage to get to the grocery store without understanding torque, horsepower or gear ratios. But there are some terms we have to be familiar with to make a wise car-buying decision and to operate the car efficiently and safely: M.P.G., M.P.H., unleaded gas, seatbelts.

10   Cars are more familiar to us than computers are. That may change someday, but until then many of us need to become familiar with such basic terms as kilobyte, disk drive and memory. So here goes.

You have a rich store of memories in your brain, and you can retrieve and process them with your mind. You may also have a library or file cabinet in which you store outside information that you need to feed to your brain from time to time. Computers "remember" and "think" in a similar fashion, with both internal and external memory.

Think of a computer's inside memory as twins: Ramulus and Romulus. RAM stands for random access memory and ROM for ready-only memory.

Ramulus is the smart twin, the one who does all the thinking. Romulus, on the other hand, is the idiot savant, the type of guy who has memorized Robert's Rules of Order and all of the subway and bus stops in New York City, but who otherwise can't tie his shoes. Many of the computer's deepest secrets are stored in ROM.

ROM is important to have around, but RAM is the guy they're probably talking about when they refer to a computer's memory, as in 640K RAM.

15   K refers to kilo, which is Greek for a thousand. A kilobyte, then, is about 1,000 bytes. A byte, in turn, is a package of eight binary digits—bits, or 0's and 1's—that make up the most common unit of information in a personal computer. (In the world of binary math a kilobyte is actually 1,024 bytes, which is a mouthful. For convenience let's switch from binary to decimal and use 1,000.) One byte is the equivalent of one character, and one K is the equiv-

alent of half a page of typed, double-spaced text. One thousand K's equal a megabyte, mega being Greek for Really Big.

If you think of RAM as I.Q., a computer with 640K RAM is smarter than a computer with 64K. Further, a computer with 2MB (megabytes) of RAM has several times the intelligence of one with 640K.

A computer with 640K RAM or more can accommodate "smarter" software than one with 128K, for example, simply because it can hold more information in its brain at one time. In general, the more complex the software, the more space in RAM it demands.

Say you ran into our friends Ramulus and Romulus at a computer party. Whoa! A power failure occurs, and when the lights come back on, Ramulus, volatile guy that he is, has vanished, while Romulus is still sitting obliviously in the closet, humming and counting his toes. Information stored in RAM is wiped out when the power is turned off. Until it is stored or saved somewhere, most commonly on a floppy disk or a hard disk, the information you've been working on is as ephemeral as campaign promises.

So save early and save often.

20   When you save data, you are moving it from one type of memory to another, just as you would jot down notes on paper during a telephone conversation and then file them in a folder or file cabinet. Sometimes memory refers to the computer equivalent of the folders and cabinets. A computer may have 640K RAM, but it probably also has a floppy disk drive (like a file folder) that can place a few hundred K's on a single disk.

Many personal computers sold today also have, in addition to a floppy drive, a "hard" disk that can store 10, 20, 40 or more megabytes of information. Hard disks used to be about the same size and cost as a Buick, but today they are small. If you can afford one, get one. The hard disk can hold more information and let you get to it faster than a floppy.

So, your computer may have lots of memories: 640K RAM, 640K ROM, 720K floppy and 20MB hard.

Since I've won a lifetime supply of jargon, I'll be passing it on from time to time in this space.

Questions

1. Most writers make assumptions about their readers: for example, their level of education, or their interest in the writer's

topic, or their previous knowledge of it. What assumptions does Lewis appear to make about his readers?

2. What *is* Lewis's topic? How soon are you aware of it? Should he have announced it earlier?

3. Lewis's essay is primarily expository (as we have defined exposition on pages 175–76). Does his essay have a thesis? (If so, what is it?) How does he attempt to *persuade* us that his essay deserves our attention?

4. Lewis explains computer terminology largely through a series of comparisons. Which do you immediately remember? Looking back through the essay list other comparisons that you find. Try to define the common principle that runs through all or most of the comparisons.

5. What devices other than comparison does Lewis use to explain computer terminology? In paragraph 15, for example? In paragraph 18?

6. In a brief paragraph, explain the following to someone who has not read Lewis's article: what his topic is, how he approaches it, and your opinion of his success.

7. In the next few weeks take note (in a journal, if you keep one) of the instances—perhaps in your textbooks, class lectures, and casual reading—when a new concept or term is explained by means of a comparison. (Note that metaphors and analogies are kinds of comparisons.) Jot down too, as they occur to you, any concepts or terms that you might explain to someone else by means of a comparison.

---

*S*tarting a Business

Alexandra Armstrong

1   Marian Strong, a 33-year-old married woman with two children, ages six and eight, worked at a bank until her first child was born. Her husband, Edward, has worked for the same corporation for the past 10 years. Paid $50,000 annually, he feels that his job is stable. Their expenses are moderate, both mortgage on their home and the car loan payments are low. Although they live on Edward's

salary, three years ago Marian went to work for H & R Block preparing tax returns. While there, she managed to save $5,000 of her earnings.

2   In addition to enjoying the work, Marian discovered that many of the company's clients needed to know how to set up and maintain financial records. A number were willing to pay a fee to have this done and some even wanted her to pay their monthly bills. As a result, Marian, who recently inherited $5,000 from an aunt, would like to use this windfall to start her own home-based business to organize and maintain financial records for clients.

3   I recommended Marian prepare a business plan describing the nature of her business, and why she believes there's a need for it. Estimates of her start-up costs, as well as projected expenses and income for the first year, must also be included. I also reminded her that people in home-based offices often find excuses not to work, and that a wise move would be to have a separate room devoted exclusively to business.

4   Having decided to give one room totally to her work, Marian needed a computer, a copying machine, some furniture and stationery. Her savings, which she estimates at $5,000, will cover these expenses. I told her not to expect to be profitable in the first year, but to plan for the worst case. Marian has her inheritance to fall back on, as well as an untapped $5,000 line of credit that she shares with her husband.

5   Marian wasn't sure whether her business should be a sole proprietorship, partnership, or a corporation. As a rule one should achieve $100,000 in revenues before incorporation is worthwhile. I recommended a sole proprietorship until her revenues become substantial, because it is less encumbering than a partnership.

6   We then discussed her marketing strategy. She needs to make sure that people find out about her business, while keeping her costs minimal. I suggested that she write letters introducing herself to estate planners and CPAs who don't want to be involved in record keeping; use personal contacts for referrals, like her former colleagues at H & R Block; and also make contact with organizations that cater to women over the age of 60, since they usually have little experience handling their own financial affairs.

7   It is important that Marian regularly review her situation to see how her sales and profits are progressing in line with projections and whether more marketing should be done or cost reduction techniques be employed.

8   Last, but not least, I stressed the importance when starting a business of getting good advisers: a lawyer to help determine poten-

tial liabilities that might be involved; an insurance agent to make sure of sufficient liability coverage; and a tax adviser who specializes in small businesses. This is not an area where one should try to save money, but on the other hand, one good initial conversation with a business lawyer or consultant at an hourly rate is often sufficient, and the same holds true for a tax adviser. Then one can continue to consult on a need-to-know basis.

9   There are also a number of organizations that Marian can turn to for advice and valuable information. The National Association of Women Business Owners, 600 South Federal Street, Suite 400, Chicago, Illinois 60605, is an excellent resource for women in sole proprietorships and has many local chapters. The National Alliance of Homebased Businesswomen, P.O. Box 306, Midland Park, New Jersey 07432, and the Small Business Administration are also useful.

Questions

1. This essay is fundamentally an essay on a process—in this case, how to start a business. Reread it, and see whether (within the severe limitations of the space allowed) it covers all the main points. And does it waste space on irrelevant matters?
2. Do you think the essay is well organized? What *is* the organization?

The Body in Question
Jonathan Miller

1   At one time or another we have all been irked by aches and pains. We have probably noticed alterations in weight, complexion and bodily function, changes in power, capability and will, unaccountable shifts of mood. But on the whole we treat these like changes in the weather: as part and parcel of living in an imperfect world. The changes they cause in our behaviour are barely noticeable—not inconvenient enough to interfere with our routine. We may retreat a little, fall silent, sigh, rub our heads, retire early, drink glasses of water, eat less, walk more, miss a meal here and there, avoid fried foods, and so on and so on. But sometimes the discomfort, alarm,

embarrassment or inconvenience begin to obstruct the flow of ordinary life; in place of modest well-being, life become so intolerably awkward, strenuous or frightening that we fall ill.

2   Falling ill is not something that happens to us, it is a choice we make as a result of things happening to us. It is an action we take when we feel unacceptably odd. Obviously, there are times when this choice is taken out of the victim's hands: he may be so over-whelmed by events that he plays no active part in what happens next and is brought to the doctor by friends or relatives, stricken and helpless. But this is rare. Most people who fall ill have chosen to cast themselves in the role of patient. Viewing their unfortunate situation, they see themselves as sick people and begin to act differently.

3   Usually this is a prelude to seeking expert advice, but falling ill can sometimes be performed as a solo act. In New Guinea, for example, the decision to fall ill is almost invariably followed by a consistent and easily recognised form of behaviour. The sufferer withdraws from the community and retires into his hut: he strips himself naked, smears himself with ash and dust, and lies down in the darkness. He also changes his tone of voice: when his friends and relatives make solicitous enquiries, he answers them in a quavering falsetto.

4   Such people are not merely suffering illness: they are performing it, thereby announcing both to themselves and to the community that they are sick people in need of care and attention. In New Guinea this is such a well-recognized form of behaviour that one is tempted to regard it as a formal ritual. Something similar, however, can often be found in more sophisticated communities. When someone falls ill but is not yet ready to summon expert help, he usually takes care to advertise his condition through the medium of a performance. In fact, such a performance is often demanded of him by those with whom he lives. Someone who takes to his bed when he has a sick headache, for instance, is not entirely prompted by the need for relief. It is a way of boosting his credibility as a sick person, and it may be the only way of getting the attention and concern which he thinks he deserves. In fact, the patient may have to abstain from activities he is quite capable of performing, if only to convince those around him that there is a good reason for his staying away from work.

5   A patient, then, is a special sort of person, rather like a recruit or a convert or a bride. By taking on the role of patient you change your social identity, turning yourself from someone who helps himself into someone who accepts the orders, routine and advice of

qualified experts. You submit to the rules and recommendations of a profession, just as a novice submits to the rules and recommendations of his or her chosen order. Ordinary life is full of such voluntary transitions—changes of social role or status which are accompanied by corresponding changes in obligation and expectation. Whenever these take place, they are accompanied by rituals which mark the event and make it clearly recognisable to all who are involved. The anthropologists have called these "rites of passage," symbolic actions which represent and dramatise significant changes in social status: they include baptisms, immersions, confirmations, all sorts of melodramatic initiations and humiliating ordeals, such as strippings, shavings, scarrings. Whenever we cross a threshold from one social role to another we take pains to advertise the fact with ceremonies which represent it in terms of vivid and memorable images.

6   The idea of "rites of passage" was first introduced by the French anthropologist Arnold Van Gennep in 1909. Van Gennep insisted that all rituals of "passing through" occurred in three successive phases: a rite of separation, a rite of transition and a rite of aggregation. The person whose status is to be changed has to undergo a ritual which marks his departure from the old version of himself: there has to be some act which symbolises the fact that he has rid himself of all his previous associations. He is washed, rinsed, sprinkled or immersed, and, in this way, all his previous obligations and attachments are symbolically untied and even annihilated. This stage is followed by a rite of transition, when the person is neither fish nor fowl; he has left his old status behind him but has not yet assumed his new one. This liminal condition is usually marked by rituals of isolation and segregation—a period of vigil, mockery perhaps, fear and trembling. There are often elaborate rites of humiliation—scourging, insults, and darkness. Finally, in the rite of aggregation, the new status is ritually conferred: the person is admitted, enrolled, confirmed and ordained.

7   This idea can be applied to the process of becoming a patient. The fact that most of the procedures involved have a rational and practical explanation doesn't prevent them from playing a very important symbolic role as well. Although one can readily understand most of what happens to someone on entering hospital in utilitarian terms, there is no doubt that both the patient and the doctor experience some of these manoeuvres as symbolic transformations. Once someone has chosen to fall ill he has to apply for the role of patient: he auditions for the part by reciting his complaint as vividly and as convincingly as he can. This can also be seen in terms

of religious confirmation: the candidate submits himself to a formal questionnaire in order to satisfy the examiner that he is a suitable person to be enrolled. If he passes the preliminary test he has to undertake the initial rites of separation. He is undressed, washed, and until quite recently, he often had to submit himself to a cleansing enema. Then come the rites of transition. No longer a person in the ordinary world, he is not yet formally accepted by his fellow patients—anxious and isolated in his novice pyjamas, he awaits the formal act of aggregation. He is introduced to the ward sister, hands over his street clothes, submits to a questionnaire by the houseman and registrar. Dressed with all the dignified credentials of a formally admitted patient, he awaits the forthcoming event.

Questions

1. What did the title lead you to expect? Evaluate the effectiveness of the title.
2. Miller has written and performed comic sketches. Where in the first paragraph do you see or hear (granted, in a subdued way) the comic performer?
3. Explain in your own words what Miller means in his sixth paragraph by "rites of passage," "rite of aggregation," and "liminal condition."
4. Miller begins his second paragraph with this sentence: "Falling ill is not something that happens to us, it is a choice we make as a result of things happening to us." Imitating Miller's essay as closely as you wish (including ideas, style, even whole sentences, or parts of sentences) write an essay of about 500 words explaining the process of "falling in love," or "becoming an adult" (or an athlete, a musician, a student), or "learning to write," or what you will.

Conversational Ballgames

Nancy Sakamoto

1   After I was married and had lived in Japan for a while, my Japanese gradually improved to the point where I could take part in simple conversations with my husband and his friends and fam-

ily. And I began to notice that often, when I joined in, the others would look startled, and the conversational topic would come to a halt. After this happened several times, it became clear to me that I was doing something wrong. But for a long time, I didn't know what it was.

2   Finally, after listening carefully to many Japanese conversations, I discovered what my problem was. Even though I was speaking Japanese, I was handling the conversation in a western way.

3   Japanese-style conversations develop quite differently from western-style conversations. And the difference isn't only in the languages. I realized that just as I kept trying to hold western-style conversations even when I was speaking Japanese, so my English students kept trying to hold Japanese-style conversations even when they were speaking English. We were unconsciously playing entirely different conversational ballgames.

4   A western-style conversation between two people is like a game of tennis. If I introduce a topic, a conversational ball, I expect you to hit it back. If you agree with me, I don't expect you simply to agree and do nothing more. I expect you to add something—a reason for agreeing, another example, or an elaboration to carry the idea further. But I don't expect you always to agree. I am just as happy if you question me, or challenge me, or completely disagree with me. Whether you agree or disagree, your response will return the ball to me.

5   And then it is my turn again. I don't serve a new ball from my original starting line. I hit your ball back again from where it has bounced. I carry your idea further, or answer your questions or objections, or challenge or question you. And so the ball goes back and forth, with each of us doing our best to give it a new twist, an original spin, or a powerful smash.

6   And the more vigorous the action, the more interesting and exciting the game. Of course, if one of us gets angry, it spoils the conversation, just as it spoils a tennis game. But getting excited is not at all the same as getting angry. After all, we are not trying to hit each other. We are trying to hit the ball. So long as we attack only each other's opinions, and do not attack each other personally, we don't expect anyone to get hurt. A good conversation is supposed to be interesting and exciting.

7   If there are more than two people in the conversation, then it is like doubles in tennis, or like volleyball. There's no waiting in line. Whoever is nearest and quickest hits the ball, and if you step back, someone else will hit it. No one stops the game to give you a turn. You're responsible for taking your own turn.

8   But whether it's two players or a group, everyone does his best to keep the ball going, and no one person has the ball for very long.

9   A Japanese-style conversation, however, is not at all like tennis or volleyball. It's like bowling. You wait for your turn. And you always know your place in line. It depends on such things as whether you are older or younger, a close friend or a relative stranger to the previous speaker, in a senior or junior position, and so on.

10   When your turn comes, you step up to the starting line with your bowling ball, and carefully bowl it. Everyone else stands back and watches politely, murmuring encouragement. Everyone waits until the ball has reached the end of the alley, and watches to see if it knocks down all the pins, or only some of them, or none of them. There is a pause, while everyone registers your score.

11   Then, after everyone is sure that you have completely finished your turn, the next person in line steps up to the same starting line, with a different ball. He doesn't return your ball, and he does not begin from where your ball stopped. There is no back and forth at all. All the balls run parallel. And there is always a suitable pause between turns. There is no rush, no excitement, no scramble for the ball.

12   No wonder everyone looked startled when I took part in Japanese conversations. I paid no attention to whose turn it was, and kept snatching the ball halfway down the alley and throwing it back at the bowler. Of course the conversation died. I was playing the wrong game.

13   This explains why it is almost impossible to get a western-style conversation or discussion going with English students in Japan. I used to think that the problem was their lack of English language ability. But I finally came to realize that the biggest problem is that they, too, are playing the wrong game.

14   Whenever I serve a volleyball, everyone just stands back and watches it fall, with occasional murmurs of encouragement. No one hits it back. Everyone waits until I call on someone to take a turn. And when that person speaks, he doesn't hit my ball back. He serves a new ball. Again, everyone just watches it fall.

15   So I call on someone else. This person does not refer to what the previous speaker has said. He also serves a new ball. Nobody seems to have paid any attention to what anyone else has said. Everyone begins again from the same starting line, and all the balls run parallel. There is never any back and forth. Everyone is trying to bowl with a volleyball.

16   And if I try a simpler conversation, with only two of us, then the other person tries to bowl with my tennis ball. No wonder foreign English teachers in Japan get discouraged.

17   Now that you know about the difference in the conversational ballgames, you may think that all your troubles are over. But if you have been trained all your life to play one game, it is no simple matter to switch to another, even if you know the rules. Knowing the rules is not at all the same thing as playing the game.

18   Even now, during a conversation in Japanese I will notice a startled reaction, and belatedly realize that once again I have rudely interrupted by instinctively trying to hit back the other person's bowling ball. It is no easier for me to "just listen" during a conversation, than it is for my Japanese students to "just relax" when speaking with foreigners. Now I can truly sympathize with how hard they must find it to try to carry on a western-style conversation.

19   If I have not yet learned to do conversational bowling in Japanese, at least I have figured out one thing that puzzled me for a long time. After his first trip to America, my husband complained that Americans asked him so many questions and made him talk so much at the dinner table that he never had a chance to eat. When I asked him why he couldn't talk and eat at the same time, he said that Japanese do not customarily think that dinner, especially on fairly formal occasions, is a suitable time for extended conversation.

20   Since westerners think that conversation is an indispensable part of dining, and indeed would consider it impolite not to converse with one's dinner partner, I found this Japanese custom rather strange. Still, I could accept it as a cultural difference even though I didn't really understand it. But when my husband added, in explanation, that Japanese consider it extremely rude to talk with one's mouth full, I got confused. Talking with one's mouth full is certainly not an American custom. We think it very rude, too. Yet we still manage to talk a lot and eat at the same time. How do we do it?

21   For a long time, I couldn't explain it, and it bothered me. But after I discovered the conversational ballgames, I finally found the answer. Of course! In a western-style conversation, you hit the ball, and while someone else is hitting it back, you take a bite, chew, and swallow. Then you hit the ball again, and then eat some more. The more people there are in the conversation, the more chances

you have to eat. But even with only two of you talking, you still have plenty of chances to eat.

22   Maybe that's why polite conversation at the dinner table has never been a traditional part of Japanese etiquette. Your turn to talk would last so long without interruption that you'd never get a chance to eat.

Questions

1. This essay, by an American woman married to a Japanese man, comes from a textbook designed to teach Japanese students to read English and to learn about American culture. Strictly speaking, the first two paragraphs are not necessary to the points that follow. Do they serve any function?
2. The writer is chiefly seeking to tell her Japanese students something about Western habits of conversation. Why, then, does she also tell them about Japanese habits?
3. Why does Sakamoto bother to use a metaphor (or figurative comparison), seeing conversations as ball games?
4. If you are familiar with a culture other than what can be called Anglo-American, what metaphor might you use to clarify differences between some Anglo-American social act—say, eating, or talking, or child care, or courting—and the corresponding act in the other culture?
5. For the next few days eavesdrop and try to take notes on a particularly lively conversation you happen to hear. As soon as possible, try to reconstruct the entire conversation in writing. Then analyze it. Does it follow the "rules" Sakamoto describes for either a Western-style or a Japanese-style conversation? Or does it resemble something other than a game, perhaps a musical composition? Whatever you find, record your observations in a paragraph. (A suggestion: if you can manage to do so, record a conversation—and the accompanying gestures—between preschool children.)

*E*lapsed Expectations

Alan P. Lightman

1   The limber years for scientists, as for athletes, generally come at a young age. Isaac Newton was in his early 20's when he discov-

ered the law of gravity, Albert Einstein was 26 when he formulated special relativity, and James Clerk Maxwell had polished off electromagnetic theory and retired to the country by 35. When I hit 35 myself, some months ago, I went through the unpleasant but irresistible exercise of summing up my career in physics. By this age, or another few years, the most creative achievements are finished and visible. You've either got the stuff and used it or you haven't.

2   In my own case, as with the majority of my colleagues, I concluded that my work was respectable but not brilliant. Very well. Unfortunately, I now have to decide what to do with the rest of my life. My 35-year-old friends who are attorneys and physicians and businessmen are still climbing toward their peaks, perhaps 15 years up the road, and blissfully uncertain of how high they'll reach. It is an awful thing, at such an age, to fully grasp one's limitations.

3   Why do scientists peak sooner than most other professionals? No one knows for sure. I suspect it has something to do with the single focus and detachment of the subject. A handiness for visualizing in six dimensions or for abstracting the motion of a pendulum favors a nimble mind but apparently has little to do with anything else. In contrast, the arts and humanities require experience with life, experience that accumulates and deepens with age. In science, you're ultimately trying to connect with the clean logic of mathematics and the physical world; in the humanities, with people. Even within science itself, a telling trend is evident. Progressing from the more pure and self-contained of sciences to the less tidy, the seminal contributions spring forth later and later in life. The average age of election to England's Royal Society is lowest in mathematics. In physics, the average age at which Nobel prize winners do their prize-winning work is 36; in chemistry it is 39, and so on.

4   Another factor is the enormous pressure to take on administrative and advisory tasks, descending on you in your mid-30's and leaving time for little else. Such pressures also occur in other professions, of course, but it seems to me they arrive sooner in a discipline where talent flowers in relative youth. Although the politics of science demands its own brand of talent, the ultimate source of approval—and invitation to supervise—is your personal contribution to the subject itself. As in so many other professions, the administrative and political plums conferred in recognition of past achievements can suffocate future ones. These plums may be politely refused, but perhaps the temptation to accept beckons more strongly when you're not constantly galloping off into new research.

5   Some of my colleagues brood as I do over this passage, many are oblivious to it, and many sail happily ahead into administration

and teaching, without looking back. Service on national advisory panels, for example, benefits the professional community and nation at large, allowing senior scientists to share with society their vides the soil that allows new ideas to take root. Most people also try to keep their hands in research, in some form or another. A favorite way is to gradually surround oneself with a large group of disciples, nourishing the imaginative youngsters with wisdom and perhaps enjoying the authority. Scientists with charisma and leadership contribute a great deal in this manner. Another, more subtle tactic is to hold on to the reins, single-handedly, but find thinner and thinner horses to ride. (This can easily be done by narrowing one's field in order to remain "the world's expert.") Or simply plow ahead with research as in earlier years, aware or not that the light has dimmed. The 1 percent of scientists who have truly illuminated their subject can continue in this manner, to good effect, well beyond their prime.

6   For me, none of these activities offers an agreeable way out. I hold no illusions about my own achievements in science, but I've had my moments, and I know what it feels like to unravel a mystery no one has understood before, sitting alone at my desk with only pencil and paper and wondering how it happened. That magic cannot be replaced. When I directed an astrophysics conference last summer and realized that most of the exciting research was being reported by ambitious young people in their mid-20's, waving their calculations and ideas in the air and scarcely slowing down to acknowledge their predecessors, I would have instantly traded my position for theirs. It is the creative element of my profession, not the exposition or administration, that sets me on fire. In this regard, I side with the great mathematician G. H. Hardy, who wrote (at age 63) that "the function of a mathematician is to do something, to prove new theorems, to add to mathematics, and not to talk about what he or other mathematicians have done."

7   In childhood, I used to lie in bed at night and fantasize about different things I might do with my life, whether I would be this or that, and what was so delicious was the limitless potential, the years shimmering ahead in unpredictability. It is the loss of that I grieve. In a way, I have gotten an unwanted glimpse of my mortality. The private discoveries of new territory are not as frequent now. Knowing this, I might make myself useful in other ways. But another 35 years of supervising students, serving on committees, reviewing others' work, is somehow too social. Inevitably, we must all reach our personal limits in whatever professions we choose. In science, this happens at an unreasonably young age, with a lot of life remaining.

Some of my older colleagues, having passed through this soul-searching period themselves, tell me I'll get over it in time. I wonder how. None of my fragile childhood dreams, my parents' ambitious encouragement, my education at all the best schools, prepared me for this early seniority, this stiffening at 35.

Questions

1. What word in the first sentence is a bit unusual in this context? Evaluate the introductory paragraph. Does it engage you? If so, why? If not, why not?

2. In a well-constructed, coherent paragraph each sentence is clearly related to the previous sentence. Analyze Lightman's third paragraph and then explain *how* the second sentence is related to the first, the third to the second, and so on. Then read his fourth paragraph. How is this paragraph related to the previous paragraph?

3. In two or three sentences characterize the writer. (Does he seem pleasant, thoughtful, conceited, crabby, or what?) Support your characterization with evidence.

4. In a sentence or two summarize Lightman's tentative explanation as to why scientists "peak sooner than most other professionals." If you can think of other explanations, briefly offer them.

5. What do you suppose was Lightman's purpose in writing this essay? It appeared in *The New York Times*, but what sort of person do you suppose he imagined his reader to be?

6. Suppose you were considering a career in science. Would reading "Elapsed Expectations" make such a career seem less attractive? Explain why or why not.

*T*he Fumblerules of Grammar
William Safire

Not long ago, I advertised for perverse rules of grammar, along the lines of "Remember to never split an infinitive" and "The passive voice should never be used." The notion of making a mistake while laying down rules ("Thimk," "We Never Make Misteakes") is highly unoriginal, and it turns out that English teachers have been circulating lists of fumblerules for years.

As owner of the world's largest collection, and with thanks to scores of readers, let me pass along a bunch of these never-say-neverisms:

- Avoid run-on sentences they are hard to read.
- Don't use no double negatives.
- Use the semicolon properly, always use it where it is appropriate; and never where it isn't.
- Reserve the apostrophe for it's proper use and omit it when its not needed.
- Do not put statements in the negative form.
- Verbs has to agree with their subjects.
- No sentence fragments.
- Proofread carefully to see if you any words out.
- Avoid commas, that are not necessary.
- If you reread your work, you will find on rereading that a great deal of repetition can be avoided by rereading and editing.
- A writer must not shift your point of view.
- Eschew dialect, irregardless.
- And don't start a sentence with a conjunction.
- Don't overuse exclamation marks!!!
- Place pronouns as close as possible, especially in long sentences, as of 10 or more words, to their antecedents.
- Hyphenate between syllables and avoid un-necessary hyphens.
- Write all adverbial forms correct.
- Don't use contractions in formal writing.
- Writing carefully, dangling participles must be avoided.
- It is incumbent on us to avoid archaisms.
- If any word is improper at the end of a sentence, a linking verb is.
- Steer clear of incorrect forms of verbs that have snuck in the language.
- Take the bull by the hand and avoid mixed metaphors.
- Avoid trendy locutions that sound flaky.
- Never, ever use repetitive redundancies.
- Everyone should be careful to use a singular pronoun with singular nouns in their writing.
- If I've told you once, I've told you a thousand times, resist hyperbole.
- Also, avoid awkward or affected alliteration.
- Don't string too many prepositional phrases together unless you are walking through the valley of the shadow of death.
- Always pick on the correct idiom.

- "Avoid overuse of 'quotation "marks." ' "
- The adverb always follows the verb.
- Last, but not least, avoid clichés like the plague; seek viable alternatives.

Question

Safire does not offer any rules concerning parentheses, capital letters, dashes, italics, or euphemisms. (For discussions of these things, consult the index.) Formulate rules for two things, such as those just listed, that Safire neglects.

7

Persuasion

To persuade is to win over, or to convince. These two are not the same thing; if we win people over by, say, an appeal to their emotions, we have not convinced them, only conquered them. To convince them we must persuade them by presenting *reasonable arguments,* supported with evidence.

But first we must present ourselves as writers worth reading.

In any kind of persuasive writing, whether it is emotional or logical or both, you must gain and then keep the audience's confidence. Unfortunately, confidence is easily lost: for instance, readers are not likely to trust (and therefore not likely to accept) the argument of a writer who spells the word "arguement." The writer's arguments may be sound, but the readers—reluctant to change their views in any case—seize on this irrelevant error and put the essay aside, supposing they have nothing to learn.

Convey your competence and your respect for your reader by

> getting the right word,
> defining crucial terms, and
> providing interesting examples.

We discuss these matters elsewhere in the book. Here we remind you to keep them in mind in writing to persuade.

ARGUMENT

Persuasive writing that, in addition to offering other evidence, relies chiefly on reasoning (rather than on appeals to the emotions) is usually called *argument*. An argument here is not a wrangle but a reasoned analysis. What distinguishes argument from explanation (for instance, the explanation of a process) is this: whereas both consist of statements, in argument some statements are offered as reasons for other statements. Another way of characterizing the difference is to say that exposition assumes there is no substantial disagreement between informed persons, but argument assumes there is or may be substantial disagreement. To overcome this disagreement, the writer tries to offer reasons that convince by their validity. Here, for example, is C. S. Lewis arguing against vivisection (experimentation on live animals for scientific research):

A rational discussion of this subject begins by inquiring whether pain is, or is not, an evil. If it is not, then the case against vivisection falls. But then so does the case for vivisection. If it is not defended on the ground that it reduces human suffering, on what ground can it be defended? And if pain is not an evil, why should human suffering be reduced? We must therefore assume as a basis for the whole discussion that pain is an evil, otherwise there is nothing to be discussed.

Now if pain is an evil then the infliction of pain, considered in itself, must clearly be an evil act. But there are such things as necessary evils. Some acts which would be bad, simply in themselves, may be excusable and even laudable when they are necessary means to a greater good. In saying that the infliction of pain, simply in itself, is bad, we are not saying that pain ought never to be inflicted. Most of us think that it can rightly be inflicted for a good purpose—as in dentistry or just and reformatory punishment. The point is that it always requires justification. On the man whom we find inflicting pain rests the burden of showing why an act which in itself would be simply bad is, in those particular circumstances, good. If we find a man giving pleasure it is for us to prove (if we criticize him) that his action is wrong. But if we find a man inflicting pain it is for him to prove that his action is right. If he cannot, he is a wicked man.

And here is Supreme Court Justice Louis Brandeis, concluding his justly famous argument that government may not use evidence illegally obtained by wiretapping:

> Decency, security and liberty alike demand that government officials shall be subjected to the same rules of conduct that are commands to the citizen. In a government of laws, existence of the government will be imperiled if it fails to observe the law scrupulously. Our Government is the potent, the omnipresent teacher. For good or for ill, it teaches the whole people by its example. Crime is contagious. If the Government becomes a lawbreaker, it breeds contempt for law; it invites every man to become a law unto himself; it invites anarchy. To declare that in the administration of the criminal law the end justifies the means—to declare that the Government may commit crimes in order to secure the conviction of a private criminal—would bring terrible retribution. Against that pernicious doctrine this Court should resolutely set its face.

Notice here that Brandeis's reasoning is highlighted by his forceful style. Note the resonant use of parallel constructions ("For good or for ill," "it breeds . . . it invites," "To declare . . . to declare") and the variation between long and short sentences. Note too the wit in his comparisons: government is a teacher, crime is like a disease.

Two Ways of Arguing: Induction and Deduction

Induction

We will begin by quoting Robert M. Pirsig's admirably brief explanation of induction, in *Zen and the Art of Motorcycle Maintenance:*

> If the cycle goes over a bump and the engine misfires, and then goes over another bump and the engine misfires, and then goes over another bump and the engine misfires, and then goes over a long smooth stretch of road and there is no misfiring, and then goes over a fourth bump and the engine misfires again, one can logically conclude that the misfiring is caused by the bumps. This is induction: reasoning from particular experiences.

Pirsig's example is pretty compelling. One can of course grant that there is a chance—an extremely improbable one—that even though the misfirings and the bumps occurred simultaneously the bumps did not cause the misfirings. Conceivably it was an amazing coincidence that the cycle misfired at each bump—but the odds are vastly in favor of the connection that Pirsig points out. The argument seems pretty sound.

Still, in proceeding by induction, that is, in offering generalizations based on experiences, one must take pains to make sure that the sample of experiences is fair. A fair sample usually means first that the number cited is sufficiently large: *one* bump certainly would not be enough, and even two or three might not be enough to make a convincing case, so Pirsig holds out for four bumps. In addition to constituting a large enough sample, the instances must also be truly representative. Take, for instance, an assertion about student opinion on intercollegiate athletics, based on a careful survey of the opinions of students living in the fraternity houses and dormitories. Such a survey leaves out those students who commute, a group that may be different (economically, religiously, and socially) from the surveyed group. Because the surveyed sample is not fully representative of student opinion, the generalizations drawn from the data may be false. The generalizations may, of course, happen to be true; they may indeed correspond to the views of the commuting students also. But that would be only a lucky accident. In short, when you offer a generalization based on induction, stand back, take another look at your evidence, and decide whether the generalization can be presented as a fact. Maybe it's only a probability or only an opinion.

Deduction

A moment ago we quoted Robert Pirsig on induction, the process of reasoning from particular experiences to general truths. Here is Pirsig again, this time commenting on *deduction*, the process of reasoning from assumptions to conclusions.

> Deductive inferences . . . start with general knowledge and predict a specific observation. For example, if from reading . . . facts about the machine, the mechanic knows the horn of the cycle

is powered exclusively by electricity from the battery, then he can logically infer that if the battery is dead the horn will not work. That is deduction.

The classic example of reasoning from assumptions (called premises) to conclusions is this one:

> *All men are mortal* (the major premise)
> *Socrates is a man* (the minor premise)
> *therefore Socrates is mortal* (the conclusion)

Such an argument, which takes two truths and joins them to produce a third truth, is called a *syllogism* (from Greek for "a reckoning together"). Deduction (from Latin "lead down from") moves from a general statement to a specific application. It is, therefore, the opposite of induction, which moves from specific instances to a general conclusion. *In*duction would note, for example, that Socrates was mortal and that all other observed people were also mortal, and it would thus arrive at the generalization that all people are mortal.

Deduction does not inevitably lead to truth. If a premise of a syllogism is not true, one can reason logically but come to a false conclusion. Example: "All teachers are members of a union"; "Jones is a teacher"; "therefore Jones is a member of a union." Although the process of reasoning is correct, the major premise is false and so the conclusion is worthless—Jones may or may not be a member of a union.

Another trap to avoid is an argument that appears logical but is not. Let's take this attempt at a syllogism: "All teachers of Spanish know that in Spanish *hoy* means *today*" (major premise); "John knows that in Spanish *hoy* means *today*" (minor premise); "therefore John is a teacher of Spanish" (conclusion). Both premises are correct, but the conclusion does not follow. After all, John may be a student taking his first term of Spanish. What's wrong with the reasoning? For a deduction to be valid, the subject or condition of the major premise (in this case, teacher of Spanish) must appear also in the minor premise, but here it does not. If the minor premise were "John is a teacher of Spanish," then the conclusion "therefore John knows that *hoy* means *today*," would be valid.

THREE KINDS OF EVIDENCE: EXAMPLES, TESTIMONY, STATISTICS

Before talking about the kinds of evidence that are especially common in argument, we want to mention again that evidence—convincing detail—is common in almost all kinds of writing. For instance, Alex Ward, writing in *The New York Times Magazine* about a grueling sled-dog race in Alaska, says:

> Next Saturday morning, sixty-three sled-dog teams will set off from Anchorage for the frontier town of Nome, Alaska, about two weeks and 1100 frozen miles to the northwest. The event is the Iditarod Trail International Sled Dog Race, billed as "the last great race on earth." These mushers and their dogs will travel through a couple of time zones, two mountain ranges, and a series of checkpoints with names like Unalakleet, Shaktoolik, McGrath and Koyuk. Just mention them and the mercury on any self-respecting thermometer will drop.

How does Ward persuade us that this race really is tough? He calls attention to "1100 frozen miles" (that's cold), to "a couple of time zones" (that's long), to "two mountain ranges" (that's arduous), and to towns whose very names sound icy. In short, the details that Ward offers help to persuade readers to accept his point of view.

Writers of arguments (like writers about sled-dog races) seek to persuade by offering evidence. The chief forms of evidence used in argument are:

examples,
testimony (the citation of authorities), and
statistics.

We'll briefly consider each of these.

Examples

"Example" is from the Latin *exemplum*, which means "something taken out." An example is the sort of thing, taken from among many similar things, that one selects and holds up for view, perhaps after saying "For example," or "For instance." A moment ago we heard Robert Pirsig illustrate inductive reasoning by means of an example involving a motorcycle. But countless other examples might have been used to make the same point. A century ago Thomas Huxley illustrated the principle of induction by saying that if one bites into a green apple and finds it hard and sour, then bites into a second and third green apple and finds them hard and sour, one may conclude that green apples are hard and sour. (Again, the point is clear, although the evidence is not strictly compelling. Perhaps all of these green apples were of one variety, and perhaps there is another variety of green apple that is mushy and sweet. In fact, Granny Smith apples are crisp and sweet.)

Three sorts of examples are especially common in written arguments:

> real examples,
> invented instances, and
> analogies.

Real examples are just what they sound like, instances that have occurred. If, for example, we are arguing that gun control won't work, we point to those states that have adopted gun control laws and that nevertheless have had no reduction in crimes using guns. Or, if one wants to support the assertion that a woman can be a capable head of state, one may find oneself pointing to the late Golda Meir and the late Indira Ghandi (prime ministers of Israel and India) and to Margaret Thatcher, the prime minister of England.

The advantage of using real examples is, clearly, that they are real. Of course an opponent might stubbornly respond that Golda Meir, Indira Gandhi, and Margaret Thatcher for some reason or other could not function as the head of state in *our* country. One might argue, for instance, that the case of Golda Meir proves nothing, since the role of women in Israeli society is different from the role of women in the United States (a country in which Protestants are the majority). And one might argue that much of Mrs. Gandhi's power came from the fact that she was the daughter of Nehru, an immensely popular Indian statesman. Even the most compelling real example inevitably will in some ways be special or particular, and in the eyes of some readers may not seem to be a fair example. Still, as the feebleness of the objections against Meir and Gandhi indicate, real examples can be very compelling.

Invented instances are exempt from the charge that, because of some detail or other, they are not relevant as evidence. Suppose, for example, you are arguing against capital punishment, on the grounds that if an innocent person is executed, there is no way of even attempting to rectify the injustice. If you point to the case of X, you may be met with the reply that X was not in fact innocent. Rather than get tangled up in the guilt or innocence of a particular person, it may be better to argue that we can suppose—we can imagine—an innocent person convicted and executed, and we can imagine that evidence later proves the person's innocence.

Invented instances have the advantage of presenting an issue clearly, free from all of the distracting particularities (and irrelevancies) that are bound up with any real instance. But invented instances have the disadvantage of being invented, and they may seem remote from the real issues being argued.

Analogies—comparisons pointing out several resemblances between two rather different things—were discussed briefly on page 72, where we cited a familiar example: a government is like a ship, and in times of stress—if the ship is to weather the storm— the authority of the captain must not be questioned.

But don't confuse an analogy with proof. An analogy is an extended comparison between two things; it can be useful in exposition, for it explains the unfamiliar by means of the familiar: "A government is like a ship, and just as a ship has a captain and a crew, so a government has . . ."; "Writing an essay is like building a house; just as an architect must begin with a plan, so the writer must . . ." Such comparisons can be useful, helping to clarify what otherwise might be obscure, but their usefulness goes only so far. Everything is what it is, and not another thing. A government is not a ship, and what is true of a captain's power need not be true of a president's power; and a writer is not an architect. Some of what is true about ships may be (roughly) true of governments, and some of what is true about architects may be (again, roughly) true of writers, but there are differences too. Consider the following analogy between a lighthouse and the death penalty:

> The death penalty is a warning, just like a lighthouse throwing its
> beams out to sea. We hear about shipwrecks, but we do not hear
> about the ships the lighthouse guides safely on their way. We do
> not have proof of the number of ships it saves, but we do not tear
> the lighthouse down.
>
> — J. Edgar Hoover

How convincing is Hoover's analogy as an argument, that is, as a
reason for retaining the death penalty?

Testimony

Testimony, or the citation of authorities, is rooted in our
awareness that some people are recognized as experts. In our daily
life we constantly turn to experts for guidance: we look up the
spelling of a word in the dictionary, we listen to the weather prediction on the radio, we take an ailing cat to the vet for a checkup.
Similarly, when we wish to become informed about controversial
matters, we often turn to experts, first to help educate ourselves,
and then to help convince our readers.

There are at least two reasons for offering testimony in an
argument. The obvious reason is that expert opinion does (and
should) carry some weight with our audience; the less obvious one
is that a change of voice in an essay may afford the reader a bit
of pleasure. No matter how engaging our own voice may be, a
fresh voice—whether that of Thomas Jefferson, Albert Einstein, or
Professor X—may provide a refreshing change of tone.

But of course in citing authorities there are dangers, the chief
of which are

1. the words of the authorities may be taken out of context or
   otherwise distorted, and,
2. the authorities may not be authorities on the present topic.

Quite rightly we are concerned with what the Founding Fathers
said, but it is not entirely clear that their words can be fairly applied, on one side or the other, to such an issue as abortion. Quite
rightly we are concerned with what Einstein said, but it is not
entirely clear that his eminence as a physicist constitutes him an

authority on, say, world peace. In a moment, when we discuss errors in reasoning, we'll have more to say about the proper and improper use of authorities.

Statistics

Statistics, another important form of evidence, are especially useful in arguments concerning social issues. If we want to argue for (or against) raising the driving age, we will probably offer statistics about the number of accidents caused by people in certain age groups.

But a word of caution: the significance of statistics may be difficult to assess. For instance, opponents of gun control legislation have pointed out, in support of the argument that such laws are ineffectual, that homicides in Florida *increased* after Florida adopted gun control laws. Supporters of gun control laws cried "Foul," arguing that in the years after adopting these laws Miami became (for reason having nothing to do with the laws) the cocaine capital of the United States, and the rise in homicide was chiefly a reflection of murders involved in the drug trade. That is, a significant change in the population has made a comparison of the figures meaningless. This objection seems plausible, and probably the statistics therefore should carry little weight.

One other example of the caution that must be used when confronted with statistics. A scholarly article concluded, on the basis of a study of self-portraits by painters, that an astounding percentage of painters were left-handed, that is, they held the brush in the left hand. The table of figures seemed irrefutable. What the author overlooked, however, is that most self-portraits are done with the aid of a mirror, so what seems to be the left hand in the portrait is in fact the right hand.

The best advice we can offer is this: check to see that the statistics are

1. up-to-date
2. compiled by an objective source
3. based on reliable (representative and sufficient) data, and,
4. capable of only one interpretation. (If they can be interpreted in more than one way, acknowledge the fact.)

How Much Evidence Is Enough?

If you allow yourself ample time to write your essay, you probably will turn up plenty of evidence to illustrate your arguments, such as examples drawn from your own experience and imagination, from your reading, and from your talks with others. Examples will not only help to clarify and to support your assertions, but they will also provide a concreteness that will be welcome in a paper that might be on the whole fairly abstract. Your sense of your audience will have to guide you in making your selection of examples. Generally speaking, a single example may not fully illuminate a difficult point, and so a second example, a clincher, may be desirable. If you offer a third or fourth example (as we sometimes do in this book, for instance where a moment ago we unnecessarily cited a flawed statistical study on supposedly left-handed artists), you probably are succumbing to a temptation to include something that tickles your fancy. If it is as good as you think it is, the reader probably will accept the unnecessary example and may even be grateful. But before you heap up examples, try to imagine yourself in your reader's place, and ask if the example is needed. If it is not needed, ask yourself if the reader will be glad to receive the overload.

One other point. On most questions, say on the value of bilingual education or on the need for rehabilitation programs in prisons, it's not possible to make a strictly logical case, in the sense of an absolutely airtight proof. Don't assume that it is your job to make an absolute proof. What you are expected to do is to offer a reasonable argument. Virginia Woolf put it this way: "When a subject is highly controversial . . . one cannot hope to tell the truth. One can only show how one came to hold whatever opinion one does hold."

Avoiding Fallacies

Let's further examine the reasoning process by considering some obvious errors in reasoning. In logic these errors are called *fallacies* (from a Latin verb meaning "to deceive"). As Tweedledee says in *Through the Looking-Glass,* "If it were so, it would be; but as it isn't, it ain't. That's logic."

To persuade readers to accept your opinions you must persuade them that you are reliable; if your argument includes fallacies, thoughtful readers will not take you seriously. More important, if your argument includes fallacies, you are misleading yourself. When you search your draft for fallacies, you are searching for ways to improve the quality of your thinking.

1. *False authority.* Don't try to borrow the prestige of authorities who are not authorities on the topic in question—for example, a heart surgeon speaking on politics. You will only discredit yourself if you think that a surgeon's opinions on redistricting or a politician's opinions on whaling have any special weight. Similarly, some former authorities are no longer authorities, because the problems have changed or because later knowledge has superseded their views. Adam Smith, Jefferson, Eleanor Roosevelt, and Einstein remain persons of genius, but an attempt to use their opinions when you are examining modern issues—even in their fields—may be questioned. Remember the last words of John B. Sedgwick, a Union Army general at the Battle of Spotsylvania in 1864: "They couldn't hit an elephant at this dist—." In short, before you rely on an authority, ask yourself if the person in question *is* an authority on the topic. And don't let stereotypes influence your idea of who is an authority. Don't assume that every black is an authority on ghetto life; many have never been in a ghetto. Remember the Yiddish proverb: "A goat has a beard, but that doesn't make him a rabbi."

2. *False quotation.* If you do quote from an authority, don't misquote. One can argue that the Bible itself says "commit adultery"—the words do occur in it—but of course the quotation is taken out of context: the Bible says "Thou shalt not commit adultery." Few writers would misquote so outrageously, but it is easy to slip into taking from an authority the passages that suit us and neglecting the rest. For example, you may find someone who grants that "there are strong arguments in favor of abolishing the death penalty"; but if she goes on to argue that, on balance, the arguments in favor of retaining it seem stronger to her, it is dishonest to quote her words so as to imply that she favors abolishing it.

3. *Suppression of evidence.* Don't neglect evidence that is contrary to your own argument. To neglect evidence is unfair—and disastrous. You will be found out and your argument will be dismissed, even if it has some merit. You owe it to yourself and your reader to present all the relevant evidence. Be especially careful not to assume that every question is simply a matter of *either/ or.* There may be some truth on both sides. Take the following thesis: "Grades encourage unwholesome competition, and should therefore be abolished." Even if the statement about the evil effect of grading is true, it may not be the whole truth, and therefore it may not follow that grades should be abolished. One might point out that grades do other things too: they may stimulate learning, and they may assist students by telling them how far they have progressed. One might nevertheless conclude, on balance, that the fault outweighs the benefits. But the argument will be more persuasive now that the benefits of grades have been considered.

Concede to the opposition what is due it, and then outscore the opposition. Failure to confront the opposing evidence will be noticed; your readers will keep wondering why you do not consider this point or that, and may consequently dismiss your argument. However, if you confront the opposition you will almost surely strengthen your own argument. As Edmund Burke said two hundred years ago, "He that wrestles with us strengthens our nerves, and sharpens our skill. Our antagonist is our helper."

4. *Generalization from insufficient evidence.* As we pointed out on page 213, in our discussion of induction, the accuracy of the generalization may vary with the size and representativeness of the sampled particulars. In rereading a draft of an argument that you have written, try to spot your own generalizations. Ask yourself if a reasonable reader is likely to agree that the generalization is based on an adequate sample.

A visitor to a college may sit in on three classes, each taught by a different instructor, and may find all three stimulating. That's a good sign, but can we generalize and say that the teaching at this college is excellent? Are three classes a sufficient sample? If all three are offered by the Biology Department, and if the Biology Department includes only five instructors, perhaps we can tentatively say that the teaching of biology at this institution is good. If the Biology Department contains twenty instructors, per-

*"Look, maybe you're right, but for the sake of argument let's
assume you're wrong and drop it."*

Drawing by Mankoff; © 1983 The New Yorker Magazine, Inc.

haps we can still say, though more tentatively, that this sample
indicates that the teaching of biology is good. But what does the
sample say about the teaching of other subjects at the college? It
probably does say something—the institution may be much concerned with teaching across the board—but then again it may not
say a great deal, since the Biology Department may be exception-
ally concerned with good teaching.

   5. *The genetic fallacy.* Don't assume that something can
necessarily be explained in terms of its birth or origin. "He wrote
the novel to make money, so it can't be any good" is palpable
nonsense. The value of the novel need not depend on the initial
pressure that motivated the author. If you think the novel is bad,
you'll have to offer better evidence. Another example: "Capital
punishment arose in days when men sought revenge, so now it
ought to be abolished." Again an unconvincing argument: capital
punishment may have some current value; for example, it may
serve as a deterrent to crime. But that's another argument, and it
needs evidence if it is to be believed. Be on guard, too, against the

thoughtless tendency to judge people by their origins: Mr. X has a foreign accent, so he is probably untrustworthy or stupid or industrious.

6. *Begging the question* and *circular reasoning.* Don't assume the truth of the point that you should prove. The term "begging the question" is a trifle odd. It means, in effect, "You, like a beggar, are asking me to grant you something at the outset."

Examples: "The barbaric death penalty should be abolished"; "This senseless language requirement should be dropped." Both of these statements assume what they should prove—that the death penalty is barbaric, and that the language requirement is senseless. You can of course make assertions such as these, but you must go on to prove them.

Circular reasoning is usually an extended form of begging the question. What ought to be proved is covertly assumed. Example: "X is the best-qualified candidate for the office, because the most informed people say so." Who are the most informed people? Those who recognize X's superiority. Circular reasoning, then, normally includes intermediate steps absent from begging the question, but the two fallacies are so closely related that they can be considered one. Another example: "I feel sympathy for her because I identify with her." Despite the "because," no reason is really offered. What follows "because" is merely a restatement, in slightly different words, of what precedes; the shift of words, from "feel sympathy" to "identify with" has misled the writer into thinking she is giving a reason. Other examples: "Students are interested in courses when the subject matter and the method of presentation are interesting"; "There cannot be peace in the Middle East because the Jews and the Arabs will always fight." In each case, an assertion that ought to be proved is reasserted as a reason in support of the assertion.

7. *Post hoc ergo propter hoc.* Latin: "after this, therefore because of this." Don't assume that because X precedes Y, X must cause Y. For example: "He went to college and came back a pothead; college corrupted him." He might have taken up pot even if he had not gone to college. (The error, like the generalizations from insufficient evidence discussed on page 213, is an error in induction.) Another example: "When a fifty-five-mile-per-hour limit

was imposed in 1974, after the Arab embargo on oil, the number of auto fatalities decreased sharply, from 55,000 deaths in 1973 to 46,000 in 1974, so it is evident that a fifty-five-mile-per-hour limit saves lives." Not quite. Because gasoline was expensive after the embargo, the number of miles traveled decreased. The number of fatalities *per mile* remained constant. The price of gas, not the speed limit, seems responsible for the decreased number of fatalities. Moreover, the national death rate has continued to fall. Why? Several factors are at work: seat-belt and child-restraint laws, campaigns against drunk driving, improved auto design, and improved roads. Medicine, too, may have improved so that today doctors can save accident victims who in 1974 would have died. In short, it probably is impossible to isolate the correlation between speed and safety.

8. *Argumentum ad hominem.* Here the argument is directed "toward the man" (or woman), rather than toward the issue. Don't shift from your topic to your opponent. A speaker argues against legalizing abortions and her opponent, instead of facing the merits of the argument, attacks the character or the associations of the opponent: "You're a Catholic, aren't you?"

9. *False assumption.* Consider the Scot who argued that Shakespeare must have been a Scot. Asked for his evidence, he replied, "The ability of the man warrants the assumption." Or take such a statement as "She goes to Yale, so she must be rich." Possibly the statement is based on faulty induction (the writer knows four Yale students, and all four are rich) but more likely he is just passing on a cliché. The Yale student in question may be on a scholarship, may be struggling to earn the money, or may be backed by parents of modest means who for eighteen years have saved money for her college education. Other examples: "I haven't heard him complain about French 10, so he must be satisfied"; "She's a writer, so she must be well read." A little thought will show how weak such assertions are; they *may* be true, but they may not.

The errors we have discussed are common, but they should never, of course, be consciously used. In revising, try to spot them and eliminate or correct them. You have a point to make, and you should make it fairly. If it can be made only unfairly, you do an

"Please forgive Edgar. He has no verbal skills."

Drawing by Lorenz; © 1980 The New Yorker Magazine, Inc.

injustice not only to your reader but to yourself; you should try to change your view of the topic. You don't want to be like the politician whose speech had a marginal note: "Argument weak; shout here."

WIT

In addition to using sound argument and other evidence, writers often use wit, especially irony, to persuade. In irony, the words convey a meaning somewhat different from what they explicitly say. Wry understatement is typical. Here, for instance, is Thoreau explaining why in *Walden,* his book about his two years in relative isolation at Walden Pond, he will talk chiefly about himself:

> In most books, the *I*, or first person, is omitted; in this it will be retained; that, in respect to egotism, is the main difference. We commonly do not remember that it is, after all, always the first person that is speaking. I should not talk so much about myself if there were anybody else whom I knew as well. Unfortunately, I am confined to this theme by the narrowness of my experience.

Notice the wry apology in his justification for talking about himself: he does not know any one else as well as he knows himself. Similarly, in "unfortunately" ("Unfortunately, I am confined to this theme by the narrowness of my experience") we again hear a wry voice. After all, Thoreau knows, as we know, that *no one* has experience so deep or broad that he or she knows others better than himself or herself. Thoreau's presentation of himself as someone who happens not to have had the luck of knowing others better than himself is playfully foxy.

Thoreau went to live at Walden Pond in order to face nature and to contemplate. In the passage quoted below, you will notice that he says he is now "a sojourner [a temporary resident] in civilized life again." But you'll also notice that, in the context of his denunciation of the materialism of his townsmen, his use of the word "civilized" is at least mildly ironic. He is indeed again living in the town among other citizens ("civilized" comes from the Latin *civis* = citizen), but this realm, at least as Thoreau presents it, is not at all a realm of an advanced society, which is the usual meaning of "civilization." (One is reminded of the shipwrecked man who, crawling from the beach to a town, saw a uniformed officer flogging a prisoner, and said, "Thank God I've landed in a civilized society.")

Let's look briefly at the first pages of Thoreau's *Walden:*

> When I wrote the following pages, or rather the bulk of them, I lived alone, in the woods, a mile from any neighbor, in a house which I had built myself, on the shore of Walden Pond, in Concord, Massachusetts, and earned my living by the labor of my hands only. I lived there two years and two months. At present I am a sojourner in civilized life again.
>
> I should not obtrude my affairs so much on the notice of my readers if very particular inquiries had not been made by my townsmen concerning my mode of life, which some would call impertinent, though they do not appear to me at all impertinent, but, con-

sidering the circumstances, very natural and pertinent. Some have asked what I got to eat; if I did not feel lonesome; if I was not afraid; and the like. Others have been curious to learn what portion of my income I devoted to charitable purposes; and some, who have large families, how many poor children I maintained. I will therefore ask those of my readers who feel no particular interest in me to pardon me if I undertake to answer some of these questions in this book. In most books, the *I*, or first person, is omitted; in this it will be retained; that, in respect to egotism, is the main difference. We commonly do not remember that it is, after all, always the first person that is speaking. I should not talk so much about myself if there were anybody else whom I knew as well. Unfortunately, I am confined to this theme by the narrowness of my experience. Moreover, I, on my side, require of every writer, first or last, a simple and sincere account of his own life, and not merely what he has heard of other men's lives; some such account as he would send to his kindred from a distant land; for if he has lived sincerely, it must have been in a distant land to me. Perhaps these pages are more particularly addressed to poor students. As for the rest of my readers, they will accept such portions as apply to them. I trust that none will stretch the seams in putting on the coat, for it may do good service to him whom it fits.

I would fain say something, not so much concerning the Chinese and Sandwich Islanders as you who read these pages, who are said to live in New England; something about your condition, especially your outward condition or circumstances in this world, in this town, what it is, whether it is necessary that it be as bad as it is, whether it cannot be improved as well as not. I have traveled a good deal in Concord; and everywhere, in shops, and offices, and fields, the inhabitants have appeared to me to be doing penance in a thousand remarkable ways. When I have heard of Bramins sitting exposed to four fires and looking in the face of the sun; or hanging suspended, with their heads downward, over flames; or looking at the heavens over their shoulders "until it becomes impossible for them to resume their natural position, while from the twist of the neck nothing but liquids can pass into the stomach"; or dwelling, chained for life, at the foot of a tree; or measuring with their bodies, like caterpillars, the breadth of vast empires; or standing on one leg on the tops of pillars—even these forms of conscious penance are hardly more incredible and astonishing than the scenes which I daily witness. The twelve labors of Hercules were trifling in comparison with those which my neighbors have undertaken; for they were only twelve, and had an end; but I could never see that these men slew or captured any monster or finished any labor. They have no friend Iolaus to burn with a hot iron the root of the hydra's head, but as soon as one head is crushed, two spring up.

I see young men, my townsmen, whose misfortune it is to have inherited farms, houses, barns, cattle, and farming tools; for these are more easily acquired than got rid of. Better if they had been born in the open pasture and suckled by a wolf, that they might have seen with clearer eyes what field they were called to labor in. Who made them serfs of the soil? Why should they eat their sixty acres, when man is condemned to eat only his peck of dirt? Why should they begin digging their graves as soon as they are born? They have got to live a man's life, pushing all these things before them, and get on as well as they can. How many a poor immortal soul have I met well nigh crushed and smothered under its load, creeping down the road of life, pushing before it a barn seventy-five feet by forty, its Augean stables never cleansed, and one hundred acres of land, tillage, mowing, pasture, and wood-lot! The portionless, who struggle with no such unnecessary inherited encumbrances, find it labor enough to subdue and cultivate a few cubic feet of flesh.

Now think about these questions.

1. In the first paragraph, how does Thoreau gain our respect?
2. Why doesn't Thoreau omit the first two paragraphs and simply begin with the first sentence of the third? And in the third paragraph, what is the small joke in "I have traveled a great deal in Concord"? And why does he refer to Bramins and to the twelve labors of Hercules, instead of simply talking about the people he sees in New England?
3. In the fourth paragraph, what does Thoreau mean when he says some men "eat their sixty acres," and what does he mean when he says "man is condemned to eat only his peck of dirt"? Explain his statement that some men on the road of life push a barn and one hundred acres of land. In fact, why does he at this point not speak merely of a man but of an "immortal soul . . . pushing before it a barn seventy-five feet by forty"? Why the statistics?

Your answers to some of these questions will help you to see how persuasive wit can be. Thoreau offers scarcely anything that in the strict sense can be called an argument, yet attracted by his shrewdness we feel compelled to share his opinions.

Almost every sentence in every piece of good writing in one way or another persuades, either by offering evidence or by keeping the reader's sympathy and attention so that the reader will stay with the writer until the end. The whole of this book, even the comments on spelling and punctuation, seeks to help you to write so that your readers are persuaded it is worth their time to listen to you.

Avoiding Sarcasm

Because writers must, among other things, persuade readers that they are humane, sarcasm has little place in persuasive writing. Although desk dictionaries usually define sarcasm as "bitter, caustic irony" or "a kind of satiric wit," if you think of a sarcastic comment that you have heard you will probably agree that "a crude, sneering remark" is a better definition. Lacking the wit of good satire and the carefully controlled mockery of irony, sarcasm usually relies on gross overstatement and intends simply to humiliate. *Sarcasm* is derived from a Greek word meaning "to tear flesh" or "to bite the lips in rage," altogether an unattractive business. Sarcasm is unfair, for it dismisses an opponent's arguments with ridicule rather than with reason; it is also unwise, for it turns the reader against you. Readers hesitate to ally themselves with a writer who apparently enjoys humiliating the opposition. A sarcastic remark can turn the hearers against the speaker and arouse sympathy for the victim. In short, sarcasm usually doesn't work.

ORGANIZING AN ARGUMENT

As we have earlier said at some length, writers find out what they think partly by means of the act of putting words on paper. But in presenting arguments for their readers, writers rarely duplicate their own acts of discovery. To put it another way, the process of setting forth ideas, and supporting them, does not follow the productive but untidy, repetitive, often haphazard process of preliminary thinking. For instance, a point that did not strike the writer until the middle of the third draft may, in the final version, appear in the opening paragraph. Or an example that seemed useful early in our thinking may, in the process of revision, be omitted in favor of a stronger example. Through a series of revisions, large and small, we try to work out the best strategy for persuading our readers to accept our reasoning as sound, our conclusion as valid. Unfortunately, we find, an argument cannot be presented either as it occurs to us or all at once.

Nor is there a simple formula that governs the organization of all effective argumentative essays. An essay may begin by announcing its thesis and then set forth the reasons that support the thesis. Or it may begin more casually, calling attention to specific cases, and then generalize from these cases. Probably it will then go on to reveal an underlying unity which brings the thesis into view, and from here it will offer detailed reasoning that supports the thesis. Nevertheless, three methods of organizing arguments are fairly common, and one or another may suit an essay you're working on.

1. Begin with a thesis statement and then work from the simplest argument up to the most complex. Such an arrangement will keep your reader with you, step by step.

2. Arrange arguments in order of increasing strength. Now, the danger in following this plan is that you may lose the reader from the start, because you begin with a weak argument. Avoid the danger by telling your reader that indeed the first argument is relatively weak (if it is terribly weak, it isn't an argument at all, so scrap it), but that you offer it for the sake of completeness or because it is often given, and that you will soon give the reader far stronger arguments. Face the opposition to this initial argument, grant that opposition as much as it deserves, and salvage what is left of the argument. Then proceed to the increasingly strong arguments, devoting at least one paragraph to each. Introduce each argument with an appropriate transition ("another reason," "even more important," "most convincing of all"). State it briefly, summarize the opposing view, and then demolish this opposition. With this organization, your discussion of each of your own arguments ends affirmatively.

3. After stating what you wish to prove in an introductory paragraph, mass all of the opposing arguments, and then respond to them one by one.

In short, when you 1) think you have done your initial thinking and your rethinking, 2) have consulted some published sources,

3) have talked with friends and perhaps with experts, and 4) have moved from random notes and lists to fairly full drafts, you are not quite done.

You still must check what you hope is your last draft to see if you have found the best possible order for the arguments, have given effective examples, and have furnished transitions. In short, you must check to see that you have produced an argument that will strike a reasonable reader as courteous, clear, and concrete.

A CHECKLIST FOR REVISING DRAFTS OF PERSUASIVE ESSAYS

1. Are the terms clearly defined?
2. Is the thesis stated promptly and clearly?
3. Are the assumptions likely to be shared by your readers? If not, are they reasonably argued rather than merely stated?
4. Are the facts verifiable? Is the evidence reliable? (No out-of-date statistics, no generalizations from insufficient evidence?)
5. Is the reasoning sound?
6. Are the authorities really authorities on this matter?
7. Are all of the substantial counterarguments recognized and effectively responded to?
8. Does the essay make use, where appropriate, of concrete examples?
9. Is the organization effective? Does the essay begin interestingly, keep the thesis in view, and end interestingly?
10. Is the tone appropriate? (Avoid sarcasm. Present yourself as fair-minded, and assume that those who hold a view opposed to yours are also fair-minded.)

EXERCISES

1. Analyze and evaluate each of the following arguments. If any of the arguments contain fallacies, name the fallacies.

    a. To the Editor:
        The recent senseless murder of a 15-year-old seminary student again emphasizes the insanity of our gun laws. No matter how

guilty the 13-year-old boy who shot into the head of the victim, it seems that our Congressmen are even more guilty by not enacting stricter gun-control laws. They are supposedly sane, rational men; and the kindest thing that can be said about them is that they are merely motivated by greed.

b. To the Editor:

Your editorial last Wednesday arguing against censorship as an infringement on freedom is full of clever arguments but it overlooks an obvious fact. We have Pure Food and Drug laws to protect us against poison, and no one believes that such laws interfere with the freedom of those who produce food and drugs. The public is entitled, then, to laws that will similarly protect us from the poison that some movie-makers produce.

c. To the Editor:

On Dec. 5 *The Times* published a story saying that Harvard has come under pressure to improve the "quality of its teaching." Unfortunately nobody knows what good teaching is, let alone how to evaluate it.

Unlike scholarship, which has a visible product, namely published reports, the results of teaching are locked in the heads of students and are usually not apparent, even to the students themselves, for a very long period.

One device which is frequently used is a poll of students, the so-called "student evaluation of teachers." This type of measurement has been studied by Rodin & Rodin, who correlated it with how much the students learned, as demonstrated on tests. The correlation was highly negative (−.75). As the Rodins put it, "Students rate most highly instructors from whom they learn least."

What invariably happens is that attempts to reward "good teaching" turn out to reward good public relations.

d. [Written shortly after the United States entered the Second World War] The Pacific Coast is in imminent danger of a combined attack from within and from without. . . . It is [true] . . . that since the outbreak of the Japanese war there has been no important sabotage on the Pacific Coast. From what we know about the fifth column in Europe, this is not, as some have liked to think, a sign that there is nothing to be feared. It is a sign that the blow is well-organized and that it is held back until it can be struck with maximum effect. . . . I am sure I understand fully and appreciate thoroughly the unwillingness of Washington to adopt a policy of mass evacuation and internment of all those who are technically enemy aliens. But I submit that Washington is not defining the problem on the coast correctly. . . . The Pacific Coast is officially a combat zone: some part of it may at any moment be a battlefield. Nobody's constitutional rights include the right to reside and do business on a battlefield. And nobody ought to be on a battlefield who has no good reason for being there.

—Walter Lippmann

2. In July 1984 President Reagan signed a bill that exerted pressure on the states to enact legislation setting the drinking age at twenty-one. The bill allows the government to withhold five percent of federal highway construction funds from states that do not set the drinking age at twenty-one by October 1986. If the age is not set at twenty-one by October 1987, ten percent of the funds can be withheld.

Read the following letter to a newspaper, and then list and evaluate the persuasive devices that it uses.

To the Editor:

Congress and the President are bullying the states into raising the drinking age.

The law is discriminatory because it withholds a right from certain people merely because of their age.

The law is unreasonable, because it seems to say that people who are old enough to vote and to fight for their country are not old enough to drink alcohol.

The law is illogical, because it takes as proof of its value the fact that those states that already have raised the drinking age to twenty-one have had a reduction in the number of nighttime driving accidents by persons under twenty-one. Of course they have—and if the age were raised to thirty-five there would be a similar reduction in the number of driving accidents by persons under thirty-five. Why not set the age at fifty? Or at sixty-five? Or a hundred?

In any case, the statistics prove nothing. The lower percent of accidents may be due to other factors, such as heightened public awareness, or stricter enforcement of speeding laws.

The real problem is not that people between eighteen and twenty-one drink, but that they do not receive adequate driver education—an education that would of course emphasize that one must never drive while intoxicated. Further, the police do not strictly enforce laws against speeding, and thus they in effect contribute to the accident rate.

Yours,
— Stephen Ohmann

3. In *The New York Times Book Review,* 24 March 1985, page 37, A. P. Thomas makes three points about handguns:

   More criminals are shot by private citizens each year than by the police.

   There are twice as many people killed by drunken drivers each year as by handguns (and ten times as many severely injured).

   In about half of the handgun murders the people know each other—so they would probably use other weapons if guns were not available.

   Trying to put aside your own views about the possession of handguns, make explicit the assumptions that lie beneath the three statements, and then evaluate each of the statements as an argument against outlawing handguns.

4. Read the brief essay below, originally published as an Op-Ed article in *The New York Times,* and the four letters written in response to it (and published two weeks later). Some questions and suggestions for writing follow.

   ### Sisters Under the Skin

   It's the beginning of April—time to put my fur coat into storage. I'll be sorry to part with the sleek brown beaver that has kept me warm all winter. The end of the season has made me think about the past winter, my first as a fur owner, and some unusual experiences.

   For example, as I walked along 57th Street in Manhattan, a woman hissed, "A lot of animals were tortured to make that coat!" I was surprised, not by her sentiment, which I understood and even respected, but by her need to express it, unsolicited, in public. In the following weeks, I discovered that my outspoken critic was not alone and that some of her compatriots were even more unabashed in proclaiming their views. One woman shouted: "Bloody fur! Shame on you!" Like it or not, I realized I was going to have to defend my coat against detractors.

   I understand the arguments against wearing fur and have decided to wear one anyway. Not only does fur solve, more efficiently than any other substance known to man, the need for warmth, it has also been with us for hundreds if not thousands of years.

   Since I eat meat, I find the distinction between wearing and eating arbitrary. Animals don't care whether their flesh is consumed or their skins are worn; the point is, they have died and we have killed them. This may sound cruel, but it is honest.

I would like to ask those women who keep shouting at me just how consistent they are. What about wearing leather and suede? Animals must be killed for those skins, too. Do all these women wear only sneakers and carry canvas bags?

What is even more offensive than the opinions is the rudeness with which they are expressed. Didn't the mothers of these women tell them that shouting at strangers shows an appalling lack of manners? Or has their love of animals so clouded their minds that they have become wholly insensitive to the feelings of others? It seems ironic that the champions of animal rights show so little regard for human rights.

What do these women think they are accomplishing by these attacks? Do they really believe that I am going to be suddenly converted, and toss my fur into the flames? What ignorance and naïveté!

On the contrary, their anti-fur campaign has made me more entrenched in my own position: I am determined to continue wearing, and delighting in, my fur. If I had the money, I'd buy another—maybe a sumptuous mink or a full-length sable.

No man has publicly upbraided me for wearing a fur coat. Why? I have some thoughts on this (which are not substantiated by research or study).

My furrier told me that the average age at which a woman picked out a mink used to be 55, and her husband footed the bill. Now, the average fur buyer is 35 and purchases the coat herself. This seems to confirm a shift in the status of women.

Women have more buying power these days. They are more likely to have well paying jobs in traditionally male fields like law, business and medicine than ever before. They work hard and know how to reward themselves: a fur coat is one way to do that.

Everything considered, I can't help but feel there's a sub rosa feminist issue lurking here. Haven't we learned something from our enormous struggle for equality? Must women resort to brutish tactics to get their point across? Hasn't every woman burned at the leering remarks offered by some man as she passed him in the street? Must she now be harangued by a woman—a sister, under the skin, so to speak—for a coat she's probably bought herself with money that would have been nearly impossible to earn 40 or even 20 years ago?

Verbal abuse was once something that men used against women in public to assert anger and their power. Shouldn't we, as women, have found a better way to express ours?

— Yona Zeldis McDonough

Letters: *Wearing Furs Isn't a Right or a Feminist Issue*

DOUBLETHINK

To the Editor:

As a writer and speaker on the principles of feminism, I found "Sisters Under the Skin" (Op-Ed, April 2) by Yona Zeldis Mc-Donough an extraordinarily good model of double-think as well as an arrogant defense of fur wearing.

Precisely because we are all the same as nonhuman individuals in important ways, such as in the desire to live unexploited and to avoid pain and death, it is immoral for us to deprive them of their basic interest in living in order to satisfy our peripheral interest in dressing a certain way. As Jeremy Bentham put it: "The number of legs, the villosity of the skin, or the termination of the os sacrum are reasons equally insufficient for abandoning a sensitive being."

Ms. McDonough's reasoning is convenient but flawed and cannot rightly be used, as she attempts to use it, to plead a woman's right to anything, particularly the "right" to wear the skins other animals were born in and were killed for.

"Since I eat meat," she says, "I find the distinction between wearing and eating arbitrary." Meat eating is not a reason to engage in a second abusive practice. Historically, thinking feminists, like Susan B. Anthony and Lucy Stone, have been vegetarians. Indeed, people like Gandhi and Cesar Chavez, whose work for the liberation of humankind is all-consuming, are vegetarians (and antivivisectionists) because they have applied the principles of their cause to their own lives. If one continues to eat animals that is no justification for beating one's dog or killing rabbits or minks to make a pretty coat.

Ms. McDonough talks of women gaining more power. What sort of power does she find it necessary to achieve? Feminists are not struggling for the power to oppress, for the right to be hunters, animal experimenters, fur wearers and buyers, and butchers. We are fighting for an ethic that embraces the right to freedom from exploitation, for all. Human chauvinism is not an acceptable replacement for male chauvinism.

Ms. McDonough is lucky that all she gets on the street are head shakes, frowns and harsh words. Were the animals on her back alive, they would consider such treatment a luxury.

— Ingrid F. Newkirk
National Director, People for the Ethical Treatment of Animals
Washington, D.C.

WOMAN WHO HISSED

To the Editor:

I think I am the woman who hissed, "A lot of animals were tortured to make that coat" on the street at Ms. McDonough. As an animal rights activist, schooled in the cruelties of the fur trade, I take my chance and confront the fur wearer in public (how else can I get her attention?) in the hope of eliciting her curiosity on the sad history of her coat.

What Ms. McDonough calls bad manners are the echoes in my mind of the screams of countless animals caught in steel-jaw leghold traps or else clubbed to death.

I know that I cannot reach a hard-hearted person such as Ms. McDonough, but maybe among those fur wearers there is a sister under the skin who will start thinking and feeling!

— Dorothy Grunebaum
Closter, N.J.

BEAVERS AND CATTLE

To the Editor:

A woman is pained that other women have hissed at her along the street because she wore a beaver coat. Don't those abusive women eat meat and wear leather shoes?

The argument offers no refuge. Beavers are wild. In swampy deep woods, they find their own lifetime mates, breed and feed their own young before being trapped and killed for their pelts. We steal beavers from their natural habitats so humans can flaunt furs when fake furs are as warm and beautiful.

Beef cattle, on the other hand, are domesticated. We breed, feed and slaughter them for their meat and hides. Even so, more and more men and women for health as well as for humane reasons have stopped eating meat.

— Malvine Cole
Jamaica, Vt.

THE SIDE OF SAVAGERY

To the Editor:

Before Yona Zeldis McDonough writes any more claptrap on the subject, I would suggest that she examine the facts of the fur trade a little more closely. Despite her blithe contention that she understands the arguments against wearing furs, I doubt very much if she has really investigated the issue.

That is because the facts are stomach churning, and include a catalogue of horrors that I'm sure would bring a blush of shame to Ms. McDonough.

Has she ever, I wonder, seen a leghold trap? Has she ever heard of the trapper's term "wring off"? Can she imagine what that involves, when an animal (like the beavers she wears) slowly wrings off its own foot or leg and limps away to bleed to death?

There's a big difference between the suede and leather trades, and the fur business. Cattle are raised for their meat and their hides. They are killed with a degree of humaneness. They certainly aren't trapped on the range and left to die there.

This subject has nothing to do with sexism, but everything to do with human cruelty. Ms. McDonough puts herself on the side of atavistic sadism and savagery for the pleasure she gets out of her fur.

— Chris Rowley
New York

Questions:

a. What issue (or issues) does McDonough raise, and what arguments does she offer? Try to list her arguments.

b. What arguments does each letter writer offer in response to McDonough?

c. In her third paragraph McDonough offers an argument not met by any of the letter writers. What is it? How might you answer it?

d. What means *other than argument* does McDonough use to persuade? Do the letter writers attempt to persuade through means other than argument?

e. Of the five pieces of writing (the original article and the four letters) which did you find most persuasive, and why?

Suggestions for Writing:

a. In an essay of approximately 500 words summarize and evaluate "Sisters Under the Skin" and the responses to it. Write for someone who has not read the article or the letters, but who is interested in animal rights, or feminism, or both.

b. In an essay of 500 words, explain your position on wearing furs. You may assume that your readers are aware of the controversy in the *Times* (although they do not have the essay or letters at hand) and you may therefore summarize, quote, or refer to "Sisters Under the Skin" and the responses to develop and support your own position.

c. In an essay of 500 words, answer question e above.

PERSUASION AT WORK

Four Letter Words Can Hurt You

Barbara Lawrence

1   Why should any words be called obscene? Don't they all describe natural human functions? Am I trying to tell them, my students demand, that the "strong, earthy, gut-honest"—or, if they are
fans of Norman Mailer, the "rich, liberating, existential"—language they use to describe sexual activity isn't preferable to "phony-
sounding, middle-class words like 'intercourse' and 'copulate'?" "Cop
You Late!" they say with fancy inflections and gagging grimaces.
"Now, what is *that* supposed to mean?"

2   Well, what is it supposed to mean? And why indeed should
one group of words describing human functions and human organs
be acceptable in ordinary conversation and another, describing presumably the same organs and functions, be tabooed—so much so,
in fact, that some of these words still cannot appear in print in
many parts of the English-speaking world?

3   The argument that these taboos exist only because of "sexual
hangups" (middle-class, middle-age, feminist), or even that they are
a result of class oppression (the contempt of the Norman conquer-
ors for the language of their Anglo-Saxon serfs), ignores a much
more likely explanation, it seems to me, and that is the sources and
functions of the words themselves.

4   The best known of the tabooed sexual verbs, for example, comes
from the German *ficken*, meaning "to strike"; combined, according
to Partridge's etymological dictionary *Origins*, with the Latin sexual verb *futuere;* associated in turn with the Latin *fustis*, "a staff or
cudgel"; the Celtic *buc*, "a point, hence to pierce"; the Irish *bot*,
"the male member"; the Latin *battuere*, "to beat"; the Gaelic *ba-
tair*, "a cudgeller"; the Early Irish *bualaim*, "I strike"; and so forth.
It is one of what etymologists sometimes call "the sadistic group of
words for the man's part in copulation."

5   The brutality of this word, then, and its equivalents ("screw,"
"bang," etc.), is not an illusion of the middle class or a crotchet of
Women's Liberation. In their origins and imagery these words carry
undeniably painful, if not sadistic, implications, the object of which

is almost always female. Consider, for example, what a "screw" actually does to the wood it penetrates; what a painful, even mutilating, activity this kind of analogy suggests. "Screw" is particularly interesting in this context, since the noun, according to Partridge, comes from words meaning "groove," "nut," "ditch," "breeding sow," "scrofula" and "swelling," while the verb, besides its explicit imagery, has antecedent associations to "write on," "scratch," "scarify," and so forth—a revealing fusion of a mechanical or painful action with an obviously denigrated object.

6   Not all obscene words, of course, are as implicitly sadistic or denigrating to women as these, but all that I know seem to serve a similar purpose: to reduce the human organism (especially the female organism) and human functions (especially sexual and procreative) to their least organic, most mechanical dimension; to substitute a trivializing or deforming resemblance for the complex human reality of what is being described.

7   Tabooed male descriptives, when they are not openly denigrating to women, often serve to divorce a male organ or function from any significant interaction with the female. Take the word "testes," for example, suggesting "witnesses" (from the Latin *testis*) to the sexual and procreative strengths of the male organ; and the obscene counterpart of this word, which suggests little more than a mechanical shape. Or compare almost any of the "rich," "liberating' sexual verbs, so fashionable today among male writers, with that much-derided Latin word "copulate" ("to bind or join together") or even that Anglo-Saxon phrase (which seems to have had no trouble surviving the Norman Conquest) "make love."

8   How arrogantly self-involved the tabooed words seem in comparison to either of the other terms, and how contemptuous of the female partner. Understandably so, of course, if she is only a "skirt," a "broad," or a "chick," a "pussycat" or a "piece." If she is, in other words, no more than her skirt, or what her skirt conceals; no more than a breeder, or the broadest part of her; no more than a piece of a human being or a "piece of tail."

9   The most severely tabooed of all the female descriptives, incidentally, are those like a "piece of tail," which suggest (either explicitly or through antecedents) that there is no significant difference between the female channel through which we are all conceived and born and the anal outlet common to both sexes—a distinction that pornographers have always enjoyed obscuring.

10   This effort to deny women their biological identity, their individuality, their humanness, is such an important aspect of obscene language that one can only marvel at how seldom, in an era preoc-

cupied with definitions of obscenity, this fact is brought to our attention. One problem, of course, is that many of the people in the best position to do this (critics, teachers, writers) are so reluctant today to admit that they are angered or shocked by obscenity. Bored, maybe, unimpressed, aesthetically displeased, but—no matter how brutal or denigrating the material—never angered, never shocked.

11   And yet how eloquently angered, how piously shocked many of these same people become if denigrating language is used about any minority group other than women; if the obscenities are racial or ethnic, that is, rather than sexual. Words like "coon," "kike," "spic," "wop," after all, deform identity, deny individuality and humanness in almost exactly the same way that sexual vulgarisms and obscenities do.

12   No one that I know, least of all my students, would fail to question the values of a society whose literature and entertainment rested heavily on racial or ethnic pejoratives. Are the values of a society whose literature and entertainment rest as heavily as ours on sexual pejoratives any less questionable?

Question

In addition to giving evidence to support her view, what persuasive devices (for example, irony, analogy) does Lawrence use?

The Colorization of Films Insults Artists and Society
Woody Allen

1   In the world of potent self-annihilation, famine and AIDS, terrorists and dishonest public servants and quack evangelists and contras and Sandinistas and cancer, does it really matter if some kid snaps on his TV and happens to see *The Maltese Falcon* in color? Especially if he can simply dial the color out and choose to view it in its original black and white?

2   I think it does make a difference and the ramifications of what's called colorization are not wonderful to contemplate. Simply put, the owners of thousands of classic American black and white films believe that there would be a larger public for the movies, and consequently more money, if they were reissued in color. Since they have computers that can change such masterpieces as *Citizen Kane* and *City Lights* and *It's A Wonderful Life* into color, it has become a serious problem for anyone who cares about these movies and has feelings about our image of ourselves as a culture.

3   I won't comment about the quality of the color. It's not good, but probably it will get better. Right now it's like elevator music. It has no soul. All faces are rendered with the same deadening pleasance. The choices of what colors people should be wearing or what colors rooms should be (all crucial artistic decisions in making a film) are left to caprices and speculations by computer technicians who are not qualified to make those choices.

4   Probably false, but not worth debating here, is the claim that young people won't watch black and white. I would think they would, judging from the amount of stylish music videos and MTV ads that are done in black and white, undoubtedly after market research. The fact that audiences of all ages have been watching Charlie Chaplin, Humphrey Bogart, Jimmy Stewart, Fred Astaire—in fact, all the stars and films of the so-called Golden Age of Hollywood—in black and white for decades with no diminution of joy also makes me wonder about these high claims for color. Another point the coloroids make is that one can always view the original if one prefers. The truth is, however, that in practical terms, what will happen is that the color versions will be aired while token copies of the original black and white will lie around preserved in a vault, unpromoted and unseen.

5   Another aspect of the problem that one should mention (although it is not the crucial ground on which I will make my stand) is that American films are a landmark heritage that do our nation proud all over the world, and should be seen as they were intended to be. One would wince at defacing great buildings or paintings, and, in the case of movies, what began as a popular entertainment has, like jazz music, developed into a serious art form. Now, someone might ask: "Is an old Abbott and Costello movie art? Should it be viewed in the same way as *Citizen Kane*?" The answer is that it should be protected, because all movies are entitled to their personal integrity and, after all, who knows what future generations will regard as art works of our epoch?

6   Yet another question: "Why were directors not up in arms about

cutting films for television or breaking them up for commercials, insulting them with any number of technical alterations to accommodate the television format?" The answer is that directors always hated these assaults on their work but were powerless to stop them. As in life, one lives with the first few wounds, because to do battle is an overwhelmingly time-consuming and pessimistic prospect.

7   Still, when the assaults come too often, there is a revolution. The outrage of seeing one's work transformed into color is so dramatically appalling, so "obvious"—as against stopping sporadically for commercials—that this time all the directors, writers and actors chose to fight.

8   But let me get to the real heart of the matter and to why I think the issue is not merely one that affronts the parties directly involved but has a larger meaning. What's at stake is a moral issue and how our culture chooses to define itself. No one should be able to alter an artist's work in any way whatsoever, for any reason, without the artist's consent. It's really as simple as that.

9   John Huston has made it clear that he doesn't want *The Maltese Falcon* seen in color. This is his right as an artist and certainly must be his choice alone. Nor would I want to see my film *Manhattan* in color. Not if it would bring in 10 times the revenue. Not if all the audiences in the world begged or demanded to see it that way.

10   I believe the people who are coloring movies have contempt for the audience by claiming, in effect, that viewers are too stupid and too insensitive to appreciate black and white photography—that they must be given, like infants or monkeys, bright colors to keep them amused. They have contempt for the artist, caring little for the moral right these directors have over their own creations. And, finally, they have contempt for society because they help define it as one that chooses to milk every last dollar out of its artists' work, even if it means mutilating the work and humiliating the culture's creative talent.

11   This is how we are viewed around the world and how we will be viewed by future generations. Most civilized governments abroad, realizing that their society is at least as much shaped and identified by its artists as by its businessmen, have laws to protect such things from happening. In our society, merchants are willing to degrade anything or anyone so long as it brings in a financial profit. Allowing the colorization of films is a good example of our country's regard for its artists, and why I think the issue of moral rights requires legislative help and protection.

12   The recent Federal copyright decision says that if a human being uses a certain minimum amount of creativity in coloring a black

and white film, the new color version is a separate work that can be copyrighted. In short, if a man colors *Citizen Kane,* it becomes a new movie that can be copyrighted. This must be changed. How? By making sure that Representative Richard A. Gephardt's film integrity bill is passed. It would legalize the moral rights of film artists and, in the process, make colorization without consent illegal.

13   It is, after all, a very short step to removing the score from *Gone With the Wind* and replacing it with a rock score under the mistaken notion that it will render it more enjoyable to young people.

Questions

1. We find Allen's argumentative strategy worth analyzing. But first, restate in a sentence or two the point he is arguing and the occasion that prompted it. (Note that Allen reports the occasion in his next-to-last paragraph.)
   Now look at Allen's opening paragraph. What does it assume about his audience? What does Allen imply about himself in relation to his audience?
2. In paragraph 2 Allen contrasts two groups. How does he make sure that you will identify yourself with one group and not with the other?
3. In paragraph 3, what words or phrases strike you as particularly lively or persuasive?
4. In paragraph 4 Allen says that "the claim that young people won't watch black and white" is "not worth debating." What does the rest of the paragraph do? Again, what particularly effective words or phrases underscore the point?
5. To what emotions does Allen appeal in paragraph 5?
6. Now consider the substance of his argument. In paragraph 8 Allen says, "No one should be able to alter an artist's work in any way whatsoever, for any reason, without the artist's consent. It's really as simple as that." Do you agree? If so, would you agree to the following propositions? Why or why not?

   a. Producers should be prohibited from showing on television films intended for the theater, unless the producers have the consent of the film director.
   b. Similarly, filmmakers should be prohibited from filming a novel, play, opera, or ballet without the consent of the au-

thor or composer. If the author or composer is dead, well, that's unfortunate, but the work cannot be adapted to a film.

What parallel strictures might govern the display of objects in museums, reproductions of works of art, and the translation of classic works of literature?

7. Finally, consider some black and white film that you admire. What do you think would be lost (or gained) by colorization? (If you have seen the original black and white film and also a colorized version, of course you are in a good position to make comparisons. But in any case you can make a "thought-experiment." You might, for example, imagine a colorized version of Woody Allen's *Manhattan*.)

Love Is a Fallacy

Max Shulman

Cool was I and logical. Keen, calculating, perspicacious, acute and astute—I was all of these. My brain was as powerful as a dynamo, as precise as a chemist's scales, as penetrating as a scalpel. And—think of it!—I was only eighteen.

It is not often that one so young has such a giant intellect. Take, for example, Petey Burch, my roommate at the University of Minnesota. Same age, same background, but dumb as an ox. A nice enough fellow, you understand, but nothing upstairs. Emotional type. Unstable. Impressionable. Worst of all, a faddist. Fads, I submit, are the very negation of reason. To be swept up in every new craze that comes along, to surrender yourself to idiocy just because everybody else is doing it—this, to me, is the acme of mindlessness. Not, however, to Petey.

One afternoon I found Petey lying on his bed with an expression of such distress on his face that I immediately diagnosed appendicitis. "Don't move," I said. "Don't take a laxative. I'll get a doctor."

"Raccoon," he mumbled thickly.

"Raccoon?" I said, pausing in my flight.

"I want a raccoon coat," he wailed.

I perceived that his trouble was not physical, but mental. "Why do you want a raccoon coat?"

"I should have known it," he cried, pounding his temples. "I should have know they'd come back when the Charleston came back. Like a fool I spent all my money for textbooks, and now I can't get a raccoon coat."

"Can you mean," I said incredulously, "that people are actually wearing raccoon coats again?"

"All the Big Men on Campus are wearing them. Where've you been?"

"In the library," I said, naming a place not frequented by Big Men on Campus.

He leaped from the bed and paced the room. "I've got to have a raccoon coat," he said passionately. "I've got to!"

"Petey, why? Look at it rationally. Raccoon coats are unsanitary. They shed. They smell bad. They weigh too much. They're unsightly. They—"

"You don't understand," he interrupted impatiently. "It's the thing to do. Don't you want to be in the swim?"

"No," I said truthfully.

"Well, I do," he declared. "I'd give anything for a raccoon coat. Anything!"

My brain, that precision instrument, slipped into high gear. "Anything?" I asked, looking at him narrowly.

"Anything," he affirmed in ringing tones.

I stroked my chin thoughtfully. It so happened that I knew where to get my hands on a raccoon coat. My father had had one in his undergraduate days; it lay now in a trunk in the attic back home. It also happened that Petey had something I wanted. He didn't *have* it exactly, but at least he had first rights on it. I refer to his girl, Polly Espy.

I had long coveted Polly Espy. Let me emphasize that my desire for this young woman was not emotional in nature. She was, to be sure, a girl who excited the emotions, but I was not one to let my heart rule my head. I wanted Polly for a shrewdly calculated, entirely cerebral reason.

I was a freshman in law school. In a few years I would be out in practice. I was well aware of the importance of the right kind of wife in furthering a lawyer's career. The successful lawyers I had observed were, almost without exception, married to beautiful, gracious, intelligent women. With one omission, Polly fitted these specifications perfectly.

Beautiful she was. She was not yet of pin-up proportions, but

I felt sure that time would supply the lack. She already had the makings.

Gracious she was. By gracious I mean full of graces. She had an erectness of carriage, an ease of bearing, a poise that clearly indicated the best of breeding. At table her manners were exquisite. I had seen her at the Kozy Kampus Korner eating the specialty of the house—a sandwich that contained scraps of pot roast, gravy, chopped nuts, and a dipper of sauerkraut—without even getting her fingers moist.

Intelligent she was not. In fact, she veered in the opposite direction. But I believed that under my guidance she would smarten up. At any rate, it was worth a try. It is, after all, easier to make a beautiful dumb girl smart than to make an ugly smart girl beautiful.

"Petey," I said, "are you in love with Polly Espy?"

"I think she's a keen kid," he replied, "but I don't know if you'd call it love. Why?"

"Do you," I asked, "have any kind of formal arrangement with her? I mean are you going steady or anything like that?"

"No. We see each other quite a bit, but we both have other dates. Why?"

"Is there," I asked, "any other man for whom she has a particular fondness?"

"Not that I know of. Why?"

I nodded with satisfaction. "In other words, if you were out of the picture, the field would be open. Is that right?"

"I guess so. What are you getting at?"

"Nothing, nothing," I said innocently, and took my suitcase out of the closet.

"Where are you going?" asked Petey.

"Home for the weekend." I threw a few things into the bag.

"Listen," he said, clutching my arm eagerly, "while you're home, you couldn't get some money from your old man, could you, and lend it to me so I can buy a raccoon coat?"

"I may do better than that," I said with a mysterious wink and closed my bag and left.

"Look," I said to Petey when I got back Monday morning. I threw open the suitcase and revealed the huge, hairy, gamy object that my father had worn in his Stutz Bearcat in 1925.

"Holy Toledo!" said Petey reverently. He plunged his hands into the raccoon coat and then his face. "Holy Toledo!" he repeated fifteen or twenty times.

"Would you like it?" I asked.

"Oh yes!" he cried, clutching the greasy pelt to him. Then a canny look came into his eyes. "What do you want for it?"

"Your girl," I said, mincing no words.

"Polly?" he said in a horrified whisper. "You want Polly?"

"That's right."

He flung the coat from him. "Never," he said stoutly.

I shrugged. "Okay. If you don't want to be in the swim, I guess it's your business."

I sat down in a chair and pretended to read a book, but out of the corner of my eye I kept watching Petey. He was a torn man. First he looked at the coat with the expression of a waif at a bakery window. Then he turned away and set his jaw resolutely. Then he looked back at the coat, with even more longing in his face. Then he turned away, but with not so much resolution this time. Back and forth his head swiveled, desire waxing, resolution waning. Finally he didn't turn away at all; he just stood and stared with mad lust at the coat.

"It isn't as though I was in love with Polly," he said thickly. "Or going steady or anything like that."

"That's right," I murmured.

"What's Polly to me, or me to Polly?"

"Not a thing," said I.

"It's just been a casual kick—just a few laughs, that's all."

"Try on the coat," said I.

He complied. The coat bunched high over his ears and dropped all the way down to his shoe tops. He looked like a mound of dead raccoons. "Fits fine," he said happily.

I rose from my chair. "Is it a deal?" I asked, extending my hand.

He swallowed. "It's a deal," he said and shook my hand.

I had my first date with Polly the following evening. This was in the nature of a survey; I wanted to find out just how much work I had to do to get her mind up to the standard I required. I took her first to dinner. "Gee, that was a delish dinner," she said as we left the restaurant. Then I took her to a movie. "Gee, that was a marvy movie," she said as we left the theater. And then I took her home. "Gee, I had a sensaysh time," she said as she bade me good night.

I went back to my room with a heavy heart. I had gravely underestimated the size of my task. This girl's lack of information was terrifying. Nor would it be enough merely to supply her with information. First she had to be taught to *think*. This loomed as a project of no small dimensions, and at first I was tempted to give her back to Petey. But then I got to thinking about her abundant physical charms and about the way she entered a room and the way she handled a knife and fork, and I decided to make an effort.

I went about it, as in all things, systematically. I gave her a course in logic. It happened that I, as a law student, was taking a course in logic myself, so I had all the facts at my finger tips. "Polly," I said to her when I picked her up on our next date, "tonight we are going over to the Knoll and talk."

"Oo, terrif," she replied. One thing I will say for this girl: you would go far to find another so agreeable.

We went to the Knoll, the campus trysting place, and we sat down under an old oak, and she looked at me expectantly. "What are we going to talk about?" she said.

"Logic."

She thought this over for a minute and decided she liked it. "Magnif," she said.

"Logic," I said, clearing my throat, "is the science of thinking. Before we can think correctly, we must first learn to recognize the common fallacies of logic. These we will take up tonight."

"Wow-dow!" she cried, clapping her hands delightedly.

I winced, but went bravely on. "First let us examine the fallacy called Dicto Simpliciter."

"By all means," she urged, batting her lashes eagerly.

"Dicto Simpliciter means an argument based on an unqualified generalization. For example: Exercise is good. Therefore everybody should exercise."

"I agree," said Polly earnestly. "I mean exercise is wonderful. I mean it builds the body and everything."

"Polly," I said gently, "the argument is a fallacy. *Exercise is good* is an unqualified generalization. For instance, if you have heart disease, exercise is bad, not good. Many people are ordered by their doctors *not* to exercise. You must *qualify* the generalization. You must say exercise is *usually* good, or exercise is good *for most people.* Otherwise you have committed a Dicto Simpliciter. Do you see?"

"No," she confessed. "But this is marvy. Do more! Do more!"

"It will be better if you stop tugging at my sleeve," I told her, and when she desisted, I continued. "Next we take up a fallacy called Hasty Generalization. Listen carefully: You can't speak French. I can't speak French. Pete Burch can't speak French. I must therefore conclude that nobody at the University of Minnesota can speak French."

"Really?" said Polly, amazed. *"Nobody?"*

I hid my exasperation. "Polly, it's a fallacy. The generalization is reached too hastily. There are too few instances to support such a conclusion."

"Know any more fallacies?" she asked breathlessly. "This is more fun than dancing even."

I fought off a wave of despair. I was getting nowhere with this girl, absolutely nowhere. Still, I am nothing if not persistent. I continued. "Next comes Post Hoc. Listen to this: Let's not take Bill on our picnic. Every time we take him out with us, it rains."

"I know somebody just like that," she exclaimed. "A girl back home—Eula Becker, her name is. It never fails. Every single time we take her on a picnic—"

"Polly," I said sharply, "it's a fallacy. Eula Becker doesn't *cause* the rain. She has no connection with the rain. You are guilty of Post Hoc if you blame Eula Becker."

"I'll never do it again," she promised contritely. "Are you mad at me?"

I sighed deeply. "No, Polly, I'm not mad."

"Then tell me some more fallacies."

"All right. Let's try Contradictory Premises."

"Yes, let's," she chirped, blinking her eyes happily.

I frowned, but plunged ahead. "Here's an example of Contradictory Premises: If God can do anything, can He make a stone so heavy that He won't be able to lift it?"

"Of course," she replied promptly.

"But if He can do anything, He can lift the stone," I pointed out.

"Yeah," she said thoughtfully. "Well, then I guess He can't make the stone."

"But He can do anything," I reminded her.

She scratched her pretty, empty head. "I'm all confused," she admitted.

"Of course you are. Because when the premises of an argument contradict each other, there can be no argument. If there is an irresistible force, there can be no immovable object. If there is an immovable object, there can be no irresistible force. Get it?"

"Tell me some more of this keen stuff," she said eagerly.

I consulted my watch. "I think we'd better call it a night. I'll take you home now, and you go over all the things you've learned. We'll have another session tomorrow night."

I deposited her at the girls' dormitory, where she assured me that she had had a perfectly terrif evening, and I went glumly home to my room. Petey lay snoring in his bed, the raccoon coat huddled like a great hairy beast at his feet. For a moment I considered waking him and telling him that he could have his girl back. It seemed clear that my project was doomed to failure. The girl simply had a logic-proof head.

But then I reconsidered. I had wasted one evening; I might as well waste another. Who knew? Maybe somewhere in the extinct crater of her mind, a few embers still smoldered. Maybe somehow I could fan them into flame. Admittedly it was not a prospect fraught with hope, but I decided to give it one more try.

Seated under the oak the next evening I said, "Our first fallacy tonight is called Ad Misericordiam."

She quivered with delight.

"Listen closely," I said. "A man applies for a job. When the boss asks him what his qualifications are, he replies that he has a wife and six children at home, the wife is a helpless cripple, the children have nothing to eat, no clothes to wear, no shoes on their feet, there are no beds in the house, no coal in the cellar, and winter is coming."

A tear rolled down each of Polly's pink cheeks. "Oh, this is awful, awful," she sobbed.

"Yes, it's awful," I agreed, "but it's no argument. The man never answered the boss's question about his qualifications. Instead he appealed to the boss's sympathy. He committed the fallacy of Ad Misericordiam. Do you understand?"

"Have you got a handkerchief?" she blubbered.

I handed her a handkerchief and tried to keep from screaming while she wiped her eyes. "Next," I said in a carefully controlled tone, "we will discuss False Analogy. Here is an example: Students should be allowed to look at their textbooks during examinations. After all, surgeons have X-rays to guide them during an operation, lawyers have briefs to guide them during a trial, carpenters have blueprints to guide them when they are building a house. Why, then, shouldn't students be allowed to look at their textbooks during an examination?"

"There now," she said enthusiastically, "is the most marvy idea I've heard in years."

"Polly," I said testily, "the argument is all wrong. Doctors, lawyers, and carpenters aren't taking a test to see how they have learned, but students are. The situations are altogether different, and you can't make an analogy between them."

"I still think it's a good idea," said Polly.

"Nuts," I muttered. Doggedly I pressed on. "Next we'll try Hypothesis Contrary to Fact."

"Sounds yummy," was Polly's reaction.

"Listen: If Madame Curie had not happened to leave a photographic plate in a drawer with a chunk of pitchblende, the world today would not know about radium."

"True, true," said Polly, nodding her head. "Did you see the movie? Oh, it just knocked me out. That Walter Pidgeon is so dreamy. I mean he fractures me."

"If you can forget Mr. Pidgeon for a moment," I said coldly, "I would like to point out that the statement is a fallacy. Maybe Madame Curie would have discovered radium at some later date. Maybe somebody else would have discovered it. Maybe any number of things would have happened. You can't start with a hypothesis that is not true and then draw any supportable conclusions from it."

"They ought to put Walter Pidgeon in more pictures," said Polly. "I hardly ever see him any more."

One more chance, I decided. But just one more. There is a limit to what flesh and blood can bear. "The next fallacy is called Poisoning the Well."

"How cute!" she gurgled.

"Two men are having a debate. The first one gets up and says, 'My opponent is a notorious liar. You can't believe a word that he is going to say.' . . . Now, Polly, think. Think hard. What's wrong?"

I watched her closely as she knit her creamy brow in concentration. Suddenly a glimmer of intelligence—the first I had seen—came into her eyes. "It's not fair," she said with indignation. "It's not a bit fair. What chance has the second man got if the first man calls him a liar before he even begins talking?"

"Right!" I cried exultantly. "One hundred percent right. It's not fair. The first man has *poisoned the well* before anybody could drink from it. He has hamstrung his opponent before he could even start. . . . Polly, I'm proud of you."

"Pshaw," she murmured, blushing with pleasure.

"You see, my dear, these things aren't so hard. All you have to do is concentrate. Think—examine—evaluate. Come now, let's review everything we have learned."

"Fire away," she said with an airy wave of her hand.

Heartened by the knowledge that Polly was not altogether a cretin, I began a long, patient review of all I had told her. Over and over and over again I cited instances, pointed out flaws, kept hammering away without let up. It was like digging a tunnel. At first everything was work, sweat, and darkness. I had no idea when I would reach the light, or even *if* I would. But I persisted. I pounded and clawed and scraped, and finally I was rewarded. I saw a chink of light. And then the chink got bigger and the sun came pouring in and all was bright.

Five grueling nights this took, but it was worth it. I had made a logician out of Polly; I had taught her to think. My job was done. She was worthy of me at last. She was a fit wife for me, a proper hostess for my many mansions, a suitable mother for my well-heeled children.

It must not be thought that I was without love for this girl. Quite the contrary. Just as Pygmalion loved the perfect woman he had fashioned, so I loved mine. I determined to acquaint her with my feelings at our very next meeting. The time had come to change our relationship from academic to romantic.

"Polly," I said when next we sat beneath our oak, "tonight we will not discuss fallacies."

"Aw, gee," she said, disappointed.

"My dear," I said, favoring her with a smile, "we have now spent five evenings together. We have gotten along splendidly. It is clear that we are well matched."

"Hasty Generalization," said Polly brightly.

"I beg your pardon," said I.

"Hasty Generalization," she repeated. "How can you say that we are well matched on the basis of only five dates?"

I chuckled with amusement. The dear child had learned her lessons well. "My dear," I said, patting her hand in a tolerant manner, "five days is plenty. After all, you don't have to eat a whole cake to know that it's good."

"False Analogy," said Polly promptly. "I'm not a cake. I'm a girl."

I chuckled with somewhat less amusement. The dear child had learned her lessons perhaps too well. I decided to change tactics. Obviously the best approach was a simple, strong, direct declaration of love. I paused for a moment while my massive brain chose the proper words. Then I began:

"Polly, I love you. You are the whole world to me, and the moon and the stars and the constellations of outer space. Please, my darling, say that you will go steady with me, for if you will not, life will be meaningless. I will languish. I will refuse my meals. I will wander the face of the earth, a shambling, hollow-eyed hulk."

There, I thought, folding my arms, that ought to do it.

"Ad Misericordiam," said Polly.

I ground my teeth. I was not Pygmalion; I was Frankenstein, and my monster had me by the throat. Frantically I fought back the tide of panic surging through me. At all costs I had to keep cool.

"Well, Polly," I said, forcing a smile, "you certainly have learned your fallacies."

"You're darn right," she said a vigorous nod.

"And who taught them to you, Polly?"

"You did."

"That's right. So you do owe me something, don't you, my dear? If I hadn't come along you never would have learned about fallacies."

"Hypothesis Contrary to Fact," she said instantly.

I dashed perspiration from my brow. "Polly," I croaked, "you mustn't take all these things so literally. I mean this is just classroom stuff. You know that the things you learn in school don't have anything to do with life."

"Dicto Simpliciter," she said, wagging her finger at me playfully.

That did it. I leaped to my feet, bellowing like a bull. "Will you or will you not go steady with me?"

"I will not," she replied.

"Why not?" I demanded.

"Because this afternoon I promised Petey Burch that I would go steady with him."

I reeled back, overcome with the infamy of it. After he promised, after he made a deal, after he shook my hand! "The rat!" I shrieked, kicking up great chunks of turf. "You can't go with him, Polly. He's a liar. He's a cheat. He's a rat."

"Poisoning the Well," said Polly, "and stop shouting. I think shouting must be a fallacy too."

With an immense effort of will, I modulated my voice. "All right," I said. "You're a logician. Let's look at this thing logically. How could you choose Petey Burch over me? Look at me—a brilliant student, a tremendous intellectual, a man with an assured future. Look at Petey—a knothead, a jitterbug, a guy who'll never know where his next meal is coming from. Can you give me one logical reason why you should go steady with Petey Burch?"

"I certainly can," declared Polly. "He's got a raccoon coat."

Questions

1. What is unusual about the first sentence? What expectation about the direction of the story does this first sentence create?

2. What other conspicuous features of the narrator's style do you find in the first paragraph? How do they help to characterize him? (How has Shulman "poisoned the well"?)

Too Many Women Are Misconstruing Feminism's Nature

Susan Jacoby

Feminism, *n*. 1. the doctrine advocating social, political, and all other rights of women equal to those of men. 2. an organized movement for the attainment of such rights for women. 3. feminine character.
    —*The Random House Dictionary of the English Language*

1   For many young women today, "feminism" is a word with a shady reputation. I first became aware of this depressing fact when I was teaching a magazine writing course at New York University and one of my brighter female students said: "I know from your lectures in class that you consider yourself a feminist. But that surprises me, because you look so feminine."

2   By "feminine" she meant what both the dictionary and ordinary people mean: that I looked the way women are usually expected to look: I wear lipstick, comb my hair (streak it, too!) and am as likely to be found in a skirt as in blue jeans. I don't wear combat boots or have bulging biceps. My student was really saying she didn't understand how someone who was committed to equal rights for women could also display conventional feminine attributes.

3   This point of view is held by a surprising number of well-educated young women in their early twenties, those who have benefited the most from the professional opportunities now open to them as a result of battles waged by the feminist movement over the past fifteen years.

4   To a woman who is proud to call herself a feminist, the most disturbing aspect of this phenomenon is not its naïveté but its adoption of the age-old patriarchal assumption that a woman who wants the same intellectual, economic and professional opportunities as a

man is rejecting her sex rather than the disabilities imposed on her because of her sex.

5   Among organized feminists of the older generation, a common response is to insist that young women are reacting not against feminism but only against the word and its "unfair" association with strident anger. This was typified by Eleanor Smeal, outgoing president of the National Organization for Women, in an interview with Susan Bolotin that appeared last fall in *The New York Times Magazine*.

6   "People don't even like the word 'discrimination,'" Mrs. Smeal said. "One of the reasons is that they don't want you to think they have a bellyache, that they are not O.K. And the word 'feminist' is still considered a militant word. The best way of dealing with all these things is not to use catchwords. Talk about actual situations."

7   This approach, which suggests that resistance to feminism is largely a question of semantics, evades the concrete issues raised by that resistance. The meanings people attach to words are of the utmost importance. When a political term becomes unpopular— whether the word is feminist, liberal, conservative, socialist or capitalist—the unpopularity arises not only from a misunderstanding of what the word actually means but from genuine distrust of the ideas it represents.

8   My students told me they objected to feminism because it made women bitter, angry and unattractive to men. They said they felt that feminists had placed too much emphasis on careers at the expense of both romance and family life. All of them planned to take 5 to 10 years off from work to raise their children and then return to rewarding, well-paid jobs.

9   Most significant, my students told me that any form of sex discrimination could be overcome by individual effort and that older feminists tend to blame personal inadequacies on "the system."

10   Many of these beliefs can, of course, be attributed entirely to insufficient life experience. Recent college graduates do not know any more about what it takes to build a career than they know about bringing up children. The idea that one can take 10 years off from work without incurring adverse professional consequences is as phantasmagorical as the notion that one will give birth to a child who never gives its mother a moment's cause for worry.

11   Furthermore, these women have not experienced the entry-level discrimination that was taken for granted in the 1950's and 60's. They do not realize that their individual abilities would have counted for very little in a system in which women made up fewer than 5

percent of first-year law and medical school classes. The feminist movement has opened those doors; women in their early 20's have not had occasion to knock on doors still closed.

12   But it is no comfort for a feminist in her 30's to sit back, secure in the knowledge that life will change the minds of young women who do not now wish to identify themselves with feminism. The whole point of movements for social change is to make it unnecessary for each new generation to learn the same lessons over again. The older generation of feminists is in roughly the same position as scientists who have been pressured to teach creationism as a respectable alternative to the theory of evolution.

13   The question is: What can be done to rectify the situation?

14   One common response is to pretend not to be angry at all. The dishonesty of this posture is quickly, and correctly, perceived by the young. Feminism is concerned with justice, and anyone who cares about justice is bound to be angry at some of the people some of the time. There is nothing wrong with anger—and we should say so with no apologies—as long as it is directed at those who are responsible for specific injustices, not at the whole world.

15   Is it also unrealistic to adopt the position that the most obvious goals of the feminist movement, like equal pay for equal work, have already been achieved and we must now concentrate on achieving the nirvana of a more "human" workplace, in which both men and women will be able to enjoy the rewards of equal rights and responsibilities. A workplace that takes family and child-rearing needs into account is a laudable goal, but, as the defeat of the proposed Federal equal rights amendment clearly demonstrated, we are far from a consensus on the desirability of the most basic forms of equality between the sexes.

16   I do not believe that the amendment was turned down solely because some people identified it with lesbian rights and unisex toilets or because the right wing spent enormous amounts of money to oppose it (although these elements certainly played a role in its defeat). The amendment was rejected because a great many people still do not believe in equal rights for women.

17   That is why I believe Eleanor Smeal is wrong in suggesting that opposition to feminism can be neutralized by avoiding the word. Feminism is considered "militant" by many members of both sexes because equal rights for women is in fact a radical idea. By "radical" I mean not the commonly used political pejorative but the original definition, derived from the Latin word for root. Feminists should not be reluctant to identify themselves with an honorable tradition rooted in issues that every woman—regardless of how much

she might prefer to be seen solely as an individual rather than as a member of her sex—must eventually face.

Questions

1. Explain the wit in Jacoby's first sentence.
2. In paragraph 13 Jacoby writes, "What can be done to rectify the situation?" Exactly what *is* "the situation"? That is, in a sentence or two, state the problem that Jacoby sees.
3. In paragraph 10 Jacoby says that it is nonsense to think that one "can take ten years off from work without incurring adverse professional consequences." Do you think she is right? Why? In this connection you may want to read Lester Thurow's essay "Why Women Are Paid Less Than Men," page 693.
4. Do you consider yourself a feminist? In an essay of 500–1000 words explain where you stand, and why, on the issues Jacoby raises.

Let's Quit the Drug War
David Boaz

1   An antiwar song that helped get the Smothers Brothers thrown off network television in the 60's went this way: "We're waist deep in the Big Muddy, and the big fool says to push on." Today we're waist-deep in another unwinnable war, and many political leaders want to push on. This time it's a war on drugs. About 23 million Americans use illicit drugs every month, despite annual Federal outlays of $3.9 billion. Even the arrests of 824,000 Americans a year don't seem to be having much effect.

2   As in the case of Vietnam—and Prohibition, another unwinnable war—many politicians can't stand losing a war. Instead of acknowledging failure, they want to escalate.

3   Mayor Edward I. Koch of New York suggests that we strip search every person entering the United States from Mexico or Southeast Asia. The White House drug adviser, Donald I. Macdonald, calls for arresting even small-time users—lawyers with a quarter-

gram of cocaine, high school kids with a couple of joints—and bringing them before a judge.

4   Where will we put those two-bit "criminals"? The Justice Department recommends doubling our prison capacity, even though President Reagan's former drug adviser Carlton E. Turner already brags about the role of drug laws in bringing about a 60 percent increase in our prison population in the last six years. Bob Dole calls for the death penalty for drug sellers.

5   Like their counterparts in Los Angeles and Chicago, the Washington, D.C., police are to be issued semiautomatic pistols so they can engage in ever bloodier shootouts with drug dealers. Members of the District of Columbia Council call for the National Guard to occupy the city. We've already pressed other governments to destroy drug crops and to help us interdict the flow of drugs into the United States. Because those measures have largely failed, the Customs Service asks authorization to "use appropriate force" to compel planes *suspected* of carrying drugs to land, including the authority to shoot them down.

6   It's time to ask ourselves: What kind of society would condone strip searches, large-scale arrests, military occupation of its capital city and the shooting of possibly innocent people in order to stop some of its citizens from using substances that others don't like?

7   Prohibition of alcohol in the 1920's failed because it proved impossible to stop people from drinking. Our 70-year effort at prohibition of marijuana, cocaine and heroin has also failed. Tens of millions of Americans, including senators, Presidential candidates, a Supreme Court nominee and conservative journalists, have broken the laws against such drugs. Preserving laws that are so widely flouted undermines respect for all laws.

8   The most dangerous drugs in the United States are alcohol, which is responsible for about 100,000 deaths a year, and tobacco, which is responsible for about 350,000. Heroin, cocaine and marijuana account for a total of 3,600 deaths a year—even though one in five people aged 20 to 40 use drugs regularly.

9   Our efforts to crack down on illegal drug use have created new problems. A Justice Department survey reports that 70 percent of those arrested for serious crimes are drug users, which may mean that "drugs cause crime." A more sophisticated analysis suggests that the high cost of drugs, a result of their prohibition, forces drug users to turn to crime to support an unnecessarily expensive habit.

10   Drug prohibition, by giving young people the thrill of breaking the law and giving pushers a strong incentive to find new custom-

ers, may actually increase the number of drug users. Moreover, our policy of pressuring friendly governments to wipe out drug cultivation has undermined many of those regimes and provoked resentment against us among their citizens and government officials.

11   We can either escalate the war on drugs, which would have dire implications for civil liberties and the right to privacy, or find a way to gracefully withdraw. Withdrawal should not be viewed as an endorsement of drug use; it would simply be an acknowledgment that the cost of this war—billions of dollars, runaway crime rates and restrictions on our personal freedom—is too high.

Questions

1. In his first paragraph, capitalizing on the frequently used expression "war on drugs," Boaz compares efforts to combat illicit drug use with the U.S. war in Vietnam. How reasonable is this comparison? Whether or not you find it reasonable, what makes the comparison effective?

2. Looking again at the first paragraph, analyze Boaz's use of statistics. How well do the statistics support his argument?

3. In his sixth paragraph Boaz refers to "citizens . . . using substances that others don't like." What substances is he probably referring to? Why do you suppose he doesn't name them? What is the effect of his use of the word "citizens" (instead of "people," for example, or "consumers," or "adults")? And what reason might you offer for why the "others don't like" the substances you have named?

4. Boaz several times compares drug use to alcohol use, and in paragraph 8 says that alcohol and tobacco (which can be legally purchased) are the most dangerous drugs in use. How does he support this claim? Whether or not you accept this argument, what counter-argument can you think of?

5. Boaz refers several times to individuals (such as Mayor Koch) and groups (such as "many political leaders") who hold opposing views to his. On the whole, how does he characterize his opponents?

6. It is considered good strategy to end a persuasive essay with one's strongest arguments. What arguments does Boaz use in his conclusion? Would you agree that they are the strongest he presents or can present? Set forth your answers to this question in an essay of about 500 words. Write for a reader who has not

read Boaz's essay, providing that reader with a brief summary of the essay's earlier arguments and strategy. (To strengthen your own argument, read Charles B. Rangel's argument against legalization, immediately following.)

Legalize Drugs? Not on Your Life

Charles B. Rangel

1   The escalating drug crisis is beginning to take its toll on many Americans. And now growing numbers of well-intentioned officials and other opinion leaders are saying that the best way to fight drugs is to legalize them. But what they're really admitting is that they're willing to abandon a war that we have not even begun to fight.

2   For example, the newly elected and promising Mayor of Baltimore, Kurt Schmoke, at a meeting of the United States Conference of Mayors, called for a full-scale study of the feasibility of legalization. His comments could not have come at a worse time, for we are in the throes of the worst drug epidemic in our history.

3   Here we are talking about legalization, and we have yet to come up with any formal national strategy or any commitment from the Administration on fighting drugs beyond mere words. We have never fought the war on drugs like we have fought other legitimate wars—with all the forces at our command.

4   Just the thought of legalization brings up more problems and concerns than already exist.

5   Advocates of legalization should be reminded, for example, that it's not as simple as opening up a chain of friendly neighborhood pharmacies. Press them about some of the issues and questions surrounding this proposed legalization, and they never seem to have any answers. At least not any logical, well thought out ones.

6   Those who tout legalization remind me of fans sitting in the cheap seats at the ballpark. They may have played the game, and they may think they know all the rules, but from where they're sitting they can't judge the action.

• Has anybody ever considered which narcotic and psychotropic drugs would be legalized?

- Would we allow all drugs to become legally sold and used, or would we select the most abused few, such as cocaine, heroin and marijuana?
- Who would administer the dosages—the state or the individual?
- What quantity of drugs would each individual be allowed to get?
- What about addicts: Would we not have to give them more in order to satisfy their craving, or would we give them enough to just whet their appetites?
- What do we do about those who are experimenting? Do we sell them the drugs, too, and encourage them to pick up the habit?
- Furthermore, will the Government establish tax-supported facilities to sell these drugs?
- Would we get the supply from the same foreign countries that support our habit now, or would we create our own internal sources and "dope factories," paying people the minimum wage to churn out mounds of cocaine and bales of marijuana?
- Would there be an age limit on who can purchase drugs, as exists with alcohol? What would the market price be and who would set it? Would private industry be allowed to have a stake in any of this?
- What are we going to do about underage youngsters—the age group hardest hit by the crack crisis? Are we going to give them identification cards? How can we prevent adults from purchasing drugs for them?
- How many people are projected to become addicts as a result of the introduction of cheaper, more available drugs sanctioned by government?

7   Since marijuana remains in a person's system for weeks, what would we do about pilots, railroad engineers, surgeons, police, cross-country truckers and nuclear plant employees who want to use it during off-duty hours? And what would be the effect on the health insurance industry?

8   Many of the problems associated with drug abuse will not go away just because of legalization. For too long we have ignored the root cause, failing to see the connection between drugs and hope lessness, helplessness and despair.

9   We often hear that legalization would bring an end to the bloodshed and violence that has often been associated with the illegal narcotics trade. The profit will be taken out of it, so to speak, as will be the urge to commit crime to get money to buy drugs. But what gives anybody the impression that legalization would deter many jobless and economically deprived people from resorting to crime to pay for their habits?

10   Even in a decriminalized atmosphere, money would still be needed to support habits. Because drugs would be cheaper and more available, people would want more and would commit more crime. Does anybody really think the black market would disappear? There would always be opportunities for those who saw profit in peddling larger quantities, or improved versions, of products that are forbidden or restricted.

11   Legalization would completely undermine any educational effort we undertake to persuade kids about the harmful effects of drugs. Today's kids have not yet been totally lost to the drug menace, but if we legalize these substances they'll surely get the message that drugs are O.K.

12   Not only would our young people realize that the threat of jail and punishment no longer exists. They would pick up the far more damaging message that the use of illegal narcotics does not pose a significant enough health threat for the Government to ban its use.

13   If we really want to do something about drug abuse, let's end this nonsensical talk about legalization right now.

14   Let's put the pressure on our leaders to first make the drug problem a priority issue on the national agenda, then let's see if we can get a coordinated national battle plan that would include the deployment of military personnel and equipment to wipe out this foreign-based national security threat. Votes by the House and more recently the Senate to involve the armed forces in the war on drugs are steps in the right direction.

15   Finally, let's take this legalization issue and put it where it belongs—amid idle chit-chat as cocktail glasses knock together at social events.

Questions

1. In the middle of his essay, beginning with paragraph 6, Rangel poses a series of questions that proponents of legalizing drugs have apparently failed to consider. Imagining for a moment that you favor legalization, which of those questions might you find easiest to answer? Which are the most difficult? (Choose three "easy" and three "difficult" questions to consider.) In the light of your experience trying to answer the questions, do you find Rangel's posing them an effective tactic?

2. In paragraph 2 Rangel says that a call for "a full scale study of the feasibility of legalization" by the Mayor of Baltimore "could not have come at a worse time." What reasons does Rangel

offer for this opinion? What reasons can you imagine to support such a study?

3. Rangel argues (paragraph 11) that legalization would undermine efforts to educate "kids about the harmful effects of drugs." Do you agree? Do you believe that the legal sale of alcohol and tobacco undermines education about their harmful effects?

4. In paragraph 14 Rangel characterizes the drug problem as a "foreign-based national security threat." What does he mean by that? Do you agree that drug use is a security threat? Do you agree that it is "foreign-based"? How consistent is Rangel's argument in this paragraph with his statement in paragraph 8 that the "root cause" of drug abuse is "hopelessness, helplessness, and despair"? If you find the arguments inconsistent, how important is it to decide in favor of one or the other?

5. What does Rangel think we should do about the drug problem? What do *you* think we should do? (For another perspective, read David Boaz's essay, pages 259–261.)

Death and Justice: How Capital Punishment Affirms Life
Edward I. Koch

---

1   Last December a man named Robert Lee Willie, who had been convicted of raping and murdering an 18-year-old woman, was executed in the Louisiana state prison. In a statement issued several minutes before his death, Mr. Willie said: "Killing people is wrong. . . . It makes no difference whether it's citizens, countries, or governments. Killing is wrong." Two weeks later in South Carolina, an admitted killer named Joseph Carl Shaw was put to death for murdering two teenagers. In an appeal to the governor for clemency, Mr. Shaw wrote: "Killing is wrong when I did it. Killing is wrong when you do it. I hope you have the courage and moral strength to stop the killing."

2   It is a curiosity of modern life that we find ourselves being lectured on morality by cold-blooded killers. Mr. Willie previously had been convicted of aggravated rape, aggravated kidnapping, and

the murders of a Louisiana deputy and a man from Missouri. Mr. Shaw committed another murder a week before the two for which he was executed, and admitted mutilating the body of the 14-year-old girl he killed. I can't help wondering what prompted these murderers to speak out against killing as they entered the death-house door. Did their newfound reverence for life stem from the realization that they were about to lose their own?

3   Life is indeed precious, and I believe the death penalty helps to affirm this fact. Had the death penalty been a real possibility in the minds of these murderers, they might well have stayed their hand. They might have shown moral awareness before their victims died, and not after. Consider the tragic death of Rosa Velez, who happened to be home when a man named Luis Vera burglarized her apartment in Brooklyn. "Yeah, I shot her," Vera admitted. "She knew me, and I knew I wouldn't go to the chair."

4   During my twenty-two years in public service, I have heard the pros and cons of capital punishment expressed with special intensity. As a district leader, councilman, congressman, and mayor, I have represented constituencies generally thought of as liberal. Because I support the death penalty for heinous crimes of murder, I have sometimes been the subject of emotional and outraged attacks by voters who find my position reprehensible or worse. I have listened to their ideas. I have weighed their objections carefully. I still support the death penalty. The reasons I maintain my position can be best understood by examining the arguments most frequently heard in opposition.

5   1. *The death penalty is "barbaric."* Sometimes opponents of capital punishment horrify with tales of lingering death on the gallows, of faulty electric chairs, or of agony in the gas chamber. Partly in response to such protests, several states such as North Carolina and Texas switched to execution by lethal injection. The condemned person is put to death painlessly, without ropes, voltage, bullets, or gas. Did this answer the objections of death penalty opponents? Of course not. On June 22, 1984, *The New York Times* published an editorial that sarcastically attacked the new "hygienic" method of death by injection, and stated that "execution can never be made humane through science." So it's not the method that really troubles opponents. It's the death itself they consider barbaric.

6   Admittedly, capital punishment is not a pleasant topic. However, one does not have to like the death penalty in order to support it any more than one must like radical surgery, radiation, or chemotherapy in order to find necessary these attempts at curing cancer. Ultimately we may learn how to cure cancer with a simple pill.

Unfortunately, that day has not yet arrived. Today we are faced with the choice of letting the cancer spread or trying to cure it with the methods available, methods that one day will almost certainly be considered barbaric. But to give up and do nothing would be far more barbaric and would certainly delay the discovery of an eventual cure. The analogy between cancer and murder is imperfect, because murder is not the "disease" we are trying to cure. The disease is injustice. We may not like the death penalty, but it must be available to punish crimes of cold-blooded murder, cases in which any other form of punishment would be inadequate and, therefore, unjust. If we create a society in which injustice is not tolerated, incidents of murder—the most flagrant form of injustice—will diminish.

7   2. *No other major democracy uses the death penalty.* No other major democracy—in fact, few other countries of any description—are plagued by a murder rate such as that in the United States. Fewer and fewer Americans can remember the days when unlocked doors were the norm and murder was a rare and terrible offense. In America the murder rate climbed 122 percent between 1963 and 1980. During that same period, the murder rate in New York City increased by almost 400 percent, and the statistics are even worse in many other cities. A study at M.I.T. showed that based on 1970 homicide rates a person who lived in a large American city ran a greater risk of being murdered than an American soldier in World War II ran of being killed in combat. It is not surprising that the laws of each country differ according to differing conditions and traditions. If other countries had our murder problem, the cry for capital punishment would be just as loud as it is here. And I daresay that any other major democracy where 75 percent of the people supported the death penalty would soon enact it into law.

8   3. *An innocent person might be executed by mistake.* Consider the work of Hugo Adam Bedau, one of the most implacable foes of capital punishment in this country. According to Mr. Bedau, it is "false sentimentality to argue that the death penalty should be abolished because of the abstract possibility that an innocent person might be executed." He cites a study of the 7,000 executions in this country from 1893 to 1971, and concludes that the record fails to show that such cases occur. The main point, however, is this. If government functioned only when the possibility of error didn't exist, government wouldn't function at all. Human life deserves special protection, and one of the best ways to guarantee that protection is to assure that convicted murderers do not kill again. Only the death penalty can accomplish this end. In a recent case in

New Jersey, a man named Richard Biegenwald was freed from prison after serving 18 years for murder; since his release he has been convicted of committing four murders. A prisoner named Lemuel Smith, who, while serving four life sentences for murder (plus two life sentences for kidnapping and robbery) in New York's Green Haven Prison, lured a woman corrections officer into the chaplain's office and strangled her. He then mutilated and dismembered her body. An additional life sentence for Smith is meaningless. Because New York has no death penalty statute, Smith has effectively been given a license to kill.

9   But the problem of multiple murder is not confined to the nation's penitentiaries. In 1981, 91 police officers were killed in the line of duty in this country. Seven percent of those arrested in the cases that have been solved had a previous arrest for murder. In New York City in 1976 and 1977, 85 persons arrested for homicide had a previous arrest for murder. Six of these individuals had two previous arrests for murder, and one had four previous murder arrests. During those two years the New York police were arresting for murder persons with a previous arrest for murder on the average of one every 8.5 days. This is not surprising when we learn that in 1975, for example, the median time served in Massachusetts for homicide was less than two and a half years. In 1976 a study sponsored by the Twentieth Century Fund found that the average time served in the United States for first-degree murder is ten years. The median time served may be considerably lower.

10   4. *Capital punishment cheapens the value of human life.* On the contrary, it can be easily demonstrated that the death penalty strengthens the value of human life. If the penalty for rape were lowered, clearly it would signal a lessened regard for the victims' suffering, humiliation, and personal integrity. It would cheapen their horrible experience, and expose them to an increased danger of recurrence. When we lower the penalty for murder, it signals a lessened regard for the value of the victim's life. Some critics of capital punishment, such as columnist Jimmy Breslin, have suggested that a life sentence is actually a harsher penalty for murder than death. This is sophistic nonsense. A few killers may decide not to appeal a death sentence, but the overwhelming majority make every effort to stay alive. It is by exacting the highest penalty for the taking of human life that we affirm the highest value of human life.

11   5. *The death penalty is applied in a discriminatory manner.* This factor no longer seems to be the problem it once was. The appeals process for a condemned prisoner is lengthy and painstaking. Every effort is made to see that the verdict and sentence were

fairly arrived at. However, assertions of discrimination are not an argument for ending the death penalty but for extending it. It is not justice to exclude everyone from the penalty of the law if a few are found to be so favored. Justice requires that the law be applied equally to all.

12   6. *Thou Shalt Not Kill.* The Bible is our greatest source of moral inspiration. Opponents of the death penalty frequently cite the sixth of the Ten Commandments in an attempt to prove that capital punishment is divinely proscribed. In the original Hebrew, however, the Sixth Commandment reads "Thou Shalt Not Commit Murder," and the Torah specifies capital punishment for a variety of offenses. The biblical viewpoint has been upheld by philosophers throughout history. The greatest thinkers of the 19th century—Kant, Locke, Hobbes, Rousseau, Montesquieu, and Mill—agreed that natural law properly authorizes the sovereign to take life in order to vindicate justice. Only Jeremy Bentham was ambivalent. Washington, Jefferson, and Franklin endorsed it. Abraham Lincoln authorized executions for deserters in wartime. Alexis de Tocqueville, who expressed profound respect for American institutions, believed that the death penalty was indispensable to the support of social order. The United States Constitution, widely admired as one of the seminal achievements in the history of humanity, condemns cruel and inhuman punishment, but does not condemn capital punishment.

13   7. *The death penalty is state-sanctioned murder.* This is the defense with which Messrs. Willie and Shaw hoped to soften the resolve of those who sentenced them to death. By saying in effect, "You're no better than I am," the murderer seeks to bring his accusers down to his own level. It is also a popular argument among opponents of capital punishment, but a transparently false one. Simply put, the state has rights that the private individual does not. In a democracy, those rights are given to the state by the electorate. The execution of a lawfully condemned killer is no more an act of murder than is legal imprisonment an act of kidnapping. If an individual forces a neighbor to pay him money under threat of punishment, it's called extortion. If the state does it, it's called taxation. Rights and responsibilities surrendered by the individual are what give the state its power to govern. This contract is the foundation of civilization itself.

14   Everyone wants his or her rights, and will defend them jealously. Not everyone, however, wants responsibilities, especially the painful responsibilities that come with law enforcement. Twenty-one years ago a woman named Kitty Genovese was assaulted and

murdered on a street in New York. Dozens of neighbors heard her cries for help but did nothing to assist her. They didn't even call the police. In such a climate the criminal understandably grows bolder. In the presence of moral cowardice, he lectures us on our supposed failings and tries to equate his crimes with our quest for justice.

15   The death of anyone—even a convicted killer—diminishes us all. But we are diminished even more by a justice system that fails to function. It is an illusion to let ourselves believe that doing away with capital punishment removes the murderer's deed from our conscience. The rights of society are paramount. When we protect guilty lives, we give up innocent lives in exchange. When opponents of capital punishment say to the state: "I will not let you kill in my name," they are also saying to murderers: "You can kill in your *own* name as long as I have an excuse for not getting involved."

16   It is hard to imagine anything worse than being murdered while neighbors do nothing. But something worse exists. When those same neighbors shrink back from justly punishing the murderer, the victim dies twice.

Questions

1. Koch is, of course, writing an argument. He wants to persuade his readers. Beginning with his fifth paragraph (his first numbered point) he states the opposition's arguments and tries to refute them. But why did he include his first four paragraphs? What, as persuasion, does each contribute?

2. In his sixth paragraph Koch compares our use of capital punishment to our use of "radical surgery, radiation, or chemotherapy." Do you find this analogy impressive—or not—and why? (Note that in this paragraph Koch goes on to say that "the analogy between cancer and murder is imperfect." Should he, then, not have used it?)

3. At the end of the paragraph we have just mentioned, Koch says, "If we create a society in which injustice is not tolerated, incidents of murder—the most flagrant form of injustice—will diminish." Has the earlier part of the paragraph prepared us for this statement?

4. Why, or why not, are you persuaded by Koch's second argument, about the likelihood that if other countries had high rates of murder they too would enact the death penalty?

5. In paragraph nine Koch speaks of "murder" and then of "homicide." Are these two the same? If not, *why* is Koch bringing in statistics about homicide?

6. In paragraph 12, Koch lists authorities who supported the death penalty. Some of these, for instance Washington and Jefferson, also supported slavery. What can be said in behalf of, and what can be said against, Koch's use of these authorities?
7. In his next-to-last paragraph, Koch puts a sentence into the mouths of his opponents. *Is* this what his opponents are in effect saying or thinking? (For the views of at least one of his opponents, see David Bruck's response to Koch, immediately below.)

The Death Penalty
David Bruck

1   Mayor Ed Koch contends that the death penalty "affirms life." By failing to execute murderers, he says, we "signal a lessened regard for the value of the victim's life." Koch suggests that people who oppose the death penalty are like Kitty Genovese's neighbors, who heard her cries for help but did nothing while an attacker stabbed her to death.

2   This is the standard "moral" defense of death as punishment: even if executions don't deter violent crime any more effectively than imprisonment, they are still required as the only means we have of doing justice in response to the worst of crimes.

3   Until recently, this "moral" argument had to be considered in the abstract, since no one was being executed in the United States. But the death penalty is back now, at least in the southern states, where every one of the more than 30 executions carried out over the last two years has taken place. Those of us who live in those states are getting to see the difference between the death penalty in theory, and what happens when you actually try to use it.

4   South Carolina resumed executing prisoners in January with the electrocution of Joseph Carl Shaw. Shaw was condemned to death for helping to murder two teenagers while he was serving as a military policeman at Fort Jackson, South Carolina. His crime, propelled by mental illness and PCP, was one of terrible brutality. It is Shaw's last words ("Killing was wrong when I did it. It is

wrong when you do it. . . .") that so outraged Mayor Koch: he finds it "a curiosity of modern life that we are being lectured on morality by cold-blooded killers." And so it is.

5   But it was not "modern life" that brought this curiosity into being. It was capital punishment. The electric chair was J. C. Shaw's platform. (The mayor mistakenly writes that Shaw's statement came in the form of a plea to the governor for clemency: actually Shaw made it only seconds before his death, as he waited, shaved and strapped into the chair, for the switch to be thrown.) It was the chair that provided Shaw with celebrity and an opportunity to lecture us on right and wrong. What made this weird moral reversal even worse is that J. C. Shaw faced his own death with undeniable dignity and courage. And while Shaw died, the TV crews recorded another "curiosity" of the death penalty—the crowd gathered outside the death-house to cheer on the executioner. Whoops of elation greeted the announcement of Shaw's death. Waiting at the penitentiary gates for the appearance of the hearse bearing Shaw's remains, one demonstrator started yelling, "Where's the beef?"

6   For those who had to see the execution of J. C. Shaw, it wasn't easy to keep in mind that the purpose of the whole spectacle was to affirm life. It will be harder still when Florida executes a cop-killer named Alvin Ford. Ford has lost his mind during his years of death-row confinement, and now spends his days trembling, rocking back and forth, and muttering unintelligible prayers. This has led to litigation over whether Ford meets a centuries-old legal standard for mental competency. Since the Middle Ages, the Anglo-American legal system has generally prohibited the execution of anyone who is too mentally ill to understand what is about to be done to him and why. If Florida wins its case, it will have earned the right to electrocute Ford in his present condition. If it loses, he will not be executed until the state has nursed him back to some semblance of mental health.

7   We can at least be thankful that this demoralizing spectacle involves a prisoner who is actually guilty of murder. But this may not always be so. The ordeal of Lenell Jeter—the young black engineer who recently served more than a year of a life sentence for a Texas armed robbery that he didn't commit—should remind us that the system is quite capable of making the very worst sort of mistake. That Jeter was eventually cleared is a fluke. If the robbery had occurred at 7 P.M. rather than 3 P.M., he'd have had no alibi, and would still be in prison today. And if someone had been killed in that robbery, Jeter probably would have been sentenced to death. We'd have seen the usual execution-day interviews with state offi-

cials and the victim's relatives, all complaining that Jeter's appeals took too long. And Jeter's last words from the gurney would have taken their place among the growing literature of death-house oration that so irritates the mayor.

8   Koch quoted Hugo Adam Bedau, a prominent abolitionist, to the effect that the record fails to establish that innocent defendants have been executed in the past. But this doesn't mean, as Koch implies, that it hasn't happened. All Bedau was saying was that doubts concerning executed prisoners' guilt are almost never resolved. Bedau is at work now on an effort to determine how many wrongful death sentences may have been imposed: his list of murder convictions since 1900 in which the state eventually *admitted* error is some 400 cases long. Of course, very few of these cases involved actual executions: the mistakes that Bedau documents were uncovered precisely because the prisoner was alive and able to fight for his vindication. The cases where someone is executed are the very cases in which we're least likely to learn that we got the wrong man.

9   I don't claim that executions of entirely innocent people will occur very often. But they will occur. And other sorts of mistakes already have. Roosevelt Green was executed in Georgia two days before J. C. Shaw. Green and an accomplice kidnapped a young woman. Green swore that his companion shot her to death after Green had left, and that he knew nothing about the murder. Green's claim was supported by a statement that his accomplice made to a witness after the crime. The jury never resolved whether Green was telling the truth, and when he tried to take a polygraph examination a few days before his scheduled execution, the state of Georgia refused to allow the examiner into the prison. As the pressure for symbolic retribution mounts, the courts, like the public, are losing patience with such details. Green was electrocuted on January 9, while members of the Ku Klux Klan rallied outside the prison.

10   Then there is another sort of arbitrariness that happens all the time. Last October, Louisiana executed a man named Ernest Knighton. Knighton had killed a gas station owner during a robbery. Like any murder, this was a terrible crime. But it was not premeditated, and is the sort of crime that very rarely results in a death sentence. Why was Knighton electrocuted when almost everyone else who committed the same offense was not? Was it because he was black? Was it because his victim and all 12 members of the jury that sentenced him were white? Was it because Knighton's court-appointed lawyer presented no evidence on his behalf at his sentence hearing? Or maybe there's no reason except bad luck. One thing is clear:

Ernest Knighton was picked out to die the way a fisherman takes a cricket out of a bait jar. No one cares which cricket gets impaled on the hook.

11   Not every prisoner executed recently was chosen that randomly. But many were. And having selected these men so casually, so blindly, the death penalty system asks us to accept that the purpose of killing each of them is to affirm the sanctity of human life.

12   The death penalty states are also learning that the death penalty is easier to advocate than it is to administer. In Florida, where executions have become almost routine, the governor reports that nearly a third of his time is spent reviewing the clemency requests of condemned prisoners. The Florida Supreme Court is hopelessly backlogged with death cases. Some have taken five years to decide, and the rest of the Court's work waits in line behind the death appeals. Florida's death row currently holds more than 230 prisoners. State officials are reportedly considering building a special "death prison" devoted entirely to the isolation and electrocution of the condemned. The state is also considering the creation of a special public defender unit that will do nothing else but handle death penalty appeals. The death penalty, in short, is spawning death agencies.

13   And what is Florida getting for all of this? The state went through almost all of 1983 without executing anyone: its rate of intentional homicide declined by 17 percent. Last year [1984] Florida executed eight people—the most of any state, and the sixth highest total for any year since Florida started electrocuting people back in 1924. Elsewhere in the U.S. last year, the homicide rate continued to decline. But in Florida, it actually rose by 5.1 percent.

14   But these are just the tiresome facts. The electric chair has been a centerpiece of each of Koch's recent political campaigns, and he knows better than anyone how little the facts have to do with the public's support for capital punishment. What really fuels the death penalty is the justifiable frustration and rage of people who see that the government is not coping with violent crime. So what if the death penalty doesn't work? At least it gives us the satisfaction of knowing that we got one or two of the sons of bitches.

15   Perhaps we want retribution on the flesh and bone of a handful of convicted murderers so badly that we're willing to close our eyes to all of the demoralization and danger that come with it. A lot of politicians think so, and they may be right. But if they are, then let's at least look honestly at what we're doing. This lottery of death both comes from and encourages an attitude toward human life that is not reverent, but reckless.

16   And that is why the mayor is dead wrong when he confuses such fury with justice. He suggests that we trivialize murder unless we kill murderers. By that logic, we also trivialize rape unless we sodomize rapists. The sin of Kitty Genovese's neighbors wasn't that they failed to stab her attacker to death. Justice does demand that murderers be punished. And common sense demands that society be protected from them. But neither justice nor self-preservation demands that we kill men whom we have already imprisoned.

17   The electric chair in which J. C. Shaw died earlier this year was built in 1912 at the suggestion of South Carolina's governor at the time, Cole Blease. Governor Blease's other criminal justice initiative was an impassioned crusade in favor of lynch law. Any lesser response, the governor insisted, trivialized the loathsome crimes of interracial rape and murder. In 1912 a lot of people agreed with Governor Blease that a proper regard for justice required both lynching and the electric chair. Eventually we are going to learn that justice requires neither.

Questions

1. In paragraph 7 Bruck cites the case of Lenell Jeter in order to show that "the system is quite capable of making the very worst sort of mistake." How relevant, and how convincing, do you find this example?

2. In paragraph 8 Bruck says that of the murder cases in which the state admitted error, "very few . . . involved actual executions." How many do you suppose is "very few?" Why do you think Bruck does not cite the exact number?

3. What precautions, if any, does Bruck take, in the essay, to indicate that he is not soft on crime? Do you regard him as soft on crime? Why, or why not?

4. Bruck argues (paragraphs 10–11) that some of the people executed are, in effect, randomly selected from the group of murderers. Do you find paragraph 10 in itself convincing? And, if so, do you take it as a strong argument against the death penalty? If not, why not?

5. Evaluate Bruck's final paragraph as an argument and as a final paragraph.

6. Bruck's article is intended as a refutation of Koch's. Which of Koch's arguments, if any, does Bruck not face?

8

Description

Looking is not as simple as it looks.
— AD REINHARDT

DESCRIPTION AS PERSUASION

Description represents in words our sensory impressions caught in a moment of time. In much descriptive writing visual imagery dominates. Look at the following example, part of a letter Vincent Van Gogh wrote to his brother, Theo.

> Twilight is falling, and the view of the yard from my window is simply wonderful, with that little avenue of poplars—their slender forms and thin branches stand out so delicately against the gray evening sky; and then the old arsenal building in the water—quiet as the "waters of the old pool" in the book of Isaiah—down by the waterside the walls of that arsenal are quite green and weather-beaten. Farther down is the little garden and the fence around it with the rosebushes, and everywhere in the yard the black figures of the workmen, and also the little dog. Just now Uncle Jan with his long black hair is probably making his rounds. In the distance the masts of the ships in the dock can be seen, in front the Atjeh, quite black, and the gray and red monitors—and just now here and there the lamps are being lit. At this moment the bell is ringing and the whole stream of workmen is pouring towards the gate; at the same time the lamplighter is coming to light the lamp in the yard behind the house.

First, notice that Van Gogh does not attempt to describe the view from the window at all times of day, but only now, when "twilight is falling." Thus, the figures of the workmen, the little dog, the masts in the distance, appear black; the evening sky is gray, and "just now here and there the lamps are being lit."

Second, notice that Vincent tells Theo that he sees not "a row of trees" but a "little avenue of poplars—their slender forms and thin branches stand out so delicately against the gray evening sky." These details, the result of close observation, help the reader to see what Van Gogh saw, and to feel as he felt.

Third, notice that while Van Gogh describes primarily what he *sees* (not surprising in a painter) he also notices and tells Theo what he *hears:* "At this moment the bell is ringing." And through every detail he communicates what he feels about the scene he describes: "the view of the yard from my window is simply wonderful."

Description is often a kind of persuasion. Writers wish to persuade us to share their judgment that what they describe is beautiful or ugly, noble or ignoble, valuable or worthless. If we are persuaded, it is as a result less of our having been told what to feel (often the judgment is not stated, but implied) than of the writer's skill in representing to us what he or she sees, or experiences through other senses.

ORGANIZING A DESCRIPTION

Patient observation of details, and willingness to search for exactly the right words with which to communicate our impressions, are both part of the secret of good descriptive writing. Still another part is organization, the translation of our disorderly, even chaotic, impressions into orderly structures. Limiting the description to what is sensed at a particular moment in time in itself imposes some order. But in addition, our descriptions must have some discernible pattern, such as from left to right, from bottom to top, from general to particular, or, as in Van Gogh's description, from near to far.

Notice this structure, from near to far, as Walt Whitman uses it in his poem "A Farm Picture."

> Through the ample open door of the peaceful country barn,
> A sunlit pasture field with cattle and horses feeding,
> And haze and vista, and the far horizon fading away.

Although the poem is only three lines long, the view is leisurely, beginning where the observer stands, inside the "ample open door," and then stretching slowly out to the "sunlit pasture field," still distinct, because still close up, then to the slightly more general "cattle and horses," and last to the indistinct "far horizon fading away." The leisurely pace persuades us that the scene is indeed "peaceful"; the orderly structure of the poem allows us to feel that it is.

Now look, by contrast, at a description not of a place, but of a phenomenon, a phenomenon not seen but felt, not peaceful, but "uneasy."

> There is something uneasy in the Los Angeles air this afternoon, some unnatural stillness, some tension. What it means is that to-night a Santa Ana will begin to blow, a hot wind from the north-east whining down through the Cajon and San Gorgonio Passes, blowing up sandstorms out along Route 66, drying the hills and the nerves to the flash point. For a few days now we will see smoke back in the canyons, and hear sirens in the night. I have neither heard nor read that a Santa Ana is due, but I know it, and almost everyone I have seen today knows it too. We know it because we feel it. The baby frets. The maid sulks. I rekindle a waning argu-ment with the telephone company, then cut my losses and lie down, given over to whatever it is in the air. To live with the Santa Ana is to accept, consciously or unconsciously, a deeply mechanistic view of human behavior.
>
> — Joan Didion

Here the governing pattern of the description is more com-plex—from the general to the specific, and back to the general. Didion begins with the relatively general statement "There is something uneasy in the Los Angeles air this afternoon." She then moves to the specific details that support the generalization: the visible effects of the unseen wind first on the landscape and then on people (the baby, the maid, Didion herself). In the final sen-tence, again a relatively general one, she summarizes a further ef-fect of what it is "to live with the Santa Ana." The organization is complex, but the passage is not disorderly. Or, we might say, it is just disorderly enough to make us feel, with the writer, "some-thing uneasy in the Los Angeles air."

Specific details and concrete language help us to imagine what the writer has observed; a suitable organization further assists us in following the writer's representation of impressions and feelings.

ESTABLISHING A POINT OF VIEW

In addition to observing closely, finding the right word, and organizing the material, there is yet another technique that helps persuade the reader to accept the writer's observations as true, and his or her judgment as sound. This technique can be discovered by comparing two descriptions of a building on fire. The first is by a student, trying her hand at description in a composition class.

> The thick, heavy smoke, that could be seen for miles, filled the blue July sky. Firemen frantically battled the blaze that engulfed Hempstead High School, while a crowd of people sadly looked on. Eyes slowly filled up with tears as the reality of having no school to go to started to sink in. Students that had once downed everything that the high school stood for and did, began to realize how much they cared for their school. But it was too late, it was going up in smoke.

The second is by a professional writer, a practiced hand.

> We were on the porch only a short time when I heard a lot of hollering coming from toward the field. The hollering and crying got louder and louder. I could hear Mama's voice over all the rest. It seemed like all the people in the field were running to our house. I ran to the edge of the porch to watch them top the hill. Daddy was leading the running crowd and Mama was right behind him.
> "Lord have mercy, my children is in that house!" Mama was screaming. "Hurry, Diddly!" she cried to Daddy. I turned around and saw big clouds of smoke booming out of the front door and shooting out of cracks everywhere. "There, Essie Mae is on the porch," Mama said. "Hurry, Diddly! Get Adline outta that house!" I looked back at Adline. I couldn't hardly see her for the smoke.
> George Lee was standing in the yard like he didn't know what to do. As Mama got closer, he ran into the house. My first thought was that he would be burned up. I'd often hoped he would get killed, but I guess I didn't really want him to die after all. I ran inside after him but he came running out again, knocking me down

as he passed and leaving me lying face down in the burning room. I jumped up quickly and scrambled out after him. He had the water bucket in his hands. I thought he was going to try to put out the fire. Instead he placed the bucket on the edge of the porch and picked up Adline in his arms.

Moments later Daddy was on the porch. He ran straight into the burning house with three other men right behind him. They opened the large wooden windows to let some of the smoke out and began ripping the paper from the walls before the wood caught on fire. Mama and two other women raked it into the fireplace with sticks, broom handles, and anything else available. Everyone was coughing because of all the smoke.

— Anne Moody

What can we learn from the professional writer? First notice her patience with detail, the concreteness of the passage. Where the student is content with "Firemen frantically battled the blaze that engulfed Hempstead High School," Anne Moody shows us individuals and exactly what each does. Where the student generalizes the reaction of the observers—"Eyes slowly filled up with tears" and "Students . . . began to realize how much they cared for their school"—in Moody's passage Mama screams, "Lord have mercy, my children is in that house!"

But equally important, the professional writer captures the reader's attention, and secures the reader's identification with the observer or narrator, by establishing the observer's physical position. At the beginning she is on the porch, looking toward the field. It is only when she hears her mother scream that she turns around and sees the smoke. And notice that she *does have to turn,* and the writer has the patience to tell us "I turned around and saw. . . ." We could, if we wished to, place the position of the observer, exactly, throughout the action, as if we were blocking a scene in a play. By contrast, notice that there is no real observer in the student's description. If there were, she would first have to be miles away from the scene and looking up into the sky to see the smoke. Then, in the second sentence she would be across the street, watching the firemen. By the third sentence she'd be closer still—not close to the fire, but close to the other observers. In fact, she'd have to be inside their heads to know what they were thinking. As readers we sense this lack of focus; we have no one to identify with. Though we may find the passage moderately interesting, it will not engage us and we will soon forget it.

In addition to the observer's physical location, a good description also provides a consistent psychological position, or *point of view*, with which we can identify ourselves. In the following passage from *Black Elk Speaks*, Black Elk, an Oglala Sioux holy man, is describing the Battle of Little Bighorn (1876).

> The valley went darker with dust and smoke, and there were only shadows and a big noise of many cries and hoofs and guns. On the left side of where I was I could hear the shod hoofs of the soldiers' horses going back into the brush and there was shooting everywhere. Then the hoofs came out of the brush, and I came out and was in among men and horses weaving in and out and going upstream, and everybody was yelling, "Hurry! Hurry!" The soldiers were running upstream and we were all mixed there in the twilight and the great noise. I did not see much; but once I saw a Lakota charge at a soldier who stayed behind and fought and was a very brave man. The Lakota took the soldier's horse by the bridle, but the soldier killed him with a six-shooter. I was small and could not crowd in to where the soldiers were, so I did not kill anybody. There were so many ahead of me, and it was all dark and mixed up.

Black Elk was an old man when he told this story. How old would you guess he was at the time it happened? How do you know?

DESCRIPTION AND NARRATION

At the beginning of this chapter we defined description as a representation, in words, of sensory impressions caught in a moment of time. Strictly speaking, description is static. The passage from Van Gogh's letter, and Whitman's poem, most nearly conform to this definition: they each describe a scene caught in a single moment, like a snapshot. Didion's paragraph about the Santa Ana is less static; it implies the passage of time. That time passes is, however, somewhat masked because Didion represents almost everything as happening simultaneously: "The baby frets. The maid sulks. I rekindle a waning argument with the telephone company." By contrast, in Moody's description of a house on fire, we not only hear (with Essie Mae) "a lot of hollering," and see "big clouds of smoke booming out of the front door and shooting out of cracks everywhere," we also know that moments have passed between the first sensory impression and the second, and that several more have passed before the passage ends with all the adults raking the burning wallpaper into the fireplace. The description is thoroughly interwoven with narration. Black Elk's account of the Battle of Little Bighorn is similarly a blend of description and narration.

Long passages of pure description are rare. The reason is simple. A description of a place will be much more interesting if the writer shows us something happening there. Similarly, descriptions of people are seldom (except briefly) static. In real life we seldom observe people at dead rest; we see them in action; we form our impressions of them from how they move, what they do. Good descriptions, then, frequently show us a person performing some action, a particularly revealing action, or a characteristic one. If, for example, you want to suggest a person's height and weight, it's much more interesting to show him maneuvering through a subway turnstile, perhaps laden with packages, than to say, "He was only five feet four but weighed 185 pounds" or "he was short and stocky." Here is Maya Angelou describing Mr. Freeman, a man who lived for a while with her mother.

> Mr. Freeman moved gracefully, like a big brown bear, and seldom spoke to us. He simply waited for Mother and put his whole self into the waiting. He never read the paper or patted his foot to the radio. He waited. That was all.
>
> If she came home before we went to bed, we saw the man come alive. He would start out of the big chair, like a man coming out of sleep, smiling. I would remember then that a few seconds before, I had heard a car door slam; then Mother's footsteps would signal from the concrete walk. When her key rattled the door, Mr. Freeman would have already asked his habitual question, "Hey, Bibbi, have a good time?"
>
> His query would hang in the air while she sprang over to peck him on the lips. Then she turned to Bailey and me with the lipstick kisses. "Haven't you finished your homework?" If we had and were just reading—"O.K., say your prayers and go to bed." If we hadn't—"Then go to your room and finish . . . then say your prayers and go to bed."
>
> Mr. Freeman's smile never grew, it stayed at the same inten-

sity. Sometimes Mother would go over and sit on his lap and the grin on his face looked as if it would stay there forever.

Notice how animated this description is, how filled not only with Mr. Freeman's physical presence but also with his mysterious inner life. We have a portrait of Mother, too, reflected in Mr. Freeman's waiting, his concentration on the slam of her car door, her footsteps, her key rattling, and, most of all, in his smile. More subtly and more pervasively, the description is animated by our identification with the observer, the small child watching the man who waits so intently for the woman who is her mother.

DESCRIPTION AND ANALYSIS

Descriptive passages are also commonly used in essays to support analysis. In the following brief essay, for example, a writer asks and answers the question "What are the functions of cemeteries for the living?" The essay is primarily analytical; reading it, we share the writer's thoughts, but these thoughts are not the random and fleeting notions of reverie. The thoughts have been organized for us; the effects of cemeteries on the living have been classified and presented to us in an orderly and coherent account made vivid by passages of description. Through them we share at least imaginatively in the experiences that gave rise to the thinking. And through them, if the communication between writer and reader has been successful, we are persuaded to share the writer's opinions.

How Cemeteries Bring Us Back to Earth
Jim Doherty

A while ago, we said goodbye to a beloved aunt in a rural Wisconsin cemetery pulsing with birdsong. It was a splendid morning, gusty and bright. Puffy white clouds went sailing across the deep blue sky and calves were bawling in the distance. Later, we would sing hymns in a pretty church that smelled of coffee and candle wax, but first we stood blinking in the sunlight while a choir of robins, red-winged blackbirds and meadowlarks lustily sere- naded the casket.

Curiously enough, graveyards often seem more alive than the places where many of us live. To soften the harshness of tomb- stones and obelisks, we plant trees and bushes, create ponds and manicure vast lawns. Even as developers transform old marshlands and forests into shopping centers and subdivisions, our forebears moulder away in lush new groves that nourish raccoons, wood- chucks, rabbits and birds.

Cemeteries are good places for living people, too. My oldest daughter attends a Connecticut college where she spends many pleasant afternoons studying in a 17th-century boneyard. I remem- ber a shady marble orchard in Mamaroneck, N.Y., where couples could usually find enough privacy for petting. Out here in south- eastern Wisconsin, rabbit hunters patrol secluded country cemeter- ies that are bounded by overgrown fence rows and cornfields.

Tombstones can teach us a little about history but the overall ambience of a cemetery tells us much more.

One snowy spring morning near a ghost town in Idaho, my wife and I happened across a cluster of faded wooden markers sur- rounded by a rusting wrought-iron fence. The wind blew mourn- fully through the tall evergreens, and off in the distance the peaks of the Rockies glowed like The Promised Land. As we meandered among the graves, we tried to imagine what kind of lives those pioneers led and gradually we seemed to absorb an impression of it—the loneliness, the uncertainty, the overpowering presence of the mountains.

Hiking in Vermont one day, we found a century-old family plot on a hillside where two generations lived and died. Most of those who perished were children—eight of them were buried side- by-side—and there were also a number of small unmarked stones. It was impossible to romanticize the past at the gravesite of a pa- triarch preceded in death by two wives and so many sons and daughters. We wondered: Was he ready to go when his time came?

Cemeteries bring us back to earth in more ways than one.

By their very presence, they remind us that the meter is run- ning. In so doing, they admonish us not to love winter less but to appreciate summer more. They reassure us, too, for if the dead can reside in such benign surroundings, then death itself somehow seems less formidable.

A man I know works as a caretaker up north. Whenever an old grave caves in, he spades off the sod and throws in enough dirt to fill the hole. Now and then he turns up a bone and simply tamps it down into the soil before replacing the sod. It bothers him not at all.

Recently, I took a 90-year-old woman to a hilltop cemetery in Johnson Creek, the small town where she grew up. It was a hot summer day and the air was sweet with the perfume of cedar trees and cut hay. Somewhere, a meadowlark was calling. My companion was looking for the headstone of a distant relative, which she did not find, but she came across many other familiar names: a neighbor, the man who ran the creamery, the banker, several childhood friends, some students from her teaching days. She stopped at each one to remember a story or two and then moved on until she grew tired, and we left.

I retain a vivid image of that windblown lady tottering gamely between the rows of mossy tombstones, full of anticipation and absolutely unafraid. It is a brave picture. I shall cherish it until the day I die.

Questions

1. Descriptive writing often falls into sentimentality, or triteness, or both. If you agree with us that Doherty avoids sentimentality (on a subject that would seem to invite it) try to explain how he avoids it. If the concluding sentence is not trite, what keeps it from being trite?
2. What were your feelings about cemeteries before you read this essay? Did the essay change your thinking in any way, or reinforce feelings and thoughts arising from your own experience? Explain.
3. Analyze the title. In what ways, according to Doherty, do "Cemeteries Bring Us Back to Earth"?

EXERCISES

1. In one paragraph, describe what you see from your window. Choose a particular time of day and describe only what you see (or might see) or otherwise sense within a moment or two.

2. In one paragraph, describe something that cannot be seen, or cannot be seen except by the effects it creates. (Something hot, or smelly, or loud?)

3. In one paragraph, describe something from the point of view of a child, or an old person, or someone of the opposite sex. (Note *person.* The point of view of a dog, or stone, or carrot is *out.*)

4. In one paragraph, describe a room, for example, a doctor's waiting room, an elementary school classroom, by showing something happening in it. Your description should reveal (without explicitly stating) your attitude toward it. The reader should be able to sense that the room is, for example, comfortable or sterile or pretentious or cozy or menacing, though no such words are used in the description.

5. First read the following two paragraphs from Saul Bellow's novel *The Victim.* Then answer the questions that follow the paragraphs.

> Leventhal's apartment was spacious. In a better neighborhood, or three stories lower, it would have rented for twice the amount he paid. But the staircase was narrow and stifling and full of turns. Though he went up slowly, he was out of breath when he reached the fourth floor, and his heart beat thickly. He rested before unlocking the door. Entering, he threw down his raincoat and flung himself on the tapestry-covered low bed in the front room. Mary had moved some of the chairs into the corners and covered them with sheets. She could not depend on him to keep the windows shut and the shades and curtains drawn during the day. This afternoon the cleaning woman had been in and there was a pervasive odor of soap powder. He got up and opened a window. The curtains waved once and then were as motionless as before. There was a movie house strung with lights across the street; on its roof a water tank sat heavily uneven on its timbers; the cowls of the chimneys, which rattled in the slightest stir of air, were still.
>
> The motor of the refrigerator began to run. The ice trays were empty and rattled. Wilma, the cleaning woman, had defrosted the machine and forgotten to refill them. He looked for a bottle of beer he had noticed yesterday; it was gone. There was nothing inside except a few lemons and some milk. He drank a glass of milk and it refreshed him. He had already taken off his shirt and was sitting on the bed unlacing his shoes when there was a short ring of the

bell. Eagerly he pulled open the door and shouted, "Who is it?" The flat was unbearably empty. He hoped someone had remembered that Mary was away and had come to keep him company. There was no response below. He called out again, impatiently. It was very probable that someone had pushed the wrong button, but he heard no other doors opening. Could it be a prank? This was not the season for it. Nothing moved in the stairwell, and it only added to his depression to discover how he longed for a visitor. He stretched out on the bed, pulling a pillow from beneath the spread and doubling it up. He thought he would doze off. But a little later he found himself standing at the window, holding the curtains with both hands. He was under the impression that he had slept. It was only eight-thirty by the whirring electric clock on the night table, however. Only five minutes had passed.

Questions: How old, approximately, is Leventhal? Of what social or economic class is he? Who is Mary? What do you know of her relationship to Leventhal? What is the weather like? What is Leventhal's mood? How did you know all these things?

6. In one or two paragraphs, describe a person by showing him or her performing some action that takes less than five minutes. From the description we should be able to infer some of the following: the time of day; the weather; and the person's height, weight, age, sex, occupation, economic or educational background, and mood.

7. Read the essay "Adman's Atlanta" (pages 293–96). Then, describe and analyze an advertisement in about 500 words. To do this, you will need a thesis, such as "This advertisement appeals to male chauvinism," or "This advertisement plays on our fear that we may lack sex appeal." Include a copy of the advertisement with your essay.

8. Choose a recent political cartoon to describe and analyze. In your first paragraph identify the cartoon (cartoonist's name, place and date of publication) and describe the drawing (including any words in it) thoroughly enough so that someone who has not seen it can visualize or even draw it fairly accurately. In a second paragraph explain the political message. Don't inject your own opinion; present the cartoonist's point objectively. Submit a copy of the cartoon with your essay. Be

sure to choose a cartoon of sufficient complexity to make the analysis worthwhile.

9. "At fifty," George Orwell wrote, "everyone gets the face he deserves." Using this sentence as your opening sentence, write a paragraph—supporting or refuting the assertion—chiefly devoted to describing one face. (Your instructor may tell you to choose a widely known face [Lincoln, Churchill, Elizabeth Taylor] or, on the other hand, a face not known to the public.)

10. Write an essay describing someone you know or have known about whom you have strongly negative feelings. The subject could be an unjust teacher; a malevolent child; a treacherous friend; a trouble-making relative; a nasty neighbor; a rude co-worker; a cruel boyfriend or girlfriend; a bad parent; a selfish acquaintance.

Your introduction (which might be a description of your subject performing some action) should yield specific information about your subject's age, location, history, job—whatever will make her or him real to the reader. Do not leave the character in some vague universe. Use a fictitious name if you wish.

The bulk of your paper should be an analysis and description of the unattractive personality, or the evil behavior, or the bad attitudes, speech, or actions of your subject.

Conclude with a summary comment, judgment, or modifying or despairing or humorous or hopeful angle that lets you come to terms with this person, or settle the score, or put it on hold, or still be troubled by the very thought of him or her . . . or at least finish the paper. (Suggested length: 750 words.)

DESCRIPTION AT WORK

The Use of Sidewalks
Jane Jacobs

1   Under the seeming disorder of the old city, wherever the old city is working successfully, is a marvelous order for maintaining the safety of the streets and the freedom of the city. It is a complex order. Its essence is intricacy of sidewalk use, bringing with it a constant succession of eyes. This order is all composed of movement and change, and although it is life, not art, we may fancifully call it the art form of the city and liken it to the dance—not to a simple-minded precision dance with everyone kicking up at the same time, twirling in unison and bowing off en masse, but to an intricate ballet in which the individual dancers and ensembles all have distinctive parts which miraculously reinforce each other and compose an orderly whole. The ballet of the good city sidewalk never repeats itself from place to place, and in any one place is always replete with new improvisations.

2   The stretch of Hudson Street where I live is each day the scene of an intricate sidewalk ballet. I make my own first entrance into it a little after eight when I put out the garbage can, surely a prosaic occupation, but I enjoy my part, my little clang, as the droves of junior high school students walk by the center of the stage dropping candy wrappers. (How do they eat so much candy so early in the morning?)

3   While I sweep up the wrappers I watch the other rituals of morning: Mr. Halpert unlocking the laundry's handcart from its mooring to a cellar door, Joe Cornacchia's son-in-law stacking out the empty crates from the delicatessen, the barber bringing out his sidewalk folding chair, Mr. Goldstein arranging the coils of wire which proclaim the hardware store is open, the wife of the tenement's superintendent depositing her chunky three-year-old with a toy mandolin on the stoop, the vantage point from which he is learning the English his mother cannot speak. Now the primary children, heading for St. Luke's, dribble through to the south; the children for St. Veronica's cross, heading to the west, and the children for P.S. 41, heading toward the east. Two new entrances are

289

being made from the wings: well-dressed and even elegant women and men with brief cases emerge from doorways and side streets. Most of these are heading for the bus and subways, but some hover on the curbs, stopping taxis which have miraculously appeared at the right moment, for the taxis are part of a wider morning ritual: having dropped passengers from midtown in the downtown financial district, they are now bringing downtowners up to midtown. Simultaneously, numbers of women in housedresses have emerged and as they crisscross with one another they pause for quick conversations that sound with either laughter or joint indignation, never, it seems, anything between. It is time for me to hurry to work too, and I exchange my ritual farewell with Mr. Lofaro, the short, thick-bodied, white-aproned fruit man who stands outside his doorway a little up the street, his arms folded, his feet planted, looking solid as earth itself. We nod; we each glance quickly up and down the street, then look back to each other and smile. We have done this many a morning for more than ten years, and we both know what it means: All is well.

4   The heart-of-the-day ballet I seldom see, because part of the nature of it is that working people who live there, like me, are mostly gone, filling the roles of strangers on other sidewalks. But from days off, I know enough of it to know that it becomes more and more intricate. Longshoremen who are not working that day gather at the White Horse or the Ideal or the International for beer and conversation. The executives and business lunchers from the industries just to the west throng the Dorgene restaurant and the Lion's Head coffee house; meat-market workers and communications scientists fill the bakery lunchroom. Character dancers come on, a strange old man with strings of old shoes over his shoulder, motor-scooter riders with big beards and girl friends who bounce on the back of the scooters and wear their hair long in front of their faces as well as behind, drunks who follow the advice of the Hat Council and are always turned out in hats, but not hats the Council would approve. Mr. Lacey, the locksmith, shuts up his shop for a while and goes to exchange the time of day with Mr. Slube at the cigar store. Mr. Koochagian, the tailor, waters the luxuriant jungle of plants in his window, gives them a critical look from the outside, accepts a compliment on them from two passers-by, fingers the leaves on the plane tree in front of our house with a thoughtful gardener's appraisal, and crosses the street for a bite at the Ideal where he can keep an eye on customers and wigwag across the message that he is coming. The baby carriages come out, and clus-

ters of everyone from toddlers with dolls to teen-agers with homework gather at the stoops.

5   When I get home after work, the ballet is reaching its crescendo. This is the time of roller skates and stilts and tricycles, and
games in the lee of the stoop with bottletops and plastic cowboys;
this is the time of bundles and packages, zigzagging from the drug
store to the fruit stand and back over to the butcher's; this is the
time when teen-agers, all dressed up, are pausing to ask if their slips
show or their collars look right; this is the time when beautiful girls
get out of MG's; this is the time when the fire engines go through;
this is the time when anybody you know around Hudson Street will
go by.

6   As darkness thickens and Mr. Halpert moors the laundry cart
to the cellar door again, the ballet goes on under lights, eddying
back and forth but intensifying at the bright spotlight pools of Joe's
sidewalk pizza dispensary, the bars, the delicatessen, the restaurant
and the drug store. The night workers stop now at the delicatessen,
to pick up salami and a container of milk. Things have settled down
for the evening but the street and its ballet have not come to a stop.

7   I know the deep night ballet and its seasons best from waking
long after midnight to tend a baby and, sitting in the dark, seeing
the shadows and hearing the sounds of the sidewalk. Mostly it is a
sound like infinitely pattering snatches of party conversation and,
about three in the morning, singing, very good singing. Sometimes
there is sharpness and anger or sad, sad weeping, or a flurry of
search for a string of beads broken. One night a young man came
roaring along, bellowing terrible language at two girls whom he
had apparently picked up and who were disappointing him. Doors
opened, a wary semicircle formed around him, not too close, until
the police came. Out came the heads, too, along Hudson Street,
offering opinion. "Drunk . . . Crazy . . . A wild kid from the suburbs."[1]

8   Deep in the night, I am almost unaware how many people are
on the street unless something calls them together, like the bagpipe.
Who the piper was and why he favored our street I have no idea.
The bagpipe just skirled out in the February night, and as if it were
a signal the random, dwindled movements of the sidewalk took on

---

[1]He turned out to be a wild kid from the suburbs. Sometimes, on
Hudson Street, we are tempted to believe the suburbs must be a difficult
place to bring up children.

direction. Swiftly, quietly, almost magically a little crowd was there, a crowd that evolved into a circle with a Highland fling inside it. The crowd could be seen on the shadowy sidewalk, the dancers could be seen, but the bagpiper himself was almost invisible because his bravura was all in his music. He was a very little man in a plain brown overcoat. When he finished and vanished, the dancers and watchers applauded, and applause came from the galleries too, half a dozen of the hundred windows on Hudson Street. Then the windows closed, and the little crowd dissolved into the random movements of the night street.

9   The strangers on Hudson Street, the allies whose eyes help us natives keep the peace of the street, are so many that they always seem to be different people from one day to the next. That does not matter. Whether they are so many always-different people as they seem to be, I do not know. Likely they are. When Jimmy Rogan fell through a plate-glass window (he was separating some scuffling friends) and almost lost his arm, a stranger in an old T shirt emerged from the Ideal bar, swiftly applied an expert tourniquet and, according to the hospital's emergency staff, saved Jimmy's life. Nobody remembered seeing the man before and no one has seen him since. The hospital was called in this way: a woman sitting on the steps next to the accident ran over to the bus stop, wordlessly snatched the dime from the hand of a stranger who was waiting with his fifteen-cent fare ready, and raced into the Ideal's phone booth. The stranger raced after her to offer the nickel too. Nobody remembered seeing him before, and no one has seen him since. When you see the same stranger three or four times on Hudson Street, you begin to nod. This is almost getting to be an acquaintance, a public acquaintance, of course.

10   I have made the daily ballet of Hudson Street sound more frenetic than it is, because writing it telescopes it. In real life, it is not that way. In real life, to be sure, something is always going on, the ballet is never at a halt, but the general effect is peaceful and the general tenor even leisurely. People who know well such animated city streets will know how it is. I am afraid people who do not will always have it a little wrong in their heads—like the old prints of rhinoceroses made from travelers' descriptions of rhinoceroses.

11   On Hudson Street, the same as in the North End of Boston or in any other animated neighborhoods of great cities, we are not innately more competent at keeping the sidewalks safe than are the people who try to live off the hostile truce of Turf in a blind-eyed city. We are the lucky possessors of a city order that makes it relatively simple to keep the peace because there are plenty of eyes on

the street. But there is nothing simple about that order itself, or the bewildering number of components that go into it. Most of those components are specialized in one way or another. They unite in their joint effect upon the sidewalk which is not specialized in the least. That is its strength.

Questions

1. Evaluate the effectiveness of the extended metaphor Jacobs uses. Did the comparison of the activity on her street with a ballet help you to share her point of view, or did you find it obtrusive and distracting? If you found the device useful or pleasing, explain why ballet is a better metaphor than, say, a concert or circus. Or, can you think of a metaphor that is better than ballet?
2. What is Jacobs's thesis? Locate the thesis sentence, or summarize the thesis in your own words.
3. Would you agree that the inherent superiority of cities over suburbs is a secondary argument or theme of the essay? If so, try to locate the passages in which this argument is stated or implied.
4. In her next-to-last paragraph, Jacobs briefly apologizes for the inadequacy of her description of life on the sidewalk. Does your experience allow you to detect inadequacies in her description? If so, what are they?
5. Explain Jacobs's next-to-last sentence.

---

*A*dman's Atlanta [2]

Lynda Martin

1   Centered in the top third of the page is a three-line, deep black headline: "Atlanta's suburban style of urban living." The first A is the only capital letter, there is a period after living, and the letters

---

[2] This essay was written by a student in response to an assignment to describe and analyze an advertisement.

are the Roman script of a regular typewriter. A round picture in black and white with a diameter the size of half the page is separated from the heading by three blocks of copy and a very small black and white rectangular picture. Each photo has a caption under it. In the round picture a beautifully gnarled tree casts its shadow over the driveway and cobblestone sidewalk that front two clean-lined, white apartment buildings at right angles to each other. In the break between the buildings a lamp of five white globes contrasts with dark trees behind it. A well-dressed businessman and businesswoman walk in the sun in front of the building on the left; at the entrance of the other building another suited man climbs into a new-looking compact car. In the other photo Atlanta's skyline glows pale in a flawless afternoon sky behind a mass of trees that covers the bottom two-thirds of the shot. The copy tells of the joys of living in Atlanta, explaining that life there combines the best of the city with the best of the suburb.

2   In attempting to persuade the reader that "Atlanta's style of living" is worth finding out about (by writing to the Atlanta Chamber of Commerce), the creators of the ad have used several techniques to associate living in Atlanta with business and with luxury; in short, with the common idea of success.

3   First to catch the reader's eye is the dark solid heading. The forceful deep black print is softened by its curved, but simple, design. Compact but not crowded, these words add up to a plain positive statement with a modestly assertive period at the end.

4   This business-like handling shows also in the picture centered below. It depicts clean white modern buildings lived in by purposeful people who are apparently going about a normal day in their successful lives. The dominance of the foreground tree and other trees in the background complement the buildings, preventing any appearance of harshness. A sense of gentleness and luxury is augmented by the blurred round border that makes the pictures seem to be surrounded by sunlight. The sun is important in this picture, and also in the rectangular picture to the left. In both, the sun heightens the contrast between the clean brightness of the buildings and the luxurious darkness of the trees, producing an atmosphere of happy leisure.

5   Lest leisure seem to be merely idleness, any emptiness created by the word "suburban" is immediately filled by the word "urban." The copy emphasizes both the convenience of living "close in"— that is, being near "necessities and pleasures: schools, shopping, churches, cultural activities . . ."—and the flexibility of being able to live in the city "in almost any manner you choose," be it some

Atlanta's suburban style of urban living.

In Atlanta you can live close in and still be close to wooded green. This blending of the urban and suburban makes Atlanta one of the most attractive and convenient big cities you'll

TREES IN ATLANTA REACH INTO THE HEART OF DOWNTOWN.

find. And you can live here in almost any manner you choose. Up in a high-rise. In a formal town house. In a garden apartment with pool and tennis courts. Or amidst a rolling lawn and garden of your own.

And no matter which you choose, you're never far from the necessities and pleasures: schools, shopping, churches, cultural activities, entertainment, and of course your office. Find out about Atlanta's style of living. Contact: Paul Miller, Atlanta Chamber of Commerce, 1314 Commerce Building, Atlanta, Ga. 30303, 404—521-0845.

TREES SURROUND LUXURY APARTMENTS ON PEACHTREE ROAD, 10 MINUTES FROM DOWNTOWN.

kind of urban apartment or a home of your own. Life in Atlanta is urban but "close to the wooded green." This idea is not only brought out in the copy, but is also emphasized in the pictures by beginning both captions with the word "trees."

6   This advertisement creates a favorable impression of city living, counteracting many readers' associations of a city with dirt, smog, and crowds. It indirectly advertises the "good life" of a prosperous businessman, be it in "a formal town house" or with "a rolling lawn and garden of your own." It also advertises middle-class values, beginning with religion and ending with business: "churches, cultural activities, entertainment, and of course your office."

Los Angeles Notebook
Joan Didion

1   There is something uneasy in the Los Angeles air this afternoon, some unnatural stillness, some tension. What it means is that tonight a Santa Ana will begin to blow, a hot wind from the northeast whining down through the Cajon and San Gorgonio Passes, blowing up sandstorms out along Route 66, drying the hills and the nerves to the flash point. For a few days now we will see smoke back in the canyons, and hear sirens in the night. I have neither heard nor read that a Santa Ana is due, but I know it, and almost everyone I have seen today knows it too. We know it because we feel it. The baby frets. The maid sulks. I rekindle a waning argument with the telephone company, then cut my losses and lie down, given over to whatever it is in the air. To live with the Santa Ana is to accept, consciously or unconsciously, a deeply mechanistic view of human behavior.

2   I recall being told, when I first moved to Los Angeles and was living on an isolated beach, that the Indians would throw themselves into the sea when the bad wind blew. I could see why. The Pacific turned ominously glossy during a Santa Ana period, and one woke in the night troubled not only by the peacocks screaming in

the olive trees but by the eerie absence of surf. The heat was sur-real. The sky had a yellow cast, the kind of light sometimes called "earthquake weather." My only neighbor would not come out of her house for days, and there were no lights at night, and her husband roamed the place with a machete. One day he would tell me that he had heard a trespasser, the next a rattlesnake.

3   "On nights like that," Raymond Chandler once wrote about the Santa Ana, "every booze party ends in a fight. Meek little wives feel the edge of the carving knife and study their husbands' necks. Anything can happen." That was the kind of wind it was. I did not know then that there was any basis for the effect it had on all of us, but it turns out to be another of these cases in which science bears out folk wisdom. The Santa Ana, which is named for one of the canyons it rushes through, is a *foehn* wind, like the *foehn* of Austria and Switzerland and the *hamsin* of Israel. There are a number of persistent malevolent winds, perhaps the best known of which are the mistral of France and the Mediterranean sirocco, but a *foehn* wind has distinct characteristics: it occurs on the leeward slope of a mountain range and, although the air begins as a cold mass, it is warmed as it comes down the mountain and appears finally as a hot dry wind. Whenever and wherever a *foehn* blows, doctors hear about headaches and nausea and allergies, about "nervousness," about "depression." In Los Angeles some teachers do not attempt to conduct formal classes during a Santa Ana, because the children become unmanageable. In Switzerland the suicide rate goes up during the *foehn,* and in the courts of some Swiss cantons the wind is considered a mitigating circumstance for crime. Surgeons are said to watch the wind, because blood does not clot normally during a *foehn.* A few years ago an Israeli physicist discovered that not only during such winds, but for the ten or twelve hours which precede them, the air carries an unusually high ratio of positive to negative ions. No one seems to know exactly why that should be; some talk about friction and others suggest solar disturbances. In any case the positive ions are there, and what an excess of positive ions does, in the simplest terms, is make people unhappy. One cannot get much more mechanistic than that.

4   Easterners commonly complain that there is no "weather" at all in Southern California, that the days and the seasons slip by relentlessly, numbingly bland. That is quite misleading. In fact the climate is characterized by infrequent but violent extremes: two periods of torrential subtropical rains which continue for weeks and wash out the hills and send subdivisions sliding toward the sea;

about twenty scattered days a year of the Santa Ana, which, with its incendiary dryness, invariably means fire. At the first prediction of a Santa Ana, the Forest Service flies men and equipment from northern California into the southern forests, and the Los Angeles Fire Department cancels its ordinary non-firefighting routines. The Santa Ana caused Malibu to burn the way it did in 1956, and Bel Air in 1961, and Santa Barbara in 1964. In the winter of 1966–67 eleven men were killed fighting a Santa Ana fire that spread through the San Gabriel Mountains.

5   Just to watch the front-page news out of Los Angeles during a Santa Ana is to get very close to what it is about the place. The longest single Santa Ana period in recent years was in 1957, and it lasted not the usual three or four days but fourteen days, from November 21 until December 4. On the first day 25,000 acres of the San Gabriel Mountains were burning, with gusts reaching 100 miles an hour. In town, the wind reached Force 12, or hurricane force, on the Beaufort Scale; oil derricks were toppled and people ordered off the downtown streets to avoid injury from flying objects. On November 22 the fire in the San Gabriels was out of control. On November 24 six people were killed in automobile accidents, and by the end of the week the Los Angeles *Times* was keeping a box score of traffic deaths. On November 26 a prominent Pasadena attorney, depressed about money, shot and killed his wife, their two sons, and himself. On November 27 a South Gate divorcée, twenty-two, was murdered and thrown from a moving car. On November 30 the San Gabriel fire was still out of control, and the wind in town was blowing eighty miles an hour. On the first day of December four people died violently, and on the third the wind began to break.

6   It is hard for people who have not lived in Los Angeles to realize how radically the Santa Ana figures in the local imagination. The city burning is Los Angeles's deepest image of itself: Nathanael West perceived that, in *The Day of the Locust;* and at the time of the 1965 Watts riots what struck the imagination most indelibly were the fires. For days one could drive the Harbor Freeway and see the city on fire, just as we had always known it would be in the end. Los Angeles weather is the weather of catastrophe, of apocalypse, and, just as the reliably long and bitter winters of New England determine the way life is lived there, so the violence and the unpredictability of the Santa Ana affect the entire quality of life in Los Angeles, accentuate its impermanence, its unreliability. The wind shows us how close to the edge we are.

Questions

1. Paraphrase or explain the last sentence of the first paragraph. What passages in the essay offer the most persuasive evidence supporting the point?
2. Beginning with the third paragraph, Didion defines the Santa Ana. Would the essay have been clearer or more effective if the definition had introduced the essay? Explain.
3. Explain the last sentence, and evaluate it as a conclusion.

9

Narration

THE USES OF NARRATIVE

Usually we think of narrative writing as the art of the novelist or short story writer, but narratives need not be fictional. Biography and autobiography, history and books of travel are all largely narrative. And of course narrative passages may appear in writings that as a whole are not themselves narratives. For instance, expository and persuasive essays may include narratives—perhaps anecdotes, or brief sketches of historical occurrences or of personal experiences—that serve to clarify the essayist's point.

Suppose, for example, that you are writing a paper for a course in ethics, arguing that it is immoral for physicians to withhold the truth (supposedly for the patients' own good) from terminally ill patients. You might include a brief narrative recounting how such a patient, when told the truth, responded not by withdrawing, but by increasing her useful activities—which included helping the members of her family to adjust to her imminent death. In writing any essay you may find that a paragraph or two of narrative helps you first to engage your readers' attention and then to make an abstract point concretely and persuasively.

In the following passage, addressed to English teachers, Paul B. Diederich, a specialist in the teaching of writing, explains mostly through narrative the "effects of excessive correction" on students in writing classes.

    I can judge one of the main effects of . . . grading by the attitudes of students who land in my remedial course in college. They hate and fear writing more than anything else they have had to do in school. If they see a blank sheet of paper on which they are expected to write something, they look as though they want to scream. Apparently they have never written anything that anyone thought was good. At least, no one ever *told* them that anything in their writing was good. All their teachers looked for were mistakes, and there are so many kinds of mistakes in writing that their students despair of ever learning to avoid them.

    The attitude toward writing that these students have developed is well illustrated by a story told by the Russian writer Chekhov about a kitten that was given to his uncle. The uncle wanted to make the kitten a champion killer of mice, so while it was still very young, he showed it a live mouse in a cage. Since the kitten's hunting instinct had not yet developed, it examined the mouse curiously but without any hostility. The uncle wanted to teach it that such fraternizing with the enemy was wrong, so he slapped the kitten, scolded it, and sent it away in disgrace. The next day the same mouse was shown to the kitten again. This time the kitten regarded it rather fearfully but without any aggressive intent. Again the uncle slapped it, scolded it, and sent it away. This treatment went on day after day. After some time, as soon as the kitten saw or smelled that mouse, it screamed and tried to climb up the walls. At that point the uncle lost patience and gave the kitten away, saying that it was stupid and would never learn. Of course the kitten had learned perfectly, and had learned exactly what it had been taught, but unfortunately not what the uncle intended to teach. "I can sympathize with that kitten," says Chekhov, "because that same uncle tried to teach me Latin."

    If everything written by our less gifted writers gets slapped down for its mistakes, and if this treatment continues year after year, can we expect that their attitude toward writing will differ from the attitude of the kitten toward that mouse? I saw the result year after year in my remedial classes. If I asked them to write anything, they reacted as though I had asked them to walk a tightrope sixty feet above the ground with no net to catch them if they fell. It took some time to build up their confidence, to convince them that writing is as simple and natural as talking, and that no reader would mind a few mistakes if he got interested in what was being written about. For some time I never commented adversely on anything they wrote but expressed appreciation of anything I found interesting, no matter how badly it was expressed. After students gained confidence I continued to express appreciation but offered one suggestion for improvement at the end of each paper. If poor writers learn one thing about writing per paper, that is far above the average.

Notice that in the brief passage, three paragraphs in all, there are two narratives. The first, a retelling of Chekhov's anecdote about a kitten, memorably illustrates Diederich's point that students subjected to excessive correction are not taught to write but taught to fear writing. The third paragraph, while mainly expository, recounts Diederich's own experiences—year after year—of restoring confidence in students in his remedial classes.

Often a short narrative provides an arresting opening to an essay. You may have noticed how often speakers rely on this device; writers, too, find it effective. Flannery O'Connor begins "The King of the Birds" (an essay on her passion for collecting and raising peacocks) with the following story:

> When I was five, I had an experience that marked me for life. Pathé News sent a photographer from New York to Savannah to take a picture of a chicken of mine. This chicken, a buff Cochin Bantam, had the distinction of being able to walk either forward or backward. Her fame had spread through the press, and by the time she reached the attention of Pathé News, I suppose there was nowhere left for her to go—forward or backward. Shortly after that she died, as now seems fitting.

What makes this anecdote arresting? First of all, we can hardly read that an experience marked a person for life without wanting to know what the experience was. We expect to learn something sensational; perhaps, human nature being what it is, we hope to learn something horrifying. But O'Connor cannily does not gratify our wish. Instead she treats us to something like a joke. The chicken, whose fame had "spread through the press," has her picture taken by Pathé News (one of the companies that made the newsreels shown regularly in movie theaters before television became popular) and then dies. If the joke is partly on us, O'Connor takes the sting out of it by turning it around on herself. In her second paragraph she explains:

> If I put this information in the beginning of an article on peacocks, it is because I am always being asked why I raise them, and I have no short or reasonable answer.

But of course her answer, contained in the first paragraph, *is* short, and about as reasonable an explanation as any of us can offer about our passion for collecting anything. If these opening paragraphs persuade us to keep reading, it is not because they deliver the melodrama they at first hinted at, but because O'Connor's irony persuades us that she is entertaining, and that she is honest about her experience. We want to learn more about her, and we may thereby be seduced into learning what she wants to teach us about peacocks. Moreover, O'Connor's explanation that she tells the story because "I have no short or reasonable answer," reveals a profound truth about the impulse to tell stories. When a writer, even the writer of an expository essay, tells a story, it is because that story happens to be the best way to make the particular point he or she wants to make.

Narrative Pace: Scene and Summary

In recounting a narrative, a storyteller usually mixes *summary* with *scene*. When we read "Two men were walking down the street," we are reading a summary (we are not told whether the street was broad or narrow, or whether the sun was shining or not). But when we read the next words, "One of them suddenly stopped, put his hand on the other man's shoulder, and said 'Wait a minute,'" we are reading a scene. The point is not that a scene requires dialogue, though in fact scenes often do include dialogue; the point is that a scene brings the characters before our eyes and lets us see or hear them in considerable detail. A summary, on the other hand, conveys necessary information ("Two men were walking down the street") without dwelling on it.

Good storytellers on the whole are sparing in their use of

summary; they know that the power of a story is in the way a certain person gesticulated, or in certain words that were spoken, or in the way members of a group responded to some happening, and the good storytellers let us see and hear these things. This does not mean that when they give us a scene they include every detail, relevant or irrelevant, in an effort to make us see the action. On the contrary, the good storyteller cuts any details or incidents that clog the action or blur the point of the story. The kitten in Chekhov's narrative is shown a live mouse "while [the kitten] was still very young," and again "the next day." Since the kitten's behavior doesn't change (nor, more significantly, does the uncle's) Chekhov swiftly summarizes what happened next: "This treatment went on day after day." We are then given only one sentence of description directly relevant to the narrative, before we are told that the uncle lost patience and gave the kitten away. It is not important to Chekhov's point, or to Diederich's, whether the kitten was gray or calico, long haired or short, cuddly or scrawny, but only that it "screamed and tried to climb up the walls" when it saw or smelled the mouse. *These* details are the relevant ones, and so Chekhov gives them to us. That is, here we get a scene (admittedly a very brief one) rather than a summary.

Similarly, O'Connor describes her chicken only enough to convince us of its reality—it was a "buff Cochin Bantam." The point of the anecdote lies not in the unremarkable chicken (who achieves her fame and dies in three sentences) but in the effect on the writer of a brief moment of celebrity. On a deeper level, the point of the anecdote is the writer's wish to secure our attention and goodwill.

ORGANIZING A NARRATIVE

The organization of a narrative is normally chronological, in accordance with the King's advice to the White Rabbit in *Alice's Adventures in Wonderland:* Begin at the beginning, and go on till you come to the end: then stop. Purposeful variations, however, are welcome. For example, fairly often narratives begin at the end, for a dramatic opening, and then present the earlier parts of the story in chronological order. Such a structure deliberately dispels surprise about the outcome, but gains suspense; the reader enjoys the pleasure of anticipating how events will move toward the known ending. In the following essay (two paragraphs in all) you'll find the end of the story foreshadowed in the word "amiable" in the first sentence.

Out in Akron, Ohio, there is an underground church called Alice's Restaurant, which figures in the most amiable story of the season just past. This group, led by unfrocked priests and unchurched ministers, was doing a deal of earnest good work in a quiet way, all to dramatize and protest the commercialization of Christmas. At shopping centers, for instance, they passed out leaflets calling upon shoppers to limit individual gifts to two-fifty and to devote the overplus to the poor. Then it occurred to one underground churchman, David Bullock by name, to demonstrate the fate that would inevitably befall the Holy Family in a society of heartless abundance. "Joseph and Mary were poor people," Mr. Bullock observed, and he proceeded to devise a scheme that would reveal "what would happen when a poor young couple dressed like Joseph and Mary tried to get a room nearly two thousand years after the birth of Christ." And so it came to pass in those days that Mr. Bullock, in beard and robe, walked out of the cold and darkness of Akron into the lobby of the Downtown Holiday Inn, accompanied by a young woman and a donkey. "I need a room for the night," he told the manager. "My wife is heavy with child." He then filled out the registration form, identifying himself as Joseph of Nazareth, travelling with his wife from Judea. Then he waited. The night manager, Mr. Robert Nagel, affably observed that they had come a long way and handed over a key to Room 101.

We picture Mr. Bullock with the key in his hand, his rented donkey lurking behind him, and his faith in human nature crumbling to the ground. To crown his discomfiture, Mr. Nagel offered the wayfarers a free meal. But, alas, in an era of affluence, satiety, like the indiscriminate rain, is apt to descend upon the just and unjust alike. "We weren't very hungry," Mr. Bullock said later, "so I asked him if we could have some drinks." Then he added, "And you know what? He sent them around." For his own part, Mr. Nagel was under no illusions about the financial standing of his new guests. "I knew they couldn't pay," he said. "I mean, a donkey is not a normal form of transportation." One would like to shake him by the hand. We thank Mr. Nagel for adding immeasurably to the merriment of our Christmas, and for his exhibition of that unpredictable, shrewd, and sometimes highly inconvenient human generosity that makes sweeping moral judgments so risky—even for the most earnest of moralists—and makes life so richly interesting for the rest of us.

— *The New Yorker*

Notice that although the narrative within the essay is organized chronologically, it is framed—at the beginning by some background information, and at the end by the writer's response to the incident, his reason for sharing it. Notice also that the writer interrupts the narrative briefly at the beginning of the second paragraph to speculate how Mr. Bullock looked and, more important, how he felt. Although the writer makes the point unobtrusively, it is clear that he was not an eyewitness to the story or an actor in it, but pieced it together from two interviews with the participants and perhaps from some additional research. Finally, notice that if you skim the essay you can easily spot the narrative portion by observing the appearance of verbs in the past tense ("walked," "told," "filled out," "waited," "observed," "handed") and by the frequency of the word "then." Narratives, however they are organized, are almost always told in the past tense; and good storytellers help us to follow the succession of events, the passage of time, by using such transitional words as *first, then, next, at last,* and *finally.*

Finally, we reprint a letter to the editor in which a college student, an assault victim, tells her experience. You may observe here too that the organization is for the most part chronological, made clear by transitions, and framed by the writer's analysis of her experience and of her reasons for revealing it. As readers, we may or may not notice these points; gripped by the story being told, we are largely unaware of the techniques of successful writers. As students of writing, however, we study these techniques.

To the Editor:
I write this letter out of concern for women of the college community. I am one of the two students who were assaulted during the winter recess. I do not feel any shame or embarrassment over what happened. Instead, I want to share some of my experience because in doing so I may help other women to think about rape and rape prevention.
First I think it is important for the community to understand

what happened to me. At my request, during the vacation a well-intentioned employee let me into my residence hall to collect some things from my room. It was after dark. I was alone in my room when a man appeared at the door with a stocking over his head and a knife in his hand. He said he was going to rape me. I had no intention of submitting, and I struggled with him for about five minutes. One of the reasons why I chose not to submit but to resist was that as a virgin I did not want my first sexual experience to be the horror of rape. While struggling I tried to get him to talk to me, saying such things as "Why do you want to rape me? Don't you understand I want no part of this? I am a woman, not an object. In God's name, please don't rape me." He finally over-powered me and attempted to rape me, but stopped when he realized I had a tampax in. Then at knife point he asked me a number of questions. He ended by threatening that if I reported and identified him he would kill me. As he was leaving he made me lie on my bed and count to five hundred, which I started to do. Then as I reached one hundred he returned and told me to start over. Thus it was good I did not get up right after he left.

It is impossible to say what should be done in all instances of assault. Each incident is different and requires a different response. I think what helped me most was my ability to remain calm, assess the situation, and then act firmly. I did struggle, I did talk, but I also did act in such a way as to ensure my own safety at knife point.

I believe there are some reasons why I was able to cope with the situation. One is that I had talked with other women about rape and self-defense. As a result I was more aware of the possibility of rape and had thought some about what I might do if confronted with an attacker. Also my active involvement in the women's movement has helped me develop confidence in myself, especially in my strength, both emotional and physical. I believe such confidence helped me not to panic. Another reason why I was able to cope was that I prayed.

I think it is important also to share with you the aftermath of the attack. The first thing I did after leaving my room was to report the incident to security and to the campus police. I did not hesitate to report the attack since I realized that reporting it was vital to protect the safety of the college community. The police were efficient and helpful in taking the report and starting search procedures. (The police also told me they did not think I was in further danger, despite the threats on my life. There seemed to be little reason for him to come back.) Also, two female members of the student services staff stayed with me most of the evening. Their presence and support were very helpful to me, especially while I talked to the police. Since the incident, I have also found support from professional staff and from friends. The residence office, the medical and psychiatric staff, the dean's office, and the chaplaincy staff have all been helpful. All have protected my confidentiality.

At first I did not realize that I would want or need to seek out people's help, but now I am glad I did. The rape experience goes beyond the assault itself. I have come to understand the importance of dealing with the complex emotions that follow. Also I now know that there is no reason for women to feel ashamed, embarrassed, or scared about seeking help.

I hope you now have a greater concern for your own safety after reading about what happened to me. I think this is the most important point of my writing. It never occurred to me that entering an unoccupied residence hall was dangerous. We all have been too accustomed to doing things on and off this campus without considering our own safety or vulnerability to attacks. But we ourselves are our own best security, so please protect yourselves and each other.

I am aware I will be working through this experience for a long time to come. I am thankful that there are people in this community to help me do that. I in turn want to be helpful in any way I can. So I invite women who are genuinely concerned about rape and assault to join me in sharing experiences and thoughts next Tuesday, February 18 at 7 P.M. in the Women's Center.

Name withheld upon request.

EXERCISES

1. In one or two paragraphs tell a story that illustrates an abstraction, such as courage, endurance, a misunderstanding, a putdown, pride, the generation gap, embarrassment, loneliness. For an example, see "Conceit" (page 538) and the brief discussion following it.
2. In 750–1000 words survey your development as a writer and explain your current attitude toward writing. Focus your essay on one narrative or on two contrasting narratives to exemplify

what you have learned and how you learned it. Whether your thesis is stated or implied, be sure that your essay makes a clear point. Your point might be, for example, that you learned more about writing from working on your school newspaper or from studying geometry than from most of your English classes, or that the different approaches of two teachers reinforced each other, or left you hopelessly confused about writing.

3. For an essay on any topic you choose, write an opening paragraph that includes an anecdote. Don't write the essay, but indicate from the anecdote and, if you wish, an additional sentence or two, the topic of your essay.

4. In 500–1000 words narrate an experience in such a way that you communicate not only the experience but the significance of it. For example, you might tell of an interview for a job which gave you some awareness of the attitude of people with jobs toward those without jobs. Or you might narrate an experience at school that seems to you to illuminate the virtues or defects or assumptions of the school. A variation: John Keats in a letter says, "Nothing ever becomes real till it is experienced— Even a proverb is no proverb to you till your life has illustrated it." Recount an experience that has made you feel the truth of a proverb.

5. Take the best movie or narrative television program that you have seen recently, and in about 100–150 words narrate the plot from the point of view of one of the main characters. Then, in another 100–150 words, narrate it from the point of view of another—preferably an opposing—character. (After all, the story of Little Red Riding Hood, told from the point of view of the wolf, is quite different from the story told from the girl's point of view.)

NARRATION AT WORK

Shooting an Elephant
George Orwell

1   In Moulmein, in Lower Burma, I was hated by large numbers of people—the only time in my life that I have been important enough for this to happen to me. I was sub-divisional police officer of the town, and in an aimless, petty kind of way anti-European feeling was very bitter. No one had the guts to raise a riot, but if a European woman went through the bazaars alone somebody would probably spit betel juice over her dress. As a police officer I was an obvious target and was baited whenever it seemed safe to do so. When a nimble Burman tripped me up on the football field and the referee (another Burman) looked the other way, the crowd yelled with hideous laughter. This happened more than once. In the end the sneering yellow faces of young men that met me everywhere, the insults hooted after me when I was at a safe distance, got badly on my nerves. The young Buddhist priests were the worst of all. There were several thousands of them in the town and none of them seemed to have anything to do except stand on street corners and jeer at Europeans.

2   All this was perplexing and upsetting. For at that time I had already made up my mind that imperialism was an evil thing and the sooner I chucked up my job and got out of it the better. Theoretically—and secretly, of course—I was all for the Burmese and all against their oppressors, the British. As for the job I was doing, I hated it more bitterly than I can perhaps make clear. In a job like that you see the dirty work of Empire at close quarters. The wretched prisoners huddling in the stinking cages of the lockups, the grey, cowed faces of the long-term convicts, the scarred buttocks of the men who had been flogged with bamboos—all these oppressed me with an intolerable sense of guilt. But I could get nothing into perspective. I was young and ill-educated and I had had to think out my problems in the utter silence that is imposed on every Englishman in the East. I did not even know that the British Empire is dying, still less did I know that it is a great deal better than the younger empires that are going to supplant it. All I knew was that

I was stuck between my hatred of the empire I served and my rage against the evil-spirited little beasts who tried to make my job impossible. With one part of my mind I thought of the British Raj as an unbreakable tyranny, as something clamped down, in *saecula saeculorum*,[1] upon the will of prostrate peoples; with another part I thought that the greatest joy in the world would be to drive a bayonet into a Buddhist priest's guts. Feelings like these are the normal by-products of imperialism; ask any Anglo-Indian official, if you can catch him off duty.

3   One day something happened which in a roundabout way was enlightening. It was a tiny incident in itself, but it gave me a better glimpse than I had had before of the real nature of imperialism— the real motives for which despotic governments act. Early one morning the sub-inspector at a police station at the other end of the town rang me up on the 'phone and said that an elephant was ravaging the bazaar. Would I please come and do something about it? I did not know what I could do, but I wanted to see what was happening and I got on to a pony and started out. I took my rifle, an old .44 Winchester and much too small to kill an elephant, but I thought the noise might be useful *in terrorem*.[2] Various Burmans stopped me on the way and told me about the elephant's doings. It was not, of course, a wild elephant, but a tame one which had gone "must." It had been chained up, as tame elephants always are when their attack of "must" is due, but on the previous night it had broken its chain and escaped. Its mahout, the only person who could manage it when it was in that state, had set out in pursuit, but had taken the wrong direction and was now twelve hours' journey away, and in the morning the elephant had suddenly reappeared in the town. The Burmese population had no weapons and were quite helpless against it. It had already destroyed somebody's bamboo hut, killed a cow and raided some fruit-stalls and devoured the stock; also it had met the municipal rubbish van and, when the driver jumped out and took to his heels, had turned the van over and inflicted violences upon it.

4   The Burmese sub-inspector and some Indian constables were waiting for me in the quarter where the elephant had been seen. It was a very poor quarter, a labyrinth of squalid bamboo huts, thatched with palmleaf, winding all over a steep hillside. I remember that it was a cloudy, stuffy morning at the beginning of the rains. We

[1] For world without end.

[2] As a warning.

began questioning the people as to where the elephant had gone and, as usual, failed to get any definite information. That is invariably the case in the East; a story always sounds clear enough at a distance, but the nearer you get to the scene of events the vaguer it becomes. Some of the people said that the elephant had gone in one direction, some said that he had gone in another, some professed not even to have heard of any elephant. I had almost made up my mind that the whole story was a pack of lies, when we heard yells a little distance away. There was a loud, scandalized cry of "Go away, child! Go away this instant!" and an old woman with a switch in her hand came round the corner of a hut, violently shooing away a crowd of naked children. Some more women followed, clicking their tongues and exclaiming; evidently there was something that the children ought not to have seen. I rounded the hut and saw a man's dead body sprawling in the mud. He was an Indian, a black Dravidian coolie, almost naked, and he could not have been dead many minutes. The people said that the elephant had come suddenly upon him round the corner of the hut, caught him with its trunk, put its foot on his back and ground him into the earth. This was the rainy season and the ground was soft, and his face had scored a trench a foot deep and a couple of yards long. He was lying on his belly with arms crucified and head sharply twisted to one side. His face was coated with mud, the eyes wide open, the teeth bared and grinning with an expression of unendurable agony. (Never tell me, by the way, that the dead look peaceful. Most of the corpses I have seen look devilish.) The friction of the great beast's foot had stripped the skin from his back as neatly as one skins a rabbit. As soon as I saw the dead man I sent an orderly to a friend's house nearby to borrow an elephant rifle. I had already sent back the pony, not wanting it to go mad with fright and throw me if it smelt the elephant.

5   The orderly came back in a few minutes with a rifle and five cartridges, and meanwhile some Burmans had arrived and told us that the elephant was in the paddy fields below, only a few hundred yards away. As I started forward practically the whole population of the quarter flocked out of the houses and followed me. They had seen the rifle and were all shouting excitedly that I was going to shoot the elephant. They had not shown much interest in the elephant when he was merely ravaging their homes, but it was different now that he was going to be shot. It was a bit of fun to them, as it would be to an English crowd; besides they wanted the meat. It made me vaguely uneasy. I had no intention of shooting the elephant—I had merely sent for the rifle to defend myself if neces-

sary—and it is always unnerving to have a crowd following you. I marched down the hill, looking and feeling a fool, with the rifle over my shoulder and an ever-growing army of people jostling at my heels. At the bottom, when you got away from the huts, there was a metalled road and beyond that a miry waste of paddy fields a thousand yards across, not yet ploughed but soggy from the first rains and dotted with coarse grass. The elephant was standing eight yards from the road, his left side towards us. He took not the slightest notice of the crowd's approach. He was tearing up bunches of grass, beating them against his knees to clean them and stuffing them into his mouth.

6   I had halted on the road. As soon as I saw the elephant I knew with perfect certainty that I ought not to shoot him. It is a serious matter to shoot a working elephant—it is comparable to destroying a huge and costly piece of machinery—and obviously one ought not to do it if it can possibly be avoided. And at that distance, peace-fully eating, the elephant looked no more dangerous than a cow. I thought then and I think now that his attack of "must" was already passing off; in which case he would merely wander harmlessly about until the mahout came back and caught him. Moreover, I did not in the least want to shoot him. I decided that I would watch him for a little while to make sure that he did not turn savage again, and then go home.

7   But at that moment I glanced round at the crowd that had followed me. It was an immense crowd, two thousand at the least and growing every minute. It blocked the road for a long distance on either side. I looked at the sea of yellow faces above the garish clothes—faces all happy and excited over this bit of fun, all certain that the elephant was going to be shot. They were watching me as they would watch a conjurer about to perform a trick. They did not like me, but with the magical rifle in my hands I was momen-tarily worth watching. And suddenly I realized that I should have to shoot the elephant after all. The people expected it of me and I had got to do it; I could feel their two thousand wills pressing me forward, irresistibly. And it was at this moment, as I stood there with the rifle in my hands, that I first grasped the hollowness, the futility of the white man's dominion in the East. Here was I, the white man with his gun, standing in front of the unarmed native crowd—seemingly the leading actor of the piece; but in reality I was only an absurd puppet pushed to and fro by the will of those yellow faces behind. I perceived in this moment that when the white man turns tyrant it is his own freedom that he destroys. He be-comes a sort of hollow, posing dummy, the conventionalized figure

of a sahib. For it is the condition of his rule that he shall spend his life in trying to impress the "natives," and so in every crisis he has got to do what the "natives" expect of him. He wears a mask, and his face grows to fit it. I had got to shoot the elephant. I had committed myself to doing it when I sent for the rifle. A sahib has got to act like a sahib; he has got to appear resolute, to know his own mind and do definite things. To come all that way, rifle in hand, with two thousand people marching at my heels, and then to trail feebly away, having done nothing—no, that was impossible. The crowd would laugh at me. And my whole life, every white man's life in the East, was one long struggle not to be laughed at.

8   But I did not want to shoot the elephant. I watched him beating his bunch of grass against his knees, with that preoccupied grandmotherly air that elephants have. It seemed to me that it would be murder to shoot him. At that age I was not squeamish about killing animals, but I had never shot an elephant and never wanted to. (Somehow it always seems worse to kill a *large* animal.) Besides, there was the beast's owner to be considered. Alive, the elephant was worth at least a hundred pounds; dead, he would only be worth the value of his tusks, five pounds, possibly. But I had got to act quickly. I turned to some experienced-looking Burmans who had been there when we arrived, and asked them how the elephant had been behaving. They all said the same thing: he took no notice of you if you left him alone, but he might charge if you went too close to him.

9   It was perfectly clear to me what I ought to do. I ought to walk up to within, say, twenty-five yards of the elephant and test his behavior. If he charged, I could shoot; if he took no notice of me, it would be safe to leave him until the mahout came back. But also I knew that I was going to do no such thing. I was a poor shot with a rifle and the ground was soft mud into which one would sink at every step. If the elephant charged and I missed him, I should have about as much chance as a toad under a steam-roller. But even then I was not thinking particularly of my own skin, only of the watchful yellow faces behind. For at that moment, with the crowd watching me, I was not afraid in the ordinary sense, as I would have been if I had been alone. A white man mustn't be frightened in front of "natives"; and so, in general, he isn't frightened. The sole thought in my mind was that if anything went wrong those two thousand Burmans would see me pursued, caught, trampled on and reduced to a grinning corpse like that Indian up the hill. And if that happened it was quite probable that some of them would laugh. That would never do. There was only one alternative. I shoved

the cartridges into the magazine and lay down on the road to get a better aim.

10   The crowd grew very still, and a deep, low, happy sigh, as of people who see the theatre curtain go up at last, breathed from innumerable throats. They were going to have their bit of fun after all. The rifle was a beautiful German thing with cross-hair sights. I did not then know that in shooting an elephant one would shoot to cut an imaginary bar running from ear-hole to ear-hole. I ought, therefore, as the elephant was sideways on, to have aimed straight at his ear-hole; actually I aimed several inches in front of this, thinking the brain would be further forward.

11   When I pulled the trigger I did not hear the bang or feel the kick—one never does when a shot goes home—but I heard the devilish roar of glee that went up from the crowd. In that instant, in too short a time, one would have thought, even for the bullet to get there, a mysterious, terrible change had come over the elephant. He neither stirred nor fell, but every line of his body had altered. He looked suddenly stricken, shrunken, immensely old, as though the frightful impact of the bullet had paralysed him without knocking him down. At last, after what seemed a long time—it might have been five seconds, I dare say—he sagged flabbily to his knees. His mouth slobbered. An enormous senility seemed to have settled upon him. One could have imagined him thousands of years old. I fired again into the same spot. At the second shot he did not collapse but climbed with desperate slowness to his feet and stood weakly upright, with legs sagging and head drooping. I fired a third time. That was the shot that did for him. You could see the agony of it jolt his whole body and knock the last remnant of strength from his legs. But in falling he seemed for a moment to rise, for as his hind legs collapsed beneath him he seemed to tower upward like a huge rock toppling, his trunk reaching skywards like a tree. He trumpeted, for the first and only time. And then down he came, his belly towards me, with a crash that seemed to shake the ground even where I lay.

12   I got up. The Burmans were already racing past me across the mud. It was obvious that the elephant would never rise again, but he was not dead. He was breathing very rhythmically with long rattling gasps, his great mound of a side painfully rising and falling. His mouth was wide open. I could see far down into caverns of pale pink throat. I waited a long time for him to die, but his breathing did not weaken. Finally I fired my two remaining shots into the spot where I thought his heart must be. The thick blood welled out of him like red velvet, but still he did not die. His body did not

even jerk when the shots hit him, the tortured breathing continued without a pause. He was dying, very slowly and in great agony, but in some world remote from me where not even a bullet could damage him further. I felt I had got to put an end to that dreadful noise. It seemed dreadful to see the great beast lying there, powerless to move and yet powerless to die, and not even to be able to finish him. I sent back for my small rifle and poured shot after shot into his heart and down his throat. They seemed to make no impression. The tortured gasps continued as steadily as the ticking of a clock.

13   In the end I could not stand it any longer and went away. I heard later that it took him half an hour to die. Burmans were bringing dahs and baskets even before I left, and I was told they had stripped his body almost to the bones by the afternoon.

14   Afterwards, of course, there were endless discussions about the shooting of the elephant. The owner was furious, but he was only an Indian and could do nothing. Besides, legally I had done the right thing, for a mad elephant has to be killed, like a mad dog, if its owner fails to control it. Among the Europeans opinion was divided. The older men said I was right, the younger men said it was a damn shame to shoot an elephant for killing a coolie, because an elephant was worth more than any damn Coringhee coolie. And afterwards I was very glad that the coolie had been killed; it put me legally in the right and it gave me a sufficient pretext for shooting the elephant. I often wondered whether any of the others grasped that I had done it solely to avoid looking a fool.

Questions

1. How does Orwell characterize himself at the time of the events he describes? What evidence in the essay suggests that he wrote it some years later?
2. Orwell says the incident was "enlightening." What does he mean? Picking up this clue, state in a sentence or two the thesis or main point of the essay.
3. Compare Orwell's description of the dead coolie (in the fourth paragraph) with his description of the elephant's death (in the eleventh and twelfth paragraphs). Why does Orwell devote more space to the death of the elephant?
4. How would you describe the tone of the last paragraph, particularly of the last two sentences? Do you find the paragraph an effective conclusion to the essay? Explain.

Just Walk On By: A Black Man Ponders His Power to Alter Public Space

Brent Staples

1   My first victim was a woman—white, well dressed, probably in her early twenties. I came upon her late one evening on a deserted street in Hyde Park, a relatively affluent neighborhood in an otherwise mean, impoverished section of Chicago. As I swung onto the avenue behind her, there seemed to be a discreet, uninflammatory distance between us. Not so. She cast back a worried glance. To her, the youngish black man—a broad six feet two inches with a beard and billowing hair, both hands shoved into the pockets of a bulky military jacket—seemed menacingly close. After a few more quick glimpses, she picked up her pace and was soon running in earnest. Within seconds she disappeared into a cross street.

2   That was more than a decade ago. I was 22 years old, a graduate student newly arrived at the University of Chicago. It was in the echo of that terrified woman's footfalls that I first began to know the unwieldy inheritance I'd come into—the ability to alter public space in ugly ways. It was clear that she thought herself the quarry of a mugger, a rapist, or worse. Suffering a bout of insomnia, however, I was stalking sleep, not defenseless wayfarers. As a softy who is scarcely able to take a knife to a raw chicken—let alone hold it to a person's throat—I was surprised, embarrassed, and dismayed all at once. Her flight made me feel like an accomplice in tyranny. It also made it clear that I was indistinguishable from the muggers who occasionally seeped into the area from the surrounding ghetto. That first encounter, and those that followed, signified that a vast, unnerving gulf lay between nighttime pedestrians—particularly women—and me. And I soon gathered that being perceived as dangerous is a hazard in itself. I only needed to turn a corner into a dicey situation, or crowd some frightened, armed person in a foyer somewhere, or make an errant move after being pulled over by a policeman. Where fear and weapons meet—and they often do in urban America—there is always the possibility of death.

3   In that first year, my first away from my hometown, I was to become thoroughly familiar with the language of fear. At dark, shadowy intersections in Chicago, I could cross in front of a car

stopped at a traffic light and elicit the *thunk, thunk, thunk, thunk* of the driver—black, white, male, or female—hammering down the door locks. On less traveled streets after dark, I grew accustomed to but never comfortable with people who crossed to the other side of the street rather than pass me. Then there were the standard unpleasantries with police, doormen, bouncers, cab drivers, and others whose business it is to screen out troublesome individuals *before* there is any nastiness.

4   I moved to New York nearly two years ago and I have remained an avid night walker. In central Manhattan, the near-constant crowd cover minimizes tense one-on-one street encounters. Elsewhere—visiting friends in SoHo, where sidewalks are narrow and tightly spaced buildings shut out the sky—things can get very taut indeed.

5   Black men have a firm place in New York mugging literature. Norman Podhoretz in his famed (or infamous) 1963 essay, "My Negro Problem—And Ours," recalls growing up in terror of black males; they "were tougher than we were, more ruthless," he writes—and as an adult on the Upper West Side of Manhattan, he continues, he cannot constrain his nervousness when he meets black men on certain streets. Similarly, a decade later, the essayist and novelist Edward Hoagland extols a New York where once "Negro bitterness bore down mainly on other Negroes." Where some see mere panhandlers, Hoagland sees "a mugger who is clearly screwing up his nerve to do more than just *ask* for money." But Hoagland has "the New Yorker's quick-hunch posture for broken-field maneuvering," and the bad guy swerves away.

6   I often witness that "hunch posture," from women after dark on the warrenlike streets of Brooklyn where I live. They seem to set their faces on neutral and, with their purse straps strung across their chests bandolier style, they forge ahead as though bracing themselves against being tackled. I understand, of course, that the danger they perceive is not a hallucination. Women are particularly vulnerable to street violence, and young black males are drastically overrepresented among the perpetrators of that violence. Yet these truths are no solace against the kind of alienation that comes of being ever the suspect, against being set apart, a fearsome entity with whom pedestrians avoid making eye contact.

7   It is not altogether clear to me how I reached the ripe old age of 22 without being conscious of the lethality nighttime pedestrians attributed to me. Perhaps it was because in Chester, Pennsylvania, the small, angry industrial town where I came of age in the 1960s, I was scarcely noticeable against a backdrop of gang warfare, street knifings, and murders. I grew up one of the good boys, had perhaps

a half-dozen fist fights. In retrospect, my shyness of combat has clear sources.

8   Many things go into the making of a young thug. One of those things is the consummation of the male romance with the power to intimidate. An infant discovers that random flailings send the baby bottle flying out of the crib and crashing to the floor. Delighted, the joyful babe repeats those motions again and again, seeking to duplicate the feat. Just so, I recall the points at which some of my boyhood friends were finally seduced by the perception of themselves as tough guys. When a mark cowered and surrendered his money without resistance, myth and reality merged—and paid off. It is, after all, only manly to embrace the power to frighten and intimidate. We, as men, are not supposed to give an inch of our lane on the highway; we are to seize the fighter's edge in work and in play and even in love; we are to be valiant in the face of hostile forces.

9   Unfortunately, poor and powerless young men seem to take all this nonsense literally. As a boy, I saw countless tough guys locked away; I have since buried several, too. They were babies, really—a teenage cousin, a brother of 22, a childhood friend in his mid-twenties—all gone down in episodes of bravado played out in the streets. I came to doubt the virtues of intimidation early on. I chose, perhaps even unconsciously, to remain a shadow—timid, but a survivor.

10   The fearsomeness mistakenly attributed to me in public places often has a perilous flavor. The most frightening of these confusions occurred in the late 1970s and early 1980s when I worked as a journalist in Chicago. One day, rushing into the office of a magazine I was writing for with a deadline story in hand, I was mistaken for a burglar. The office manager called security and, with an ad hoc posse, pursued me through the labyrinthine halls, nearly to my editor's door. I had no way of proving who I was. I could only move briskly toward the company of someone who knew me.

11   Another time I was on assignment for a local paper and killing time before an interview. I entered a jewelry store on the city's affluent Near North Side. The proprietor excused herself and returned with an enormous red Doberman pinscher straining at the end of a leash. She stood, the dog extended toward me, silent to my questions, her eyes bulging nearly out of her head. I took a cursory look around, nodded, and bade her good night. Relatively speaking, however, I never fared as badly as another black male journalist. He went to nearby Waukegan, Illinois, a couple of summers ago to work on a story about a murderer who was born there. Mistaking the reporter for the killer, police hauled him from his car

at gunpoint and but for his press credentials would probably have tried to book him. Such episodes are not uncommon. Black men trade tales like this all the time.

12   In "My Negro Problem—And Ours," Podhoretz writes that the hatred he feels for blacks makes itself known to him through a variety of avenues—one being his discomfort with that "special brand of paranoid touchiness" to which he says blacks are prone. No doubt he is speaking here of black men. In time, I learned to smother the rage I felt at so often being taken for a criminal. Not to do so would surely have led to madness—via that special "paranoid touchiness" that so annoyed Podhoretz at the time he wrote the essay.

13   I began to take precautions to make myself less threatening. I move about with care, particularly late in the evening. I give a wide berth to nervous people on subway platforms during the wee hours, particularly when I have exchanged business clothes for jeans. If I happen to be entering a building behind some people who appear skittish, I may walk by, letting them clear the lobby before I return, so as not to seem to be following them. I have been calm and extremely congenial on those rare occasions when I've been pulled over by the police.

14   And on late-evening constitutionals along streets less traveled by, I employ what has proved to be an excellent tension-reducing measure: I whistle melodies from Beethoven and Vivaldi and the more popular classical composers. Even steely New Yorkers hunching toward nighttime destinations seem to relax, and occasionally they even join in the tune. Virtually everybody seems to sense that a mugger wouldn't be warbling bright, sunny selections from Vivaldi's *Four Seasons*. It is my equivalent of the cowbell that hikers wear when they know they are in bear country.

Questions

1. What did Staples learn, from the first experience that he narrates, about other people? What did he learn about himself?
2. In the third paragraph Staples gives a second example (the response of people in cars) of the effect that he has on others. Why do you suppose he bothered to give a second example, since it illustrates a point already made by the first example?
3. In the third paragraph from the end, Staples quotes Norman Podhoretz's remark about the "special brand of paranoid touchiness" that Podhoretz finds in many blacks. What would you say is Staples's view of Podhoretz's idea?

4. In his next-to-last paragraph Staples discusses the "precautions" he takes to make himself "less threatening." Are these precautions reasonable? Or do they reveal that he is, in Podhoretz's word, "paranoid"? Do you think he ought to be less concerned with taking precautions? Why, or why not?

5. Evaluate Staples's final paragraph as a way of ending the essay.

6. The success of a narrative as a piece of writing often depends on the reader's willingness to identify with the narrator. From an analysis of "Just Walk On By," what explanation can you give for your willingness (or unwillingness) to identify yourself with Staples?

---

*G*raduation

Maya Angelou

1   The children in Stamps trembled visibly with anticipation. Some adults were excited too, but to be certain the whole young population had come down with graduation epidemic. Large classes were graduating from both the grammar school and the high school. Even those who were years removed from their own day of glorious release were anxious to help with preparations as a kind of dry run. The junior students who were moving into the vacating classes' chairs were tradition-bound to show their talents for leadership and management. They strutted through the school and around the campus exerting pressure on the lower grades. Their authority was so new that occasionally if they pressed a little too hard it had to be overlooked. After all, next term was coming, and it never hurt a sixth grader to have a play sister in the eighth grade, or a tenth-year student to be able to call a twelfth grader Bubba. So all was endured in a spirit of shared understanding. But the graduating classes themselves were the nobility. Like travelers with exotic destinations on their minds, the graduates were remarkably forgetful. They came to school without their books, or tablets or even pencils. Volunteers fell over themselves to secure replacements for the missing equipment. When accepted, the willing workers might or might not be thanked, and it was of no importance to the pregraduation rites. Even teachers were respectful of the now quiet and aging seniors, and tended to speak to them, if not as equals, as beings only slightly

lower than themselves. After tests were returned and grades given, the student body, which acted like an extended family, knew who did well, who excelled, and what piteous ones had failed.

2   Unlike the white high school, Lafayette County Training School distinguished itself by having neither lawn, nor hedges, nor tennis court, nor climbing ivy. Its two buildings (main classrooms, the grade school and home economics) were set on a dirt hill with no fence to limit either its boundaries or those of bordering farms. There was a large expanse to the left of the school which was used alternately as a baseball diamond or a basketball court. Rusty hoops on the swaying poles represented the permanent recreational equipment, although bats and balls could be borrowed from the P. E. teacher if the borrower was qualified and if the diamond wasn't occupied.

3   Over this rocky area relieved by a few shady tall persimmon trees the graduating class walked. The girls often held hands and no longer bothered to speak to the lower students. There was a sadness about them, as if this old woman was not their home and they were bound for higher ground. The boys, on the other hand, had become more friendly, more outgoing. A decided change from the closed attitude they projected while studying for finals. Now they seemed not ready to give up the old school, the familiar paths and classrooms. Only a small percentage would be continuing on to college—one of the South's A & M (agricultural and mechanical) schools, which trained Negro youths to be carpenters, farmers, handymen, masons, maids, cooks and baby nurses. Their future rode heavily on their shoulders, and blinded them to the collective joy that had pervaded the lives of the boys and girls in the grammar school graduating class.

4   Parents who could afford it had ordered new shoes and ready-made clothes for themselves from Sears and Roebuck or Montgomery Ward. They also engaged the best seamstresses to make the floating graduating dresses and to cut down secondhand pants which would be pressed to a military slickness for the important event.

5   Oh, it was important, all right. Whitefolks would attend the ceremony, and two or three would speak of God and home, and the Southern way of life, and Mrs. Parsons, the principal's wife, would play the graduation march while the lower-grade graduates paraded down the aisles and took their seats below the platform. The high school seniors would wait in empty classrooms to make their dramatic entrance.

6   In the Store I was the person of the moment. The birthday girl. The center. Bailey had graduated the year before, although to do

so he had had to forfeit all pleasures to make up for his time lost in Baton Rouge.

7   My class was wearing butter-yellow piqué dresses, and Momma launched out on mine. She smocked the yoke into tiny crisscrossing puckers, then shirred the rest of the bodice. Her dark fingers ducked in and out of the lemony cloth as she embroidered raised daisies around the hem. Before she considered herself finished she had added a crocheted cuff on the puff sleeves, and a pointy crocheted collar.

8   I was going to be lovely. A walking model of all the various styles of fine hand sewing and it didn't worry me that I was only twelve years old and merely graduating from the eighth grade. Besides, many teachers in Arkansas Negro schools had only that diploma and were licensed to impart wisdom.

9   The days had become longer and more noticeable. The faded beige of former times had been replaced with strong and sure colors. I began to see my classmates' clothes, their skin tones, and the dust that waved off pussy willows. Clouds that lazed across the sky were objects of great concern to me. Their shiftier shapes might have held a message that in my new happiness and with a little bit of time I'd soon decipher. During that period I looked at the arch of heaven so religiously my neck kept a steady ache. I had taken to smiling more often, and my jaws hurt from the unaccustomed activity. Between the two physical sore spots, I suppose I could have been uncomfortable, but that was not the case. As a member of the winning team (the graduating class of 1940) I had outdistanced unpleasant sensations by miles. I was headed for the freedom of open fields.

10   Youth and social approval allied themselves with me and we trammeled memories of slights and insults. The wind of our swift passage remodeled my features. Lost tears were pounded to mud and then to dust. Years of withdrawal were brushed aside and left behind, as hanging ropes of parasitic moss.

11   My work alone had awarded me a top place and I was going to be one of the first called in the graduating ceremonies. On the classroom blackboard, as well as on the bulletin board in the auditorium, there were blue stars and white stars and red stars. No absences, no tardinesses, and my academic work was among the best of the year. I could say the preamble to the Constitution even faster than Bailey could say it. We timed ourselves often: "WethepeopleoftheUnitedStatesinordertoformamoreperfectunion . . ." I had memorized the Presidents of the United States from Washington to Roosevelt in chronological as well as alphabetical order.

12   My hair pleased me too. Gradually the black mass had length-
ened and thickened, so that it kept at last to its braided pattern,
and I didn't have to yank my scalp off when I tried to comb it.

13   Louise and I had rehearsed the exercises until we tired out ourselves. Henry Reed was class valedictorian. He was a small, very
black boy with hooded eyes, a long, broad nose and an oddly shaped
head. I had admired him for years because each term he and I vied
for the best grades in our class. Most often he bested me, but instead of being disappointed I was pleased that we shared top places
between us. Like many Southern black children, he lived with his
grandmother, who was as strict as Momma and as kind as she
knew how to be. He was courteous, respectful and soft-spoken to
elders, but on the playground he chose to play the roughest games.
I admired him. Anyone, I reckoned, sufficiently afraid or sufficiently
dull could be polite. But to be able to operate at a top level with
both adults and children was admirable.

14   His valedictory speech was entitled "To Be or Not to Be." The
rigid tenth-grade teacher had helped him write it. He'd been working on the dramatic stresses for months.

15   The weeks until graduation were filled with heady activities. A
group of small children were to be presented in a play about buttercups and daisies and bunny rabbits. They could be heard
throughout the building practicing their hops and their little songs
that sounded like silver bells. The older girls (non-graduates, of
course) were assigned the task of making refreshments for the night's
festivities. A tangy scent of ginger, cinnamon, nutmeg and choco-
late wafted around the home economics building as the budding
cooks made samples for themselves and their teachers.

16   In every corner of the workshop, axes and saws split fresh tim-
ber as the woodshop boys made sets and stage scenery. Only the
graduates were left out of the general bustle. We were free to sit in
the library at the back of the building or look in quite detachedly,
naturally, on the measures being taken for our event.

17   Even the minister preached on graduation the Sunday before.
His subject was, "Let your light so shine that men will see your
good works and praise your Father, Who is in Heaven." Although
the sermon was purported to be addressed to us, he used the occasion to speak to backsliders, gamblers and general ne'er-do-wells.
But since he had called our names at the beginning of the service
we were mollified.

18   Among Negroes the tradition was to give presents to children
going only from one grade to another. How much more important
this was when the person was graduating at the top of the class.

Uncle Willie and Momma had sent away for a Mickey Mouse watch like Bailey's. Louise gave me four embroidered handkerchiefs. (I gave her three crocheted doilies.) Mrs. Sneed, the minister's wife, made me an underskirt to wear for graduation, and nearly every customer gave me a nickel or maybe even a dime with the instruction "Keep on moving to higher ground," or some such encouragement.

19   Amazingly the great day finally dawned and I was out of bed before I knew it. I threw open the back door to see it more clearly, but Momma said, "Sister, come away from that door and put your robe on."

20   I hoped the memory of that morning would never leave me. Sunlight was itself still young, and the day had none of the insistence maturity would bring it in a few hours. In my robe and barefoot in the backyard, under cover of going to see about my new beans, I gave myself up to the gentle warmth and thanked God that no matter what evil I had done in my life He had allowed me to live to see this day. Somewhere in my fatalism I had expected to die, accidentally, and never have the chance to walk up the stairs in the auditorium and gracefully receive my hard-earned diploma. Out of God's merciful bosom I had won reprieve.

21   Bailey came out in his robe and gave me a box wrapped in Christmas paper. He said he had saved his money for months to pay for it. It felt like a box of chocolates, but I knew Bailey wouldn't save money to buy candy when we had all we could want under our noses.

22   He was as proud of the gift as I. It was a soft-leather-bound copy of a collection of poems by Edgar Allan Poe, or, as Bailey and I called him, "Eap." I turned to "Annabel Lee" and we walked up and down the garden rows, the cool dirt between our toes, reciting the beautifully sad lines.

23   Momma made a Sunday breakfast although it was only Friday. After we finished the blessing, I opened my eyes to find the watch on my plate. It was a dream of a day. Everything went smoothly and to my credit I didn't have to be reminded or scolded for anything. Near evening I was too jittery to attend to chores, so Bailey volunteered to do all before his bath.

24   Days before, we had made a sign for the Store, and as we turned out the lights Momma hung the cardboard over the doorknob. It read clearly: CLOSED. GRADUATION.

25   My dress fitted perfectly and everyone said that I looked like a sunbeam in it. On the hill, going toward the school, Bailey walked behind with Uncle Willie, who muttered, "Go on, Ju." He wanted

him to walk ahead with us because it embarrassed him to have to walk so slowly. Bailey said he'd let the ladies walk together, and the men would bring up the rear. We all laughed, nicely.

26   Little children dashed by out of the dark like fireflies. Their crepe-paper dresses and butterfly wings were not made for running and we heard more than one rip, dryly, and the regretful "uh uh" that followed.

27   The school blazed without gaiety. The windows seemed cold and unfriendly from the lower hill. A sense of ill-fated timing crept over me, and if Momma hadn't reached for my hand I would have drifted back to Bailey and Uncle Willie, and possibly beyond. She made a few slow jokes about my feet getting cold, and tugged me along to the now-strange building

28   Around the front steps, assurance came back. There were my fellow "greats," the graduating class. Hair brushed back, legs oiled, new dresses and pressed pleats, fresh pocket handkerchiefs and little handbags, all homesewn. Oh, we were up to snuff, all right. I joined my comrades and didn't even see my family go in to find seats in the crowded auditorium.

29   The school band struck up a march and all classes filed in as had been rehearsed. We stood in front of our seats, as assigned, and on a signal from the choir director, we sat. No sooner had this been accomplished than the band started to play the national anthem. We rose again and sang the song, after which we recited the pledge of allegiance. We remained standing for a brief minute before the choir director and the principal signaled to us, rather desperately I thought, to take our seats. The command was so unusual that our carefully rehearsed and smooth-running machine was thrown off. For a full minute we fumbled for our chairs and bumped into each other awkwardly. Habits change or solidify under pressure, so in our state of nervous tension we had been ready to follow our usual assembly pattern: the American national anthem, then the pledge of allegiance, then the song every Black person I knew called the Negro National Anthem. All done in the same key, with the same passion and most often standing on the same foot.

30   Finding my seat at last, I was overcome with a presentiment of worse things to come. Something unrehearsed, unplanned, was going to happen, and we were going to be made to look bad. I distinctly remember being explicit in the choice of pronoun. It was "we," the graduating class, the unit, that concerned me then.

31   The principal welcomed "parents and friends" and asked the Baptist minister to lead us in prayer. His invocation was brief and

punchy, and for a second I thought we were getting back on the high road to right action. When the principal came back to the dais, however, his voice had changed. Sounds always affected me profoundly and the principal's voice was one of my favorites. During assembly it melted and lowed weakly into the audience. It had not been in my plan to listen to him, but my curiosity was piqued and I straightened up to give him my attention.

32   He was talking about Booker T. Washington, our "late great leader," who said we can be as close as the fingers on the hand, etc. . . . Then he said a few vague things about friendship and the friendship of kindly people to those less fortunate than themselves. With that his voice nearly faded, thin, away. Like a river diminishing to a stream and then to a trickle. But he cleared his throat and said, "Our speaker tonight, who is also our friend, came from Texarkana to deliver the commencement address, but due to the irregularity of the train schedule, he's going to, as they say, 'speak and run.' " He said that we understood and wanted the man to know that we were most grateful for the time he was able to give us and then something about how we were willing always to adjust to another's program, and without more ado—"I give you Mr. Edward Donleavy."

33   Not one but two white men came through the door offstage. The shorter one walked to the speaker's platform, and the tall one moved over to the center seat and sat down. But that was our principal's seat, and already occupied. The dislodged gentleman bounced around for a long breath or two before the Baptist minister gave him his chair, then with more dignity than the situation deserved, the minister walked off the stage.

34   Donleavy looked at the audience once (on reflection, I'm sure that he wanted only to reassure himself that we were really there), adjusted his glasses and began to read from a sheaf of papers.

35   He was glad "to be here and to see the work going on just as it was in the other schools."

36   At the first "Amen" from the audience I willed the offender to immediate death by choking on the word. But Amens and Yes, sir's began to fall around the room like rain through a ragged umbrella.

37   He told us of the wonderful changes we children in Stamps had in store. The Central School (naturally, the white school was Central) had already been granted improvements that would be in use in the fall. A well-known artist was coming from Little Rock to teach art to them. They were going to have the newest microscopes and chemistry equipment for their laboratory. Mr. Donleavy didn't

leave us long in the dark over who made these improvements available to Central High. Nor were we to be ignored in the general betterment scheme he had in mind.

38   He said that he had pointed out to people at a very high level that one of the first-line football tacklers at Arkansas Agricultural and Mechanical College had graduated from good old Lafayette County Training School. Here fewer Amen's were heard. Those few that did break through lay dully in the air with the heaviness of habit.

39   He went on to praise us. He went on to say how he had bragged that "one of the best basketball players at Fisk sank his first ball right here at Lafayette County Training School."

40   The white kids were going to have a chance to become Galileos and Madame Curies and Edisons and Gauguins, and our boys (the girls weren't even in on it) would try to be Jesse Owenses and Joe Louises.

41   Owens and the Brown Bomber were great heroes in our world, but what school official in the white-goddom of Little Rock had the right to decide that those two men must be our only heroes? Who decided that for Henry Reed to become a scientist he had to work like George Washington Carver, as a bootblack, to buy a lousy microscope? Bailey was obviously always going to be too small to be an athlete, so which concrete angel glued to what county seat had decided that if my brother wanted to become a lawyer he had to first pay penance for his skin by picking cotton and hoeing corn and studying correspondence books at night for twenty years?

42   The man's dead words fell like bricks around the auditorium and too many settled in my belly. Constrained by hard-learned manners I couldn't look behind me, but to my left and right the proud graduating class of 1940 had dropped their heads. Every girl in my row had found something new to do with her handkerchief. Some folded the tiny squares into love knots, some into triangles, but most were wadding them, then pressing them flat on their yellow laps.

43   On the dais, the ancient tragedy was being replayed. Professor Parsons sat, a sculptor's reject, rigid. His large, heavy body seemed devoid of will or willingness, and his eyes said he was no longer with us. The other teachers examined the flag (which was draped stage right) or their notes, or the windows which opened on our now-famous playing diamond.

44   Graduation, the hush-hush magic time of frills and gifts and congratulations and diplomas, was finished for me before my name was called. The accomplishment was nothing. The meticulous maps,

drawn in three colors of ink, learning and spelling decasyllabic words, memorizing the whole of *The Rape of Lucrece*—it was for nothing. Donleavy had exposed us.

45   We were maids and farmers, handymen and washerwomen, and anything higher than we aspired to was farcical and presumptuous.

46   Then I wished that Gabriel Prosser and Nat Turner had killed all whitefolks in their beds and that Abraham Lincoln had been assassinated before the singing of the Emancipation Proclamation, and that Harriet Tubman had been killed by that blow on her head and Christopher Columbus had drowned in the *Santa María.*

47   It was awful to be Negro and have no control over my life. It was brutal to be young and already trained to sit quietly and listen to charges brought against my color with no chance of defense. We should all be dead. I thought I should like to see us all dead, one on top of the other. A pyramid of flesh with the whitefolks on the bottom, as the broad base, then the Indians and their silly tomahawks and tepees and wigwams and treaties, the Negroes with their mops and recipes and cotton sacks and spirituals sticking out of their mouths. The Dutch children should all stumble in their wooden shoes and break their necks. The French should choke to death on the Louisiana Purchase (1803) while silkworms ate all the Chinese with their stupid pigtails. As a species, we are an abomination. All of us.

48   Donleavy was running for election, and assured our parents that if he won we could count on having the only colored paved playing field in that part of Arkansas. Also—he never looked up to acknowledge the grunts of acceptance—also, we were bound to get some new equipment for the home economics building and the workshop.

49   He finished, and since there was no need to give any more than the most perfunctory thank-you's, he nodded to the men on the stage, and the tall white man who was never introduced joined him at the door. They left with the attitude that now they were off to something really important. (The graduation ceremonies at Lafayette County Training School had been a mere preliminary.)

50   The ugliness they left was palpable. An uninvited guest who wouldn't leave. The choir was summoned and sang a modern arrangement of "Onward, Christian Soldiers," with new words pertaining to graduates seeking their place in the world. But it didn't work. Elouise, the daughter of the Baptist minister, recited "Invictus," and I could have cried at the impertinence of "I am the master of my fate, I am the captain of my soul."

51   My name had lost its ring of familiarity and I had to be nudged to go and receive my diploma. All my preparations had fled. I neither marched up to the stage like a conquering Amazon, nor did I look in the audience for Bailey's nod of approval. Marguerite Johnson, I heard the name again, my honors were read, there were noises in the audience of appreciation, and I took my place on the stage as rehearsed.

52   I thought about colors I hated: ecru, puce, lavender, beige and black.

53   There was shuffling and rustling around me, then Henry Reed was giving his valedictory address, "To Be or Not to Be." Hadn't he heard the whitefolks? We couldn't *be,* so the question was a waste of time. Henry's voice came out clear and strong. I feared to look at him. Hadn't he got the message? There was no "nobler in the mind" for Negroes because the world didn't think we had minds, and they let us know it. "Outrageous fortune"? Now, that was a joke. When the ceremony was over I had to tell Henry Reed some things. That is, if I still cared. Not "rub," Henry, "erase." "Ah, there's the erase." Us.

54   Henry had been a good student in elocution. His voice rose on tides of promise and fell on waves of warnings. The English teacher had helped him to create a sermon winging through Hamlet's soliloquy. To be a man, a doer, a builder, a leader, or to be a tool, an unfunny joke, a crusher of funky toadstools. I marveled that Henry could go through with the speech as if we had a choice.

55   I had been listening and silently rebutting each sentence with my eyes closed; then there was a hush, which in an audience warns that something unplanned is happening. I looked up and saw Henry Reed, the conservative, the proper, the A student, turn his back to the audience and turn to us (the proud graduating class of 1940) and sing, nearly speaking,

> Lift ev'ry voice and sing
> Till earth and heaven ring
> Ring with the harmonies of Liberty . . .[4]

It was the poem written by James Weldon Johnson. It was the music composed by J. Rosamond Johnson. It was the Negro national anthem. Out of habit we were singing it.

---

[4] "Lift Ev'ry Voice and Sing"—words by James Weldon Johnson and music by J. Rosamond Johnson. Copyright by Edward B. Marks Music Corporation. Used by permission.

56   Our mothers and fathers stood in the dark hall and joined the hymn of encouragement. A kindergarten teacher led the small children onto the stage and the buttercups and daisies and bunny rabbits marked time and tried to follow:

> Stony the road we trod
> Bitter the chastening rod
> Felt in the days when hope, unborn, had died.
> Yet with a steady beat
> Have not our weary feet
> Come to the place for which our fathers sighed?

57   Every child I knew had learned that song with his ABC's and along with "Jesus Loves Me This I Know." But I personally had never heard it before. Never heard the words, despite the thousands of times I had sung them. Never thought they had anything to do with me.

58   On the other hand, the words of Patrick Henry had made such an impression on me that I had been able to stretch myself tall and trembling and say, "I know not what course others may take, but as for me, give me liberty or give me death."

59   And now I heard, really for the first time:

> We have come over a way that with tears has been watered,
> We have come, treading our path through the blood of the slaughtered.

60   While echoes of the song shivered in the air, Henry Reed bowed his head, said "Thank you," and returned to his place in the line. The tears that slipped down many faces were not wiped away in shame.

61   We were on top again. As always, again. We survived. The depths had been icy and dark, but now a bright sun spoke to our souls. I was no longer simply a member of the proud graduating class of 1940; I was a proud member of the wonderful beautiful Negro race.

62   Oh, Black known and unknown poets, how often have your auctioned pains sustained us? Who will compute the lonely nights made less lonely by your songs, or by the empty pots made less tragic by your tales?

63   If we were a people much given to revealing secrets, we might raise monuments and sacrifice to the memories of our poets, but slavery cured us of that weakness. It may be enough, however, to

have it said that we survive in exact relationship to the dedication of our poets (include preachers, musicians and blues singers).

Questions

1. In the first paragraph, notice such overstatements as "glorious release," "the graduating classes themselves were the nobility," and "exotic destinations." Find some additional examples of similar statements in the next few pages. Why did Angelou use such words?
2. Characterize the writer as you perceive her up through paragraph 20. Support your characterization with references to specific passages. Next, characterize her in the paragraph beginning "It was awful to be Negro" (paragraph 47). Next, characterize her on the basis of the entire essay. Finally, in a sentence, try to describe the change, indicating the chief attitudes or moods that she goes through.
3. How would you define "poets," as Angelou uses the word in the last sentence?

High Horse's Courting
Black Elk

---

1   You know, in the old days, it was not so very easy to get a girl when you wanted to be married. Sometimes it was hard work for a young man and he had to stand a great deal. Say I am a young man and I have seen a young girl who looks so beautiful to me that I feel all sick when I think about her. I can not just go and tell her about it and then get married if she is willing. I have to be a very sneaky fellow to talk to her at all, and after I have managed to talk to her, that is only the beginning.

2   Probably for a long time I have been feeling sick about a certain girl because I love her so much, but she will not even look at me, and her parents keep a good watch over her. But I keep feeling worse and worse all the time; so maybe I sneak up to her tepee in the dark and wait until she comes out. Maybe I just wait there all

night and don't get any sleep at all and she does not come out. Then I feel sicker than ever about her.

3   Maybe I hide in the brush by a spring where she sometimes goes to get water, and when she comes by, if nobody is looking, then I jump out and hold her and just make her listen to me. If she likes me too, I can tell that from the way she acts, for she is very bashful and maybe will not say a word or even look at me the first time. So I let her go, and then maybe I sneak around until I can see her father alone, and I tell him how many horses I can give him for his beautiful girl, and by now I am feeling so sick that maybe I would give him all the horses in the world if I had them.

4   Well, this young man I am telling about was called High Horse, and there was a girl in the village who looked so beautiful to him that he was just sick all over from thinking about her so much and he was getting sicker all the time. The girl was very shy, and her parents thought a great deal of her because they were not young any more and this was the only child they had. So they watched her all day long, and they fixed it so that she would be safe at night too when they were asleep. They thought so much of her that they had made a rawhide bed for her to sleep in, and after they knew that High Horse was sneaking around after her, they took rawhide thongs and tied the girl in bed at night so that nobody could steal her when they were asleep, for they were not sure but that their girl might really want to be stolen.

5   Well, after High Horse had been sneaking around a good while and hiding and waiting for the girl and getting sicker all the time, he finally caught her alone and made her talk to him. Then he found out that she liked him maybe a little. Of course this did not make him feel well. It made him sicker than ever, but now he felt as brave as a bison bull, and so he went right to her father and said he loved the girl so much that he would give two good horses for her—one of them young and the other one not so very old.

6   But the old man just waved his hand, meaning for High Horse to go away and quit talking foolishness like that.

7   High Horse was feeling sicker than ever about it; but there was another young fellow who said he would loan High Horse two ponies and when he got some more horses, why, he could just give them back for the ones he had borrowed.

8   Then High Horse went back to the old man and said he would give four horses for the girl—two of them young and the other two not hardly old at all. But the old man just waved his hand and would not say anything.

9   So High Horse sneaked around until he could talk to the girl

again, and he asked her to run away with him. He told her he thought he would just fall over and die if she did not. But she said she would not do that; she wanted to be bought like a fine woman. You see she thought a great deal of herself too.

10   That made High Horse feel so very sick that he could not eat a bite, and he went around with his head hanging down as though he might just fall down and die any time.

11   Red Deer was another young fellow, and he and High Horse were great comrades, always doing things together. Red Deer saw how High Horse was acting, and he said: "Cousin, what is the matter? Are you sick in the belly? You look as though you were going to die."

12   Then High Horse told Red Deer how it was, and said he thought he could not stay alive much longer if he could not marry the girl pretty quick.

13   Red Deer thought awhile about it, and then he said: "Cousin, I have a plan, and if you are man enough to do as I tell you, then everything will be all right. She will not run away with you; her old man will not take four horses; and four horses are all you can get. You must steal her and run away with her. Then afterwhile you can come back and the old man cannot do anything because she will be your woman. Probably she wants you to steal her anyway."

14   So they planned what High Horse had to do, and he said he loved the girl so much that he was man enough to do anything Red Deer or anybody else could think up.

15   So this is what they did.

16   That night late they sneaked up to the girl's tepee and waited until it sounded inside as though the old man and the old woman and the girl were sound asleep. Then High Horse crawled under the tepee with a knife. He had to cut the rawhide thongs first, and then Red Deer, who was pulling up the stakes around that side of the tepee, was going to help drag the girl outside and gag her. After that, High Horse could put her across his pony in front of him and hurry out of there and be happy all the rest of his life.

17   When High Horse had crawled inside, he felt so nervous that he could hear his heart drumming, and it seemed so loud he felt sure it would 'waken the old folks. But it did not, and afterwhile he began cutting the thongs. Every time he cut one it made a pop and nearly scared him to death. But he was getting along all right and all the thongs were cut down as far as the girl's thighs, when he became so nervous that his knife slipped and stuck the girl. She gave a big, loud yell. Then the old folks jumped up and yelled too.

By this time High Horse was outside, and he and Red Deer were running away like antelope. The old man and some other people chased the young men but they got away in the dark and nobody knew who it was.

18   Well, if you ever wanted a beautiful girl you will know how sick High Horse was now. It was very bad the way he felt, and it looked as though he would starve even if he did not drop over dead sometime.

19   Red Deer kept thinking about this, and after a few days he went to High Horse and said: "Cousin, take courage! I have another plan, and I am sure, if you are man enough, we can steal her this time." And High Horse said: "I am man enough to do anything anybody can think up, if I can only get that girl."

20   So this is what they did.

21   They went away from the village alone, and Red Deer made High Horse strip naked. Then he painted High Horse solid white all over, and after that he painted black stripes all over the white and put black rings around High Horse's eyes. High Horse looked terrible. He looked so terrible that when Red Deer was through painting and took a good look at what he had done, he said it scared even him a little.

22   "Now," Red Deer said, "if you get caught again, everybody will be so scared they will think you are a bad spirit and will be afraid to chase you."

23   So when the night was getting old and everybody was sound asleep, they sneaked back to the girl's tepee. High Horse crawled in with his knife, as before, and Red Deer waited outside, ready to drag the girl out and gag her when High Horse had all the thongs cut.

24   High Horse crept up by the girl's bed and began cutting at the thongs. But he kept thinking, "If they see me they will shoot me because I look so terrible." The girl was restless and kept squirming around in bed, and when a thong was cut, it popped. So High Horse worked very slowly and carefully.

25   But he must have made some noise, for suddenly the old woman awoke and said to her old man: "Old Man, wake up! There is somebody in this tepee!" But the old man was sleepy and didn't want to be bothered. He said: "Of course there is somebody in this tepee. Go to sleep and don't bother me." Then he snored some more.

26   But High Horse was so scared by now that he lay very still and as flat to the ground as he could. Now, you see, he had not been sleeping very well for a long time because he was so sick about the

girl. And while he was lying there waiting for the old woman to snore, he just forgot everything, even how beautiful the girl was. Red Deer who was lying outside ready to do his part, wondered and wondered what had happened in there, but he did not dare call out to High Horse.

27 Afterwhile the day began to break and Red Deer had to leave with the two ponies he had staked there for his comrade and girl, or somebody would see him.

28 So he left.

29 Now when it was getting light in the tepee, the girl awoke and the first thing she saw was a terrible animal, all white with black stripes on it, lying asleep beside her bed. So she screamed, and then the old woman screamed and the old man yelled. High Horse jumped up, scared almost to death, and he nearly knocked the tepee down getting out of there.

30 People were coming running from all over the village with guns and bows and axes, and everybody was yelling.

31 By now High Horse was running so fast that he hardly touched the ground at all, and he looked so terrible that the people fled from him and let him run. Some braves wanted to shoot at him, but the others said he might be some sacred being and it would bring bad trouble to kill him.

32 High Horse made for the river that was near, and in among the brush he found a hollow tree and dived into it. Afterwhile some braves came there and he could hear them saying that it was some bad spirit that had come out of the water and gone back in again.

33 That morning the people were ordered to break camp and move away from there. So they did, while High Horse was hiding in his hollow tree.

34 Now Red Deer had been watching all this from his own tepee and trying to look as though he were as much surprised and scared as all the others. So when the camp moved, he sneaked back to where he had seen his comrade disappear. When he was down there in the brush, he called, and High Horse answered, because he knew his friend's voice. They washed off the paint from High Horse and sat down on the river bank to talk about their troubles.

35 High Horse said he never would go back to the village as long as he lived and he did not care what happened to him now. He said he was going to go on the war-path all by himself. Red Deer said: "No, cousin, you are not going on the war-path alone, because I am going with you."

36 So Red Deer got everything ready, and at night they started out on the war-path all alone. After several days they came to a

Crow camp just about sundown, and when it was dark they sneaked up to where the Crow horses were grazing, killed the horse guard, who was not thinking about enemies because he thought all the Lakotas were far away, and drove off about a hundred horses.

37   They got a big start because all the Crow horses stampeded and it was probably morning before the Crow warriors could catch any horses to ride. Red Deer and High Horse fled with their herd three days and nights before they reached the village of their people. Then they drove the whole herd right into the village and up in front of the girl's tepee. The old man was there, and High Horse called out to him and asked if he thought maybe that would be enough horses for his girl. The old man did not wave him away this time. It was not the horses that he wanted. What he wanted was a son who was a real man and good for something.

38   So High Horse got his girl after all, and I think he deserved her.

Questions

1. The story "High Horse's Courting" is told by Black Elk, an Oglala Sioux holy man. Though High Horse's behavior is amusing and at times ridiculous, how does Black Elk make it clear that he is not ridiculing the young man, but is instead sympathetic with him? Consider the following questions:

   a. What is the effect of the first three paragraphs? Consider the first two sentences, and then the passage beginning "Say I am a young man . . ." and ending ". . . I would give him all the horses in the world if I had them."

   b. Describe the behavior of the young girl, and of her father and mother. How do they contribute to the comedy? How does their behavior affect your understanding of Black Elk's attitude toward High Horse?

   c. What is the function of Red Deer?

   d. The narrative consists of several episodes. List them in the order in which they occur, and then describe the narrative's structure. How does the structure of the narrative affect the tone?

   e. What is the effect of the last two sentences?

2. What similarities, if any, are there between the courting customs and attitudes toward courting that Black Elk describes and those

you are familiar with? Consider the behavior and attitudes not only of High Horse, the girl, her parents, and his friend, but also of the old man who tells the story.

Coming to Grips with Death
Russell Baker

1   Supper was almost ready when we arrived that night at Uncle Miller's. In the few minutes before we sat down Uncle Miller asked my father to come out to the pigpen for a look at the porkers to be slaughtered in the morning. I heard them outside talking and laughing and knew they were having a drink in the darkness. In Morrisonville you learned the symptoms young. There was a certain change in the level of the voice, a laughter slightly more enthusiastic than laughter usually sounded. But they were only outside a few minutes, not long enough to overdo it, and when they returned and we all sat at the table, they looked fine.

2   We started with fried oysters. Presently my father put his fork down, rose from the table, and went into the yard; we all sat there not saying a word, listening to him outside vomiting. Uncle Miller and my mother went outside then, and after a while my mother returned and took Doris and me off to the bedroom where Audrey was already asleep.

3   The house was unnaturally quiet next morning. The butchering festival I'd expected was not in progress, and my father was not in the bedroom with us. My mother said he was in Uncle Miller's bedroom, because a doctor was coming to see him.

4   I wandered around the backyard until the sun burned off the frost. After a while my mother came out.

5   "The doctor's here," she said. "He's going to take Daddy to the hospital in Frederick so he can get better. Come and kiss him good-bye."

To my surprise my father was fully dressed and seated in the doctor's small roadster at the front of the house. He was wearing his blue serge suit, white shirt, and necktie, and looked all right to me. I walked across the lawn to the car, and he leaned out the window on the passenger's side and smiled, but he didn't have much to say to me. Just, "Daddy'll be home in a day or two. Be a good boy till I get back."

My mother held me up, and he gave me a kiss.

"We'd better get going," the doctor said.

My mother set me down and leaned into the car and kissed him. She and I watched the roadster together until it passed over the brow of the hill headed for the Maryland side of the Potomac.

10   By afternoon we were back in Morrisonville. Next day before sunup she rose to visit the hospital. Uncle Irvey would drive her.

"Is Daddy coming home today?"

"Maybe we'll bring him back with us," she said.

It was a gentle Indian summer morning, and my grandmother told me to go out and play while she minded Doris and Audrey. I set off on one of my daily wandering expeditions, taking the road down toward the creek.

I was down there by myself. You could always find something entertaining to do around Morrisonville. Climb a fence. Take a stick and scratch pictures in the dirt. There were always cows around, or a horse. Throw pebbles at a locust tree. I was busy at this sort of thing when I saw my cousins, Kenneth and Ruth Lee, coming down the road.

15   Besides Doris, Audrey, and me, they were the only other children living in Morrisonville. Kenneth, two years older than I, was our leader. He was coming down the road with Ruth Lee following as usual. I was happy to see them. We usually played in the fields and around the barns and straw ricks together. Sometimes we ripped open a burlap grain sack to build a tepee in the apple orchard, or picked through the junk pile behind Liz Virts's house to collect enough tin cans and broken dishes to play store. I was glad now to have company.

When Kenneth walked right up to me, though, he stared at me with such a stare as I'd never seen.

"Your father's dead," he said.

It was like an accusation that my father had done something criminal, and I came to my father's defense.

"He is not," I said.

20   But of course they didn't know the situation. I started to explain. He was sick. In the hospital. My mother was bringing him home right now. . . .

"He's dead," Kenneth said.

His assurance slid an icicle into my heart.

"He is not either!" I shouted.

"He is too," Ruth Lee said. "They want you to come home right away."

25   I started running up the road screaming, "He is not!"

It was a weak argument. They had the evidence and gave it to me as I hurried home crying, "He is not. . . . He is not. . . . He is not. . . ."

I was almost certain before I got there that he was.

And I was right. Arriving at the hospital that morning, my mother was told he had died at four A.M. in "acute diabetic coma." He was thirty-three years old.

When I came running home, my mother was still not back from Frederick, but the women had descended on our house, as women there did in such times, and were already busy with the housecleaning and cooking that were Morrisonville's ritual response to death. With a thousand tasks to do, they had no time to handle a howling five-year-old. I was sent to the opposite end of town, to Bessie Scott's house.

30   Poor Bessie Scott. All afternoon she listened patiently as a saint while I sat in her kitchen and cried myself out. For the first time I thought seriously about God. Between sobs I told Bessie that if God could do things like this to people, then God was hateful and I had no more use for Him.

Bessie told me about the peace of Heaven and the joy of being among the angels and the happiness of my father who was already there. This argument failed to quiet my rage.

"God loves us all just like His own children," Bessie said.

"If God loves me, why did He make my father die?"

Bessie said I would understand someday, but she was only partly right. That afternoon, though I couldn't have phrased it this way then, I decided that God was a lot less interested in people than anybody in Morrisonville was willing to admit. That day I decided that God was not entirely to be trusted.

35   After that I never cried again with any real conviction, nor expected much of anyone's God except indifference, nor loved deeply without fear that it would cost me dearly in pain. At the age of five I had become a skeptic and began to sense that any happiness that came my way might be the prelude to some grim cosmic joke.

While I came to grips with death in Bessie's kitchen, its rites were being performed by other Morrisonville women in my father's house. Our floors were being scrubbed, windows washed, furniture dusted, beds made. Visitors would be arriving by the dozen. It was a violation of the code to show them anything but a spotless house.

Prodigies of cooking were already under way in surrounding houses. Precious hams were being removed from smokehouses, eggs and butter were being beaten in cake bowls, pie crusts were being rolled, canning jars of pickles and preserved fruits were being lifted from pantry shelves. Death was also a time for feasting.

It was growing dark when, pretty well cried out and beginning to respond to the holiday excitement in the air, I left Bessie Scott's and walked back down the road to home. The place sparkled with cleanliness, and the women sat clustered in the kitchen, exhausted, I suppose. The men had just begun to arrive, looking uncomfortable in their good dark suits, their shirts and neckties and low shoes. I went outside and stood around with the men in the road. So late in November, the dusk came early. The men seemed unusually quiet. I did not know many of them. They stood in little groups talking quietly, almost in whispers, probably not saying anything very interesting, just feeling self-conscious in their Sunday suits with nothing to do but stand. The men standing and waiting and talking quietly with nothing to do in their good dark suits was part of the ritual too. It was important to have a powerful turnout of humanity. That showed the dead man had been well liked in the community, and it was therefore considered an important source of comfort to the widow.

It was fully dark when someone told me to move around and wait in the backyard, which I did. After a while Annie Grigsby came out and hugged me and said it was all right to come into the kitchen. "They've brought your daddy home," she said.

40   My mother was in the kitchen, but most of the other women had left now. It was the first time I had seen her since she left for the hospital that morning. She was sitting on a chair looking very tired. Annie took a chair beside her. It was terribly quiet. I wondered where my father was. Annie finally broke the silence.

"Maybe he'd like to see his father."

"Do you want to see your father?" my mother asked.

"I guess so," I said.

The undertaker had come and gone while I was in the backyard, and now that most of the bustle was over and most of the people had gone home for supper, the house felt empty and still. My mother did not seem up to showing me the undertaker's handiwork.

45   "I'll take him in," Annie said, rising in her weary fashion, taking my hand.

She led me into the adjoining living room. The blinds were drawn. A couple of kerosene lamps were burning. Annie lifted me in her arms so I could look down. For some reason there was an American flag.

"There's your daddy, child," Annie said. "Doesn't he look nice?"

He was wearing his blue serge suit and a white shirt and necktie.

"Yes. He looks nice," I told Annie, knowing that was what I was supposed to say. But it wasn't the niceness of the way he was dressed and the way his hair was so carefully combed that impressed me. It was his stillness. I gazed at the motionless hand laid across his chest, thinking no one can lie so still for so long without moving a finger. I waited for the closed eyelids to flutter, for his chest to move in a slight sigh to capture a fresh breath of air. Nothing. His motionlessness was majestic and terrifying. I wanted to be away from that room and never see him like that again.

50   "Do you want to kiss your daddy?" Annie asked.

"Not now," I said.

Then I went back to the warmth of the kitchen with Annie, born in slavery, and sat there until bedtime with my mother and Doris while the neighbors came back and stood whispering in the living room.

Questions

1. If the first paragraph of this narrative were omitted, what would be lost?
2. In paragraph 6, we learn that the writer's father "was fully dressed, . . . wearing his blue serge suit, white shirt, and necktie." Why was the boy surprised, and why do you suppose the father was dressed up? And why is this passage about clothing included in the narrative?
3. In an essay of about 1000 words, recount the most painful experience of your childhood or adolescence. Tell not only what happened and how you responded but also what other people did and said.

10

The Research Paper

Knowledge is of two kinds. We know a subject
ourselves, or we know where we can find information upon it.
— SAMUEL JOHNSON, in a conversation in 1775

WHAT RESEARCH IS

Research consists of collecting evidence to develop and support ideas. The evidence usually includes the opinions of others,
reported in such sources as books, articles, lectures, and interviews. A "research paper" is an essay based in part on such evidence. It is the kind of paper that you will write in most of your
college courses.

In this chapter we explain how to

frame a suitable topic for research,
find and evaluate evidence,
take useful notes, and
acknowledge the work of others.

It is in the careful acknowledgment of sources, explained on pages
362–64, that scholarly writing, for which writing research papers
prepares you, may differ from other kinds of writing. When you
acknowledge sources, giving credit where credit is due for your
use of the ideas and words of others, you do two things:

1. You provide a kind of roadmap for the researcher who comes after you and who may want to retrace some of your steps.
2. You publicly thank those who have helped you on your way.

There are some conventions to learn about the form of acknowledgments, and we'll offer some rules to guide you. But the rules make sense only when you bear in mind the reasons for acknowledgment: courtesy to your readers on the one hand, and to your sources on the other.

Because a research paper requires its writer to collect the available evidence—usually including the opinions of earlier investigators—one sometimes hears that a research paper, unlike a critical essay, is not the expression of personal opinion. But such a view is unjust both to criticism and to research. A critical essay is not a mere expression of personal opinion; to be any good it must offer evidence that supports the opinions, thus persuading the reader of their objective rightness. And a research paper is largely personal, because the author continuously uses his or her own judgment to evaluate the evidence, deciding what is relevant and convincing. A research paper is not merely an elaborately documented presentation of what a dozen scholars have already said about a topic; it is a thoughtful evaluation of the available evidence, and so it is, finally, an expression of what the author thinks the evidence adds up to.

Before we talk at some length about writing a research paper, we should mention that you may want to do some research even for a paper that is primarily critical. Consider the difference between a paper on Bob Dylan's emergence as a popular singer, and a paper on Bob Dylan's songs of social protest. The first of these, necessarily a research paper, will require you to dig into magazines and newspapers to find out about his reception in clubs in New York; but even if you are writing an analysis of his songs of social protest you may want to do a little research into Dylan's indebtedness to Woody Guthrie. You may, for example, study Dylan's record jackets and read some interviews in magazines and newspapers to find out if he has anything to say about his relation to Guthrie. Our point is that writers must learn to use source material thoughtfully, whether they expect to work with few sources or with many.

PRIMARY AND SECONDARY MATERIALS

The materials of most research can be conveniently divided into two sorts, primary and secondary. The primary materials or sources are the real subject of study; the secondary materials are critical and historical accounts already written about these primary materials. For example, if you want to know whether Shakespeare's attitude toward Julius Caesar was highly traditional or highly original, or a little of each, you would read *Julius Caesar,* other Elizabethan writings about Caesar, and Roman writings known to the Elizabethans; and in addition to these primary materials you would also read secondary material such as modern books on Shakespeare and on Elizabethan attitudes toward Rome and toward monarchs.

The line between these two kinds of sources, of course, is not always clear. For example, if you are concerned with the degree to which Joyce's *Portrait of the Artist as a Young Man* is autobiographical, primary materials include not only *A Portrait* and Joyce's letters, but perhaps also his brother Stanislaus's diary and autobiography. Although the diary and autobiography might be considered secondary sources—certainly a scholarly biography about Joyce or his brother would be a secondary source—because Stanislaus's books are more or less contemporary with your subject they can reasonably be called primary sources.

FROM SUBJECT TO THESIS

First, a subject. No subject is unsuited. Perhaps sports, war, art, dreams, food. As G. K. Chesterton said, "There is no such thing on earth as an uninteresting subject; the only thing that can exist is an uninterested person." Even a subject so apparently unpromising as the corset has been the material of research—and, what is more, of research that is fascinating, as readers of David Kunzle's *Fashion and Fetishism* know. By the way, Kunzle's thesis—the argument that holds together his wide-ranging findings—is this: the tightly-laced corset gave "positive and erotic pleasures" and thus was an image not of repression but of bodily freedom.

Males who crusaded against tight-lacing spoke of freeing women from sexual tyranny but they were often, Kunzle suggests, really seeking to restrict sexuality and to enslave women to regular childbearing and to domestic labor.

Research, then, can be done on almost anything that interests you, though you should keep in mind two limitations. First, materials on current events may be extremely difficult to get hold of, since crucial documents may not yet be in print and you may not have access to the people involved. And, second, materials on some subjects may be unavailable to you because they are in languages you can't read or in publications that your library doesn't have. So you probably won't try to work on the stuff of today's headlines, and (because almost nothing in English has been written on it) you won't try to work on Japanese attitudes toward the hunting of whales. But no subject is too trivial for study: Newton, according to legend, wondered why an apple fell to the ground.

You cannot, however, write a research paper on subjects as broad as sports, war, art, dreams, or food. You have to focus on a much smaller area within such a subject. Let's talk about food. You might want to study the dietary laws of the Jews, the food of American Indians before the arrival of the whites, the consumption of whale meat, subsidies to hog farmers, or legislation governing the purity of food. Your own interests will guide you to the topic—the part of the broad subject—that you wish to explore.

But of course, though you have an interest in one of these narrow topics, you don't know a great deal about it; that's one of the reasons you are going to do research on it. Let's say that you happened to read a stomach-turning essay by Ralph Nader on frankfurters, in which Nader reports that although today's frankfurters contain only 11.7 percent protein (the rest is water, salt, spices, and preservatives), they contain a substantial dose of sodium nitrate to inhibit the growth of bacteria and to keep the meat from turning gray.

Assuming that your appetite for research on food continues, you decide that you want to know something more about additives, that is, substances (such as sodium nitrate) added to preserve desirable properties—color, flavor, freshness—or to suppress undesirable properties. You want to do some reading, and you must now find the articles and books. Of course, as you do the reading, your focus may shift a little; you may stay with frankfurters, you may shift to the potentially dangerous effects, in various foods, of sodium nitrate, or to the controversy over the effects of saccharin (an artificial sweetener), or you may concentrate on so-called enriched bread, which is first robbed of many nutrients by refining and bleaching the four and is then enriched by the addition of some of the nutrients in synthetic form. Exactly what you will focus on, and exactly what your *thesis* or point of view will be, you may not know until you do some more reading. But how do you find the relevant material?

FINDING THE MATERIAL

Although most research papers that students write are largely based on materials they find in libraries, research can draw also on other sources. Don't neglect the expertise that friends can provide in conversation, or the material that you can garner from

attending lectures,
interviewing experts, and
distributing questionnaires.

Field trips, too, may be invaluable; for some topics, a visit to a day-care center or to a political convention may be immensely informative. They are the equivalent of primary sources found in the library.

We will, however, concentrate on ways of getting familiar with material in the library. You may happen already to know of some relevant material that you have been intending to read, but if you are at a loss where to begin, consult the card catalog of your library and the appropriate guides to articles in journals. Many libraries have transferred the information formally in their catalogs to computer files. If you use computerized files, what you find on the screen will closely resemble the catalog cards that we describe.

The Card Catalog

The card catalog has cards arranged alphabetically not only by author and by title but also by subject. It probably won't have a subject heading for "frankfurter," but it will have one for "food," followed by cards listing books on this topic. And on the "food"

```
    FOOD

      see also

    COOKERY
    DIET
    DIETARIES
    FARM PRODUCE
    FRUIT
    GASTRONOMY
    GRAIN
    MARKETS
    MEAT
    NUTRITION
    POULTRY                        see next card
```

card will be a note telling you of relevant subjects to consult. In fact, even before you look at the catalog you can know what subject headings it contains by checking one of two books: *Sears List of Subject Headings* (for libraries that use the Dewey decimal system of arranging books) and *Subject Headings Used in the Dictionary Catalogs of the Library of Congress,* 7th edition. (Because most academic libraries use the Library of Congress system, the second of these is probably the book you'll use.) If you look for "food" in *Subject Headings,* you will find two pages of listings, including cross references such as *"sa* [= see also] Animal Food." Among the subject headings that sound relevant are Bacteriology, Food Contamination, and Preservation. Notice also the abbreviation "xx," referring to broader headings you may want to look at. If you make use of some of these subject headings you will probably find that the library has a fair amount of material on your topic.

Whether you went to *Subject Headings* or to the "food" card, you have now gathered a number of subject headings that seem relevant. With this information you can locate useful books—even though you began without knowing the author or title of even one book—simply by turning to the subject heading in the card file,

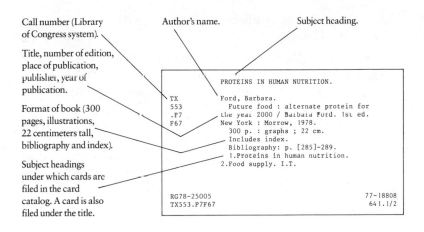

Call number (Library of Congress system).

Title, number of edition, place of publication, publisher, year of publication.

Format of book (300 pages, illustrations, 22 centimeters tall, bibliography and index).

Subject headings under which cards are filed in the card catalog. A card is also filed under the title.

Author's name.

Subject heading.

```
                    PROTEINS IN HUMAN NUTRITION.
     TX
     553            Ford, Barbara.
     .P7                Future food : alternate protein for
     F67             the year 2000 / Barbara Ford. 1st ed.
                    New York : Morrow, 1978.
                       300 p. : graphs ; 22 cm.
                       Includes index.
                       Bibliography: p. [285]-289.
                       1.Proteins in human nutrition.
                    2.Food supply. I.T.

     RG78-25005                                77-18808
     TX553.P7F67                               641.1/2
```

and writing down the information on the books filed under that subject. For example, if you look up "Diet," "Nutrition," and "Proteins in Human Nutrition" you will find cards for whatever books the library has on each of these topics. A card for a book listed under the subject is called a *subject card*. Notice, in the illustrated example, the following points:

1. The subject is given at the top of the card.
2. The classification number at the left enables you to find the book in the library.
3. The card gives the author's name, title, and other information, such as the fact that this book includes a bibliography.
4. Below this information there is a list of other subject headings under which this card is filed. By checking these other subject headings (called *tracings* by librarians), you will be able to find additional books that probably are relevant to your research.

An *author card,* that is, a card filed alphabetically under the author's last name, is identical with a subject card except that the subject is not given at the top of the card. If you know the author's name, just look for it in the catalog.

Finally, a *title card* is identical with an author card, except that the title is added to the top of the card and the card is indexed under the first word of the title, or the second word if the first is *A, An,* or *The,* or a foreign equivalent.

Three Notes on the Alphabetic Arrangement of the Card Catalog

1. The catalog is arranged alphabetically from A to Z, of course, but the arrangement is word by word, not letter by letter. This means, for example, that "ion implantation" *precedes* "ionic crystals," because "i-o-n" precedes "i-o-n-i-c." (If the catalog were letter by letter instead of word by word, of course "i-o-n-i-c" would precede "i-o-n-i-m. . . .") Similarly, in the card catalog "folk tales" precedes "folklorists." Here is a short list of cards in the order they are in the catalog:

> Good, Emanual
> *Good Men and True*
> *Good Old Days*
> Goodall, Ann
> Goodman, Paul

2. Under the author's name, books are usually arranged alphabetically by title, but for highly prolific authors the cards listing the collected works may be grouped before those listing individual works. Cards for books *about* the author follow cards for books *by* the author. Note that authors whose surnames begin *Mc* or *Mac* are all listed—in most libraries—as though spelled *Mac;* authors whose surnames begin with a prefix (for example, *De, Le, Van*) are listed as though the prefixes and surname formed a single word: De Lisle would come after Delano and before Delos.

3. Under the title, remember that books are alphabetized under the *second* word if the first word is *A, An,* or *The,* or a foreign equivalent. Note, too, that words normally abbreviated are spelled out in the catalog: *Doctor Zhivago, Mister Roberts, Saint Joan.*

Scanning Books, Book Reviews, and Encyclopedias

Having checked the card catalog and written down the relevant data (author, title, call number), you can begin to scan the books, or you can postpone looking at the books until you have found some relevant articles in periodicals. For the moment, let's postpone the periodicals.

Put a bunch of books in front of you, and choose one as an introduction. How do you choose one from half a dozen? Partly by its size—choose a thin one—and partly by its quality. Roughly speaking, it should be among the more recent publications, and it should strike you as fair. A pamphlet published by a meat-packers association is desirably thin but you have a hunch that it may be biased. Roger John Williams' *Nutrition in a Nutshell* is published by a well-known commercial press (Doubleday), and it is only 171 pages, but because it was published in 1962 it may not reflect current food chemistry. Though it is rather big (260 pages), Michael Jacobson's *Eater's Digest: The Consumer's Factbook of Food Additives* (Washington: Center for Science in the Public Interest, 1987) probably is about right.

When you have found the book that you think may serve as your introductory study:

> read the preface in order to get an idea of the author's purpose and outlook
>
> scan the table of contents in order to get an idea of the organization and the coverage
>
> scan the final chapter or the last few pages, where you may be lucky enough to find a summary

The index, too, may let you know if the book will suit your purpose, by showing you what topics are covered and how much coverage they get. If the book still seems suitable, scan it.

At this stage it is acceptable to trust one's hunches—you are only going to scan the book, not buy it or even read it—but you may want to look up some book reviews to assure yourself that the book has merit. There are five especially useful indexes to book reviews:

> *Book Review Digest* (published from 1905 onward)
> *Book Review Index* (1965–)
> *Index to Book Reviews in the Humanities* (1960–)
> *Humanities Index* (1974–)
> *Social Sciences Index* (1974–)

The last two publications are chiefly indexes to articles, but at the rear of each issue you'll find indexes to book reviews, arranged alphabetically under the name of the author of the book.

Most reviews of books will come out in the same year as the book, or within the next two years. If, for example, a book was published in 1984, look in the 1984 volume of the appropriate index and see what is there. If you want some more reviews, look in 1985 and 1986. Begin with *Book Review Digest,* because it includes excerpts from and synopses of the reviews; if it has your book, the excerpts and synopses may be enough, and you won't have to dig out the reviews themselves. But *Book Review Digest* does not have as broad coverage as the other indexes, and you may have to turn to them for citations, and then to the journals to which they refer you. Read the synopses in *Book Review Digest,* or some reviews in journals, and draw some conclusions about the merit of the book in question. Of course you cannot assume that every review is fair, but a book that on the whole gets good reviews is probably at least good enough for a start.

By quickly reading such a book (take few or no notes at this stage) you will probably get an overview of your topic, and you will see exactly what part of the topic you wish to pursue.

Sometimes, too, you can get a quick general view of a subject from an encyclopedia. The chief encyclopedias are

Chambers's Encyclopaedia (1973)

Collier's Encyclopedia (1972; and the annual *Collier's Encyclopedia Year Book*)

Encyclopedia Americana (1974; and the annual yearbook, *The Americana Annual*)

Encyclopaedia Britannica (1974, revised 1985; and the annual *Encyclopaedia Britannica: Book of the Year*)

The first three of these encyclopedias simply use an alphabetic arrangement: *aardvark* is in the first volume, *zoo* in the last. But the organization of the *Encyclopaedia Britannica* requires a brief explanation.

The 1985 revision of the fifteenth edition of the *Britannica* (1974) comprises thirty volumes, divided into three parts. (1) *Propaedia: Outline of Knowledge and Guide to the Britannica.* This is one volume. It divides all knowledge into ten categories, with many subdivisions. It is an outline or a table of contents for the remaining volumes. (2) *Micropaedia: Ready Reference and Index.* This is twelve volumes, containing some eighty-six thousand short entries (few are longer than 750 words), which means that only the most essential points get mentioned. (3) *Macropaedia: Knowledge in Depth.* Seventeen volumes contain 681 long articles, many of which are equivalent in length to short books. All of the subjects treated in the *Macropaedia* are also treated, more briefly, in the *Micropaedia*.

Finding Bibliographies

Many researchers have published bibliographies, that is, lists of the works they have consulted. Sometimes the bibliographies appear as articles in scholarly journals or as appendices to books, or even as entire books. All of these kinds of bibliographies are listed in *Bibliographic Index,* which is issued three times a year and cumulates in an annual volume. Begin, of course, with the most recent issue, check it for your subject, and then work back for a few years.

For the use of computers in bibliographic searches, see pages 424–26.

Indexes to Periodicals

An enormous amount is published in magazines and scholarly journals; you can start thumbing through them at random, but such a procedure is monstrously inefficient. Fortunately there are indexes to publications. We have already suggested that you can locate bibliographies listing articles and books on your topic, but it is possible that there is no relevant bibliography. You can still find material—books, of course, by consulting the card catalog, and articles by consulting indexes to periodicals. Among the most widely used indexes are

Readers' Guide to Periodical Literature (1900–)
Humanities Index (1974–)
Social Sciences Index (1974–)
Social Sciences and Humanities Index (1965–74)
International Index (1907–64)

Readers' Guide indexes more than one hundred of the more familiar magazines—such as *Atlantic, Ebony, Nation, Scientific American, Sports Illustrated, Time.* The other indexes are guides to many of the less popular, more scholarly journals, for example journals published by learned societies. Notice that *Humanities Index* and *Social Sciences Index* are fairly new; for indexes to older articles in these two fields, look in *Social Sciences and Humanities Index* (1965–74), and for still older ones look in *International Index*.

The names of the periodicals indexed in these volumes are printed at the front of the volumes. All of these invaluable indexes include subject headings as well as entries listed alphabetically by author. If you know that you are looking for a piece by Ralph Nader, look it up under Nader. But if you don't know the author, look under the subject. For example, if you look up "additives" in the *Readers' Guide* you will find: "Additives, *See* Food additives," and so you next turn to "Food additives," where you will find a listing (by title) of the relevant articles. You will also find, under "Food," a note referring you to other subject headings that may be relevant, for example "Food, Organic," and "Food adulteration."

FOOD additives
    See also
Monosodium glutamate
Nitrites
In science we trust (unless it involves sugarless
    soda) [survey by National Science Founda-
    tion] R. W. Miller. il FDA Consumer 15:27 My
    '81
Yesterday's additives—generally   safe   [GRAS
    (generally recognized as safe) list] FDA Con-
    sumer 15:14-15 Mr '81
            Laws   and   regulations
    See Food laws and regulations

This material is not attractive reading, but it is useful. From the front of the *Readers' Guide* you will learn what the abbreviations mean. The first item here, for example, is an essay called "In Science We Trust (Unless It Involves Sugarless Soda)," by R. W. Miller. This essay, which has illustrations (note "il"), was published in *FDA Consumer,* volume 15, page 27, which is the May 1981 issue.

Another index that you are likely to use is *The New York Times Index* (covering from 1851 to the present). This index, enabling you to locate articles that were published in *The Times* newspaper, is especially useful if you are working on a recent public event.

The National Newspaper Index (1979 to the present, alas only on microfilm and microfiche) indexes articles from five newspapers:

The Christian Science Monitor
The Los Angeles Times
The New York Times
The Wall Street Journal
The Washington Post

Even if your library does not have a file of these newspapers, once you have learned from these indexes the date of an event, you can locate material about it in other newspapers or in weekly magazines such as *Time* or *Newsweek*.

The indexes just mentioned (along with the indexes to book reviews mentioned on page 351) are the ones you are most likely to use, but here are some others that may be valuable, depending on what your topic is:

Accountant's Index (1944–)

Applied Science and Technology Index (1958–); formerly *Industrial Arts Index* (1913–57)

Art Index (1929–)

Biography Index (1947–)

Biological and Agricultural Index (1964–); before 1964 it was known as *Agricultural Index* (1942–64)

Business Periodicals Index (1958–)

Chemical Abstracts (1907–)

Congressional Digest (1921)

Congressional Quarterly Weekly Reports (1955–)

Dramatic Index (1909–49)

Education Index (1929–)

Engineering Index Monthly and Author Index (1906–)

Film Literature Index (1973–)

Historical Abstracts (1955–)

Index to Legal Periodicals (1908–)

International Index to Film Periodicals (1972–)

MLA International Bibliography (1921–); an annual listing of books and scholarly articles on linguistics and on literature in modern languages

Monthly Catalog of United States Government Publications (1895–)

Music Index (1949–)

Poole's Index for Periodical Literature (1802–1907)

Psychology Abstracts (1927–)

Public Affairs Information Service Bulletin (1915–)

Statistical Yearbook (1949–)

United Nations Documents Index (1950–)

Whichever indexes you use, begin with the most recent years and work your way back. If you collect the titles of articles published in the last five years you will probably have as much as you can read. These articles will probably incorporate the significant points of earlier writings. But of course it depends on the topic; for instance, if you are writing about the Lindbergh kidnapping, you may have to—and want to—go back fifty or more years before you find a useful body of material.

Caution: Indexes drastically abbreviate the titles of periodicals. Before you put the indexes back on the shelf, be sure to check the key to the abbreviations, so that you know the full titles of the periodicals you are looking for.

Other Guides to Published Material

There are a great many reference books—not only general dictionaries and encyclopedias but dictionaries of technical words, and encyclopedias of special fields. For example, Leslie Halliwell, *The Filmgoer's Companion,* 8th edition (1988), has thousands of brief entries, listing films, directors, motifs, and so forth. Some of these entries conclude with references to books for further reading. There are also books chiefly devoted to telling you where to find material in special fields. Examples: Helen J. Poulton, *The Historian's Handbook: A Descriptive Guide to Reference Works* (1972); Elizabeth Miller and Mary Fisher, eds., *The Negro in America: A Bibliography,* revised edition (1970); Bernard Klein and Daniel Icolari, eds., *Reference Encyclopedia of the American Indian,* 2nd edition (1971); James Monaco, *Film: How and Where to Find Out What You Want to Know* (1976). The best guides to such guides—books telling you about such books—are:

> Eugene P. Sheehy, *Guide to Reference Books,* 10th ed. (1986)
> *American Reference Books Annual* (1970–).

There are also guides to all of these guides: reference librarians. If you don't know where to turn to find something, turn to the librarian.

TAKING BIBLIOGRAPHIC NOTES

Practice and theory differ. In theory, one should write down each citation (whether a book or an article) on a separate three-by-five index card, giving complete information. Our own practice at the start of any research is more shoddy. Instead of carefully recording all of this information from the card catalog (for a book that may be lost) or from an index to periodicals (for a periodical that may not be in the library) we usually jot down the citations of books on one sheet of paper, and of articles on another sheet. Then we see how much of this material is available. When we actually get hold of the material, we make out a card, as illustrated, with the library call number in the upper right-hand corner. True, we sometimes regret our attempted shortcut if we later find that on the sheet we forgot to write the year of the periodical and we must now hunt through indexes again to locate it. We recall the wisdom of the Chinese proverb, "It is foolish to go to bed early to save the candle if the result is twins," but we have never been able to resist economizing at the start.

Caution: Because it is easy to misspell names, turning unfamiliar forms into familiar ones (Barnet into Barnett, Stubbs into Stubbes), it is advisable to *print* the name in block letters, and,

TX
553.83
J23

Jacobson, Michael F.
<u>Eater's Digest</u>   Washington:
Center for Science in the
Public Interest, 1982

Bibliographic card for a book

Zwerdling, Daniel. "Death for
Dinner," <u>The New York Review</u>,"
21, no. 1 (21 Feb. 1974), 22-24.

Bibliographic card for an article in a periodical

having done so, to check your version against the original. Check also to see that the other information—title (and subtitle, if any), place of publication, and date are correctly written on your card.

READING AND TAKING NOTES

Preliminaries

Almost all researchers—professionals as well as beginners— find that they end up with some notes that are irrelevant, and, on the other hand, find that when drafting the paper they vaguely remember certain material that they now wish they had taken notes on. Especially in the early stages of one's research, when the topic and thesis may still be relatively unfocused, it's hard to know what is noteworthy and what is not. One simply has to flounder a bit.

We cannot overemphasize two points: 1) a certain amount of inefficiency is inevitable (and therefore plenty of time should be allowed), and 2) different people work differently.

Our own practice in reading an article or a chapter of a book is to read it through, *not* taking notes. By the time you reach the end, you may find it isn't noteworthy. Or you may find a useful summary near the end that will contain most of what you can get from the piece. Or you will find that, having a sense of the whole, you can now quickly reread the piece and take notes on the chief points.

When you take notes use four-by-six-inch cards, and write on one side only; material on the back of a card is usually neglected when you come to write the paper. Use four-by-six cards because the smaller cards, suitable for bibliographic notes, do not provide enough space for your summaries of useful material. Here is a guide to note taking:

A Guide to Note Taking

1. We suggest summaries rather than paraphrases (that is, abridgments rather than restatements which in fact may be as long as or longer than the original) because there is rarely any point to paraphrasing. Generally speaking, either quote exactly (and put

the passage in quotation marks, with a notation of the source, including the page number or numbers) or summarize, reducing a page or even an entire article or chapter of a book to a single four-by-six card. Even when you summarize, indicate your source (including the page numbers) on the card, so that you can give appropriate credit in your paper.

2. Of course in your summary you will sometimes quote a phrase or a sentence—putting it in quotation marks—but quote sparingly. You are not doing stenography; rather you are assimilating knowledge and you are thinking, and so for the most part your source should be digested rather than engorged whole. Thinking now, while taking notes, will also help you later to avoid plagiarism. If, on the other hand, when you take notes you mindlessly copy material at length, later when you are writing the paper you may be tempted to copy it yet again, perhaps without giving credit. Similarly, if you photocopy pages from articles or books, and then merely underline some passages, you probably will not be thinking; you will just be underlining. But if you make a terse summary on a note card you will be forced to think and to find your own words for the idea. Quote directly only those passages that are particularly effective, or crucial, or memorable. In your finished paper these quotations will provide authority and emphasis.

3. If you quote but omit some material within the quotation, be sure to indicate the omission by three spaced periods, as explained on page 371. After copying a quotation, check your card against the original, correct any misquotation, and then put a checkmark after your quotation to indicate that it is accurate. Verify the page number also, and then put a check on your card, after the page number. If a quotation runs from the bottom of, say, page 306 to the top of 307, on your card put a distinguishing mark (for instance two parallel vertical lines after the last word of the first page), so that if you later use only part of the quotation, you will know the page on which it appeared.

4. *Never* copy a passage by changing an occasional word, under the impression that you are thereby putting it into your own words. Notes of this sort may find their way into your paper, your reader will sense a style other than your own, and suspicions of plagiarism may follow. (For a detailed discussion of plagiarism, see pages 362–65).

5. Feel free to jot down your own responses to the note. Indeed, consider it your obligation to *think* about the material, evaluating it and using it as a stimulus to further thought. For example, you may want to say "Gold seems to be generalizing from insufficient evidence," or "Corsa made the same point five years earlier"; but make certain that later you will be able to distinguish between these comments and the notes summarizing or quoting your source. A suggestion: surround all comments recording your responses with double parentheses, thus: ((. . .)).

6. In the upper corner of each note card, write a brief key— for example "effect on infants' blood"—so that later you can tell at a glance what is on the card. The sample card shown here summarizes a few pages; notice that it includes a short quotation and records the source. The source is not given in full bibliographic form because the full form is recorded on a bibliography card.

As you work, especially if you are working on a literary or historical topic, you'll of course find yourself returning again and again to the primary materials—and you'll probably find to your surprise that a good deal of the secondary material is unconvinc-

Verrett, pp. 152-154 ✓   botulism argument
                               search for substitute

p.152 Industry and gov't approved nitrite as color fixer. Now shifting ground, saying it prevents botulism. Verrett points out "legal snag." New approval needed for new use.
(Thus public hearing and unwanted attention)

p.154 "... the industry--USDA-FDA coalition seems firm in its position that there is no substitute for nitrate, now or ever. Their posture is misdirected at defending nitrites devising ways to keep it in food rather than ways to get it out. ✓

Verrett and Carper, *Eating May Be Hazardous*

ing or even wrong, despite the fact that it is printed in a handsome book. One of the things we learn from research is that not everything in print is true; one of the pleasures we get from research results from this discovery.

ACKNOWLEDGING SOURCES

Borrowing without Plagiarizing

As we suggested earlier, respect for your readers and for your sources requires that you acknowledge your indebtedness for material when

1. you quote directly from a work, or
2. you paraphrase or summarize someone's words (the words of your paraphrase or summary are your own, but the points are not), or
3. you appropriate an idea that is not common knowledge.

Let's suppose you are going to make use of Ralph Linton's comment on definitions of primitive art:

> The term "primitive art" has come to be used with at least three distinct meanings. First and most legitimate is its use with reference to the early stages in the development of a particular art, as when one speaks of the Italian primitives. Second is its use to designate works of art executed by persons who have not had formal training in our own art techniques and aesthetic canons. Third is its application to the art works of all but a small group of societies which we have chosen to call civilized. The present discussion will deal only with the last.
>
> —Ralph Linton, Preface to Eliot Elisofon,
> *The Sculpture of Africa*
> (New York: Frederick A. Praeger, 1958), p. 9.

1. *Acknowledging a direct quotation.* You may want to use some or all of Linton's words, in which case you will write something like this:

```
As Ralph Linton says, ''The term 'primitive art' has
come to be used with at least three distinct meanings. First
and most legitimate is its use with reference to the early
```

```
stages in the development of a particular art, as when one
speaks of the Italian primitives'' (Elisofon 9).
```

2. *Acknowledging a paraphrase or summary.* We have already suggested (page 359) that summaries (abridgments) are usually superior to paraphrases (rewordings, of approximately the same length as the original) because summaries are briefer; but occasionally you may find that you cannot greatly abridge a passage in your source and yet don't want to quote it word for word— perhaps because it is too technical or poorly written. Even though you are changing some or all of the words, you must give credit to the source because the idea is not yours. Here is an example of a summary:

```
Ralph Linton, in his Preface to Eliot Elisofon's The
Sculpture of Africa, suggests that there are at least three
common but distinct meanings of the term ''primitive art'':
the early stages of a particular art; the art of untrained
artists; and the art of societies that we consider unciva-
lized (Elisofon 9).
```

Not to give credit to Linton is to plagiarize, even though the words are yours. And of course if you say something like this, and do not give credit, you are also plagiarizing:

```
''Primitive art'' is used in three different senses.
First and most reasonable is the use of the word to refer to
the early years of a certain art. . . .
```

It is pointless to offer this sort of rewording; if there is a point, it is to conceal the source and to take credit for thinking that is not your own.

3. *Acknowledging an idea.* Let us say that you have read an essay in which Irving Kristol argues that journalists who pride themselves on being tireless critics of national policy are in fact irresponsible critics because they have no policy they prefer. If this strikes you as a new idea and you adopt it in an essay—even though you set it forth entirely in your own words and with examples not

offered by Kristol—you should acknowledge your debt to Kristol. Not to acknowledge such borrowing is plagiarism. Your readers will not think the less of you for naming your source; rather, they will be grateful to you for telling them about an interesting writer.

In short, acknowledge your source
(1) if you quote directly, and put the quoted words in quotation marks,
(2) if you summarize or paraphrase someone's material, even though not one word of your source is retained, and
(3) if you borrow a distinctive idea, even though the words and the concrete application are your own.

Fair Use of Common Knowledge

If in doubt as to whether or not to give credit (either with formal documentation or merely in a phrase such as "Ralph Linton says . . ."), give credit. But as you begin to read widely in your field or subject, you will develop a sense of what is considered common knowledge. Unsurprising definitions in a dictionary can be considered common knowledge, and so there is no need to say "According to Webster, a novel is a long narrative in prose." (That's weak in three ways: it's unnecessary, it's uninteresting, and it's unclear, since "Webster" appears in the titles of several dictionaries, some good and some bad.) Similarly, the date of Freud's death can be considered common knowledge. Few can give it when asked, but it can be found out from innumerable sources, and no one need get the credit for providing you with the date. Again, if you simply *know,* from your reading of Freud, that Freud was interested in literature, you need not cite a specific source for an assertion to that effect, but if you know only because some commentator on Freud said so, and you have no idea whether the fact is well known or not, you should give credit to the source that gave you the information. Not to give credit—for ideas as well as for quoted words—is to plagiarize.

"But How Else Can I Put It?"

If you have just learned—say from an encyclopedia—something that you sense is common knowledge, you may wonder, How can I change into my own words the simple, clear words that this source uses in setting forth this simple fact? For example, if before writing about the photograph of Buffalo Bill and Sitting Bull (page 79), you look up these names in the *Encyclopaedia Britannica,* you will find this statement about Buffalo Bill (William F. Cody): "In 1883 Cody organized his first Wild West exhibition." You cannot use this statement as your own, word for word, without feeling uneasy. But to put in quotation marks such a routine statement of what can be considered common knowledge, and to cite a source for it, seems pretentious. After all, the *Encyclopedia Americana* says much the same thing in the same routine way: "In 1883, . . . Cody organized Buffalo Bill's Wild West." It may be that the word "organized" is simply the most obvious and the best word, and perhaps you will end up using it. Certainly to change "Cody organized" into "Cody presided over the organization of" or "Cody assembled" or some such thing, in an effort to avoid plagiarizing, would be to make a change for the worse and still to be guilty of plagiarism. But you won't get yourself into this mess of wondering whether to change clear, simple wording into awkward wording if in the first place, when you take notes, you summarize your sources, thus: "1883: organized Wild West," or "first Wild West: 1883." Later (even if only thirty minutes later), when drafting your paper, if you turn this nugget—probably combined with others—into the best sentence you can, you will not be in danger of plagiarizing, even if the word "organized" turns up in your sentence.

Of course, even when dealing with material that can be considered common knowledge—and even when you have put it into your own words—you probably *will* cite your source if you are drawing more than just an occasional fact from a source. If, for instance, your paragraph on Buffalo Bill uses half a dozen facts from a source, cite the source. You do this both to avoid charges of plagiarism and to protect yourself in case your source contains errors of fact.

WRITING THE PAPER

There remains the difficult job of writing up your findings. Beyond referring you to the rest of this book, we can offer only seven pieces of advice.

1. With a tentative thesis in mind, begin by rereading your note cards and sorting them into packets by topic. Put together what belongs together. Don't hesitate to reject material that—however intersting—now seems irrelevant or redundant. In doing your research you quite properly took lots of notes (as William Blake said, "You never know what is enough unless you know what is more than enough"), but now, in looking over your material, you see that some of it is unnecessary, and so you reject it. Your finished paper should not sandbag the reader. After sorting, resorting, and rejecting, you will have a kind of first draft without writing a draft.

If you use a word processor, you can type your notes onto the same disk you'll use for writing your paper. You will still, of course, have to think about how to classify your notes, but the computer will reduce most of the physical effort of sorting, resorting, and rejecting, and all of the clutter.

2. From your packets of cards you can make a first outline. In arranging the packets into a sequence, and then in sketching an outline, of course you will be guided by your *thesis*. As you worked, you probably modified your tentative ideas in the light of what your further research produced, but by now you ought to have a firm idea of what you think the evidence adds up to. Without a thesis you will have only a lot of note cards, not a potential essay.

Do not, however, confuse this tentative outline with a paragraph outline; when you come to write your essay, a single heading may require two or three or even more paragraphs. Although you can't yet make a paragraph outline, you may find it useful to make a fairly full outline, indicating, for example, not only the sequence of points but also the quotations that you will use.

Do not confuse this tentative outline with a formal outline, discussed on pages 434–36. An example of an outline preceding a research paper is given on pages 398–99.

3. When you write your first draft, leave lots of space at the top and bottom of each page so that you can add material, which will be circled and connected by arrows to the proper place. For example, as you are drafting page 6, from perhaps your tenth packet, you may find a note card that now seems more appropriate to a point you made back on page 2. Write it on page 2,

and put the card in the appropriate earlier packet so that if for some reason you later have to check your notes you can find it easily.

Again, a word processor makes all this shifting of material from one place to another easy. You can try out and store several versions of page 6; you can print out whatever versions you want to see on a typed page; you can revise on the screen, or on the page. The possibilities are endless.

4. Write or type your quotations, even in the first draft, exactly as you want them to appear in the final version. Of course this takes some time, and the time will be wasted if, as may well turn out, you later see that the quotation is not really useful. (On the other hand, the time has not really been wasted, since it helped you ultimately to delete the unnecessary material.)

If at this early stage you just write a summary of the quotation—something like "here quote Jackson on undecided voters"—when you re-read the draft you won't really know how the page sounds. You won't, for instance, know how much help your reader needs by way of a lead-in to the quotation, or how much discussion should follow. Only if you actually see the quotation are you in the position of your readers—and all good writers try to imagine their readers.

Short quotations (fewer than three lines of poetry or fewer than five lines of prose) are enclosed within quotation marks but are not otherwise set off; longer quotations, however, are set off: they begin a new line, are indented ten spaces, and are *not* within quotation marks.

For a comment on ways to introduce quotations, see point 7.

For the form of embedded quotations and of set-off quotations, see pages 374–75.

5. Include, right in the body of the draft, all of the relevant citations so that when you come to revise you don't have to start hunting through your notes to find who said what, and where. You can, for the moment, enclose these citations within diagonal lines, or within double parentheses—anything at all to remind you that they will be your documentation.

6. Beware of the compulsion to include every note card in your essay. You have taken all these notes, and there is a strong

temptation to use them all. But, truth to tell, in hindsight many are useless. By now you will probably have a clearer sense of your thesis. You may have modified it in the light of your research. Consequently, you will probably find, as you write your draft, that some of what you have accumulated is irrelevant, and, on the other hand, here and there you need to do more research, to check a quotation or to collect additional examples. Probably it is best to continue writing your draft if possible, and to incorporate new material in a later draft.

7. As you revise your draft, make sure that you do not merely tell the reader "A says . . . B says . . . C says. . . ." Rather, by such expressions as "A claims," "B provides evidence that," "C gives the usual view," "D concedes that," you help the reader to see the role of the quotation in your paper. When you write a research paper, you are not merely dumping on the table the contents of a shopping-cart filled at the scholar's supermarket, the library. You are cooking a meal. You must have a point, an opinion, a thesis; you are working toward a conclusion, and your readers should always feel they are moving toward that conclusion (by means of your thoughtful evaluation of the evidence) rather than reading an anthology of commentary on the topic.

While you were doing your research you may have noticed that the more interesting writers persuade the reader of the validity of their opinions by

1. letting the reader see that they know what of significance has been written on the topic;
2. letting the reader hear the best representatives of the chief current opinions, whom they correct or confirm;
3. advancing their opinions, by offering generalizations supported by concrete details; and
4. using quotations effectively—not as padding and not in place of the essayist's own words—to support and emphasize the essayist's words.

Adopt these techniques in your own writing. Thus, because you have a focus, we should get things like: "There are three common views on. . . . The first two are represented by A and B; the third, and by far the most reasonable, is C's view that . . ." or "A argues . . . but . . ." or "Although the third view, C's, is not conclusive, still . . ." or "Moreover, C's point can be strengthened when we consider a piece of evidence that he does not make use of." We have already mentioned that you cannot merely say "A says . . ., B says . . ., C says . . .," because your job is not to report what everyone says but to establish the truth of a thesis. When you introduce a quotation, then, try to let the reader see the use to which you are putting it. "A says" is of little help; giving the quotation and then following it with "thus says A" is even worse. You need a lead-in such as "A concisely states the common view," "B shrewdly calls attention to a fatal weakness," "Without offering any proof, C claims that. . . ." In short, it is usually advisable to let the reader know why you are quoting, or, to put it a little differently, how the quotation fits into your organization.

Your overall argument, then, is fleshed out with careful summaries and with effective quotations and with judicious analyses of your own, so that by the end of the paper the readers not only have read a neatly typed paper, but they also are persuaded that under your guidance they have seen the evidence, heard the arguments justly summarized, and reached a sound conclusion. They may not become better persons but they are better informed.

A CHECKLIST FOR READING DRAFTS

1. Is the tentative title informative and focused?
2. Does the paper make a point, or does it just accumulate other people's ideas?
3. Does it reveal the thesis early?
4. Are generalizations supported by evidence?
5. Are quotations introduced adequately?
6. Are all of the long quotations necessary, or can some of them be effectively summarized?
7. Are quotations discussed adequately?
8. Are all sources given?
9. Does the paper advance in orderly stages? Can your imagined reader easily follow your thinking?
10. Is the documentation in the correct form?

When you have finished your paper prepare a final copy that will be easy to read. Type the paper or clearly handwrite it on

8½-by-11 inch paper of decent weight. (If you write with a word processor, you already have a final copy in the computer, and you need only print it.) Write on one side only, and leave a one-inch margin all around (much more, of course, for the title page if you have one). For additional details about manuscript form, see pages 000–00; for additional details about documentation, see the comments immediately following.

A list entitled "Works Cited" in MLA style (see page 412) is appended to the research paper. This list has three important purposes: it enables you to add authority to your paper, to give credit to those writers who have helped you to develop your thoughts, and to assist the interested reader who may wish to look further into the primary and secondary material. APA style titles this list "References."

DOCUMENTATION

Until recently, sources were regularly acknowledged in footnotes or endnotes, but in 1984 the Modern Language Association, which had established the footnote form used in hundreds of journals, university presses, and classrooms, substituted a new form. It is this new form—parenthetical citations *within* the text (rather than at the foot of the page or the end of the essay)—that we explain here, and that we illustrate in a research paper called "Nitrites: Cancer for Many, Money for Few" (pages 397–412). But notice that at the end of this section, on pages 380–82, we include "A Note on Footnotes," explaining the uses to which footnotes may still be put.

Notice, too, that later, on pages 394–96, we list some manuals that set forth other styles of documentation, and on pages 413–23 we include a research paper ("Beyond the Institution: The Effects of Labeling on Ex-Mental Patients") that uses the form recommended by the American Psychological Association.

Citations within the Text (MLA Format)

Brief parenthetic citations within the body of the essay are made clear by a list of your sources, entitled Works Cited, appended to the essay. This list usually cites books and articles, and films, television programs, interviews, and the like. Thus, an item in your list of Works Cited will clarify such a sentence in your essay as

> The Food and Drug Administration depends heavily for research
> and advice on the food committees of the National Academy of
> Sciences, which Daniel Zwerdling claims are a ''Who's Who of
> the food industry'' (34).

This citation means that Zwerdling wrote the quoted words on page 34 of a source listed in Works Cited. More often than not the parenthetic citation appears at the end of a sentence, as in the example just given, but it can appear elsewhere in the sentence; its position will depend chiefly on your ear. You might, for instance, write the sentence thus:

> Daniel Zwerdling says that the food committees of the Na-
> tional Academy of Sciences are a ''Who's Who of the food in-
> dustry'' (34), and it is on these committees that the Food
> and Drug Administration depends.

Six points must be made about these examples:

1. Quotation marks. The closing quotation mark appears after the last word of the quotation, *not* after the parenthetic citation. Since the citation is not part of the quotation, the citation is not included within the quotation marks.

2. Omission of words (ellipsis). If the quoted words are merely a phrase, as in the example above, you do not need to indicate (by three spaced periods) that you are omitting material before or after the quotation, but if the quotation is longer than a phrase, and is not a complete sentence, you must indicate that you are omitting material. If you are omitting material from the beginning of the sentence, after the opening quotation mark put three spaced periods, and then give the quotation; if you are omitting material from the end of the sentence, put three spaced periods after the quoted words, or four periods if you are ending your sentence, and then close the quotation with a quotation mark, and add a final period. See pages 727–29.

3. Punctuation with parenthetic citations. Look again at the two examples given a moment ago, both referring to Zwerdling's book. Notice that if you follow a quotation with a parenthetic citation, any necessary period, semicolon, or comma *follows* the parenthetic citation. In the first example, a period follows the citation; in the second, a comma. In the next example, notice that the comma follows the citation.

```
Jackson insists that ''the figures can be interpreted in dif-
ferent ways'' (72), but he offers no further discussion.
```

If, however, the quotation itself uses a question mark or an exclamation mark, this mark of punctuation appears *within* the closing quotation mark; even so, a period follows the parenthetic citation.

```
Jackson is the only one to suggest doubt: ''How can we accept
such inadequate data?'' (78). He therefore rejects the en-
tire argument.
```

4. Two or more titles by one author. If your list of Works Cited includes more than one work by an author, you will have to give additional information (either in your sentence or within the parentheses) in order to indicate *which* of the titles you are referring to. We will go further into this in a moment (on page 374).

5. Long (set off) quotations. We have been talking about short quotations, which are not set off but are embedded within your own sentences. Long quotations, usually defined as more than four typed lines, are set off, as in the example below.

```
Michael Jacobson explains the preservative action of nitrite:
     Nitrite makes botulinum spores sensitive to heat. When
     foods are treated with nitrite and then heated, any botu-
     linum spores that may be present are killed. In the ab-
     sence of nitrite, spores can be inactivated only at tem-
     peratures that ruin the meat products. . . . Nitrite's
```

        preservative action is particularly important in foods

        that are not cooked after they leave the factory, such as

        ham, because these offer an oxygen-free environment, the

        kind in which bo<u>tulinum</u> can grow.　(165)

It seems unlikely that sodium nitrite is really necessary as a preservative. After extensive hearings in 1971, a congressional subcommittee . . .

In introducing a long quotation, keep in mind that a reader will have trouble reading a sentence that consists of a lead-in, a long quotation, and then a continuation of your own sentence. It's better to have a short lead-in ("Michael Jacobson explains the preservative action of nitrite"), and then set off a long quotation that is a complete sentence or group of sentences and therefore ends with a period. The quotation that is set off begins on a new line, is indented ten spaces from the left margin, and is *not* enclosed within quotation marks. Put a period at the end of the quotation (since the quotation is a complete sentence or group of sentences and is not embedded within a longer sentence of your own), hit the space bar three times, and then, on the same line, give the citation in parenthesis. Do *not* put a period after the parenthetic citation that follows a long quotation. Next, doublespace, and offer your comment flush with the left margin, or indent the first line of your comment if you are beginning a new paragraph. (Look back at the preceding example.)

6. Citing a summary or a paraphrase. Even if you don't quote a source directly, but use its point in a paraphrase or a summary, you will give a citation:

        Daniel Zwerdling points out (34) that the Food and Drug Ad-

        ministration relies for advice on committees which consist of

        the most eminent people in the food business.

The basic point, then, is that the system of in-text citation gives the documentation parenthetically. Notice that in all of the previous examples the author's name is given in the text (rather than within the parenthetic citation). But there are several other ways of giving the citation, and we shall now look at them.

Author and Page Number in Parenthetic Citation

```
As early as 1899, scientists discovered that nitrate breaks
down into nitrite and that it is the nitrite which actually
preserves the red color in meats (Jacobson 164-65).
```

It doesn't matter whether you summarize (as in this example) or quote directly; the parenthetic citation means that your source is pages 164–65 of a work by Jacobson, listed in Works Cited, at the end of your essay.

Title and Page Number in Parentheses

If, as we mentioned earlier, your list of Works Cited includes two or more titles by an author, you cannot in the text simply give a name and a page reference; the reader would not know to which of the titles you are referring. Let's assume that Works Cited includes two items by William Robbins. If in a sentence in your essay you don't specify one title—that is, if you don't say something like, "Robbins, in *The American Food Scandal*, says . . ." —you will have to give the title (in a shortened form) in the parenthetic citation:

```
William Robbins (American 2) characterizes as a ''big lie''
the assertion that Americans have better food than the people
of any other nation.
```

Notice in this example that *American* is a short title for Robbins's book *The American Food Scandal*. The full title is given in Works Cited, as is the title of another work by Robbins, but the short title in the parenthetic citation is enough to direct the reader to page 2 of the correct source in Works Cited.

Notice also that when a short title and a page reference are given in parentheses, a comma is *not* used after the title.

Author, Title, and Page Number in Parentheses

We have just seen that if Works Cited includes two or more works by an author, and if in your lead-in you do not specify which work you are at the moment making use of, you will have to give the title as well as the page number in parentheses. Similarly, if for some reason you do not in your lead-in mention the name of the author, you will have to add this bit of information to the parenthetic citation, thus:

```
That Americans are the best fed people is a ''big lie'' (Rob-
bins, American 2).
```

Notice that, as in the previous example, a comma does *not* separate the title from the page reference; but notice, too, that a comma *does* separate the author's name from the title. (Don't ask us why; ask the Modern Language Association, or, on the other hand, just obey orders.)

A Government Document or a Work of Corporate Authorship

Treat the issuing body as the author. Thus, you will probably write something like this:

```
The Commission on Food Control, in Food Resources Today, con-
cludes that there is no danger (36—37).
```

A Work by Two or More Authors

If a work is by *two authors,* give the names of both, either in the parenthetic citation (the first example below) or in a lead-in (the second example below):

```
The Food and Drug Administration found nitrosamines in salmon
''at levels up to twenty-six parts per billion'' (Verrett and
Carper 146—47).
```

or

```
Verrett and Carper point out that the Food and Drug Adminis-
tration found nitrosamines in salmon ''at levels up to
twenty-six parts per billion'' (146—47).
```

If there are *three or more authors,* give the last name of the first
author, followed by "et al." (an abbreviation for *et alii,* Latin for
"and others"), thus:

```
Gardner et al. found that . . .
```

or

```
Sometimes even higher levels are found (Gardner et al. 83).
```

Parenthetic Citation of an Indirect Source (Citation of Material that Itself was Quoted or Summarized in Your Source)

Suppose you are reading a book by Jones, and she quotes
Smith, and you wish to use Smith's material. Your citation will be
to Jones—the source you are using—but of course you cannot attribute the words to Jones. You will have to make it clear that
you are quoting not Jones but Smith, and so your parenthetic citation will look like this:

```
(qtd. in Jones 84-85)
```

Parenthetic Citation of Two or More Works

```
In microorganisms, nitrite enters the blood (Hervey 72; Led-
erer 195).
```

Note that a semicolon, followed by a space, separates the
two sources.

A Work in More than One Volume

This is a bit tricky.

a. If you have used only one volume, in Works Cited you
will specify the volume, and so in your parenthetic in-text citation
you will need to give only a page number—the very sort of thing
illustrated by most of the examples that we have been giving.

b. If you have used more than one volume, your parenthetic citation will have to specify the volume as well as the page, thus:

```
Landsdale points out that nitrite combines with hemoglobin to
form a pigment which cannot carry oxygen (2: 370).
```

The reference is to page 370 of volume 2 of a work by Landsdale.

c. If, however, you are citing not a page but an entire volume—let's say volume 2—your parenthetic citation would be

```
(vol. 2)
```

Or, if you did not name the author in your lead-in, it would be

```
(Landsdale, vol. 2)
```

Notice that

1. in citing a volume and page, the volume number, like the page number, is given in arabic (not roman) numerals;
2. the volume number is followed by a colon, then a space, then the page number;
3. abbreviations such as "vol." and "p." and "pg." are *not* used, except when citing a volume number without a page number, as illustrated in the last two examples.

An Anonymous Work

For an anonymous work, give the title in your lead-in, or give it in a shortened form in your parenthetic citation:

```
Official Guide to Food Standards includes a statistical table
on nitrates (362).
```

or

```
A statistical table on nitrites is available (Official Guide
362).
```

But double-check to make sure that the work is truly anonymous. Some encyclopedias, for example, give the authors' names quietly. If initials follow the article, these are the initials of the author's name. Check the alphabetic list of authors given at the front of the encyclopedia.

A Literary Work

You will specify the edition in Works Cited—let's say Alvin Kernan's edition of *Othello,* or an edition of Conrad's *Heart of Darkness* with a preface by Albert Guerard, but because classic works of literature are widely available, and your reader may have at hand an edition different from the one that you have read, it is customary to use the following forms:

A Novel

In parentheses give the page number of the edition you specify in Works Cited, followed by a semicolon, a space, and helpful additional information, thus:

    (181; ch.6)

or

    (272; part 1, ch. 7).

A Play

Most instructors want the act, scene, and (if the lines are numbered) the line numbers, rather than a page reference. Until recently, the act was given in capital roman numerals, the scene in lower-case roman numerals, and the line(s) in arabic numerals, without spaces between them. Thus,

    (II.iv.18-23)

would refer to lines 18–23 of the fourth scene of the second act. Recently, however, at the urging of the Modern Language Association, there has been a tendency to use arabic numerals throughout:

(2.4.18–23)

If you are quoting a few words within a sentence of your own, immediately after closing the brief quotation give the citation (enclosed within parentheses), and, if your sentence ends with the quotation, put the period after the closing parenthesis.

```
That Macbeth fully understands that killing Duncan is not a
manly act but a villainous one is clear from his words to
Lady Macbeth: ''I dare do all that may become a man''
(1.7.46). Moreover, even though he goes on to kill Duncan,
he does not go on to deceive himself into thinking that his
act was noble.
```

If, however, your sentence continues beyond the citation, after the parenthetic citation put whatever punctuation may be necessary (for instance, a comma may be needed), complete your sentence, and end it with a period.

```
This is clear from his words, ''I dare do all that does be-
come a man'' (1.7.46), and he never loses his awareness of
true manliness.
```

A Poem

Preferences vary, and you can't go wrong in citing the page, but for a poem longer than, say, a sonnet (fourteen lines), most instructors find it useful if students cite the line numbers, in parentheses, after the quotations. In your first use, preface the numerals with "line" or "lines" (not in quotation marks, of course); in subsequent citations simply give the numerals. For very long poems that are divided into books, such as Homer's *Odyssey*, give the page, a semicolon, a space, the book number, and the line number(s). The following example refers to page 327 of a title listed in Works Cited; it goes on to indicate that the passage occurs in the ninth book of the poem, lines 130–35.

    (327; 9.130–35).

Long quotations (more than three lines of poetry) are indented ten spaces. As we explained on page 373, if you give a long quotation, try to give one that can correctly be concluded with a period. After the period, hit the space bar three times, and then, on the same line, give the citation in parentheses.

An Interview

Probably you won't need a parenthetic citation, because you'll say something like

    Cyril Jackson, in an interview, said . . .

or

    According to Cyril Jackson, . . .

and when your reader turns to Works Cited, he or she will see that Jackson is listed, along with the date of the interview. But if you do not mention the source's name in the lead-in, you will have to give it in the parentheses, thus:

    It has been estimated that chemical additives earn the drug

    companies well over five hundred million dollars annually

    (Jackson).

A Note on Footnotes in an Essay Using Parenthetic Citations

In a research paper you will of course draw on many sources, but in other kinds of papers you may be using only one source, and yet within the paper you may often want to specify a reference to a page or (for poetry) a line number, or (for a play) to an act, scene, and line number. In such a case, to append a page headed Works Cited, with a single title, is silly; it is better to use a single footnote when you first allude to the source. Such a note can run something like this:

> [1]All references are to Mary Shelley, <u>Frankenstein</u>, after word by Harold Bloom (New York: Signet, 1965).

Here's another example of this sort of footnote:

> [2]All experiments described in this paper were performed in January 1989 in the laboratory of Dr. Jan Pechenik, of Tufts University.

Footnotes can also be used in another way in a paper that documents sources by giving parenthetic citations. If you want to include some material that might seem intrusive in the body of the essay, you may relegate it to a footnote. For example, in a footnote you might translate a quotation given in a foreign language, or in a footnote you might write a paragraph—a sort of mini-essay—in which you offer an amplification of some point. By putting the amplification in a footnote you are signaling to the reader that it is dispensable; it is, so to speak, thrown in as something extra, something relevant but not essential to your argument. On the whole, it's a bad habit to write this sort of note, but there are times when it is appropriate.

To indicate in the body of your text that you are adding a footnote at this point, place a raised arabic numeral (without a period, and not enclosed in parentheses) by raising the typewriter carriage half a line.

> Joachim Jeremias's <u>The Parables of Jesus</u> is probably the best example of this sort of book.[1]

Usually the number is put at the end of a sentence, immediately after the period, but put it earlier if clarity requires you to do so.

> Helen Cam[1] as well as many lesser historians hold this view.

After you have typed the last line of text on the page, double-space twice, then indent five spaces, elevate the carriage half a line, type the digit (without a period and without parentheses), lower the carriage to the regular position, hit the space bar once, and type the note. If the note runs more than one line, type it single-spaced (unless your instructor tells you to the contrary), flush with the left margin. Double-space between notes, and begin each note with an indented raised numeral and then a capital letter. End each note with a period or, if the sentence calls for one, a question mark.

The List of Works Cited (MLA Format)

As we have just explained, your parenthetic documentation consists of references that become meaningful when the reader consults a list entitled Works Cited, given at the end of your essay. We give sample entries below, but see also the list of Works Cited at the end of a student's research paper, on page 412.

The list of Works Cited continues the pagination of the essay; if the last page of text is 10, then the list begins on page 11. Type your last name and the page number in the upper right corner, half an inch from the top of the sheet. Next, type "Works Cited," centered, one inch from the top, then double-space and type the first entry. Here are the governing conventions.

Alphabetic Order

1. Arrange the list alphabetically by author, with the author's last name first.
2. List an anonymous work alphabetically under the first word of the title, or under the second word if the first word is *A, An,* or *The,* or a foreign equivalent.
3. If your list includes two or more works by one author, the work whose title comes earlier in the alphabet precedes the work whose title comes later in the alphabet.

Form on the Page

1. Begin each entry flush with the left margin, but if an entry runs to more than one line, indent five spaces for each succeeding line of the entry.
2. Double-space each entry, and double-space between entries.

From here on, things get complicated. We will begin with

books, then

films, television and radio programs (page 392), and finally

articles in journals and newspapers and database sources (pages 392–94).

The forms for books are as follows.

The Author's Name

Note that the last name is given first, but otherwise the name is given as on the title page. Do not substitute initials for names written out on the title page.

If your list includes two or more works by an author, the author's name is not repeated for the second title, but is represented by three hyphens followed by a period and two spaces. Note, too, that the sequence of the works is determined by the alphabetic order of the titles, as in the example below (page 384), listing two books by Northrop Frye, where *Fables* precedes *Fools*.

We have already discussed the treatment of an anonymous work; in a few moments we will discuss books by more than one author, government documents, and works of corporate authorship.

The Title

Take the title from the title page, not from the cover or the spine, but disregard any unusual typography—for instance, the use of only capital letters, or the use of *&* for *and*. Underline title and subtitle (separate them by a colon) with one continuous underline, to indicate italics, but do not underline the period that concludes this part of the entry. Example:

```
Frankenstein: Or, The Modern Prometheus.
```

A peculiarity: underlining is used to indicate the title of a book, but if a title of a book itself includes the title of a book (for instance, a book about Mary Shelley's *Frankenstein* might include the title of her novel in its own title), the title-within-the-title is *not* underlined. Thus, the title would be given as

The Endurance of Frankenstein.

Place of Publication, Publisher, and Date

For the place of publication, give the name of the city (you can usually find it either on the title page or on the reverse of the title page). If several cities are listed, give only the first. If the city is not likely to be widely known, or if it may be confused with another city of the same name (for instance, Cambridge, Massachusetts, and Cambridge, England), add the name of the state.

The name of the publisher is abbreviated. Usually the first word is enough (Random House becomes Random; Little, Brown and Co. becomes Little), but if the first word is a first name, such as in Alfred A. Knopf, the surname (Knopf) is used instead. University presses are abbreviated thus: Yale UP, U of Chicago P, State U of New York P.

The date of publication of a book is given when known; if no date appears on the book, write n.d. to indicate "no date."

Here are sample entries, illustrating the points we have covered thus far:

Douglas, Ann.   The Feminization of American Culture.   New

   York: Knopf, 1977.

Frye, Northrop.   Fables of Identity: Studies in Poetic My-

   thology.   New York: Harcourt, 1963.

———   Fools of Time: Studies in Shakespearian Tragedy.   To-

   ronto: U of Toronto P, 1967.

Hartman, Chester.   The Transformation of San Francisco.   To-

   towa, N. J.: Rowman, 1984.

Kellerman, Barbara.   The Political Presidency: Practice of

   Leadership from Kennedy through Reagan.   New York: Ox-

   ford UP, 1984.

Notice that a period follows the author's name, and another period follows the title. If a subtitle is given, as it is for Kellerman's book, it is separated from the title by a colon and a space. A colon follows the place of publication, a comma follows the publisher, and a period follows the date.

A Book by More than One Author

The book is alphabetized under the last name of the first author named on the title page. If there are *two or three authors,* the names of these are given (after the first author's name) in the normal order, *first name first.*

Honour, Hugh, and John Fleming. The Visual Arts: A History.

Englewood Cliffs: Prentice-Hall, 1982.

Notice, again, that although the first author's name is given *last name first,* the second author's name is given in the normal order. Notice, too, that a comma is put after the first name of the first author, separating the authors.

If there are *more than three authors,* give the name of only the first, and then add (but *not* enclosed within quotation marks) "et al." (Latin for "and others").

Altshuler, Alan, et al. The Future of the Automobile. Cam-

bridge, Mass.: MIT P, 1984.

Government Documents

If the writer is not known, treat the government and the agency as the author. Most federal national documents are issued by the Government Printing Office (abbreviated to GPO) in Washington.

United States Congress. Office of Technology Assessment.

Computerized Manufacturing Automation: Employment, Edu-

cation, and the Workplace. Washington: GPO, 1984.

Works of Corporate Authorship

Begin the citation with the corporate author, even if the same body is also the publisher, as in the first example:

```
American Psychiatric Association.  Psychiatric Glossary.

    Washington: American Psychiatric Association, 1984.


Carnegie Council on Policy Studies in Higher Education.  Giv-

    ing Youth a Better Chance: Options for Education, Work,

    and Service.  San Francisco: Jossey, 1980.
```

A Reprint, for Instance a Paperback Version of an Older Clothbound Book

```
Rourke, Constance.  American Humor.  1931.  Garden City, New

    York: Doubleday, 1953.
```

After the title, give the date of original publication (it can usually be found on the reverse of the title page of the reprint you are using), then a period, and then the place, publisher, and date of the edition you are using. The example indicates that Rourke's book was originally published in 1931 and that the student is using the Doubleday reprint of 1953.

A Book in Several Volumes

```
Friedel, Frank.  Franklin D. Roosevelt.  4 vols.  Boston:

    Little, 1973.
```

If you have used more than one volume, in your essay you will (as has been explained on page 376) indicate a reference to, say, page 250 of volume 3 thus: (3: 250).

If, however, you have used only one volume of the set—let's say volume 3—in your entry in Works Cited write, after the period following the date, "Vol. 3," as in the next entry:

```
Friedel, Frank.  Franklin D. Roosevelt.  4 vols.  Boston:

    Little, 1973.  Vol. 3.
```

In this case, the parenthetic citation would be to the page only, not to the volume and page, since a reader will understand that the page reference must be to this volume. But notice that in Works Cited, even though you say you used only volume 3, you also give the total number of volumes.

One Book with a Separate Title in a Set of Volumes

Sometimes a set with a title makes use also of a separate title for each book in the set. If you are listing such a book, use the following form:

```
Churchill, Winston.  The Age of Revolution.  Vol. 3 of A His-
     tory of the English-Speaking Peoples.  New York: Dodd,
     1957.
```

A Book with an Author and an Editor

```
Shakespeare, William  The Sonnets.  Ed. William Burto.  New
     York: NAL, 1965.

Churchill, Winston, and Franklin D. Roosevelt.  The Complete
     Correspondence.  3 vols.  Ed. Warren F. Kimball.
     Princeton: Princeton UP, 1985.
```

If the book has one editor, the abbreviation is "ed."; if two or more editors, "eds."

If you are making use of the editor's introduction or other editorial material, rather than of the author's work, list the book under the name of the editor, rather than of the author, following the form on page 388 for "An introduction, foreword, or afterword."

A Revised Edition of a Book

```
Chaucer, Geoffrey.  The Works of Geoffrey Chaucer.  Ed.
     F. N. Robinson.  2nd ed.  Boston: Houghton, 1957.
```

A Translated Book

Franqui, Carlos. Family Portrait with Fidel: A Memoir.

   Trans. Alfred MacAdam. New York: Random, 1984.

But if you are discussing the translation itself, as opposed to the book, list the work under the translator's name, then put a comma, a space, and "trans." After the period following "trans." skip two spaces, then give the title of the book, a period, two spaces, and then "By" and the author's name, first name first. Continue with information about the place of publication, publisher, and date, as in any entry for a book.

An Introduction, Foreword, or Afterword

Clark, Kenneth. Introduction. Dictionary of Subjects and

   Symbols in Art. By James Hall. New York: Harper, 1974.

Usually a book with an introduction or some such comparable material is listed under the name of the author of the book (here Hall), rather than under the name of the writer of the introduction (here Clark), but if you are referring to the apparatus rather than to the book itself, use the form just given. The words Introduction, Preface, Foreword, and Afterword are neither enclosed within quotation marks nor underlined.

A Book with an Editor but No Author

Anthologies of literature fit this description, but here we have in mind a book of essays written by various people but collected by an editor (or editors), whose name appears on the collection.

LaValley, Albert J., ed. Focus on Hitchcock. Englewood

   Cliffs: Prentice, 1972.

A Work in a Volume of Works by One Author

The following entry indicates that a short work by Susan Sontag—an essay called "The Aesthetics of Science"—appears in a book by Sontag entitled *Styles of Radical Will.* Notice that the inclusive page numbers of the short work are cited—not merely page numbers that you may happen to refer to, but the page numbers of the entire piece.

```
Sontag, Susan.  ''The Aesthetics of Science.''  In Styles of
    Radical Will.  New York: Farrar, 1969.  3-34.
```

A Work in an Anthology—That Is, in a Collection of Works by Several Authors

There are several possibilities here. Let's assume, for a start, that you have made use of one work in an anthology. In Works Cited, begin with the author (last name first) and title of the work you are citing, not with the name of the anthologist or the title of the anthology. Here is an entry for Coleridge's poem "Kubla Khan," which the student found on pages 353–55 in the second volume of a two-volume anthology edited by M. H. Abrams and several others.

```
Coleridge, Samuel Taylor.  ''Kubla Khan.''  Norton Anthology
    of English Literature.  Ed. M. H. Abrams et al.  4th ed.
    2 vols.  New York: Norton, 1979.  2:353-55.
```

Now let's assume that during the course of your essay you refer to several, rather than to only one work in this anthology. You can, of course, list each work in the form just given. Or you can have an entry in Works Cited for Abrams's anthology, under Abrams's name, and then in each entry for a work in the anthology you can eliminate some of the data by simply referring to Abrams, thus:

```
Coleridge, Samuel Taylor.  ''Kubla Khan.''  Abrams 2:353-55.
```

Again, this requires that you also list Abrams's volume, thus:

```
Abrams, M. H. et al., eds.  The Norton Anthology of English
    Literature.  4th ed.  2 vols.  New York: Norton, 1979.
```

The advantage of listing the anthology separately is that if you are using a dozen works from the anthology, you can shorten the dozen entries in Works Cited merely by adding one entry, that of the anthology itself. Notice, of course, that in the body of the essay you would still refer to Coleridge and to your other eleven authors, not to the editor of the anthology—but the entries in Works Cited will guide the reader to the book you have used.

A Book Review

```
Vendler, Helen.   Rev. of Essays on Style.   Ed. Roger

    Fowler.   Essays in Criticism 16 (1966): 457-63.
```

If the review has a title, give it between the period following the reviewer's name and "Rev."

If a review is anonymous, list it under the first word of the title, or under the second word if the first word is *A, An,* or *The.* If an anonymous review has no title, begin the entry with "Rev. of" and then give the title of the work reviewed; alphabetize the entry under the title of the work reviewed.

An Article or Essay—Not a Reprint—in a Collection

A book may consist of a collection (edited by one or more persons) of new essays by several authors. Here is a reference to one essay in such a book. (The essay, by Balmforth, occupies pages 19–35 in a collection edited by Bevan.)

```
Balmforth, Henry.   ''Science and Religion.''   Steps to Chris-

    tian Understanding.   Ed.   R. J. W. Bevan.   London: Ox-

    ford UP, 1958.   19-35.
```

An Article or Essay Reprinted in a Collection

The previous example (Balmforth's essay in Bevan's collection) was for an essay written for a collection. But some collections reprint earlier material, for example essays from journals, or chapters from books. The following example cites an essay that was originally printed in a book called *The Cinema of Alfred Hitchcock*. This essay has been reprinted in a later collection of essays on Hitchcock, edited by Arthur J. LaValley, and it was LaValley's collection that the student used.

```
Bogdanovich, Peter.  ''Interviews with Alfred Hitchcock.''

    The Cinema of Alfred Hitchcock.  New York: Museum of

    Modern Art, 1963. 15-18.  Rpt. in Focus on Hitchcock.

    Ed.  Albert J. LaValley.  Englewood Cliffs: Prentice,

    1972.  28-31.
```

The student has read Bogdanovich's essay or chapter, but not in Bogdanovich's book, where it occupied pages 15–18. The material was actually read on pages 28–31 in a collection of writings on Hitchcock, edited by LaValley. Details of the original publication—title, date, page numbers, and so forth—were found in LaValley's collection. Almost all editors will include this information, either on the copyright page or at the foot of the reprinted essay, but sometimes they do not give the original page numbers. In such a case, the original numbers need not be included in the entry.

Notice that the entry begins with the author and the title of the work you are citing (here, Bogdanovich's interviews), not with the name of the editor of the collection or the title of the collection. In the following example, the student used an essay by Arthur Sewell; the essay was originally on pages 53–56 in a book by Sewell entitled *Character and Society in Shakespeare*, but the student encountered the piece on pages 36–38 in a collection of essays, edited by Leonard Dean, on Shakespeare's *Julius Caesar*. Here is how the entry should run:

```
Sewell, Arthur.  ''The Moral Dilemma in Tragedy: Brutus.''

    Character and Society in Shakespeare.  Oxford: Claren-

    don, 1951.  53 56.  Rpt. in Twentieth Century Interpre-

    tations of Julius Caesar.  Ed. Leonard F. Dean.  Engle-

    wood Cliffs: Prentice, 1968.  36-38.
```

An Encyclopedia or Other Alphabetically Arranged Reference Work

The publisher, place of publication, volume number, and page number do *not* have to be given. For such works, list only the edition (if it is given) and the date.

For a *signed* article, begin with the author's last name. (If the article is signed with initials, check the volume for a list of abbreviations, which will say what the initials stand for, and use the following form.)

```
Messer, Thomas.  ''Picasso.''  Encyclopedia Americana.  1980

     ed.
```

For an *unsigned article,* begin with the title of the article.

```
''Picasso, Pablo (Ruiz y).''  Encyclopaedia Britannica:

     Macropaédia.  1985 ed.

''Automation.''  The Business Reference Book.  1977 ed.
```

A Film

Begin with the director's name (last name first), followed by "dir." Next give the title of the film, underlined, then a period, two spaces, the name of the studio, the date, and a period.

```
Lean, David, dir.  A Passage to India.  Columbia, 1984.
```

A Television or Radio Program

```
Sixty Minutes.  CBS.  17 Feb. 85.
```

An Article in a Scholarly Journal

The title of the article is enclosed within quotation marks, and the title of the journal is underlined to indicate italics.

Some journals are paginated consecutively—the pagination of the second issue begins where the first issue leaves off; but other journals begin each issue with page 1. The forms of the citations

differ slightly. First, an article in a *journal that is paginated consecutively:*

> Jacobus, Mary.   ''Tess's Purity.''   Essays in Criticism 26
>   (1976): 318–38.

Jacobus's article occupies pages 318–38 of volume 26, which was
published in 1976. (Note that the volume number is followed by
a space, and then by the year, in parentheses, and then by a colon,
a space, and the page numbers of the entire article. Because the
journal is paginated consecutively, the issue number does *not* need
to be specified.

For a *journal that begins each issue with page 1* (there will
be four page 1's each year if such a journal is a quarterly), the
issue number must be given. After the volume number, type a period and (without hitting the space bar) the issue number, as in
the next example.

> Spillers, Hortense J.   ''Martin Luther King and the Style of
>   the Black Sermon.''   The Black Scholar 3.1 (1971): 14–
>   27.

Spillers's article on King appeared in the first issue of volume 3 of
The Black Scholar.

An Article in a Weekly, Biweekly, or Monthly Publication

The date and page numbers are given, but volume numbers
and issue numbers are usually omitted for these publications. The
first example is for an article in a weekly publication:

> McCabe, Bernard.   ''Taking Dickens Seriously.''   Commonweal
>   14 May 1965: 245–46.

An Article in a Newspaper

Because a newspaper usually consists of several sections, a
section number or a capital letter may precede the page number.
The example indicates that an article begins on page 1 of section
2 and is continued on a later page.

```
Takayanagi, Peter.  ''Museum Appoints New Director.''  New
     York Times 15 Jan. 1986, Sec. 2:1 +.
```

A Database Source

Treat material obtained from a computer service, such as Bibliographies Retrieval Service (BRS), like other printed material, but at the end of the entry add the name of the service and the identification number of the item.

```
Jackson, Morton.  ''A Look at Profits.''  Harvard Business
     Review 40 (1962): 106—13.  Bibliographies Retrieval Ser-
     vice, 1984, Accession No. 621081.
```

Caution: although we have covered the most usual kinds of sources, it is entirely possible that you will come across a source that does not fit any of the categories that we have discussed. For two hundred pages of explanation of these matters, covering the proper way to cite all sorts of troublesome and unbelievable (but real) sources, see Joseph Gibaldi and Walter S. Achtert, *MLA Handbook for Writers of Research Papers,* 3rd ed. (New York: Modern Language Association of America, 1988).

Documentation in Fields Other Than the Humanities

We have given the system of documentation (footnotes and bibliography) used in the humanities, but the sciences and some of the social sciences use different systems. If you are writing a paper for a course other than one in the humanities, history, or political science, follow the style set forth in the appropriate manual.

The systems differ in many details, but one significant way in which most of them differ from the MLA system is their greater emphasis on the date, an emphasis based on the fact that research in the sciences and social sciences dates more quickly than work in the humanities. Thus, a passage might run along these lines:

```
Jones (1985) dismissed Thompson's findings as statistically

    worthless (pp. 84—85), but his own interpretation of the

    data has been seriously questioned (Smith, 1986, p. 84;

    Rizullo, 1986, pp. 200—01; Yanagi and Hunter, 1986, pp.

    99—101).
```

Moreover, in the list at the end of the paper (usually headed "References" instead of "Works Cited") the date is given immediately after the author's name. And in this list, if one author has written two or more papers, the papers are arranged not alphabetically (as in the MLA system) but chronologically.

On pages 413–23 we print a research paper by a student who used the system endorsed by the American Psychological Association.

Biology:

Council of Biology Editors, Style Manual Committee. *CBE Style Manual.* 5th ed. Bethesda: Council of Biology Editors, 1983.

Chemistry:

American Chemical Society. *Handbook for Authors of Papers in the Journals of the American Chemical Society.* Washington: American Chemical Society, 1978.

Engineering:

Engineers Joint Council, Committee of Engineering Society Editors. *Recommended Practice for Style of References in Engineering Publications.* New York: Engineers Joint Council, 1966.

Geology:

U.S. Geological Survey. *Suggestions to Authors of Reports of the United States Geological Survey.* 6th ed. Washington: GPO, Department of the Interior, 1978.

Mathematics:

American Mathematical Society. *Manual for Authors of Mathematical Papers.* 7th ed. Providence, R.I.: American Mathematical Society, 1980.

Medicine:

American Medical Association, Scientific Publications Division. *Stylebook.* 6th ed. Acton, Mass.: Publishing Sciences Group, 1976.

Physics:

American Institute of Physics, Publications Board. *Style Manual.* 3rd ed. New York: American Institute of Physics, 1978.

Psychology:

American Psychological Association. *Publication Manual of the American Psychological Association.* 3rd ed. Washington: American Psychological Association, 1983.

Two Sample Research Papers

Here are two sample papers. The first uses the MLA form of in-text citations, which are clarified by a list headed "Works Cited." The second paper, beginning on page 413, uses the APA (American Psychological Association) form of in-text citations, which are clarified by a list headed "References."

Notice that the first paper includes a thesis statement and an outline, helpful but not obligatory additions.

Nitrites: Cancer for Many, Money for Few

by

Jacob Alexander

English 1B

Mr. Cavitch

May 10, 1989

Alexander   i

Thesis

Sodium nitrite and sodium nitrate, added to cured meats and smoked
fish as a color fixative, combine in meat and in the stomach to
form a powerful carcinogen (cancer-producing substance). This fact
puts the profit motive of the food industry and the health of the
American public squarely into opposition, and thus far the government regulatory agencies are supporting the food industry.

Outline

I. Sodium nitrite and nitrate can be poison.

   A. Nitrites combine with blood to form a pink pigment which
      does not carry oxygen.

   B. They have a number of other ominous side-effects.

II. Nitrites combine with amines to form nitrosamines, among the
    most potent carcinogens known.

   A. Nitrites are likely to combine with amines in the human
      stomach to form nitrosamines.

   B. Animals of all kinds, fed nitrites and amines, develop can-
      cer in various parts of their bodies.

   C. Nitrosamines are sometimes present in nitrited food even
      before we ingest it.

III. Why are nitrites used in food?

   A. Nitrites are traditionally used as color fixers.

   B. Producers argue that they are also preservatives.

IV. Why does the government allow nitrites?

   A. Nitrites and nitrates have a very long history of use.

   B. Government regulatory mechanisms are full of loopholes.

     1. Delaney Clause in Food Additive Amendment (1958) does
        not apply.

     2. FDA controls fish; USDA controls meats.

     3. Both depend on industry-oriented NAS.

    C. The agencies defend themselves.

       1. They find fault with the experiments.

       2. They claim nitrites prevent botulism.

       3. They claim that there is a ''no-effect'' level of use for carcinogens, though doctors disagree.

V. American government is serving the food industry rather than the people.

    A. Food industry's enormous profits enable them to bring pressure to bear on regulatory agencies.

    B. Hazy patriotic optimism contributes to inaction.

VI. Stop eating nitrated fish and meat.

Alexander   1

Americans eat between three thousand and ten thousand additives in their food today, most of them untested (Zwerdling, ''Food''
34) and many of them known to be dangerous. Of these, nitrites are
among the most hazardous of all. In this country, ham, bacon,
corned beef, salami, bologna, lox, and other cold cuts and smoked
fish almost invariably contain sodium nitrite (or sodium nitrate,
which readily converts to nitrite in the human body). In fact,
one-third of the federally inspected meat and fish we consume—more
than seven billion pounds of it every year—contains this chemical
(Jacobson 169).

       To begin with, nitrite is just plain poison in amounts only
slightly greater than those allowed in cured meats. Jacqueline
Verrett, who worked for the Food and Drug Administration (FDA) for
fifteen years, and Jean Carper list in their book, Eating May Be
Hazardous to Your Health, recent instances of people poisoned by
accidental overdoses.

              In Buffalo, New York, six persons were hospitalized with
       ''cardiovascular collapse'' after they ate blood sausage
       which contained excessive amounts of nitrites. . . . In
       New Jersey, two persons died and many others were criti-
       cally poisoned after eating fish illegally loaded with
       nitrites. In New Orleans, ten youngsters between the
       ages of one and a half and five became seriously ill
       . . . after eating wieners or bologna overnitrited by a
       local meat-processing firm; one wiener that was obtained
       later from the plant was found to contain a whopping
       6,570 parts per million of nitrate, whereas the federal
       limitation is 200 parts per million. In Florida, a
       three-year-old boy died after eating hot dogs with three
       times greater nitrite concentration than the government
       allows. (138–39)

The chemical has the usual and difficult-to-replace quality of keeping meat a fresh-looking pink throughout the cooking, curing, and storage process (Assembly of Life Sciences 3). The nitrous acid from the nitrite combines with the hemoglobin in the blood of the meat, fixing its red color so that the meat does not turn the tired brown or gray natural to cured meats.

Unfortunately, it does much the same thing in humans. Although most of the nitrite passes through the body unchanged, a small amount is released into the bloodstream. This combines with the hemoglobin in the blood to form a pigment called methemoglobin, which cannot carry oxygen. If enough oxygen is incapacitated, a person dies. The allowable amount of nitrite in a quarter pound of meat can incapacitate between 1.4 and 5.7 percent of the hemoglobin in an average-sized adult (Verrett and Carper 138-39). When 10 to 20 percent is incapacitated, a victim discolors and has difficulty breathing (Jacobson 166). One of the problems with nitrite poisoning is that infants under a year, because of the quantity and makeup of their blood, are especially susceptible to it.

If the consumer of nitrite is not acutely poisoned, his blood soon returns to normal and this particular danger passes; the chemical, however, has long-term effects. Nitrite can cause headaches in people who are especially sensitive to it, an upsetting symptom in light of the fact that in rats who ate it regularly for a period of time it has produced lasting ''epileptic-like'' changes in the brain—abnormalities which showed up when the rats were fed only a little more than an American fond of cured meats might eat (Wellford 173). Experiments with chickens, cattle, sheep, and rats have shown that nitrite, when administered for several days, inhibits the ability of the liver to store vitamin A and carotene (Hunter 90). And, finally, Nobel laureate Joshua Lederberg points out that, in microorganisms, nitrite enters the DNA. ''If it does the

same thing in humans,'' he says, ''it will cause mutant genes.''
Geneticist Bruce Ames adds, ''If out of one million people, one
person's genes are mutant, that's a serious problem. . . . If
we're filling ourselves now with mutant genes, they're going to be
around for generations'' (qtd. in Zwerdling, ''Food'' 34–35).

By far the most alarming characteristic of nitrite, however,
is that in test tubes, in meats themselves, in animal stomachs, and
in human stomachs—wherever a mildly acidic solution is present—it
can and does combine with amines to form nitrosamines. And nitrosamines are carcinogens. They cause cancer. Even the food industry and the agencies responsible for allowing the use of nitrite in
foods admit that nitrosamines cause cancer. Those people who have
studied them feel, in fact, that they are among the surest and most
deadly of all the carcinogens currently recognized.

Now it is important to note that nitrite <u>alone</u>, when fed to
rats on an otherwise controlled diet, does not induce cancer. It
must first combine with amines to form nitrosamines. Considering,
however, that the human stomach has the kind of acidic solution in
which amines and nitrites readily combine, and considering as well
that amines are present in beer, wine, cereals, tea, fish, cigarette smoke, and a long list of drugs including antihistamines,
tranquilizers, and even oral contraceptives, it is hardly surprising to find that nitrosamines have been found in human stomachs.

When animals are fed amines in combination with nitrite, they
develop cancer with a statistical consistency that is frightening,
even to scientists. Verrett and Carper report that William Lijinsky, a scientist at Oak Ridge National Laboratory who has been
studying the effects of nitrite in food since 1961, after feeding
animals 250 parts per million (ppm) of nitrites and amines—an
amount comparable to what some Americans are taking in today—

found malignant tumors in 100 percent of the test animals
within six months, and he thinks they all will be dead in
the next three months. ''Unheard of,'' he says. . . .
''You'd usually expect to find 50 percent at the most.
And the cancers are all over the place--in the brain,
lung, pancreas, stomach, liver, adrenals, intestines. We
open up the animals and they are a bloody mess.''
[He] believes that nitrosamines, because of their incredible versatility in inciting cancer, may be the key to an
explanation of the mass production of cancer in seemingly
dissimilar populations. In other words, nitrosamines may
be a common factor in cancer that has been haunting us
all these years. (136)

Lijinsky, in a statement before the Intergovernmental Relations Subcommittee of the Committee on Government Operations, U.S.
House of Representatives, 16 March 1971 said that nitrites ''seem
to be most effective in eliciting tumors when they are applied in
small doses over a long period, rather than as large single doses''
(qtd. in Wellford 1972).[1]

Verrett and Carper (143--46) list still more damning evidence.
Nitrosamines have caused cancer in rats, hamsters, mice, guinea
pigs, dogs, and monkeys. It has been proven that nitrosamines of
over a hundred kinds cause cancer. Nitrosamines have been shown to
pass through the placenta from the mother to cause cancer in the
offspring. Even the lowest levels of nitrosamines ever tested have
produced cancer in animals. When animals are fed nitrite and
amines separately over a period of time, they develop cancers of

----

[1]To the best of my knowledge, Lijinsky's statement has never
been challenged.

the same kind and at the same frequency as animals fed the corresponding nitrosamines already formed.   In a part of South Africa
where the people drink a locally distilled liquor containing a high
concentration of nitrosamines, there is an ''extraordinarily high
incidence of human esophageal cancer.''   Finally, Verrett and Carper quote Lijinsky again:

> We have evidence that while the amount of carcinogen
> might not build up, the effect in the animal body does
> build up.   In other words, the more carcinogen you are
> exposed to, the more cells are damaged and the more
> likely you are to develop a tumor within your lifetime.
> So I feel no amount of a nitrosamine can be ignored.
>
> (144)

The question, then, is why nitrite continues to be used in a
third of the meat Americans consume.   Although nitrite adds a small
amount to flavor, it is used primarily for cosmetic purposes, and
is, in fact, legally sanctioned <u>only</u> as a color fixative.   United
States meat processors, however, are allowed to use up to twenty
times as much nitrite as is needed to fix color.

Recently, as controversy over nitrite has accelerated, food
producers are arguing that nitrite also prevents the growth of <u>bot-</u>
<u>ulinum</u>, an argument to which the public is particularly susceptible
because of a number of recent botulism scares.   Michael Jacobson
explains the preservative action of nitrite:

> Nitrite makes <u>botulinum</u> spores sensitive to heat.   When
> foods are treated with nitrite and then heated, any <u>botu-</u>
> <u>linum</u> spores that may be present are killed.   In the ab-
> sence of nitrite, spores can be inactivated only at tem-
> peratures that ruin the meat products. . . .   Nitrite's
> preservative action is particularly important in foods

that are not cooked after they leave the factory, such as
ham, because these offer an oxygen-free environment, the
kind in which <u>botulinum</u> can grow. The toxin does not
pose a danger in foods that are always well cooked, such
as bacon, because the toxin would be destroyed in cooking. Laboratory studies demonstrate clearly that nitrite
<u>can</u> kill <u>botulinum</u>, but whether it actually does in com-
mercially processed meat is now being questioned. Frequently, the levels used may be too low to do anything
but contribute to the color. (165)

It seems unlikely that sodium nitrite is really necessary as a
preservative. After extensive hearings in 1971, a congressional
subcommittee concluded it was not, except possibly in a few cases
like that of canned ham (Verrett and Carper 138). Bratwurst and
breakfast sausage are manufactured now without nitrite because they
don't need to be colored pink; bacon is always cooked thoroughly
enough to kill off any <u>botulinum</u> spores present; and the Maple
Crest Sausage Company has been distributing frozen nitrite-free hot
dogs, salami, and bologna to health food stores since 1966 without
poisoning anyone. Certainly there are other ways of dealing with
botulism. High or low temperature prevents botulism. What nitrite undoubtedly does lower, however, is the level of care and
sanitation necessary in handling meat.

The use of nitrite in smoked fish is particularly frivolous.
If the fish is heated to 180° for thirty minutes, as it is supposed
to be by law, and then distributed with adequate refrigeration,
there should be no need for nitrite. The fish industry has appealed to the government with the argument that it should be allowed to use nitrite in more products precisely because some plants
do not possess the facilities to process fish at properly high tem-

peratures.   Furthermore, the government exercises little control
over nitrite in fish.   In 1969, three out of six food packaging
firms surveyed were putting dangerously high levels of nitrite into
their fish, yet only in the most extreme case did the FDA confis-
cate the fish (Verrett and Carper 149–50).

    Clearly, the use of nitrite adds immeasurably to the profit-
making potential of the meat industry, but why does the federal
government allow this health hazard in our food––that same government which stands firmly behind the message that ''Americans . . .
are blessed with better food at lower costs than anyone in any
other country,'' a message William Robbins calls the ''big lie.''
(2)?

    In the first place, nitrite and nitrate have been used for so
long that it is hard for lawmakers to get past their instinctive
reaction, ''But that's the way we've always done it.''   Indeed, the
Romans used saltpeter, a nitrate, to keep meat and, as early as
1899, scientists discovered that the nitrate breaks down into nitrite and that it is the nitrite which actually preserves the red
color in meats (Jacobson 164–65).   Thus, by the time the U.S. Department of Agriculture and the Food and Drug Administration got
into the business of regulating food, they tended to accept nitrite
and nitrate as givens.   For example, the tolerance level of nitrite
set by these agencies is based, not on experiment, but on the level
found, in 1925, to be the maximum level usually found in cured ham.
Following this government standard, a representative of the fish
industry, petitioning to use nitrite, claimed that ''no extensive
reports of investigations to establish safety are required in view
of the long history in common use and the previously accepted
safety of these curing agents in the production of meat and fish

products within the already established tolerances'' (Verrett and
Carper 148).

A second reason for the inadequacy of regulation is that government mechanisms for protecting the consumer are full of curious
loopholes.   In 1958 Congress passed the Food Additive Amendment,
including the Delaney Clause, which clearly states that additives
should be banned if they induce cancer in laboratory animals.   Unfortunately, however, the amendment does not apply to additives
that were in use before it was passed, so, since nitrite and nitrate had already been in use for a long time, they were automatically included on the list of chemicals ''Generally Recognized as
Safe.''   To complicate matters further, nitrite in meat is regu-
lated by the USDA, while nitrite in fish is under the jurisdiction
of the FDA.   And these agencies generally leave it to industry--the
profit-maker--to determine whether or not an additive is safe.   The
final irony in this long list of governmental errors is that the
FDA depends heavily, for ''independent'' research and advice, on
the food committees of the National Academy of Sciences, which Daniel Zwerdling claims are ''like a Who's Who of the food and chemical industry'' (''Food'' 34).

Nevertheless, as they have come under fire in recent years on
the subject of nitrite and nitrate, the FDA and the USDA have found
it necessary to give reasons for their continued sanction of these
chemicals.   First, they find fault with the experiments done to
date.   According to the USDA, for example,

> The Department was aware that under certain conditions,
> nitrites do interact with secondary amines to form nitro-
> samines and that some nitrosamines are carcinogenic.
> However, knowledge in this area was limited and analyti-

cal methods available to study the possibility of nitro-
samine formation in meat food products containing the
permissible amount of sodium nitrate lacked the necessary
accuracy and reliability to give conclusive results.
(Verrett and Carper 152)

Despite the Delaney Clause, moreover, the FDA points out,
''Man is the most important experimental animal and nitrites have
not been linked to cancer in all the years that man has been eating
the chemical'' (qtd. in Wellford 179). This is an almost foolproof
argument, since cancer usually shows up only after its inception,
and it is extremely difficult to trace it to any source. And certainly it is unlikely that any sizable group will offer to serve as
guinea pigs for nitrite experiments. In evaluating this argument,
it is significant that humans are generally <u>more</u> susceptible to
chemical damage than animals--ten times more so than rats, for example (Verrett and Carper 59). Following through on its own logic,
however, since nitrite has indeed been proven to cause cancer in
dogs, the FDA has dutifully and responsibly banned its use in dog
food.

The industry's second argument is that nitrite prevents botulism. However, the USDA regulations approve the use of nitrite and
nitrate <u>only</u> as color fixers. If they are being used as preservatives, this is a new use and comes squarely under the auspices of
the Delaney Clause, which would have them banned outright because
they cause cancer in animals.

The last argument is that small enough doses of carcinogens
are not dangerous. Dr. Leo Friedman, director of the FDA's Division of Toxicology, puts it this way:

> . . . There is always a threshold level below which the
> substance does not exert any physiologically significant
> effect. . . . The design of a safety evaluation study is

to determine a level at which there is no demonstrable
effect. This level, when divided by a suitable safety
factor, is then considered to be a safe level, in that
there is a practical certainty that no harm will result
from the use of the substance at that level. (Qtd. in
Wellford 180)

The medical community does not agree. The Surgeon General's committee stated in 1970, ''The principle of a zero tolerance for carcinogenic exposures should be retained in all areas of legislation
presently covered by it and should be extended to cover other exposures as well'' (Wellford 181). Hughes Ryser stated in the New
England Journal of Medicine: ''. . . weak carcinogenic exposures
have irreversible and additive effects and cannot be dismissed
lightly as standing 'below a threshold of action.' '' He also commented that, until the carcinogens are removed from the environment, ''efforts must continue to educate populations and government
about their presence'' (qtd. in Wellford 181). Even with this, the
FDA Commissioner, Charles Edwards, strenuously disagrees: ''We
can't deluge the public with scare items based on our suspicions.
. . . The pendulum swings too far in most cases, and consumers tend
to boycott a product . . . even though we might feel that continued
use within certain limits is entirely justified'' (qtd. in Wellford
18).

Something has gone wrong. The issue is one of what we eat.
It makes no sense at all to eat a substance until it is proven to
be poison. Even a starving man is reluctant to eat mushrooms unless he knows what he's doing. Nitrite is banned altogether in
Norway, and forbidden in fish in Canada. European allowances are
generally lower than ours, and even the Germans make their ''wursts''
without nitrite.

One is forced to a radical conclusion. The American govern-

ment is, in this instance, clearly serving the interests of the industry rather than the people.   The fact is that the food industry
is willing to spend millions every year to make sure the regulatory
agencies act in ways that please them.   Each time an additive is
banned, the food industry finds itself in the spotlight.   It feels
an implicit threat to all its other additives, and ultimately to
the immense profits Daniel Zwerdling describes:

> This marvelous chemical additive technology has earned
> $500 million a year for the drug companies . . . and it
> has given the food manufacturers enormous control over
> the mass market.   Additives like preservatives enable
> food that might normally spoil in a few days or a week to
> endure unchanged for weeks, months, or even years.   A few
> central manufacturers can saturate supermarket shelves
> across the country with their products because there's no
> chance the food will spoil.   Companies can buy raw ingre-
> dients when they're cheap, produce and stock-pile vast
> quantities of the processed result, then withhold the
> products from the market for months, hoping to manipulate
> prices upward and make a windfall.   (''Death'', 22)

Under pressure from the food industry, and probably influenced
as well by a sincere, if hazy, patriotic optimism, the FDA issued a
fact sheet in May 1967, stating unequivocally that our soil is not
being poisoned by fertilizers, that pesticide residues are entirely
safe, that our soil is the ''envy of every nation,'' and that food
processing is a ''modern marvel because the natural value of the
food is not lost in the process.''   It concludes, ''Today's scientific knowledge, working through good laws to protect consumers,
assures the safety and wholesomeness of every component of our food
supply.''   The FDA's continuing support for nitrite allowances, de-

spite increasing evidence that nitrite is lethal, indicates that
the FDA has not removed its rose-colored glasses.

A recent extended discussion, <u>The Health Effects of Nitrate,</u>
<u>Nitrite and N-Nitroso Compounds</u>, issued in 1981 under the auspices
of the National Academy of Sciences, offers no new information but
by saying that nitrites in cured meats may be no more harmful than
those in vegetables, baked goods, and cereals, it seems to suggest
that cured meats may be less dangerous than has been thought.
Still, as Marian Burros pointed out in <u>The New York Times</u>, many
specialists feel that <u>The Health Effects</u> offers no new evidence.
And in fact, an even more recent study by a committee organized by
the National Academy of Science strongly implies (Assembly 12) that
the government should develop a safe alternate to nitrites.

Until the FDA and other regulatory agencies begin to see
clearly, then, the American consumer has little choice other than
to give up eating the nitrited cured meats and smoked fish on the
market today. If we do so, we will be following the practice of
Dr. William Lijinsky, a biologist who has studied the problem for
fifteen years. ''I don't touch any of that stuff when I know nitrite has been added'' (qtd. in Sheraton 26).

Works Cited

Assembly of Life Science. <u>Alternatives to the Current Use of Ni-
    trite in Food</u>. Washington: National Academy Press, 1982.

Burros, Marian. ''Do I Dare to Eat a Peach?'' <u>The New York
    Times</u>, 22 November 1988, p. C33.

Hunter, Beatrice Trum. <u>Fact/Book on Food Additives and Your
    Health</u>. New Canaan, Conn.: Keats, 1972.

Jacobson, Michael F. <u>Eater's Digest</u>. Washington: Center for Sci-
    ence in the Public Interest, 1987.

Robbins, William. <u>The American Food Scandal</u>. New York: Morrow,
    1974.

Sheraton, Mimi. ''Take Away the Preservatives, and How Do Meats
    Taste?'' <u>The New York Times</u>, 13 June 1985, p. 26.

Verrett, Jacqueline, and Jean Carper. <u>Eating May Be Hazardous to
    Your Health</u>. New York: Simon and Schuster, 1974.

Wellford, Harrison. <u>Sowing the Wind</u>. New York: Bantam, 1973.

Zwerdling, Daniel. ''Death for Dinner.'' <u>The New York Review</u>,
    21, No. 1 (21 Feb. 1974): 22–24.

———. ''Food Pollution.'' <u>Ramparts</u>, 9, No. 11 (June 1971), 31–
    37, 53–54.

Beyond the Institution:

The Effects of Labeling on Ex-Mental Patients

by

Lisa Temple

May 10, 1989

Writing 125 S

When mental health professionals decide that an individual is mentally ill and should be hospitalized, the public usually agrees with this judgment. However, when the same professionals determine that a person is no longer mentally ill and has the competence and the right to return to normal society, the public does not generally defer to their decision. Instead, they continue to view the individual under the constraints of his previous label. Thus, they see the ex-mental patient through the bias of a label which is no longer professionally accurate and which places the former patient at a disadvantage in most, if not all, aspects of social integration into the community.

Those social psychologists and others who subscribe to ''Labeling Theory'' hold that a label does not merely describe a condition; rather, a label helps to produce behavior appropriate to the label. That is, persons who are labeled deviants may, because of the label, behave in the expected way. If we accept this theory, there is reason to doubt the widely accepted assumption that social control is a preventative response to deviance. Rather, it can be maintained, this cause-and-effect relationship is in reality reversed; social control causes deviance. According to labeling theorists, when rule breakers are labeled and forced to adopt society's view of themselves as deviant, they begin to act in a manner that conforms to the stereotype commonly associated with this label. Scheff makes this point when he states that ''. . . among residual rule breakers, labeling is the single most important cause of careers of residual deviance'' (Scheff, 1966, pp. 92-93). In short, supporters of labeling theory claim that societal efforts to control deviance not only fail to effectively reduce deviance but actually increase it.

The potential effects of labeling can be placed into three

distinct categories: 1) the creation of deviance, 2) the stabiliza-
tion of deviant behavior, and 3) the consequences of a label in relation to other areas of an individual's life, such as employment,
friendships, family relations, and mate selection (Link, 1982). It
is the third category which most affects ex—mental patients as they
attempt to reenter conventional society while confronting the effects of their past label on their immediate community, family, and
employer.

An important consideration for ex—mental patients is how they
are viewed by the community in which they live. Jones and Cochrane
of the University of Birmingham found in an experiment (1981) that
a stereotype of mental illness exists and that the stereotype is a
reasonably accurate impression of the behavior of the mentally ill.
Most people believe that mental patients are excessively intro-
verted and are given to rapid, unprovoked mood swings from one emotional extreme to the other. This stereotype closely resembles the
behavior of psychiatric patients described in objective studies.

According to labeling theory, this close relationship between
stereotype and reality occurs because the cultural stereotype of
mental illness acts as a ''self-fulfilling prophecy.'' That is,
others react toward the potential patient in a way that leads him
or her to fulfill the expected role, which in turn reinforces the
original label. This reaction and counterreaction become a cycle
which can lead to the point where alternative roles are no longer
available to the prospective patient; adopting the role of a mentally ill person may become the only possible way the person can
cope with the label. As Jones's and Cochrane's study shows, the
general population has a negative attitude toward the mentally ill,
and mental patients' attitudes concerning themselves reflect those
of the public.

Another experiment, done by Phillips (1966), demonstrates the effect a label can have on ''attitudinal social distance,'' which is a measure of rejection. In this study, several short descriptions of various individuals were given to subjects, and psychiatric hospitalization was mentioned in some of the descriptions to measure the amount of rejection provoked by the label psychiatric hospitalization suggested. Various questions were asked about the individuals described in each vignette, ranging from questions about the desirability of having the person as a neighbor, of working with him, and of the degree to which one should discourage one's children from marrying him. The results showed that a person with a label is very likely to have more difficulty finding a job, friends, a marriage partner, and a place to live than would a person without a label, even if both have exactly the same mental characteristics. Thus it seems that a label has a substantial effect upon the individual it concerns.

It follows, then, that many of us also hold a certain stereotypical attitude toward mental patients after they have left the institution and that this public attitude has an effect on the self-concept and behavior of the ex-mental patient. The relationship between label and self-concept is demonstrated quite effectively in an experiment by Farina et al. (1968). The purpose of this experiment was to show that a label can have a great effect, even when the label in question has no factual basis. In this study, unacquainted male college students were paired randomly. Each member of the pair was led to believe that the other was told that the former was in some way deviant. The results showed that merely believing that one is viewed as stigmatized can influence a person's behavior; the labeled individual is likely to become less confident and thus less capable of adequately fulfilling normal ex-

pectations. This failure in turn leads to rejection by the other
individuals and to increased feeling of stigmatization.

Another study (Stensrud and Stensrud, 1980) was performed specifically to determine whether the stigma attached to a person who
once received psychiatric hospitalization persists over time, even
after the individual has shown that he has successfully reinte-
grated into the society and that the stigma is inappropriate. In
this experiment subjects were asked to rate several unknown persons
on amount of internal control versus tendency to be controlled by
chance and ''powerful others.'' In the study a successful individual who was described as having once experienced depression, and as
having sought treatment as a psychiatric inpatient was evaluated by
subjects as possessing less internal control than an equally successful person who had experienced depression, but who hadn't
sought treatment, even though both had current personal histories
that were considered very successful. In other words, a person who
had been a psychiatric patient but who had since then stabilized
his disability and successfully integrated himself into the culture
was still perceived as mentally ill by others. This finding supports the hypothesis that once the label of mental illness is attached to an individual, all future interactions with others are
influenced by this label. Regardless of the person's current status, a previous label continues to influence how others perceive
the person.

Family is another sphere of the ex-mental patient's life that
is affected by a previous label. Although relatives are closer to
the former patient, they do not necessarily place less stigma on
the patient's label than does the rest of society. This was shown
in a study by Vannicelli et al. (1980), in which the relatives of
schizophrenic patients fostered attitudes that were more similar to

those prevalent in their own social class than to those held by
mental health professionals. Like other members of society, relatives of ex-mental patients tend to associate this label with
strong negative connotations. Although one study (Hollingshead and
Redlich, 1958) showed a technical difference in the attitudes of
family members in differing social classes--higher class relatives
were more likely to experience shame and guilt while lower class
relatives felt more resentment and fear toward the former patient--
all of these attitudes are very clearly negative ones.

    Similarly, several other experiments have shown that ''. . .
the stigma of mental illness is reflected in the shame and rejection experienced by patients [as well as] . . . the sensitivity and
embarrassment experienced by close friends and family'' (Nuehring,
1979, p. 626; Freeman and Simmons, 1963; Siassi et al., 1973; Yarrow et al., 1955). One experiment in particular (Nuehring, 1979)
concentrated on feelings of stigma among discharged state mental
hospital patients as well as the stigmatizing attitudes held by
family and close friends toward these ex-patients. Nuehring discovered that a stigma is not, to any great degree, a result of patients' social characteristics, environment, or functioning. Instead, there are two specific dependent variables which affect
feelings of stigma and stigmatizing attitudes: the patient's degree
of depression and the degree to which he is seen as a burden to his
''significant others.''

    This study suggests that ex-patients who feel relatively more
depressed are more likely to experience stigma, perhaps because
feeling depressed and feeling stigmatized are negatively reinforcing. The study also suggests that former patients who receive af-
tercare are thought of as a burden, especially if they are depressed, or show a lack of anxiety, or are male. It seems possible

that these cases are considered more stigmatizing because they are individuals who failed in fulfilling society's norms to an even greater extent than did other ex-mental patients. All mental patients are usually considered deviant, but former mental patients who receive treatment may be more stigmatized than other ex-patients because, although living in the outside community, they are still receiving treatment. Male ex-patients may be more stigmatized than female ex-patients simply because, in our society, males are typically thought of as the stronger and less emotional of the two sexes; thus, male ex-patients seem to stray more from the norm and are more likely to be stigmatized. In addition, the ex-patients most likely to be seen as burdens by family and friends are those who seek high degrees of social interaction. This seems to imply that the more integrated into a community a former patient tries to become, the more unfavorably he is looked upon by the community.

The ex-mental patient's previous label also affects his chances of finding and keeping a job. According to Link (1982), there are two major ways in which former mental patients are harmed in the world of work. One of these is through direct discrimination by employers. As documented in a study done by Olshansky et al. (1958), employers openly admit that they would prefer not to hire former mental patients. Furthermore, it has been shown that ''. . . employers are less friendly in an interview situation and rate the applicant's chance of getting the job significantly lower when he reveals a history of mental illness'' (Farina and Felner, 1973, p. 270). In fact, individuals with a history of mental hospitalization are automatically prohibited in many states from pursuing certain careers such as firefighter, teacher, or police officer (Ennis and Siegal, 1973). In addition, former mental patients

can be refused privileges to which others have access, such as a
driver's license, which de facto excludes them from certain jobs.
Thus a label, as well as being a source of direct discrimination,
can indirectly affect a person's ability to find a job. In other
words, a label such as that of the ex-mental patient increases
one's chances of being unemployed and decreases one's chances of
obtaining a well-paying job.

In addition to increasing discrimination, the label of the
former mental patient in another way negatively affects chances of
employment. This concerns the ''. . . mechanisms which operate
through the individual's expectations of rejection'' (Link, 1982,
p. 204). Even before treatment, most patients fear rejection because of their own beliefs about mental illness and their knowledge
of the public's attitude. During treatment, the ''mortification
process'' (Goffman, 1961) strengthens the fears of patients, who
come to believe that they need certain restrictions and thus deserve to be regarded negatively. This fear of rejection then becomes a self-fulfilling prophecy. Ex-patients act more defen-
sively, less confidently, or totally avoid threatening contact
because they fear and expect rejection. The ex-patient internal-
izes this negative view and begins to think of himself as ''. . .
totally ineffective . . . [or as a hopeless case]'' (Link, 1982, p.
204). As a result, these former mental patients appear to prospective employers as unconfident and incompetent.

In summary, the previous label of the ex-mental patient negatively affects the former patient's life. Specifically, this label
increases environmental stresses such as unemployment and rejection
by family and friends, reduces the individual's access to social
supports, and produces a tentativeness and lack of confidence which
greatly weaken the person's usual means of coping. Moreover, these

effects are exactly those which have been found by environmentally oriented researchers to be of most importance in the origins of mental illness.   It is entirely possible then, that a previous psychiatric label plays a significant role in the maintenance of mental disorder (Link, 1982).   Any attempt to improve the plight of the ex–mental patient, therefore, must include educational programs not only for ex–patients but also for the community in which they live.   Before former mental patients can be expected to integrate successfully into society, there must first be a significant and necessary change in society's view of these individuals.

Temple   9

References

Bord, R.   (1971).   Rejection of the Mentally Ill: Continuities and Further Developments.   Social Problems, 18, 496–509.

Cumming, E., and Cumming, J.   (1957).   Closed Ranks: An Experiment in Mental Health.   Cambridge: Harvard.

Ennis, B., and Siegal, L.   (1973).   The Rights of Mental Patients. New York: Avon.

Farina, A., Allen, J., and Saul, B.   (1968).   The Role of the Stigmatized in Affecting Social Relationships.   Journal of Personality, 36, 169–82.

Freeman, H., and Simmons, O.   (1963).   The Mental Patient Comes Home.   New York: Wiley.

Goffman, E.   (1961).   Asylums.   Garden City, New York: Doubleday.

Hollingshead, H., and Redlich, F.   (1958).   Social Change and Mental Illness.   New York: Wiley.

Jones, L., and Cochrane, R.   (1981).   Stereotypes of Mental Illness: A Test of the Labeling Hypothesis.   International Journal of Social Psychiatry, 27, 99–107.

Link, B.   (1982).   Mental Patient Status, Work, and Income: An Examination of the Effects of a Psychiatric Label.   American Sociological Review, 47, 202–15.

Nuehring, E. M.   (1979).   Stigma and State Hospital Patients. American Journal of Orthopsychiatry, 49, 626–33.

Nunnally, J.   (1961).   Popular Conceptions of Mental Health: Their Development and Change.   New York: Holt.

Olshansky, S., Grob, S., and Malmud, I. T.   (1958).   Employers' Attitudes and Practices in the Hiring of Ex–Mental Patients. Mental Hygiene, 42, 391–401.

Temple 10

Phillips, D. (1966). Public Identification and Acceptance of the Mentally Ill. <u>American Journal of Public Health</u>, <u>56</u>, 755–63.

Scheff, T. (1966). <u>Being Mentally Ill: A Sociological Theory</u>. Chicago: Aldine.

Siassi, I., Spiro, H., and Crocetti, G. (1973). The Social Acceptance of the Ex–Mental Patient. <u>Community Mental Health Journal</u>, 233–43.

Star, S. (1955). <u>The Public's Ideas About Mental Illness</u>. Chicago: National Opinion Research Center.

Stensrud, R., and Stensrud, K. (1980). Attitudes Toward Successful Individuals with and without Histories of Psychiatric Hospitalization. <u>Psychological Reports</u>, <u>47</u>, 495–498.

Vannicelli, M., Washburn, S. L., and Scheff, B. J. (1980). Family Attitudes Toward Mental Illness: Immutable with Respect to Time, Treatment Setting, and Outcome. <u>American Journal of Orthopsychiatry</u>, <u>50</u>, 151–55.

Yarrow, M., Clausen, J., and Robbins, P. (1955). The Social Meaning of Mental Illness. <u>Journal of Social Issues</u>, <u>11</u>, 33–48.

A NOTE ON THE USE OF COMPUTERS IN RESEARCH AND WRITING

We've all become familiar in recent years with computers and their seemingly limitless uses: from guiding space vehicles to computing a day's business receipts. When you make an airline reservation, cash a check at a bank, or register as a student in college, the chances are that a computer has assisted (or impeded) you in reserving your air space, checking your balance, or electing your courses. Computers are also being used increasingly in research and writing.

Computers are used in research in at least two ways. First, computer services available at some libraries help scholars to generate bibliographies and refine research problems. If, for example, you are interested in the possibility that some food additives cause cancer, and if your library subscribes to Bibliographic Retrieval Services (a database that provides bibliographies and abstracts from more than one hundred databases in business, the social sciences, the physical sciences, and the life sciences), you will log into BRS and instruct the computer to search databases under such headings as *cancer, nitrites,* and *food additives* in order to find articles concerned with your specific topic. If you merely search for *food additives* you will find that one database alone, *Medline* (a computer-based system operated by the National Library of Medicine), can provide some 1500 references for the last three years. Such a search is far too broad for your purposes. It is important, then, to formulate the right group of key words—they are called *descriptors*—so that the computer will make a narrow search and will produce only the most relevant articles. A reference librarian will help you to formulate the terminology. The computer will then inform you of the number of articles with your descriptors in each database, and you can then instruct the computer to list the titles. Although the hourly cost of the service is fairly high, if you have carefully planned your search, the search with the computer will probably take only a few minutes.

If a title sounds relevant, you can then ask the computer to print the full citation (author, journal, pages, date) and a summary of about fifty words (called an abstract). When you have read the

*"Please, Daddy. I don't want to learn to use a computer. I want
to learn to play the violin."*

Drawing by Weber; © 1984 The New Yorker Magazine, Inc.

abstract, you have a pretty clear idea of whether or not you should
go on to read the article itself. Some, but not all, of the articles
will themselves be available on the computer, and in a minute or
two you can have an entire article put onto your disk, which you
can read later at your leisure. Thus, you pay only for the time of
the search and for the time it takes to copy the article, not for the
much longer time it will take to read from the disk. But note that
although the abstracts of many articles are on line, only some of
these articles are themselves on line; for those that are not, you
will have to read the journal in the library.

Computers are frequently used not only for bibliographic
searches but also for statistical analyses, mathematical computa-
tions, or simulated experiments. With access to a computer and
knowledge of its language, you might, for example, use, modify,

or devise a computer program to analyze election data, calculate the weight of a star, or simulate the air flow over an airplane wing.

When you come to write a report, a computer with a text-editing program can further assist you. You will again have to invest some time learning to use it, but you will find your time well spent. With a text-editing program, or word processor—which functions something like a smart typewriter with a faultless memory—you can compose, revise, and edit your writing and then make copies of the finished essay, all on the same machine. You can, for example, start by typing a rough draft, then delete whole paragraphs or sections, and continue by adding new material. When you want to check your revisions, you can request a clean copy of any part of your text. If you discover that you have misspelled a word a dozen times, you can, with one command to the computer, correct the error every place it appears. Some programs will discover the misspelled word for you, but since they cannot distinguish between pairs such as *there/their,* you can't depend exclusively on them.

When you have the final version of your essay stored in the computer's memory, you can request as many copies as you want; and, with a sophisticated program, your computer will present them to you correctly paged, footnotes in place, left and right margins adjusted, and all neatly typed.

Computer facilities vary greatly from place to place; those we describe here—automated bibliographic searches and mathematical, scientific, and text-editing programs—are only examples of some of the current uses of computers in research and writing. Computers and their applications are proliferating, as computers become not only more powerful and more versatile but also smaller and cheaper; and every year they are more commonly available. If any facilities are available to you now, we suggest that you find out about them and acquire some computer literacy, even if you must take a course, invent a project, or apply for a grant to do it. Look in your college catalog to see what opportunities exist, and ask your instructors and the reference librarian. Sometimes even where computer facilities exist, it takes some persistence to find out about them.

EXERCISES

1. If you have trouble finding material in the library, don't hesitate to ask a librarian for assistance. But you will soon learn to solve many of the commonest problems yourself. Here are a few.

   a. You want to do some research for a paper on Mexican immigrants in the United States. You look in the card catalog and find only one card, reprinted below. How can you find other books on the subject?

   ```
               The Mexican immigrant.

   JV          Gamio, Manuel, 1883-1960, comp.
   6798           The Mexican immigrant.  New York,
   .M6          Arno Press, 1969.
   G28             xiii, 288 p. map. 22 cm.  (The
   1969         American immigration collection)
                   Reprint of the 1931 ed.
                     1.United States-Emigration and
                immigration. 2.Mexico-Emigration and
                immigration. 3.Mexicans in the United
                States. I.T.

   RG77-115225 r                          69-18778
   JV6798.M6G28 1969                       301.453/72/
   ```

   b. You want to do a paper on Richard Wright's short stories, and the catalog lists several relevant books, but when you check the stacks you find none of these books is on the shelf. What do you do, short of abandoning the topic or going to another library?
   c. You are looking for a book by David McCord, called *Far and Few*. You look under the author's name, but find that a card for "Mbunda (Bantu tribe)" is followed not by a card for McCord

but by a card for "Mchedishvili, Georgii." You next look for the book by its title; you find a card for an author named "Faral," and you assume that *Far and Few* should be the next card or so, but in fact the next card is for an author named "Fararo, T. J." Yet you know that the library has McCord's *Far and Few*. Where did you go wrong?

d. You need reviews of a film released a few months ago. There are no books on this film, and the *Readers' Guide* lists nothing under the film's title. What do you do?

e. You find references to *CQ Weekly Report*, the *Department of State Bulletin*, and the *Journal of the American Oriental Society*, but these journals don't seem to be listed alphabetically in the periodical file. Still, you have heard that the library does have them. How can that be?

f. You are looking for an issue of a journal published a few months ago. It is not on the shelf with the current issues, and it is not on the shelf with the bound volumes. Where is it?

g. You want to write a paper on bilingual education, or, more exactly, on bilingual education of Mexican Americans. What do you look for in the card catalog? And what periodical indexes do you consult?

h. You want to know if juvenile delinquency in the Soviet Union increased during the 1970s, but you can't find anything on the topic. What do you do?

2. Using the MLA form, list the following items in Works Cited.

a. A book entitled *Areas of Challenge for Soviet Foreign Policy,* with an introduction by Adam B. Ulam. The book, published in 1985 by the Indiana University Press, in Bloomington, is written by three authors: Gerrit W. Gong, Angela E. Stent, and Rebecca V. Strode. Write *two* entries for Works Cited, the first entry indicating that you referred only to Ulam's introduction, the second entry indicating that you referred to material written by the three authors of the book.

b. *Journal of Political and Military Strategy* paginates its issues continuously; the second issue takes up where the first issue leaves off. The issues of 1984 constitute volume 12. Issue number 2 (the fall issue) contains an article that runs from page 229 to page 241. The article, written by James Burke, is entitled "Patriotism and the All-Volunteer Force."

c. *International Security* begins the pagination of each issue with page 1. The issues of 1985 constitute volume 9. Issue number 4 (the spring issue) contains an article that runs from page 79 to page 98. The article, written by Klaus Knorr, is entitled "Controlling Nuclear War."

d. On page 89 of the book you are now holding in your hand you will find an essay by Jeff Greenfield. How would you list the essay in Works Cited?

3. Go to your library and prepare entries for Works Cited for each of the following:

   a. A signed article in a recent issue of a journal devoted to some aspect of psychology.
   b. A signed article in a newspaper.
   c. A signed article in a recent issue of *Time*.
   d. An unsigned article in a recent issue of *Newsweek*.
   e. An unsigned article from the Macropaedia portion of *Encyclopaedia Britannica*.
   f. A signed article from the Micropaedia portion of *Encyclopaedia Britannica*.
   g. A catalog from your college.
   h. A book (one of your textbooks will do) written by one author.

11

Special Assignments, Special Forms

Making an Outline

When you write an outline, you do pretty much what artists do whey they draw an outline: you give, without detail and shading, the general shape of your subject.

An outline is a kind of blueprint, a diagram showing the arrangement of the parts. It is, then, essentially an analysis of your essay, a classification of its parts. Not all writers use outlines, but those who use them report that an outline helps to make clear to them, before or while they labor through a first draft, what their thesis is, what the main points are, and what the subordinate points are. When the outline is drawn, they have a guide that will help them subordinate what is subordinate, and they can easily see if development from part to part is clear, consistent, and reasonable.

An outline drafted before you write, however, is necessarily tentative. Don't assume that once you have constructed an outline your plan is fixed. If, as you begin to write, previously neglected points come to mind, or if you see that in any way the outline is unsatisfactory, revise or scrap the outline. One other caution: an outline does not indicate connections. In your essay be sure to use transitions like "equally important," "less important but still worth mentioning," and "on the other hand" to make clear the relationships between your points.

Scratch Outline

The simplest outline is a *scratch outline,* half a dozen phrases jotted down, revised, rearranged, listing the topics to be covered in the most effective and logical order. Here is an example.

> travel common in blues--
> disappointed lover
> travel to a job
> from the South
> fantasy travel
> back to the South
> life is a trip
> ~~my first trip out of the state~~
> jail

These phrases serve as milestones rather than as a road map. Most writers do at least this much.

Paragraph Outline

A *paragraph outline* is more developed. It begins with a sentence or a phrase, stating the thesis—this will ensure that you know where you are going—and then it gives the topic sentence (or a phrase summarizing the topic idea) of each paragraph. Thus, a paragraph outline of Jeff Greenfield's "Columbo Knows the Butler Didn't Do It" (page 89) might begin like this:

> Thesis: *Columbo* is popular because it shows a privileged, undeserving elite brought down by a fellow like us.
> I. *Columbo* is popular.
> II. Its popularity is largely due to its hostility toward a social and economic elite.

III. The killers are all rich and white.

IV. Their lives are privileged.

And so on, one roman numeral for each remaining paragraph. A paragraph outline has its uses, especially for papers under, say, a thousand words; it can help you to write unified paragraphs, and it can help you to write a reasonably organized essay. But after you write your essay, check to see if your paragraphs really are developments of what you assert to be the topic sentences, and check to see if you have made the organization clear to the reader, chiefly by means of transitional words and phrases (see pages 118–19). If your essay departs from your outline, the departures should be improvements.

As this last point suggests, your first paragraph outline, worked out after some preliminary thinking, should be a guide, not a straitjacket. As you jot down what you think may be your topic sentences, you will probably find that the jottings help you to get further ideas, but once you draft your essay you may find that the outline has served its initial purpose and has been superseded by a better organization than you had originally imagined. Of course you should then sketch a new outline, one that corresponds to your draft, to make sure that the pattern of the essay as it now stands really is more effective than the earlier pattern.

Formal Outline

For longer papers, such as a research paper (usually at least eight pages of double-speced typing), a more complicated outline is usually needed. As you can see from the outline preceding the sample research paper on pages 398–99, the *formal outline* shows relationships, distinguishing between major parts of the essay and subordinate parts. Major parts are indicated by capital roman numerals. The parts should clearly bear on the thesis. Chief divisions within a major part are indicated by indented capital letters. Subdivisions within these divisions are indicated by arabic numerals, further indented. Smaller subdivisions are indicated by lowercase letters, indented still further. Still smaller subdivisions—although they are rarely needed, because they are apt to provide too much detail for an outline—are indicated by small roman numerals, again indented.

The point of indenting is to make clear to a reader, in a visual form, the relationships of the parts. If you use I, II, and III, these are three big points, at least roughly equal. Under point I, A and B are parts roughly equal to each other, and so on. The outline is a sort of table of contents.

Notice that you cannot have a single subdivision. In the example that follows, part I is divided into parts A and B; it cannot have only a part A. Similarly, part B cannot be "divided" into 1 without there being a 2. In effect, you can't say, as a naturalist did say, "The snakes in this district may be divided into one species—the venomous." If you have a single subdivision, eliminate it and work the material into the previous heading.

Note also that some authorities require that an outline be consistent in using either sentences or phrases, not a mixture. (Look again at the outline on pages 398–99.)

Here is a formal outline of Greenfield's "Columbo." Other versions are, of course, possible. In fact, in order to illustrate the form of divisions and subdivisions, we have written a much fuller outline than is usual for such a short essay.

Thesis: *Columbo* is popular because it shows the undeserving rich brought low by a member of the working class.
   I. Popularity of *Columbo*
      A. What it is *not* due to
         1. Acting
         2. Clever detection of surprising criminal plot
      B. What it is due to
         1. Hostility to privileged elite
         2. Columbo is poor and shoddy.
         3. The high are brought low.
            a. No black (minority) villains
            b. The villains live far above us.
   II. The hero
      A. Physical appearance
         1. Dress
         2. Hair, beard
      B. Manner
      C. Success as an investigator
         1. Adversaries mistakenly treat him as negligible.
            a. They assume his lack of wealth indicates lack of intelligence.

b. They learn too late.
2. Columbo understands the elite.
   a. They are not superior mentally or in diligence.
   b. They are in a shaky position.
III. Our satisfaction with the program
   A. The villains do not deserve their privileges.
   B. Villains are undone by a man in the street.
   C. We look forward to an episode when Columbo visits the most privileged house.

There is, of course, no evidence that Greenfield wrote an outline before he wrote his essay. But he may have roughed out something along these lines, thereby providing himself with a ground plan or a roadmap. And while he looked at it he may have readjusted a few parts to give more emphasis here (changing a subdivision into a major division) or to establish a more reasonable connection there (say, reversing A and B in one of the parts).

Even if you don't write from an outline, when you complete your final draft you ought to be able to outline it—you ought to be able to sketch its parts. If you have trouble outlining the draft, your reader will certainly have trouble following your ideas. Even a paragraph outline made from what you hope is your final draft may help to reveal disproportion or faulty organization (for example, an anticlimactic arrangement of the material) that you can remedy before you write your final copy.

Exercise

Write a paragraph outline of "A Note on the Use of Computers in Research and Writing" (pages 424–26).

WRITING AN EXPLICATION

An explication (literally, unfolding or spreading out) is a commentary, usually line by line, on what is going on in a poem or in a short passage of prose. An explication is not concerned with the writer's life or times, nor is it a paraphrase, a rewording—though it may include paraphrase; it is a commentary revealing your sense of the meaning of the work. To this end it calls attention, as it proceeds, to the implications of words, the function of rhymes, the shifts in point of view, the development of contrasts, and any other contributions to the meaning.

Take for example, the short poem by William Butler Yeats that opens this book, "The Balloon of the Mind":

> Hands, do what you're bid:
> Bring the balloon of the mind
> That bellies and drags in the wind
> Into its narrow shed.

Now, if we have done research on the work of Yeats we may remember that in an autobiography, *Reveries over Childhood and Youth,* Yeats already had used the figure of a balloon (dirigible) to represent mental activity: "My thought were a great excitement, but when I tried to do anything with them, it was like trying to pack a balloon into a shed in a high wind." But because explication usually confronts the work itself, without relating it to biography, we can pass over this interesting anticipation and confine ourselves to the poem's four lines.

Here is the final version of an explication that went through several drafts after many readings (some aloud) of the poem. After reading this explication do not chastise yourself for not having seen all the subtleties when you read the poem. The writer himself did not see them all during the first, or even the fifth, reading. Notice that among the topics discussed are the tone (of the first line), the lengths of the lines, and the effect of patterns of sound, including rhythm, rhyme, and alliteration.

> Yeats's "Balloon of the Mind" is about poetry, specifically about the difficulty of getting one's floating thoughts down into lines on the page. The first line, a short, stern, heavily stressed command to the speaker's hands, implies by its impatient tone that these hands will be disobedient or inept or careless if not watched closely: the poor bumbling body so often fails to achieve the goals of the mind. The bluntness of the command in the first line ("Hands, do what you're bid") is emphasized by the fact that it has fewer syllables than each of the subsequent lines. Furthermore, the first line is a grammatically complete sentence, whereas the thought of line 2 spills over into the subsequent lines, implying the difficulty of fitting ideas

into confining spaces. Lines 2 and 3 amplify the metaphor already stated in the title (a thought is an airy but unwieldy balloon) and they also contain a second command, "Bring." Alliteration ties this command, "Bring," to the earlier "*bid*"; it also ties both of these verbs to their object, "*balloon*," and to the verb that most effectively describes the balloon, "*bellies*." In comparison with the peremptory first line of the poem, lines 2 and 3 themselves seem almost swollen, bellying and dragging, an effect aided by using adjacent unstressed syllables ("of the," "[bell]ies and," "in the") and by using an eye rhyme ("mind" and "wind") rather than an exact rhyme. And then comes the short last line: almost before we could expect it, the cumbersome balloon—here, the idea that is to be packed into the stanza—is successfully lodged in its "narrow shed." Aside from the relatively colorless "into," the only words of more than one syllable in the poem are "narrow," "balloon," and "bellies," and all three of them emphasize the difficulty of the task. But after "narrow" (the word itself almost looks long and narrow, in this context like a hangar) we get the simplicity of the monosyllable "shed," and the difficult job is done, the thought is safely packed away, the poem is completed—but again with an off rhyme ("bid" and "shed"), for neatness can go only so far when hands and the mind and a balloon are involved.

Because the language of a literary work is denser (richer in associations or connotations) than the language of discursive prose, such as this paragraph, explication is concerned with bringing to the surface the meanings that are in the words but not be immediately apparent. Explication, in short, seeks to make explicit the implicit.

The reader of an explication needs to see the text. Since the explicated text is usually short, it is advisable to quote the entire text. You can quote it, complete, at the outset, or you can quote the first unit (for example, a stanza) and then explicate the unit, and then quote the next unit and explicate it, and so on. If the poem or passage of prose is longer than say, six lines, number each line at the right for easy reference.

WRITING A BOOK REVIEW

Because book reviews in newspapers or magazines are usually about a newly published work, reviewers normally assume that their readers will be unfamiliar with the book. Reviewers take it as their job to acquaint readers with the book, its contents and its value, and to help them decide whether or not they wish to read it. Since most reviews are brief (500–1500 words) they cannot, like explications, comment on everything. On the other hand they cannot, like analyses, focus on one aspect of the writing; they usually attempt in some way to cover the book. Reviews, then, usually contain more summary and more evaluation than explications or analyses. Nevertheless, reviewers must approach the task analytically if they are to accomplish it in the relatively small space allotted. And if they are to be convincing, they must support their opinion by quotations (usually indispensable), examples, and specific references to the text so that readers may think and feel the way the reviewer thinks and feels.

A review commonly has a structure something like this:

1. an opening paragraph that names the author and the title, gives the reader some idea of the nature and scope of the work (a children's book; a book for the general reader; a book for specialists), and establishes the tone of the review (more about tone in a moment)
2. a paragraph or two of plot summary if the book is a novel; some summary of the contents if it is not
3. a paragraph on the theme, purpose, idea, or vision embodied in the book, perhaps within the context of related works
4. a paragraph or two on the strengths, if any (for instance, the book fulfills its purpose)
5. a paragraph or two on the weaknesses, if any
6. a concluding paragraph in which the reviewer delivers his or her point—but the point in some degree has probably been implied from the beginning, because the concluding paragraph is a culmination rather than a surprise.

Tone, as we suggest elsewhere in this book (see pages 553–56, usually refers to the writer's attitude toward the subject, the readers, and the writer's self. The tone of a review is therefore somewhat dependent on the publicaton in which it will appear. A review in *Scientific American* will have a different tone from one in *Ms.* Since you have not been commissioned to write your review and are essentially playing a game, you must *imagine* your reader. It's a reasonable idea to imagine that your classmates are your readers, forgetting of course that they may be reviewing the same book you are. (It's a very bad idea to imagine that your teacher is your reader.) And it's always productive to treat both your reader and your subject with respect. This does not mean you need to be solemn or boring; on the contrary, the best way to show your respect for your reader is to write something you would be interested in reading yourself.

Here is a book review from *The New York Times.* Although some reviews are untitled, this one has a title "The Tough Got Going"; unless your instructor tells you otherwise, give your review a title. (Finding your title will help you to see if you have focused your essay.)

SIGNIFICANT SISTERS

The Grassroots of Active Feminism:
1839–1939
By Margaret Forster

By Carole Klein

A poem by Marge Piercy, called "Rough Times," begins:

We are trying to live
as if we were an experiment
conducted by the future.

The eight women whose lives form *Significant Sisters* were selected for the ways in which their separately courageous breaks with tradition set the future of feminism in motion. Having decided that feminist history can be divided into eight areas of changed experience, Margaret Forster provides narrative biographies of the women responsible for starting each change that has taken place.

Some of these British and American pioneers are familiar to us, such as Margaret Sanger, who made birth control a feminist issue, and Emma Goldman, who served as a bridge between feminist ideologies of the 19th and late 20th centuries. Some other sisters are relatively unknown, and I for one am indebted to Miss Forster for bringing them to my attention. I confess to having scarcely heard, for example, of Caroline Norton. A bitterly unhappy marriage gave her, a well-connected woman and popular writer, the impetus to fight for the reform of English marriage and divorce laws—laws which had made married women powerless chattels, completely at their husbands' mercy. In another sphere of experience, education, we find Emily Davies, who challenged the entrenched belief that education for British girls should be shorter and softer than for boys, and eventually established Girton College for women at Cambridge University in 1873.

What is particularly provocative in this history is how different these women were from each other in temperament and ideology. By no means were all even purposefully advancing a feminist cause as they fought their separate battles. Indeed, Elizabeth Blackwell, the first woman doctor, born in Britain, educated there and in the United States, was decidedly unsympathetic to organized feminism. She saw her own ambitions as atypical, her success due to special gifts. Other women, she thought, should devote themselves to life's highest calling—being good wives and mothers. Of course, as Miss Forster points out, by establishing the principle that gender doesn't rule out professional achievement, Elizabeth Blackwell was in fact a feminist, indeed one who made immense contributions to feminist history.

I must note here that Miss Forster appears to be a bit insensitive to the feminist commitments of many contemporary women physicians. After discussing Blackwell's hope that future female doctors would devote themselves to humanizing medicine, paying particular attention to the medical problems of women, Miss Forster writes: "There are no measurable signs that the entry of women into the medical profession has significantly humanized it. No broad changes exist for the better which are the result of female medical action." Such categorical dismissal seems to ignore the various and well-organized advances female doctors continue to make by, for example, demystifying the physician's role, helping women to participate in their own health care, and in making childbirth a far less clinical and isolating affair. For the most part, however, Miss Forster seems to be quite clear-eyed about her subjects and their legacies, neither romanticizing motives nor being unduly critical of what, from a modern perspective, might seem contradictory or naïve behavior.

Margaret Forster has written two biographies, one a highly acclaimed study of Thackeray. She is also the author of 12 novels, among them the sprightly "Georgy Girl." Her substantial research for *Significant Sisters* draws on diaries, private and published papers and autobiographies. But in constructing her profiles from these historical sources, she employes the novelist's tools of evocative language and skillful rendering of character, story and theme.

Perhaps the most persistent theme in these pages is the conflict between being feminine and feminist. Marriage and motherhood, even love and sex, more often than not eroded a woman's strength. Miss Forster does not believe this conflict is over. Many women still fear that a separate self will be submerged in the roles of wife and mother. But she suggests that in the arc of feminist history we are headed towards a time when such integration really will be possible. As a result of reading this engaging book, we shall certainly know which ancestral sisters to thank when that time arrives.

Questions

1. Characterize or describe the tone of Klein's review.
2. Write a one-sentence summary of each paragraph. Your list of sentences should resemble an outline.
3. How well does your outline correspond with the structure we say reviews commonly have? (See page 437.)
5. If there are discrepancies between what we have said about reviews and the review by Klein, can you offer a reasonable explanation for these discrepancies? Or would you argue that we revise our discussion, or that we choose a different review as an example?
5. Write a brief argument (one or two paragraphs) defending your answer to question 4.

WRITING OTHER REVIEWS

Our suggestions for writing a book review, with obvious modifications, can serve as guidelines for other reviews you may be assigned or choose to write: of a play, a movie, a concert, or other performance. Again, it is the reviewer's job to acquaint readers, real or imagined, with a performance they are assumed to be unfamiliar with (although in fact reviews are often read by readers who want to see their own judgments confirmed, or their small talk improved). And again, you must adopt an appropriate tone, suggesting both your own expert knowledge of your topic and your respect for your readers' intelligence and taste.

Your best preparation for writing a review is to read reviews in publications you trust, consciously noting what you find informative, interesting, and persuasive. Then, if you are covering a live event, you'll find it useful to ask to see in advance the promotional material usually in the hands of the organization sponsoring the event. You'll want to be skeptical of some of the rave reviews you'll find quoted (and of course you mustn't use them in your own review without acknowledging their sources), but you may well find biographical and other background information that will prepare you for the performance and make notetaking easier. And you must go prepared to take notes—often in the dark—and allow yourself sufficient time immediately after the event to type or rewrite your notes legibly.

Reviewing a record or tape obviously has some advantages. You can listen to it many times, you may have access to the score or lyrics and previous recordings, and you can choose your own time and place for listening. Or perhaps the relaxed and witty style of the review we print below just makes it seem easier. The review was written by a student for a college newspaper.

Jimmy Buffett Is Going Coconuts?!
Pat Bellanca

This is what Jimmy Buffett used to do: sail around the Caribbean with his friends, smoke a lot of pot, drink a lot of tequila, write some songs—and every year or so return (rather unwillingly, he would have had us believe) to the mainland to record an album, tour the country and make some money so that he could afford to keep his sailboat running and himself pleasantly numbed to the realities of humdrum, everyday American existence.

Romantically melancholy escapism is the theme that Buffett has consistently examined, espoused and re-examined in all of the albums he has released since he first achieved a kind of pop stardom with "Margaritaville," the single from his 1977 album *Changes in Latitudes, Changes in Attitudes.* In that album he developed a formula that worked commercially.

In his most recent effort, *Coconut Telegraph,* released several weeks ago, he reworks an extremely watered-down version of the formula into yet another of his silly celebrations of sailing, smoking and drinking with fellow "expatriated Americans." But now, in keeping with his absorption into the mainstream of pop music, he writes noticeably less about smoking, drinking and wandering than he did before. It sounds like he's raising a family.

Coconut Telegraph is a cleanly produced country-rock-pop album which, despite Buffett's latest change in attitude, almost entirely consists of musical and thematic clones of songs he has previously recorded.

There is the song about the escapades of the businessman in the islands: "The Weather Is Here, Wish You Were Beautiful," which was recycled from "American Friend," a track from *Son of a Son of a Sailor,* Buffett's seventh album. There's the gee-I-kinda-wish-I could-go-home song, "Incommunicado," this year's model of "Miss You So Badly" from *Changes.* And there's the campy crooner song, "Stars Fell on Alabama" (a 1934 Parish/Perkins song, actually one of the brighter moments on the album), reminiscent of "Pencil Thin Moustache" which Buffett wrote for his 1974 album, *Living and Dying in 3/4 Time.*

With *Coconut Telegraph,* Buffett has completed his transformation from a cult songwriter of nutty hippie anthems (check out "God's Own Drunk" and "The Great Filling Station Hold-up" on two of his earlier albums) to an unambitious, unfunny middle of the middle of the road pop craftsman. In the year in which Christopher Cross walked away with multiple Grammy Awards, it's hardly surprising.

In "Growing Older But Not Up" Buffett tells us, "My metabolic rate is pleasantly stuck/So let the winds of change blow over my head. . . ." And that's probably the best summation of the attitude behind the album. It's entirely pleasant.

The combined effect of the ever-present congas, steel drums, acoustic guitars, unobtrusive strings and effortlessly wailing harmonica is pleasantly mellow. The song about Buffett's daughter, "Little Miss Magic," is pleasantly sentimental without being overly gooey. The hooks are pleasantly "catchy," particularly in "The Weather Is Here, Wish You Were Beautiful," a single from the album which seems to be getting a fair amount of airplay on WEEI-FM. Even the photo of the star on the cover of the album is pleasantly unassuming—he is wearing topsiders, chinos and an off-white crew-neck.

Of course, all of this is about as relevant and meaningful as sitting in a wad of bubblegum, but if one could prevent oneself from becoming bored and irritated by the unrelieved "pleasantness" of *Coconut Telegraph,* one might find it—a-hem—enjoyable.

Questions

1. Characterize the writer's tone. Is it appropriate to her material and her audience? Explain.
2. On the basis of this review, would you buy *Coconut Telegraph?* If you didn't have to pay for the record, would you be interested, because of the review, in listening to it? Explain why, or why not.
3. If you saw this writer's byline in your newspaper would you read the article? Explain.
4. Write a review of a current album. Or, attend a concert and review it. In a note appended to your review, define your intended audience.

WRITING AN ESSAY BASED ON AN INTERVIEW

We have all been treated to the television interview with (and perhaps by) a celebrity: Question: "Which fight was the toughest that you have ever lost?" Answer: "Uh, well, Howard, that's a tough question." Question: "When did you have your first sexual experience?" Answer: "Oh, Barbara, I knew you'd ask me that!" And we've read similarly inspiring transcriptions in popular magazines (while standing in the checkout line at a supermarket). But the interview is also an important tool of social science research and serious journalism. Sociologists and psychologists regularly use interviews, and biographers and historians often rely heavily on interviews when they write about recent events. Interviews with poets and fiction writers in literary magazines help us to learn not only about the writers and their work but also about the craft of poetry or fiction. For the apprentice writer, interviews provide excellent sources for interesting expository essays about the person being interviewed or about issues and ideas.

A college campus is an ideal place to practice interviewing. Faculties are composed of experts in a variety of fields and distinguished visitors are a regular part of extracurricular life. In the next few pages, we'll offer some advice on conducting interviews and writing essays based on them. If you take our advice, you'll acquire a skill you may well put to further, more specialized use in social science courses; at the same time you'll be developing skill in asking questions and shaping materials relevant to all research and writing.

Before we list the steps for you to follow, we offer two examples, essays based largely on interviews. First read "The Einstein of Happiness." Then answer the questions that follow it.

---

*T*he Einstein of Happiness
By Patricia Freeman

If the truth be known, being a professor of happiness is no picnic. People deride your research, trivialize your interests—then badger you for the secret of eternal bliss. Nevertheless, Allen Parducci, fifty-seven-year-old professor of psychology at UCLA, has been exploring the fabric of human felicity for over forty years.

Parducci became a happiness scholar because of his father, a stern architectural sculptor in Grosse Pointe, Michigan, who voiced a vexing conviction that "things balance out" between happiness and woe—or, as Mark Twain put it, "Every man is a suffering machine and a happiness machine combined, and for every happiness turned out in one department, the other stands ready to modify it with a sorrow or pain." Young Parducci, wondering why he ought to bother getting out of bed in the morning if that were true, set out to debunk the theory.

He conducted his research everywhere. He quizzed his college roommates as to the completeness of their contentment. He grilled his fellow sailors during World War II: "As the ship rolled back and forth and they retched, I'd ask them, 'How happy are you now? Are you really unhappy?' "

Eventually he received a graduate degree in psychology from Berkeley, where he could finally study the phenomenon scientifically. Today, he is known around the world for his work in "the relativism of absolute judgments"—a fancy phrase meaning that how we evaluate a thing depends on what we compare it to. (Though his work was an outgrowth of his search for the answers to human happiness, hardly anybody in academia has applied it that way). To back up his ideas, he devised several studies to show that judgments of all kinds depend on the context in which they are made.

For one study, he gave a "test" of moral judgments to college students, who were asked to assign each item in a list of behaviors a ranking of from "1—not particularly bad or wrong" to "5—extremely evil." Half of the students were given a list of comparatively mild acts of wrongdoing, including such items as "cheating at solitaire," "wearing shorts on the street where it is illegal" and "stealing towels from a hotel room." The other half were given a much nastier list, including such acts as "selling to a hospital milk from diseased cattle." Both lists contained six of the same items. The crucial feature of the test was that the students were to judge the items according to their own personal values and not to judge them in comparison to one another. Nonetheless, the experiment showed that students' moral judgments depended on how the list was "skewed"—the six acts appearing on both lists were rated more leniently by students who judged them in the context of the nasty list than by those who encountered them on the mild list. "Poisoning a neighbor's barking dog," for example, got a rather harsh score of 4.19 when it appeared along with "playing poker on a Sunday" and a less disapproving 3.65 when it came just after "murdering your mother without justification or provocation."

According to the same principle, which Parducci calls a "negatively skewed distribution," our judgments of personal satisfaction depend on how often we experience the things we deem most satisfying. To demonstrate this, he devised a study in which two groups of students selected cards from two different decks and won money based on the value assigned to each card. One group played with cards marked from 1 cent to 21 cents, with the higher values predominating, and the other groups with cards marked from 7 cents to 27 cents, with low sums predominating. Every player won the same total of money for the series, but group one, which garnered its winnings primarily from the higher end of the scale, reported themselves happier with their winnings.

What does all of this mean for us? It means, Parducci says, that just as the cardplayers were happiest when most of their winnings were close to the maximum that could be earned, we will likely be most satisfied if our lives are arranged so that the best of what we experience happens more frequently. The happy person, who finds "zest, fun and joy in life," says Parducci, is one for whom "the things he's experiencing are high relative to his standards." And conversely, the unhappy person—whose life is marked by "terror, anxiety and misery"—sets inappropriate standards for himself, often comparing his life to an impossible ideal.

Parducci will venture a few tips on living the happy life, but only with prodding. If we want to be happy, he says, we ought not to live in the future, thinking that we'd be happy if only we could double our income, marry this person or get that job; instead we should learn to delight in what we have and look forward to things that happen every day. Above all, we should let go of what's impossible.

"We all know people who have had a great love affair break up and their friends say, 'Get it out of your head,' but they can't. But if they could, in effect, drop that relationship out of their context altogether, then the best of their experience with someone new would seem good and wonderful. They could experience the same high even with a lesser person."

The happiest person Parducci has ever known (though he doesn't think he's particularly good at telling whether people are happy or not) was a woman who died of cancer in her mid-thirties. "The six months before she died was like a party every night," he recalls. "Her friends would come over, her ex-husbands would visit, and everybody would have a great time. I asked her, 'Joanne, how do you feel about death?' and she said, 'I know I could die any time, but I'm very happy.' " Joanne was married approximately five times if you count both legal and informal spouses. "She'd meet these men anybody would say she shouldn't marry," Parducci says, "and it would be disastrous. She'd see virtues in people that no one else could see. It seemed that she was living in a dream world. I would have said, looking at her life, that she should see things the way they are. But sometimes I think some people are just born to be happy."

Most Americans, in fact, say that they are happy. According to national polls the average citizen gives himself a happiness rating of seven on a scale of one to ten. Parducci gives himself a six, a rating he believes actually makes him significantly more sanguine than most Americans. "People's reports of their own happiness show an astonishing positive bias," he says. He thinks people make themselves out to be happier than they really are because "there's the implication that there's something wrong with you if you can't somehow arrange your life to be satisfying."

In fact, unhappiness seems to be a national personality trait. "The success credo of American business is that you're supposed to always be setting higher standards," Parducci says. "And in setting inappropriately high standards, we can't help but doom ourselves to unhappiness. Society is pyramidal. There's only one position at the top, and if everyone is pushing toward that one position, the great majority must inevitably fall by the wayside." But still we push our children to aim for medical school or sports superstardom.

Does Parducci hope, in some small way, to make the world a happier place to live? "I'm very skeptical about the possibility of doing that," he says. Still, there are those who would make him into a guru of good cheer. But, unlike Leo Buscaglia, psychologist to the masses and a fixture on the best-seller lists, Parducci is uninterested in providing road maps to felicity and pointers to pleasure. "I've been approached by several literary agents," he says. "There's always a pressure toward self-help. You know. 'The Ten Rules for Happiness.' But if it were that simple, it would have been discovered by now."

People tell him that he could make a fortune if only he would become at least a bit of a happiness hawker. "I ask myself, if lightning struck in that way, if I made a million dollars, would I be happier? But friends of mine who have made that kind of money say that it hasn't made them happy," he says.

Even though Parducci says he'd like to be "more happy," in the end there's something he considers more important—and that is, "being good." He will readily declare that religion—particularly Christianity—has fostered unhappiness by holding up an ideal of goodness that is impossible to live up to. Still, he says, "I think there are rules that people ought to follow, rules that may be difficult. Suppose Mephistopheles came and said, 'If you kill a few people I'll make you very happy,' I hope I would be strong enough to turn him down. I don't want to be identified with the 'me first' psychology that says we're all out for ourselves."

If he can't make people happier and he doesn't consider happiness the most important thing in the world anyway, why does Parducci press on with his work? "There's a satisfaction," he submits, "in just understanding things. We can understand how the planets move around the sun, though we can't affect them. We get satisfaction out of understanding happiness, even though we can't do much about it."

Questions

1. What homework do you think Patricia Freeman did in preparation for the interview?
2. List the questions Freeman might have posed to elicit the information in each paragraph or group of paragraphs. Were there any paragraphs for which you had difficulty imagining questions? Can you explain why? (Or, what information do you suppose did not come from Professor Parducci's own words? Who or what do you imagine to be the source of this information?)
3. Through much of the article we hear Parducci's voice, either paraphrased or directly quoted. Where do we hear the interviewer's voice as well?
4. Suppose you had begun with only the information that Allen Parducci is a professor of psychology at an American university. What library sources might tell you his age, education, major field of interest, publications, and current academic post? (See if you can find this information in your own library.)

Now read the second article and answer the questions following it.

Ethnobotanists Race Against Time to Save Useful Plants
Eileen Garred

Although a white lab coat hangs from a bookshelf in his cramped office and an IBM personal computer sits on a nearby table, these are not the tools Mark Plotkin prefers to use. As an ethnobotanist, Plotkin has spent months in the tropical forests of South America, bringing along newspapers and moth balls to press and preserve plant specimens he then hauls back to the Botanical Museum at Harvard.

In annual visits over the past eight years, Plotkin has been patiently cultivating the trust of tribal medicine men in the Suriname jungle in order to learn how the native people use forest plants in their cultures. It is a race against time and the steadily increasing influences of civilization.

Tropical forests the world over are shrinking as deforestation escalates and development spurred by rapid population growth reaches further into the jungle. The Amazon region alone contains approximately 80,000 species of plants, a vast resource of living organisms, many of which are yet unknown to science. Plants of great potential value for medical, agricultural, and industrial uses are vanishing even before they are identified.

Perhaps more important, knowledge about plants long used by native Indians for beneficial purposes is dying out with the witch doctors. "Within one generation after civilization arrives, aboriginal peoples will forget most of their plant lore," predicts Richard Schultes, Director of the Botanical Museum.

The Westerners who arrive to build roads or preach the Gospel also bring with them Western medicines. "Our medicines are effective, cheap, and easy to get," Schultes adds. "The natives are not going to run through the forest to look for a leaf their ancestors used to alleviate sickness if they don't have to."

Few of the witch doctors today have young apprentices from the tribe because visiting missionaries have strongly discouraged shamanism. The last of the medicine men in the tribes must be coaxed to reveal their secrets to a new breed of botanist like Plotkin.

Last year, for example, Plotkin returned from Suriname with a small tree limb called *doubredwa*. The South American Indians scrape the bark into rum and claim the resulting drink is a powerful male aphrodisiac. "The world doesn't need more people," explains Plotkin. "What it needs is a treatment for impotence—and there it is in a woody vine from the Amazon."

Curare, a native arrow poison, has been used for a number of years in hospitals as an anesthetic and muscle relaxant during surgery. Another plant poison that stupefies fish and forces them to the water's surface where they are easy targets for spearfishers is the basis for the pesticide rotenone. Because it is biodegradable, rotenone is widely used in the United States.

Fruit from a common Amazonian palm produces oil that is very similar to olive oil, and the fruit from still another species is extremely rich in vitamins C and A.

"The so-called 'wonder drugs,' including penicillin, cortisone, and reserpine, that have revoluntionized the practice of medicine came from plants that had some use in primitive societies that called the attention of a chemist to the plant," says Schultes.

According to Schultes, tribes of the northwest Amazon utilize just under 2000 different plant species for "medicinal" purposes. "In these plants there is a tremendous storehouse of new chemicals," he explains. "In the hands of a chemist, a naturally occurring chemical can be changed to form the basis of many new semi-synthetic chemicals. So if you find in a plant one useful chemical, you are finding literally hundreds that chemists can make using that natural structure as a base. How can chemists hope to procure and analyze 80,000 species of plants?

"One shortcut for the chemist is to concentrate on the plants that native peoples by trial and error over thousands of years have found to have some biological activity," he says.

Although it often takes two decades or more of research from discovery of a plant to a packaged drug, ethnobotanists who provide chemists with the material must work quickly since the varieties of jungle plants and the numbers of medicine men who know how to identify and use them are disappearing at an alarming rate.

As a defined field of study, ethnobotany is more than a century old, but it has received greater attention only in recent years. Schultes, a pioneer in the field, lived and worked in Colombia and Peru from 1941 to 1954. During that time, he collected 24,000 plants and filled dozens of field notebooks, which he is still trying to put into publishable form.

"We call this work an 'ethnobotanical salvage operation,' " says Plotkin, "which just means that we are documenting the plants the Indians use and the ways in which they use them." The U.S. Division of the World Wildlife Fund is sponsoring Plotkin's work at the Harvard Botanical Museum. As part of the Tropical South American Conservation and Ethnobotany Project, Plotkin has compiled a catalog of more than 1000 useful plant species, which includes Latin and vernacular names, data on distribution, aboriginal use, chemical composition and economic potential. Previously, much of this information was widely scattered and not available to botanists, conservationists and development planners.

Plotkin, whose initial interest in the beneficial uses of plants was cultivated by Schultes, is now primarily concerned with tying ethnobotany to conservation. Money, he says, is the bottom line. In fighting for preservation of the Amazon's tropical forest with its large reserve of natural resources, Plotkin aims to put conservation in economic terms.

"The ill-planned development in the tropics by local governments and transnational corporations is causing serious damage," he says. "But you can't tell Brazil, a country with the largest foreign debt in the world, 'Don't cut down the forest because you've got the cutest little monkey living there.' You have to explain that plant A is worth 'x' number of dollars and plant B, if you manage it right, will be worth 'y' number of dollars."

"You have to convince the government that it is worth more as a forest than as an agricultural area, which is probably going to fail anyway over the long term. Until you can put it in concrete economic terms, it's just talk."

As an example, Plotkin points to the irony that Brazil imports $20 million worth of olive oil a year, although there are millions of the palm trees that produce a similar edible oil within its borders.

One of the most common trees in the Amazon, the *buriti* palm, has a multitude of uses discovered by the Indians. Its fruit is rich in vitamins, an extract from the stem can be used to make bread, the fibers can be used to make twine, houses are built from its wood, and it grows only in swampy areas that could not otherwise be used for agriculture. However, says Plotkin, the Brazilian government has yet to step in to look for high yielding strains of the *buriti*, or "tap into what is a potential gold mine" by putting it into plantations.

"Conservation works best if it's in that country's self-interest." says Plotkin. "Ethnobotany"—the study of the use of plants by native peoples who have intimate knowledge of forests and the useful products they contain—"is really in the forefront of international conservation efforts."

"For thousands of years, aboriginal peoples have been living with and depending on the native vegetation. Now civilization is destroying that knowledge," says Schultes. "Much more endangered than any species is the knowledge about plant lore. If we don't pick it up now, we'll never get it."

Questions

1. Is the article primarily about Plotkin or about Schultes? If neither, what is it about?
2. What is ethnobotany? Where in the article is it defined? Should Garred have defined it earlier? Why or why not?
3. Garred is on the editorial staff of the *Harvard Gazette*, a weekly devoted to news of the Harvard community. How do you sup-

pose Garred came upon her story? Reconstruct the steps she probably took to research her article.

4. From what office or offices at your institution might you learn of an activity of more than usual interest engaged in by a faculty member, an administrator, a student, an alumnus, or a trustee? (Check your college catalog and directory for possible leads.)

Guidelines for Conducting the Interview and Writing the Essay

As these two essays illustrate, writers use interviews in writing about people, and they also use interviews in writing about issues. For either purpose, an interview produces, and the writer reproduces, more than information. By skillful selection of the most interesting remarks for quotation and by reporting gestures and settings, the writer allows us to experience both the writer's and the speaker's interest in the topic under discussion.

Here are some steps to follow in conducting an interview and writing an essay based on it.

1. *Finding a subject for an interview.* As with all writing projects, the best place to start is with your own interests. If you are taking a course from a particularly interesting professor, you might end your search, and begin your research, there. Or, you might use an interview as a way of investigating a department you're thinking of majoring in. Your college catalog lists the names of all faculty members, by department.

Scan the list in the department that interests you and begin to ask questions of upperclassmen. Then, with a name or two in mind, check your library for appropriate biographical reference works. *Directory of American Scholars* contains the most names of academicians, but also check various Who's Who volumes. In addition to *Who's Who in America,* you'll also find such works as *Who's Who in the West,* (and similar titles for the East, South, Southwest, and Midwest), *Who's Who Among Black Americans, Who's Who in Religion, Who's Who of American Women.* In addition, the circulation desk or the research librarian may have a list of current publications by faculty members. In some libraries, current publications by faculty and alumni are on display. Department secretaries are good sources of information not only about the special interests of the faculty, but also about guest speakers scheduled by the department in the near future. Investigate the athletic department if you're interested in sports; or the departments of music, art, and drama, for the names of resident or visiting performing artists. Other sources of newsworthy personalities or events: the publicity office, the president's office, the college newspaper. All are potential sources for information about recent awards, or achievements, or upcoming events that may lead you to a subject for an interview, and a good story.

2. *Preliminary homework.* Find out as much as you can about your potential interviewee's work, from the sources we mentioned above. If the subject of your interview is a faculty member, ask the department secretary if you may see a copy of that person's vita (pronounced vee-ta). Many departments have these brief biographical sketches on file for publicity purposes. The vita will list, among other things, publications and current research interests.

3. *Requesting the interview.* In making your request, don't hesitate to mention that you are fulfilling an assignment, but also make evident your own interest in the person's work or area of expertise. (Showing that you already know something about the work, that you've done some preliminary homework, is persuasive evidence of your interest.) Request the interview, preferably in writing, at least a week in advance, and ask for ample time (probably an hour to an hour and a half) for a thorough interview.

4. *Preparing thoroughly.* If your subject is a writer, read and take notes on the publications that most interest you. Read book reviews, if available; read reviews of performances if your subject is a performing artist. As you read, write out the questions that occur to you. As you work on them, try to phrase your questions so that they require more than a yes or no answer. A "why" or "how" question is likely to be productive, but don't be afraid of a general question such as "Tell me something about. . . ."

Revise your questions and put them in a reasonable order. Work on an opening question that you think your subject will find both easy and interesting to answer. "How did you get interested in . . ." is often a good start. Type your questions or write them boldly so that you will find them easy to refer to.

Think about how you will record the interview. Although a tape recorder may seem like a good idea, there are good reasons not to rely on one. First of all, your subject may be made uneasy by its presence and freeze up. Second, the recorder (or the operator) may malfunction, leaving you with a partial record, or nothing at all. Third, even if all goes well, when you prepare to write you will face a mass of material, some of it inaudible, and all of it daunting to transcribe.

If, despite these warnings, you decide (with your subject's permission) to tape, expect to take notes anyway. It's the only way you can be sure you will have a record of what was important to you out of all that was said. Think beforehand, then, of how you will take notes, and if you can manage to, practice by interviewing a friend. You'll probably find that you'll want to devise some system of shorthand, perhaps no more than using initials for names that frequently recur, dropping the vowels in words that you transcribe—whatever assists you to write quickly but legibly. But don't think you must transcribe every word. Be prepared to do a lot more listening than writing.

5. *Presenting yourself for the interview.* Dress appropriately, bring your prepared questions and a notebook or pad for your notes, and appear on time.

6. *Conducting the interview.* At the start of the interview, try to engage briefly in conversation, without taking notes, to put your subject at ease. Even important people can be shy. Remembering that will help keep you at ease, too. If you want to use a tape recorder, ask your subject's permission, and if it is granted, ask where the microphone may be conveniently placed.

As the interview proceeds, keep your purpose in mind. Are you trying to gain information about an issue or topic, or are you trying to get a portrait of a personality? Listen attentively to your subject's answers and be prepared to follow up with your own responses and spontaneous questions. Here is where your thorough preparation will pay off.

A good interview develops like a conversation. Keep in mind that your prepared questions, however essential, are not sacred. At the same time don't hesitate to steer your subject, courteously, from apparent irrelevancies (what one reporter calls "sawdust") to something that interests you more. "I'd like to hear a little more about . . ." you can say. Or, "Would you mind telling me about how you . . ." It's also perfectly acceptable to ask your subject to repeat a remark so that you can record it accurately, and if you don't understand something, don't be afraid to admit it. Experts are accustomed to knowing more than others do and are particularly happy to explain even the most elementary parts of their lore to an interested listener.

7. *Concluding the interview*. Near the end of the time you have agreed upon, ask your subject if he or she wishes to add any material, or to clarify something said earlier. Express your thanks and, at the appointed time, leave promptly.

8. *Preparing to write*. As soon as possible after the interview, review your notes, amplify them with details you wish to remember but might have failed to record, and type them up. You might have discovered during the interview, or you might see now, that there is something more that you want to read by or about your subject. Track it down and take further notes.

9. *Writing the essay*. In writing your first draft, think about your audience. Unless a better idea occurs to you, consider your college newspaper or magazine, or a local newspaper, as the place you hope to publish your story. Write with the readers of that publication in mind. Thinking of your readers will help you to be clear—for instance to identify names that have come up in the interview but which may be unfamiliar to your readers.

As with other writing, begin your draft with any idea that strikes you, and write at a fast clip until you have exhausted your material (or yourself).

When you revise, remember to keep your audience in mind; your material should, as it unfolds, tell a coherent and interesting story. Interviews, like conversations, tend to be delightfully circular or disorderly. But an essay, like a story, should reveal its contents in a sequence that captures and holds attention.

If you've done a thorough job of interviewing you may find that you have more notes than you can reasonably incorporate without disrupting the flow of your story. Don't be tempted to plug them in anyway. If they're really interesting, save them, perhaps by copying them into your journal; if not, chuck them out. (For a wretched example of a story that ends with a detail the writer couldn't bear to let go, see "Fish Eats Brazilian Fisherman," page 125.)

In introducing direct quotations from your source, choose those that are paticularly characteristic, or vivid, or memorable. Paraphrase or summarize the rest of what is usable. Although the focus of your essay is almost surely the person you interviewed, it is your story, and most of it should be in your own words. Even though you must keep yourself in the background, your writing will gain in interest if your reader hears your voice as well as your subject's.

You might want to use a particularly good quotation for your conclusion. (Notice that both essays we've chosen as examples conclude this way.) Now make sure that you have an attractive opening paragraph. Identifying the subject of your interview and describing the setting is one way to begin. (Again, look at the sample essays.) Give your essay an attractive title. Before you prepare your final draft, read your essay aloud. You're almost certain to catch phrases you can improve, and places where a transition will help your reader to follow you without effort. Check your quotations for accuracy; check with your subject any quotations or other details you're in doubt about. Type your final draft, then edit and proofread carefully.

10. *Going public.* Make two copies of your finished essay, one for the person you interviewed, one for yourself. The original is for your instructor; hand it in on time.

EXERCISE

Write an essay based on an interview. You needn't be limited in your choice of subject by the examples we've given. A very old person, a recent immigrant, the owner or manager of an interesting store or business, a veteran of the Vietnam war, a gardner, are only a few of the possibilities. If you can manage to do so, include a few photographs of your subject, with appropriate captions.

TAKING ESSAY EXAMINATIONS

What Examinations Are

An examination not only measures learning and thinking but stimulates them. Even so humble an examination as a short-answer quiz—chiefly a device to coerce the student to do the assigned reading—is a sort of push designed to move the student forward. Of course internal motivation is far superior to external, but even such crude external motivation as a quiz can have a beneficial effect. Students know this; indeed they often seek external compulsion, choosing a course "because I want to know something about it, and I know that I won't do the reading on my own." (Teachers often teach a new course for the same reason; we want to become knowledgeable about, say, communism in China, and we know that despite our lofty intentions we may not seriously confront the subject unless we are under the pressure of facing a class.) In short, however ignoble it sounds, examinations force the student to acquire learning and then to convert learning into thinking.

Sometimes it is not until preparing for the final examination that the student—rereading the chief texts and classroom notes—sees what the course was really about; until this late stage, the trees obscured the forest, but now, as the student reviews and sorts things out, a pattern emerges. The experience of reviewing and then of writing an examination, though fretful, can be highly exciting as connections are made and ideas take on life. Such discoveries about the whole subject matter of a course can almost never be made by writing critical essays on topics of one's own construction, for such topics rarely require a view of the whole. Furthermore, most of us are more likely to make imaginative leaps when trying to answer questions that other people pose to us than when we are trying to answer questions we pose to ourselves. And although questions posed by others cause anxiety, when they have been confronted and responded to on an examination students often make yet another discovery—a self-discovery, a sudden and satisfying awareness of powers they didn't know they had.

Writing Essay Answers

We assume that before the examination you have read the assigned material, made notes in the margins of your books, made summaries of the reading and of the classroom comments, reviewed all of this material, and had a decent night's sleep. Now you are facing the examination sheet.

Here are eight obvious but important practical suggestions.

1. Take a moment to jot down, as a kind of outline or source of further inspiration, a few ideas that strike you after you have thought a little about the question. You may at the outset realize there are three points you want to make: unless you jot these down—three key words will do—you may spend all the allotted time on only one.

2. Don't bother to copy the question in the examination booklet, but if you have been given a choice of questions do indicate the question number, or write a word or two that will serve as a cue to the reader.

3. Answer the question. Consider this question: "Fromm and Lorenz try to explain aggression. Compare their theories, and discuss the extent to which they assist us in understanding the Arab-Israeli conflict." Notice that you must compare—not just summarize—two theories, and that you must also evaluate their relevance to a particular conflict. In short, take seriously such words as *compare, define, evaluate,* and *summarize.* And don't waste time generalizing about aggression; again, answer the question.

4. You can often get a good start merely by turning the question into an affirmation, for example by turning "In what ways is the poetry of Allen Ginsberg influenced by Whitman?" into "The poetry of Ginsberg is influenced by Whitman in at least . . . ways."

5. Don't waste time summarizing at length what you have read, unless asked to do so—but of course occasionally you may have to give a brief summary in order to support a point. The instructor wants to see that you can *use* your reading, not merely that you have done the reading.

6. Budget your time. Do not spend more time on a question than the allotted time—at least, not *much* more.

7. Be concrete. Illustrate your arguments with facts—names, dates, and quotations if possible.

8. Leave space for last minute additions. Either skip a page between essays, or write only on the right-hand pages so that on rereading you can add material at the appropriate place on the left-hand pages.

Beyond these general suggestions, we can best talk about essay examinations by looking at specific types of questions.

Questions on Literature

The five most common sorts of questions encountered in literature examinations are

1. a passage to explicate
2. a historical question, such as "Trace T. S. Eliot's religious development," "Trace the development of Shakespeare's conception of the tragic hero," or "What are Virginia Woolf's contributions to feminist criticism?"
3. a critical quotation to be evaluated
4. a comparison, such as "Compare the dramatic monologues of Browning with those of T. S. Eliot"
5. a wild question, such as "What would Dickens think of Vonnegut's *Cat's Cradle?*" or "What would Juliet do if she were in Ophelia's position?"

A few remarks on each of these types may be helpful:

1. For a discussion of how to write an explication, see pages 434–36. As a short rule, look carefully at the tone (speaker's attitude toward self, subject, and audience) and at the implications of the words (the connotations or associations), and see if there is a pattern of imagery. For example, religious language ("adore," "saint") in a secular love poem may define the nature of the lover and of the beloved. Remember, *an explication is not a paraphrase* (a putting into other words) but an attempt to show the relations of the parts, especially by calling attention to implications. Organization of such an essay is rarely a problem, since most explications begin with the first line and go on to the last.

2. A good essay on a historical question will offer a nice combination of argument and evidence; the thesis will be supported by concrete details (names, dates, perhaps even brief quotations). A discussion of Eliot's movement toward the Church of England cannot be convincing if it does not specify certain works as representative of Eliot in certain years. If you are asked to relate a writer or a body of work to an earlier writer or period, list the chief characteristics of the earlier writer or the period and then show *specifically* how the material you are discussing is related to these characteristics. And if you can quote some relevant lines from the works, your reader will feel that you know not only titles and stock phrases but also the works themselves.

3. If you are asked to evaluate a critical quotation, read it carefully and in your answer take account of *all* of the quotation. If the critic has said, "Eliot in his plays always   . . . but in his poems rarely . . ." you will have to write about both the plays and the poems; it will not be enough to talk only about the plays (unless, of course, the instructions on the examination ask you to take only as much of the quotation as you wish). Watch especially for words like "always," "for the most part," "never"; although the passage may on the whole approach the truth, you may feel that some important qualifications are needed. This is not being picky; true thinking involves making subtle distinctions, yielding assent only so far and no further. And, again, be sure to give concrete details, supporting your argument with evidence.

4. Comparisons are discussed on pages 60–72. Because comparisons are especially difficult to write, be sure to take a few moments to jot down a sort of outline so that you can know where you will be going. A comparison of Browning's and Eliot's monologues might treat three poems by each, devoting alternate paragraphs to one author; or it might first treat one author's poems and then turn to the other. But if it adopts this second strategy, the essay may break into two parts. You can guard against this weakness by announcing at the outset that you will treat the authors separately, then by reminding your reader during your treatment of the first author that certain points will be picked up when you get to the second author, and again by briefly reminding your reader during the second part of the essay of certain points already made.

5. Curiously, a wild question such as "What would Dickens think of *Cat's Cradle?*" or "What would Juliet do in Ophelia's position?" usually produces tame answers: a half dozen ideas about Dickens or Juliet are neatly applied to Vonnegut or Ophelia, and the gross incompatibilities are thus revealed. But, as the previous paragraph suggests, it may be necessary to do more than to set up bold and obvious oppositions. The interest in such a question and in the answer to it may largely be in the degree to which superficially different figures *resemble* each other in some important ways. And remember that the wildness of the question does not mean that all answers are equally acceptable; as usual, a good answer will be supported by concrete details.

Questions on the Social Sciences

First, an obvious statement: courses in the social sciences almost always require lots of reading. Do the reading when it is assigned, rather than try to do it the night before the examination. Second, when confronted with long reading assignments, you probably will read more efficiently if you scan the table of contents of a book to see the layout of the material, and then read the first and last chapters, where the authors usually summarize their theses. Books and articles on history, psychology, and sociology are not whodunits; there is nothing improper about knowing at the start how it will all turn out. Indeed, if at the start you have a clear grasp of the author's thesis, you may have the pleasure of catching the author perpetrating the crime of arguing from insufficient evidence. The beginning and the end of an article in a journal also may offer summaries that will assist you to read the article with relative ease. But only a reading of the entire work (perhaps with a little skimming) will offer you all of the facts and—no less important—the fully developed view or approach that the instructor believes is essential to an understanding of the course.

The techniques students develop in answering questions on literature may be transferred to examinations in the social sciences. A political science student, for example, can describe through explication the implicit tone or attitude in some of the landmark decisions of the Supreme Court. Similarly, the student of history who has learned to write an essay with a good combination of argument and evidence will not simply offer generalizations or present a list of facts unconnected by some central thesis, but will use relevant facts to support a thesis. The student who is able to evaluate a critical quotation or to compare literary works can also evaluate and compare documents in all the social sciences. Answers to wild questions can be as effective or as trite in the social sciences as in literature. "You are the British ambassador in Petrograd in November 1918. Write a report to your government about the Bolshevik revolution of that month" is to some instructors and students an absurd question but to others it is an interesting and effective way of ascertaining whether a student has not only absorbed the facts of an event but has also learned how to interpret them.

Questions on the Physical Sciences and Mathematics

Although the answer to an examination question in the physical sciences usually requires a mathematical computation, a few sentences may be useful in explaining the general plan of the computation, the assumptions involved, and sometimes the results.

It is particularly valuable to set down at the outset in a brief statement, probably a single sentence, your plan for solving the problem posed by the examination question. The statement is equivalent to the topic sentence of a paragraph. For instance, if the examination question is "What is the time required for an object to fall from the orbit of the moon to the earth?" the statement of your plan might be: "The time required for an object to fall from the orbit of the moon to the earth can be obtained by integration from Newton's law of motion, taking account of the increasing gravitational force as the object approaches the earth." Explicitly setting down your plan in words is useful first in clarifying your thought: is the plan a complete one leading to the desired answer? Do I know what I need to know to implement the plan? If your plan doesn't make sense you can junk it right away before wasting more time on it.

The statement of plan is useful also in communicating with the instructor. Your plan of solution, although valid, may be a surprise to the instructor. (She may have expected a solution to the problem posed above starting from Kepler's laws without any integration.) When this is so, the instructor will need your explanation to become oriented to your plan, and to properly assess its merits. Then if you botch the subsequent computation or can't remember how the gravitational force varies with the distance you will still have demonstrated that you have some comprehension of the problem. If on the other hand you present an erroneous computation without any explanation, the instructor will see nothing but chaos in your effort.

Further opportunities to use words will occur when you make assumptions or simplifications: "I assume the body is released with zero velocity and accordingly set $b = 0$," or "The third term is negligible and I drop it."

Finally, the results of your computation should be summarized or interpreted in words to answer the question asked. "The object will fall to the earth in five days." (The correct answer, for those who are curious.) Or, if you arrive at the end of your computation and of the examination hour and find you have a preposterous result, you can still exit gracefully (and increase your partial credit) with an explanation: "The answer of 53 days is clearly erroneous since the fall time of an object from the moon's orbit must be less than the 7 days required for the moon to travel a quarter orbit."

WRITING RÉSUMÉS, LETTERS FOR JOBS, AND APPLICATIONS FOR GRADUATE AND PROFESSIONAL PROGRAMS

In writing for a job, you need to send not only a letter but also a résumé (French for summary). The letter will be addressed to a specific person and may be an application for a specific job, but the résumé should give as full a picture of you as is possible to give in one page.

The Résumé

Make every effort to keep your résumé down to one page, so that the reader can get the whole picture—education, experience, interests, and so forth—at a single glance. You need not include any statement about race, religioin, weight, sex, marital status, or age, but if you think such information may be to your advantage, include it. Several formats are acceptable, but on page 466 we illustrate the most common. Notice that information in each category is given in *reverse chronological order*—the most recent experience first.

After your name, address, and telephone number (if you live at a college, give your home number as well as your local number, with dates of residence, so that you can be reached during vacations), give a "job objective" *if* you know exactly what you are looking for. Examples:

```
Entry-level sales position with a firm that provides opportu-
nity to meet people who work with computer systems

Editorial work with publisher of social science textbooks

To work in customer relations in a department store, to con-
tinue my education part time, and eventually to assume a man-
agerial position
```

You may, of course, want to prepare two or even three résumés, varying the job objective in order to suit different kinds of potential employers.

If you can't state a job objective, begin with either "Education" or with "Work Experience," whichever seems stronger to you. The point, of course, is to begin with your chief credentials.

Notice that under "Work Experience" you do not simply list names of employers, or even titles of jobs; you also specify the kind of work done, the responsibilities fulfilled. Thus, if you worked at a ski shop you might say:

```
sales: assisted buyer at spring ski show
```

If you were a sports medicine intern at the Lahey Clinic, you might add

```
administered prescribed treatment for physical therapy outpa-
tients
```

If honesty allows, use such words as "administered," "developed," "initiated," "installed," "operated," "responsible for," "supervised," "advanced to," and "promoted to."

Similarly, under "Education" you should not only give the reader a sense of the program you studied but should also specify any academic awards, including scholarships, that you received.

The heading called "Personal Interests" (or "Personal Data") gives you an additional chance to convey what sort of person you are. Don't hesitate to list hobbies; hobbies often suggest important traits. For example, if you are an amateur magician, you probably are at ease with audiences, and if you are a Go player (Go is a sort of Japanese chess) you probably like to solve problems. But if you have a collection of snakes, keep that information to yourself unless you are applying for a job in a pet store or on a snake farm.

The last heading in a résumé usually is "References." Before you list a name (with an address and telephone number, of course), be sure to get permission; if the person seems cool when you ask if you may give his or her name, find someone else. In fact, since you don't want a lukewarm letter, don't simply ask people if you may list their names as references. Rather, ask if they feel that they know you and your work well enough to write a helpful recommendation. If you state the matter this way, someone who otherwise might write a dutiful but unenthusiastic (and therefore unhelpful and perhaps even damaging) letter can gracefuly decline, saying that you ought to turn to someone else who knows you better.

Be sure, also, to allow the letter writer ample time to write a thoughtful, unhurried letter. Ten days is a minimum; two weeks is better. And provide what help you can—a transcript, a résumé, a draft of your letter applying for a job, and possibly copies of course papers that you had submitted.

After you have drafted and typed your résumé, show it to a couple of friends and, if possible, to someone who has had experience in reading résumés. Revise it in the light of their suggestions. In typing the final copy, keep an eye on the design: don't crowd your material into the upper two-thirds of the sheet. Make sure that there are no typographical errors (a prospective employer will take a typo as evidence that you are careless) and no spelling errors.

Finally, take the résumé to a photocopy shop or an offset printer and have it reproduced on 8½-by-11-inch paper. Never use carbon, thermofax, or mimeographed copies.

The Cover Letter

Employers, even if they are philanthropic institutions such as churches, schools, and museums, are not engaged in philanthropy when they hire employees. They are looking to get rather than to give; that is, they are looking for people who can be useful to

[Sample Résumé]

Howard Saretta

School Address
(until 16 May 1989)
Buckminster Hall, #202
Redding College
Woodmere, MA 02156
(617) 864-2964

Home Address
(after 17 May 1989)
38 Barker's Road
Somerville, MA 02150
(617) 352-6650

JOB OBJECTIVE   Marketing or advertising trainee

EDUCATION

1985-89   Redding College, Woodmere, MA
                                Degree: BA (expected in June 1989)
                                Major: Business administration
                                Minor: English

1981-85   Somerville High School

WORK EXPERIENCE

Summer 1988   Acting Assistant Manager, O'Neill's Sports
                                  Center, Medford, MA. Responsible for
                                  checking inventory, dealing with retail
                                  customers, assisting buyers

Summer 1987   Salesclerk, O'Neill's Sports Center

1985-88   Part-time work in shipping office of Blackston's
                                  Department Store. Processed orders. Respon-
                                  sible for insuring valuable parcels.

EXTRACURRICULAR   Undergraduate Senate, Redding College (1987-88)
ACTIVITIES   Debating Society, Redding College (1986-87;
                                  Vice President, 1988)
                                Drama Club, Somerville High School (1985)

PERSONAL INTERESTS   Drama, photography, crossword puzzles

REFERENCES   Academic References:
                                  Office of Student Placement
                                  Redding College
                                  Woodmere, MA 02156

                                Mr. Bert Williams
                                  O'Neill's Sports Center
                                  200 Main Street
                                  Medford, MA 02155

them. Your letter of application, therefore, must indicate what you can contribute.

Unlike your résumé, your letter should be an original, not a copy. Address it to a specific person, not to "Dear Sir," "Dear Sir or Madam," "Director of Personnel," or "To Whom It May Concern." A vague address means that you haven't bothered to make a telephone call to find out the name of the person to whom you are writing. And be sure to spell the name correctly; a misspelling (Bergman for Bergmann) will be taken as a sign of carelessness. Getting the right name, and spelling it right, shows that you have done at least a little homework; it suggests that you are conscientious, and that you know something about the institution that you are seeking to join. If you are aware of an opening in a particular department, it usually is best to send your letter and résumé to the head of the department rather than to the personnel office. Probably the head will routinely route your material to Personnel, but possibly he or she will scan it, notice something of interest, and may at least scrawl "looks good" at the top of the letter before sending it on to Personnel.

Try to keep the letter down to one page; since your résumé will accompany the letter, there is no need to repeat much of the information given in the résumé. But there is no harm in stating your job objective early in the letter even though it is also in the résumé. Similarly, you can mention your strongest point (possibly your academic major, or possibly some experience on the job) in the letter as well as in the résumé. Encountering this information near the outset, the reader of the letter may feel that you are indeed the person that the company is looking for. If someone already working for the company suggested that you write—and has given you permission to use his or her name—it's not a bad idea to begin by saying, "Jane Doe has suggested that I write to you. . . ." If Doe is respected, your letter will get extra attention, especially because the reader will assume that Doe is endorsing your candidacy.

The gist of the letter should suggest, if possible, that you are especially interested in this job and in this company. For instance, if you are writing to a small company you may indicate that you are especially interested because you will have the opportunity to work in several departments and thus be able to get a sense of the overall activities of the company. On the other hand, if your interests are fairly specialized and you are writing to a large company, you may want to indicate that you prefer such a company because it can use all of your time in a single sort of activity. If you are writing for a particular job—let's say for one that has been advertised—say so. The implication in the letter should be that you believe the company can use you, perhaps because you have the necessary experience, or, if experience is lacking, because you have the necessary brains and interest. Notice the "you believe" in the previous sentence. You letter should be affirmative, but it should not be arrogant. Statements such as "I am fully qualified to do . . ." and "I am expert at . . ." will probably turn most readers off. It's better to say something like "My experience as an assistant manager at Pizza Hut taught me to be patient with customers and to make demands on myself," or "The manager of Pizza Hut has recommended me for the position of night manager, but I have decided to. . . ."

When you read and reread your draft, try to imagine what sort of person it reveals. It ought to reveal someone diligent and competent, but not a braggart and not a clown (unless you are applying for a job as a clown). It's difficult, of course, to avoid bragging and yet at the same time to convey the impression that it's to the employer's self-interest to invite you for an interview, but it can be done. If your letter is clear and direct, and if it suggests that the job and the company are just the sort of thing you are keenly interested in, you will have a chance.

Let's assume the letter is one page long, probably with three or four paragraphs so that it can be read easily. The last paragraph usually includes a polite request for an interview. Show your draft of the letter to a friend or two, to an instructor, and if possible to an employer, with an eye toward revising it, and then type up your final version on 8½-by-11-inch paper. (Smaller, personal stationery—especially with fancy lettering or with a flower in a corner—will not do.) Single-space all of the writing, but double-space between units—for instance, between the date and the name of the recipient—and double-space between paragraphs, as in the example on page 469. Be sure to check the spelling and the typing; it's not a bad idea to ask a friend to do a second check.

If you do get an interview, and after the interview are still

[Sample Letter Applying for a Job]

29 Cleveland Street
Waltham, MA 02254
20 May, 1989

Mr. William C. Bliss, Personnel Director
Conway Products, Inc.
17 Main Street
Worcester, MA 01610

Dear Mr. Bliss:

Dr. Helen Stone, who serves as a writing consultant to Conway Products and who is one of my professors at Hewson College, has suggested that I write to you about the possibility of a position in the junior management training program at Conway. I will graduate from Hewson, with a major in English, in May 1989, and will then be available for full-time work.

In the second term of my junior year I served as an aide in the Writing Program, assisting freshmen whose native language was not English to improve their writing. I am now an assistant supervisor in this program, guiding ten other upperclass students in their work with freshmen. I am also the assistant advertising manager of The Observer, the college's weekly newspaper, with special responsibility for generating new accounts.

I enjoy working with others and meeting challenges, and these activities have given me experience in dealing with people and in responding to minor crises. Certainly the challenge (successfully met) to double our advertising revenue was a stimulant. I believe that my background would enable me, after training in the management program, to work effectively at Conway Products.

I enclose a résumé so that you may have a more detailed idea of my interests and my qualifications. I can be reached at 628-5000, and I can arrange my schedule so that I will be available for an interview at almost any time.

Sincerely yours,

Doris Curson

Doris Curson

interested in the job, write a follow-up letter immediately. In this letter, reaffirm your interest, include any information that you wish you had mentioned during the interview, and thank the interviewer for having given you the opportunity to present yourself. Proofread it carefully and mail it promptly.

EXERCISE

Clip out an advertisement for a job that is of some interest to you, and write a letter of application. (For the purposes of this exercise, assume that you are in the last year of schooling; thus, you can invent reasonable accomplishments for yourself.) Hand in a copy of the advertisement with your letter.

Applying to Graduate and Professional Programs

Our comments on writing a letter applying for a job are applicable to writing for admission to a graduate or professional program. Most programs receive far more applicants—even qualified applicants—than they can admit, and so they admit only those applicants who seem able to make a contribution because they are especially strong. A person who seeks admission to the law school at New York University "because my wife has just taken a job in New York" is revealing not strength but naivete.

Carefully study the catalog to see if you have any special strengths that will suit the program, and if you do, call attention to them. For instance, if you have had a course or two in folklore and are applying to do graduate work in English in a department that is especially strong in folklore, you might want to indicate that one of the reasons you are applying is the chance to do more work in this field. If you speak Spanish, call attention to this strength, which equips you to study Hispanic folklore. Similarly, if you have had some teaching experience, and you notice that the department awards teaching assistantships to first-year students, mention your experience and perhaps specify the name of the professor who supervised your work. If an alumnus of the program is one of the persons who is recommending you, be sure to mention this point, and indicate (if true) that Professor X's comments on the program have suggested to you that it is a program in which you would especially like to participate, perhaps because the program emphasizes interdisciplinary studies, or because it is small, or because it is innovative, or whatever.

Finding out about programs by studying catalogs and by talking to people who have been through the programs is not merely a way of writing an application that will help to get you accepted; it is a way of finding the program that will in fact best suit you.

PART TWO

*R*evising

The friends that have it I do wrong
When ever I remake a song.
Should know what issue is at stake:
It is myself that I remake.
— WILLIAM BUTLER YEATS

473

12

Revising for Conciseness

Excess is the common substitute for energy.
— MARIANNE MOORE

All writers who want to keep the attention and confidence of their readers revise for conciseness. The general rule is to say everything relevant in as few words as possible. The conclusion of the Supreme Court's decision in *Brown v. The Board of Education of Topeka,* for example—"Separate educational facilities are inherently unequal"—says it all in six words.

The writers of the following sentences talk too much; they bore us because they don't make every word count.

There are two pine trees which grow behind this house.

On his left shoulder is a small figure standing. He is about the size of the doctor's head.

The judge is seated behind the bench and he is wearing a judicial robe.

Compare those three sentences with these revisions:

Two pine trees grow behind this house.

On his left shoulder stands a small figure, about the size of the doctor's head.

The judge, wearing a robe, sits behind the bench.

We will soon discuss in some detail the chief patterns of wordiness, but here it is enough to say that if you prefer the revisions you already have a commendable taste for conciseness. What does your taste tell you to do with the following sentences?

> A black streak covers the bottom half. It appears to have been painted with a single stroke of a large brush.

The time to begin revising for conciseness is when you think you have an accpetable draft in hand—something that pretty much covers your topic and comes reasonably close to saying what you believe about it. As you go over it, study each sentence to see what, without loss of meaning or emphasis, can be deleted. (Delete by crossing out, not erasing; this saves time, and keeps a record of something you may want to reintroduce.) Read each paragraph, preferably aloud, to see if each sentence supports the topic sentence or idea and clarifies the point you are making. Leave in the concrete and specific details and examples that support your ideas (you may in fact be adding more) but cut out all the deadwood that chokes them: extra words, empty or pretentious phrases, weak qualifiers, redundancies, negative constructions, wordy uses of the verb *to be,* and other extra verbs and verb phrases. We'll discuss these problems in the next pages, but first we offer some examples of sentences that cannot be improved upon; they're so awful there's nothing to do but cross them out and start over. Zonker, in Garry Trudeau's cartoon, is a master of what we call Instant Prose (stuff that sounds like the real thing, but isn't).

INSTANT PROSE (ZONKERS)

Here are some examples of Instant Prose from students' essays:

> Frequently a chapter title in a book reveals to the reader the main point that the author desires to bring out during the course of the chapter.

We could try revising this, cutting the twenty-seven words down to seven:

> A chapter's title often reveals its thesis.

But why bother? Unless the title is an exception, is the point worth making?

> The two poems are basically similar in many ways, yet they have their significant differences.

True; all poems are both similar to and different from other poems. Start over with your next sentence, perhaps something like: "The two poems, superficially similar in rough paraphrase, are strikingly different in diction."

> Although the essay is simple in plot, the theme encompasses many vital concepts of emotional makeup.

> Following a transcendental vein, the nostalgia in the poem takes on a spiritual quality.

> Cassell only presents a particular situation concerning the issue, and with clear descriptions and a certain style sets up an interesting article.

Pure zonkers. Not even the writers of these sentences now know what they mean.

Writing Instant Prose is an acquired habit, like smoking cigarettes or watching soap operas; fortunately it's easier to kick. It often begins in high school, sometimes earlier, when the victim is assigned a ten-page paper, or is told that a paragraph *must* contain at least three sentences, or that a thesis is stated in the introduction to an essay, elaborated in the body, and repeated in the conclusion. If the instructions appear arbitrary, and the student is bored or intimidated by them, the response is likely to be, like Zonker's, meaningless and mechanical.

Students like Zonker have forgotten or have never learned, the true purpose of writing—the discovery and communication of ideas, attitudes, and judgments. They concentrate instead on the word count: stuffing sentences, padding paragraphs, stretching and repeating points, and adding flourishes. Rewarded by a satisfactory grade, they repeat the performance, and in time, through practice, develop some fluency in spilling out words without thought or commitment, and almost without effort. Such students enter, as Zonker would say, the college of their choice, feeling somehow inauthentic, perhaps even aware that they don't really mean what they write: symptoms of habitual use of, or addiction to, Instant Prose.

How to Avoid Instant Prose

1. Trust yourself. Writing Instant Prose is not only a habit; it's a form of alienation. If you habitually write zonkers you probably don't think of what you write as your own but as something you produce on demand for someone else. (Clearly Zonker is writing for that unreasonable authority, the teacher, whose mysterious whims and insatiable appetite for words he must somehow satisfy.) Breaking the habit begins with recognizing it, and then acknowledging the possibility that you can take yourself and your work seriously. It means learning to respect your ideas and experiences (unlearning the passive habits that got you through childhood) and determining that when you write you'll write what you mean—nothing more, nothing less. This involves taking some risks, of course; habits offer some security or they would have no grip on us. Moreover, we all have moments when we doubt that our ideas are worth taking seriously. Keep writing honestly anyway. The self-doubts will pass; accomplishing something—writing one clear sentence—can help make them pass.

2. Distrust your first draft. Learn to recognize Instant Prose Additives when they crop up in your writing, and in what you read. And you *will* find them in what you read—in textbooks and in academic journals, notoriously.

Here's an example from a recent book on contemporary theater:

> One of the principal and most persistent sources of error that tends to bedevil a considerable proportion of contemporary literary analysis is the assumption that the writer's creative process is a wholly conscious and purposive type of activity.

Notice all the extra stuff in the sentence: "principal and most persistent," "tends to bedevil," "considerable proportion," "type of activity." Cleared of deadwood the sentence might read:

> The assumption that the writer's creative process is wholly conscious bedevils much contemporary criticism.

3. Acquire two things: a new habit, Revising for Conciseness; and what Isaac Singer calls "the writer's best friend," a wastebasket.

REVISING FOR CONCISENESS

Extra Words and Empty Words

Extra words should, by definition, be eliminated; vague, empty, or pretentious words and phrases may be replaced by specific and direct language.

Wordy
However, it must be remembered that Ruth's marriage could have positive effects on Naomi's situation.

Concise
Ruth's marriage, however, will also provide security for Naomi.

In the second version, the unnecessary "it must be remembered that" has been eliminated; for the vague "positive effects" and "situation," specific words communicating a precise point have been substituted. The revision, though briefer, says more.

Wordy
In high school, where I had the opportunity for three years of working with the student government, I realized how significantly a person's enthusiasm could be destroyed merely by the attitudes of his superiors.

Concise
In high school, during three years on the student council, I saw students' enthusiasm destroyed by insecure teachers and cynical administrators.

Again, the revised sentence gives more information in fewer words. How?

Wordy
The economic situation of Miss Moody was also a crucial factor in the formation of her character.

Concise
Anne Moody's poverty also helped to form her character.

"Economic situation" is evasive for poverty; "crucial factor" is pretentious. Both are Instant Prose.

Wordy
It creates a better motivation of learning when students can design

their own programs involving education. This way students' interests can be focused on.

Concise
Motivation improves when students design their own programs, focused on their own interests.

Now revise the following wordy sentences:

1. Perhaps they basically distrusted our capacity to judge correctly.
2. The use of setting is also a major factor in conveying a terrifying type atmosphere.

Notice how, in the examples provided, the following words crop up: "basically," "significant," "situation," "factor," "involving," "effect," "type." These words have legitimate uses, but are often no more than Instant Prose Additives. Cross them out whenever you can. Similar words to watch out for: *aspect, facet, fundamental, manner, nature, ultimate, utilization, viable, virtually, vital.* If they make your writing sound good, don't hesitate—cross them out at once.

Weak Intensifiers and Qualifiers

Words like *very, quite, rather, completely, definitely,* and *so* can usually be struck from a sentence without loss. Paradoxically, sentences are often more emphatic without intensifiers. Try reading the following sentences both with and without the bracketed words:

At that time I was [very] idealistic.
We found the proposal [quite] feasible.
The remark, though unkind, was [entirely] accurate.
It was a [rather] fatuous statement.
The scene was [extremely] typical.
Both films deal with disasters [virtually] beyond our control.
The death scene is [truly] grotesque.
What she did next was [completely] inexcusable.
The first line [definitely] establishes that the father had been drinking.

Always avoid using intensifiers with *unique*. Either something is unique—the only one of its kind—or it is not. It can't be very, quite, so, pretty, or fairly unique.

Circumlocutions

Roundabout ways of saying things enervate your prose and tire your reader. Notice now each circumlocution in the first column is matched by a concise expression in the second.

I came to the realization that	I realized that
She is of the opinion that	She thinks that
The quotation is supportive of	The quotation supports
Concerning the matter of	About
During the course of	During
For the period of a week	For a week
In the event that	If
In the process of	During, while
Regardless of the fact that	Although
Due to the fact that	Because
For the simple reason that	Because
The fact that	That
Inasmuch as	Since
If the case was such that	If
It is often the case that	Often
In all cases	Always
I made contact with	I called, saw, phoned, wrote
At that point in time	Then
At this point in time	Now

Now revise this sentence:

These movies have a large degree of popularity for the simple reason that they give the viewers insight in many cases.

Wordy Beginnings

Vague, empty words and phrases clog the beginnings of some sentences. They're like elaborate windups before the pitch.

1. *Wordy*
By analyzing carefully the last lines in this stanza, you find the connections between the loose ends of the poem.

Concise
The last lines of the stanza connect the loose ends of the poem.

2. *Wordy*
What the cartoonist is illustrating and trying to get across is the greed of the oil producers.

Concise
The cartoon illustrates the greed of the oil producers.

3. *Wordy*
Dealing with the crucial issue of the year, the editorial is expressing ironical disbelief in any of the possible solutions to the Middle East crisis.

Concise
The editorial ironically expresses disbelief in the proposed solutions to the Middle East crisis.

4. *Wordy*
In the last stanza is the conclusion (as usual) and it tells of the termination of the dance.

Concise
The last stanza concludes with the end of the dance.

5. *Wordy*
In opposition to the situation of the younger son is that of the elder who remained in his father's house, working hard and handling his inheritance wisely.

Concise
The elder son, by contrast, remained in his father's house, worked hard, and handled his inheritance wisely.

Notice in the above examples that when the deadwood is cleared from the beginning of the sentence, the subject appears early, and the main verb appears close to it:

1. The last lines . . . connect . . .
2. The cartoon illustrates . . .
3. The editorial . . . expresses . . .
4. The last stanza concludes . . .
5. The elder son . . . remained . . .

Locating the right noun for the subject, and the right verb for the predicate, is the key to revising sentences with wordy beginnings. Try revising the following sentences:

1. The way that Mabel reacts toward her brother is a fine representation of her nature.
2. In Langston Hughes's case he was "saved from sin" when he was going on thirteen.

Empty Conclusions

Often a sentence that begins well has an empty conclusion. The words go on but the sentence seems to stand still; if it's not revised, it requires another sentence to explain it. A short sentence is not necessarily concise.

1. *Empty*
"Those Winter Sundays" is composed so that a reader can feel what the poet was saying. (How is it composed? What is he saying?)

Concise
"Those Winter Sundays" describes the speaker's anger as a child, and his remorse as an adult.

2. *Empty*
In both Orwell's and Baldwin's essays the feeling of white supremacy is very important. (Why is white supremacy important?)

Concise
Both Orwell and Baldwin trace the insidious consequences of white supremacy.

3. *Empty*
Being the only white girl among about ten black girls was quite a learning experience. (What did she learn?)

Concise
As the only white girl among about ten black girls, I began to understand the experiences of isolation, helplessness, and rage regularly reported by minority students.

Wordy Uses of the Verbs "To Be," "To Have," and "To Make"

Notice that in the preceding unrevised sentences a form of the verb *to be* introduces the empty conclusion: "*was* saying," "*is* very important," "*was* quite a learning experience." In each revision, the right verb added and generated substance. In the following sentences, substitutions for the verb *to be* both invigorate and shorten otherwise substantial sentences.

1. *Wordy*
The scene is taking place at night, in front of the capitol building.

Concise
The scene takes place at night, in front of the capitol building.

2. *Wordy*
In this shoeshining and early rising there are indications of church attendance.

Concise
The early rising and shoeshining indicate church attendance.

3. *Wordy*
The words "flashing," "rushing," "plunging," and "tossing" are suggestive of excitement.

Concise
The words "flashing," "rushing," "plunging," and "tossing" suggest excitement.

The rule is, whenever you can, replace a form of the verb *to be* with a stronger verb.

To Be	*Strong Verb*
1. and a participle ("is taking")	1. takes
2. and a noun ("are indications")	2. indicate
3. and an adjective ("are suggestive")	3. suggest

Try revising the following sentence:

The rising price of oil is reflective of the spiraling cost of all goods.

Sentences with the verbs *to have* and *to make* can similarly be reduced:

1. *Wordy*
The Friar has knowledge that Juliet is alive.

Concise
The Friar knows that Juliet is alive.

2. *Wordy*
The stanzas make a vivid contrast between Heaven and Hell.

Concise
The stanzas vividly contrast Heaven and Hell.

Like all rules, this one has exceptions. We don't list them here; you'll discover them by listening to your sentences.

Redundancy

This term, derived from a Latin word meaning "overflowing, overlapping," refers to unnecessary repetition in the expression of ideas. "Future plans," after all, are only plans, and "to glide smoothly" or "to scurry rapidly" is only to glide or to scurry. Unlike repetition, which often provides emphasis or coherence (for example, "government of the people, by the people, for the people"), redundancy can always be eliminated.

1. *Redundant*
Any student could randomly sit anywhere. (If the students could sit anywhere, the seating was random.)

Concise
Students could sit anywhere.
Students chose their seats at random.

2. *Redundant*
I have no justification with which to excuse myself.

Concise
I have no justification for my action.
I can't justify my action.
I have no excuse for my action.
I can't excuse my action.

3. *Redundant*
In the orthodox Cuban culture, the surface of the female role seemed degrading. (Perhaps this sentence means what it says. More probably "surface" and "seemed" are redundant.)

Concise
In the orthodox Cuban culture, the female role seemed degrading.
In the orthodox Cuban culture, the female role was superficially degrading.

4. *Redundant*
In "Araby" the boy feels alienated emotionally from his family.

Concise
In "Araby" the boy feels alienated from his family.

Try eliminating redundancy from the following sentences:

1. The reason why she hesitates is because she is afraid.
2. Marriage in some form has long existed since prehistoric times.

What words can be crossed out of the following phrases?

1. throughout the entire article
2. her attitude of indifference
3. a conservative type suit
4. all the different tasks besides teaching
5. his own personal opinion
6. elements common to both of them
7. emotions and feelings
8. shared together
9. falsely padded expense accounts
10. alleged suspect

Many phrases in common use are redundant. For example, there is no need to write "blare noisily," since the meaning of the adverb "noisily" is already in the verb "blare." Watch for phrases like these when you revise:

round in shape	resulting effect
purple in color	close proximity
poetic in nature	connected together
tall in stature	prove conclusively
autobiography of her life	must necessarily
basic fundamentals	very unique
true fact	very universal
free gift	the reason why is because

Negative Constructions

Negative constructions are often wordy and sometimes pretentious.

1. *Wordy*
Housing for married students is *not unworthy of* consideration.

Concise
Housing for married students is worthy of consideration.

Better
The trustees should earmark funds for married students' housing. (Probably what the author meant)

2. *Wordy*
After reading the second paragraph *you aren't left with* an immediate reaction as to how the story will end.

*"See what I mean? You're never sure just where you stand
with them."*

Drawing by Rossi; © 1971 The New Yorker Magazine, Inc.

Concise
The first two paragraphs create suspense.

The following example from a syndicated column is not untypical:

> Although it is not reasonably to be expected that someone who
> fought his way up to the Presidency is less than a largely political
> animal and sometimes a beast, it is better not to know—really—
> exactly what his private conversations were composed of.

The Golden Rule of writing is "Write for others as you would
have them write for you," not "Write for others in a manner not
unreasonably dissimilar to the manner in which you would have
them write for you." (But see the discussion of *not . . . un-* in the
Glossary for effective use of the negative.)

Extra Sentences, Extra Clauses: Subordination

Sentences are sometimes wordy because ideas are given more
elaborate grammatical constructions than they need. In revising,
these constructions can be grammatically subordinated, or re-

duced. Two sentences, for example, may be reduced to one, or a clause may be reduced to a phrase.

1. *Wordy*

The Book of Ruth was probably written in the fifth century B.C. It was a time when women were considered the property of men.

Concise

The Book of Ruth was probably written in the fifth century B.C., when women were considered the property of men.

2. *Wordy*

The first group was the largest. This group was seated in the center of the dining hall.

Concise

The first group, the largest, was seated in the center of the dining hall.

3. *Wordy*

The colonists were upset over the tax on tea and they took action against it.

Concise

The colonists, upset over the tax on tea, took action against it.

Watch particularly for clauses beginning with *who, which,* and *that.* Often they can be shortened.

1. *Wordy*

George Orwell is the pen name of Eric Blair, who was an English writer.

Concise

George Orwell is the pen name of Eric Blair, an English writer.

2. *Wordy*

They are seated at a table which is covered with a patched and tattered cloth.

Concise

They are seated at a table, covered with a patched and tattered cloth.

3. *Wordy*

There is one feature that is grossly out of proportion.

Concise

One feature is grossly out of proportion.

Also watch for sentences and clauses beginning with *it is, this is, there are.* (Again, wordy uses of the verb *to be.*) These expressions often lead to a *which* or a *that,* but even when they don't they may be wordy.

1. *Wordy*
The trail brings us to the timberline. This is the point where the trees become stunted from lack of oxygen.

Concise
The trail brings us to the timberline, the point where the trees become stunted from lack of oxygen.

2. *Wordy*
This is a quotation from Black Elk's autobiography which discloses his prophetic powers.

Concise
This quotation from Black Elk's autobiography discloses his prophetic powers.

3. *Wordy*
It is frequently considered that *Hamlet* is Shakespeare's most puzzling play.

Concise
Hamlet is frequently considered Shakespeare's most puzzling play.

4. *Wordy*
In Notman's photograph of Buffalo Bill and Sitting Bull there are definite contrasts between the two figures.

Concise
Notman's photograph of Buffalo Bill and Sitting Bull contrasts the two figures.

Try revising the following sentences:

1. There are many writers who believe that writing can't be taught.
2. Always take more clothes than you think you will need. This is so that you will be prepared for the weather no matter what it is.
3. This is an indication that the child has a relationship with his teacher which is very respectful.

(For further discussion of subordination see pages 541–45. On *which* clauses, see also page 768.)

SOME CONCLUDING REMARKS

We spoke earlier about how students learn to write Instant Prose and acquire other wordy habits—by writing what they think the teacher has asked for. We haven't forgotten that teachers assign papers of a certain length in college too. But the length given is not an arbitrary limit that must be reached—the teacher who asks for a five-page or twenty-page paper is probably trying to tell you the degree of elaboration expected on the assignment. Such, apparently, was the intention of William Randolph Hearst, the newspaper publisher, who cabled an astronomer, "Is there life on Mars? Cable reply 1000 words." The astronomer's reply was, "Nobody knows," repeated five hundred times.

What do you do when you've been asked to produce a ten-page paper and after diligent writing and revising you find you've said everything relevant to your topic in seven and a half pages? Our advice is, hand it in. We can't remember ever counting the words or pages of a substantial, interesting essay; we assume that our colleagues elsewhere are equally reasonable and equally overworked. If we're wrong, tell us about it—in writing, and in the fewest possible words.

EXERCISE

A. First identify the fault or faults that make the following sentences wordy, and then revise them for conciseness.

1. There were quite a number of contrasts that White made between the city school and the country school which was of a casual nature all throughout.

2. The study of political topics involves a careful researching of the many components of the particular field.

3. Virtually the most significant feature of any field involving science is the vital nature of the technical facilities, the fundamental factor of all research.

4. Like a large majority of American people, I, too, have seen the popular disaster films.

5. Something which makes this type of film popular (disaster) is

the kind of subconscious aspect of "Can man overcome this problem?" Horror films, on the other hand, produce the aspects of whether or not man can make amends for his mistakes.

6. The average American becomes disappointed and downtrodden due to the fact that he can't help himself and is at the mercy of inflation and unemployment.

7. Some relationships have split up because of the simple fear of having an abnormal child, while perhaps there might have been other alternatives for these couples.

8. Reading has always been a fascinating and exciting pastime for me for as long as I can remember.

9. This cartoon appeared in the 17 September 1989 issue of *Newsweek*. This political cartoon was originally taken from the *Tulsa Tribune*. The cartoonist is Simpson.

10. Only once in the first two sentences does the author make reference to the first person.

11. The length of the sentences are similar in moderation and in structural clarity.

12. The magnitude of student satisfaction with the program ranged from total hatred to enthusiastic approval.

13. Taking a look at the facial expressions of the man and the woman in both pictures one can see a difference in mood.

14. One drawing is done in watercolor and the other is done in chalk which is a revision of the watercolor.

15. The dialogue places the role of the two gods on a believable basis.

16. Senseless crimes such as murder and muggings are committed on a daily basis.

17. One must specify that the current heavy metal craze which is so very popular today is not considered to be black music.

18. The two major aspects behind the development of a performer are technique and musicianship.

19. I remember my first desire to smoke cigarettes as I watched my father smoke. My father often sat in his favorite easy chair idly smoking cigarettes.

20. Christopher Stone's article "Putting the Outside Inside the Fence of Law" is concerning the legal rights of the environment. He comments on the legal rights of other inanimate

entities which seem to be acceptable. Just as these entities are represented, so should the environment be represented.

B. In the following paragraph, circle all forms of the verbs "to be," "to have," and "to make." Then, wherever possible, eliminate these verbs by reducing clauses or by substituting stronger, more exact, or active verbs.

"Confidential Chat" is a column in the *Boston Globe* that anonymously publishes letters from readers and then publishes subsequent responses. In one letter, submitted by Mrs. Mike, advice is sought on a moral issue. Mrs. Mike, a landlord and mother of teenage children, has a tenant who "has been having her boyfriend sleep over almost every night." Mrs. Mike feels that her tenant's behavior could make an undesirable impression upon her children whom she is trying to "raise with a strong sense of Christian morality" and thus has resolved that eviction would be a solution. Her dilemma being stated as "being basically spiritual in nature" receives several responses which address the moral conflict and make suggestions for handling the situation.

13

Revising for Clarity

Here's to plain speaking and clear understanding.
— SIDNEY GREENSTREET,
The Maltese Falcon

CLARITY

We have seen new realities created by the advance of physics. But
this chain of creation can be traced back far beyond the starting
point of physics. One of the most primitive concepts is that of an
object. The concepts of a tree, a horse, any material body, are creations gained on the basis of experience, though the impressions
from which they arise are primitive in comparison with the world
of physical phenomena. A cat teasing a mouse also creates, by
thought, its own primitive reality. The fact that the cat reacts in a
similar way toward any mouse it meets shows that it forms concepts and theories which are its guide through its own world of
sense impressions.

— ALBERT EINSTEIN AND LEOPOLD INFELD

Skills constitute the manipulative techniques of human goal attainment and control in relation to the physical world, so far as artifacts or machines especially designed as tools do not yet supplement
them. Truly human skills are guided by organized and codified
knowledge of both the things to be manipulated and the human
capacities that are used to manipulate them. Such knowledge is an
aspect of cultural-level symbolic processes, and, like other aspects
to be discussed presently, requires the capacities of the human cen-

tral nervous system, particularly the brain. This organic system is clearly essential to all of the symbolic processes; as we well know, the human brain is far superior to the brain of any other species.
— TALCOTT PARSONS

Why is the first passage easier to understand than the second?

Both passages discuss the relationship between the brain and the physical world it attempts to understand. The first passage, by Einstein and Infeld, is, if anything, more complex both in what it asserts and in what it suggests than the second, by Parsons. Both passages explain that the brain organizes sense impressions. But Einstein and Infeld further explain that the history of physics can be understood as an extension of the simplest sort of organization, such as we all make in distinguishing a tree from a horse, or such as even a cat makes in teasing a mouse. Parsons only promises that "other aspects" will "be discussed presently." How many of us are eager for those next pages?

Good writing is clear, not because it presents simple ideas, but because it presents ideas in the simplest form the subject permits. A clear analysis doesn't falsely reduce a complex problem to a simple one; it breaks it down into its simple, comprehensible parts and discusses them, one by one, in a logical order. A clear paragraph explains one of these parts coherently, thoroughly, and in language as simple and as particular as the reader's understanding requires and the context allows. Where Parsons writes of "organized and codified *knowledge* of . . . the things to be manipulated," Einstein and Infeld write simply of the concept of an object. And even "object," a simple but general word, is further clarified by the specific, familiar examples, "tree" and "horse." Parsons writes of "the manipulative techniques of . . . goal attainment and control in relation to the physical world, so far as artifacts or machines especially designed as tools do not yet supplement them." Einstein and Infeld show us a cat teasing a mouse.

Notice also the clear organization of Einstein and Infeld's paragraph. The first sentence, clearly transitional, refers to the advance of physics traced in the preceding pages. The next sentence, introduced by "But," reverses our direction: we are now going to look not at an advance, but at primitive beginnings. And the following sentences, to the end of the paragraph, fulfill that promise. We move back to primitive human concepts, clarified by examples, and finally to the still more primitive example of the cat. Parsons's paragraph is also organized, but the route is much more difficult to follow.

Why do people write obscurely? Surely some students learn to write obscurely by trying to imitate the style of their teachers or textbooks. The imitation may spring from genuine admiration for these authorities, mixed perhaps with an understandable wish to be one of Us (the authorities) not one of Them (the dolts). Or students may feel that a string of technical-sounding words is what the teacher expects. If this thought has crossed your mind, we can't say you're entirely wrong. Learning a new discipline often involves acquiring a specialized vocabulary. But we add the following cautions:

1. What teachers expect is that your writing show thought and make sense. They are likely to be puzzled by the question "Do you want me to use technical terms in this paper?"
2. If you try to use technical terms appropriate to one field when you write about another, you are likely to write nonsense. Don't write "the machine was viable" if you mean only that it worked.
3. When you do write for specialists in a particular field use technical terms precisely. Don't write in an art history paper "This print of Van Gogh's *Sunflowers*" if you mean "This reproduction of Van Gogh's *Sunflowers*."
4. No matter what you are writing, don't become so enamored of technical words that you can't write a sentence without peppering it with *input, interface, death-symbol, parameter, feedback,* and so on.

But to return to the question, "Why do people write obscurely?" It's difficult to write clearly.[1] Authorities may be unintelligible not because they want to tax you with unnecessary difficulties, but because they don't know how to avoid them. In our era, when we sometimes seem to be drowning in a flood of print, few persons who write know how to write well. If you have ever tried to assemble a mechanical toy or to thread an unfamiliar sew-

---

[1] Our first draft of this sentence read "Writing clearly is difficult." Can you see why we changed it?

ing machine by following the "easy instructions," you know that the simplest kind of expository writing, giving instructions, can foil the writers most eager for your goodwill (that is, those who want you to use their products). Few instructions, unfortunately, are as unambiguous as "Go to jail. Go directly to jail. Do not pass Go. Do not collect $200."

You can, though, learn to write clearly, by learning to recognize common sources of obscurity in writing and by consciously revising your own work. We offer, to begin with, three general rules:

1. Use the simplest, most exact, most specific language your subject allows.
2. Put together what belongs together, in the essay, in the paragraph, and in the sentence.
3. Keep your reader in mind, particularly when you revise.

Now for more specific advice, and examples—the cats and mice of revising for clarity.

CLARITY AND EXACTNESS: USING THE RIGHT WORD

Denotation

Be sure the word you choose has the right *denotation* (explicit meaning). Did you mean sarcastic or ironic? Fatalistic or pessimistic? Disinterested or uninterested? Biannual or semiannual? Enforce or reinforce? Use or usage? If you're not sure, check the dictionary. You'll find some of the most commonly misused words discussed in Chapter 20. Here are examples of a few others.

1. Daru faces a dilemma between his humane feelings and his conceptions of justice. (Strictly speaking, a dilemma requires a choice between two equally unattractive alternatives. "Conflict" would be a better word here.)
2. However, as time dragged on, exorcising seemed to lose its charisma. (What is charisma? Why is it inexact here?)
3. Ms. Wu's research contains many symptoms of depression which became evident during the reading period. (Was Ms. Wu de-

pressed by her research? We hope not. Probably she described or listed the symptoms.)
4. When I run I don't allow myself to stop until I have reached my destiny. (Which word is inexact?)

Connotation

Be sure the word you choose has the right *connotation* (association, implication). As Mark Twain said, the difference between the right word and the almost right word is the difference between lightning and the lightning bug.

1. Boston politics has always upheld the reputation of being especially crooked. ("Upheld" inappropriately suggests that Boston has proudly maintained its reputation. "Has always had" would be appropriate here, but pale. "Deserved" would, in this context, be ironic, implying—accurately—the writer's scorn.)
2. This book, unlike many other novels, lacks tedious descriptive passages. ("Lacks" implies a deficiency. How would you revise the sentence?)
3. New Orleans, notorious for its good jazz and good food. . . . (Is "notorious" the word here? or "famous"?)
4. Sunday, Feb. 9. Another lingering day at Wellesley. (In this entry from a student's journal, "lingering" strikes us as right. What does "lingering" imply about Sundays at Wellesley that "long" would not?)

Because words have connotations, most writing—even when it pretends to be objective—conveys attitudes as well as facts. Consider, for example, this passage by Jessica Mitford, describing part of the procedure used today for embalming:

> A long, hollow needle attached to a tube   . . . is jabbed into the abdomen, poked around the entrails and chest cavity, the contents of which are pumped out. . . .

Here, as almost always, the writer's *purpose* in large measure determines the choice of words. Probably the sentence accurately describes part of the procedure, but it also, of course, records Mitford's contempt for the procedure. Suppose she wanted to be more respectful—suppose, for example, she were an undertaker writing an explanatory pamphlet. Instead of the needle being "jabbed" it

*"I'm not quite clear on this, Fulton. Are you moaning about
your prerequisites, your requisites, or your perquisites?"*

Drawing by Richter; © 1976 The New Yorker Magazine, Inc.

would be "inserted," and instead of being "poked around the entrails" it would be "guided around the viscera," and the contents would not be "pumped out" but would be "drained." Mitford's words would be the wrong words for an undertaker explaining embalming to apprentices or to the general public, but, given her purpose, they are exactly the right ones because they convey her attitude with great clarity.

Notice, too, that many words have social, political, or sexist overtones. We read for example of the *children* of the rich, but the *offspring* of the poor. What is implied by the distinction? Consider the differences in connotation in each of the following series:

1. friend, boyfriend, young man, lover (What age is the speaker?)
2. dine, eat (What was on the menu? Who set the table?)
3. spinster, bachelor (Which term is likely to be considered an insult?)
4. underdeveloped nations, developing nations, emerging nations
5. preference, bias, prejudice
6. upbringing, conditioning, brainwashing
7. message from our sponsor, commercial, ad, plug
8. intelligence gathering, espionage, spying
9. emigrate, defect, seek asylum
10. anti-abortion, pro-life; pro-abortion, pro-choice

Quotation Marks as Apologies

When you have used words with exact meanings (denotations) and appropriate associations (connotations) for your purpose, don't apologize for them by putting quotation marks around them. If the words *copped a plea, ripped off,* or *kids* suit your purpose better than *plea-bargained, stolen,* or *children,* use them. If they are inappropriate, don't put them in quotation marks; find the right words.

Being Specific

In writing descriptions, catch the richness, complexity, and uniqueness of things. Suppose, for example, you are describing a scene from your childhood, a setting you loved. There was, in particular, a certain tree . . . and you write: "Near the water there was a big tree that was rather impressive." Most of us would produce something like that sentence. Here is the sentence Ernesto Galarza wrote in *Barrio Boy:*

> On the edge of the pond, at the far side, there was an enormous walnut tree, standing like an open umbrella whose ribs extended halfway across the still water of the pool.

We probably could not have come up with the metaphor of the umbrella because we wouldn't have seen the similarity. (As Aristotle observed, the gift for making metaphors distinguishes the poet from the rest of us.) But we can all train ourselves to be accurate observers and reporters. For "the water" (general) we can *specify* "pond"; for "near" we can say how near, "on the edge of the pond," and add the specific location, "at the far side"; for "tree" we can give the *species*, "walnut tree"; and for "big" we can provide a picture, its branches "extended halfway across" the pond: it was, in fact, "enormous."

Galarza does not need to add limply, as we did, that the tree "was rather impressive." The tree he describes *is* impressive. That he accurately remembered it persuades us that he was impressed, without his having to tell us he was. For writing descriptions, a good general rule is: show, don't tell.

Be as specific as you can be in all forms of exposition too. Take the time, when you revise, to find the exact word to replace vague, woolly phrases or clichés. (In the following examples we have had to guess or invent what the writer meant.)

1. *Vague*
The clown's part in *Othello* is very small.

Specific
The clown appears in only two scenes in *Othello*
The clown in *Othello* speaks only thirty lines.
(Notice the substitution of the verb "appears" or "speaks" for the frequently debilitating "is." And in place of the weak intensifier "very" we have specific details to tell us how small the role is.)

2. *Vague*
He feels uncomfortable at the whole situation. (Many feelings are uncomfortable. Which one does he feel? What's the situation?)

Specific
He feels guilty for having distrusted his father.

3. *Vague*
The passage reveals a somewhat calculating aspect behind Antigone's noble motives. ("A somewhat calculating aspect" is vague—and wordy—for "calculation." Or did the writer mean "shrewdness"? What differences in connotation are there between "shrewd" and "calculating"?)

4. *Vague*
She uses simplicity in her style of writing. (Do we know, exactly, what simplicity in style means?)

Specific
She uses familiar words, normal word order, and conversational phrasing.

5. Vague Cliché
Then she criticized students for living in an ivory tower. (Did she criticize them for being detached or secluded? For social irresponsibility or studiousness?)

Specific
Then she criticized students for being socially irresponsible.

Using Examples

In addition to exact words and specific details, illustrative examples make for clear writing. Einstein and Infeld, in the passage quoted on page 494, use as an example of a primitive concept a cat teasing not only its first mouse, but "any mouse it meets." Here are two paragraphs which clarify their topic sentences through examples; the first is again from *Barrio Boy*.

> In Jalco people spoke in two languages—Spanish and with gestures. These signs were made with the face or hands or a combination of both. If you bent one arm and tapped the elbow with the other hand, it meant "He is stingy." When you sawed one arm across the other you were saying that someone you knew played the fiddle terribly. To say that a man was a tippler you made a set of cow's horns with the little finger and the thumb of one hand, bending the three middle fingers to the palm and pointing the thumb at your mouth. And if you wanted to indicate, without saying so for the sake of politeness, that a mutual acquaintance was daffy, you tapped three times on your forehead with your middle finger.
>
> — Ernesto Galarza

In the next paragraph, Northrop Frye, writing about the perception of rhythm, illustrates his point:

> Ideally, our literary education should begin, not with prose, but with such things as "this little pig went to market"—with verse rhythm reinforced by physical assault. The infant who gets bounced on somebody's knee to the rhythm of "Ride a cock horse" does not need a footnote telling him that Banbury Cross is twenty miles northeast of Oxford. He does not need the information that "cross"

and "horse" make (at least in the pronunciation he is most likely to hear) not a rhyme but an assonance. . . . All he needs is to get bounced.

Frye does not say our literary education should begin with "simple rhymes" or with "verse popular with children." He says "with such things as 'this little pig went to market,' " and then he goes on to add "Ride a cock horse." We know exactly what he means. Notice, too, that we do not need a third example. Be detailed, but know when to stop.

Your reader is likely to be brighter and more demanding than Lady Pliant, who in a seventeenth-century play says to a would-be seducer, "You are very alluring—and say so many fine Things, and nothing is so moving to me as a fine Thing." "Fine Things," of course, are what is wanted, but only exact words and apt illustrations will convince intelligent readers that they are hearing fine things.

Now look at a paragraph from a student's essay whose thesis is that rage can be a useful mechanism for effecting change. Then compare the left-hand paragraph with the same paragraph, revised, at the right. Note the specific ways, sentence by sentence, the student revised for clarity.

In my high school we had little say in the learning processes that were used. The subjects that we were required to take were irrelevant. One had to take them to earn enough points to graduate. Some of the teachers were sympathetic to our problem. They would tell us about when they were young, how they tried to oppose their school system. But when they were young it was a long time ago, for most of them. The principal would call	In my high school we had little say about our curriculum. We were required, for example, to choose either American or European History to earn enough points for graduation. We wanted, but were at first refused, the option of Black History. Some of our teachers were sympathetic with us; one told me about her fight opposing the penmanship course required in her school. Nor was the principal totally indifferent—he called assem-

assemblies to speak on the subject. They were entitled, ''The
Value of an Education'' or ''Get
a Good Education to Have a Bright
Future.'' The titles were not
inviting. They had nothing to do
with our plight. Most students
never came to any agreements with
the principal because most of his
thoughts and views seemed old and
outdated.

blies. I remember one talk he
gave called ''The Value of an
Education in Today's World,'' and
another, ''Get a Good Education
to Have a Bright Future.'' I
don't recall hearing about a
Black History course in either
talk. Once, he invited a group of
us to meet with him in his office, but we didn't reach any
agreement. He solemnly showed us
an American History text (not the
one we used) that had a whole
chapter devoted to Black History.

Using Analogies

In the revised essay that we have just quoted, the writer clarified his point about the academic program by citing specific examples, for instance by mentioning a particular course (Black History) that the students wanted to study. But sometimes the topic
is such that examples of this sort cannot be given, and the writer
may be forced to clarify the topic by giving an analogy, that is by
giving an extended comparison which makes the unfamiliar more
familiar. Earlier, on pages 217–18, we illustrated analogy with
this example: "A government is like a ship, and just as a ship has
a captain and a crew, so a government. . . ." Or one can construct an analogy between the mind and the body: as the body is
fed with food, so the mind is fed with ideas. The mind's diet, one
might explain, must be taken at appropriate intervals, in proper
amounts, and it must be balanced.

In an effort to explain the part that law plays in settling
disputes, K. N. Llewellyn sets forth an analogy, comparing the law
to an umpire in a game:

Strikes are called and fought through and settled. Often some phases of them reach the courts. Often none do. Almost never does the main question in a strike occupy a court. But perhaps the case of the strike is as good as any to bring out the part that law does play. Law (in the person of judges, police and sheriffs) does lay down rules within which strike and lockout and struggle of employer and employee are to be worked out. "Rules" of the game: no beating, no shooting, no intimidation, no blacklisting. Does it follow that these rules of the game are always observed? It does not. The games are few in number in which the rules are *always* observed. But what is vital is to see that the law official functions somewhat like an umpire in *attempting to see* that they are. Somewhat like an umpire, but not wholly. Like an umpire in that he does not always see the breach of the rules. Like an umpire in that at times he is severely partial to one side, or stubborn, or ignorant, or ill tempered. Like an umpire, at least on the criminal side, in that he reaches in to decide and control on his own motion. But on the civil side, on the side of private law, less like an umpire in this: that he does not reach in on his own motion, but waits to be called upon. Always, however, and on both civil and criminal sides, like an umpire, I repeat, in that when acting he tries in the main, and in the main with some success, to insist that the rules of the game shall be abided by; in that he takes the rules of the game in the main not from his own inner consciousness, but from existing practice, and again in the main from authoritative sources (which in the case of the law are largely statutes and the decisions of the courts). Like an umpire finally in that his decision is made only after the event, and that play is held up while he is making it, and that he is cursed roundly by the losing party and gets little enough thanks from the winner.

Notice, by the way, that Llewellyn is not taken in by his own analogy. That is, he realizes that the comparison goes only so far and no further. As we said in our earlier discussion of analogy, an analogy cannot prove anything, it can only hope to clarify. After all, the relation between employer and striker is *not* a game; there are essential differences between a strike and a baseball game. Still, the relationship between (on the one hand) employer, striker, and law and (on the other hand) rival teams and the umpire can be clarified or made easy and familiar through the comparison. As Sigmund Freud said, "Analogies prove nothing, but they can make one feel at home." If, then, you are trying to clarify a point, consider the possibility that an analogy, in which you compare the unfamiliar with the familiar, will help your reader to see what you are getting at.

Jargon and Technical Language

Jargon is the unnecessary, inappropriate, or inexact use of technical or specialized language. Look at this passage:

Dodgers Keep Perfect Record in Knocking Out Southpaws

NEW YORK (AP)—The Brooklyn Dodgers didn't win the first World Series game yesterday, but they got a measure of comfort in that they maintained one of their season records.

No left-hander went the distance in beating them the past season. Six lefties got the decision but none was around at the end.

New York hurler Whitey Ford made No. 7, but he, too, went the way of the other southpaws . . . empty consolation, to be sure, in view of the Yanks' 6–5 victory in the World Series opener.

Consider the diction of this sports story: "went the distance," "lefties," "got the decision," "around at the end," "hurler," "southpaws," "opener," "made No. 7." Do you understand the individual words? Most of them, probably. Do you know what the item is about? Some of us do, some don't. Is it written in technical language, or jargon?

The answer depends, as we define jargon, on where the story appeared, and for whom it was intended. Because it appeared on the sports page of a newspaper, we would classify the diction as technical language, not jargon. Properly used, technical language communicates information concisely and clearly, and can, as it does here, create a comfortable bond between reader and writer. Both are having fun. If the same story appeared on the front page of the newspaper, we would classify the language as jargon because it would baffle the general reader.

If the baseball story makes perfect sense to you, as an exercise, try to explain it in nontechnical language to someone who does not understand it. And while you're at it, can you explain why baseball fans are particularly interested in left-handed pitchers—in other words, what makes the statistic here a statistic? Why are baseball fans so interested in statistics anyway—more interested, say, than football or hockey fans? Is it because baseball is intrinsically boring?

Let's move quickly to another example:

> For many years Boston parents have tried to improve the public schools. But any input the parents might have desired has been stifled by the Boston School Committee.

What does "input" mean in this sentence? Is the term used as technical language here, or jargon? (And by the way, how would you go about stifling an input?)

A student wrote the passage just quoted. But recently in Dallas, parents of children in kindergarten through third grade received a twenty-eight page manual written by a professional educator to help them decipher their children's report cards. The title of the manual: *Terminal Behavioral Objectives for Continuous Progression Modules in Early Childhood Education.* Terminal objectives, it seems, means goals. What does the rest mean? If you were one of the parents, would you expect much help from the manual?

Here's a film critic discussing the movie *Last Tango in Paris:*

> The failure of the relationship between Paul and Jeanne is a function of the demands placed on the psyche by bourgeois society, and it is the family as mediator of psychological and social repression which provides the dialectic of Bertolucci's film.

Perhaps some film criticism should be x-rated?

And finally, a deliberate parody. A. P. Herbert in his book *What a Word!* tells us how a social scientist might write a familiar Biblical command:

"With you, I think I've found a maximization of experience."

Drawing by Donald Reilly; © 1978. The New Yorker Magazine, Inc.

In connection with my co-citizens, a general standard of mutual good will and reciprocal non-aggression is obviously incumbent upon me.

What is the command? (See Leviticus 19.18.)

In general, when you write for nonspecialists, avoid technical terms; if you must use them, define them. If you use a technical term when writing for specialists, be sure you know its precise meaning. But whenever you can, even among specialists, use plain English.

Clichés

Clichés (literally, in French, molds from which type is cast) are trite expressions, mechanically—that is, mindlessly—produced. Since they are available without thought they are great Instant Prose Additives (see pages 476–78). Writers who use them are usually surprised to be criticized: they find the phrases attractive, and may even think them exact. (Phrases become clichés precisely because they have wide appeal and therefore wide use.) But clichés, by their very nature, cannot communicate the uniqueness of your thoughts. Furthermore, because they come instantly to mind, they tend to block the specific detail or exact expression that will let the reader know what precisely is in your mind. When, in revising, you strike out a cliché, you force yourself to do the work of writing clearly. The following examples are full of clichés:

> Finally, the long awaited day arrived. Up bright and early. . . . She peered at me with suspicion; then a faint smile crossed her face.

Other examples:

first and foremost	time honored
the acid test	bustled to and fro
fatal flaw	short but sweet
budding genius	few and far between
slowly but surely	D-day arrived
little did I know	sigh of relief
the big moment	last but not least

In attempting to avoid clichés, however, don't go to the other extreme of wildly original, super-vivid writing—" 'Well then, say something to her,' he roared, his whole countenance gnarled in rage." It's often better to simply say, "he said." (Anyone who intends to write dialogue should memorize Ring Lardner's intentionally funny line, " 'Shut up!' he explained.") Note also that such common expressions as "How are you?" "Please pass the salt," and "So long" are not clichés; they make no claim to be colorful.

Metaphors and Mixed Metaphors

Ordinary speech abounds with metaphors (implied comparisons). We speak or write of the foot of a mountain, the germ (seed) of an idea, the root of a problem. Metaphors so deeply embedded in the language that they no longer evoke pictures in our minds are called *dead metaphors*. Ordinarily, they offer us, as writers, no problems: we need neither seek them nor avoid them; they are simply there. (Notice, for example, "embedded" two sen-

*"You're right as rain. It's the dawn of history, and there are no
clichés as yet. I'll drink to that."*

Drawing by Handelsman; © 1972 The New Yorker Magazine, Inc.

tences back.) Such metaphors become problems, however, when
we unwittingly call them back to life. Howard Nemerov observes:
"That these metaphors may be not dead but only sleeping, or that
they may arise from the grave and walk in our sentences, is something that has troubled everyone who has ever tried to write plain
expository prose. . . ."

Dead metaphors are most likely to haunt us when they are
embodied in clichés. Since we use clichés without attention to what
they literally say or point to, we are unlikely to be aware of the
dead metaphors buried in them. But when we attach one cliché to
another, we may raise the metaphors from the grave. The result is
likely to be a mixed metaphor; the effect is almost always absurd.

Water seeks its own level whichever way you want to slice it.

Traditional liberal education has run out of gas and educational soup kitchens are moving into the vacuum.

The low ebb has been reached and hopefully it's turned the corner.

Her energy, drained through a stream of red tape, led only to closed doors.

We no longer ask for whom the bell tolls but simply chalk it up as one less mouth to feed.

As comedian Joe E. Lewis observed, "Show me a man who builds castles in the air and I'll show you a crazy architect."

Fresh metaphors, on the other hand, imaginatively combine accurate observations. They are not prefabricated ideas; they are a means of discovering or inventing new ideas. They enlarge thought and enliven prose. Here are two examples from students' journals:

```
I have some sort of sporadic restlessness in me, like the pen
on a polygraph machine. It moves along in curves, then sud-
denly shoots up, blowing a bubble in my throat, making my
chest taut, forcing me to move around. It becomes almost un-
bearable and then suddenly it will plunge, leaving something
that feels like a smooth orange wave.
```

```
Time is like wrapping papers. It wraps memories, decorates
them with sentiment. No matter (almost) what's inside, it's
remembered as a beautiful piece of past time. That's why I
even miss my high school years, which were filled with tired-
ness, boredom, confusion. . . .
```

And here is a passage from an essay in which a student analyzes the style of a story he found boring:

```
Every sentence yawns, stretches, shifts from side to side,
and then quietly dozes off.
```

Experiment with metaphors, let them surface in the early drafts of your essays and in your journals, and by all means, introduce original and accurate comparisons in your essays. But leave the mixed metaphors to politicians and comedians.

Euphemisms

Euphemisms are words substituted for other words thought to be offensive. In deodorant advertisements there are no armpits, only *underarms,* which may *perspire,* but not sweat, and even then they don't smell. A parent reading a report card is likely to learn not that his child got an F in conduct, but that she "experiences difficulty exercising self-control: (a) verbally (b) physically." And where do old people go? To Sun City, "a retirement community for senior citizens."

Euphemisms are used for two reasons: to avoid giving offense, and, sometimes unconsciously, to disguise fear or animosity. We do not advise you to write or speak discourteously; we do advise you, though, to use euphemisms consciously and sparingly, when tact recommends them. It's customary in a condolence letter to avoid the word *"death,"* and, depending both on your own feelings and those of the bereaved, you may wish to follow that custom. But there's no reason on earth to write "Hamlet passes on." You should be aware, moreover, that some people find euphemisms themselves offensive. There may be more comfort for your friend in "I'm sorry about his death" than in "I regret to hear of your loss." And Margaret Kuhn argues that the word "old" is preferable to "senior." "Old," she says "is the right word. . . . I think we should wear our gray hair, wrinkles, and crumbling joints as badges of distinction. After all, we worked damn hard to get them." She has organized a militant group called the Gray Panthers to fight agism.

In revising, replace needless euphemisms with plain words. Your writing will be sharper, and you might, in examining and confronting them, free yourself of a mindless habit, an unconscious prejudice, or an irrational fear.

A Digression on Public Lying

There is a kind of lying which, in the words of Walker Gibson, we may call *public lying.* Its rules are to avoid substance, direct answers, and plain words. Its tendency is to subvert the

English language. It employs and invents euphemisms, but the public liar intends to protect not his listeners, but himself and his friends, and he misleads and deceives consciously. Public lying was not invented during the Vietnam War (in 1946 George Orwell had already written the definitive essay on it, "Politics and the English Language"). But the war produced some classic examples, from which we select a few.

Feiffer

The war, of course, was not a war, but a "conflict" or an "era." "Our side" never attacked "the other side," we made "protective reaction raids"; we didn't invade, we "incursed." We didn't bomb villages, we "pacified" them; peasants were not herded into concentration camps, but "relocated." We didn't spray the countryside with poisons, destroying forests, endangering or killing plant, animal, and human life, we "practiced vegetation control." When American intelligence agents drowned a spy they referred to their action as "termination with extreme prejudice."

More recently, it was disclosed that the CIA published a manual for insurgents in Nicaragua instructing that "It is possible to neutralize carefully selected and planned targets, such as court judges, police and state security officials, etc." And the State Department now substitutes for the word "killing," in reports on human rights, "unlawful or arbitrary deprivation of life." A national committee of English teachers gave the State Department its 1984 Doublespeak Award for that.

There is a Gresham's law in rhetoric as there is in economics: bad language drives out good. Bad language is contagious; learn to detect the symptoms: use of vague words for clear words; use of sentences or phrases where words suffice; evasive use of the passive voice; and outright lying.

Passive or Active Voice?

1. I baked the bread. (Active voice)
2. The bread was baked by me. (Passive voice)
3. The bread will be baked. (Passive voice)

Although it is the verb that is in the active or the passive voice, notice that the words *active* and *passive* describe the subjects of the sentences. That is, in the first sentence the verb "baked" is in the active voice; the subject "I" acts. In the second and third sentences the verbs "was baked" and "will be baked" are in the passive voice; the subject "bread" is acted upon. Notice also the following points:

1. The *voice* of the verb is distinct from its *tense*. Don't confuse the passive voice with the past tense. (Sentence 2 above happens to be in the past tense, but 3 is not; both 2 and 3 are in the passive voice.)
2. The passive voice uses more words than the active voice. (Compare sentences 1 and 2.)
3. A sentence with a verb in the passive voice may leave the doer of the action unidentified. (See sentence 3.)
4. Finally, notice that in each of the three sentences the emphasis is different.

In revising, take a good look at each sentence in which you have used the passive voice. If the passive clarifies your meaning, retain it; if it obscures your meaning, change it. More often than not, the passive voice obscures meaning.

1. *Obscure*
The revolver given Daru by the gendarme is left in the desk drawer. (Left by whom? The passive voice here obscures the point.)

Clear
Daru leaves the gendarme's revolver in the desk drawer.

2. *Obscure*
Daru serves tea and the Arab is offered some. (Confusing shift from the active voice "serves" to the passive voice "is offered.")

Clear
Daru serves tea and offers the Arab some.

3. *Appropriate*
For over fifty years *Moby-Dick* was neglected. ("Was neglected" suggests that the novel was neglected by almost everyone. The passive voice catches the passivity of the response. Changing the sentence to "For over fifty years few readers read *Moby-Dick*" would make "readers" the subject of the sentence, but the true subject is—as in the original—*Moby-Dick*.)

Finally, avoid what has been called the Academic Passive: "In this essay it has been shown that. . . ." This cumbersome form used to be common in academic writing (to convey scientific objectivity) but *I* is usually preferable to such stuffiness.

The Writer's "I"

It is seldom necessary in writing an essay (even on a personal experience) to repeat "I think that" or "in my opinion." Your reader knows that what you write is your opinion. Nor is it necessary, if you've done your job well, to apologize. "After reading the story over several times I'm not really sure what it is about, but. . . ." Write about something you are reasonably sure of. Occasionally, though, when there is a real problem in the text, for example the probable date of the Book of Ruth, it is not only permissible to disclose doubts and to reveal tentative conclusions; it may be necessary to do so.

Note also that there is no reason to avoid the pronoun *I* when you are in fact writing about yourself. Attempts to avoid *I* ("this writer," "we," expressions in the passive voice such as "it has been said above" and "it was seen") are noticeably awkward and distracting. And sometimes you may want to focus on your subjective response to a topic in order to clarify a point. The following opening paragraph of a movie review provides an example:

I take the chance of writing about Bergman's *Persona* so long after its showing because this seems to me a movie there's no hurry about. It will be with us a long time, just as it has been on my mind for a long time. Right now, when I am perhaps still under its spell, it seems to me Bergman's masterpiece, but I can't imagine ever thinking it less than one of the great movies. This of course is opinion; what I know for certain is that *Persona* is also one of the most difficult movies I will ever see; and I am afraid that in this case there is a direct connection between difficulty and value. It isn't only that *Persona* is no harder than it has to be; its peculiar haunting power, its spell, and its value come directly from the fact that it's so hard to get a firm grasp on.

                                         — Robert Garis

Students who have been taught not to begin sentences with *I* often produce sentences that are eerily passive even when the verbs are in the active voice. For example:

1. Two reasons are important to my active participation in dance.
2. The name of the program that I enrolled in is the Health Careers Summer Program.
3. An eager curiosity overcame my previous feeling of fear to make me feel better.

But doesn't it make more sense to say:

1. I dance for two reasons.
2. I enrolled in the Health Careers Summer Program.
3. My curiosity aroused, I was no longer afraid.

A good rule: make the agent of the action the subject of the sentence. A practical suggestion: to avoid a boring series of sentences all beginning with *I*, subordinate for conciseness and emphasis. (See pages 488–90 and 541–42.)

CLARITY AND COHERENCE

Writing a coherent essay is hard work; it requires mastery of a subject and skill in presenting it; it always takes a lot of time. Writing a coherent paragraph often takes more fussing and patching than you expect, but once you have the hang of it, it's relatively easy and pleasant. Writing a coherent sentence requires only that you stay awake until you get to the end of it.

We all do nod sometimes, even over our own prose. But if you make it a practice to read your work over several times, at least once aloud, you give yourself a chance to spot the incoherent sentence before your reader does, and to revise it. Once you see that a sentence is incoherent, it's usually easy to recast it.

Cats Are Dogs

In some sentences a form of the verb *to be* asserts that one thing is in a class with another. Passover is a Jewish holiday. Dartmouth is a college. But would anyone not talking in his sleep say "Dartmouth is a Jewish Holiday"? Are cats dogs? Students did write the following sentences:

1. *Incoherent*
X. J. Kennedy's poem "Nothing in Heaven Functions as It Ought" is a contrast between Heaven and Hell. (As soon as you ask yourself the question "Is a poem a contrast?" you have, by bringing the two words close together, isolated the problem. A poem may be a sonnet, an epic, an ode—but not a contrast. The writer was trying to say what the poem does, not what it is.)

Coherent
X. J. Kennedy's poem "Nothing in Heaven Functions as It Ought" contrasts Heaven and Hell.

2. *Incoherent*
Besides, he tells himself, a matchmaker is an old Jewish custom. (Is a matchmaker a custom?)

Coherent
Besides, he tells himself, consulting a matchmaker is an old Jewish custom.

Try revising the following:

The essay is also an insight into imperialism.

In a related problem, one part of the sentence doesn't know what the other is doing:

1. *Incoherent*
Ruth's devotion to Naomi is rewarded by marrying Boaz. (Does devotion marry Boaz?)

Coherent
Ruth's marriage to Boaz rewards her devotion to Naomi.

2. *Incoherent*
He demonstrates many human frailties, such as the influence of others' opinions upon one's actions. (Is influence a frailty? How might this sentence be revised?)

False Series

If you were given a shopping list that mentioned apples, fruit, and pears, you would be puzzled and possibly irritated by the inclusion of "fruit." Don't puzzle or irritate your reader. Analyze sentences containing items in a series to be sure that the items are of the same order of generality. For example:

> *False Series*
> His job exposed him to the "dirty work" of the British and to the evils of imperialism. ("The 'dirty work' of the British" is a *specific* example of the more *general* "evils of imperialism." The false series makes the sentence incoherent.)
>
> *Revised*
> His job, by exposing him to the "dirty work" of the British, brought him to understand the evils of imperialism.

In the following sentence, which item in the series makes the sentence incoherent?

> Why should one man, no matter how important, be exempt from investigation, arrest, trial, and law enforcing tactics?

Modifiers

A modifier should appear close to the word it modifies (that is, describes or qualifies). Three kinds of faulty modifiers are common: misplaced, squinting, and dangling.

Misplaced Modifiers

If the modifier seems to modify the wrong word, it is called *misplaced.* Misplaced modifiers are often unintentionally funny. The judo parlor that advertised "For $20 learn basic methods of protecting yourself from an experienced instructor" probably attracted more amused readers than paying customers.

1. *Misplaced*
Orwell shot the elephant under pressured circumstances. (Orwell was under pressure, not the elephant. Put the modifier near what it modifies.)

Revised
Orwell, under pressure, shot the elephant.

2. *Misplaced*
Orwell lost his individual right to protect the elephant as part of the imperialistic system. (The elephant was not part of the system; Orwell was.)

Revised
As part of the imperialistic system, Orwell lost his right to protect the elephant.

3. *Misplaced*
Amos Wilder has been called back to teach at Harvard Divinity School after ten years retirement due to a colleague's illness. (Did Wilder retire for ten years because a colleague was ill? Revise the sentence.)

Revise the following:

1. Sitting Bull and William Cody stand side by side, each supporting a rifle placed beween them with one hand.
2. Complete with footnotes the author has provided her readers with some background information.

Sometimes other parts of sentences are misplaced:

1. *Misplaced*
We learn from the examples of our parents who we are. (The sentence appears to say we are our parents.)

Revised
We learn who we are from the examples of our parents.

2. *Misplaced*
It is up to the students to revise the scheme, not the administrators. (We all know you can't revise administrators. Revise the sentence.)

Squinting Modifiers

If the modifier is ambiguous, that is, if it can be applied equally to more than one term, it is sometimes called a *squinting modifier:* it seems to look forward, and it seems to look backward.

1. *Squinting*
Being with Jennifer more and more enrages me. (Is the writer spending more time with Jennifer, or is she more enraged? Probably more enraged.)

Revised
Being with Jennifer enrages me more and more.

2. *Squinting*
Writing clearly is difficult. (The sentence may be talking about writing—it's clearly difficult to write—or about writing clearly—it's difficult to write clearly.)

3. *Squinting*
Students only may use this elevator. (Does "only" modify students? If so, no one else may use the elevator. Or does it modify elevator? If so, students may use no other elevator.)

Revised
Only students may use this elevator.
Students may use only this elevator.

Note: the word *only* often squints. In general, put *only* immediately before the word or phrase it modifies. Often it appears too early in the sentence. (See Glossary.)

Dangling Modifiers

If the term it should modify appears nowhere in the sentence, the modifier is called *dangling*.

1. *Dangling*
Being small, his ear scraped against the belt when his father stumbled. (The writer meant that the boy was small, not the ear. But the boy is not in the sentence.)

Revised
Because the boy was small his ear scraped against the belt when his father stumbled.
Being small, the boy scraped his ear against the belt when his father stumbled.

2. *Dangling*
A meticulously organized person, his suitcase could be tucked under an airplane seat. (How would you revise the sentence?)

The general rule: *when you revise sentences, put together what belongs together.*

Reference of Pronouns

A pronoun is used in place of a noun. Because the noun usually precedes the pronoun, the noun to which the pronoun refers is called the antecedent (Latin: "going before"). For example: in "When Sheriff Johnson was on a horse, he was a big man" the noun, "Sheriff Johnson," precedes the pronoun, "he." But the noun can also follow the pronoun, as in "When he was on a horse, Sheriff Johnson was a big man."

Be sure that whenever possible a pronoun has a clear reference. Sometimes it isn't possible: *it* is commonly used with an unspecified reference, as in "It's hot today," and "Hurry up please, it's time"; and there can be no reference for interrogative pronouns: "What's bothering you?" and "Who's on first?" But otherwise always be sure that you've made clear what noun the pronoun is standing for.

Vague References

1. *Vague*

Apparently, they fight physically and it can become rather brutal. ("It" doubtless refers to "fight," but "fight" in this sentence is the verb, not an antecedent noun.)

Clear

Their fights are apparently physical, and sometimes brutal.

2. *Vague*

I was born in Colon, the second largest city in the Republic of Panama. Despite this, Colon is still an undeveloped town. ("This" has no specific antecedent. It appears to refer to the writer's having been born in Colon.)

Clear

Although Colon, where I was born, is the second largest city in Panama, it remains undeveloped.

(On *this,* see also Glossary.)

Revise the following sentence:

> They're applying to medical school because it's a well-paid profession.

Shift in Pronouns

This common error is easily corrected.

1. In many instances the child was expected to follow the profession of your father. (Expected to follow the profession of whose father, "yours" or "his"?)
2. Having a tutor, you can get constant personal encouragement and advice that will help me budget my time. (If "you" have a tutor will that help "me"?)
3. If one smokes, you should at least ask permission before you light up. (If "one" smokes, why should "you" ask permission? But here the change to "If one smokes, one should at least ask permission before one lights up," though correct, sounds inappropriately formal. Omit a "one": "If one smokes, one should at least ask permission before lighting up." Or forget about "one" and use "you" throughout the sentence.)

Revise the following sentences:

1. Schools bring people of the same age together and teach you how to get along with each other.
2. If asked why you went to the mixer, one might say they were simply curious.

Ambiguous Reference of Pronouns

A pronoun normally refers to the first appropriate noun or pronoun preceding it. Same-sex pronouns and nouns, like dogs, often get into scraps.

1. *Ambiguous*
Her mother died when she was eighteen. (Who was eighteen, the mother or the daughter?)

Clear
Her mother died when Mabel was eighteen.
Her mother died at the age of eighteen. (Note the absence of ambiguity in "His mother died when he was eighteen.")

2. *Ambiguous*

Daru learns that he must take an Arab to jail against his will. (Both Daru and the Arab are male. The writer of the sentence meant that Daru learns he must act against his will.)

Clear

Daru learns that he must, against his will, take an Arab to jail.

The general rule: *put together what belongs together.*

Agreement

Noun and Pronoun

Everyone knows that a singular noun requires a singular pronoun, and a plural noun requires a plural pronoun, but writers sometimes slip.

1. *Faulty*

A dog can easily tell if people are afraid of them.

Correct

A dog can easily tell if people are afraid of it.

2. *Faulty*

Every student feels that Wellesley expects them to do their best.

Correct

Every student feels that Wellesley expects her to do her best.

Each, everybody, nobody, no one, and *none* are especially troublesome. See the entries on these words in the glossary.

Subject and Verb

A singular subject requires a singular verb, a plural subject a plural verb.

Faulty

Horror films bring to light a subconscious fear and shows a character who succeeds in coping with it.

Correct

Horror films bring to light a subconscious fear and show a character who succeeds in coping with it.

The student who wrote "shows" instead of "show" thought that the subject of the verb was "fear," but the subject really is "Horror films," a plural.

Faulty
The manager, as well as the pitcher and the catcher, were fined.

Correct
The manager, as well as the pitcher and the catcher, was fined.

If the sentence had been "The manager and the pitcher . . . ," the subject would have been plural and the required verb would be *were:*

The manager and the pitcher were fined.

But in the sentence as it was given, "as well as" (like *in addition to, with,* and *together with*) does *not* add a subject to a subject and thereby make a plural subject. "As well as" merely indicates that what is said about the manager applies to the pitcher and the catcher.

Revise the following:

About mid-morning during Spanish class the sound of jeeps were heard.

Three Additional Points:

1. A *collective noun*—that is, a noun that is singular in form but that denotes a collection of individuals, such as "mob," "audience," "jury"—normally takes a *singular* verb:

Correct
The mob is at the gate.

Correct
An audience of children *is* easily bored.

(The subject is "an audience," *not* "children.")

Correct
The jury is seated.

But when the emphasis is on the individuals within the group—for instance when you are calling attention to a division within the group—you can use a plural verb:

The jury disagree.

Still, because this sounds a bit odd, it is probably better to recast the sentence:

The jurors disagree.

2. Sometimes a sentence that is grammatically correct may nevertheless sound awkward:

One of its most noticeable features is the lounges.

Because the subject is "one"—*not* "features"—the verb must be singular, "is," but "is" sounds odd when it precedes the plural "lounges." The solution: revise the sentence.

Among the most noticeable features are the lounges.

3. When a singular and a plural subject are joined by *or,* *either . . . or,* or *neither . . . nor,* use a verb that agrees in number with the subject closest to the verb. Examples:

Correct
Either the teacher or the students are mistaken.

Correct
Either the students or the teacher is mistaken.

The first revision uses "are" because the verb is nearer to "students" (plural) than to "teacher" (singular); the second uses "is" because the verb is nearer to "teacher" than to "students."

Repetition and Variation

1. *Don't be afraid to repeat a word if it is the best word.* The following paragraph repeats "interesting," "paradox," "Salinger," "What makes," and "book"; notice also "feel" and "feeling." Repetition, a device necessary for continuity and clarity, holds the paragraph together.

The reception given to *Franny and Zooey* in America has illustrated again the interesting paradox of Salinger's reputation there: great public enthusiasm, of the *Time* magazine and Best Seller List kind, accompanied by a repressive coolness in the critical journals. What makes this a paradox is that the book's themes are among the most ambitiously highbrow, and its craftsmanship most uncompromisingly virtuoso. What makes it an interesting one is that those who are most patronizing about the book are those who most resemble its characters: people whose ideas and language in their best moments resemble Zooey's. But they feel they ought not to enjoy the book. There is a very strong feeling in American literary circles that Salinger and love of Salinger must be discouraged.

— Martin Green

2. *Use pronouns, when their reference is clear, as substitutes for nouns.* Notice Green's use of pronouns; notice also his substitution of "the book," for *"Franny and Zooey,"* and then "its" for "the book's." Substitutions that neither confuse nor distract keep a paragraph from sounding like a broken phonograph record.

3. *Do not, however, confuse the substitutions we have just spoken of with the fault called Elegant Variation.* A groundless fear of repetition sometimes leads students to write first, for example, of "Salinger," then of "the writer," then of "our author." Such variations strike the reader as silly. They can, moreover, be confusing. Does "the writer" mean "Salinger," or the person writing about him? Substitute "he" for "Salinger" if "he" is clear and sounds better. Otherwise, repeat "Salinger."

4. *But don't repeat a word if it is being used in two different senses.*

1. *Confusing*
Green's theme focuses on the theme of the book. (The first "theme" means "essay"; the second means "underlying idea" or "motif.")

Clear
Green's essay focuses on the theme of the book.

2. *Confusing*
Caesar's character is complex. The comic characters, however, are simple. (The first "character" means "personality"; the second means "persons" or "figures in the play.")

Clear
Caesar is complex; the comic characters, however, are simple.

5. *Finally, eliminate words repeated unnecessarily.* Use of words like *surely, in all probability, it is noteworthy* may become

habitual. If they don't help your reader to follow your thoughts, they are Instant Prose Additives. Cross them out.

In general, when you revise, decide if a word should be repeated, varied, or eliminated, by testing sentences and paragraphs for both sound and sense.

Euphony

The word is from the Greek, "sweet voice," and though you need not aim at sweetness, try to avoid cacophony, or "harsh voice." Avoid distracting repetitions of sound, as in "The story is marked by a remarkable mystery," and "This is seen in the scene in which. . . ." Such echoes call attention to themselves, getting in the way of the points you are making. When you revise, tune out irrelevant sound effects.

Not all sound effects are irrelevant; some contribute meaning. James Baldwin, in his essay "Stranger in the Village," argues that the American racial experience has permanently altered black and white relationships throughout the world. His concluding sentence is

This world is white no longer, and it will never be white again.

As the sentence opens, the repetition of sounds in "*w*orld is *w*hite" binds the two words together, but the idea that they are permanently bound is swiftly denied by the most emphatic repetition of sounds in "*no*," "*never*," "*again*," as the sentence closes. Or take another example:

America, Love It or Leave It.

If it read "America, Love It or Emigrate," would the bumper sticker still imply, as clearly and menacingly, that there are only two choices, and for the patriot only one?

Transitions

Repetition holds a paragraph together by providing continuity and clarity. Transitions such as *next, on the other hand,* and *therefore* also provide continuity and clarity. Because we discuss transitions at length on pages 118–20, in our chapter on paragaphs, we here only remind you to make certain that the relation between one sentence and the next, and one paragaph and the next, is clear. Often it will be clear without an explicit transition: "She was desperately unhappy. She quit school."

But do not take too much for granted; relationships between sentences may not be as clear to your readers as they are to you. You know what you are talking about; they don't. After reading the passage readers may see, in retrospect, that you have just given an example, or a piece of contrary evidence, or an amplification, but readers like to know in advance where they are going; brief transitions such as *for example, but, finally* (readers are keenly interested in knowing when they are getting near the end) are enormously helpful.

CLARITY AND SENTENCE STRUCTURE: PARALLELISM

Make the structure of your sentence reflect the structure of your thought. This is not as formidable as it sounds. If you keep your reader in mind, remembering that you are explaining something to someone who understands it less well than you, you will almost automatically not only say *what* you think but show *how* you think.

Almost automatically. In revising, read your work as if you were not the writer of it, but your intended reader. If you reach a bump or snag, where the shape or direction of your thought isn't clear, revise your sentence structure. Three general rules help:

1. Put main ideas in main (independent) clauses.
2. Subordinate the less important elements in the sentence to the more important.
3. Put parallel ideas and details in parallel constructions.

The time to consult these rules consciously is not while you write, but while you revise. (The first two rules are amplified in the next chapter, "Revising for Emphasis." Clarity and emphasis are closely related, as the following discussion of parallel construction makes evident.)

Consider the following sentence and the revision:

Awkward
He liked eating and to sleep.

Parallel
He liked to eat and sleep.

In the first version, "eating" and "to sleep" are not grammatically parallel; the difference in grammatical form blurs the writer's point that there is a similarity. Use parallel constructions to clarify relationships—for instance to emphasize similarities or to define differences.

> I divorce myself from my feelings and immerse myself in my obligations.
>
> — From a student journal

> She drew a line between respect, which we were expected to show, and fear, which we were not.
>
> — Ernesto Galarza

> I will not accept if nominated and will not serve if elected.
> — William Tecumseh Sherman

> Fascist art glorifies surrender; it exalts mindlessness; it glamorizes death.
>
> — Susan Sontag

In the following examples, the parallel construction is printed in italic type.

1. *Awkward*
The dormitory rules needed revision, a smoking area was a necessity, and a generally more active role for the school in social affairs were all significant to her.

Parallel
She recommended that the school *revise* its dormitory rules, *provide* a smoking area, and *organize* more social activities.

2. *Awkward*
Most Chinese parents disapprove of interracial dating or they just do not permit it.

Parallel
Most Chinese parents *disapprove* of interracial dating, and many *forbid* it.

Revise the following sentence:

The rogallo glider is recommended for beginners because it is easy to assemble, to maintain, and it is portable.

In parallel constructions, be sure to check the consistency of articles, prepositions, and conjunctions. For example, "He wrote papers on a play by Shakespeare, a novel by Dickens, and a story by Oates," *not* "He wrote papers on a play by Shakespeare, a novel of Dickens, and a story by Oates." The shift from "by" to "of" and back to "by" serves no purpose and is merely distracting.

Let's study this matter a little more, using a short poem as our text.

Love Poem
Robert Bly

When we are in love, we love the grass,
And the barns, and the lightpoles,
And the small mainstreets abandoned all night.

Suppose we change "Love Poem" by omitting a conjunction or an article here and there:

When we are in love, we love the grass,
Barns, and lightpoles,
And the small mainstreets abandoned all night.

We've changed the rhythm, of course, but we still get the point: the lover loves all the world. In the original poem, however, the syntax of the sentence, the consistent repetition of "and the . . ." "and the . . ." makes us feel, without our thinking about it, that when we are in love we love the world, everything in it, equally. The list could extend infinitely, and everything in it would give us identical pleasure. In our altered version, we sacrifice this unspoken assurance. We bump a little, and stumble. As readers, without consciously being aware of it, we wonder if there's some distinction being made, some qualification we've missed. We still get the point of the poem, but we don't feel it the same way.

To sum up:

> A pupil once asked Arthur Schnabel [the noted pianist] whether it was better to play in time or to play as one feels; his characteristic mordant reply was another question: "Why not feel in time?"
> — David Hamilton

EXERCISES

1. In the following sentences, underline phrases in which you find the passive voice. Recast the sentences, using the active voice:

    a. The phrases in which the passive voice is found should be underlined.
    b. The active voice should be used.
    c. In the letter from Mrs. Mike advice was sought regarding her problem with her tenant.
    d. The egg is guarded, watched over, and even hatched by the male penguin.
    e. After the Industrial Revolution, the workers' daylight hours were spent in factories.
    f. Tyler found that sexual stereotyping was reinforced in the kindergarten: the girls were encouraged to play with dolls and the boys with Mack trucks.
    g. Insufficient evidence was given in the report to prove her hypothesis that reading problems originate in peer relationships.

2. Revise the following sentences to eliminate faults in modifiers:

    a. At the age of ten years, my family moved to Zierenberg, West Germany.
    b. Without knowing the reason, my father's cheeks became red with embarrassment.
    c. Buffalo Bill became friends with Sitting Bull while performing together in the Wild West Show.
    d. During a drought, annual plants will succumb without help.
    e. Looking out from my window, the sky was inky black.

    f. Mr. Karajan conducted the orchestra three times during the weekend before returning to his home in the Alps to the delight of the audience.

    g. "Some of it is sitting down with the most powerful single person in the free world." (John Glenn, alluding to President Reagan)

3. In the following sentences, locate the errors in agreement and correct them.

    a. Locate the error and correct them.

    b. One must strive hard to reach their goal.

    c. I would recommend the book to anyone who wants to improve their writing.

    d. Her collection of antique toys fill the house.

4. Recast the following sentences, using parallel constructions to express parallel ideas:

    a. Jacoby's aim in writing is to disgrace the passively committed and opposition to feminism.

    b. The boys segregated themselves less, the girls showed broader career interests, and unromantic, cross-sex relationships were achieved.

    c. The study shows parents and educators that it is important to change and it can be done.

    d. I do believe that there should be equality between men and women: equal pay for equal work; everybody should have an equal chance to attain whatever goals they may have set for themselves; and everybody should share the same responsibilities toward society.

5. Identify the specific faults that make the following sentences unclear, then revise each sentence for clarity. (Note that you will often have to invent what the writer thought he or she had said.)

    a. Actually, she was aging, and quite average in other respects.

    b. If technology cannot sort out its plusses and minuses, and work to improve them, man must.

    c. Brooks stresses the farm workers' strenuous way of life and the fact that they have the bare necessities of life.

    d. Instead of movable furniture, built-in ledges extend into the center of the room to be used as tables or to sit on.

    e. The issue has been saved for my final argument because it is controversial.

  f. I am neither indifferent nor fond of children.
  g. When the students heard that their proposal was rejected a meeting was called.
  h. A viable library is the cornerstone of any college campus.
  i. Her main fault was that she was somewhat lacking in decision-making capabilities.
  j. After industrialization a swarm of immigrants came bantering to our shores.
  k. Each group felt there was very personal rapport and thus very candid feedback resulted.
  l. He can tolerate crowding and pollution and seems disinterested or ignorant of these dangers.
  m. The wooden door occupies the majority of the stone wall.
  n. Yale students frequently write to Ann Landers telling her fictional stories of their so-called troubles as a childish prank.
  o. At my grandmother's house vegetables were only served because meat was forbidden.
  p. My firm stand seemed to melt a little.
  q. The conclusion leaves the conflict neatly tied in smooth knots.
  r. The paragraph reeks of blandness.

6. The following sentences, published in *AIDE*, a magazine put out by an insurance company, were written to the company by various policyholders. The trouble is that the writers mean one thing but their sentences say another. Make each sentence clearly say what the writer means.

  a. The other car collided with mine without giving warning of its intentions.
  b. I collided with a stationary truck coming the other way.
  c. The guy was all over the road; I had to swerve a number of times before I hit him.
  d. I pulled away from the side of the road, glanced at my mother-in-law, and headed over the embankment.
  e. In my attempt to kill a fly, I drove into a telephone pole.
  f. I had been driving for forty years when I fell asleep at the wheel and had the accident.
  g. To avoid hitting the bumper of the car in front, I struck the pedestrian.
  h. The pedestrian had no idea which direction to run, so I ran over him.
  i. The indirect cause of this accident was a little guy in a small car with a big mouth.

534 Chapter 13 Revising for Clarity

7. In 1983, while conflicting reports were being broadcast about an invasion of Grenada by U.S. troops, Admiral Wesley L. McDonald, in the Pentagon, answered a reporter's question thus: "We were not micromanaging Grenada intelligencewise until about that time frame." Bruce Felknor, director of year-books for the *Encyclopaedia Britannica,* says that he was "in-spired" by that answer to translate "a small selection of earlier admirals' heroic prose for the edification, indeed enjoyment, of our young." Below we list Felknor's translations and, in parentheses, the names of the admirals, the battles, and the dates of their heroic prose. What were the original words?

   a. "Combatwise, the time frame is upcoming." (John Paul Jones, off the English coast, September 23, 1779)
   b. "Area accessed in combat mode; mission finished." (Oliver Haz-ard Perry, after the Battle of Lake Erie, September 10, 1813)
   c. "Disregard anticipated structural damage. Continue as pro-grammed." (David Farragut, Mobile Bay, August 5, 1864)
   d. "Implementation of aggressive action approved; time frame to be selected by fire control officer." (George Dewey, Manila Bay, May 1, 1898)

8. Translate the following euphemisms into plain English:

   a. micromanaging Grenada intelligencewise
   b. revenue enhancement
   c. atmospheric deposition of anthropogenically derived acidic sub-stances
   d. resize our operations to the level of profitable opportunities (spo-ken by a business executive)
   e. reconcentrate (or redeploy) our forces

14

*R*evising for *E*mphasis

In revising for conciseness and clarity we begin to discover what we may have been largely unaware of in the early stages of writing: what in our topic most concerns us and precisely why it interests us. That moment of discovery (or those several discrete moments) yields more pleasure than any other in writing. From there on we work, sometimes as if inspired, to make our special angle of vision seem as inevitable to our readers as it is to us. Now as we tighten sentences or expand them, as we shift the position of a word or a paragraph, or as we subordinate a less important idea to a more important one, we are assigning relative value and weight to each of our statements. The expression of value and weight is what is meant by emphasis.

Inexperienced writers may *try* to achieve emphasis as Queen Victoria did, by a style consisting *almost entirely* of italics and—dashes—and—exclamation marks!!! Or they may spice their prose with clichés ("little did I realize," "believe it or not") or with a liberal sprinkling of intensifiers ("really beautiful," "definitely significant," and so on). But experienced writers abandon these unconvincing devices, preferring to exploit the possibilities of position, of brevity and length, of repetition, and of subordination.

EMPHASIS BY POSITION

First, let's see how a word or phrase may be emphasized. If it appears in an unusual position it gains emphasis, as in "This course he liked." Because in English the object of the verb usually comes after the verb (as in "He liked this course"), the object is emphasized if it appears first. But this device is tricky; words in an unusual position often seem ludicrous, the writer fatuous: "A mounted Indian toward the forest raced."

Let's now consider a less strained sort of emphasis by position. The beginning and the end of a sentence or a paragraph are emphatic positions; of these two positions, the end is usually the more emphatic. What comes last is what stays most in the mind. Compare these two sentences:

> The essay is brief but informative.
> The essay is informative but brief.

The first sentence leaves the reader with the impression that the essay, despite its brevity, is worth looking at. The second, however, ends more negatively, leaving the reader with the impression that the essay is so brief that its value is fairly slight. Because the emphasis in each sentence is different, the two sentences say different things.

The rule: it usually makes sense to put the important point near the end, lest the sentence become anticlimactic. Here is a sentence that properly moves to an emphatic end:

> Although I could not read its six hundred pages in one sitting, I never willingly put it down.

If the halves are reversed the sentence trails off:

> I never willingly put it down, although I could not read its six hundred pages in one sitting.

This second version straggles away from the real point—that the book was interesting.

Anticlimactic
Besides not owning themselves women also could not own property.

Emphatic
Women could not own property; in fact, they did not own themselves.

The commonest anticlimaxes are caused by weak qualifiers *(in my opinion, it seems to me, in general, etc.)* tacked on to interesting statements. Weak qualifiers usually can be omitted. Even useful ones rarely deserve an emphatic position.

Anticlimactic
Poodles are smart but they are no smarter than pigs, I have read.

Emphatic
Poodles are smart, but I have read that they are no smarter than pigs.

The rule: try to bury dull but necessary qualifiers in the middle of the sentence.

EMPHASIS BY BREVITY AND LENGTH: SHORT AND LONG SENTENCES

How long should a sentence be? One recalls Lincoln's remark to a heckler who asked him how long a man's legs should be: "Long enough to reach the ground." No rules about length can be given, but be careful not to bore your reader with a succession of short sentences (say, under ten words) and be careful not to tax your reader with a monstrously long sentence. Victor Hugo's sentence in *Les Misérables* containing 823 words punctuated by ninety-three commas, fifty-one semicolons, and four dashes, is not a good model for beginners.

Consider this succession of short sentences:

The purpose of the refrain is twofold. First, it divides the song into stanzas. Second, it reinforces the theme of the song.

These sentences are clear, but since the points are simple, readers may feel they are being addressed as if they were children. There is too much emphasis (too many heavy pauses) on too little. The reader can take all three sentences at once:

The purpose of the refrain is twofold: it divides the song into stanzas and it reinforces the theme.

The three simple sentences have been turned into one compound sentence, allowing the reader to keep going for a while.

Now compare another group of sentences with a revision.

Hockey is by far the fastest moving team sport in America. The skaters are constantly on the go. They move at high speeds. The action rarely stops.

These four sentences, instead of suggesting motion, needlessly stop us. Here is a revision:

Hockey is by far the fastest moving team sport in America. The skaters, constantly on the go, move at high speeds, and the action rarely stops.

By combining the second, third, and fourth sentences, the writer keeps the reader on the go, like the players.

Next, a longer example that would be thoroughly delightful if parts of it were less choppy.

Conceit

At my high school graduation we had two speakers. One was a member of our class, and the other was a faculty member. The student speaker's name was Alva Reed. The faculty speaker's name was Mr. Williams. The following conversation took place after the graduation ceremony. Parents, relatives, faculty, and friends were all outside the gymnasium congratulating the class of 1989. Alva was surrounded by her friends, her parents, and some faculty members who were congratulating her on her speech. Not standing far from her was Mr. Williams with somewhat the same crowd.

"Alva dear, you were wonderful!"

"Thanks Mom. I sure was scared though; I'm glad it's over."

At that moment, walking towards Alva were her grandparents. They both were wearing big smiles on their faces. Her grandfather said rather loudly, "That was a good speech dear. Nicely done, nicely done." Walking past them at that moment was Mr. Williams.

He stuck his head into their circle and replied, "Thank you," and walked away.

The first four sentences seem to be written in spurts. They can easily be combined and improved thus:

> At my high school graduation we had two speakers. One was a member of our class, Alva Reed, and the other was a faculty member, Mr. Williams.

If we think that even this version, two sentences instead of four, is a little choppy, we can rewrite it into a single sentence:

> At my high school graduation we had two speakers, Alva Reed, a member of our class, and Mr. Williams, a faculty member.

or:

> The two speakers at my high school graduation were Alva Reed, a member of our class, and Mr. Williams, a faculty member.

The rest of the piece is less choppy, but reread it and see if you don't discover some other sentences that should be combined. Revise them.

Sometimes, however, the choppiness of a succession of short sentences is effective. Look at this description of the methods by which George Jackson, in prison, resisted efforts to destroy his spirit:

> He trains himself to sleep only three hours a night. He studies Swahili, Chinese, Arabic and Spanish. He does pushups to control his sexual urge and to train his body. Sometimes he does a thousand a day. He eats only one meal a day. And, always, he is reading and thinking.
>
> — Julius Lester

These six sentences add up to only fifty-one words. The longest sentence—the one about pushups—contains only thirteen words. That the author is at ease also with longer and more complicated sentences is evident in the next paragraph, which begins with a sentence of forty-two words.

> Yet, when his contact with the outside world is extended beyond his family to include Angela Davis, Joan, a woman who works with the Soledad defense committee, and his attorney, he is able to find within himself feelings of love and tenderness.

Can we account for the success of the passage describing Jackson's prison routine? First, the short sentences, with their repeated commonplace form (subject, verb, object) in some degree imitate Jackson's experience: they are almost monotonously disciplined, almost as regular as the pushups the confined Jackson does.

> He trains himself. . . .
>
> He studies Swahili. . . .
>
> He does pushups. . . .
>
> Sometimes he does a thousand. . . .
>
> He eats only one meal a day.

Later, when Jackson makes contact with Angela Davis and others, the long sentence (forty-two words) helps to suggest the expansion of his world. Second, the brevity of the sentences suggests their enormous importance, certainly to Jackson and to Julius Lester and, Lester hopes, to the reader.

Keep in mind this principle: *any one sentence in your essay is roughly equal to any other sentence.* If a sentence is short, it must be relatively weighty. A lot is packed into a little. Less is more. (The chief exceptions are transitional sentences such as, "Now for the second point.") Consider the following passage:

> It happened that in September of 1933 Lord Rutherford, at the British Association meeting, made some remark about atomic energy never becoming real. Leo Szilard was the kind of scientist, perhaps just the kind of good-humored, cranky man, who disliked any statement that contained the word "never," particularly when made by a distinguished colleague. So he set his mind to think about the problem.
>
> — Jacob Bronowski

The first two sentences are relatively long (twenty-three words and thirty-one words); the third is relatively short (ten words), and its brevity—its weight or density—emphasizes Szilard's no-nonsense attitude.

EMPHASIS BY REPETITION

Don't be afraid to repeat a word if it is important. The repetition will add emphasis. Notice in these lucid sentences by Helen Gardner the effective repetition of "end" and "beginning."

> *Othello* has this in common with the tragedy of fortune, that the end in no way blots out from the imagination the glory of the beginning. But the end here does not merely by its darkness throw up into relief the brightness that was. On the contrary, beginning and end chime against each other. In both the value of life and love is affirmed.

The substitution of "conclusion" or "last scene" for the second "end" would be worse than pointless; it would destroy Miss Gardner's point that there is *identity* or correspondence between beginning and end.

EMPHASIS BY SUBORDINATION

Five Kinds of Sentences

Before we can discuss the use of subordination for emphasis, we must first talk about what a sentence is, and about five kinds of sentences.

If there is an adequate definition of a sentence, we haven't found it. Perhaps the best definition is not the old one, "a complete thought," but "a word or group of words that the reader takes to be complete." This definition includes such utterances as "Who?" and "Help!" and "Never!" and "Maybe." Now, in speaking, "While he was walking down the street" may be taken as a complete thought, if it answers the question "When did the car hit him?" In writing, however, it would be a sentence fragment that probably should be altered to, say, "While he was walking down the street he was hit by a car." We will discuss intentional fragments on pages 542–43. But first we should take a closer look at complete sentences.

Usually a sentence names someone or something (this is the subject) and it tells us something about the subject (this is the predicate); that is, it "predicates" something about the subject. Let us look at five kinds of sentences: simple, compound, complex, compound-complex, and sentence fragments.

1. A *simple sentence* has one predicate, here italicized:

Shakespeare *died.*

Shakespeare and Jonson *were contemporaries.*

542   *Chapter 14   Revising for Emphasis*

The subject can be elaborated ("Shakespeare and Jonson, England's chief Renaissance dramatists, were contemporaries"), or the predicate can be elaborated ("Shakespeare and Jonson were contemporaries in the Renaissance England of Queen Elizabeth"); but the sentence remains technically a simple sentence, consisting of only one main (independent) clause with no dependent (subordinate) clause.

2. A *compound sentence* has two or more main clauses, each containing a subject and a predicate. It is then, two or more simple sentences connected by a coordinating conjunction *(and, but, for, nor, or, yet)* or by *not only . . . but also,* or by a semicolon or colon or, rarely, by a comma.

> Shakespeare died in 1616, and Jonson died in 1637.
>
> Shakespeare not only wrote plays, but he also acted in them.
>
> Shakespeare died in 1616; Jonson died twenty-one years later.

3. A *complex sentence* has one main (independent) clause and one or more subordinate (dependent) clauses. The main clause (here italicized) can stand as a sentence by itself.

> Although Shakespeare died, *England survived.*
>
> *Jonson did not write a commemorative poem* when Shakespeare died.

The parts not italicized are subordinate or dependent because they cannot stand as sentences by themselves.

4. A *compound-complex sentence* has two or more main clauses (here italicized) and one or more subordinate clauses.

> *In 1616 Shakespeare died* and *his wife inherited the second-best bed* because he willed it to her.

Each of the two italicized passages could stand by itself as a sentence, but "because he willed it to her" could not (except as the answer to a question). Each italicized passage, then, is a main (independent) clause, and "because he willed it to her" is a subordinate (dependent) clause.

We will return to subordination, but let us first look at the fifth kind of sentence, the sentence fragment.

5. A *sentence fragment* does not fit the usual definition of a sentence, but when the fragment is intended the thought is often

clear and complete enough. Intentional fragments are common in advertisements:

> Made of imported walnut. For your pleasure. At finer stores.

> More native than the Limbo. More exciting than the beat of a steel drum. Tia Maria. Jamaica's haunting liqueur.

And yet another example, this one not from an advertisement but from an essay on firewood:

> Piles of it. Right off the sidewalk. Split from small logs of oak or ash or maple. Split. Split again.
>
> — John McPhee

All these examples strike us as pretentious in their obviously studied efforts at understatement. Words are hoarded, as though there is much in little, and as though to talk more fully would demean the speaker and would desecrate the subject. A few words, and then a profound silence. Here less is not more; it is too much. The trouble with these fragmentary sentences is not that they don't convey complete thoughts but that they attract too much attention to themselves; they turn our minds too emphatically to their writers, and conjure up images of unpleasantly self-satisfied oracles.

Here, however, is a passage from a student's essay, where the fragmentary sentences seem satisfactory to us. The passage begins with a simple sentence, and then gives three fragmentary sentences.

```
        The film has been playing to sellout audiences.  Even
    though the acting is inept.  Even though the sound is poorly
    synchronized.  Even though the plot is incoherent.
```

If this passage is successful, it is because the emphasis is controlled. The author is dissatisfied, and by means of parallel fragments (each beginning with the same words) she conveys a moderately engaging weariness and a gentle exasperation.

Then, too, we see that if the first three periods were changed to commas we would have an orthodox complex sentence. In short, because the fragments are effective we find them acceptable.

For ways to correct ineffective or unacceptable fragments, see pages in ch. 19.

Subordination

Having surveyed the kinds of sentences, we can at last talk about using subordination to give appropriate emphasis.

Make sure that the less important element is subordinate to the more important. Consider this sentence, about the painter Vincent van Gogh, who was supported by his brother Theo.

> Supported by Theo's money, van Gogh painted at Arles.

The writer puts van Gogh in the independent clause, subordinating the relatively unimportant Theo. Notice, by the way, that emphasis by subordination often works along with emphasis by position. Here the independent clause comes after the subordinate clause; the writer appropriately puts the more important material at the end, that is, in the more emphatic position.

Had the writer wished to give Theo more prominence, the passage might have run:

> Theo provided money, and van Gogh painted at Arles.

Here Theo (as well as van Gogh) stands in an independent clause, linked to the next clause by "and." The two clauses, and the two people, are now of approximately equal importance.

If the writer had wanted to emphasize Theo and to deemphasize van Gogh, he might have written:

> While van Gogh painted at Arles, Theo provided the money.

Here van Gogh is reduced to the subordinate clause, and Theo is given the dignity of the only independent clause. (And again notice that the important point is also in the emphatic position, near the end of the sentence. A sentence is likely to sprawl if an independent clause comes first, preceding a long subordinate clause of lesser importance, such as the sentence you are now reading.)

In short, though simple sentences and compound sentences have their place, they make everything of equal importance. Since everything is not of equal importance, you must often write complex and compound-complex sentences, subordinating some things to other things. Look again at the first four sentences of "Conceit" (page 538), and at the suggested revisions.

Having made the point that subordination reduces monotony and conveys appropriate emphasis, we must again say that there are times when a succession of simple or compound sentences is effective, as in the passage on page 539 describing George Jackson. As a rough rule, however, don't write more than two consecutive simple sentences unless you know what you are doing.

EXERCISE

1. Here is one way to test your grasp of the relationship of independent and subordinate elements in a sentence. This *haiku*
   (a Japanese poetic form) consists of one sentence that can be
   written as prose: "After weeks of watching the roof leak, I
   fixed it tonight by moving a single board."

   ### Hitch Haiku

   Gary Snyder

   After weeks of watching the roof leak
      I fixed it tonight
   by moving a single board.

   a. Identify the independent clause and the subordinate elements in
      the poem.
   b. The "I" in the poem's sentence does or has done three things.
      Write three simple sentences, each expressing one of the actions.
   c. Write one sentence in which all three of the poem's actions are
      expressed, but put in the independent clause one of the two ac-
      tions that appear in a subordinate element in the poem.
   d. Compare your sentence with the poem's. Both sentences should
      be clear. How do they vary in emphasis?
   e. Optional: Compare the original sentence written as poetry and
      written as prose.

2. First identify the fault or faults that make the following sentences unemphatic, and then revise them for emphasis.

   a. He lists some of the rights given to humans and things and both
      admits and accounts for the oddity of his proposal well by citing
      examples.
   b. Rights for women, blacks and the insane were granted though
      many couldn't see the value in it and so now our environment
      should be granted rights even though it takes some getting used
      to the idea.
   c. Thus Creon's pride forces Antigone's death which drives his son
      to suicide and then his wife.
   d. Stock breeding will give the same result as population evolution,
      defenders of positive eugenics claim.

e. The family today lacks the close relationship it had before the industrial age, for example.

f. The woman's face is distraught, her hair is unkempt, and her dress is rumpled.

g. There is probably no human being who would enjoy being eaten by a shark.

3. Analyze the ways Theodore Roosevelt achieved emphasis in the following passage on Grand Canyon.

> In Grand Canyon Arizona has a natural wonder which, so far as I know, is in kind absolutely unparalleled throughout the rest of the world. . . . Leave it as it is. You cannot improve upon it. The ages have been at work on it, and man can only mar it. What you can do is to keep it for your children, your children's children, and for all those who come after you as one of the great sights which every American, if he can travel at all, should see.

PART THREE

Style

Two monks were arguing about a flag. One said: "The flag is moving."

The other said: "The wind is moving."

The sixth patriarch happened to be passing by. He told them: "Not the wind, not the flag: mind is moving."

— ZEN ANECDOTE

15

Defining Style

The style is the man.
          — Buffon
(or the woman)
— BARNET AND STUBBS

Style is not simply a flower here and some gilding there; it pervades the whole work. Van Gogh's style, or Walt Disney's, let us say, consists in part of features recurring throughout a single work and from one work to the next: angular or curved lines, hard or soft edges, strong or gentle contrasts, and so on. Pictures of a seated woman by each of the two artists are utterly different, and if we have seen a few works by each, we can readily identify who did which one. Artists leave their fingerprints, so to speak, all over their work; writers leave their voiceprints.

The word *style* comes from the Latin *stilus*, a Roman writing instrument. Even in Roman times *stilus* had acquired a figurative sense, referring not only to the instrument but also to the writer's choice of words and arrangement of words into sentences. But is it simply the choice and arrangement of words we comment on when we speak of a writer's style, or are we also commenting on the writer's mind? Don't we feel that a piece of writing, whether it's on Civil War photographs or on genetics and intelligence, is also about the writer? The writing, after all, sets forth the writer's views of his or her topic. It sets forth perceptions and responses to something the writer has thought about. The writer has, from the start, from the choice of a topic, revealed that he or she found it worth thinking about. The essay, in attempting to persuade us to think as the writer does, reveals not only how and what the writer thinks, but what he or she values.

When we write about things "out there," our writing always reveals the form and likeness of our minds, just as every work of art reveals the creator as well as the ostensible subject. A portrait painting, for example, is not only about the sitter, it is about the artist's perceptions of the sitter; hence the saying that every portrait is a self-portrait. Even photographs are as much about the photographer as they are about the subject. Richard Avedon said of his portraits of famous people, "They are all pictures of me, of the way I feel about the people I photograph." A student's essay similarly, if it is truly written, is not exclusively about "*La Causa and the New Chicana*"; it is also about her perceptions and responses to both racism and sexism.

Still, a useful distinction can be made between the author and the speaker of an essay. The flesh-and-blood author creates, through words, a particular speaker or voice or (to use the term common in literary criticism) persona. The persona is the author in a role adopted for a specific audience. When Abraham Lincoln wrote, he sometimes did so in the persona of the commander in chief of the Union Army, but he sometimes did so in the very different persona of the simple man from Springfield, Illinois. The persona is a mask put on for a performance (*persona* is the Latin word for mask). If "mask" suggests insincerity, we should remember that whenever we speak or write we do so in a specific role—as friend, or parent, or teacher, or applicant for a job, or whatever. The audience determines, to some degree, what we will say and how we will say it. Although Lincoln was a husband, a father, a politician, a president, and many other things, when he wrote a letter to his son, Lincoln's consciousness of his audience caused him to write in the persona (or, we might say, personality) of the father, not the persona of the commander in chief.

The distinction between the writer (who necessarily fills many roles) and the persona who writes or speaks a given work is especially useful in talking about satire, because the satirist often invents a mouthpiece very different from himself or herself. The satirist—say Jonathan Swift—may be strongly opposed to a view, but the persona (the invented essayist) may favor the view; the reader must perceive that the real writer is ridiculing the invented essayist.

STYLE AND TONE

The style is the man. Rather say the
style is the way the man takes himself.
— ROBERT FROST

Suppose we take a page of handwriting, or even a signature.
We need not believe that graphology is an exact science to believe
that the shape of the ink-lines on paper (apart from the meaning
of the words) often tells us something about the writer. We look
at a large, ornate signature, and we sense that the writer is confident; we look at a tiny signature written with the finest of pens,
and we wonder why anyone is so self-effacing.

More surely than handwriting, the writer's style reveals, among
other things, his or her attitude toward the self (as Frost's addition
to Buffon's epigram suggests), toward the reader, and toward the
subject. The writer's attitudes are reflected in what is usually called
tone. It is difficult to separate style from tone but we can try. Most
discussions of style concentrate on what might be thought of as
ornament: figurative language ("a sea of troubles"), inversion ("A
leader he is not"), repetition and parallelism ("government of the
people, by the people, for the people"), balance and antithesis ("It
was the best of times, it was the worst of times"). Indeed, for
centuries style has been called "the dress of thought," implying
that the thought is something separate from the expression; the
thought, in this view, is dressed up in stylistic devices. But in most
of the writing that we read with interest and pleasure the stylistic
devices are not ornamental and occasional but integral and per-
vasive. When we talk about wit, sincerity, tentativeness, self-assurance, aggressiveness, objectivity, and so forth, we can say we are
talking about style, but we should recognize that style now is not
a matter of ornamental devices that dress up some idea, but part
of the idea itself. And "the idea itself" includes the writer's unified
yet appropriately varied tone of voice.

To take a brief example: the famous English translation of
Caesar's report of a victory,

I came, I saw, I conquered,

might be paraphrased thus:

> After getting to the scene of the battle, I studied the situation. Then I devised a strategy that won the battle.

But this paraphrase loses much of Caesar's message; the brevity and the parallelism of the famous version, as well as the alliteration (*c*ame, *c*onquered), convey tight-lipped self-assurance—convey, that is, the tone that reveals Caesar to us. And this tone is a large part of Caesar's message. Caesar is really telling us not only about what he did, but about what sort of person he is. He is perceptive, decisive, and effective. The three actions, Caesar in effect tells us, are (for a man like Caesar) one. (The Latin original is even more tight-lipped and more unified by alliteration: *veni, vidi, vici.*)

Let's look now at a longer sentence, the opening sentence of Lewis Thomas's essay called "On Natural Death":

> There are so many new books about dying that there are now special shelves set aside for them in bookstores, along with the health-diet and home-repair paperbacks and the sex manuals.

This sentence could have ended where the comma is placed: the words after "bookstores" are, it might seem, not important. One can scarcely argue that by specifying some kinds of "special shelves" Thomas clarifies an otherwise difficult or obscure concept. What, then, do these additional words do? They tell us nothing about death and almost nothing about bookshops, but they tell us a great deal about Thomas's *attitude* toward the new books on death. He suggests that such books are faddish and perhaps (like "the sex manuals") vulgar. After all, if he had merely wanted to call up a fairly concrete image of a well-stocked bookstore he could have said "along with books on politics and the environment," or some such thing. His next sentence runs:

> Some of them are so packed with detailed information and step-by-step instructions for performing the function you'd think this was a new sort of skill which all of us are now required to learn.

Why "you'd think" instead of, say, "one might believe"? Thomas uses a colloquial form, and a very simple verb, because he wants to convey to us his common-sense, homely, down-to-earth view that these books are a bit pretentious—a pretentiousness conveyed in his use of the words "performing the function," words that might come from the books themselves. In short, when we read Thomas's paragraph we are learning as much about Thomas as we are about books on dying. We are hearing a voice, perceiving an attitude, and we want to keep reading, not only because we are interested in death but also because Thomas has managed to make us interested in Thomas, a thoughtful but unpretentious fellow.

Now listen to a short paragraph from John Szarkowski's *Looking at Photographs*. Szarkowski is writing about one of Alexander Gardner's photographs of a dead Confederate sharpshooter.

> Among the pictures that Gardner made himself is the one reproduced here. Like many Civil War photographs, it showed that the dead of both sides looked very much the same. The pictures of earlier wars had not made this clear.

Try, in a word or two, to characterize the tone (the attitude, as we sense it in the inflection of the voice) of the first sentence. Next, the tone of the second, and then of the third. Suppose the second and third sentences had been written thus:

> It showed that the dead of both sides looked very much the same. This is made clear in Civil War photographs, but not in pictures of earlier wars.

How has the tone changed? What word can you find to characterize the tone of the whole, as Szarkowski wrote it?

Now another passage from Szarkowski's book:

> Jacob A. Riis was a newspaper reporter by occupation and a social reformer by inclination. He was a photographer rather briefly and apparently rather casually; it seems beyond doubt that he considered photography a useful but subservient tool for his work as reporter and reformer. It is clear that he had no interest in "artistic" photography, and equally clear that the artistic photographers of his time had no interest in him.

Do you find traces of Szarkowski's voiceprint here?

Finally, a longer passage by the same writer. After you read it, try to verbalize the resemblances between this and the other passages—the qualities that allow us to speak of the writer's tone.

> There are several possible explanations for the fact that women have been more important to photography than their numbers alone

would warrant. One explanation might be the fact that photography has never had licensing laws or trade unions, by means of which women might have been effectively discriminated against. A second reason might be the fact that the specialized technical preparation for photography need not be enormously demanding, so that the medium has been open to those unable to spend long years in formal study.

A third possible reason could be that women have a greater natural talent for photography than men do. Discretion (or cowardice) suggests that this hypothesis is best not pursued, since a freely speculative exploration of it might take unpredictable and indefensible lines. One might for example consider the idea that the art of photography is in its nature receptive, or passive, thus suggesting that women are also.

STYLE AND LEVELS OF USAGE

Although the dividing lines between levels of usage cannot always be drawn easily, tradition recognizes three: *formal, informal,* and *popular* or *vulgar.* Sometimes *popular* is used to designate a level between informal and vulgar. (*Vulgar* here doesn't mean dirty words; rather, it refers to the speech characteristic of uneducated people, speech that uses such expressions as *ain't, nohow,* and *he don't.*)

Formal writing, found mostly in scholarly articles, textbooks, ceremonial speeches, and scientific reports, assumes an audience not only generally well educated but also with special knowledge of or interest in the writer's subject. The writer can therefore use a wide vocabulary (including words and references that in another context would be pretentious or obscure) and sentence patterns that demand close attention.

A noted figure, say a distinguished historian of science, addressing the world of thoughtful readers, may use a formal style, as Evelyn Fox Keller does here in a discussion of the accomplishments of women in science. Keller assumes an attentive reader, a reader who is capable of holding in mind a long sentence (about sixty words) with some fairly specialized terms ("differential," "conceptual," "innate").

The central theme of my discussion is that the differential performance of men and women in science, the apparent differences between conceptual styles of men and women everywhere, are the result, not so much of innate differences between the sexes, but rather of the myth that prevails throughout our culture identifying certain kinds of thinking as male and others as female. The consequent compartmentalization of our minds is as effective as if it had been biologically, and not socially, induced.
— Evelyn Fox Keller,
"Women in Science: An Analysis of a Social Problem"

Notice that the meaning of the sentence is suspended or withheld for quite a while. The first half of this long sentence tells us that something is *not* the result of "innate differences between the sexes," but not until later in the sentence do we learn what it *is* the result of.

But a formal sentence need not be long. Here is a fairly short formal sentence by W. H. Auden:

Owing to its superior power as a mnemonic, verse is superior to prose as a medium for didactic instruction.

In another frame of mind Auden might have written something less formal, along these lines:

Because it stays more easily in the memory, verse is better than prose for teaching.

This revision of Auden's sentence can be called informal, but it is high on the scale, the language of an educated person writing courteously to an audience he or she conceives of as his or her peers. It is the level of almost all academic writing. A low informal version might be:

Poetry sticks in the mind better than prose; so if you want to teach something, poetry is better.

This is the language any of us might use in conversation; it is almost never the language used in writing to our peers.

In textbooks, the most obvious purpose of discussions of levels has been to dislodge older, more rigid ideas about "good" and "bad" or "correct" and "incorrect" English, and to replace them with the more flexible and more accurate standard of appropriateness. The labels *formal* and *informal* (we can for the moment drop *vulgar,* since few essays are written in it) attempt to describe the choices that writers make under particular circumstances, rather than to prescribe those they ought to make under all circumstances. The choices, often unconscious, include those of vocabulary, sentence structure, and tone.

Finding the Appropriate Level

What is appropriate in writing, as in dress, is subject to change, and the change recently has been to greater informality in both. Students who attend classes, concerts, and even their own weddings in the blue jeans might experiment with similar freedom in writing college essays, and work toward a style that feels comfortable and natural to them. Developing a natural style, writing at an appropriate level, does take work. Consider, for example, the following opening paragraph from a student's theme:

> The college experience is traumatic, often because one must adjust not only to new academic horizons and new friends but also to the new physical environment constituted by the college and by the community surrounding it. One might think that, coming from a city only sixty miles from Wellesley, I would be exempt from this aspect of adaptation. However, this assumption has proven to be false.

"Traumatic"? "Academic horizons"? "Constituted"? "Exempt from this aspect of adaptation"? "Assumption . . . proven to be false"? There's nothing wrong with the language here, that is, nothing ungrammatical. But the paragraph has a hollow ring, a tone of insincerity, because the diction and syntax—the writer's level of usage—so ill suit the theme: a personal and spirited defense of the writer's lower-middle-class industrial home town, whose liveliness, friendliness, and above all, informality, she emphatically prefers to the aloofness of suburban Wellesley.

By contrast, in a review of *Soledad Brother—The Prison Letters of George Jackson,* another student described Jackson's style as "clear, simple, expressive, and together." The word "together," though technically incorrect (an adverb, here used as an adjective), strikes us, in context, as exactly right. And, when later in the essay we read "Surviving on glasses of water, crumbs of bread, deep concentration, daily push-ups, and cigarettes, Jackson shouts to the black world to wake up: get off your knees and start kicking asses," we feel that the deliberately inconsistent use of the formal series of parallels with the colloquial or vulgar "kicking asses" exactly expresses both Jackson's discipline and rage, and the writer's empathy with them.

In most of your college writing you are addressing people like yourself; use a language that you would like to read, neither stuffy nor aggressively colloquial. Probably it will stand somewhere in between the levels of "aspects of adaptation" and "kicking asses."

Tone: Four Examples

The first two excerpts are the opening paragraphs of two speeches. The third, though not an opening paragraph, is also from a speech. The fourth, by Pauline Kael, is the beginning of an essay on the tedium of most modern films.

> 1. It is indeed both an honor and a challenge to be invited to participate in this most significant occasion, the observation of the one hundredth anniversary of the birth of Max Weber. It is also a great pleasure to revisit the University of Heidelberg, though not quite for the first time, just short of forty years after my enrollment here as a student in 1925. This was too late to know Max Weber in person, but of course his intellectual influence was all-pervasive in the Heidelberg of that time, constituting the one primary point of reference about which all theoretical and much empirical discussion in the social and cultural fields revolved. I was also privileged to know his gracious and highly intelligent widow, Marianne Weber, in particular to attend a number of her famous "sociological teas" on Sunday afternoons. It was an extraordinarily stimulating intellectual environment, participation in which was one of the most important factors in determining my whole intellectual and professional career.
>
> — Talcott Parsons

> 2. It has been suggested that I discuss what it is like to be a poet these days (the only days in which my opinion could possibly be useful), or, if that is immodest, what it is like to write poetry,

what one thinks about the art, what its relation is to the life we supposedly live these days, and so on. This is a fascinatingly large range in which to wander, and I shall be interested to find out what I do think. I hope you will be interested, too. But I must advise you that this will not be a coherently organized essay running in a smooth and logical progression from question to conclusion. Nor will the views expressed necessarily be consistent. I have consulted with my selves, and come up, as usual, with a number of fragmentary notions, many of them aphoristic in expression, and I believe I will do best simply to put these before you without much in the way of explanation or connective tissue.

— Howard Nemerov

3. Style, in its finest sense, is the last acquirement of the educated mind; it is also the most useful. It pervades the whole being. The administrator with a sense for style hates waste; the engineer with a sense for style economizes his material; the artisan with a sense for style prefers good work. Style is the ultimate morality of mind. . . . With style the end is attained without side issues, without raising undesirable inflammations. With style you attain your end and nothing but your end. With style the effect of your activity is calculable, and foresight is the last gift of gods to men. With style your power is increased, for your mind is not distracted with irrelevancies, and you are more likely to attain your object.

— Alfred North Whitehead

4. Early this year, the most successful of the large-circulation magazines for teen-age girls took a two-page spread in the *Times* for an "interview" with its editor-in-chief, and after the now ritual bulling (Question: "You work with young people—what is your view of today's generation?" Answer: "My faith in them is enormous. They make a sincere attempt at being totally honest, at sharing. They're happily frank about their experiences. They're the most idealistic generation in history. . . . When you consider the vast problems confronting us, their optimism and activism is truly inspirational"), and after the obeissance to the new myths ("They are the best-educated and most aware generation in history"), the ad finally got to the come-on. Question: "Is it true that your readers don't differentiate between your ads and your editorials?" Answer: "Yes, that's true. Our readers are very impressionable, not yet cynical about advertising . . . eager to learn . . . to believe." The frightening thing is, it probably is true that the teen-agers don't differentiate between the ads and the editorials, and true in a much more complex sense than the delicately calculated Madison Ave-

nue-ese of the editor's pitch to advertisers indicates. Television is blurring the distinction for all of us; we don't know what we're reacting to anymore, and beyond that, it's becoming just about impossible to sort out the con from the truth because a successful con makes its lies come true.

— Pauline Kael

EXERCISES

1. What is Parsons's attitude toward himself? Exactly how do you know?
2. What is Nemerov's attitude toward himself? How do you know?
3. Suppose that the first sentence of Whitehead's passage began thus: "I want to point out to you today that style may be regarded not only as the last acquirement of what I consider the mind that has been well educated, but it is also the most useful, I definitely believe." What is lost?
4. Do you think that Pauline Kael knows what she is talking about? Why?
5. Read a political speech (you can find lots of examples in a periodical called *Vital Speeches*), and in a paragraph analyze the speaker's attitude toward himself or herself. In another paragraph analyze his or her attitude toward the audience.

A RANGE OF STYLES

Professions for Women[1]
Virginia Woolf

1   When your secretary invited me to come here, she told me that your Society is concerned with the employment of women and she suggested that I might tell you something about my own profes-

[1]This essay was originally a talk delivered in 1931 to the Women's Service League.

sional experiences. It is true I am a woman; it is true I am employed; but what professional experiences have I had? It is difficult to say. My profession is literature; and in that profession there are fewer experiences for women than in any other, with the exception of the stage—fewer, I mean, that are peculiar to women. For the road was cut many years ago—by Fanny Burney, by Aphra Behn, by Harriet Martineau, by Jane Austen, by George Eliot—many famous women, and many more unknown and forgotten, have been before me, making the path smooth, and regulating my steps. Thus, when I came to write, there were very few material obstacles in my way. Writing was a reputable and harmless occupation. The family peace was not broken by the scratching of a pen. No demand was made upon the family purse. For ten and sixpence one can buy paper enough to write all the plays of Shakespeare—if one has a mind that way. Pianos and models, Paris, Vienna and Berlin, masters and mistresses, are not needed by a writer. The cheapness of writing paper is, of course, the reason why women have succeeded as writers before they have succeeded in the other professions.

2   But to tell you my story—it is a simple one. You have only got to figure to yourselves a girl in a bedroom with a pen in her hand. She had only to move that pen from left to right—from ten o'clock to one. Then it occurred to her to do what is simple and cheap enough after all—to slip a few of those pages into an envelope, fix a penny stamp in the corner, and drop the envelope into the red box at the corner. It was thus that I became a journalist; and my effort was rewarded on the first day of the following month—a very glorious day it was for me—by a letter from an editor containing a check for one pound ten shillings and sixpence. But to show you how little I deserve to be called a professional woman, how little I know of the struggles and difficulties of such lives, I have to admit that instead of spending that sum upon bread and butter, rent, shoes and stockings, or butcher's bills, I went out and bought a cat—a beautiful cat, a Persian cat, which very soon involved me in bitter disputes with my neighbors.

3   What could be easier than to write articles and to buy Persian cats with the profits? But wait a moment. Articles have to be about something. Mine, I seem to remember, was about a novel by a famous man. And while I was writing this review, I discovered that if I were going to review books I should need to do battle with a certain phantom. And the phantom was a woman, and when I came to know her better I called her after the heroine of a famous poem, The Angel in the House. It was she who used to come between me and my paper when I was writing reviews. It was she who bothered

me and wasted my time and so tormented me that at last I killed her. You who come of a younger and happier generation may not have heard of her—you may not know what I mean by the Angel in the House. I will describe her as shortly as I can. She was intensely sympathetic She was immensely charming. She was utterly unselfish. She excelled in the difficult arts of family life. She sacrificed herself daily. If there was chicken, she took the leg; if there was a draught she sat in it—in short she was so constituted that she never had a mind or a wish of her own, but preferred to sympathize always with the minds and wishes of others. Above all—I need not say it—she was pure. Her purity was supposed to be her chief beauty—her blushes, her great grace. In those days—the last of Queen Victoria—every house had its Angel. And when I came to write I encountered her with the very first words. The shadow of her wings fell on my page; I heard the rustling of her skirts in the room. Directly, that is to say, I took my pen in hand to review that novel by a famous man, she slipped behind me and whispered: "My dear, you are a young woman. You are writing about a book that has been written by a man. Be sympathetic; be tender; flatter; deceive; use all the arts and wiles of our sex. Never let anybody guess that you have a mind of your own. Above all, be pure." And she made as if to guide my pen. I now record the one act for which I take some credit to myself, though the credit rightly belongs to some excellent ancestors of mine who left me a certain sum of money— shall we say five hundred pounds a year?—so that it was not necessary for me to depend solely on charm for my living. I turned upon her and caught her by the throat. I did my best to kill her. My excuse, if I were to be had up in a court of law, would be that I acted in self-defense. Had I not killed her she would have killed me. She would have plucked the heart out of my writing. For, as I found, directly I put pen to paper, you cannot review even a novel without having a mind of your own, without expressing what you think to be the truth about human relations, morality, sex. And all these questions, according to the Angel in the House, cannot be dealt with freely and openly by women; they must charm, they must conciliate, they must—to put it bluntly—tell lies if they are to succeed. Thus, whenever I felt the shadow of her wing or the radiance of her halo upon my page, I took up the inkpot and flung it at her. She died hard. Her fictitious nature was of great assistance to her. It is far harder to kill a phantom than a reality. She was always creeping back when I thought I had despatched her. Though I flatter myself that I killed her in the end, the struggle was severe; it took much time that had better have been spent upon learning Greek grammar; or in roaming the world in search of adventures. But it was a real experience; it was an experience that was bound to befall all women writers at the time. Killing the Angel in the House was part of the occupation of a woman writer.

4   But to continue my story. The Angel was dead; what then remained? You may say that what remained was a simple and common object—a young woman in a bedroom with an inkpot. In other words, now that she had rid herself of falsehood, that young woman had only to be herself. Ah, but what is "herself"? I mean, what is a woman? I assure you, I do not know. I do not believe that you know. I do not believe that anybody can know until she has expressed herself in all the arts and professions open to human skill. That indeed is one of the reasons why I have come here—out of respect for you, who are in process of showing us by your experiments what a woman is, who are in process of providing us, by your failures and successes, with that extremely important piece of information.

5   But to continue the story of my professional experiences. I made one pound ten and six by my first review; and I bought a Persian cat with the proceeds. Then I grew ambitious. A Persian cat is all very well, I said; but a Persian cat is not enough. I must have a motor car. And it was thus that I became a novelist—for it is a very strange thing that people will give you a motor car if you will tell them a story. It is a still stranger thing that there is nothing so delightful in the world as telling stories. It is far pleasanter than writing reviews of famous novels. And yet, if I am to obey your secretary and tell you my professional experiences as a novelist, I must tell you about a very strange experience that befell me as a novelist. And to understand it you must try first to imagine a novelist's state of mind. I hope I am not giving away professional secrets if I say that a novelist's chief desire is to be as unconscious as possible. He has to induce in himself a state of perpetual lethargy. He wants life to proceed with the utmost quiet and regularity. He wants to see the same faces, to read the same books, to do the same things day after day, month after month, while he is writing, so that nothing may break the illusion in which he is living—so that nothing may disturb or disquiet the mysterious nosings about, feelings round, darts, dashes and sudden discoveries of that very shy and illusive spirit, the imagination. I suspect that this state is the same both for men and women. Be that as it may, I want you to imagine me writing a novel in a state of trance. I want you to figure to yourselves a girl sitting with a pen in her hand, which for minutes, and indeed for hours, she never dips into the inkpot. The im-

age that comes to my mind when I think of this girl is the image of a fisherman lying sunk in dreams on the verge of a deep lake with a rod held out over the water. She was letting her imagination sweep unchecked round every rock and cranny of the world that lies submerged in the depths of our unconscious being. Now came the experience, the experience that I believe to be far commoner with women writers than with men. The line raced through the girl's fingers. Her imagination had rushed away. It had sought the pools, the depths, the dark places where the largest fish slumber. And then there was a smash. There was an explosion. There was foam and confusion. The imagination had dashed itself against something hard. The girl was roused from her dream. She was indeed in a state of the most acute and difficult distress. To speak without figure she had thought of something, something about the body, about the passions which it was unfitting for her as a woman to say. Men, her reason told her, would be shocked. The consciousness of what men will say of a woman who speaks the truth about her passions had roused her from her artist's state of unconsciousness. She could write no more. This I believe to be a very common experience with women writers—they are impeded by the extreme conventionality of the other sex. For though men sensibly allow themselves great freedom in these respects, I doubt that they realize or can control the extreme severity with which they condemn such freedom in women.

6   These then were two very genuine experiences of my own. These were two of the adventures of my professional life. The first—killing the Angel in the House—I think I solved. She died. But the second, telling the truth about my own experiences as a body, I do not think I solved. I doubt that any woman has solved it yet. The obstacles against her are still immensely powerful—and yet they are very difficult to define. Outwardly, what is simpler than to write books? Outwardly, what obstacles are there for a woman rather than for a man? Inwardly, I think, the case is very different; she has still many ghosts to fight, many prejudices to overcome. Indeed it will be a long time still, I think, before a woman can sit down to write a book without finding a phantom to be slain, a rock to be dashed against. And if this is so in literature, the freest of all professions for women, how is it in the new professions which you are now for the first time entering?

7   Those are the questions that I should like, had I time, to ask you. And indeed, if I have laid stress upon these professional experiences of mine, it is because I believe that they are, though in different forms, yours also. Even when the path is nominally open—

when there is nothing to prevent a woman from being a doctor, a lawyer, a civil servant—there are many phantoms and obstacles, as I believe, looming in her way. To discuss and define them is I think of great value and importance; for thus only can the labor be shared, the difficulties be solved. But besides this, it is necessary also to discuss the ends and the aims for which we are fighting, for which we are doing battle with these formidable obstacles. Those aims cannot be taken for granted; they must be perpetually questioned and examined. The whole position, as I see it—here in this hall surrounded by women practising for the first time in history I know not how many different professions—is one of extraordinary interest and importance. You have won rooms of your own in the house hitherto exclusively owned by men. You are able, though not without great labor and effort, to pay the rent. You are earning your five hundred pounds a year. But this freedom is only a beginning; the room is your own, but it is still bare. It has to be furnished; it has to be decorated; it has to be shared. How are you going to furnish it, how are you going to decorate it? With whom are you going to share it, and upon what terms? These, I think, are questions of the utmost importance and interest. For the first time in history you are able to ask them; for the first time you are able to decide for yourselves what the answers should be. Willingly would I stay and discuss those questions and answers—but not tonight. My time is up; and I must cease.

Questions

1. The first two paragraphs seem to describe the ease with which women enter writing as a profession. What difficulties or obstacles for women do these paragraphs imply?
2. Try to characterize Woolf's tone, especially her attitude toward her subject and herself, in the first paragraph.
3. What do you think Woolf means when she says (page 563), "It is far harder to kill a phantom than a reality"?
4. Woolf conjectures (page 565) that she has not solved the problem of "telling the truth about my own experiences as a body." Is there any reason to believe that today a woman has more difficulty than a man in telling the truth about the experiences of the body?
5. In her final paragraph, Woolf suggests that phantoms as well as obstacles impede women from becoming doctors and lawyers. What might some of these phantoms be?

6. This essay is highly metaphoric. Speaking roughly (or, rather, as precisely as possible), what is the meaning of the metaphor of "rooms" in the final paragraph? What does Woolf mean when she says, "The room is your own, but it is still bare. . . . With whom are you going to share it, and upon what terms?"
7. Explain, to a reader who doesn't understand it, the analogy making use of fishing on page 565.
8. Evaluate the last two sentences. Are they too abrupt and mechanical? Or do they provide a fitting conclusion to the speech?

Education

E. B. White

1   I have an increasing admiration for the teacher in the country school where we have a third-grade scholar in attendance. She not only undertakes to instruct her charges in all the subjects of the first three grades, but she manages to function quietly and effectively as a guardian of their health, their clothes, their habits, their mothers, and their snowball engagements. She has been doing this sort of Augean task for twenty years, and is both kind and wise. She cooks for the children on the stove that heats the room, and she can cool their passions or warm their soup with equal competence. She conceives their costumes, cleans up their messes, and shares their confidences. My boy already regards his teacher as his great friend, and I think tells her a great deal more than he tells us.

2   The shift from city school to country school was something we worried about quietly all last summer. I have always rather favored public school over private school, if only because in public school you meet a greater variety of children. This bias of mine, I suspect, is partly an attempt to justify my own past (I never knew anything but public schools) and partly an involuntary defense against getting kicked in the shins by a young ceramist on his way to the kiln. My wife was unacquainted with public schools, never having been exposed (in her early life) to anything more public than the washroom of Miss Winsor's. Regardless of our backgrounds, we both knew that the change in schools was something that concerned not us but the scholar himself. We hoped it would work out all right. In New York our son went to a medium-priced private institution

with semi-progressive ideas of education, and modern plumbing. He learned fast, kept well, and we were satisfied. It was an electric, colorful, regimented existence with moments of pleasurable pause and giddy incident. The day the Christmas angel fainted and had to be carried out by one of the Wise Men was educational in the highest sense of the term. Our scholar gave imitations of it around the house for weeks afterward, and I doubt if it ever goes completely out of his mind.

3   His days were rich in formal experience. Wearing overalls and an old sweater (the accepted uniform of the private seminary), he sallied forth at morn accompanied by a nurse or a parent and walked (or was pulled) two blocks to a corner where the school bus made a flag stop. This flashy vehicle was as punctual as death: seeing us waiting at the cold curb, it would sweep to a halt, open its mouth, suck the boy in, and spring away with an angry growl. It was a good deal like a train picking up a bag of mail. At school the scholar was worked on for six or seven hours by half a dozen teachers and a nurse, and was revived on orange juice in mid-morning. In a cinder court he played games supervised by an athletic instructor, and in a cafeteria he ate lunch worked out by a dietitian. He soon learned to read with gratifying facility and discernment and to make Indian weapons of a semi-deadly nature. Whenever one of his classmates fell low of a fever the news was put on the wires and there were breathless phone calls to physicians, discussing periods of incubation and allied magic.

4   In the country all one can say is that the situation is different, and somehow more casual. Dressed in corduroys, sweatshirt, and short rubber boots, and carrying a tin dinner-pail, our scholar departs at crack of dawn for the village school, two and a half miles down the road, next to the cemetery. When the road is open and the car will start, he makes the journey by motor, courtesy of his old man. When the snow is deep or the motor is dead or both, he makes it on the hoof. In the afternoons he walks or hitches all or part of the way home in fair weather, gets transported in foul. The schoolhouse is a two-room frame building, bungalow type, shingles stained a burnt brown with weather-resistant stain. It has a chemical toilet in the basement and two teachers above stairs. One takes the first three grades, the other the fourth, fifth, and sixth. They have little or no time for individual instruction, and no time at all for the esoteric. They teach what they know themselves, just as fast and as hard as they can manage. The pupils sit still at their desks in class, and do their milling around outdoors during recess.

5   There is no supervised play. They play cops and robbers (only they call it "Jail") and throw things at one another—snowballs in winter, rose hips in fall. It seems to satisfy them. They also construct darts, pinwheels, and "pick-up sticks" (jackstraws), and the school itself does a brisk trade in penny candy, which is for sale right in the classroom and which contains "surprises." The most highly prized surprise is a fake cigarette, made of cardboard, fiendishly lifelike.

6   The memory of how apprehensive we were at the beginning is still strong. The boy was nervous about the change too. The tension, on that first fair morning in September when we drove him to school, almost blew the windows out of the sedan. And when later we picked him up on the road, wandering along with his little blue lunch-pail, and got his laconic report "All right" in answer to our inquiry about how the day had gone, our relief was vast. Now, after almost a year of it, the only difference we can discover in the two school experiences is that in the country he sleeps better at night—and *that* probably is more the air than the education. When grilled on the subject of school-in-country *vs.* school-in-city, he replied that the chief difference is that the day seems to go so much quicker in the country. "Just like lightning," he reported.

Questions

1. Which school, city or country, does White prefer?
2. How do you know which school he prefers?
3. How does he persuade you to accept his evaluation?
4. What are some of the notable features of the essay's style? Cite a passage or two illustrating each.

*T*he Iks

Lewis Thomas

1   The small tribe of Iks, formerly nomadic hunters and gatherers in the mountain valleys of northern Uganda, have become celebrities, literary symbols for the ultimate fate of disheartened, heartless

mankind at large. Two disastrously conclusive things happened to them: the government decided to have a national park, so they were compelled by law to give up hunting in the valleys and become farmers on poor hillside soil, and then they were visited for two years by an anthropologist who detested them and wrote a book about them.

2   The message of the book is that the Iks have transformed themselves into an irreversibly disagreeable collection of unattached, brutish creatures, totally selfish and loveless, in response to the dismantling of their traditional culture. Moreover, this is what the rest of us are like in our inner selves, and we will all turn into Iks when the structure of our society comes all unhinged.

3   The argument rests, of course, on certain assumptions about the core of human beings, and is necessarily speculative. You have to agree in advance that man is fundamentally a bad lot, out for himself alone, displaying such graces as affection and compassion only as learned habits. If you take this view, the story of the Iks can be used to confirm it. These people seem to be living together, clustered in small, dense villages, but they are really solitary, unrelated individuals with no evident use for each other. They talk, but only to make ill-tempered demands and cold refusals. They share nothing. They never sing. They turn the children out to forage as soon as they can walk, and desert the elders to starve whenever they can, and the foraging children snatch food from the mouths of the helpless elders. It is a mean society.

4   They breed without love or even casual regard. They defecate on each other's doorsteps. They watch their neighbors for signs of misfortune, and only then do they laugh. In the book they do a lot of laughing, having so much bad luck. Several times they even laughed at the anthropologist, who found this especially repellent (one senses, between the lines, that the scholar is not himself the world's luckiest man). Worse, they took him into the family, snatched his food, defecated on his doorstep, and hooted dislike at him. They gave him two bad years.

5   It is a depressing book. If, as he suggests, there is only Ikness at the center of each of us, our sole hope for hanging on to the name of humanity will be in endlessly mending the structure of our society, and it is changing so quickly and completely that we may never find the threads in time. Meanwhile, left to ourselves alone, solitary, we will become the same joyless, zestless, untouching lone animals.

6   But this may be too narrow a view. For one thing, the Iks are

extraordinary. They are absolutely astonishing, in fact. The anthropologist has never seen people like them anywhere, nor have I. You'd think, if they were simply examples of the common essence of mankind, they'd seem more recognizable. Instead, they are bizarre, anomalous. I have known my share of peculiar, difficult, nervous, grabby people, but I've never encountered any genuinely, consistently detestable human beings in all my life. The Iks sound more like abnormalities, maladies.

7   I cannot accept it. I do not believe that the Iks are representative of isolated, revealed man, unobscured by social habits. I believe their behavior is something extra, something laid on. This unremitting, compulsive repellence is a kind of complicated ritual. They must have learned to act this way; they copied it, somehow.

8   I have a theory, then. The Iks have gone crazy.

9   The solitary Ik, isolated in the ruins of an exploded culture, has built a new defense for himself. If you live in an unworkable society you can make up one of your own, and this is what the Iks have done. Each Ik has become a group, a one-man tribe on its own, a constituency.

10   Now everything falls into place. This is why they do seem, after all, vaguely familiar to all of us. We've seen them before. This is precisely the way groups of one size or another, ranging from committees to nations, behave. It is, of course, this aspect of humanity that has lagged behind the rest of evolution, and this is why the Ik seems so primitive. In his absolute selfishness, his incapacity to give anything away, no matter what, he is a successful committee. When he stands at the door of his hut, shouting insults at his neighbors in a loud harangue, he is city addressing another city.

11   Cities have all the Ik characteristics. They defecate on doorsteps, in rivers and lakes, their own or anyone else's. They leave rubbish. They detest all neighboring cities, give nothing away. They even build institutions for deserting elders out of sight.

12   Nations are the most Iklike of all. No wonder the Iks seem familiar. For total greed, rapacity, heartlessness, and irresponsibility there is nothing to match a nation. Nations, by law, are solitary, self-centered, withdrawn into themselves. There is no such thing as affection between nations, and certainly no nation ever loved another. They bawl insults from their doorsteps, defecate into whole oceans, snatch all the food, survive by detestation, take joy in the bad luck of others, celebrate the death of others, live for the death of others.

13   That's it, and I shall stop worrying about the book. It does not

signify that man is a sparse, inhuman thing at his center. He's all right. It only says what we've always known and never had enough time to worry about, that we haven't yet learned how to stay human when assembled in masses. The Ik, in his despair, is acting out this failure, and perhaps we should pay closer attention. Nations have themselves become too frightening to think about, but we might learn some things by watching these people.

Questions

1. Find the grim joke in the first paragraph.
2. Suppose that "of course" were omitted from the first sentence of the third paragraph. Would anything significant be lost? Suppose in the second sentence of the third paragraph, instead of "You have to agree," Thomas had written "One has to agree." What would be gained or lost?
3. In the third and fourth paragraphs, what is the effect of repeating the structure of subject and verb: "They talk . . . ," "They share . . . ," "They never sing," "They turn . . . ," "They breed . . . ," and so on?
4. Point to a few colloquial expressions, and to a few notably informal sentences. Do you find them inappropriate to a discussion of a serious topic?
5. What is Thomas's attitude toward the anthropologist and his book? Cite some passages that convey his attitude, and explain how they convey it, or how they attempt to persuade us to share it.

My Wood

E. M. Forster

1   A few years ago I wrote a book which dealt in part with the difficulties of the English in India. Feeling that they would have had no difficulties in India themselves, the Americans read the book freely. The more they read it the better it made them feel, and a cheque to the author was the result. I bought a wood with the

cheque. It is not a large wood—it contains scarcely any trees, and it is intersected, blast it, by a public footpath. Still, it is the first property that I have owned, so it is right that other people should participate in my shame, and should ask themselves, in accents that will vary in horror, this very important question: What is the effect of property upon the character? Don't let's touch economics; the effect of private ownership upon the community as a whole is another question—a more important question, perhaps, but another one. Let's keep to psychology. If you own things, what's their effect on you? What's the effect on me of my wood?

2   In the first place, it makes me feel heavy. Property does have this effect. Property produces men of weight, and it was a man of weight who failed to get into the Kingdom of Heaven. He was not wicked, that unfortunate millionaire in the parable, he was only stout; he stuck out in front, not to mention behind, and as he wedged himself this way and that in the crystalline entrance and bruised his well-fed flanks, he saw beneath him a comparatively slim camel passing through the eye of a needle and being woven into the robe of God. The Gospels all through couple stoutness and slowness. They point out what is perfectly obvious, yet seldom realized: that if you have a lot of things you cannot move about a lot, that furniture requires dusting, dusters require servants, servants require insurance stamps, and the whole tangle of them makes you think twice before you accept an invitation to dinner or go for a bathe in the Jordan. Sometimes the Gospels proceed further and say with Tolstoy that property is sinful; they approach the difficult ground of asceticism here, where I cannot follow them. But as to the immediate effects of property on people, they just show straightforward logic. It produces men of weight. Men of weight cannot, by definition, move like the lightning from the East unto the West, and the ascent of a fourteen-stone bishop into a pulpit is thus the exact antithesis of the coming of the Son of Man. My wood makes me feel heavy.

3   In the second place, it makes me feel it ought to be larger.

4   The other day I heard a twig snap in it. I was annoyed at first, for I thought that someone was blackberrying, and depreciating the value of the undergrowth. On coming nearer, I saw it was not a man who had trodden on the twig and snapped it, but a bird, and I felt pleased. My bird. The bird was not equally pleased. Ignoring the relation between us, it took fright as soon as it saw the shape of my face, and flew straight over the boundary hedge into a field, the property of Mrs. Henessy, where it sat down with a loud squawk.

It had become Mrs. Henessy's bird. Something seemed grossly amiss here, something that would not have occurred had the wood been larger. I could not afford to buy Mrs. Henessy out, I dared not murder her, and limitations of this sort beset me on every side. Ahab did not want that vineyard—he only needed it to round off his property, preparatory to plotting a new curve—and all the land around my wood has become necessary to me in order to round off the wood. A boundary protects. But—poor little thing—the boundary ought in its turn to be protected. Noises on the edge of it. Children throw stones. A little more, and then a little more, until we reach the sea. Happy Canute! Happier Alexander! And after all, why should even the world be the limit of possession? A rocket containing a Union Jack, will, it is hoped, be shortly fired at the moon. Mars. Sirius. Beyond which . . . But these immensities ended by saddening me. I could not suppose that my wood was the destined nucleus of universal dominion—it is so very small and contains no mineral wealth beyond the blackberries. Nor was I comforted when Mrs. Henessy's bird took alarm for the second time and flew clean away from us all, under the belief that it belonged to itself.

5   In the third place, property makes its owner feel that he ought to do something to it. Yet he isn't sure what. A restlessness comes over him, a vague sense that he has a personality to express—the same sense which, without any vagueness, leads the artist to an act of creation. Sometimes I think I will cut down such trees as remain in the wood, at other times I want to fill up the gaps between them with new trees. Both impulses are pretentious and empty. They are not honest movements towards money-making or beauty. They spring from a foolish desire to express myself and from an inability to enjoy what I have got. Creation, property, enjoyment form a sinister trinity in the human mind. Creation and enjoyment are both very very good, yet they are often unattainable without a material basis, and at such moments property pushes itself in as a substitute, saying, "Accept me instead—I'm good enough for all three." It is not enough. It is, as Shakespeare said of lust, "The expense of spirit in a waste of shame": it is "Before, a joy proposed; behind, a dream." Yet we don't know how to shun it. It is forced on us by our economic system as the alternative to starvation. It is also forced on us by an internal defect in the soul, by the feeling that in property may lie the germs of self-development and of exquisite or heroic deeds. Our life on earth is, and ought to be, material and carnal. But we have not yet learned to manage our materialism and carnality prop-

erly; they are still entangled with the desire for ownership, where (in the words of Dante) "Possession is one with loss."

6   And this brings us to our fourth and final point: the blackberries.

7   Blackberries are not plentiful in this meagre grove, but they are easily seen from the public footpath which traverses it, and all too easily gathered. Foxgloves, too—people will pull up the foxgloves, and ladies of an educational tendency even grub for toadstools to show them on the Monday in class. Other ladies, less educated, roll down the bracken in the arms of their gentlemen friends. There is paper, there are tins. Pray, does my wood belong to me or doesn't it? And, if it does, should I not own it best by allowing no one else to walk there? There is a wood near Lyme Regis, also cursed by a public footpath, where the owner has not hesitated on this point. He has built high stone walls each side of the path, and has spanned it by bridges, so that the public circulate like termites while he gorges on the blackberries unseen. He really does own his wood, this able chap. Dives in Hell did pretty well, but the gulf dividing him from Lazarus could be traversed by vision, and nothing traverses it here.[1] And perhaps I shall come to this in time. I shall wall in and fence out until I really taste the sweets of property. Enormously stout, endlessly avaricious, pseudo-creative, intensely selfish, I shall wear upon my forehead the quadruple crown of possession until those nasty Bolshies come and take it off again and thrust me aside into the outer darkness.

Question

Much of the strength of the essay is in its concrete presentation of generalities. Note, for example, that the essay is called "My Wood," but we might say that the general idea of the essay is "The Effect of Property on Owners." Forster gives four effects, chiefly through concrete statements. What are they? Put these four effects in four general statements.

---

[1] Editors' note: According to Christ's parable in Luke xvi. 19–26, the rich man (unnamed, but traditionally known as Dives), at whose gate the poor man Lazarus had begged, was sent to hell, from where he could see Lazarus in heaven.

16

*A*cquiring Style

Draw lines, young man,
draw many lines
— OLD INGRES TO THE
   YOUNG DEGAS

In the preceding pages on style we said that your writing reveals not only where you stand (your topic) and how you think (the structure of your argument), but also who you are and how you take yourself (your tone). To follow our argument to its limit, we might say that everything in this book—including rules on the comma (where you breathe)—is about style. We do. What more is there to say?

CLARITY AND TEXTURE

First, a distinction Aristotle makes between two parts of style: that which gives *clarity,* and that which gives *texture.* Exact words, concrete illustrations of abstractions, conventional punctuation, and so forth—matters we treat in some detail in the sections on revising and editing—make for clarity. On the whole, this part of style is inconspicuous when present; when absent the effect ranges from mildly distracting to ruinous. Clarity is the foundation of style. It can be achieved by anyone willing to make the effort.

Among the things that give texture, or individuality, are effective repetition, variety in sentence structure, wordplay, and so forth. This second group of devices, on the whole more noticeable, makes the reader aware of the writer's particular voice. These devices can be learned too, but seldom by effort alone. In fact playfulness helps here more than doggedness. Students who work at this part of style usually enjoy hanging around words. At the same time, they're likely to feel that when they put words on paper, even in a casual letter to a friend, they're putting themselves on the line. Serious, as most people are about games they really care about, but not solemn, they'll come to recognize the rules of play in John Holmes's advice to young poets: "You must believe that your feelings and your words for your feelings are important. . . . That they are unique is a fact; that you believe they are unique is necessary."

A REPERTORY OF STYLES

We make a second distinction: between style as the reader perceives it from the written word, and style as the writer experiences it. The first is static: it's fixed in writing or print; we can point to it, discuss it, analyze it. The second, the writer's experience of his or her own style, changes as the writer changes. In his essay "Why I Write" George Orwell said, "I find that by the time you have perfected any style of writing, you have always outgrown it." An exaggeration that deposits a truth. The essay concludes, however, "Looking back through my work, I see that it is invariably where I lacked a *political* purpose that I wrote lifeless books and was betrayed into purple passages, sentences without meaning, decorative adjectives and humbug generally." A suggestion surely, that through trial and error, and with maturity, a writer comes to a sense of self, a true style, not static and not constantly changing, but achieved.

Undergraduates seldom know what purpose, in Orwell's sense, they will have. You may be inclined toward some subjects and against others, you may have decided on a career—many times. But if your education is worth anything like the money and time invested in it, your ideas and feelings will change more rapidly in the next few years than ever before in your memory, and perhaps more than they ever will again. Make use of the confusion you're in. Reach out for new experiences to assimilate; make whatever connections you can from your reading to your inner life, reaching back into your past and forward into your future. And keep writing: "Draw lines . . . draw many lines."

To keep pace with your changing ideas—and here is our main point—you'll need to acquire not one style, but a repertory of styles, a store of writing habits on which you can draw as the need arises.

ORIGINALITY AND IMITATION

Finally, a paradox: one starts to acquire an individual style by studying and imitating the style of others. The paradox isn't limited to writing. Stylists in all fields begin as apprentices. The young ball player imitates the movements of Reggie Jackson, the potter joins a workshop in California to study under Marguerite Wildenhain, the chess player hangs around the park or club watching the old pros, then finds a book that probably recommends beginning with Ruy Lopez's opening. When Michelangelo was an apprentice he copied works by his predecessors; when Millet was young he copied works by Michelangelo; when Van Gogh was young he copied works by Millet. The would-be writer may be lucky enough to have a teacher, one he can imitate; more likely he will, in W. H. Auden's words, "serve his apprenticeship in the library."

PRACTICE IN ACQUIRING STYLE

Benjamin Franklin's Exercise

Benjamin Franklin says in his *Autobiography*, "Prose writing has been of great use to me in the course of my life, and was a principal means of my advancement," and he reveals how he acquired his ability in it. (He had just abandoned, at about the age of eleven, his ambition to be a great poet—after his father told him that "verse-makers were generally beggars.")

About this time I met with an odd volume of the *Spectator*. It was the third. I had never before seen any of them. I bought it, read it over and over, and was much delighted with it. I thought the writing excellent, and wished, if possible, to imitate it. With that view I took some of the papers, and making short hints of the sentiment in each sentence, laid them by a few days, and then, without looking at the book, tried to complete the papers again by expressing each sentiment at length, and as fully as it had been expressed before, in any suitable words that should come to hand. Then I compared my *Spectator* with the original, discovered some of my faults, and corrected them.

A few pages later Franklin confides, with characteristic understatement (which he learned, he thought, by imitating Socrates), "I sometimes had the pleasure of fancying that in certain particulars of small import I had been lucky enough to improve the method or the language."

EXERCISES

1. Outline, in a list of brief notes, Franklin's exercise.
2. Choose a passage of current prose writing whose style you admire and follow Franklin's method. (Don't forget the last step: where you've improved on your model, congratulate yourself with becoming modesty.)

Paraphrasing

Do not confuse a paraphrase with a summary.

A summary is always much shorter than the original; a paraphrase is often a bit longer. To paraphrase a sentence, replace each word or phrase in it with one of your own. (Articles, pronouns, and conjunctions need not be replaced.) Your sentence should say substantially what the original says, but in your own words, and in a fluent, natural style. Consider the following sentence by W. H. Auden, and the paraphrase that follows it:

> Owing to its superior power as a mnemonic, verse is superior to prose as a medium for didactic instruction.
> — W. H. Auden

Because it is more easily memorized and can be retained in the mind for a longer time, poetry is better than prose for teaching moral lessons.

Paraphrasing is useful for several reasons. First, paraphrasing helps you to increase your vocabulary. (Many students say that a limited vocabulary is their chief source of difficulty in writing.) You may know, for example, that "didactic" means "intended for instruction, or instructive." But why then does Auden say "didactic instruction"? Are the words redundant, or is Auden stipulating a kind of instruction? Your dictionary, which may list "tending to teach a moral lesson" as one of three or four meanings of didactic, will help you understand Auden's sentence. But notice, first, that you'll have to choose the appropriate definition, and second, that you won't be able to insert that definition as is into your sentence. To paraphrase "didactic instruction" you'll have to put "didactic" in your own words. (If you look up "mnemonic" you'll find an even more complex puzzle resolved in our paraphrase.) Paraphrasing, then, expands your vocabulary because to paraphrase accurately and gracefully you must actively understand the use of an unfamiliar word, not simply memorize a synonym for it.

Paraphrasing also helps you to focus your attention on what you read. If you want, for example, to become a better reader of poetry, the best way is to *pay attention,* and the best way of paying attention is to try paraphrasing a line whose meaning escapes you. So too with understanding art history or economics or any specialized study. If you come across a difficult passage, don't just stare at it, paraphrase it. (If you don't have time to stop and puzzle through a sentence that is not entirely clear to you, you can always make time to jot it down on a three-by-five card. As Stanislav Andreski says, "Paper is patient.")

Finally, in paraphrasing, you are observing closely and actively the way another mind works. You are, in effect, serving as an apprentice stylist. (Some masters, of course, are not worth serving or emulating. Be discriminating.)

EXERCISE

Try paraphrasing the following sentences:

> Generally speaking and to a varying extent, scientists follow their temperaments in their choice of problems.
> — Charles Hermite

> To commit violent and unjust acts, it is not enough for a government to have the will or even the power; the habits, ideas, and passions of the time must lend themselves to their committal.
> — Alexis de Tocqueville

> The most intolerable people are provincial celebrities.
> — Anton Chekhov

> A distinction must be made between my uncle's capricious brutality and my aunt's punishments and repressions, which seem to have been dictated to her by her conscience.
> — Mary McCarthy

> Consciousness reigns but doesn't govern.
> — Paul Valéry

> The more extensive your acquaintance is with the works of those who have excelled, the more extensive will be your powers of invention, and what may appear still more like a paradox, the more original will be your composition.
> — Sir Joshua Reynolds

> The fashion wears out more apparel than the man.
> — William Shakespeare

> What is expressed is impressed.
> — Aristotle

> All the road to heaven is heaven.
> — Saint Teresa of Avila

> When the shoe fits, the foot is forgotten.
> — Chuang Tzu

Imitating the Cumulative Sentence

When you write, you make a point, not by subtracting as though you sharpened a pencil, but by adding. When you put one word after another, your statement should be more precise the more you add. If the result is otherwise, you have added the wrong thing, or you have added more than was needed.

— John Erskine

In *Notes Toward a New Rhetoric* Francis Christensen cites "Erskine's principle" and argues that "the cumulative sentence" best fulfills it. The cumulative sentence makes a statement in the main clause; the rest of the sentence consists of modifiers *added* to make the meaning of the statement more precise. The cumulative sentence adds *texture* to writing because as the writer adds modifiers she is examining her impressions, summarized in the main clause. At the same time she reveals to the reader how those impressions impinged on her mind. Here are some of Christensen's examples:

He dipped his hands in the bichloride solution and shook them, a quick shake, fingers down, like the fingers of a pianist above the keys.

— Sinclair Lewis

The jockeys sat bowed and relaxed, moving a little at the waist with the movement of their horses.

— Katherine Anne Porter

The Texan turned to the nearest gatepost and climbed to the top of it, his alternate thighs thick and bulging in the tight trousers, the butt of the pistol catching and losing the sun in pearly gleams.

— William Faulkner

George was coming down in the telemark position, kneeling, one leg forward and bent, the other trailing, his sticks hanging like some insect's thin legs, kicking up puffs of snow, and finally the whole kneeling, trailing figure coming around in a beautiful right curve like points of light, all in a wild cloud of snow.

— Ernest Hemingway

EXERCISE

Try writing a cumulative sentence. First, reread Christensen's sample sentences out loud. Then, during a second reading, try to sense the similarities in structure. For the next few days train yourself to observe people closely, the way they walk, move, gesture, smile, speak. Take notes when you can. Then, after reading the sentences again, try writing one. Either imitate one of the sentences closely, word by word (substituting your own words) or start with your subject, imitating the structure you have detected or have simply absorbed.

Transformations

If you take a proverb, an epigram, or any interesting, suggestive sentence and change it enough to make it say something else, something on *your* mind, you have a transformation. To cite a famous example, G. K. Chesterton transformed

> If a thing is worth doing it is worth doing well

to

> If a thing is worth doing it is worth doing badly.

Professor Marion Levy transformed Leo Durocher's

> Nice guys finish last

to

> Last guys don't finish nice.

A student transformed Marianne Moore's

> We must be as clear as our natural reticence allows us to be

to

> We must be as outspoken as our adversaries would forbid us to be.

EXERCISE

How can you transform one or more of the following?

> When a poor man eats a chicken, one of them is sick.
> — Yiddish proverb

> The Battle of Waterloo was won on the playing fields of Eton.
> — Attributed to the Duke of Wellington

You can't step into the same river twice.

— Heraclitus

Mañana es otro día.

— Proverb

Finding Poems

Finding poems is a variation of the language game called acquiring style. It amuses the student who enjoys hanging around words but who is tired of writing, tired of pulling words out of his mind and making them shape up—weary too, very weary, of reading "fine things." Still, he hungers for print, consuming the words on the cereal box along with the cereal, reading last week's classified ads when he has nothing to sell, no money to buy. What can be made of such an affliction? A poem.

Here are X. J. Kennedy's directions for finding a poem.

In a newspaper, magazine, catalogue, textbook, or advertising throwaway, find a sentence or passage that (with a little artistic manipulation on your part) shows promise of becoming a poem. Copy it into lines like poetry, being careful to place what seem to be the most interesting words at the ends of lines to give them greatest emphasis. According to the rules of found poetry you may excerpt, delete, repeat, and rearrange elements but not add anything.

Here are examples of "found poems." The first, "And All Those Others," was found by Jack S. Margolis in the Watergate transcripts; he published it in *The Poetry of Richard Milhous Nixon.*

I'm the President
Of the country—
And I'm going
To get on with it
  And meet
  Italians
  and
  Germans,
And all those others.

Below you will find a passage from a textbook. The paragraph talks of symbols, what they are and what they are not. After the student read that passage, she wrote the poem which follows the prose discussion and is entitled "Symbolism."

> A symbol, then, is an image so loaded with significance that it is not simply literal, and it does not simply stand for something else; it is both itself *and* something else that it richly suggests, a kind of manifestation of something too complex or too elusive to be otherwise revealed.

An image
so loaded with
   significance
that it is not
   simply literal,
and it does not
   simply stand
for
   something else;
it is both
   itself
and
   something else
that it
   richly suggests,
a kind of
   manifestation
of
   something
   too complex
or
   too elusive
to be
   otherwise revealed,
is a
   symbol.

Finally, a poem found by a student in an advertisement in *Newsweek:*

Winchester model 101
made for hands
that know the difference
There's more
than meets the eye
to any fine
shotgun

EXERCISES

1. Find a poem.
2. Explain in one sentence (a) how finding poems might help you acquire style or (b) why such an exercise is a waste of time.

*A*dditional Readings

The Flag

Russell Baker

1   At various times when young, I was prepared to crack skulls, kill and die for Old Glory. I never wholly agreed with the LOVE IT OR LEAVE IT bumper stickers, which held that everybody who didn't love the flag ought to be thrown out of the country, but I wouldn't have minded seeing them beaten up. In fact, I saw a man come very close to being beaten up at a baseball park one day because he didn't stand when they raised the flag in the opening ceremonies, and I joined the mob screaming for him to get to his feet like an American if he didn't want lumps all over his noodle. He stood up, all right. I was then thirteen, and a Boy Scout, and I knew you never let the flag touch the ground, or threw it out with the trash when it got dirty (you burned it), or put up with disrespect for it at the baseball park.

2   At eighteen, I longed to die for it. When World War II ended in 1945 before I could reach the combat zone, I moped for months about being deprived of the chance to go down in flames under the guns of a Mitsubishi Zero. There was never much doubt that I would go down in flames if given the opportunity, for my competence as a pilot was such that I could barely remember to lower the plane's landing gear before trying to set it down on a runway.

3   I had even visualized my death. It was splendid. Dead, I would be standing perhaps 4,000 feet up in the sky. (Everybody knew that heroes floated in those days.) Erect and dashing, surrounded by beautiful cumulus clouds, I would look just as good as ever, except for being slightly transparent. And I would smile, devil-may-care, at the camera—oh, there would be cameras there—and the American flag would unfurl behind me across 500 miles of glorious American sky, and back behind the cumulus clouds the Marine Band would be playing "The Stars and Stripes Forever," but not too fast.

4   Then I would look down at June Allyson and the kids, who had a gold star in the window and brave smiles shining through their tears, and I would give them a salute and one of those brave, wistful Errol Flynn grins, then turn and mount to Paradise, becoming more transparent with each step so the audience could get a great view of the flag waving over the heavenly pastures.

5   Okay, so it owes a lot to Louis B. Mayer in his rococo period. I couldn't help that. At eighteen, a man's imagination is too busy

with sex to have much energy left for fancy embellishments of patriotic ecstasy. In the words of a popular song of the period, there was a star-spangled banner waving somewhere in The Great Beyond, and only Uncle Sam's brave heroes got to go there. I was ready to make the trip.

6   All this was a long time ago, and, asinine though it now may seem, I confess it here to illustrate the singularly masculine pleasures to be enjoyed in devoted service to the Stars and Stripes. Not long ago I felt a twinge of the old fire when I saw an unkempt lout on a ferryboat with a flag sewed in the crotch of his jeans. Something in me wanted to throw him overboard, but I didn't since he was a big muscular devil and the flag had already suffered so many worse indignities anyhow, having been pinned in politicians' lapels, pasted on cars to promote gasoline sales and used to sanctify the professional sports industry as the soul of patriotism even while the team owners were instructing their athletes in how to dodge the draft.

7   For a moment, though, I felt some of the old masculine excitement kicked up by the flag in the adrenal glands. It's a man's flag, all right. No doubt about that. Oh, it may be a scoundrel's flag, too, and a drummer's flag, and a fraud's flag, and a thief's flag, but first and foremost, it is a man's flag.

8   Except for decorating purposes—it looks marvelous on old New England houses—I cannot see much in it to appeal to women. Its pleasures, in fact, seem so exclusively masculine and its sanctity so unassailable by feminist iconoclasts that it may prove to be America's only enduring, uncrushable male sex symbol.

9   Observe that in my patriotic death fantasy, the starring role is not June Allyson's, but mine. As defender of the flag, I am able to leave a humdrum job, put June and the kids with all their humdrum problems behind me, travel the world with a great bunch of guys, do exciting things with powerful flying machines, and, fetchingly uniformed, strut exotic saloons on my nights off.

10   In the end, I walk off with all the glory and the big scene.

11   And what does June get? Poor June. She gets to sit home with the kids the rest of her life dusting my photograph and trying to pay the bills, with occasional days off to visit the grave.

12   No wonder the male pulse pounds with pleasure when the Stars and Stripes comes fluttering down the avenue with the band smashing out those great noises. Where was Mrs. Teddy Roosevelt when Teddy was carrying it up San Juan Hill? What was Mrs. Lincoln doing when Abe was holding it aloft for the Union? What was Martha up to while George Washington was carrying it across the

Delaware? Nothing, you may be sure, that was one-tenth as absorbing as what their husbands were doing.

13   Consider some of the typical masculine activities associated with Old Glory: Dressing up in medals. Whipping cowards, slackers and traitors within an inch of their miserable lives. Conquering Mount Suribachi. Walking on the moon. Rescuing the wagon train. Being surrounded by the whole German Army and being asked to surrender and saying, "You can tell Schicklgruber my answer is 'Nuts.' " In brief, having a wonderful time. With the boys.

14   Yes, surely the American flag is the ultimate male sex symbol. Men flaunt it, wave it, punch noses for it, strut with it, fight for it, kill for it, die for it.

15   And women—? Well, when do you see a woman with the flag? Most commonly when she is wearing black and has just received it, neatly folded, from coffin of husband or son. Later, she may wear it to march in the Veterans Day parade, widows' division.

16   Male pleasures and woman's sorrow—it sounds like the old definition of sex. Yet these are the immemorial connotations of the flag, and women, having shed the whalebone girdle and stamped out the stag bar, nevertheless accept it, ostensibly at least, with the same emotional devotion that men accord it.

17   There are good reasons, of course, why they may be reluctant to pursue logic to its final step and say, "To hell with the flag, too." In the first place, it would almost certainly do them no good. Men hold all the political trumps in this matter. When little girls first toddle off to school, does anyone tell them the facts of life when they stand to salute the flag? Does anyone say, "You are now saluting the proud standard of the greatest men's club on earth?" You bet your chewing gum nobody tells them that. If anyone did, there would be a joint session of Congress presided over by the President of the United States to investigate the entire school system of the United States of America.

18   What little girls have drilled into them is that the flag stands for one nation indivisible, with liberty and justice for all. A few years ago, the men of the Congress, responding to pressure from the American Legion (all men) and parsons (mostly all men), all of whom sensed perhaps that women were not as gullible as they used to be, revised the Pledge of Allegiance with words intimating that it would be ungodly not to respect the flag. The "one nation indivisible" became "one nation *under God*, indivisible," and another loophole for skeptics was sealed off. The women's movement may be brave, but it will not go far taking on national indivisibility, liberty, justice and God, all in one fight. If they tried it, a lot of us

men would feel perfectly justified in raising lumps on their lovely noodles.

19   Philosophically speaking, the masculinity of the American flag is entirely appropriate. America, after all, is not a motherland—many places still are—but a fatherland, which is to say a vast nation-state of disparate people scattered over great distances, but held together by a belligerent, loyalty-to-the-death devotion to some highly abstract political ideas. Since these ideas are too complex to be easily grasped, statesmen have given us the flag and told us it sums up all these noble ideas that make us a country.

20   Fatherland being an aggressive kind of state, the ideas it embodies must be defended, protected and propagated, often in blood. Since the flag is understood to represent these ideas, in a kind of tricolor shorthand, we emote, fight, bleed and rejoice in the name of the flag.

21   Before fatherland there was something that might be called motherland. It still exists here and there. In the fifties, when Washington was looking for undiscovered Asiatic terrain to save from un-American ideologies, somebody stumbled into an area called Laos, a place so remote from American consciousness that few had ever heard its name pronounced. (For the longest time, Lyndon Johnson, then Democratic leader of the Senate, referred to it as "Low Ass.") Federal inspectors sent to Laos returned with astounding information. Most of the people living there were utterly unaware that they were living in a country. Almost none of them knew the country they were living in was called Laos. All they knew was that they lived where they had been born and where their ancestors were buried.

22   What Washington had discovered, of course, was an old-fashioned motherland, a society where people's loyalties ran to the place of their birth. It was a Pentagon nightmare. Here were these people, perfectly happy with their home turf and their ancestors' graves, and they had to be put into shape to die for their country, and they didn't even know they had a country to die for. They didn't even have a flag to die for. And yet, they were content!

23   The point is that a country is only an idea and a fairly modern one at that. Life would still be going on if nobody had ever thought of it, and would probably be a good deal more restful. No flags. Not much in the way of armies. No sharing of exciting group emotions with millions of other people ready to do or die for national honor. And so forth. Very restful, and possibly very primitive, and almost surely very nasty on occasion, although possibly not as nasty as occasions often become when countries disagree.

24   I hear my colleagues in masculinity protesting. "What? No country? No flag? But there would be nothing noble to defend, to fight for, to die for, in the meantime having a hell of a good time doing all those fun male things in the name of!"

25   Women may protest, too. I imagine some feminists may object to the suggestion that fatherland's need for prideful, warlike and aggressive citizens to keep the flag flying leaves women pretty much out of things. Those who hold that sexual roles are a simple matter of social conditioning may contend that the flag can offer the same rollicking pleasures to both sexes once baby girls are trained as thoroughly as baby boys in being prideful, warlike and aggressive.

26   I think there may be something in this, having seen those harridans who gather outside freshly desegregated schools to wave the American flag and terrify children. The question is whether women really want to start conditioning girl babies for this hitherto largely masculine sort of behavior, or spend their energies trying to decondition it out of the American man.

27   In any case, I have no quarrel with these women. Living in a fatherland, they have tough problems, and if they want to join the boys in the flag sports, it's okay with me. The only thing is, if they are going to get a chance, too, to go up to Paradise with the Marine Band playing "The Stars and Stripes Forever" back behind the cumulus clouds, I don't want to be stuck with the role of sitting home dusting their photographs the rest of my life after the big scene is ended.

Questions

1. Baker's first five paragraphs are devoted to his childhood and adolescence. On what attitudes does he focus our attention? Do you think that his attitudes during those years were exceptional, or was he pretty much like other male adolescents?

2. How does Baker make it clear in the first five paragraphs, where he is describing his youthful ideals, that these *were* youthful ideals, ideals he no longer holds?

3. After saying that the flag "is a man's flag," Baker reminds us that we don't associate it with Mrs. Teddy Roosevelt, Mrs. Lincoln, or Martha Washington. But let's say that Baker's wife, reading his manuscript, reminded him of the tradition that Betsy Ross ("with a single snip of her scissors") cut the five-pointed star for the flag. Using Baker's style, write the paragraph that Baker might then have been tempted (or pressured) to add.

4. How is Baker's last sentence connected to the rest of the essay? Why is the sentence amusing?

5. Baker is kidding around, and the essay amuses, but one can argue that it is also serious. Make the case.

6. If someone, having skimmed Baker's essay, were to charge that Baker is unpatriotic, how (on the basis of this essay) would you defend him from that charge?

7. In a paragraph, explain, for someone who has not read this essay, what Baker means by calling the American flag "the ultimate male sex symbol."

---

*H*ow to Get Things Done
Robert Benchley

1   A great many people have come up to me and asked me how I manage to get so much work done and still keep looking so dissipated. My answer is "Don't you wish you knew?" and a pretty good answer it is, too, when you consider that nine times out of ten I didn't hear the original question.

2   But the fact remains that hundreds of thousands of people throughout the country are wondering how I have time to do all my painting, engineering, writing and philanthropic work when, according to the rotogravure sections and society notes, I spend all my time riding to hounds, going to fancy-dress balls disguised as Louis XIV or spelling out GREETINGS TO CALIFORNIA in formation with three thousand Los Angeles school children. "All work and all play," they say.

3   The secret of my incredible energy and efficiency in getting work done is a simple one. I have based it very deliberately on a well-known psychological principle and have refined it so that it is now almost *too* refined. I shall have to begin coarsening it up again pretty soon.

4   The psychological principle is this: anyone can do any amount of work, provided it isn't the work he is *supposed* to be doing at that moment.

5   Let us see how this works out in practice. Let us say that I

have five things which have to be done before the end of the week: (1) a basketful of letters to be answered, some of them dating from October 1928, (2) some bookshelves to be put up and arranged with books (3) a hair-cut to get (4) a pile of scientific magazines to go through and clip (I am collecting all references to tropical fish that I can find, with the idea of some day buying myself one) and (5) an article to write for this paper.

6   *Now.* With these five tasks staring me in the face on Monday morning, it is little wonder that I go right back to bed as soon as I have had breakfast, in order to store up health and strength for the almost superhuman expenditure of energy that is to come. *Mens sana in corpore sano*[1] is my motto, and, not even to be funny, am I going to make believe that I don't know what the Latin means. I feel that the least that I can do is to treat my body right when it has to supply fuel for an insatiable mind like mine.

7   As I lie in bed on Monday morning storing up strength, I make out a schedule. "What do I have to do first?" I ask myself. Well, those letters really should be answered and the pile of scientific magazines should be clipped. And here is where my secret process comes in. Instead of putting them first on the list of things which have to be done, I put them last. I practice a little deception on myself and say: "First you must write that article for the newspaper." I even say this out loud (being careful that nobody hears me, otherwise they would *keep* me in bed) and try to fool myself into really believing that I must do the article that day and that the other things can wait. I sometimes go so far in this self-deception as to make out a list in pencil, with "No. 1. Newspaper article" underlined in red. (The underlining in red is rather difficult, as there is never a red pencil on the table beside the bed, unless I have taken one to bed with me on Sunday night.)

8   Then, when everything is lined up, I bound out of bed and have lunch. I find that a good, heavy lunch, with some sort of glutinous dessert, is good preparation for the day's work as it keeps one from getting nervous and excitable. We workers must keep cool and calm, otherwise we would just throw away our time in jumping about and fidgeting.

9   I then seat myself at my desk with my typewriter before me and sharpen five pencils. (The sharp pencils are for poking holes in the desk-blotter, and a pencil has to be pretty sharp to do that. I find that I can't get more than six holes out of one pencil.) Follow-

---

[1] Editors' note: Latin for "A sound mind in a sound body."

ing this I say to myself (again out loud, if it is practical), "Now, old man! Get at this article!"

10   Gradually the scheme begins to work. My eye catches the pile of magazines, which I have artfully placed on a near-by table beforehand. I write my name and address at the top of the sheet of paper in the typewriter and then sink back. The magazines being within reach (also part of the plot) I look to see if anyone is watching me and get one off the top of the pile. Hello, what's this! In the very first one is an article by Dr. William Beebe, illustrated by horrifying photographs! Pushing my chair away from my desk, I am soon hard at work clipping.

11   One of the interesting things about the Argyopelius, or "Silver Hatchet" fish, I find, is that it has eyes in its wrists. I would have been sufficiently surprised just to find out that a fish had wrists, but to learn that it has eyes in them is a discovery so astounding that I am hardly able to cut out the picture. What a lot one learns simply by thumbing through the illustrated weeklies! It is hard work, though, and many a weaker spirit would give it up half-done, but when there is something else of "more importance" to be finished (you see, I still keep up the deception, letting myself go on thinking that the newspaper article is of more importance) no work is too hard or too onerous to keep one busy.

12   Thus, before the afternoon is half over, I have gone through the scientific magazines and have a neat pile of clippings (including one of a Viper Fish which I wish you could see. You would die laughing). Then it is back to the grind of the newspaper article.

13   This time I get as far as the title, which I write down with considerable satisfaction until I find that I have misspelled one word terribly, so that the whole sheet of paper has to come out and a fresh one be inserted. As I am doing this, my eye catches the basket of letters.

14   Now, if there is one thing that I hate to do (and there is, you may be sure) it is to write letters. But somehow, with the magazine article before me waiting to be done, I am seized with an epistolary fervor which amounts to a craving, and I slyly sneak the first of the unanswered letters out of the basket. I figure out in my mind that I will get more into the swing of writing the article if I practice a little on a few letters. This first one, anyway, I really must answer. True, it is from a friend in Antwerp asking me to look him up when I am in Europe in the summer of 1929, so he can't actually be watching the incoming boats for an answer, but I owe something to politeness after all. So instead of putting a fresh sheet of copy-

paper into the typewriter, I slip in one of my handsome bits of personal stationery and dash off a note to my friend in Antwerp. Then, being well in the letter-writing mood, I clean up the entire batch. I feel a little guilty about the article, but the pile of freshly stamped envelopes and the neat bundle of clippings on tropical fish do much to salve my conscience. Tomorrow I will do the article, and no fooling this time either.

15　　When tomorrow comes I am up with one of the older and more sluggish larks. A fresh sheet of copy-paper in the machine, and my name and address neatly printed at the top, and all before eleven A.M.! "A human dynamo" is the name I think up for myself. I have decided to write something about snake-charming and am already more than satisfied with the title "These Snake-Charming People." But, in order to write about snake-charming, one has to know a little about its history, and where should one go to find history but to a book? Maybe in that pile of books in the corner is one on snake-charming! Nobody could point the finger of scorn at me if I went over to those books for the avowed purpose of research work for the matter at hand. No writer could be supposed to carry all that information in his head.

16　　So, with a perfectly clear conscience, I leave my desk for a few minutes and begin glancing over the titles of the books. Of course, it is difficult to find any book, much less one on snake-charming, in a pile which has been standing in the corner for weeks. What really is needed is for them to be on a shelf where their titles will be visible at a glance. And there is the shelf, standing beside the pile of books! It seems almost like a divine command written in the sky: "If you want to finish that article, first put up the shelf and arrange the books on it!" Nothing could be clearer or more logical.

17　　In order to put up the shelf, the laws of physics have decreed that there must be nails, a hammer and some sort of brackets to hold it up on the wall. You can't just wet a shelf with your tongue and stick it up. And, as there are no nails or brackets in the house (or, if there are, they are probably hidden somewhere) the next thing to do is put on my hat and go out to buy them. Much as it disturbs me to put off the actual start of the article, I feel that I am doing only what is in the line of duty to put on my hat and go out to buy nails and brackets. And, as I put on my hat, I realize to my chagrin that I need a hair-cut badly. I can kill two birds with one stone, or at least with two, and stop in at the barber's on the way back. I will feel all the more like writing after a turn in the fresh air. Any doctor would tell me that.

18   So in a few hours I return, spick and span and smelling of lilac, bearing nails, brackets, the evening papers and some crackers and peanut butter. Then it's ho! for a quick snack and a glance through the evening papers (there might be something in them which would alter what I was going to write about snake-charming) and in no time at all the shelf is up, slightly crooked but up, and the books are arranged in a neat row in alphabetical order and all ready for almost instantaneous reference. There does not happen to be one on snake-charming among them, but there is a very interesting one containing some Hogarth prints and one which will bear even closer inspection dealing with the growth of the Motion Picture, illustrated with "stills" from famous productions. A really remarkable industry, the motion-pictures. I might want to write an article on it sometime. Not today, probably, for it is six o'clock and there is still the one on snake-charming to finish up first. Tomorrow morning sharp! Yes, *sir!*

19   And so, you see, in two days I have done four of the things I had to do, simply by making believe that it was the fifth that I *must* do. And the next day, I fix up something else, like taking down the bookshelf and putting it somewhere else, that I *have* to do, and then I get the fifth one done.

20   The only trouble is that, at this rate, I will soon run out of things to do, and will be forced to get at that newspaper article the first thing Monday morning.

Questions

1. In the first sentence, what did you expect after the words "looking so"? Why didn't Benchley say what you expected?
2. In paragraph 7 Benchley claims that he is deliberately practicing self-deception when he lists writing an article as the first thing he must do, and that "the other things can wait." How do we know that he is being ironic—that writing the article really is the most urgent task? Write a 500-word essay, due Monday, explaining your answer (or answer the next question).
3. Why did you turn to this question?
4. Write an essay setting down in meticulous detail everything you do when you go about writing an essay. Play it straight, but don't be surprised if it comes out sounding like a spoof.

*P*ay Equity—How to Argue Back

Barbara R. Bergmann

1   Thanks to the pay equity campaign, state and local governments around the country are taking steps to raise the pay scales in the traditionally female occupations. The drumbeat of criticism continues, however, with that raucous, mocking tone that we are used to hearing in response to any proposal to improve women's status. Some of it comes from the same folks who oppose shelters for battered women—they are against anything that would make women more uppity. But some of the criticism is serious and needs answering.

2   The first count of the indictment is that pay equity adjustments tamper with "wage scales set in the marketplace." Of course they do. The pay that the market decrees for women's labor is badly depressed by discrimination. Pay equity adjustments, along with affirmative action for hiring and promoting women, are attempts to get away from the sex discrimination that most employers practice and that now dominates the "market." The real question is, what harm would be done?

3   If women's wages are raised, then employers will want to employ fewer of them, say pay equity's critics. For a response we can point to the example of Australia, where government pay boards handed out equity raises in the traditional women's occupations amounting to about 30 percent. Australian economists fully expected to see women's unemployment rates rise significantly as a result. After thorough study, they had to report that the bad effects hadn't materialized. In Sweden, Britain, West Germany, Holland, and Denmark, women workers have had significant gains in pay. In terms of equity with men, they are way ahead of American women. In none of these countries are there reports of special unemployment problems for women. There is no reason to think that American women will experience such problems either.

4   Another complaint against pay equity is that, apart from the market, there is no really good way to compare men's and women's occupations, so how could we decide which ones should have comparable pay? "How can you compare a secretary to a truck driver, or a nurse to a tree trimmer?" the opponents of pay equity ask plaintively in mock anguish. The answer is that employers do have

a method that they rely on to make comparisons between very different occupations. It is called "job evaluation."

5   Many large employers already use job evaluation techniques in setting pay, and well-respected consulting firms help in the implementation. These employers use job evaluation because the idea of a "market" that will tell them the wage for each of hundreds of job titles is sheer fantasy. However, these firms have wanted to avoid paying male-level salaries to women, so they never directly compared the qualities of traditional women's jobs and traditional men's jobs. They set up a job evaluation system for the jobs labeled "clerical" and an entirely different one for the jobs labeled "administrative." It is as if they were doing job evaluations on blue paper for the men and on pink paper for the women, taking care not to compare the pink and blue sheets. The idea of pay equity is that men's and women's jobs should be evaluated by a unified system, and then pay scales adjusted accordingly. The basic methodology already exists, and already is in widespread use in business and in government. It just needs to be cleaned up a bit.

6   Another allegation about pay equity is that the costs will be huge—billions of dollars. That's true, but since there are millions of women involved, billions of dollars are needed to make a dent in the problem. Where can we get the billions for pay equity? They will come out of the billions that are handed out every year as wage increases to workers. At most, for a few years, women will get larger-than-average increases, and for a few years men will get smaller-than-average increases. Nobody's pay need go down. Nor will profits or budgets be wiped out.

7   The silliest argument the pay equity critics have come up with is that women will be so satisfied with their pay in the traditional female jobs that they will stop trying to get into the better jobs reserved for men. That argument is an insult to every secretary who has been passed over for a promotion to a job she could do better than the man who got it. Better pay has never prevented men or women from wanting promotions.

8   Pay equity is going forward for the women employees of state and local governments because a combination of political and union pressure is being exerted behind it. For it to spread to the private sector, unions must confront the issue at the bargaining table. Where there is no union, or where the union is indifferent to women's issues, women employees must organize on their own. Whether pay equity lawsuits will be worthwhile depends on the Supreme Court.

9   One of the economic effects of pay equity that seldom gets mentioned is its effect on poverty. A healthy boost in the pay of the

traditional women's occupations is the best and may be the only way that we have of reducing poverty among women in the near future. It might rescue from poverty some of the millions of children dependent on those women. When you come to think about it, it's women's current salaries that make poor economic sense. Pay equity makes good economic sense.

Questions

1. From the title and first paragraph of this essay, would you say that Bergmann is addressing proponents or opponents of pay equity? Considering that the article was published in *Ms.*, does she strike an appropriate opening note? Does she risk alienating readers?

2. What Bergmann and many other people call "pay equity" is called, by still others, "comparable worth." If you advocate the idea, which term do you prefer? Why?

3. In paragraph 4 Bergmann mentions the opposition's belief that the only way to compare the value of a nurse with the value of a tree trimmer is to see what the market offers. Bergmann says there is an alternative, "job evaluation." In her next paragraph she offers a comment on job evaluations. If you were evaluating the two jobs she mentions in paragraph 4—nurse and tree trimmer—which job would you find deserving of higher pay? Why? What criteria would you use? Possible criteria might be the amount of education or training, or the skill level, required; the degree of responsibility; the amount of initiative (or intelligence?) required; and work conditions (e.g., congenial or uncongenial).

4. Why is the choice of criteria important in establishing pay equity? Try to explain your answer by again comparing the jobs of the secretary and the tree trimmer, this time using criteria other than those listed in question 3.

5. In paragraph 7 Bergmann speaks of certain "better jobs [that are] reserved for men." What are some examples of such jobs? What makes them "better"? Money, and nothing else?

6. In rejecting the request of Denver nurses that they be paid as much as Denver tree trimmers, a federal judge noted that such a change in pay involved "the possibility of disrupting the entire economic system in the United States." Is the possibility of such disruption a sound reason for rejecting the change? Why, or why not?

7. If you have ever been underpaid, or overpaid, because of sexual

or racial discrimination, explain the circumstances and then argue the case that might have been made for pay equity.

8. If you have read Lester C. Thurow's "Why Women Are Paid Less Than Men" (page 693), set forth what you think would be Bergmann's response to Thurow's analysis of the problem and her response to his two proposals for equalizing male and female earnings.

To Lie or Not to Lie?— The Doctor's Dilemma
Sissela Bok

---

1   Should doctors ever lie to benefit their patients—to speed recovery or to conceal the approach of death? In medicine as in law, government, and other lines of work, the requirements of honesty often seem dwarfed by greater needs: the need to shelter from brutal news or to uphold a promise of secrecy; to expose corruption or to promote the public interest.

2   What should doctors say, for example, to a forty-six-year-old man coming in for a routine physical checkup just before going on vacation with his family who, though he feels in perfect health, is found to have a form of cancer that will cause him to die within six months? Is it best to tell him the truth? If he asks, should the doctors deny that he is ill, or minimize the gravity of the prognosis? Should they at least conceal the truth until after the family vacation?

3   Doctors confront such choices often and urgently. At times, they see important reasons to lie for the patient's own sake; in their eyes, such lies differ sharply from self-serving ones.

4   Studies show that most doctors sincerely believe that the seriously ill do not want to know the truth about their condition, and that informing them risks destroying their hope, so that they may recover more slowly, or deteriorate faster, perhaps even commit suicide. As one physician wrote: "Ours is a profession which traditionally has been guided by a precept that transcends the virtue of uttering the truth for truth's sake, and that is 'as far as possible do no harm.'"

5   Armed with such a precept, a number of doctors may slip into deceptive practices that they assume will "do no harm" and may well help their patients. They may prescribe innumerable placebos, sound more encouraging than the facts warrant, and distort grave news, especially to the incurably ill and the dying.

6   But the illusory nature of the benefits such deception is meant to bestow is now coming to be documented. Studies show that, contrary to the belief of many physicians, an overwhelming majority of patients do want to be told the truth, even about grave illness, and feel betrayed when they learn that they have been misled. We are also learning that truthful information, humanely conveyed, helps patients cope with illness: helps them tolerate pain better, need less medication, and even recover faster after surgery.

7   Not only do lies not provide the "help" hoped for by advocates of benevolent deception; they invade the autonomy of patients and render them unable to make informed choices concerning their own health, including the choice of whether to *be* a patient in the first place. We are becoming increasingly aware of all that can befall patients in the course of their illness when information is denied or distorted.

8   Dying patients especially—who are easiest to mislead and most often kept in the dark—can then not make decisions about the end of life: about whether or not to enter a hospital, or to have surgery; about where and with whom to spend their remaining time; about how to bring their affairs to a close and take leave.

9   Lies also do harm to those who tell them: harm to their integrity and, in the long run, to their credibility. Lies hurt their colleagues as well. The suspicion of deceit undercuts the work of the many doctors who are scrupulously honest with their patients; it contributes to the spiral of litigation and of "defensive medicine," and thus it injures, in turn, the entire medical profession.

10   Sharp conflicts are now arising. Patients are learning to press for answers. Patients' bills of rights require that they be informed about their condition and about alternatives for treatment. Many doctors go to great lengths to provide such information. Yet even in hospitals with the most eloquent bill of rights, believers in benevolent deception continue their age-old practices. Colleagues may disapprove but refrain from remonstrating. Nurses may bitterly resent having to take part, day after day, in deceiving patients, but feel powerless to take a stand.

11   There is urgent need to debate this issue openly. Not only in medicine, but in other professions as well, practitioners may find themselves repeatedly in straits where serious consequences seem

avoidable only through deception. Yet the public has every reason to be wary of professional deception, for such practices are peculiarly likely to become ingrained, to spread, and to erode trust. Neither in medicine, nor in law, government, or the social sciences can there be comfort in the old saw, "What you don't know can't hurt you."

Questions

1. Is there anything in Bok's opening paragraph that prepares the reader for Bok's own position on whether or not lying is ever justifiable?
2. List the reasons Bok offers on behalf of telling the truth to patients. Are some of these reasons presented more convincingly than others? If any are unconvincing, rewrite them to make them more convincing.
3. Suppose Bok's last sentence was revised to read thus: "In medicine, law, government, and the social sciences, what you don't know *can* hurt you." Which version do you prefer, and why?
4. "What you don't know can't hurt you." Weigh the truth of this assertion in your own life. Were there instances of a truth being withheld from you that did hurt you? Were there occasions when you were told a truth that you now judge would have been better withheld? On the whole, do you come out in favor of the assertion, against it, or somewhere in between?
5. How much should adopted children be told about their biological parents? Consider reasons both for and against telling all. Use not only your own experiences and opinions but those of others, such as friends and classmates. If you read some relevant books or articles, see pages 362–94 on acknowledging sources.

The Gaucho and the City: Stories of Horsemen

Jorge Luis Borges

---

1   They are many and they may be countless. My first story is quite modest; those that follow will lend it greater depth.

2   A rancher from Uruguay had bought a country establishment

(I am sure this is the word he used) in the province of Buenos Aires. From Paso de los Toros, in the middle of Uruguay, he brought a horse breaker, a man who had his complete trust but was extremely shy. The rancher put the man up in an inn near the Once markets. Three days later, on going to see him, the rancher found his horseman brewing maté in his room on the upper floor. When asked what he thought of Buenos Aires, the man admitted that he had not once stuck his head out in the street.

3   The second story is not much different. In 1903, Aparicio Saravia staged an uprising in the Uruguayan provinces; at a certain point of the campaign, it was feared that his men might break into Montevideo. My father, who happened to be there at the time, went to ask advice of a relative of his, the historian Luis Melián Lafinur, only to be told that there was no danger "because the gaucho stands in fear of cities." In fact, Saravia's troops did change their route, and somewhat to his amazement my father found out that the study of history could be useful as well as pleasurable.

4   My third story also belongs to the oral tradition of my family. Toward the end of 1870, forces of the Entre Ríos caudillo, López Jordán, commanded by a gaucho who was called (because he had a bullet embedded in him) "El Chumbiao," surrounded the city of Paraná. One night, catching the garrison off guard, the rebels broke through the defenses and rode right around the central square, whooping like Indians and hurling insults. Then, still shouting and whistling, they galloped off. To them war was not a systematic plan of action but a manly sport.

5   The fourth of these stories, and my last, comes from the pages of an excellent book, *L'Empire des Steppes* (1939), by the Orientalist René Grousset. Two passages from the second chapter are particularly relevant. Here is the first:

> Genghis Khan's war against the Chin, begun in 1211, was the last—with brief periods of truce—until his death (1227), only to be finished by his successor (1234). With their mobile cavalry, the Mongols could devastate the countryside and open settlements, but for a long time they knew nothing of the art of taking towns fortified by Chinese engineers. Besides, they fought in China as on the steppe, in a series of raids, after which they withdrew with their booty, leaving the Chinese behind them to reoccupy their towns, rebuild the ruins, repair the breaches in the walls, and reconstruct the fortifications, so that in the course of that war the Mongol generals found themselves obliged to reconquer the same places two or three times.

Here is the second passage:

> The Mongols took Peking, massacred the whole population, looted
> the houses, and then set fire to them. The devastation lasted a
> month. Clearly, the nomads had no idea what to do with a great
> city or how to use it for the consolidation and expansion of their
> power. We have here a highly interesting case for specialists in
> human geography: the predicament of the peoples of the steppe
> when, without a period of transition, chance hands them old
> countries with an urban civilization. They burn and kill not out
> of sadism but because they find themselves out of their element
> and simply know no better.

6   I now give a story that all the authorities agree upon. During
Genghis Khan's last campaign, one of his generals remarked that
his new Chinese subjects were of no use to him, since they were
inept in war, and that, consequently, the wisest course was to ex-
terminate them all, raze the cities, and turn the almost boundless
Middle Kingdom into one enormous pasture for the Mongol horses.
In this way, at least, use could be made of the land, since nothing
else was of any value. The Khan was about to follow this counsel
when another adviser pointed out to him that it would be more
advantageous to levy taxes on the land and on goods. Civilization
was saved, the Mongols grew old in the cities that they had once
longed to destroy, and doubtless they ended up, in symmetrical gardens, appreciating the despised and peaceable arts of prosody and
pottery.

7   Distant in time and space, the stories I have assembled are really
one. The protagonist is eternal, and the wary ranch hand who spends
three days behind a door that looks out into a backyard—although
he has come down in life—is the same one who, with two bows, a
lasso made of horse hair, and a scimitar, was poised to raze and
obliterate the world's most ancient kingdom under the hooves of
his steppe pony. There is a pleasure in detecting beneath the masks
of time the eternal species of horseman and city. This pleasure, in
the case of these stories, may leave the Argentine with a melancholy
aftertaste, since (through Hernández's gaucho, Martín Fierro, or
through the weight of our past) we identify with the horseman,
who in the end is the loser. The centaurs defeated by the Lapiths;
the death of the shepherd Abel at the hand of Cain, who was a
farmer; the defeat of Napoleon's cavalry by British infantry at Wa-
terloo are all emblems and portents of such a destiny.

8   The horseman vanishing into the distance with a hint of defeat
is, in our literature, the gaucho. And so we read in *Martín Fierro:*

Cruz y Fierro de una estancia
una tropilla se arriaron;
por delante se la echaron
como criollos entendidos,
y pronto, sin ser sentidos,
por la frontera cruzaron.

Y cuando la habían pasao,
una madrugada clara,
le dijo Cruz que mirara
las últimas poblaciones;
y a Fierro dos lagrimones
le rodaron por la cara.

Y siguiendo el fiel del rumbo
se entraron en el desierto . . .

From a ranch, Cruz and Fierro rounded up a herd of horses and, being practical gauchos, drove it before them. Undetected, they soon crossed over the border.

After this was done, early one morning Cruz told Fierro to look back on the last settlements. Two big tears rolled down Fierro's face.

Then, continuing on their course, the men set off into the wilderness . . .

And in Lugones's *El Payador:*

In the fading twilight, turning brown as a dove's wing, we may have seen him vanish beyond the familiar hillocks, trotting on his horse, slowly, so that no one would think him afraid, under his gloomy hat and the poncho that hung from his shoulders in the limp folds of a flag at half mast.

And in *Don Segundo Sombra:*

Still smaller now, my godfather's silhouette appeared on the slope. My eyes concentrated on that tiny movement on the sleepy plain. He was about to reach the crest of the trail and vanish. He grew smaller and smaller, as if he were being whittled away from below. My gaze clung to the black speck of his hat, trying to preserve that last trace of him.

9   In the texts just quoted, space stands for time and history.

10   The figure of the man on the horse is, secretly, poignant. Under Attila, the "Scourge of God," under Genghis Khan, and under Tamerlane, the horseman tempestuously destroys and founds extensive empires, but all he destroys and founds is illusory. His work, like him, is ephemeral. From the farmer comes the word "culture" and from cities the word "civilization," but the horseman is a storm that fades away. In his book *Die Germanen der Völkerwanderung* (Stuttgart, 1939), Capelle remarks apropos of this that the Greeks, the Romans, and the Germans were agricultural peoples.

Questions

1. Are you a city person or a country (farm, mountain) person? Explain, in an essay of 250–500 words.
2. Briefly set forth a narrative of a kind of person (again, city, farm, mountain, or similar category) and then offer a paragraph of reflection on the kind. (If, like Borges, you can give more than one narrative, do so.)

---

*T*he Girls' Room

Laura Cunningham

1   When I heard she was coming to stay with us I was pleased. At age eight I thought of "grandmother" as a generic brand. My friends had grandmothers who seemed permanently bent over cookie racks. They were a source of constant treats and sweets. They were pinchers of cheeks, huggers and kissers. My own grandmother had always lived in a distant state; I had no memory of her when she decided to join the household recently established for me by my two uncles.

2   But with the example of my friends' grandmothers before me, I could hardly wait to have a grandmother of my own—and the cookies would be nice too. For while my uncles provided a cuisine that ranged from tuna croquettes to Swedish meatballs, they showed no signs of baking anything more elegant than a potato.

3   My main concern on the day of my grandmother's arrival was: How soon would she start the cookies? I remember her arrival, my uncles flanking her as they walked down the apartment corridor. She wore a hat, a tailored navy blue suit, an ermine stole. She held, tucked under her arm, the purple leather folder that contained her work in progress, a manuscript entitled "Philosophy for Women." She was preceded by her custom-made white trunk packed with purses, necklaces, earrings, dresses and more purple-inked pages that stress "the spiritual above the material."

4   She was small—at 5 feet 1 inch not much taller than I was— thin and straight, with a pug nose, one brown eye (the good eye) and one blue eye (the bad eye, frosted by cataracts). Her name was "Esther in Hebrew, Edna in English, and Etka in Russian." She preferred the Russian, referring to herself as "Etka from Minsk." It was not at once apparent that she was deaf in her left ear (the bad ear) but could hear with the right (the good ear). Because her good ear happened to be on the opposite side from the good eye, anyone who spoke to her had to run around her in circles, or sway to and fro, if eye contact and audibility were to be achieved simultaneously.

5   Etka from Minsk had arrived not directly from Minsk, as the black-eyed ermine stole seemed to suggest, but after many moves. She entered with the draft of family scandal at her back, blown out of her daughter's home after assaults upon her dignity. She held the evidence: an empty-socketed peacock pin. My cousin, an eleven-year-old boy, had surgically plucked out the rhinestone eyes. She could not be expected to stay where such acts occurred. She had to be among "human beings," among "real people" who could understand. We seemed to understand. We—my two uncles and I—encircled her, studied her vandalized peacock pin and vowed that such things would never happen with "us."

6   She patted my head—a good sign—and asked me to sing the Israeli national anthem. I did, and she handed me a dollar. My uncles went off to their jobs, leaving me alone with my grandmother for the first time. I looked at her, expecting her to start rolling out the cookie dough. Instead she suggested: "Now maybe you could fix me some lunch?"

7   It wasn't supposed to be this way, I thought, as I took her order: "toasted cheese and a sliced orange." Neither was she supposed to share my pink and orange bedroom, but she did. The bedroom soon exhibited a dual character—stuffed animals on one side, a hospital bed on the other. Within the household this cham-

ber was soon referred to as "the girls' room." The name, given by Uncle Abe, who saw no incongruity, only the affinity of sex, turned out to be apt, for what went on in the girls' room could easily have been labeled sibling rivalry if she had not been eighty and I eight. I soon found that I had acquired not a traditional grandmother but an aged kid sister.

8   The theft and rivalry began within days. My grandmother had given me her most cherished possession, a violet beaded bag. In return I gave her my heart-shaped "ivory" pin and matching earrings. That night she stole back the purse but insisted on keeping the pin and earrings. I turned to my uncles for mediation and ran up against unforeseen resistance. They thought my grandmother should keep the beaded bag; they didn't want to upset her.

9   I burned at the injustice of it and felt the heat of an uncomfortable truth: where I once had my uncles' undivided indulgence, they were now split as my grandmother and I vied for their attention. The household, formerly geared to my little-girl needs, was rearranged to accommodate hers. I suffered serious affronts—my grandmother, in a fit of frugality, scissored all the household blankets, including what a psychiatrist would have dubbed my "security" blanket, in half. "Now," she said, her good eye gleaming, "we have twice as many." I lay under my narrow slice of blanket and stared hopelessly up at the ceiling. I thought evilly of ways of getting my grandmother out of the apartment.

10   Matters worsened, as more and more of my trinkets disappeared. One afternoon I came home from school to find her squeezed into my unbuttoned favorite blouse. Rouged and beribboned, she insisted that the size 3 blouse was hers. Meanwhile, I was forced to adapt to her idiosyncracies: she covered everything black—from the dog to the telephone—with white doilies. She left saucers balanced on top of glasses. She sang nonstop. She tried to lock my dog out of the apartment.

11   The word that explained her behavior was "arteriosclerosis." She had forgotten so much that sometimes she would greet me with "You look familiar." At other times she'd ask, "What hotel is this?" My answer, shouted in her good ear, was: "We're not in a hotel! This is our apartment!" The response would be a hoot of laughter: "Then why are we in the ballroom?"

12   Finally we fought: arm-to-arm combat. I was shocked at her grip, steely as the bars that locked her into bed at night. Her good eye burned into mine and she said, "I'll tell." And she did. For the first time I was scolded. She had turned their love to disapproval, I thought, and how it chafed.

13   Eventually our rivalry mellowed into conspiracy. Within months we found we had uses for each other. I provided the lunches and secret, forbidden ice cream sundaes. She rewarded me with cold cash. She continued to take my clothes; I charged her competitive prices. I hated school; she paid me not to go. When I came home for lunch I usually stayed.

14   Our household endured the status quo for eight years: my uncles, my grandmother and I. Within the foursome rivalries and alliances shifted. I became my grandmother's friend and she became mine. We were the source of all the family comedy. When she said she wanted a college diploma we gave her one—with tinfoil stars and a "magna magna summa summa cum laude" inscription. We sang and performed skits. We talcum-powdered hair and wearing one of her old dresses, I would appear as her "long-lost friend." We had other themes, including a pen pal, "The Professor."

15   Of course, living with an elderly person had its raw aspects. When she was ill our girls' room took on the stark aura of a geriatrics ward. I imagined, to my shame, that neighbors could stare in through curtainless windows as I tended to my grandmother's most personal needs.

16   Yet, in these times of age segregation, with grandmothers sent off to impersonal places, I wonder if the love and the comedy weren't worth the intermittent difficulties? Certainly I learned what it might be to become old. And I took as much comfort as my grandmother did in a nightly exchange of Russian endearments—"Ya tebya lyublyu," "Ya tebya tozhe lyublyu—"I love you," "I love you, too."

17   If I sold my grandmother blouses and baubles, maybe she gave me the truth in exchange. Once, when we were alone in the girls' room, she turned to me, suddenly lucid, her good eye as bright as it would ever be—a look I somehow recognized as her "real" gaze—and said, "My life passes like a dream."

Questions

1. In the second sentence, what does Cunningham mean by "a generic brand"?
2. What is the title of Esther's manuscript? What is it about? Do you detect any irony in the way Cunningham conveys this information? Explain.
3. In the second sentence of paragraph 4, what is conveyed by putting the names within quotation marks?
4. Is paragraph 4—about Esther's physical disabilities—in bad taste? Explain.

5. In her last paragraph Cunningham says that perhaps her grand-mother gave her "the truth." What does she mean?
6. "I burned at the injustice of it and felt the heat of an uncom-fortable truth." Where in the narrative does Cunningham say this? What was the "truth"? If you remember a similar experi-ence, write a narrative that discloses both the experience and the truth on which it was based. Or, write an essay of 500 words on your own most potent experience of living with or near an elderly person.

On Keeping a Notebook

Joan Didion

1   " 'That woman Estelle,' " the note reads, " 'is partly the reason why George Sharp and I are separated today.' *Dirty crepe-de-Chine wrapper, hotel bar, Wilmington RR, 9:45 a.m. August Monday morning.*"

2   Since the note is in my notebook, it presumably has some meaning to me. I study it for a long while. At first I have only the most general notion of what I was doing on an August Monday morning in the bar of the hotel across from the Pennsylvania Rail-road station in Wilmington, Delaware (waiting for a train? missing one? 1960? 1961? why Wilmington?), but I do remember being there. The woman in the dirty crepe-de-Chine wrapper had come down from her room for a beer, and the bartender had heard be-fore the reason why George Sharp and she were separated today. "Sure," he said, and went on mopping the floor. "You told me." At the other end of the bar is a girl. She is talking, pointedly, not to the man beside her but to a cat lying in the triangle of sunlight cast through the open door. She is wearing a plaid silk dress from Peck & Peck, and the hem is coming down.

3   Here is what it is: the girl has been on the Eastern Shore, and now she is going back to the city, leaving the man beside her, and all she can see ahead are the viscous summer sidewalks and the 3 a.m. long-distance calls that will make her lie awake and then sleep drugged through all the steaming mornings left in August (1960? 1961?). Because she must go directly from the train to lunch in

New York, she wishes that she had a safety pin for the hem of the plaid silk dress, and she also wishes that she could forget about the hem and the lunch and stay in the cool bar that smells of disinfectant and malt and make friends with the woman in the crepe-de-Chine wrapper. She is afflicted by a little self-pity, and she wants to compare Estelles. That is what that was all about.

4   In fact I have abandoned altogether that kind of pointless entry; instead I tell what some would call lies. "That's simply not true," the members of my family frequently tell me when they come up against my memory of a shared event. "The party was *not* for you, the spider was *not* a black widow, *it wasn't that way at all.*" Very likely they are right, for not only have I always had trouble distinguishing between what happened and what merely might have happened, but I remain unconvinced that the distinction, for my purposes, matters. The cracked crab that I recall having for lunch the day my father came home from Detroit in 1945 must certainly be embroidery, worked into the day's pattern to lend verisimilitude; I was ten years old and would not now remember the cracked crab. The day's events did not turn on cracked crab. And yet it is precisely that fictitious crab that makes me see the afternoon all over again, a home movie run all too often, the father bearing gifts, the child weeping, an exercise in family love and guilt. Or that is what it was to me. Similarly, perhaps it never did snow that August in Vermont; perhaps there never were flurries in the night wind, and maybe no one else felt the ground hardening and summer already dead even as we pretended to bask in it, but that was how it felt to me, and it might as well have snowed, could have snowed, did snow.

5   *How it felt to me:* that is getting closer to the truth about a notebook. I sometimes delude myself about why I keep a notebook, imagine that some thrifty virtue derives from preserving everything observed. See enough and write it down, I tell myself, and then some morning when the world seems drained of wonder, some day when I am only going through the motions of doing what I am supposed to do, which is write—on that bankrupt morning I will simply open my notebook and there it will all be, a forgotten account with accumulated interest, paid passage back to the world out there: dialogue overheard in hotels and elevators and at the hat-check counter in Pavillon (one middle-aged man shows his hat check to another and says, "That's my old football number"); impressions of Bettina Aptheker and Benjamin Sonnenberg and Teddy ("Mr. Acapulco") Stauffer; careful *aperçus* about tennis bums and failed fashion models and Greek shipping heiresses, one of whom taught

me a significant lesson (a lesson I could have learned from F. Scott Fitzgerald, but perhaps we all must meet the very rich for ourselves) by asking, when I arrived to interview her in her orchid-filled sitting room on the second day of a paralyzing New York blizzard, whether it was snowing outside.

6   Why did I write it down? In order to remember, of course, but exactly what was it I wanted to remember? How much of it actually happened? Did any of it? Why do I keep a notebook at all? It is easy to deceive oneself on all those scores. The impulse to write things down is a peculiarly compulsive one, inexplicable to those who do not share it, useful only accidentally, only secondarily, in the way that any compulsion tries to justify itself. I suppose that it begins or does not begin in the cradle. Although I have felt compelled to write things down since I was five years old, I doubt that my daughter ever will, for she is a singularly blessed and accepting child, delighted with life exactly as life presents itself to her, unafraid to go to sleep and unafraid to wake up. Keepers of private notebooks are a different breed altogether, lonely and resistant rearrangers of things, anxious malcontents, children afflicted apparently at birth with some presentiment of loss.

7   My first notebook was a Big Five tablet, given to me by my mother with the sensible suggestion that I stop whining and learn to amuse myself by writing down my thoughts. She returned the tablet to me a few years ago; the first entry is an account of a woman who believed herself to be freezing to death in the Arctic night, only to find, when day broke, that she had stumbled onto the Sahara Desert, where she would die of the heat before lunch. I have no idea what turn of a five-year-old's mind could have prompted so insistently "ironic" and exotic a story, but it does reveal a certain predilection for the extreme which has dogged me into adult life; perhaps if I were analytically inclined I would find it a truer story than any I might have told about Donald Johnson's birthday party or the day my cousin Brenda put Kitty Litter in the aquarium.

8   So the point of my keeping a notebook has never been, nor is it now, to have an accurate factual record of what I have been doing or thinking. That would be a different impulse entirely, an instinct for reality which I sometimes envy but do not possess. At no point have I ever been able successfully to keep a diary; my approach to daily life ranges from the grossly negligent to the merely absent, and on those few occasions when I have tried dutifully to record a day's events, boredom has so overcome me that the results are mysterious at best. What is this business about "shopping, typing piece, dinner with E, depressed"? Shopping for what? Typing

what piece? Who is E? Was this "E" depressed, or was I depressed? Who cares?

9   I imagine, in other words, that the notebook is about other people. But of course it is not. I have no real business with what one stranger said to another at the hat-check counter in Pavillon; in fact I suspect that the line "That's my old football number" touched not my own imagination at all, but merely some memory of something once read, probably "The Eighty-Yard Run." Nor is my concern with a woman in a dirty crepe-de-Chine wrapper in a Wilmington bar. My stake is always, of course, in the unmentioned girl in the plaid silk dress. *Remember what it was to be me:* that is always the point.

10   It is a difficult point to admit. We are brought up in the ethic that others, any others, all others, are by definition more interesting than ourselves; taught to be diffident, just this side of self-effacing. ("You're the least important person in the room and don't forget it," Jessica Mitford's governess would hiss in her ear on the advent of any social occasion; I copied that into my notebook because it is only recently that I have been able to enter a room without hearing some such phrase in my inner ear.) Only the very young and the very old may recount their dreams at breakfast, dwell upon self, interrupt with memories of beach picnics and favorite Liberty lawn dresses and the rainbow trout in a creek near Colorado Springs. The rest of us are expected, rightly, to affect absorption in other people's favorite dresses, other people's trout.

11   And so we do. But our notebooks give us away, for however dutifully we record what we see around us, the common denominator of all we see is always, transparently, shamelessly, the implacable "I." We are not talking here about the kind of notebook that is patently for public consumption, a structural conceit for binding together a series of graceful *pensées;* we are talking about something private, about bits of the mind's string too short to use, an indiscriminate and erratic assemblage with meaning only for its maker.

12   And sometimes even the maker has difficulty with the meaning. There does not seem to be, for example, any point in my knowing for the rest of my life that, during 1964, 720 tons of soot fell on every square mile of New York City, yet there it is in my notebook, labeled "FACT." Nor do I really need to remember that Ambrose Bierce liked to spell Leland Stanford's name "£eland $tanford" or that "smart women almost always wear black in Cuba," a fashion hint without much potential for practical application. And does not the relevance of these notes seem marginal at best?:

In the basement museum of the Inyo County Courthouse in Independence, California, sign pinned to a mandarin coat: "This MANDARIN COAT was often worn by Mrs. Minnie S. Brooks when giving lectures on her TEAPOT COLLECTION."

Redhead getting out of car in front of Beverly Wilshire Hotel, chinchilla stole, Vuitton bags and tags reading:

MRS. LOU FOX

HOTEL SAHARA

VEGAS

13   Well, perhaps not entirely marginal. As a matter of fact, Mrs. Minnie S. Brooks and her MANDARIN COAT pull me back into my own childhood, for although I never knew Mrs. Brooks and did not visit Inyo County until I was thirty, I grew up in just such a world, in houses cluttered with Indian relics and bits of gold ore and ambergris and the souvenirs my Aunt Mercy Farnsworth brought back from the Orient. It is a long way from that world to Mrs. Lou Fox's world, where we all live now, and is it not just as well to remember that? Might not Mrs. Minnie S. Brooks help me to remember what I am? Might not Mrs. Lou Fox help me to remember what I am not?

14   But sometimes the point is harder to discern. What exactly did I have in mind when I noted down that it cost the father of someone I know $650 a month to light the place on the Hudson in which he lived before the Crash? What use was I planning to make of this line by Jimmy Hoffa: "I may have my faults, but being wrong ain't one of them"? And although I think it interesting to know where the girls who travel with the Syndicate have their hair done when they find themselves on the West Coast, will I ever make suitable use if it? Might I not be better off just passing it on to John O'Hara? What is a recipe for sauerkraut doing in my notebook? What kind of magpie keeps this notebook? *"He was born the night the Titanic went down."* That seems a nice enough line, and I even recall who said it, but is it not really a better line in life than it could ever be in fiction?

15   But of course that is exactly it: not that I should ever use the line, but that I should remember the woman who said it and the afternoon I heard it. We were on her terrace by the sea, and we were finishing the wine left from lunch, trying to get what sun there was, a California winter sun. The woman whose husband was born the night the *Titanic* went down wanted to rent her house, wanted to go back to her children in Paris. I remember wishing that I could

afford the house, which cost $1,000 a month. "Someday you will," she said lazily. "Someday it all comes." There in the sun on her terrace it seemed easy to believe in someday, but later I had a low-grade afternoon hangover and ran over a black snake on the way to the supermarket and was flooded with inexplicable fear when I heard the checkout clerk explaining to the man ahead of me why she was finally divorcing her husband. "He left me no choice," she said over and over as she punched the register. "He has a little seven-month-old baby by her, he left me no choice." I would like to believe that my dread then was for the human condition, but of course it was for me, because I wanted a baby and did not then have one and because I wanted to own a house that cost $1,000 a month to rent and because I had a hangover.

16   It all comes back. Perhaps it is difficult to see the value in having one's self back in that kind of mood, but I do see it; I think we are well advised to keep on nodding terms with the people we used to be, whether we find them attractive company or not. Otherwise they turn up unannounced and surprise us, come hammering on the mind's door at 4 a.m. of a bad night and demand to know who deserted them, who betrayed them, who is going to make amends. We forget all too soon the things we thought we could never forget. We forget the loves and the betrayals alike, forget what we whispered and what we screamed, forget who we were. I have already lost touch with a couple of people I used to be; one of them, a seventeen-year-old, presents little threat, although it would be of some interest to me to know again what it feels like to sit on a river levee drinking vodka-and-orange-juice and listening to Les Paul and Mary Ford and their echoes sing "How High the Moon" on the car radio. (You see I still have the scenes, but I no longer perceive myself among those present, no longer could even improvise the dialogue.) The other one, a twenty-three-year-old, bothers me more. She was always a good deal of trouble, and I suspect she will reappear when I least want to see her, skirts too long, shy to the point of aggravation, always the injured party, full of recriminations and little hurts and stories I do not want to hear again, at once saddening me and angering me with her vulnerability and ignorance, an apparition all the more insistent for being so long banished.

17   It is a good idea, then, to keep in touch, and I suppose that keeping in touch is what notebooks are all about. And we are all on our own when it comes to keeping those lines open to ourselves: your notebook will never help me, nor mine you. *"So what's new in the whiskey business?"* What could that possibly mean to you?

To me it means a blonde in a Pucci bathing suit sitting with a couple of fat men by the pool at the Beverly Hills Hotel. Another man approaches, and they all regard one another in silence for a while. "So what's new in the whiskey business?" one of the fat men finally says by way of welcome, and the blonde stands up, arches one foot and dips it in the pool, looking all the while at the cabaña where Baby Pignatari is talking on the telephone. That is all there is to that, except that several years later I saw the blonde coming out of Saks Fifth Avenue in New York with her California complexion and a voluminous mink coat. In the harsh wind that day she looked old and irrevocably tired to me, and even the skins in the mink coat were not worked the way they were doing them that year, not the way she would have wanted them done, and there is the point of the story. For a while after that I did not like to look in the mirror, and my eyes would skim the newspapers and pick out only the deaths, the cancer victims, the premature coronaries, the suicides, and I stopped riding the Lexington Avenue IRT because I noticed for the first time that all the strangers I had seen for years—the man with the Seeing Eye dog, the spinster who read the classified pages every day, the fat girl who always got off with me at Grand Central—looked older than they once had.

18   It all comes back. Even that recipe for sauerkraut: even that brings it back. I was on Fire Island when I first made that sauerkraut, and it was raining, and we drank a lot of bourbon and ate the sauerkraut and went to bed at ten, and I listened to the rain and the Atlantic and felt safe. I made the sauerkraut again last night and it did not make me feel any safer, but that is, as they say, another story.

Questions

1. In the sixth paragraph, beginning "Why did I write it down?" Didion says that "it is easy to deceive oneself" about the reasons for keeping a notebook. What self-deceptive reasons does she go on to give? What others can be added? And exactly why *does* she keep a notebook? (Didion in her last three paragraphs—and especially in the first two of these—makes explicit her reasons, but try to state her reasons in a paragraph of your own.)

2. In paragraph 5 Didion refers to a lesson she might have learned from F. Scott Fitzgerald and goes on to say, "but perhaps we all must meet the very rich for ourselves." If you have read a

book by Fitzgerald, explain (in a paragraph) the point to someone who doesn't get it.
3. In paragraph 13 Didion says, "It is a long way from that world
to Mrs. Lou Fox's world, where we all live now." What does
she mean?
4. If you keep a notebook (or diary or journal), explain in one to
three paragraphs why you keep it. Following Didion's example,
use one entry or two to illustrate the notebook's usefulness to
you. If you don't keep a notebook, explain in one to three paragraphs why you don't, and explain what effect, if any, Didion's
essay had on you. Do you now think it would be a good idea
to keep a notebook? Or did the essay reinforce your belief that
there's nothing useful in it for you? Explain.

A Few Words About Breasts: Shaping Up Absurd
Nora Ephron

1   I have to begin with a few words about androgyny. In grammar school, in the fifth and sixth grades, we were all tyrannized by
a rigid set of rules that supposedly determined whether we were
boys or girls. The episode in *Huckleberry Finn* where Huck is disguised as a girl and gives himself away by the way he threads a
needle and catches a ball—that kind of thing. We learned that the
way you sat, crossed your legs, held a cigarette and looked at your
nails, your wristwatch, the way you did these things instinctively
was absolute proof of your sex. Now obviously most children did
not take this literally, but I did. I thought that just one slip, just
one incorrect cross of my legs or flick of an imaginary cigarette ash
would turn me from whatever I was into the other thing; that would
be all it took, really. Even though I was outwardly a girl and had
many of the trappings generally associated with the field of girl-
dom—a girl's name, for example, and dresses, my own telephone,
an autograph book—I spent the early years of my adolescence absolutely certain that I might at any point gum it up. I did not feel
at all like a girl. I was boyish. I was athletic, ambitious, outspoken,
competitive, noisy, rambunctious. I had scabs on my knees and my

socks slid into my loafers and I could throw a football. I wanted desperately not to be that way, not to be a mixture of both things but instead just one, a girl, a definite indisputable girl. As soft and as pink as a nursery. And nothing would do that for me, I felt, but breasts.

2   I was about six months younger than everyone in my class, and so for about six months after it began, for six months after my friends had begun to develop—that was the word we used, develop—I was not particularly worried. I would sit in the bathtub and look down at my breasts and know that any day now, any second now, they would start growing like everyone else's. They didn't. "I want to buy a bra," I said to my mother one night. "What for?" she said. My mother was really hateful about bras, and by the time my third sister had gotten to that point where she was ready to want one, my mother had worked the whole business into a comedy routine. "Why not use a Band-Aid instead?" she would say. It was a source of great pride to my mother that she had never even had to wear a brassiere until she had her fourth child, and then only because her gynecologist made her. It was incomprehensible to me that anyone would ever be proud of something like that. It was the 1950's, for God's sake. Jane Russell. Cashmere sweaters. Couldn't my mother see that? *"I am too old to wear an undershirt."* Screaming. Weeping. Shouting. "Then don't wear an undershirt," said my mother. "But I want to buy a bra." "What for?"

3   I suppose that for most girls, breasts, brassieres, that entire thing, has more trauma, more to do with the coming of adolescence, of becoming a woman, than anything else. Certainly more than getting your period, although that too was traumatic, symbolic. But you could *see* breasts; they were there; they were visible. Whereas a girl could claim to have her period for months before she actually got it and nobody would ever know the difference. Which is exactly what I did. All you had to do was make a great fuss over having enough nickels for the Kotex machine and walk around clutching your stomach and moaning for three to five days a month about The Curse and you could convince anybody. There is a school of thought somewhere in the women's lib/women's mag/ gynecology establishment that claims that menstrual cramps are purely psychological, and I lean toward it. Not that I didn't have them finally. Agonizing cramps, heating-pad cramps, go-down-to-the-school-nurse-and-lie-on-the-cot cramps. But unlike any pain I had ever suffered, I adored the pain of cramps, welcomed it, wallowed in it, bragged about it. "I can't go. I have cramps." "I can't do that. I have cramps." And most of all, gigglingly, blushingly: "I

can't swim. I have cramps." Nobody ever used the hard-core word. Menstruation. God, what an awful word. Never that. "I have cramps."

4   The morning I first got my period, I went into my mother's bedroom to tell her. And my mother, my utterly-hateful-about-bras mother, burst into tears. It was really a lovely moment, and I remember it so clearly not just because it was one of the two times I ever saw my mother cry on my account (the other was when I was caught being a six-year-old kleptomaniac), but also because the incident did not mean to me what it meant to her. Her little girl, her firstborn, had finally become a woman. That was what she was crying about. My reaction to the event, however, was that I might well be a woman in some scientific, textbook sense (and could at least stop faking every month and stop wasting all those nickels). But in another sense—in a visible sense—I was as androgynous and as liable to tip over into boyhood as ever.

5   I started with a 28AA bra. I don't think they made them any smaller in those days, although I gather that now you can buy bras for five year olds that don't have any cups whatsoever in them; trainer bras they are called. My first brassiere came from Robinson's Department Store in Beverly Hills. I went there alone, shaking, positive they would look me over and smile and tell me to come back next year. An actual fitter took me into the dressing room and stood over me while I took off my blouse and tried the first one on. The little puffs stood out on my chest. "Lean over," said the fitter (to this day I am not sure what fitters in bra departments do except to tell you to lean over). I leaned over, with the fleeting hope that my breasts would miraculously fall out of my body and into the puffs. Nothing.

6   "Don't worry about it," said my friend Libby some months later, when things had not improved. "You'll get them after you're married."

7   "What are you talking about?" I said.

8   "When you get married," Libby explained, "your husband will touch your breasts and rub them and kiss them and they'll grow."

9   That was the killer. Necking I could deal with. Intercourse I could deal with. But it had never crossed my mind that a man was going to touch my breasts, that breasts had something to do with all that, petting, my God they never mentioned petting in my little sex manual about the fertilization of the ovum. I became dizzy. For I knew instantly—as naïve as I had been only a moment before—that only part of what she was saying was true: the touching, rubbing, kissing part, not the growing part. And I knew that no one

would ever want to marry me. I had no breasts. I would never have breasts.

10   My best friend in school was Diana Raskob. She lived a block from me in a house full of wonders. English muffins, for instance. The Raskobs were the first people in Beverly Hills to have English muffins for breakfast. They also had an apricot tree in the back, and a badminton court, and a subscription to *Seventeen* magazine, and hundreds of games like Sorry and Parcheesi and Treasure Hunt and Anagrams. Diana and I spent three or four afternoons a week in their den reading and playing and eating. Diana's mother's kitchen was full of the most colossal assortment of junk food I have ever been exposed to. My house was full of apples and peaches and milk and homemade chocolate-chip cookies—which were nice, and good for you, but-not-right-before-dinner-or-you'll-spoil-your-appetite. Diana's house had nothing in it that was good for you, and what's more, you could stuff it in right up until dinner and nobody cared. Bar-B-Q potato chips (they were the first in them, too), giant bottles of ginger ale, fresh popcorn with melted butter, hot fudge sauce on Baskin-Robbins jamoca ice cream, powdered-sugar doughnuts from Van de Kamps. Diana and I had been best friends since we were seven; we were about equally popular in school (which is to say, not particularly), we had about the same success with boys (extremely intermittent) and we looked much the same. Dark. Tall. Gangly.

11   It is September, just before school begins. I am eleven years old, about to enter the seventh grade, and Diana and I have not seen each other all summer. I have been to camp and she has been somewhere like Banff with her parents. We are meeting, as we often do, on the street midway between our two houses and we will walk back to Diana's and eat junk and talk about what has happened to each of us that summer. I am walking down Walden Drive in my jeans and my father's shirt hanging out and my old red loafers with the socks falling into them and coming toward me is . . . I take a deep breath . . . a young woman. Diana. Her hair is curled and she has a waist and hips and a bust and she is wearing a straight skirt, an article of clothing I have been repeatedly told I will be unable to wear until I have the hips to hold it up. My jaw drops, and suddenly I am crying, crying hysterically, can't catch my breath sobbing. My best friend has betrayed me. She has gone ahead without me and done it. She has shaped up.

12   Here are some things I did to help:

13   Bought a Mark Eden Bust Developer.

14   Slept on my back for four years.

15   Splashed cold water on them every night because some French actress said in *Life* magazine that that was what *she* did for her perfect bustline.

16   Ultimately, I resigned myself to a bad toss and began to wear padded bras. I think about them now, think about all those years in high school I went around in them, my three padded bras, every single one of them with different sized breasts. Each time I changed bras I changed sizes: one week nice perky but not too obtrusive breasts, the next medium-sized slightly pointed ones, the next week knockers, true knockers; all the time, whatever size I was, carrying around this rubberized appendage on my chest that occasionally crashed into a wall and was poked inward and had to be poked outward—I think about all that and wonder how anyone kept a straight face through it. My parents, who normally had no restraints about needling me—why did they say nothing as they watched my chest go up and down? My friends, who would periodically inspect my breasts for signs of growth and reassure me—why didn't they at least counsel consistency?

17   And the bathing suits. I die when I think about the bathing suits. That was the era when you could lay an uninhabited bathing suit on the beach and someone would make a pass at it. I would put one on, an absurd swimsuit with its enormous bust built into it, the bones from the suit stabbing me in the rib cage and leaving little red welts on my body, and there I would be, my chest plunging straight downward absolutely vertically from my collarbone to the top of my suit and then suddenly, wham, out came all that padding and material and wiring absolutely horizontally.

18   Buster Klepper was the first boy who ever touched them. He was my boyfriend my senior year of high school. There is a picture of him in my high-school yearbook that makes him look quite attractive in a Jewish, horn-rimmed glasses sort of way, but the picture does not show the pimples, which were air-brushed out, or the dumbness. Well, that isn't really fair. He wasn't dumb. He just wasn't terribly bright. His mother refused to accept it, refused to accept the relentlessly average report cards, refused to deal with her son's inevitable destiny in some junior college or other. "He was tested," she would say to me, apropos of nothing, "and it came out 145. That's near-genius." Had the word underachiever been coined, she probably would have lobbed that one at me, too. Anyway, Buster was really very sweet—which is, I know, damning with faint praise, but there it is. I was the editor of the front page of the high-school newspaper and he was editor of the back page; we had to work together, side by side, in the print shop, and that was how it started.

On our first date, we went to see *April Love* starring Pat Boone. Then we started going together. Buster had a green coupe, a 1950 Ford with an engine he had handchromed until it shone, dazzled, reflected the image of anyone who looked into it, anyone usually being Buster polishing it or the gas-station attendants he constantly asked to check the oil in order for them to be overwhelmed by the sparkle on the valves. The car also had a boot stretched over the back seat for reasons I never understood; hanging from the rear-view mirror, as was the custom, was a pair of angora dice. A previous girl friend named Solange who was famous throughout Beverly Hills High School for having no pigment in her right eyebrow had knitted them for him. Buster and I would ride around town, the two of us seated to the left of the steering wheel. I would shift gears. It was nice.

19   There was necking. Terrific necking. First in the car, overlooking Los Angeles from what is now the Trousdale Estates. Then on the bed of his parents' cabana at Ocean House. Incredibly wonderful, frustrating necking, I loved it, really, but no further than necking, please don't, please, because there I was absolutely terrified of the general implications of going-a-step-further with a near-dummy and also terrified of his finding out there was next to nothing there (which he knew, of course; he wasn't that dumb).

20   I broke up with him at one point. I think we were apart for about two weeks. At the end of that time I drove down to see a friend at a boarding school in Palos Verdes Estates and a disc jockey played *April Love* on the radio four times during the trip. I took it as a sign. I drove straight back to Griffith Park to a golf tournament Buster was playing in (he was the sixth-seeded teen-age golf player in Southern California) and presented myself back to him on the green of the 18th hole. It was all very dramatic. That night we went to a drive-in and I let him get his hand under my protuberances and onto my breasts. He really didn't seem to mind at all.

21   *"Do you want to marry my son?" the woman asked me.*

"Yes," I said.

I was nineteen years old, a virgin, going with this woman's son, this big strange woman who was married to a Lutheran minister in New Hampshire and pretended she was Gentile and had this son, by her first husband, this total fool of a son who ran the hero-sandwich concession at Harvard Business School and whom for one moment one December in New Hampshire I said—as much out of politeness as anything else—that I wanted to marry.

"Fine," she said. "Now, here's what you do. Always make sure you're on top of him so you won't seem so small. My bust is very

large, you see, so I always lie on my back to make it look smaller,
but you'll have to be on top most of the time."
   I nodded. *"Thank you,"* I said.
   "I have a book for you to read," she went on. *"Take it with*
you when you leave. Keep it." She went to the bookshelf, found it,
and gave it to me. It was a book on frigidity.
   "Thank you," I said.

22   That is a true story. Everything in this article is a true story,
but I feel I have to point out that that story in particular is true. It
happened on December 30, 1960. I think about it often. When it
first happened, I naturally assumed that the woman's son, my boyfriend, was responsible. I invented a scenario where he had had a
little heart-to-heart with his mother and had confessed that his only
objection to me was that my breasts were small; his mother then
took it upon herself to help out. Now I think I was wrong about
the incident. The mother was acting on her own, I think: that was
her way of being cruel and competitive under the guise of being
helpful and maternal. You have small breasts, she was saying;
therefore you will never make him as happy as I have. Or you
have small breasts; therefore you will doubtless have sexual problems.
Or you have small breasts; therefore you are less woman than I
am. She was, as it happens, only the first of what seems to me to
be a never-ending string of women who have made competitive remarks to me about breast size. "I would love to wear a dress like
that," my friend Emily says to me, "but my bust is too big." Like
that. Why do women say these things to me? Do I attract these
remarks the way other women attract married men or alcoholics or
homosexuals? This summer, for example, I am at a party in East
Hampton and I am introduced to a woman from Washington. She
is a minor celebrity, very pretty and Southern and blonde and outspoken and I am flattered because she has read something I have
written. We are talking animatedly, we have been talking no more
than five minutes, when a man comes up to join us. "Look at the
two of us," the woman says to the man, indicating me and her.
"The two of us together couldn't fill an A cup." Why does she say
that? It isn't even true, dammit, so why? Is she even more addled
than I am on this subject? Does she honestly believe there is something wrong with her size breasts, which, it seems to me, now that
I look hard at them, are just right. Do I unconsciously bring out
competitiveness in women? In that form? What did I do to deserve
it?

23   As for men.

24   There were men who minded and let me know they minded.

There were men who did not mind. In any case, I always minded.

25   And even now, now that I have been countlessly reassured that my figure is a good one, now that I am grown up enough to understand that most of my feelings have very little to do with the reality of my shape, I am nonetheless obsessed by breasts. I cannot help it. I grew up in the terrible Fifties—with rigid stereotypical sex roles, the insistence that men be men and dress like men and women be women and dress like women, the intolerance of androgyny—and I cannot shake it, cannot shake my feelings of inadequacy. Well, that time is gone, right? All those exaggerated examples of breast worship are gone, right? Those women were freaks, right? I know all that. And yet, here I am, stuck with the psychological remains of it all, stuck with my own peculiar version of breast worship. You probably think I am crazy to go on like this: here I have set out to write a confession that is meant to hit you with the shock of recognition and instead you are sitting there thinking I am thoroughly warped. Well, what can I tell you? If I had had them, I would have been a completely different person. I honestly believe that.

26   After I went into therapy, a process that made it possible for me to tell total strangers at cocktail parties that breasts were the hang-up of my life, I was often told that I was insane to have been bothered by my condition. I was also frequently told, by close friends, that I was extremely boring on the subject. And my girl friends, the ones with nice big breasts, would go on endlessly about how their lives had been far more miserable than mine. Their bra straps were snapped in class. They couldn't sleep on their stomachs. They were stared at whenever the word "mountain" cropped up in geography. And *Evangeline,* good God what they went through every time someone had to stand up and recite the Prologue to Longfellow's *Evangeline:* ". . . *stand like druids of eld . . . With beards that rest on their bosoms."* It was much worse for them, they tell me. They had a terrible time of it, they assure me. I don't know how lucky I was, they say.

27   I have thought about their remarks, tried to put myself in their place, considered their point of view. I think they are full of shit.

Questions

1. In her first paragraph Ephron says that Huck Finn gives himself away by his manner of threading a needle and catching a ball. In what ways does a boy supposedly differ from a girl in performing these activities? And how do they supposedly differ in the other activities that Ephron mentions in this paragraph?

2. Toward the end of the second paragraph Ephron writes several sentence fragments. How can you justify them?
3. Is the essay offensive? If so, why, and if not, why not?
4. On the basis of this essay characterize Nora Ephron, quoting a few words or phrases to support your characterization.

A *Proposal to Abolish Grading*

Paul Goodman

1   Let half a dozen of the prestigious Universities—Chicago, Stanford, the Ivy League—abolish grading, and use testing only and entirely for pedagogic purposes as teachers see fit.

2   Anyone who knows the frantic temper of the present schools will understand the transvaluation of values that would be effected by this modest innovation. For most of the students, the competitive grade has come to be the essence. The naïve teacher points to the beauty of the subject and the ingenuity of the research; the shrewd student asks if he is responsible for that on the final exam.

3   Let me at once dispose of an objection whose unanimity is quite fascinating. I think that the great majority of professors agree that grading hinders teaching and creates a bad spirit, going as far as cheating and plagiarizing. I have before me the collection of essays, *Examining in Harvard College,* and this is the consensus. It is uniformly asserted, however, that the grading is inevitable; for how else will the graduate schools, the foundations, the corporations *know* whom to accept, reward, hire? How will the talent scouts know whom to tap?

4   By testing the applicants, of course, according to the specific task-requirements of the inducting institution, just as applicants for the Civil Service or for licenses in medicine, law, and architecture are tested. Why should Harvard professors do the testing *for* corporations and graduate-schools?

5   The objection is ludicrous. Dean Whitla, of the Harvard Office of Tests, points out that the scholastic-aptitude and achievement tests used for *admission* to Harvard are a super-excellent index for all-around Harvard performance, better than high-school grades or

particular Harvard course-grades. Presumably, these college-entrance tests are tailored for what Harvard and similar institutions want. By the same logic, would not an employer do far better to apply his own job-aptitude test rather than to rely on the vagaries of Harvard section-men? Indeed, I doubt that many employers bother to look at such grades; they are more likely to be interested merely in the fact of a Harvard diploma, whatever that connotes to them. The grades have most of their weight with the graduate schools—here, as elsewhere, the system runs mainly for its own sake.

6   It is really necessary to remind our academics of the ancient history of Examination. In the medieval university, the whole point of the grueling trial of the candidate was whether or not to accept him as a peer. His disputation and lecture for the Master's was just that, a master-piece to enter the guild. It was not to make comparative evaluations. It was not to weed out and select for an extramural licensor or employer. It was certainly not to pit one young fellow against another in an ugly competition. My philosophic impression is that the medievals thought they knew what a good job of work was and that we are competitive because we do not know. But the more status is achieved by largely irrelevant competitive evaluation, the less will we ever know.

7   (Of course, our American examinations never did have this purely guild orientation, just as our faculties have rarely had absolute autonomy; the examining was to satisfy Overseers, Elders, distant Regents—and they as paternal superiors have always doted on giving grades, rather than accepting peers. But I submit that this set-up itself makes it impossible for the student to *become* a master, to *have* grown up, and to commence on his own. He will always be making A or B for some overseer. And in the present atmosphere, he will always be climbing on his friend's neck.)

8   Perhaps the chief objectors to abolishing grading would be the students and their parents. The parents should be simply disregarded; their anxiety has done enough damage already. For the students, it seems to me that a primary duty of the university is to deprive them of their props, their dependence on extrinsic valuation and motivation, and to force them to confront the difficult enterprise itself and finally lose themselves in it.

9   A miserable effect of grading is to nullify the various uses of testing. Testing, for both student and teacher, is a means of structuring, and also of finding out what is blank or wrong and what has been assimilated and can be taken for granted. Review—including high-pressure review—is a means of bringing together the fragments, so that there are flashes of synoptic insight.

10   There are several good reasons for testing, and kinds of test. But if the aim is to discover weakness, what is the point of down-grading and punishing it, and thereby inviting the student to con-ceal his weakness, by faking and bulling, if not cheating? The nat-ural conclusion of synthesis is the insight itself, not a grade for having had it. For the important purpose of placement, if one can establish in the student the belief that one is testing *not* to grade and make invidious comparisons but for his own advantage, the student should normally seek his own level, where he is challenged and yet capable, rather than trying to get by. If the student dares to accept himself as he is, a teacher's grade is a crude instrument compared with a student's self-awareness. But it is rare in our uni-versities that students are encouraged to notice objectively their vast confusion. Unlike Socrates, our teachers rely on power-drives rather than shame and ingenuous idealism.

11   Many students are lazy, so teachers try to goad or threaten them by grading. In the long run this must do more harm than good. Laziness is a character-defense. It may be a way of avoiding learning, in order to protect the conceit that one is already perfect (deeper, the despair that one *never* can). It may be a way of avoid-ing just the risk of failing and being down-graded. Sometimes it is a way of politely saying, "I won't." But since it is the authoritarian grown-up demands that have created such attitudes in the first place, why repeat the trauma? There comes a time when we must treat people as adult, laziness and all. It is one thing courageously to fire a do-nothing out of your class; it is quite another thing to evaluate him with a lordly F.

12   Most important of all, it is often obvious that balking in doing the work, especially among bright young people who get to great universities, means exactly what it says: The work does not suit me, not this subject, or not at this time, or not in this school, or not in school altogether. The student might not be bookish; he might be school-tired; perhaps his development ought now to take an-other direction. Yet unfortunately, if such a student is intelligent and is not sure of himself, he *can* be bullied into passing, and this obscures everything. My hunch is that I am describing a common situation. What a grim waste of young life and teacherly effort! Such a student will retain nothing of what he has "passed" in. Sometimes he must get mononucleosis to tell his story and be be-lieved.

13   And ironically, the converse is also probably commonly true. A student flunks and is mechanically weeded out, who is really ready and eager to learn in a scholastic setting, but he has not quite caught

on. A good teacher can recognize the situation, but the computer wreaks its will.

Questions

1. In his opening paragraph Goodman limits his suggestion about grading and testing to "half a dozen of the prestigious Universities." Does he offer any reason for this limitation? Can you?
2. In the third paragraph Goodman says that "the great majority of professors agree that grading hinders teaching." What evidence does he offer to support this claim? What arguments might be offered that grading assists teaching? Should Goodman have offered them?
3. Have grades helped you to learn or hindered you? Explain.

Women's Brains

Stephen Jay Gould

1   In the Prelude to *Middlemarch*, George Eliot lamented the unfulfilled lives of talented women:

> Some have felt that these blundering lives are due to the inconvenient indefiniteness with which the Supreme Power has fashioned the natures of women: if there were one level of feminine incompetence as strict as the ability to count three and no more, the social lot of women might be treated with scientific certitude.

2   Eliot goes on to discount the idea of innate limitation, but while she wrote in 1872, the leaders of European anthropometry were trying to measure "with scientific certitude" the inferiority of women. Anthropometry, or measurement of the human body, is not so fashionable a field these days, but it dominated the human sciences for much of the nineteenth century and remained popular until intelligence testing replaced skull measurement as a favored device for making invidious comparisons among races, classes, and sexes. Craniometry, or measurement of the skull, commanded the most attention and respect. Its unquestioned leader, Paul Broca (1824–

80), professor of clinical surgery at the Faculty of Medicine in Paris, gathered a school of disciples and imitators around himself. Their work, so meticulous and apparently irrefutable, exerted great influence and won high esteem as a jewel of nineteenth-century science.

3   Broca's work seemed particularly invulnerable to refutation. Had he not measured with the most scrupulous care and accuracy? (Indeed, he had. I have the greatest respect for Broca's meticulous procedure. His numbers are sound. But science is an inferential exercise, not a catalog of facts. Numbers, by themselves, specify nothing. All depends upon what you do with them.) Broca depicted himself as an apostle of objectivity, a man who bowed before facts and cast aside superstition and sentimentality. He declared that "there is no faith, however respectable, no interest, however legitimate, which must not accommodate itself to the progress of human knowledge and bend before truth." Women, like it or not, had smaller brains than men and, therefore, could not equal them in intelligence. This fact, Broca argued, may reinforce a common prejudice in male society, but it is also a scientific truth. L. Manouvrier, a black sheep in Broca's fold, rejected the inferiority of women and wrote with feeling about the burden imposed upon them by Broca's numbers:

> Women displayed their talents and their diplomas. They also invoked philosophical authorities. But they were opposed by *numbers* unknown to Condorcet or to John Stuart Mill. These numbers fell upon poor women like a sledge hammer, and they were accompanied by commentaries and sarcasms more ferocious than the most misogynist imprecations of certain church fathers. The theologians had asked if women had a soul. Several centuries later, some scientists were ready to refuse them a human intelligence.

4   Broca's argument rested upon two sets of data: the larger brains of men in modern societies, and a supposed increase in male superiority through time. His most extensive data came from autopsies performed personally in four Parisian hospitals. For 292 male brains, he calculated an average weight of 1,325 grams; 140 female brains averaged 1,144 grams for a difference of 181 grams, or 14 percent of the male weight. Broca understood, of course, that part of this difference could be attributed to the greater height of males. Yet he made no attempt to measure the effect of size alone and actually stated that it cannot account for the entire difference because we know, a priori, that women are not as intelligent as men (a premise that the data were supposed to test, not rest upon):

We might ask if the small size of the female brain depends exclusively upon the small size of her body. Tiedemann has proposed this explanation. But we must not forget that women are, on the average, a little less intelligent than men, a difference which we should not exaggerate but which is, nonetheless, real. We are therefore permitted to suppose that the relatively small size of the female brain depends in part upon her physical inferiority and in part upon her intellectual inferiority.

5   In 1873, the year after Eliot published *Middlemarch,* Broca measured the cranial capacities of prehistoric skulls from L'Homme Mort cave. Here he found a difference of only 99.5 cubic centimeters between males and females, while modern populations range from 129.5 to 220.7. Topinard, Broca's chief disciple, explained the increasing discrepancy through time as a result of differing evolutionary pressures upon dominant men and passive women:

> The man who fights for two or more in the struggle for existence, who has all the responsibility and the cares of tomorrow, who is constantly active in combating the environment and human rivals, needs more brain than the woman whom he must protect and nourish, the sedentary woman, lacking any interior occupations, whose role is to raise children, love, and be passive.

6   In 1879, Gustave Le Bon, chief misogynist of Broca's school, used these data to publish what must be the most vicious attack upon women in modern scientific literature (no one can top Aristotle). I do not claim his views were representative of Broca's school, but they were published in France's most respected anthropological journal. Le Bon concluded:

> In the most intelligent races, as among the Parisians, there are a large number of women whose brains are closer in size to those of gorillas than to the most developed male brains. This inferiority is so obvious that no one can contest it for a moment; only its degree is worth discussion. All psychologists who have studied the intelligence of women, as well as poets and novelists, recognize today that they represent the most inferior forms of human evolution and that they are closer to children and savages than to an adult, civilized man. They excel in fickleness, inconstancy, absence of thought and logic, and incapacity to reason. Without doubt there exist some distinguished women, very superior to the average man, but they are as exceptional as

the birth of any monstrosity, as, for example, of a gorilla with two heads; consequently, we may neglect them entirely.

7   Nor did Le Bon shrink from the social implications of his views. He was horrified by the proposal of some American reformers to grant women higher education on the same basis as men:

> A desire to give them the same education, and, as a consequence, to propose the same goals for them, is a dangerous chimera. . . . The day when, misunderstanding the inferior occupations which nature has given her, women leave the home and take part in our battles; on this day a social revolution will begin, and everything that maintains the sacred ties of the family will disappear.

Sound familiar? *

8   I have reexamined Broca's data, the basis for all this derivative pronouncement, and I find his numbers sound but his interpretation ill-founded, to say the least. The data supporting his claim for increased difference through time can be easily dismissed. Broca based his contention on the samples from L'Homme Mort alone—only seven male and six female skulls in all. Never have so little data yielded such far ranging conclusions.

9   In 1888, Topinard published Broca's more extensive data on the Parisian hospitals. Since Broca recorded height and age as well as brain size, we may use modern statistics to remove their effect. Brain weight decreases with age, and Broca's women were, on average, considerably older than his men. Brain weight increases with height, and his average man was almost half a foot taller than his average woman. I used multiple regression, a technique that allowed me to assess simultaneously the influence of height and age upon brain size. In an analysis of the data for women, I found that, at average male height and age, a woman's brain would weigh 1,212 grams. Correction for height and age reduces Broca's measured difference of 181 grams by more than a third, to 113 grams.

10   I don't know what to make of this remaining difference because I cannot assess other factors known to influence brain size in a major way. Cause of death has an important effect: degenerative

---

* When I wrote this essay, I assumed that Le Bon was a marginal, if colorful, figure. I have since learned that he was a leading scientist, one of the founders of social psychology, and best known for a seminal study on crowd behavior, still cited today (*La psychologie des foules*, 1895), and for his work on unconscious motivation.

disease often entails a substantial diminution of brain size. (This effect is separate from the decrease attributed to age alone.) Eugene Schreider, also working with Broca's data, found that men killed in accidents had brains weighing, on average, 60 grams more than men dying of infectious diseases. The best modern data I can find (from American hospitals) records a full 100-gram difference between death by degenerative arteriosclerosis and by violence or accident. Since so many of Broca's subjects were very elderly women, we may assume that lengthy degenerative disease was more common among them than among the men.

11   More importantly, modern students of brain size still have not agreed on a proper measure for eliminating the powerful effect of body size. Height is partly adequate, but men and women of the same height do not share the same body build. Weight is even worse than height, because most of its variation reflects nutrition rather than intrinsic size—fat versus skinny exerts little influence upon the brain. Manouvrier took up this subject in the 1880s and argued that muscular mass and force should be used. He tried to measure this elusive property in various ways and found a marked difference in favor of men, even in men and women of the same height. When he corrected for what he called "sexual mass," women actually came out slightly ahead in brain size.

12   Thus, the corrected 113-gram difference is surely too large; the true figure is probably close to zero and may as well favor women as men. And 113 grams, by the way, is exactly the average difference between a 5 foot 4 inch and a 6 foot 4 inch male in Broca's data. We would not (especially us short folks) want to ascribe greater intelligence to tall men. In short, who knows what to do with Broca's data? They certainly don't permit any confident claim that men have bigger brains than women.

13   To appreciate the social role of Broca and his school, we must recognize that his statements about the brains of women do not reflect an isolated prejudice toward a single disadvantaged group. They must be weighed in the context of a general theory that supported contemporary social distinctions as biologically ordained. Women, blacks, and poor people suffered the same disparagement, but women bore the brunt of Broca's argument because he had easier access to data on women's brains. Women were singularly denigrated but they also stood as surrogates for other disenfranchised groups. As one of Broca's disciples wrote in 1881: "Men of the black races have a brain scarcely heavier than that of white women." This juxtaposition extended into many other realms of

anthropological argument, particularly to claims that, anatomically and emotionally, both women and blacks were like white children—and that white children, by the theory of recapitulation, represented an ancestral (primitive) adult stage of human evolution. I do not regard as empty rhetoric the claim that women's battles are for all of us.

14   Maria Montessori did not confine her activities to educational reform for young children. She lectured on anthropology for several years at the University of Rome, and wrote an influential book entitled *Pedagogical Anthropology* (English edition, 1913). Montessori was no egalitarian. She supported most of Broca's work and the theory of innate criminality proposed by her compatriot Cesare Lombroso. She measured the circumference of children's heads in her schools and inferred that the best prospects had bigger brains. But she had no use for Broca's conclusions about women. She discussed Manouvrier's work at length and made much of his tentative claim that women, after proper correction of the data, had slightly larger brains than men. Women, she concluded, were intellectually superior, but men had prevailed heretofore by dint of physical force. Since technology has abolished force as an instrument of power, the era of women may soon be upon us: "In such an epoch there will really be superior human beings, there will really be men strong in morality and in sentiment. Perhaps in this way the reign of women is approaching, when the enigma of her anthropological superiority will be deciphered. Woman was always the custodian of human sentiment, morality and honor."

15   This represents one possible antidote to "scientific" claims for the constitutional inferiority of certain groups. One may affirm the validity of biological distinctions but argue that the data have been misinterpreted by prejudiced men with a stake in the outcome, and that disadvantaged groups are truly superior. In recent years, Elaine Morgan has followed this strategy in her *Descent of Woman,* a speculative reconstruction of human prehistory from the woman's point of view—and as farcical as more famous tall tales by and for men.

16   I prefer another strategy. Montessori and Morgan followed Broca's philosophy to reach a more congenial conclusion. I would rather label the whole enterprise of setting a biological value upon groups for what it is: irrelevant and highly injurious. George Eliot well appreciated the special tragedy that biological labeling imposed upon members of disadvantaged groups. She expressed it for people like herself—women of extraordinary talent. I would apply

it more widely—not only to those whose dreams are flouted but also to those who never realize that they may dream—but I cannot match her prose. In conclusion, then, the rest of Eliot's prelude to *Middlemarch*:

> The limits of variation are really much wider than anyone would imagine from the sameness of women's coiffure and the favorite love stories in prose and verse. Here and there a cygnet is reared uneasily among the ducklings in the brown pond, and never finds the living stream in fellowship with its own oary-footed kind. Here and there is born a Saint Theresa, foundress of nothing, whose loving heartbeats and sobs after an unattained goodness tremble off and are dispersed among hindrances instead of centering in some long-recognizable deed.

Questions

1. In paragraph 3, what does Gould mean when he says, "But science is an inferential exercise, not a catalog of facts"?
2. Gould quotes (paragraph 5) Topinard's explanation for the increasing discrepancy in the size of brains. Given your own understanding of evolution, what do you think of Topinard's explanation?
3. In paragraph 9 Gould says, "Brain weight decreases with age." Do you believe this? Why? How would one establish the truth or falsity of the assertion?
4. In paragraph 12 Gould says, "Thus, the corrected 113-gram difference is surely too large; the true figure is probably close to zero and may as well favor women as men." Why "thus"? What evidence or what assumptions prompt Gould to say that the figure is surely too large?
5. In paragraph 13 Gould says, "I do not regard as empty rhetoric the claim that women's battles are for all of us." What does this mean?
6. Also in paragraph 13 Gould refers to the "social role of Broca and his school." What does he mean by that? On the basis of this essay (and other essays of Gould's you may have read) try to formulate in a sentence or two the social role of Gould.

A Message *to* Garcia
Elbert Hubbard

---

1   In all this Cuban business[1] there is one man stands out on my memory like Mars at perihelion.[2]

When war broke out between Spain and the United States, it was very necessary to communicate quickly with the leader of the Insurgents. Garcia was somewhere in the mountain fastnesses of Cuba—no one knew where. No mail nor telegraph message could reach him. The President must secure his cooperation, and quickly.

What to do!

Some one said to the President, "There is a fellow by the name of Rowan will find Garcia for you, if anybody can."

5   Rowan was sent for and given a letter to be delivered to Garcia.

6   How "the fellow by the name of Rowan" took the letter, sealed it up in an oil-skin pouch, strapped it over his heart, in four days landed by night off the coast of Cuba from an open boat, disappeared into the jungle, and in three weeks came out on the other side of the Island, having traversed a hostile country on foot, and delivered his letter to Garcia, are things I have no special desire now to tell in detail. The point I wish to make is this: McKinley gave Rowan a letter to be delivered to Garcia; Rowan took the letter and did not ask "Where is he at?"

7   By the Eternal! there is a man whose form should be cast in deathless bronze and the statue placed in every college of the land. It is not book-learning young men need, nor instruction about this and that, but a stiffening of the vertebrae which will cause them to be loyal to a trust, to act promptly, concentrate their energies: do the thing—"Carry a message to Garcia."

---

[1] Hubbard wrote the essay in 1899, hence "all this Cuban business" refers to the Spanish-American War (1898) and to the peace settlement. Calixto Garcia y Iñigues (1839–1898) was a Cuban revolutionary whose advice was sought by President McKinley. Andrew S. Rowan located Garcia, who then conferred with McKinley in Washington, D.C., where Garcia died. (Editors' note)

[2] Mars at perihelion, i.e., Mars when it is nearest to the sun. (Editors' note)

8   General Garcia is dead now, but there are other Garcias. No man who has endeavored to carry out an enterprise where many hands were needed but has been well-nigh appalled at times by the imbecility of the average man—the inability or unwillingness to concentrate on a thing and do it. Slip-shod assistance, foolish inattention, dowdy indifference, & half-hearted work seem the rule; and no man succeeds, unless by hook or crook, or threat, he forces or bribes other men to assist him; or mayhap, God in his goodness performs a miracle, and sends him an Angel of Light for an assistant. You, reader, put this matter to a test: You are sitting now in your office—six clerks are within call. Summon any one and make this request: "Please look in the encyclopedia and make a brief memorandum for me concerning the life of Correggio."

9   Will the clerk quietly say, "Yes sir," and go do the task?

10   On your life he will not. He will look at you out of a fishy eye and ask one or more of the following questions:

Who was he?

Which encyclopedia?

Where is the encyclopedia?

Was I hired for that?

15   Don't you mean Bismarck?

What's the matter with Charlie doing it?

Is he dead?

Is there any hurry?

Shan't I bring you the book and let you look it up yourself?

20   What do you want to know for?

And I will lay you ten to one that after you have answered the questions, & explained how to find the information, and why you want it, the clerk will go off and get one of the other clerks to help him try to find Garcia—and then come back and tell you there is no such man. Of course I may lose my bet, but according to the Law of Average I will not.

Now if you are wise you will not bother to explain to your "assistant" that Correggio is indexed under the C's, not in the K's, but you will smile sweetly and say, "Never mind," and go look it up yourself.

And this incapacity for independent action, this moral stupidity, this infirmity of the will, this unwillingness to cheerfully catch hold and lift, are the things that put pure Socialism so far into the future. If men will not act for themselves, what will they do when the benefit of their effort is for all? A first-mate with knotted club seems necessary; and the dread of getting "the bounce" Saturday night, holds many a worker to his place. Advertise for a stenographer, and nine out of ten who apply can neither spell nor punctuate—and do not think it necessary to.

Can such a one write a letter to Garcia?

25   "You see that book-keeper," said the foreman to me in a large factory.

"Yes, what about him?"

"Well, he's a fine accountant, but if I'd send him up town on an errand, he might accomplish the errand all right, and on the other hand, might stop at four saloons on the way, and when he got to Main Street, would forget what he had been sent for."

Can such a man be entrusted to carry a message to Garcia?

We have recently been hearing much maudlin sympathy expressed for the "down-trodden denizen of the sweatshop" and the "homeless wanderer searching for honest employment," and with it all often go many hard words for the men in power.

30   Nothing is said about the employer who grows old before his time in a vain attempt to get frowsy ne'er-do-wells to do intelligent work, and his long, patient striving with "help" that does nothing but loaf when his back is turned. In every store and factory there is a constant weeding-out process going on. The employer is constantly sending away "help" that have shown their incapacity to further the interests of the business, and others are being taken on. No matter how good times are, this sorting continues, only if times are hard and work is scarce, the sorting is done finer—but out and forever out the incompetent and unworthy go. It is the survival of the fittest. Self-interest prompts every employer to keep the best—those who can carry a message to Garcia.

31   I know one man of really brilliant parts who has not the ability to manage a business of his own, and yet who is absolutely worthless to any one else, because he carries with him constantly the insane suspicion that his employer is oppressing, or intending to oppress him. He cannot give orders; and he will not receive them. Should a message be given him to take to Garcia, he would probably at once refer to you as a greedy, grasping Shylock, and tell you to "Take it yourself!" He regards all business men as rogues, and constantly uses the term "commercial" as an epithet. To-night this man walks the streets looking for work, the wind whistling through his thread-bare coat. No one who knows him dare employ him, for he is a regular fire-brand of discontent. He is impervious to reason, and the only thing that can impress him is the toe of a thick-soled No. 9 boot.

32   Of course I know that one so morally deformed is no less to be pitied than a physical cripple: but in our pitying, let us drop a tear, too, for the men who are striving to carry on a great enterprise, whose working hours are not limited by the whistle, and whose hair is fast turning white through the struggle to hold in line dowdy indifference, slip-shod imbecility, and the heartless ingratitude, which, but for their enterprise, would be both hungry and homeless.

33   Have I put the matter too strongly? Possibly I have; but when all the world has gone a-slumming I wish to speak a word of sympathy for the man who succeeds—the man who, against great odds, has directed the efforts of others, and having succeeded, finds there's nothing in it: nothing but bare board and clothes. I have carried a dinner pail and worked for day's wages, and I have also been an employer of labor, and I know there is something to be said on both sides. There is no excellence, per se, in poverty; rags are no recommendation; and all employers are not rapacious and high handed, any more than all poor men are virtuous. My heart goes out to the man who does his work when the "boss" is away, as well as when he is at home. And the man, who, when given a letter for Garcia, quietly takes the missive, without asking any idiotic questions, and with no lurking intention of chucking it into the nearest sewer, or of doing aught else but deliver it, never gets "laid off," nor has to go on a strike for higher wages. Civilization is one long anxious search for just such individuals. Anything such a man asks shall be granted. He is wanted in every city, town and village—in every office, shop, store and factory. The world cries out for such: he is needed, and is needed badly—the man who can carry a message to Garcia.

Questions

1. In paragraph 30 Hubbard invokes the phrase "survival of the fittest." Why? What does he mean?
2. In the first third of the twentieth century employers distributed to their employees millions of copies of this essay. The essay is apparently almost unknown today. Why?
3. If you did not know who Correggio was when you began this essay, did you look him up while reading the essay or immediately after finishing it? Why, or why not? If you didn't look him up, do you plan to? If you do look him up, you might think about whether Hubbard would offer him a job.

4. Under what circumstances would you go to work for Hubbard? Would you hire him to work for you? Why?

Soaps, Cynicism, and Mind Control: Randomness in Everyday Life

Elizabeth Janeway

1 What does the powerful teaching tool of television have to say to its viewers about desirable attitudes toward life and its problems? And what does the Media Establishment assume that *we* assume about the way this world functions? With these questions, I approached soap operas and evening series—programs that claimed to present ordinary existence, though heightened for drama and catering to everyone's curiosity about how the other half lives.

2 In between commercial breaks, I noted a deeply disturbing factor in so many of the dramas: the lack of any sense of process, of the eternal truth that events have consequences, and that people can and do influence what happens to them and to others. What I saw instead was a consistent, insistent demonstration of *randomness,* a statement that life is unpredictable and out of control. With rare exceptions what happens on-screen suggests that no one can trust her or his own judgment and (the other side of the same coin) that no one, friend, kin, or lover, is really trustworthy.

3 We may identify with the actors because we all face unpredictable events, but we get no clues to coping with them. No one seems talented at solving the puzzles of life: even J. R. Ewing was shot. Nobody shows us how to decide on the fidelity of kin or associates, no love is certain. Let a wedding date be set and you can be pretty sure the ceremony won't come off. Report a death and expect the corpse to show up in a future segment fleeing crime, amnesiac, or as survivor of a "fatal" plane crash. Says one of a pair of embracing lovers, "I don't know anything about you." Par for the course. Later in the same segment (of *Another World*) a young woman tells a young man she doesn't love him. But wait a minute! She has been hypnotized, it seems, in a program I missed, and here she is on tape

declaring she *does* love him to the hypnotist. Not only don't we/
they know anything about the others in their lives, they/we don't
understand ourselves either. The Guiding Lights we seek are shrouded
in fog.

4   Now drama, and indeed fiction as a whole, has always aimed
at surprising its audiences. But those surprises end by showing us
something we hadn't known, some truth, about existence. It may
be a tragic truth, but tragedy can strengthen us to face the future
because it explains and illustrates the processes that lead to defeat
instead of victory. And knowledge is power. Even when it tells us
some things can't be changed, it differentiates inevitability from po-
tentiality; and moreover, it gives us a chance to plan our own responses: we can't change the weather, but we can take an umbrella
when we go out. Our intervention in ongoing existence is shown to
be possible. Beginning with childhood fables and fairy tales, such
stories bring us useful messages about the workings of the real world
and what human beings can do to influence it.

5   That's not what the TV programs say. The people on the screen
are adrift in a world of happenstance, and the messages warn that
no action will do any good.

6   Certainly there's a lot of randomness in the world. Stable unchanging small-town life is fading from the American scene and
close ties to extended families are rare. Most of us meet a lot of
strangers from unfamiliar backgrounds. Women who have moved
into formerly all-male preserves have had to learn or invent patterns of relationships as well as new processes of doing things. These
women have begun to take risks and forget old lessons in helplessness. But daily there appears on the screen counsel that the world
is unpredictable, that one can't hope to plan or gain control of
events. Moreover when we see the rare realistic portrayal of work-
life (where competence, daring, and imagination may be rewarded),
attention is concentrated on the personal. Intimate relationships are
chancy and dangerous, comes the word, but they're the only things
that matter.

7   Randomness, like guilt, is a powerful tool for social control.
Survivors of the Holocaust and refugees from Stalin's "Gulag Ar-
chipelago" record how personality was deliberately broken down
by those in control disrupting their prisoners' normal expectations.
Guards separated consequences from action and thus persuaded
prisoners that it was hopeless for them to plan a particular behavior, hopeless for them to imagine a future. Survival became a matter
of utter chance. Inmates of the camps were thus reduced to subhu-
man, mindless robots who moved as they were told to.

8   Today in El Salvador (and who can say how many other places?), terror activates the randomness of danger. No one knows where the death squads will strike next, and therefore people can't take any reasonable action and expect to ensure greater safety. If safety exists at all, it lies in passivity and hiding. *Time* magazine quotes an expert on Central America in a recent issue: "Anybody can be killed with virtual impunity. You do not want to investigate because you might find out, and finding out can itself be fatal."

9   But it's not only in extreme situations that randomness can be used to promote self-policing. If the powerful can divide the majority of ordinary folk into disconnected, self-protecting individuals, they need not fear organized resistance. And when television suggests to a woman that even her friends had better not be trusted, it is denying comradeship, sisterhood—and joint action.

10   I don't suggest that this is a conscious media conspiracy intended to keep women and other groups in their subordinate places. *It doesn't need to be.* Standard practice and the mythic ideology that enforces it have always played up individual effort as a way of establishing one's value and one's deserts. For instance, the Supreme Court has underlined that message by limiting affirmative action remedies that can be awarded to a group or class. Legal recourse must now be sought by *individuals* rather than on a group basis. When the media repeats this message, it need only appeal to what we've often heard before: success means learning the rules and following them. Don't trust your colleagues. The big world of action is both dangerous and mysterious, you'll never really understand it. Stay out of it, sit still, don't try.

11   Will we follow that message more than two generations after women won the ballot? . . . Let us refuse the posture of the powerless. People who have begun to feel strong don't have to accept victimization.

Questions

1. In her second paragraph Janeway asserts that soap operas generally depict a world of randomness. Let's assume that you agree. Write a new third paragraph, in which you support this assertion by offering concrete examples drawn from a soap opera with which you are familiar. Or, if you disagree, write a paragraph in which you offer evidence to show that a particular program does not support Janeway's argument.
2. In her fourth paragraph Janeway moves from soaps to "fiction as a whole." Why does she seem to desert her topic?

3. Formulate a thesis-sentence for Janeway's essay.
4. In the course of commenting on soaps, Janeway states or implies certain assumptions about real life. List these assumptions. Are they irrelevant to a discussion of soap operas? Explain.
5. This essay first appeared in *Ms* magazine. Where in the essay does Janeway appear to address the special interests of *Ms* readers? Does the essay as a whole seem to exclude a wider audience?

Vivisection
C. S. Lewis

1   It is the rarest thing in the world to hear a rational discussion of vivisection. These who disapprove of it are commonly accused of "sentimentality," and very often their arguments justify the accusation. They paint pictures of pretty little dogs on dissecting tables. But the other side lies open to exactly the same charge. They also often defend the practice by drawing pictures of suffering women and children whose pain can be relieved (we are assured) only by the fruits of vivisection. The one appeal, quite as clearly as the other, is addressed to emotion, to the particular emotion we call pity. And neither appeal proves anything. If the thing is right—and if right at all, it is a duty—then pity for the animal is one of the temptations we must resist in order to perform that duty. If the thing is wrong, then pity for human suffering is precisely the temptation which will most probably lure us into doing that wrong thing. But the real question—*whether* it is right or wrong—remains meanwhile just where it was.

2   A rational discussion of this subject begins by inquiring whether pain is, or is not, an evil. If it is not, then the case against vivisection falls. But then so does the case for vivisection. If it is not defended on the ground that it reduces human suffering, on what ground can it be defended? And if pain is not an evil, why should human suffering be reduced? We must therefore assume as a basis for the whole discussion that pain is an evil, otherwise there is nothing to be discussed.

3   Now if pain is an evil then the infliction of pain, considered in itself, must clearly be an evil act. But there are such things as necessary evils. Some acts which would be bad, simply in themselves, may be excusable and even laudable when they are necessary means to a greater good. In saying that the infliction of pain, simply in itself, is bad, we are not saying that pain ought never to be inflicted. Most of us think that it can rightly be inflicted for a good purpose—as in dentistry or just and reformatory punishment. The point is that it always requires justification. On the man whom we find inflicting pain rests the burden of showing why an act which in itself would be simply bad is, in those particular circumstances, good. If we find a man giving pleasure it is for us to prove (if we criticize him) that his action is wrong. But if we find a man inflicting pain it is for him to prove that his action is right. If he cannot, he is a wicked man.

4   Now vivisection can only be defended by showing it to be right that one species should suffer in order that another species should be happier. And here we come to the parting of the ways. The Christian defender and the ordinary "scientific" (i.e., naturalistic) defender of vivisection, have to take quite different lines.

5   The Christian defender, especially in the Latin countries, is very apt to say that we are entitled to do anything we please to animals because they "have no souls." But what does this mean? If it means that animals have no consciousness, then how is this known? They certainly behave as if they had, or at least the higher animals do. I myself am inclined to think that far fewer animals than is supposed have what we should recognize as consciousness. But that is only an opinion. Unless we know on other grounds that vivisection is right we must not take the moral risk of tormenting them on a mere opinion. On the other hand, the statement that they "have no souls" may mean that they have no moral responsibilities and are not immortal. But the absence of "soul" in that sense makes the infliction of pain upon them not easier but harder to justify. For it means that animals cannot deserve pain, nor profit morally by the discipline of pain, nor be recompensed by happiness in another life for suffering in this. Thus all the factors which render pain more tolerable or make it less totally evil in the case of human beings will be lacking in the beasts. "Soullessness," in so far as it is relevant to the question at all, is an argument against vivisection.

6   The only rational line for the Christian vivisectionist to take is to say that the superiority of man over beast is a real objective fact, guaranteed by Revelation, and that the propriety of sacrificing beast

to man is a logical consequence. We are "worth more than many sparrows,"[1] and in saying this we are not merely expressing a natural preference for our own species simply because it is our own but conforming to a hierarchical order created by God and really present in the universe whether any one acknowledges it or not. The position may not be satisfactory. We may fail to see how a benevolent Deity could wish us to draw such conclusions from the hierarchical order He has created. We may find it difficult to formulate a human right of tormenting beasts in terms which would not equally imply an angelic right of tormenting men. And we may feel that though objective superiority is rightly claimed for men, yet that very superiority ought partly to *consist in* not behaving like a vivisector: that we ought to prove ourselves better than the beasts precisely by the fact of acknowledging duties to them which they do not acknowledge to us. But on all these questions different opinions can be honestly held. If on grounds of our real, divinely ordained, superiority a Christian pathologist thinks it right to vivisect, and does so with scrupulous care to avoid the least dram or scruple of unnecessary pain, in a trembling awe at the responsibility which he assumes, and with a vivid sense of the high mode in which human life must be lived if it is to justify the sacrifices made for it, then (whether we agree with him or not) we can respect his point of view.

7   But of course the vast majority of vivisectors have no such theological background. They are most of them naturalistic and Darwinian. Now here, surely, we come up against a very alarming fact. The very same people who will most contemptuously brush aside any consideration of animal suffering if it stands in the way of "research" will also, on another context, most vehemently deny that there is any radical difference between man and the other animals. On the naturalistic view the beasts are at bottom just the same *sort* of thing as ourselves. Man is simply the cleverest of the anthropoids. All the grounds on which a Christian might defend vivisection are thus cut from under our feet. We sacrifice other species to our own not because our own has any objective metaphysical privilege over others, but simply because it is ours. It may be very natural to have this loyalty to our own species, but let us hear no more from the naturalists about the "sentimentality" of antivivisectionists. If loyalty to our own species, preference for man simply because we are men, is not a sentiment, then what is? It may

[1] Matthew x.31

be a good sentiment or a bad one. But a sentiment it certainly is. Try to base it on logic and see what happens!

8   But the most sinister thing about modern vivisection is this. If a mere sentiment justifies cruelty, why stop at a sentiment for the whole human race? There is also a sentiment for the white man against the black, for a *Herrenvolk*[2] against the non-Aryans, for "civilized" or "progressive" peoples against "savages" or "backward" peoples. Finally, for our own country, party or class against others. Once the old Christian idea of a total difference in kind between man and beast has been abandoned, then no argument for experiments on animals can be found which is not also an argument for experiments on inferior men. If we cut up beasts simply because they cannot prevent us and because we are backing our own side in the struggle for existence, it is only logical to cut up imbeciles, criminals, enemies or capitalists for the same reasons. Indeed, experiments on men have already begun. We all hear that Nazi scientists have done them. We all suspect that our own scientists may begin to do so, in secret, at any moment.

9   The alarming thing is that the vivisectors have won the first round. In the nineteenth and eighteenth centuries a man was not stamped as a "crank" for protesting against vivisection. Lewis Carroll protested, if I remember his famous letter correctly, on the very same ground which I have just used.[3] Dr. Johnson—a man whose mind had as much *iron* in it as any man's—protested in a note on *Cymbeline* which is worth quoting in full. In Act I, scene v, the Queen explains to the Doctor that she wants poisons to experiment on "such creatures as We count not worth the hanging,—but none human."[4] The Doctor replies:

> Your Highness
> Shall from this practice but make hard your heart.[5]

Johnson comments: "The thought would probably have been more amplified, had our author lived to be shocked with such experiments as have been published in later times, by a race of men that have practised tortures without pity, and related them without shame, and are yet suffered to erect their heads among human beings."[6]

[2]Editors' note: German for "master race."
[3]"Vivisection as a Sign of the Times," *The Works of Lewis Carroll*, ed. Roger Lancelyn Green (London, 1965), pp. 1089–92. See also "Some Popular Fallacies about Vivisection," ibid., pp. 1092–1100.
[4]Shakespeare, *Cymbeline*, I, v, 19–20.
[5]Ibid., 23.
[6]*Johnson on Shakespeare: Essays and Notes Selected and Set Forth with an Introduction* by Sir Walter Raleigh (London, 1908), p. 181.

10   The words are his, not mine, and in truth we hardly dare in these days to use such calmly stern language. The reason why we do not dare is that the other side has in fact won. And though cruelty even to beasts is an important matter, their victory is symptomatic of matters more important still. The victory of vivisection marks a great advance in the triumph of ruthless, non-moral utilitarianism over the old world of ethical law; a triumph in which we, as well as animals, are already the victims, and of which Dachau and Hiroshima mark the more recent achievements. In justifying cruelty to animals we put ourselves also on the animal level. We choose the jungle and must abide by our choice.

11   You will notice I have spent no time in discussing what actually goes on in the laboratories. We shall be told, of course, that there is surprisingly little cruelty. That is a question with which, at present, I have nothing to do. We must first decide what should be allowed: after that it is for the police to discover what is already being done.

Questions

1. What purpose does Lewis's first paragraph serve? Is his implied definition of sentimentality adequate for his purpose?
2. By the end of the second paragraph are you willing to agree, at least for the sake of argument, that pain is an evil?
3. In the third paragraph Lewis gives two examples (dentistry and reformatory punishment) to prove that the infliction of pain "always requires justification." Are these two examples adequate and effective?
4. By the end of the fifth paragraph (the paragraph beginning "The Christian defender") are we more or less convinced that Lewis is fully aware of both sides of the argument? Do we feel he is fairly presenting both sides?
5. Characterize the tone (Lewis's attitude) implied in "The position may not be satisfactory" (paragraph 6). Notice also the effect of the repetition (in the same paragraph) of "We may fail to see," "We may find it difficult," "And we may feel. . . ." How tentative do you think Lewis really is?
6. The eighth paragraph begins, "But the most sinister thing about modern vivisection is this." How surprising is the word "sinister"? And why does Lewis bring in (drag in?) racist and religious persecution?
7. Late in his essay (paragraph 9) Lewis quotes Lewis Carroll,

Shakespeare, and Dr. Johnson. Except for a phrase from the Bible, these are the first quotations he uses. Should he have introduced these quotations, or others, earlier?

8. Analyze the final paragraph. Is Lewis correct in dismissing the question of how much cruelty there is in laboratories? Characterize the tone of the last sentence.

---

*T*otal Effect and the Eighth Grade
Flannery O'Connor

1   In two recent instances in Georgia, parents have objected to their eighth- and ninth-grade children's reading assignments in modern fiction. This seems to happen with some regularity in cases throughout the country. The unwitting parent picks up his child's book, glances through it, comes upon passages of erotic detail or profanity, and takes off at once to complain to the school board. Sometimes, as in one of the Georgia cases, the teacher is dismissed and hackles rise in liberal circles everywhere.

2   The two cases in Georgia, which involved Steinbeck's *East of Eden* and John Hersey's *A Bell for Adano,* provoked considerable newspaper comment. One columnist, in commending the enterprise of the teachers, announced that students do not like to read the fusty works of the nineteenth century, that their attention can best be held by novels dealing with the realities of our own time, and that the Bible, too, is full of racy stories.

3   Mr. Hersey himself addressed a letter to the State School Superintendent in behalf of the teacher who had been dismissed. He pointed out that his book is not scandalous, that it attempts to convey an earnest message about the nature of democracy, and that it falls well within the limits of the principle of "total effect," that principle followed in legal cases by which a book is judged not for isolated parts but by the final effect of the whole book upon the general reader.

4   I do not want to comment on the merits of these particular cases. What concerns me is what novels ought to be assigned in the eighth and ninth grades as a matter of course, for if these cases

indicate anything, they indicate the haphazard way in which fiction is approached in our high schools. Presumably there is a state reading list which contains "safe" books for teachers to assign; after that it is up to the teacher.

5   English teachers come in Good, Bad, and Indifferent, but too frequently in high schools anyone who can speak English is allowed to teach it. Since several novels can't easily be gathered into one textbook, the fiction that students are assigned depends upon their teacher's knowledge, ability, and taste: variable factors at best. More often than not, the teacher assigns what he thinks will hold the attention and interest of the students. Modern fiction will certainly hold it.

6   Ours is the first age in history which has asked the child what he would tolerate learning, but that is a part of the problem with which I am not equipped to deal. The devil of Educationism that possesses us is the kind that can be "cast out only by prayer and fasting." No one has yet come along strong enough to do it. In other ages the attention of children was held by Homer and Virgil, among others, but, by the reverse evolutionary process, that is no longer possible; our children are too stupid now to enter the past imaginatively. No one asks the student if algebra pleases him or if he finds it satisfactory that some French verbs are irregular, but if he prefers Hersey to Hawthorne, his taste must prevail.

7   I would like to put forward the proposition, repugnant to most English teachers, that fiction, if it is going to be taught in the high schools, should be taught as a subject and as a subject with a history. The total effect of a novel depends not only on its innate impact, but upon the experience, literary and otherwise, with which it is approached. No child needs to be assigned Hersey or Steinbeck until he is familiar with a certain amount of the best work of Cooper, Hawthorne, Melville, the early James, and Crane, and he does not need to be assigned these until he has been introduced to some of the better English novelists of the eighteenth and nineteenth centuries.

8   The fact that these works do not present him with the realities of his own time is all to the good. He is surrounded by the realities of his own time, and he has no perspective whatever from which to view them. Like the college student who wrote in her paper on Lincoln that he went to the movies and got shot, many students go to college unaware that the world was not made yesterday; their studies began with the present and dipped backward occasionally when it seemed necessary or unavoidable.

9   There is much to be enjoyed in the great British novels of the nineteenth century, much that a good teacher can open up in them for the young student. There is no reason why these novels should be either too simple or too difficult for the eighth grade. For the simple, they offer simple pleasures; for the more precocious, they can be made to yield subtler ones if the teacher is up to it. Let the student discover, after reading the nineteenth-century British novel, that the nineteenth-century American novel is quite different as to its literary characteristics, and he will thereby learn something not only about these individual works but about the sea-change which a new historical situation can effect in a literary form. Let him come to modern fiction with this experience behind him, and he will be better able to see and to deal with the more complicated demands of the best twentieth-century fiction.

10   Modern fiction often looks simpler than the fiction that preceded it, but in reality it is more complex. A natural evolution has taken place. The author has for the most part absented himself from direct participation in the work and has left the reader to make his own way amid experiences dramatically rendered and symbolically ordered. The modern novelist merges the reader in the experience; he tends to raise the passions he touches upon. If he is a good novelist, he raises them to effect by their order and clarity a new experience—the total effect—which is not in itself sensuous or simply of the moment. Unless the child has had some literary experience before, he is not going to be able to resolve the immediate passions the book arouses into any true, total picture.

11   It is here the moral problem will arise. It is one thing for a child to read about adultery in the Bible or in *Anna Karenina,* and quite another for him to read about it in most modern fiction. This is not only because in both the former instances adultery is considered a sin, and in the latter, at most, an inconvenience, but because modern writing involves the reader in the action with a new degree of intensity, and literary mores permit him to be involved in any action a human being can perform.

12   In our fractured culture, we cannot agree on morals; we cannot even agree that moral matters should come before literary ones when there is a conflict between them. All this is another reason why the high schools would do well to return to their proper business of preparing foundations. Whether in the senior year students should be assigned modern novelists should depend both on their parents' consent and on what they have already read and understood.

13   The high-school English teacher will be fulfilling his responsibility if he furnishes the student a guided opportunity, through the best writing of the past, to come, in time, to an understanding of the best writing of the present. He will teach literature, not social studies or little lessons in democracy or the customs of many lands.

14   And if the student finds that this is not to his taste? Well, that is regrettable. Most regrettable. His taste should not be consulted; it is being formed.

Questions

1. What is the function of the first three paragraphs of "Total Effect and the Eighth Grade"? Can you justify O'Connor's abrupt dismissal ("I do not want to comment on the merits of these particular cases") of the opposing argument summarized in the second and third paragraphs? How?
2. "English teachers come in Good, Bad, and Indifferent, but too frequently in high schools anyone who can speak English is allowed to teach it." Can you, from your own experience, support this view?
3. Is the tone of the sixth paragraph, beginning "Ours is the first age," sarcastic? If not, how would you characterize it?
4. Which of O'Connor's arguments might be used to support the rating of movies X, R, PG, and G? Are you for or against these ratings? How would you support your position?

Politics and the English Language
George Orwell

1   Most people who bother with the matter at all would admit that the English language is in a bad way, but it is generally assumed that we cannot by conscious action do anything about it. Our civilization is decadent and our language—so the argument runs—must inevitably share in the general collapse. It follows that any struggle against the abuse of language is a sentimental archaism, like preferring candles to electric light or hansom cabs to aeroplanes. Underneath this lies the half-conscious belief that language

is a natural growth and not an instrument which we shape for our own purposes.

2   Now, it is clear that the decline of a language must ultimately have political and economic causes: it is not due simply to the bad influence of this or that individual writer. But an effect can become a cause, reinforcing the original cause and producing the same effect in an intensified form, and so on indefinitely. A man may take to drink because he feels himself to be a failure, and then fail all the more completely because he drinks. It is rather the same thing that is happening to the English language. It becomes ugly and inaccurate because our thoughts are foolish, but the slovenliness of our language makes it easier for us to have foolish thoughts. The point is that the process is reversible. Modern English, especially written English, is full of bad habits which spread by imitation and which can be avoided if one is willing to take the necessary trouble. If one gets rid of these habits one can think more clearly, and to think clearly is a necessary first step towards political regeneration: so that the fight against bad English is not frivolous and is not the exclusive concern of professional writers. I will come back to this presently, and I hope that by that time the meaning of what I have said here will have become clearer. Meanwhile, here are five specimens of the English language as it is now habitually written.

3   These five passages have not been picked out because they are especially bad—I could have quoted far worse if I had chosen—but because they illustrate various of the mental vices from which we now suffer. They are a little below the average, but are fairly representative samples. I number them so that I can refer back to them when necessary:

> (1) I am not, indeed, sure whether it is not true to say that the Milton who once seemed unlike a seventeenth-century Shelley had not become, out of an experience ever more bitter in each year, more alien [sic] to the founder of that Jesuit sect which nothing could induce him to tolerate.
>
> — Professor Harold Laski (Essay in *Freedom of Expression*)

> (2) Above all, we cannot play ducks and drakes with a native battery of idioms which prescribes such egregious collocations of vocables as the basic *put up with* for *tolerate* or *put at a loss* for *bewilder*.
>
> — Professor Lancelot Hogben (*Interglossa*)

> (3) On the one side we have the free personality: by definition it is not neurotic, for it has neither conflict nor dream. Its desires, such as they are, are transparent, for they are just what

institutional approval keeps in the forefront of consciousness; another institutional pattern would alter their number and intensity; there is little in them that is natural, irreducible, or culturally dangerous. But *on the other side,* the social bond itself is nothing but the mutual reflection of these self-secure integrities. Recall the definition of love. Is not this the very picture of a small academic? Where is there a place in this hall of mirrors for either personality or fraternity?

— Essay on psychology in *Politics* (New York)

(4) All the "best people" from the gentlemen's clubs, and all the frantic fascist captains, united in common hatred of Socialism and bestial horror of the rising tide of the mass evolutionary movement, have turned to acts of provocation, to foul incendiarism, to medieval legends of poisoned wells, to legalize their own destruction of proletarian organizations, and rouse the agitated petty-bourgeoisie to chauvinistic fervor on behalf of the fight against the revolutionary way out of the crisis.

— Communist Pamphlet

(5) If a new spirit is to be infused into this old country, there is one thorny and contentious reform which must be tackled, and that is the humanization and galvanization of the B.B.C. Timidity here will bespeak canker and atrophy of the soul. The heart of Britain may be sound and of strong beat, for instance, but the British lion's roar at present is like that of Bottom in Shakespeare's *Midsummer Night's Dream*—as gentle as any sucking dove. A virile new Britain cannot continue indefinitely to be traduced in the eyes or rather ears, of the world by the effete languors of Langham Place, brazenly masquerading as "standard English." When the voice of Britain is heard at nine o'clock, better far and infinitely less ludicrous to hear aitches honestly dropped than the present priggish, inflated, school-ma'amish arch braying of blameless bashful mewing maidens!

— Letter in *Tribune*

4   Each of these passages has faults of its own, but, quite apart from avoidable ugliness, two qualities are common to all of them. The first is staleness of imagery; the other is lack of precision. The writer either has a meaning and cannot express it, or he inadvertently says something else, or he is almost indifferent as to whether his words mean anything or not. This mixture of vagueness and sheer incompetence is the most marked characteristic of modern English prose, and especially of any kind of political writing. As

soon as certain topics are raised, the concrete melts into the abstract and no one seems able to think of turns of speech that are not hackneyed: prose consists less and less of *words* chosen for the sake of their meaning, and more and more of *phrases* tacked together like the sections of a prefabricated hen-house. I list below, with notes and examples, various of the tricks by means of which the work of prose-construction is habitually dodged:

5   *Dying metaphors.* A newly invented metaphor assists thought by evoking a visual image, while on the other hand a metaphor which is technically "dead" (e.g., *iron resolution*) has in effect reverted to being an ordinary word and can generally be used without loss of vividness. But in between these two classes there is a huge dump of worn-out metaphors which have lost all evocative power and are merely used because they save people the trouble of inventing phrases for themselves. Examples are: *Ring the changes on, take up the cudgels for, toe the line, ride roughshod over, stand shoulder to shoulder with, play into the hands of, no axe to grind, grist to the mill, fishing in troubled waters, on the order of the day, Achilles' heel, swan song, hotbed.* Many of these are used without knowledge of their meaning (what is "grist," for instance?), and incompatible metaphors are frequently mixed, a sure sign that the writer is not interested in what he is saying. Some metaphors now current have been twisted out of their original meaning without those who use them even being aware of the fact. For example, *toe the line* is sometimes written *tow the line.* Another example is the *hammer and the anvil,* now always used with the implication that the anvil gets the worst of it. In real life it is always the anvil that breaks the hammer, never the other way about: a writer who stopped to think what he was saying would be aware of this, and would avoid perverting the original phrase.

6   *Operators* or *verbal false limbs.* These save the trouble of picking out appropriate verbs and nouns, and at the same time pad each sentence with extra syllables which give it an appearance of symmetry. Characteristic phrases are *render inoperative, militate against, make contact with, be subjected to, give rise to, give grounds for, have the effect of, plays a leading part (role) in, make itself felt, take effect, exhibit a tendency to, serve the purpose of,* etc., etc. The keynote is the elimination of simple verbs. Instead of being a single word, such as *break, stop, spoil, mend, kill,* a verb becomes a *phrase,* made up of a noun or adjective tacked on to some general-purpose verb such as *prove, serve, form, play, render.* In addition, the passive voice is wherever possible used in preference to the active, and noun constructions are used instead of gerunds *(by ex-*

amination of instead of *by examining).* The range of verbs is further cut down by means of the *-ize* and *de-* formations, and the banal statements are given an appearance of profundity by means of the *not un-* formation. Simple conjunctions and prepositions are replaced by such phrases as *with respect to, having regard to, the fact that, by dint of, in view of, in the interests of, on the hypothesis that;* and the ends of sentences are saved from anticlimax by such resounding common-places as *greatly to be desired, cannot be left out of account, a development to be expected in the near future, deserving of serious consideration, brought to a satisfactory conclusion,* and so on and so forth.

7   *Pretentious diction.* Words like *phenomenon, element, individual* (as noun), *objective, categorical, effective, virtual, basic, primary, promote, constitute, exhibit, exploit, utilize, eliminate, liquidate,* are used to dress up simple statements and give an air of scientific impartiality to biased judgments. Adjectives like *epochmaking, epic, historic, unforgettable, triumphant, age-old, inevitable, inexorable, veritable,* are used to dignify the sordid processes of international politics, while writing that aims at glorifying war usually takes on an archaic color, its characteristic words being: *realm, throne, chariot, mailed fist, trident, sword, shield, buckler, banner, jackboot, clarion.* Foreign words and expressions such as *cul de sac, ancien régime, deus ex machina, mutatis mutandis, status quo, gleichschaaltung, weltanschauung,* are used to give an air of culture and elegance. Except for the useful abbreviations *i.e., e.g.,* and *etc.,* there is no real need for any of the hundreds of foreign phrases now current in English. Bad writers, and especially scientific, political and sociological writers, are nearly always haunted by the notion that Latin or Greek words are grander than Saxon ones, and unnecessary words like *expedite, ameliorate, predict, extraneous, deracinated, clandestine, subaqueous* and hundreds of others constantly gain ground from their Anglo-Saxon opposite numbers.[1] The jargon peculiar to Marxist writing *(hyena, hangman, cannibal, petty bourgeois, these gentry, lacquey, flunkey, mad dog, White Guard,* etc.) consists largely of words and phrases

---

[1] An interesting illustration of this is the way in which the English flower names which were in use till very recently are being ousted by Greek ones, *snapdragon* becoming *antirrhinum, forget-me-not* becoming *myosotis,* etc. It is hard to see any practical reason for this change of fashion: it is probably due to an instinctive turning-away from the more homely word and a vague feeling that the Greek word is scientific.

translated from Russian, German or French; but the normal way of coining a new word is to use a Latin or Greek root with the appropriate affix and, where necessary, the *-ize* formation. It is often easier to make up words of this kind (*deregionalize, impermissible, extramarital, non-fragmentary* and so forth) than to think up the English words that will cover one's meaning. The result, in general, is an increase in slovenliness and vagueness.

8   *Meaningless words.* In certain kinds of writing, particularly in art criticism and literary criticism, it is normal to come across long passages which are almost completely lacking in meaning.[2] Words like *romantic, plastic, values, human, dead, sentimental, natural, vitality,* as used in art criticism, are strictly meaningless, in the sense that they not only do not point to any discoverable object, but are hardly ever expected to do so by the reader. When one critic writes, "The outstanding feature of Mr. X's work is its living quality," while another writes, "The immediately striking thing about Mr. X's work is its peculiar deadness," the reader accepts this as a simple difference of opinion. If words like *black* and *white* were involved, instead of the jargon words *dead* and *living,* he would see at once that language was being used in an improper way. Many political words are similarly abused. The word *Fascism* has now no meaning except in so far as it signifies "something not desirable." The words *democracy, socialism, freedom, patriotic, realistic, justice,* have each of them several different meanings which cannot be reconciled with one another. In the case of a word like *democracy,* not only is there no agreed definition, but the attempt to make one is resisted from all sides. It is almost universally felt that when we call a country democratic we are praising it: consequently the defenders of every kind of régime claim that it is a democracy, and fear that they might have to stop using the word if it were tied down to any one meaning. Words of this kind are often used in a consciously dishonest way. That is, the person who uses them has his own private definition, but allows his hearer to think he means something quite different. Statements like *Marshal Pétain was a true patriot, The Soviet Press is the freest in the world, The Catholic*

---

[2]Example: "Comfort's catholicity of perception and image, strangely Whitmanesque in range, almost the exact opposite in aesthetic compulsion, continues to evoke that trembling atmospheric accumulative hinting at a cruel, an inexorably serene timelessness. . . . Wrey Gardiner scores by aiming at simple bull's-eyes with precision. Only they are not so simple, and through this contented sadness runs more than the surface bittersweet of resignation." *(Poetry Quarterly.)*

Church is opposed to persecution, are almost always made with intent to deceive. Other words used in variable meanings, in most cases more or less dishonestly, are: *class, totalitarian, science, progressive, reactionary, bourgeois, equality.*

9   Now that I have made this catalogue of swindles and perversions, let me give another example of the kind of writing that they lead to. This time it must of its nature be an imaginary one. I am going to translate a passage of good English into modern English of the worst sort. Here is a well-known verse from *Ecclesiastes:*

> I returned and saw under the sun, that the race is not to the swift, nor the battle to the strong, neither yet bread to the wise, nor yet riches to men of understanding, nor yet favor to men of skill; but time and chance happeneth to them all.

Here it is in modern English:

> Objective consideration of contemporary phenomena compels the conclusion that success or failure in competitive activities exhibits no tendency to be commensurate with innate capacity, but that a considerable element of the unpredictable must invariably be taken into account.

10   This is a parody, but not a very gross one. Exhibit (3), above, for instance, contains several patches of the same kind of English. It will be seen that I have not made a full translation. The beginning and ending of the sentence follow the original meaning fairly closely, but in the middle the concrete illustrations—race, battle, bread—dissolve into the vague phrase "success or failure in competitive activities." This had to be so, because no modern writer of the kind I am discussing—no one capable of using phrases like "objective consideration of contemporary phenomena"—would ever tabulate his thoughts in that precise and detailed way. The whole tendency of modern prose is away from concreteness. Now analyse these two sentences a little more closely. The first contains forty-nine words but only sixty syllables, and all its words are those of everyday life. The second contains thirty-eight words of ninety syllables: eighteen of its words are from Latin roots, and one from Greek. The first sentence contains six vivid images, and only one phrase ("time and chance") that could be called vague. The second contains not a single fresh, arresting phrase, and in spite of its ninety syllables it gives only a shortened version of the meaning contained in the first. Yet without a doubt it is the second kind of sentence that is gaining ground in modern English. I do not want to exaggerate. This kind

of writing is not yet universal, and outcrops of simplicity will occur here and there in the worst-written page. Still, if you or I were told to write a few lines on the uncertainty of human fortunes, we should probably come much nearer to my imaginary sentence than to the one from *Ecclesiastes*.

11   As I have tried to show, modern writing at its worst does not consist in picking out words for the sake of their meaning and inventing images in order to make the meaning clearer. It consists in gumming together long strips of words which have already been set in order by someone else, and making the results presentable by sheer humbug. The attraction of this way of writing is that it is easy. It is easier—even quicker, once you have the habit—to say *In my opinion it is not an unjustifiable assumption that* than to say *I think*. If you use ready-made phrases, you not only don't have to hunt about for words; you also don't have to bother with the rhythms of your sentences, since these phrases are generally so arranged as to be more or less euphonious. When you are composing in a hurry—when you are dictating to a stenographer, for instance, or making a public speech—it is natural to fall into a pretentious, Latinized style. Tags like *a consideration which we should do well to bear in mind* or *a conclusion to which all of us would readily assent* will save many a sentence from coming down with a bump. By using stale metaphors, similes and idioms, you save much mental effort, at the cost of leaving your meaning vague, not only for your reader but for yourself. This is the significance of mixed metaphors. The sole aim of a metaphor is to call up a visual image. When these images clash—as in *The Fascist octopus has sung its swan song, the jackboot is thrown into the melting pot*—it can be taken as certain that the writer is not seeing a mental image of the objects he is naming; in other words he is not really thinking. Look again at the examples I gave at the beginning of this essay. Professor Laski (1) uses five negatives in fifty-three words. One of these is superfluous, making nonsense of the whole passage, and in addition there is the slip *alien* for *akin*, making further nonsense, and several avoidable pieces of clumsiness which increase the general vagueness. Professor Hogben (2) plays ducks and drakes with a battery which is able to write prescriptions, and, while disapproving of the everyday phrase *put up with*, is unwilling to look *egregious* up in the dictionary and see what it means; (3), if one takes an uncharitable attitude towards it, is simply meaningless: probably one could work out its intended meaning by reading the whole of the article in which it occurs. In (4), the writer knows more or less what he wants to say, but an accumulation of stale phrases chokes him like tea leaves blocking a

sink. In (5), words and meaning have almost parted company. People who write in this manner usually have a general emotional meaning—they dislike one thing and want to express solidarity with another—but they are not interested in the detail of what they are saying. A scrupulous writer, in every sentence that he writes, will ask himself at least four questions, thus: What am I trying to say? What words will express it? What image or idiom will make it clearer? Is this image fresh enough to have an effect? And he will probably ask himself two more: Could I put it more shortly? Have I said anything that is avoidably ugly? But you are not obliged to go to all this trouble. You can shirk it by simply throwing your mind open and letting the ready-made phrases come crowding in. They will construct your sentences for you—even think your thoughts for you, to a certain extent—and at need they will perform the important service of partially concealing your meaning even from yourself. It is at this point that the special connection between politics and the debasement of language becomes clear.

12   In our time it is broadly true that political writing is bad writing. Where it is not true it will generally be found that the writer is some kind of rebel, expressing his private opinions and not a "party line." Orthodoxy, of whatever color, seems to demand a lifeless, imitative style. The political dialects to be found in pamphlets, leading articles, manifestos, White Papers and the speeches of undersecretaries do, of course, vary from party to party, but they are all alike in that one almost never finds in them a fresh, vivid, homemade turn of speech. When one watches some tired hack on the platform mechanically repeating the familiar phrase—*bestial atrocities, iron heel, bloodstained tyranny, free peoples of the world, stand shoulder to shoulder*—one often has a curious feeling that one is not watching a live human being but some kind of dummy: a feeling which suddenly becomes stronger at moments when the light catches the speaker's spectacles and turns them into blank discs which seem to have no eyes behind them. And this is not altogether fanciful. A speaker who uses that kind of phraseology has gone some distance towards turning himself into a machine. The appropriate noises are coming out of his larynx but his brain is not involved as it would be if he were choosing his words for himself. If the speech he is making is one that he is accustomed to make over and over again, he may be almost unconscious of what he is saying, as one is when one utters the responses in church. And this reduced state of consciousness, if not indispensable, is at any rate favorable to political conformity.

13   In our time, political speech and writing are largely the defence of the indefensible. Things like the continuance of British rule in India, the Russian purges and deportations, the dropping of the atom bombs on Japan, can indeed be defended, but only by argu ments which are too brutal for most people to face, and which do not square with the professed aims of political parties. Thus political language has to consist largely of euphemism, question-begging and sheer cloudy vagueness. Defenceless villages are bombarded from the air, the inhabitants driven out into the countryside, the cattle machine-gunned, the huts set on fire with incendiary bullets: this is called *pacification.* Millions of peasants are robbed of their farms and sent trudging along the roads with no more than they can carry: this is called *transfer of population* or *rectification of frontiers.* People are imprisoned for years without trial, or shot in the back of the neck or sent to die of scurvy in Arctic lumber camps: this is called *elimination of unreliable elements.* Such phraseology is needed if one wants to name things without calling up mental pictures of them. Consider for instance some comfortable English professor defending Russian totalitarianism. He cannot say outright, "I believe in killing off your opponents when you can get good results by doing so." Probably, therefore, he will say something like this:

> While freely conceding that the Soviet régime exhibits certain features which the humanitarian may be inclined to deplore, we must, I think, agree that a certain curtailment of the right to political opposition is an unavoidable concomitant of transitional periods, and that the rigors which the Russian people have been called upon to undergo have been amply justified in the sphere of concrete achievement.

14   The inflated style is itself a kind of euphemism. A mass of Latin words falls upon the facts like soft snow, blurring the outlines and covering up all the details. The great enemy of clear language is insincerity. When there is a gap between one's real and one's declared aims, one turns as it were instinctively to long words and exhausted idioms, like a cuttlefish squirting out ink. In our age there is no such thing as "keeping out of politics." All issues are political issues, and politics itself is a mass of lies, evasions, folly, hatred and schizophrenia. When the general atmosphere is bad, language must suffer. I should expect to find—this is a guess which I have not sufficient knowledge to verify—that the German, Russian and Italian languages have all deteriorated in the last ten to fifteen years, as a result of dictatorship.

15   But if thought corrupts language, language can also corrupt thought. A bad usage can spread by tradition and imitation, even among people who should and do know better. The debased language that I have been discussing is in some ways very convenient. Phrases like *a not unjustifiable assumption, leaves much to be desired, would serve no good purpose, a consideration which we should do well to bear in mind,* are a continuous temptation, a packet of aspirins always at one's elbow. Look back through this essay, and for certain you will find that I have again and again committed the very faults I am protesting against. By this morning's post I have received a pamphlet dealing with conditions in Germany. The author tells me that he "felt impelled" to write it. I open it at random, and here is almost the first sentence that I see: "[The Allies] have an opportunity not only of achieving a radical transformation of Germany's social and political structure in such a way as to avoid a nationalistic reaction in Germany itself, but at the same time of laying the foundations of a cooperative and unified Europe." You see, he "feels impelled" to write—feels, presumably, that he has something new to say—and yet his words, like cavalry horses answering the bugle, group themselves automatically into the familiar dreary pattern. This invasion of one's mind by ready-made phrases *(lay the foundations, achieve a radical transformation)* can only be prevented if one is constantly on guard against them, and every such phrase anesthetizes a portion of one's brain.

16   I said earlier that the decadence of our language is probably curable. Those who deny this would argue, if they produced an argument at all, that language merely reflects existing social conditions, and that we cannot influence its development by any direct tinkering with words and constructions. So far as the general tone or spirit of a language goes, this may be true, but it is not true in detail. Silly words and expressions have often disappeared, not through any evolutionary process but owing to the conscious action of a minority. Two recent examples were *explore every avenue* and *leave no stone unturned,* which were killed by the jeers of a few journalists. There is a long list of flyblown metaphors which could similarly be got rid of if enough people would interest themselves in the job; and it should also be possible to laugh the *not un-* formation out of existence,[3] to reduce the amount of Latin and Greek

---

[3] One can cure oneself of the *not un-* formation by memorizing this sentence: *A not unblack dog was chasing a not unsmall rabbit across a not ungreen field.*

in the average sentence, to drive out foreign phrases and strayed scientific words, and, in general, to make pretentiousness unfashionable. But all these are minor points. The defence of the English language implies more than this, and perhaps it is best to start by saying what it does *not* imply.

17   To begin with it has nothing to do with archaism, with the salvaging of obsolete words and turns of speech, or with the setting up of a "standard English" which must never be departed from. On the contrary, it is especially concerned with the scrapping of every word or idiom which has outworn its usefulness. It has nothing to do with correct grammar and syntax, which are of no importance so long as one makes one's meaning clear, or with the avoidance of Americanisms, or with having what is called a "good prose style." On the other hand it is not concerned with fake simplicity and the attempt to make written English colloquial. Nor does it even imply in every case preferring the Saxon word to the Latin one, though it does imply using the fewest and shortest words that will cover one's meaning. What is above all needed is to let the meaning choose the word, and not the other way about. In prose, the worst thing one can do with words is to surrender to them. When you think of a concrete object, you think wordlessly, and then, if you want to describe the thing you have been visualizing you probably hunt about till you find the exact words that seem to fit it. When you think of something abstract you are more inclined to use words from the start, and unless you make a conscious effort to prevent it, the existing dialect will come rushing in and do the job for you, at the expense of blurring or even changing your meaning. Probably it is better to put off using words as long as possible and get one's meaning as clear as one can through pictures or sensations. Afterwards one can choose—not simply *accept*—the phrases that will best cover the meaning, and then switch round and decide what impression one's words are likely to make on another person. This last effort of the mind cuts out all stale or mixed images, all prefabricated phrases, needless repetitions, and humbug and vagueness generally. But one can often be in doubt about the effect of a word or a phrase, and one needs rules that one can rely on when instinct fails. I think the following rules will cover most cases:

(i)   Never use a metaphor, simile or other figure of speech which you are used to seeing in print.

(ii)   Never use a long word where a short one will do.

(iii)   If it is possible to cut a word out, always cut it out.

 (iv) Never use the passive where you can use the active.

 (v) Never use a foreign phrase, a scientific word or a jargon word if you can think of an everyday English equivalent.

 (vi) Break any of these rules sooner than say anything outright barbarous.

These rules sound elementary, and so they are, but they demand a deep change of attitude in anyone who has grown used to writing in the style now fashionable. One could keep all of them and still write bad English, but one could not write the kind of stuff that I quoted in those five specimens at the beginning of this article.

18 I have not here been considering the literary use of language, but merely language as an instrument for expressing and not for concealing or preventing thought. Stuart Chase and others have come near to claiming that all abstract words are meaningless, and have used this as a pretext for advocating a kind of political quietism. Since you don't know what Fascism is, how can you struggle against Fascism? One need not swallow such absurdities as this, but one ought to recognize that the present political chaos is connected with the decay of language, and that one can probably bring about some improvement by starting at the verbal end. If you simplify your English, you are freed from the worst follies of orthodoxy. You cannot speak any of the necessary dialects, and when you make a stupid remark its stupidity will be obvious, even to yourself. Political language—and with variations this is true of all political parties, from Conservatives to Anarchists—is designed to make lies sound truthful and murder respectable, and to give an appearance of solidity to pure wind. One cannot change this all in a moment, but one can at least change one's own habits, and from time to time one can even, if one jeers loudly enough, send some worn-out and useless phrase—some *jackboot, Achilles' heel, hotbed, melting pot, acid test, veritable inferno* or other lump of verbal refuse—into the dustbin where it belongs.

Questions

1. Revise one or two of Orwell's examples of bad writing.
2. Examine Orwell's metaphors. Do they fulfill his requirements for good writing?
3. Look again at Orwell's grotesque revision (paragraph 9) of a passage from the Bible. Write a similar version of another passage from the Bible.

4. Examine an editorial on a political issue. Analyze the writing as Orwell might have.

What Have 60 Million Readers Found in Nancy Drew?

Patricia Meyer Spacks

1   I had quite a lot of trouble managing to reread Nancy Drew. First I went to the New Haven Public Library. They didn't have any Nancy Drew books; the librarian said that kind of reading wasn't good for children. Then I asked my secretary if *she* owned any Nancy Drew. She said she had had all eighty volumes, she'd read them and her children read them, but she'd sold them three weeks before at a garage sale. She lives in a small town outside New Haven; she thought her public library might be able to supply me with some books. The next day she brought me a pile, with copyrights ranging from 1935 to 1985. Every book in the stack had been taken out consistently about once a month. If Nancy Drew isn't good ₁ur children, it's clear that the children don't realize that.

2   I started asking people at random whether they'd ever read Nancy Drew. Each woman in my arbitrary sample of highly intellectual types said yes; all remembered their childhood experience of Nancy with great pleasure. More surprisingly, several men had also enjoyed Nancy Drew. More surprising still, one of my colleagues reported that his six year old daughter's favorite bedtime reading-aloud books at the moment are Nancy Drew mysteries. And a colleague from another institution revealed that he teaches Nancy Drew in his course on mystery novels.

3   In this context of official disapproval and unofficial enthusiasm, I began my own rereading, feeling rather dutiful about it, expecting to be bored. Not at all: the more I read, the more interested I became in how these reiterative, simple plots and sketchily defined characters worked on their readers. For what it's worth, I concluded that Nancy Drew—the old-fashioned, "out-of-date" version of Nancy Drew—is probably rather good for children.

4   Some of you may remember Bruno Bettelheim's book on fairy-tales, *The Use of Enchantment*. Analyzing the effect of fairytales on child readers, Bettelheim concludes that such stories provide developmental models. His accounts of individual tales make clear that they offer little boys patterns of mastery. For girls, on the other hand, the most familiar stories reinforce images of passivity and dependence. Sleeping Beauty must await in a state of literal unconsciousness the coming of her prince. Goodness is rewarded in girls—think of Cinderella's domestic virtues!—while courage, independence, and adventurousness (as well as generosity and compassion) win success for boys. Girls are constantly warned (in "Snow White," for instance) of the dangers of their own sexuality. The fairytales, in other words, reinforce cultural stereotypes about male and female roles. Bettelheim doesn't put it this way, but feminist critics after him have repeatedly made the point, often suggesting in what ways women's fairytales might be different. Usually their proposals for useful tales emphasize expression of rage at male domination and of attachment among females.

5   The Nancy Drew stories aren't fairytales or versions of fairy-tales. Nor do they provide developmental models. On the contrary, Nancy remains staggeringly the same—eighteen years old, "titian-haired," driving her convertible—through one book after another. And no one reads *one* Nancy Drew book: it would be like eating one peanut. (An academic father told me that his eight year old currently has a list of fifty-two more Nancy Drew books she's determined to read.) In an utterly unthreatening way, though, these books generate imaginative power by creating images of female mastery that clearly and directly address little girls' wishes and fears without encouraging their rage. Let me remind you in some detail of the characters who inhabit these books, the kinds of situations they confront, and the typical outcomes of those situations; then I'll try to say more about how these elements may work to instruct and reassure child readers.

6   Nancy, the perpetual eighteen year old, lives with her father, a prosperous and generous lawyer who has great respect for her abilities and who interferes not at all with her plans. Indeed, if someone steals Nancy's car, her father will promptly provide her with a new and better one (*The Haunted Showboat,* 1957). Her mother having died when Nancy was three, there is no one to come between her and her father; no mother makes restrictive rules or keeps a penetrating eye on Nancy's activities. Nor does she have a cruel step-mother. Instead, a kindly housekeeper (often described as "moth-

erly") exclaims at the girls's cleverness and provides her and her friends with hot cocoa and apple pie. As much of the last two centuries' literature testifies, this is a little girl's dream situation.

7   . Nancy has two female allies her own age: Bess, always characterized either as "a little plump" or as "slightly overweight," with blonde hair and occasional feminine fears; and George, Bess's "spunky cousin, an attractive brunette, who liked athletics and was proud of her boy's name" (*The Clue in the Crumbling Wall*, 1945). Although Nancy originates the most useful tactics for solving mysteries, all solutions result from the combined efforts of the three girls. There is also a boyfriend, Ned Nickerson, who often inhabits the remote peripheries of the narratives. Occasionally someone in the stories will suggest romantic feeling betwen Nancy and Ned; on such occasions, Ned blushes, and Nancy says "Don't be silly."

8   Always competent, Nancy possesses a surprising range of knowledge. If a car starts making ominous noises, Nancy will look underneath and announce "the whole rear housing has given way!" (*The Haunted Showboat*). On the basis of artistic style, she can decide (correctly) that the creator of a given painting was female (*The Strange Message in the Parchment*, 1977). She makes her own travel arrangements, checks into hotels by herself with aplomb (*The Eskimo's Secret*, 1985), goes off on airplane trips alone. If one path is blocked, literally or metaphorically, she can always figure out another.

9   Whether she is asked to solve a mystery or simply finds herself in the middle of one, she invariably discovers and analyzes the evidence that leads to the solution. Along the way to that solution, she often acquires new funds of knowledge: about the nature of sheep-raising, for instance, including the realities of slaughter, unsentimentally treated; or about how buttons are made; or how you tell good from bad mink pelts. (The reader, of course, learns the same facts.)

10   Each mystery conforms to a single pattern, with variations. Someone appeals to Nancy for help: an inheritance will be forfeited if the missing heir doesn't show up within a month; a New Orleans family wants to tow an old showboat from a bayou for Mardi Gras, but mysterious forces prevent the boat's being moved. Alternatively, something happens to Nancy herself: two rosebushes disappear from her yard; a sheepskin coat is stolen from her living room. In either case, she sets out, with paternal approval, to solve the problem, which typically becomes increasingly complicated as she investigates it. Soon she finds a clue, most often a scrap of paper

with a cryptic, usually fragmentary message on it. It takes some time to decipher these messages, but all eventually yield to Nancy's common sense and acumen, with a little help from her friends. And to her dogged persistence. As the housekeeper remarks on one occasion, "I can see why you're a good detective. If you don't find hidden gold under one stone, you turn up another" (*Nancy's Mysterious Letter,* 1968).

11   Each book has its "scary parts," but no threatening situation lasts very long—sometimes only from one sentence to the next. The most common form of menace consists in something being thrown at Nancy. Stones, concrete blocks, bottles come whizzing through the air, from no immediately comprehensible source. Sometimes Nancy is locked up somewhere, but soon she gets away. Sometimes a bridge collapses, or a ladder, or a car tries to run her down. Occasionally cars are tampered with or boats sink; once in a while the heroine faces less definable forms of danger, like the strange sounds that come from the haunted showboat. In the end, always, Nancy discovers the source of every threat and arranges the capture of all threateners. And each book concludes with the promise of its successor, in a formulation of this sort: "Nancy was thoughtful for a moment [sometimes, more forthrightly, she is *sad*] as she realized this mystery was solved. Little did she know that she would soon become involved in the exciting *Mystery of Crocodile Island*" (*The Strange Message in the Parchment*).

12   All mysteries provide the satisfaction of problems solved and allow their readers vicarious participation in the process of solution. At this level, one can readily explain the appeal of the Nancy Drew books to a young audience. They are just scary enough, just difficult enough, to supply titillation and stimulation without making excessive demands on intelligence or endurance. Reading one Nancy Drew book educates the reader in how to approach the next. Soon a child grows into awareness of the pattern and can almost expect without quite knowing what's going to happen. The combination of familiarity and novelty generates a potent source of pleasure.

13   But the pleasure goes deeper than this, and the meaning of mysteries stated and resolved has special weight for youthful readers. The Nancy Drew stories, over and over, insist that growing up provides no unmanageable difficulties, that adolescence is even for girls a time of freedom and power, not a time of dangerous sexuality, and that young people can play a meaningful part in society. The reassurance of these messages, I suspect, accounts for the enduring popularity of this series—and for the fact that boys as well as girls read them.

14   At no time in the series' history, I suspect, have eighteen year olds read Nancy Drew. The form of identification invited by these books depends on more remote varieties of fantasy than that produced by interaction between a fictional and a literal teen ager. For eight year olds, on the other hand, the fantasy is utterly satisfying: keeping your loving, approving father all to yourself; not having to endure obscure, troubling rivalries with a mother, yet retaining the forms of maternal comfort; living in conflict-free egalitarian relationship to boys without suspicion or rivalry or teasing from other girls. Lots of love, no overt sex—an ideal situation.

15   The near sexlessness of these narratives must contribute to their appeal for some boys as well. Gender is almost never an explicit issue here. The narrator assumes that girls take care of themselves as boys do, that girls and boys alike face problems and solve them. The freedom of a world in which gender is suppressed as a category manifestly extends to boys as well as girls.

16   So the fables of mastery can apply to both sexes. Over and over, these stories tell child-readers the same thing; if you persist, you can figure it out—"it" being not only the individual mystery that concerns Nancy at any given moment, but the larger mystery of grown-up existence. Nancy never needs to be aggressive and she feels angry only at injustices, but she can rarely be scared. No one succeeds in bullying her. Although she's by no means remarkably articulate, she knows what she thinks and she has a solid sense of self-confidence, presumably based on her repeated successes.

17   The notion of "growing up" that Nancy and her friends epitomize offers all kinds of reassurance to a child. It's a kind of up-to-date version of *Peter Pan:* instead of remaining forever a child, to be taken care of by big dogs and charming female fairies, one can imagine retaining the innocence of childhood, the father who pays the bills, the housekeeper who worries about you just enough and offers warm cookies when they're needed—but also fulfilling, without undue pain, the responsibilities of adulthood and enjoying some of adulthood's privileges. Indeed, Nancy excels most of the literal adults around her. The police, for instance, in these fables turn out to be kindly and helpful, but *they* never solve the crime or find the heiress. Over and over, apparent complexity becomes simple as Nancy works at it. What could be more comforting?

18   Children see around them, and hear about, dangers and difficulties of adolescence. In the Nancy Drew stories, they can read about adolescence in which all danger is externalized and objectified. If someone sneaks into your house while you're giving the poor old mailman a cup of hot cocoa and steals a mailbag containing letters of value, that someone can be found and punished. It's a

far easier problem to locate and punish him than it is to deal with internal conflicts or external demands for conformity with troubling norms. Even if the mail-thief interests young readers because at some level they recognize in themselves fleeting impulses to make off with someone else's letters, such impulses are usually less worrisome to little boys and girls than, say, their fantasies about sex. After all, they already know that they're not supposed to steal mail, so it's satisfying to them to learn that the person who breaks the prohibition gets his comeuppance.

19   The adult reader of Nancy Drew notices a striking contrast in these books between the sparseness of realistic detail and the elaboration of plot. The narrator seems more interested in button-making and mink-raising than in the appearance of people or of the physical world, or in details of what people say, wear, and do in day-to-day contact. But she also has a rather intricate conception of plot. Although no single episode takes long to develop and be resolved, a dizzying sequence of events occurs in virtually all Nancy Drew stories. In the first eight pages of *The Clue in the Crumbling Wall*, a policewoman asks Nancy to find a dancer who has disappeared, two rosebushes vanish from the front yard, a clamseller shows up. Nancy finds a pearl, she goes to the jeweler to sell it, encounters an "unpleasant man," and has her purse snatched. (And one of those eight pages is occupied by an illustration; and some space is taken up by explanations of Nancy's situation, with housekeeper and father, and her history of successful mystery-solving.) Eventually all these happenings will interlock: for the moment, several seem to promise different directions. And Nancy's life continues at a comparable pace. The stories make considerable demands on a child-reader's attention, moving from one episode to another at breakneck speed and connecting episodes in complicated ways. Although the large outlines of plot, as I've already suggested, remain constant from one book to another, it would be difficult to summarize in adequate detail the intricacies of any individual plot.

20   Perhaps it's my training as an eighteenth-century scholar that makes this conjunction of generalized scene and highly specified plot so interesting to me: it's a very eighteenth-century combination. Dr. Johnson, you may remember, suggested through a fictional character that the poet should not try to describe the streaks on the tulip; he should, instead, evoke the type of the tulip, reminding every reader of his or her own direct knowledge of the flower. I have a hunch that that's how the Nancy Drew books work for

children. The sketches of scene, character, and conversation create vague outlines for the reader to fill in from personal experience. Dark hair, blonde hair, titian hair: most readers can identify quite straightforwardly with one or another of the girls, given the lack of detail in their characterizations. The father, the housekeeper, the boyfriend, the houses and gardens, the clothes: they could be *anyone's* father or clothes or whatever. On the other hand, details about sheepshearing or the feeding of minks provide a sense of solid information, imaginably useful in the real world.

21   Those complicated plots also involve the process of working things out; they declare that no matter how fast or how crazily things happen, they always turn out to make sense, given persistent effort to fathom them. When you know that everything *will* eventually make sense, it becomes delightful to indulge in the vicarious experience of utter confusion.

22   It might be argued—I'm sure it has been argued—that the unrealistic aspects of this fiction make it useless if not dangerous for children. After all, if I'm right, these books suggest what is neither psychologically nor literally true. Adolescents do not have so much effectual power as Nancy and her friends wield: they do not lead lives free of familial and of internal conflict; they are not always readily able to figure things out; they often feel troubled by their own and other people's sexuality; they sometimes fight with their friends, they sometimes feel depressed, they rarely get to have their fathers all to themselves (if there's no mother, there's usually a girlfriend). Many recent stories for children are predicated on the assumption that useful fictions provide realistic accounts of dangers to be faced in the world. You tell the little girl about drug dealers and divorce, the theory goes, and she'll be better prepared to deal with them when she confronts them herself.

23   Maybe so; I don't know. I wouldn't want children to read *only* about the idealized white middle-class harmonies depicted in the Nancy Drew books. But I suspect that it's useful for a white middle-class eight year old—and such, obviously, is the intended audience of the series—to be reassured about what lies ahead, to be told that she can solve problems by using available resources, that cooperative models of accomplishment are meaningful, and that she doesn't have to grow up until she wants to. Nancy Drew as she exists on the page resembles an eight year old's idealized self-image more than a realistic portrayal of an eighteen year old. But it's eight year olds who like to read about her, and I strongly suspect that a more up-to-date, "realistic" version of the character will enjoy less

popular success than her implausible predecessor. Harriet Stratemeyer Adams took pride in having created an early version of the independent woman. Her achievement—the degree to which she causes young readers to feel deeply involved with that figure of the independent woman—may depend partly on exactly the aspects of her fictions that make them seem unrealistic and uncompelling to adults.

Questions

1. Spacks offers an explanation of why the Nancy Drew books interest children. If you read such books when you were a child, do you now agree with Spacks's analysis of their appeal?
2. If as a child you read some other sort of books designed for children—for example, the kind Spacks refers to in the last two sentences of paragraph 22—what were its appeals?
3. In paragraph 20 Spacks says that "most readers can identify . . . with" Nancy or one of her friends. But in paragraph 23 she refers to the "white middle-class eight year old" as the "intended audience of the series." Does Spacks contradict herself? Or, though she doesn't address the question directly, does her analysis suggest reasons that the books might also appeal to eight-year-olds of other races and classes?
4. In her first paragraph, and in the next-to-last paragraph, Spacks suggests that some people find the Nancy Drew books not good for children, or even dangerous for them. She clearly disagrees. Whether or not you are convinced by her argument, imagine some books that might be, in your opinion, "not good" or "dangerous" for children to read. What would they be like? What would you do about them? Would you try to keep them out of children's libraries (as the Nancy Drew books have been kept out of the New Haven library)? Or put pressure on publishers not to publish them? Or what?
5. Spacks does not discuss the illustrations in the Nancy Drew books. Consider (in these books or in some others with which you are familiar) the episodes illustrated and also the style of the illustrations. (You may find it helpful to compare the style with other styles used in other books designed for children.)

Mobile Homes
John Steinbeck

1   I can only suspect that the lonely man peoples his driving dreams with friends, that the loveless man surrounds himself with lovely loving women, and that children climb through the dreaming of the childless driver. And how about the areas of regrets? If only I had done so-and-so, or had not said such-and-such—my God, the damn thing might not have happened. Finding this potential in my own mind, I can suspect it in others, but I will never know, for no one ever tells. And this is why, on my journey which was designed for observation, I stayed as much as possible on secondary roads where there was much to see and hear and smell, and avoided the great wide traffic slashes which promote the self by fostering daydreams. . . .

2   On these roads out of the manufacturing centers there moved many mobile homes, pulled by specially designed trucks, and since these mobile homes comprise one of my generalities, I may as well get to them now. Early in my travels I had become aware of these new things under the sun, of their great numbers, and since they occur in increasing numbers all over the nation, observation of them and perhaps some speculation is in order. They are not trailers to be pulled by one's own car but shining cars long as pullmans. From the beginning of my travels I had noticed the sale lots where they were sold and traded, but then I began to be aware of the parks where they sit down in uneasy permanence. In Maine I took to stopping the night in these parks, talking to the managers and to the dwellers in this new kind of housing, for they gather in groups of like to like.

3   They are wonderfully built homes, aluminum skins, doublewalled, with insulation, and often paneled with veneer of hardwood. Sometimes as much as forty feet long, they have two to five rooms, and are complete with air-conditioners, toilets, baths, and invariably television. The parks where they sit are sometimes landscaped and equipped with every facility. I talked with the park men, who were enthusiastic. A mobile home is drawn to the trailer park and installed on a ramp, a heavy rubber sewer pipe is bolted underneath, water and electricity power connected, the television an-

tenna raised, and the family is in residence. Several park managers agreed that last year one in four new housing units in the whole country was a mobile home. The park men charge a small ground rent plus fees for water and electricity. Telephones are connected in nearly all of them simply by plugging in a jack. Sometimes the park has a general store for supplies, but if not the supermarkets which dot the countryside are available. Parking difficulties in the towns have caused these markets to move to the open country where they are immune from town taxes. This is also true of the trailer parks. The fact that these homes can be moved does not mean that they do move. Sometimes their owners stay for years in one place, plant gardens, build little walls of cinder blocks, put out awnings and garden furniture. It is a whole way of life that was new to me. These homes are never cheap and often are quite expensive and lavish. I have seen some that cost $20,000 and contained all the thousand appliances we live by—dishwashers, automatic clothes washers and driers, refrigerators and deep freezes.

4   The owners were not only willing but glad and proud to show their homes to me. The rooms, while small, were well proportioned. Every conceivable unit was built in. Wide windows, some even called picture windows, destroyed any sense of being closed in; the bedrooms and beds were spacious and the storage space unbelievable. It seemed to me a revolution in living and on a rapid increase. Why did a family choose to live in such a home? Well, it was comfortable, compact, easy to keep clean, easy to heat.

5   In Maine: "I'm tired of living in a cold barn with the wind whistling through, tired of the torment of little taxes and payments for this and that. It's warm and cozy and in the summer the air-conditioner keeps us cool."

"What is the usual income bracket of the mobiles?"

"That is variable but a goodly number are in the ten-thousand-to twenty-thousand-dollar class."

"Has job uncertainty anything to do with the rapid increase of these units?"

"Well perhaps there may be some of that. Who knows what is in store tomorrow? Mechanics, plant engineers, architects, accountants, and even here and there a doctor or a dentist live in the mobile. If a plant or a factory closes down, you're not trapped with property you can't sell. Suppose the husband has a job and is buying a house and there's a layoff. The value goes out of his house. But if he has a mobile home he rents a trucking service and moves on and he hasn't lost anything. He may never have to do it, but the fact that he can is a comfort to him."

10.   "How are they purchased?"

"On time, just like an automobile. It's like paying rent."

And then I discovered the greatest selling appeal of all—one that crawls through nearly all American life. Improvements are made on these mobile homes every year. If you are doing well you turn yours in on a new model just as you do with an automobile if you can possibly afford to. There's status to that. And the turn-in value is higher than that of automobiles because there's a ready market for used homes. And after a few years the once expensive home may have a poorer family. They are easy to maintain, no need to paint since they are usually of aluminum, and are not tied to fluctuating land values.

"How about schools?"

The school buses pick the children up right at the park and bring them back. The family car takes the head of the house to work and the family to a drive-in movie at night. It's a healthy life out in the country air. The payments, even if high and festooned with interest, are no worse than renting an apartment and fighting the owner for heat. And where could you rent such a comfortable ground-floor apartment with a place for your car outside the door? Where else could the kids have a dog? Nearly every mobile home has a dog, as Charley discovered to his delight. Twice I was invited to dinner in a mobile home and several times watched a football game on television. A manager told me that one of the first considerations in his business was to find and buy a place where television reception is good. Since I did not require any facilities, sewer, water, or electricity, the price to me for stopping the night was one dollar.

15   The first impression forced on me was that permanence is neither achieved nor desired by mobile people. They do not buy for the generations, but only until a new model they can afford comes out. The mobile units are by no means limited to the park communities. Hundreds of them will be found sitting beside a farm house, and this was explained to me. There was a time when, on the occasion of a son's marriage and the addition of a wife and later of children to the farm, it was customary to add a wing or at least a lean-to on the home place. Now in many cases a mobile unit takes the place of additional building. A farmer from whom I bought eggs and home-smoked bacon told me of the advantages. Each family has a privacy it never had before. The old folks are not irritated

by crying babies. The mother-in-law problem is abated because the new daughter has a privacy she never had and a place of her own in which to build the structure of a family. When they move away, and nearly all Americans move away, or want to, they do not leave unused and therefore useless rooms. Relations between the generations are greatly improved. The son is a guest when he visits the parents' house, and the parents are guests in the son's house.

16   Then there are the loners, and I have talked with them also. Driving along, you see high on a hill a single mobile home placed to command a great view. Others nestle under trees fringing a river or a lake. These loners have rented a tiny piece of land from the owner. They need only enough for the unit and the right of passage to get to it. Sometimes the loner digs a well and a cesspool, and plants a garden, but others transport their water in fifty-gallon oil drums. Enormous ingenuity is apparent with some of the loners in placing the water supply higher than the unit and connecting it with plastic pipe so that a gravity flow is insured.

17   One of the dinners that I shared in a mobile home was cooked in an immaculate kitchen, walled in plastic tile, with stainless-steel sinks and ovens and stoves flush with the wall. The fuel is butane or some other bottled gas which can be picked up anywhere. We ate in a dining alcove paneled in mahogany veneer. I've never had a better or a more comfortable dinner. I had brought a bottle of whisky as my contribution, and afterward we sat in deep comfortable chairs cushioned in foam rubber. This family liked the way they lived and wouldn't think of going back to the old way. The husband worked as a garage mechanic about four miles away and made good pay. Two children walked to the highway every morning and were picked up by a yellow school bus.

18   Sipping a highball after dinner, hearing the rushing of water in the electric dishwasher in the kitchen, I brought up a question that had puzzled me. These were good, thoughtful, intelligent people. I said, "One of our most treasured feelings concerns roots, growing up rooted in some soil or some community." How did they feel about raising their children without roots? Was it good or bad? Would they miss it or not?

19   The father, a good-looking, fair-skinned man with dark eyes, answered me. "How many people today have what you are talking about? What roots are there in an apartment twelve floors up? What roots are in a housing development of hundreds and thousands of small dwellings almost exactly alike? My father came from Italy," he said. "He grew up in Tuscany in a house where his family had

lived maybe a thousand years. That's roots for you, no running water, no toilet, and they cooked with charcoal or vine clippings. They had just two rooms, a kitchen and a bedroom where everybody slept, grandpa, father and all the kids, no place to read, no place to be alone, and never had had. Was that better? I bet if you gave my old man the choice he'd cut his roots and live like this." He waved his hands at the comfortable room. "Fact is, he cut his roots away and came to America. Then he lived in a tenement in New York—just one room, walk-up, cold water and no heat. That's where I was born and I lived in the streets as a kid until my old man got a job upstate in New York in the grape country. You see, he knew about vines, that's about all he knew. Now you take my wife. She's Irish descent. Her people had roots too."

20   "In a peat bog," the wife said. "And lived on potatoes." She gazed fondly through the door at her fine kitchen.

21   "Don't you miss some kind of permanence?"

22   "Who's got permanence? Factory closes down, you move on. Good times and things opening up, you move on where it's better. You got roots you sit and starve. You take the pioneers in the history books. They were movers. Take up land, sell it, move on. I read in a book how Lincoln's family came to Illinois on a raft. They had some barrels of whisky for a bank account. How many kids in America stay in the place where they were born, if they can get out?"

23   "You've thought about it a lot."

24   "Don't have to think about it. There it is. I've got a good trade. Long as there's automobiles I can get work, but suppose the place I work goes broke. I got to move where there's a job. I get to my job in three minutes. You want I should drive twenty miles because I got roots?"

25   Later they showed me magazines designed exclusively for mobile dwellers, stories and poems and hints for successful mobile living. How to stop a leak. How to choose a place for sun or coolness. And there were advertisements for gadgets, fascinating things, for cooking, cleaning, washing clothes, furniture and beds and cribs. Also there were full-page pictures of new models, each one grander and more shiny than the next.

26   "There's thousands of them," said the father, "and there's going to be millions."

27   "Joe's quite a dreamer," the wife said. "He's always figuring something out. Tell him your ideas, Joe."

28   "Maybe he wouldn't be interested."

29   "Sure I would."

30   "Well, it's not a dream like she said, it's for real, and I'm going to do it pretty soon. Take a little capital, but it would pay off. I been looking around the used lots for the unit I want at the price I want to pay. Going to rip out the guts and set it up for a repair shop. I got enough tools nearly already, and I'll stock little things like windshield wipers and fan belts and cylinder rings and inner tubes, stuff like that. You take these courts are getting bigger and bigger. Some of the mobile people got two cars. I'll rent me a hundred feet of ground right near and I'll be in business. There's one thing you can say about cars, there's nearly always something wrong with them that's got to be fixed. And I'll have my house, this here one right beside my shop. That way I would have a bell and give twenty-four-hour service."

31   "Sounds like a good deal," I said. And it does.

32   "Best thing about it," Joe went on, "if business fell off, why, I'd just move on where it was good."

33   His wife said, "Joe's got it all worked out on paper where everything's going to go, every wrench and drill, even an electric welder. Joe's a wonderful welder."

34   I said, "I take back what I said, Joe. I guess you've got your roots in a grease pit."

35   "You could do worse. I even worked that out. And you know, when the kids grow up, we can even work our way south in the winter and north in the summer."

36   "Joe does good work," said his wife. "He's got his own steady customers where he works. Some men come fifty miles to get Joe to work on their cars because he does good work."

37   "I'm a real good mechanic," said Joe.

38   Driving the big highway near Toledo I had a conversation with Charley on the subject of roots. He listened but he didn't reply. In the pattern-thinking about roots I and most other people have left two things out of consideration. Could it be that Americans are a restless people, a mobile people, never satisfied with where they are as a matter of selection? The pioneers, the immigrants who peopled the continent, were the restless ones in Europe. The steady rooted ones stayed home and are still there. But every one of us, except the Negroes forced here as slaves, are descended from the restless ones, the wayward ones who were not content to stay at home. Wouldn't it be unusual if we had not inherited this tendency? And the fact is that we have. But that's the short view. What are roots and how long have we had them? If our species has existed for a couple of million years, what is its history? Our remote ancestors

followed the game, moved with the food supply, and fled from evil weather, from ice and the changing seasons. Then after millennia beyond thinking they domesticated some animals so that they lived with their food supply. Then of necessity they followed the grass that fed their flocks in endless wanderings. Only when agriculture came into practice—and that's not very long ago in terms of the whole history—did a place achieve meaning and value and permanence. But land is a tangible, and tangibles have a way of getting into few hands. Thus it was that one man wanted ownership of land and at the same time wanted servitude because someone had to work it. Roots were in ownership of land, in tangible and immovable possessions. In this view we are a restless species with a very short history of roots, and those not widely distributed. Perhaps we have overrated roots as a psychic need. Maybe the greater the urge, the deeper and more ancient is the need, the will, the hunger to be somewhere else.

Questions

1   In paragraph 1 Steinbeck explains why he preferred secondary roads to heavily used roads. Explain his reason, in your own words. Exactly what does he mean when he says that "the great wide traffic slashes . . . promote the self by fostering daydreams"?

2. If you have ever lived in a mobile home, what do you consider its advantages? Its disadvantages? If you have never lived in one, on the basis of this essay do you think someday you might give it a try? Why, or why not?

3. In paragraphs 18–22 Steinbeck raises the question of whether the residents of mobile homes may be "without roots." The father, in paragraph 19, suggests that people who live in apartments, or in housing developments, also probably lack roots. Do you find his argument compelling? Why, or why not?

4. In paragraph 34 Steinbeck says, "I take back what I said, Joe. I guess you've got your roots in a grease pit." What does he mean? Does his response have any relevance to other members of Joe's family?

5. In the last paragraph Steinbeck writes, "We are a restless species with a very short history of roots." What can you add to his meditation?

*F*athers and Sons
Studs Terkel

Glenn Stribling[1]

1   *A casual encounter on a plane; a casual remark: he and his wife are returning from a summer cruise. It was their first vacation in twenty-five years. He is forty-eight.*

2   *He and his son are partners in the business: Glenn & Dave's Complete Auto Repair. They run a Texaco service station in a fairly affluent community some thirty miles outside Cleveland. "There's eight of us on the payroll, counting my son and I. Of course, the wife, she's the bookkeeper." There are three tow trucks.*

3   *"Glenn & Dave's is equipped to do all nature of repair work: everything from transmission, air conditioning, valves, all . . . everything. I refer to it as a garage because we do everything garages do.*

4   *"We have been here four years." He himself has been at it "steady" for twenty-nine years. "When I was a kid in high school I worked at the Studebaker garage part-time for seven dollars a week. And I paid seven dollars a week board and room." (Laughs.) "It more or less runs in our family. My great-grandfather used to make spokes for automobiles back in Pennsylvania when they used wooden wheels. I have a brother, he's a mechanic. I have another brother in California, he's in the same business as I'm in. My dad, he was a steam engine repairman.*

5   *"Another reason I went into this business: it's Depression-proof. A good repairman will always have a job. Even though they're making cars so they don't last so long and people trade 'em in more often, there's still gonna be people that have to know what they're doing."*

6   I work eight days a week. (Laughs.) My average weeks usually run to eighty, ninety hours. We get every other Sunday off, my son and I. Alternate, you know. Oh, I love it. There's never a day long enough. We never get through. And that's a good way to have it,

---

[1]Terkel's book *Working* consists of edited versions of more than a hundred interviews with workers of all sorts. Here we reprint an interview with Glenn Stribling and another with Stribling's son, Dave.

'cause people rely on you and you rely on them, and it's one big business. Sometimes, they're all three trucks goin'. All we sell is service, and if you can't give service, you might as well give up.

7   All our business has come to us from mouth to mouth. We've never run a big ad in the paper. That itself is a good sign that people are satisfied. Of course, there's some people that nobody could satisfy. I've learned: Why let one person spoil your whole day?

8   A new customer comes to town, he would say, "So-and-so, I met him on the train and he recommended you folks very highly." Oh, we've had a lot of compliments where people, they say they've never had anything like that done to a car. They are real happy that we did point out things and do things. Preventive maintenance I call it.

9   A man come in, we'd Xed his tires, sold him a set of shocks, repacked his wheel bearings, aligned his front, serviced his car—by service I mean lubricate, change oil, filter . . . But he had only one tail light working and didn't know it. So we fixed that and he'll be grateful for it. If it's something big, a matter of a set of tires or if he needs a valve job, we call the customer and discuss it with him.

10   Sometimes, but not very often, I've learned to relax. When I walk out of here I try to leave everything, 'cause we have a loud bell at home. If I'm out in the yard working, people call. They want to know about a car, maybe make a date for next week, or maybe there's a car here that we've had and there's a question on it. The night man will call me up at home. We have twenty-four-hour service, too, towing. My son and I, we take turns. So this phone is hooked up outside so you can hear it. And all the neighbors can hear it too. (Laughs.)

11   Turn down calls? No, never. Well, if it's some trucking outfit and they don't have an account with us—they're the worst risk there is. If they don't have a credit card or if the person they're delivering won't vouch for them, there's gotta be some sort of agreement on payment before we go out. Of course, if it's a stranger, if it's broke down, naturally we have the car.

12   Sometimes if we're busy, bad weather and this and that, why we won't get any lunch, unless the wife runs uptown and grabs a sandwich. I usually go home, it varies anywhere between six thirty, seven, eight. Whatever the public demands. In the wintertime, my God, we don't get out of here till nine. I have worked thirty-seven hours non-stop.

13   I don't do it for the money. People are in trouble and they call

you and you feel obligated enough to go out there and straighten them out as much as you can. My wife tells me I take my business more serious than a doctor. Every now and then a competitor will come down and ask me to diagnose something. And I go ahead and do it. I'll tell anybody anything I know if it'll help him. That's a good way to be. You might want a favor from them sometime. Live and let live.

14   You get irritated a lot of times, but you keep it within yourself. You can't be too eccentric. You gotta be the same. Customers like people the same all the time. Another thing I noticed: the fact that I got gray hair, that helps in business. Even though my son's in with me and we have capable men working for us, they always want to talk to Glenn. They respect me and what I tell 'em.

15   If I'm tensed up and there'll be somebody pull in on the driveway, ring all the bells, park right in front of the door, then go in and use the washroom—those kind of people are the most inconsiderate kind of people there is. If you're out there in the back, say you're repacking wheel bearings. Your hands are full of grease. In order to go out in that drive, you have to clean your hands. And all the customer wanted to know was where the courtroom is. When I travel, if I want information, I'll park out on the apron. Sometimes we have as high as fifty, sixty people a day in here for information. They pull up, ring all the bells . . . You can imagine how much time it takes if you go out fifty, sixty times and you don't pump gas. I call 'em IWW: Information, wind, and water. It's worse the last four years we've been here. People don't care. They don't think of us. All they think of is themself.

16   Oh, I lose my temper sometimes. You wouldn't be a red-blooded American if you wouldn't, would you? At the same time you're dealing with the public. You have to control yourself. Like I say, people like an even-tempered person. When I do lose my temper, the wife, she can't get over it. She says, "Glenn, I don't know how you can blow your stack at one person and then five minutes later you're tellin' him a joke." I don't hold grudges. Why hold a grudge? Let people know what you think, express your opinion, and then forget it. Of course, you don't forget, you just don't keep harpin' on it.

17   In the summertime, when I get home I don't even go in the house. I grab a garden tool and go out and work till dark. I have a small garden—lettuce, onions, small vegetables. By the time you're on your feet all day you're ready to relax, watch television, sometimes have a fire in the fireplace. At social gatherings, if somebody's

in the same business, we compare notes. If we run into something that's a time saver, we usually exchange. But not too much. Because who likes to talk shop?

18   There's a few good mechanics left. Most of 'em in this day and age, all they are is parts replacers. This is a new trend. You need an air conditioner, you don't repair 'em any more. You can get exchange units, factory guaranteed and much cheaper, much faster. People don't want to lay up their car long enough to get it fixed. If they can't look out and see their car in the driveway, they feel like they've lost something. They get nervous. It's very seldom people will overhaul a car. They'll trade it in instead.

19   This is something hard to find any more, a really good, conscientious worker. When the whistle blows, they're all washed up, ready to go before they're punched out. You don't get a guy who'll stay two or three hours later, just to get a job done.

20   Take my son, Dave. Say a person's car broke down. It's on a Sunday or a Saturday night. Maybe it would take an hour to fix. Why, I'll go ahead and fix it. Dave's the type that'll say, "Leave it sit till Monday." I put myself in the other guy's boots and I'll go ahead and fix his car, because time don't mean that much to me. Consequently we got a lot of good customers. Last winter we had a snowstorm. People wanted some snow tires. I put 'em on. He's a steady customer now. He just sold his house for $265,000.

21   When we took this last cruise, my customers told me Dave did a terrific job. "Before, we didn't think much of him. But he did a really good job this last time." I guess compared to the average young person Dave is above average as far as being conscientious. Although he does sleep in the morning. Today's Wednesday? Nine o'clock this morning. It was ten o'clock yesterday morning. He's supposed to be here at seven. Rather than argue and fight about it, I just forget it.

22   Another thing I trained myself: I know the address and phone number of all the places we do business with and a lot of our customers. I never even look in the phone book. (Dave had just made a phone call after leafing through the directory.) If he asked me, I coulda told him.

Dave Stribling

23   *He is twenty-three, married, and has two baby children. He has been working with his father "more or less since I was twelve years old. It's one of those deals where the son does carry on the family tradition.*

24   *"I actually worked full-time when I was in junior high school.*
School was a bore. But when you stop and look back at it you wish
to hell you'd done a lot more. I wanted to go get that fast buck.
Some people are fortunate to make it overnight. My dad and I had
a few quarrels and I quit him. I used to work down at Chrysler
while I was in high school. I worked at least eight hours a day.
That was great. You don't work Saturdays and you don't work
Sundays. Then I came back and worked for my dad."

25   How would I describe myself? Mixed up really. (Laughs.) I
like my work. (Sighs.) But I wish I hadn't started that early. I wish
I would have tried another trade, actually. At my age I could quit
this. I could always come back. But I'm pretty deep now. If I were
to walk out, it would be pretty bad. (Laughs.) I don't think I'll
change my occupation, really.

26   I think I'da tried to be an architect or, hell, maybe even a real
top-notch good salesman. Or maybe even a farmer. It's hard to say.
The grass is always greener on the other side of the fence. You turn
around and there's an attorney. It makes you feel different. You
work during the day and you're dirty from this and that. The majority of the people overlook the fact as long as you're established
and this and that. They don't really care what your occupation is
as long as you're a pretty good citizen.

27   Where it really gets you down is, you're at some place and
you'll meet a person and strike up a conversation with 'em. Naturally, sometime during that conversation he's going to ask about
your occupation, what you do for a living. So this guy, he manages
this, he manages that, see? When I tell him—and I've seen it happen
lots of times—there's a kind of question mark in his head. Just
what is this guy? You work. You just sweat. It's not mental. 'Cause
a lot of these jobs that you do, you do so many of the same thing,
it just becomes automatic. You know what you're doing blind-
folded.

28   It's made me a pretty good livin' so far. But I don't have a lot
of time that a lot of these guys do that are in my age and in the
same status that I am. I put in every week at least sixty, sixty-five
hours. And then at night, you never know. If somebody breaks
down, you can't tell 'em no. You gotta go. My friends work forty
hours a week and they're done. Five days a week. I work seven,
actually. Every other Sunday. I have to come and open up.

29   I don't really like to talk about my work with my friends. They
don't really seem to, either. A lot of times somebody will ask me
something about their car. How much will this cost? How much

will that cost? I don't really even want to quote my price to them. A couple of 'em work for the state, in an office. A couple of 'em are body men. One's a carpenter, one's a real estate salesman. A few of 'em, they just work.

30   I come home, I gotta go in the back door, 'cause I've got on greasy boots. (Laughs.) If it does happen to be about six thirty, then I won't get cleaned up before I eat. I'll sit down and eat with the wife and kids. If they've already eaten, I'll take a shower and I'll get cleaned up and I'll come down and eat. If it's a nice night, I might go out and putz around the yard. If it's not nice outside, I'll just sit and watch the TV. I don't really read that much. I probably read as much as the average American. But nothing any more. Sometimes you really put out a lot of work that day—in general, I'm tired. I'm asleep by ten o'clock at night. I come to work, it varies, I might come in between eight and nine, maybe even ten o'clock in the morning. I like my sleep. (Laughs.)

31   He's the one that opens it up. He believes the early bird gets the worm. But that's not always true either. I might come in late, but actually I do more work than he does here in a day. Most of it probably is as careful as his. I can't understand a lot of the stuff he does. But he can't understand a lot of the stuff I do either. (Laughs.) He's getting better. He's kinda come around. But he still does think old-fashioned.

32   Like tools. You can buy equipment, it might cost a lot more money but it'll do the job faster and easier. He'll go grab hand tools, that you gotta use your own muscle. He doesn't go in for power tools.

33   Like judging people. Anybody with long hair is no good to him—even me. If he caught me asleep, he'd probably give me a Yul Brynner. Hair doesn't have anything to do with it. I've met a lot of people with hair really long, just like a female. They're still the same. They still got their ideas and they're not hippies or anything. They go to work every day just like everybody else does. It gets him. Especially if someone will come in and ask him to do something, he'll let them know he doesn't like them. I don't give people that much static.

34   When somebody comes in and they're in a rage and it's all directed at you. I either go get the hell out of there or my rage is brought up towards them. I've definitely lost customers by tellin' 'em. I don't know how to just slough it off. In the majority of cases you're sorry for it.

35   I've seen my father flare up a lot of times. Somebody gives him

a bad time during the day, he'll take it home. Whereas instead of tellin' 'em right there on the spot, he'll just keep it within himself. Then half-hour later he might be mumblin' somethin'. When I used to live at home, you could tell by thirty seconds after he got in the door that he either didn't feel good or somebody gave him a bad time. He just keeps it going through his mind. He won't forget it. Whereas when I go home to the wife and the two kids, I just like to forget it. I don't want to talk about it at all.

36   I yell a lot, cuss a lot. I might throw things around down here, take a hammer and hit the bench as hard as it'll go, I'm getting better though, really. I used to throw a lot of stuff. I'd just grab and throw a wrench or something. But I haven't done that in a long time now. When you get older and you start thinking about it, you really have changed a lot in the last few years. (Laughs.) It'll stay inside me. You learn to absorb more of it. More so than when you were a kid. You realize you're not doing any good. Lotta times you might damage something. It's just gonna come out of your pocket.

37   When I was younger, if there was something I didn't agree upon, I was ready to go right then against it. But now I don't. I kinda step back a half a step and think it out. I've gotten into pretty good arguments with my buddies. It never really comes down to fists, but if you're with somebody long enough, it's bound to happen, you're gonna fight. You had a hard day and somebody gave you a hard time and, say you went out to eat and the waitress, she screwed something up? Yeah, it'll flare up. But not as much as it used to be.

38   As far as customers goes, there's not too many of 'em I like. A lot of customers, you can joke with, you can kid with. There are a lot of 'em, they don't want to hear any of it. They don't want to discuss anything else but the business while they're here. Older people, yeah, they're pretty hard. Because they've gone through a change from a Model T to what you got nowadays. Nowadays a lot of 'em will put up the hood and they just shake their heads. They just can't figure it out.

39   Some of 'em, when they get old they get real grumpy. Anything you say, you're just a kid and you don't know what you're doin'. (Laughs.) They don't want to listen to you, they want to talk to somebody else. There's a lot of 'em that'll just talk to him. But there's a lot of 'em that want to talk to me and don't want to talk to him. My-age people. It's a mixed-up generation. (Laughs.)

40   ˙ I have pride in what I do. This day and age, you don't always repair something. You renew. Whereas in his era you could buy a kit to rebuild pretty near anything. Take a water pump. You can

buy 'em. You can put on a new one. I wouldn't even bother to repair a water pump. You can buy rebuilts, factory rebuilts. Back in his time you rebuilt water pumps.

41   His ideas are old, really. You gotta do this a certain way and this a certain way. There's short cuts found that you could just eliminate half the stuff you do. But he won't. A lot of the new stuff that comes out, he won't believe anybody. He won't even believe me. He might call three or four people before he'll believe it. Why he won't believe me I don't know. I guess he must figure I bull him a lot. (Laughs.)

42   When he was working for a living as a mechanic, his ability was pretty good. Actually, he doesn't do that much work. I mean, he more or less is a front. (Laughs.) Many people come in here that think he does work on their car. But he doesn't. He's mostly the one that meets people. He brings the work in. In his own mind he believes he's putting out the work. But we're the ones that put out the work.

43   He's kind of funny to figure out. (Laughs.) He has no hobbies, really. When he's out he'll still talk his trade. He just can't forget it, leave it go.

44   I'd like to go bigger in this business, but father says no for right now. He's too skeptical. We're limited here. He doesn't want to go in debt. But you gotta spend money to make money. He's had to work harder than I have. There's nobody that ever really gave him anything. He's had to work for everything he's got. He's given me a lot. Sometimes he gives too much. His grand-kids, they've got clothes at home still in boxes, brand-new as they got 'em. He just goes overboard. If I need money, he'll loan it to me. He's lent me money that I haven't even paid back, really. (Laughs.)

45   (Sighs.) I used to play music. I used to play in a rock group. Bass. I didn't know very much on the bass. Everybody that was in the band really didn't know all that much. We more or less progressed together. We played together for a year and a half, then everything just broke up. Oh yeah, we enjoyed it. It was altogether different. I like to play music now but don't have the time . . . I like to play, but you can't do both. This is my living. You have to look at it that way.

Questions

1. How accurate do you think Glenn Stribling's view of his son is?
2. How accurate do you think Dave Stribling's view of his father is?

3. How does Dave see himself? How do his views contrast with his father's?

O*n Natural Death*

Lewis Thomas

---

1   There are so many new books about dying that there are now special shelves set aside for them in bookshops, along with the health-diet and home-repair paperbacks and the sex manuals. Some of them are so packed with detailed information and step-by-step instructions for performing the function that you'd think this was a new sort of skill which all of us are now required to learn. The strongest impression the casual reader gets, leafing through, is that proper dying has become an extraordinary, even an exotic experience, something only the specially trained get to do.

2   Also, you could be led to believe that we are the only creatures capable of the awareness of death, that when all the rest of nature is being cycled through dying, one generation after another, it is a different kind of process, done automatically and trivially, more "natural," as we say.

3   An elm in our backyard caught the blight this summer and dropped stone dead, leafless, almost overnight. One weekend it was a normal-looking elm, maybe a little bare in spots but nothing alarming, and the next weekend it was gone, passed over, departed, taken. Taken is right, for the tree surgeon came by yesterday with his crew of young helpers and their cherry picker, and took it down branch by branch and carted it off in the back of a red truck, everyone singing.

4   The dying of a field mouse, at the jaws of an amiable household cat, is a spectacle I have beheld many times. It used to make me wince. Early in life I gave up throwing sticks at the cat to make him drop the mouse, because the dropped mouse regularly went ahead and died anyway, but I always shouted unaffections at the cat to let him know the sort of animal he had become. Nature, I thought, was an abomination.

5   Recently I've done some thinking about that mouse, and I wonder if his dying is necessarily all that different from the passing of our elm. The main difference, if there is one, would be in the matter of pain. I do not believe that an elm tree has pain receptors, and even so, the blight seems to me a relatively painless way to go even if there were nerve endings in a tree, which there are not. But the mouse dangling tail-down from the teeth of a gray cat is something else again, with pain beyond bearing, you'd think, all over his small body.

6   There are now some plausible reasons for thinking it is not like that at all, and you can make up an entirely different story about the mouse and his dying if you like. At the instant of being trapped and penetrated by teeth, peptide hormones are released by cells in the hypothalamus and the pituitary gland; instantly these substances, called endorphins, are attached to the surfaces of other cells responsible for pain perception; the hormones have the pharmacologic properties of opium; there is no pain. Thus it is that the mouse seems always to dangle so languidly from the jaws, lies there so quietly when dropped, dies of his injuries without a struggle. If a mouse could shrug, he'd shrug.

7   I do not know if this is true or not, nor do I know how to prove it if it is true. Maybe if you could get in there quickly enough and administer naloxone, a specific morphine antagonist, you could turn off the endorphins and observe the restoration of pain, but this is not something I would care to do or see. I think I will leave it there, as a good guess about the dying of a cat-chewed mouse, perhaps about dying in general.

8   Montaigne had a hunch about dying, based on his own close call in a riding accident. He was so badly injured as to be believed dead by his companions, and was carried home with lamentations, "all bloody, stained all over with the blood I had thrown up." He remembers the entire episode, despite having been "dead, for two full hours," with wonderment:

> It seemed to me that my life was hanging only by the tip of my lips. I closed my eyes in order, it seemed to me, to help push it out, and took pleasure in growing languid and letting myself go. It was an idea that was only floating on the surface of my soul, as delicate and feeble as all the rest, but in truth not only free from distress but mingled with that sweet feeling that people have who have let themselves slide into sleep. I believe that this is the same state in which people find themselves whom we see

fainting in the agony of death, and I maintain that we pity them
without cause. . . . In order to get used to the idea of death, I
find there is nothing like coming close to it.

Later, in another essay, Montaigne returns to it:

If you know not how to die, never trouble yourself; Nature will
in a moment fully and sufficiently instruct you; she will exactly
do that business for you; take you no care for it.

9   The worst accident I've ever seen was on Okinawa, in the early
days of the invasion, when a jeep ran into a troop carrier and was
crushed nearly flat. Inside were two young MPs, trapped in bent
steel, both mortally hurt, with only their heads and shoulders visible. We had a conversation while people with the right tools were
prying them free. Sorry about the accident, they said. No, they said,
they felt fine. Is everyone else okay, one of them said. Well, the
other one said, no hurry now. And then they died.

10   Pain is useful for avoidance, for getting away when there's time
to get away, but when it is end game, and no way back, pain
is likely to be turned off, and the mechanisms for this are wonderfully precise and quick. If I had to design an ecosystem in which
creatures had to live off each other and in which dying was an
indispensable part of living, I could not think of a better way to
manage.

Questions

1. We find the first paragraph witty, in a quiet way. In a paragraph
   point out the wit to a friend who missed it.
2. Make a rough outline of Thomas's essay—perhaps a sentence
   for each paragraph or group of closely related paragraphs—and
   then, on the basis of this outline, explain the organization of
   the essay. In particular, account for the relation between the
   first paragraph and the last.
3. Thomas uses "I" fairly often. Does he talk too much about himself? Explain.

Why Women Are Paid
Less Than Men
Lester C. Thurow

1   In the 40 years from 1939 to 1979 white women who work full time have with monotonous regularity made slightly less than 60 percent as much as white men. Why?

2   Over the same time period, minorities have made substantial progress in catching up with whites, with minority women making even more progress than minority men. Black men now earn 72 percent as much as white men (up 16 pecentage points since the mid-1950's) but black women earn 92 percent as much as white women. Hispanic men make 71 percent of what their white counterparts do, but Hispanic women make 82 percent as much as white women. As a result of their faster progress, fully employed black women make 75 percent as much as fully employed black men while Hispanic women earn 68 percent as much as Hispanic men.

3   This faster progress may, however, end when minority women finally catch up with white women. In the bible of the New Right, George Gilder's *Wealth and Poverty*, the 60 percent is just one of Mother Nature's constants like the speed of light or the force of gravity. Men are programmed to provide for their families economically while women are programmed to take care of their families emotionally and physically. As a result men put more effort into their jobs than women. The net result is a difference in work intensity that leads to that 40 percent gap in earnings. But there is no discrimination against women—only the biological facts of life.

4   The problem with this assertion is just that. It is an assertion with no evidence for it other than the fact that white women have made 60 percent as much as men for a long period of time.

5   "Discrimination against women" is an easy answer but it also has its problems as an adequate explanation. Why is discrimination against women not declining under the same social forces that are leading to a lessening of discrimination against minorities? In recent years women have made more use of the enforcement provisions of the Equal Employment Opportunities Commission and the courts than minorities. Why do the laws that prohibit discrimination against women and minorities work for minorities but not for women?

6   When men discriminate against women, they run into a problem. To discriminate against women is to discriminate against your own wife and to lower your own family income. To prevent women from working is to force men to work more.

7   When whites discriminate against blacks, they can at least think that they are raising their own incomes. When men discriminate against women they have to know that they are lowering their own family income and increasing their own work effort.

8   While discrimination undoubtedly explains part of the male-female earnings differential, one has to believe that men are monumentally stupid or irrational to explain all of the earnings gap in terms of discrimination. There must be something else going on.

9   Back in 1939 it was possible to attribute the earnings gap to large differences in educational attainments. But the educational gap between men and women has been eliminated since World War II. It is no longer possible to use education as an explanation for the lower earnings of women. Some observers have argued that women earn less money since they are less reliable workers who are more apt to leave the labor force. But it is difficult to maintain this position since women are less apt to quit one job to take another and as a result they tend to work as long, or longer, for any one employer. From any employer's perspective they are more reliable, not less reliable, than men.

10   Part of the answer is visible if you look at the lifetime earnings profile of men. Suppose that you were asked to predict which men in a group of 25-year-olds would become economically successful. At age 25 it is difficult to tell who will be economically successful and your predictions are apt to be highly inaccurate. But suppose that you were asked to predict which men in a group of 35-year-olds would become economically successful. If you are successful at age 35, you are very likely to remain successful for the rest of your life. If you have not become economically successful by age 35, you are very unlikely to do so later.

11   The decade between 25 and 35 is when men either succeed or fail. It is the decade when lawyers become partners in the good firms, when business managers make it onto the "fast track," when academics get tenure at good universities, and when blue collar workers find the job opportunities that will lead to training opportunities and the skills that will generate high earnings. If there is any one decade when it pays to work hard and to be consistently in the labor force, it is the decade between 25 and 35. For those

who succeed, earnings will rise rapidly. For those who fail, earnings will remain flat for the rest of their lives.

12   But the decade between 25 and 35 is precisely the decade when women are most apt to leave the labor force or become part-time workers to have children. When they do, the current system of promotion and skill acquisition will extract an enormous lifetime price.

13   This leaves essentially two avenues for equalizing male and female earnings. Families where women who wish to have successful careers, compete with men, and achieve the same earnings should alter their family plans and have their children either before 25 or after 35. Or society can attempt to alter the existing promotion and skill acquisition system so that there is a longer time period in which both men and women can attempt to successfully enter the labor force. Without some combination of these two factors, a substantial fraction of the male-female earnings differentials are apt to persist for the next 40 years, even if discrimination against women is eliminated.

Questions

1. Thurow assumes that discrimination against women can't possibly be the whole explanation for their lower earnings. On what does he base this assumption? Do you agree with his assumption?

2. Evaluate Thurow's opening paragraph, explaining why you find it effective or ineffective.

3. After giving his analysis, Thurow ends the essay by suggesting two ways in which the differential in earnings may be decreased. Does he convey enthusiasm? Optimism? Is the tone of the ending consistent with the tone of the rest of the essay?

4. If you have read Bergmann's "Pay Equity—How to Answer Back" (page 601), set forth what you think would be Bergmann's response to Thurow's analysis of the problem and her response to his two proposals for equalizing male and female earnings.

PART FIVE

*E*diting

No iron can stab the heart
with such force as a period
put just at the right place.
— ISAAC BABEL

17

Manuscript Form

To edit a manuscript is to refine it for others to read. When your essay at last says what you want to say, you are ready to get it into good physical shape, into an edited manuscript.

BASIC MANUSCRIPT FORM

Much of what follows is nothing more than common sense. Unless your instructor specifies something different, you can adopt these principles as a guide.

1. Use 8½-by-11-inch paper of good weight. Do not use paper torn out of a spiral notebook; the ragged edges will distract the reader. If you have written your essay on a computer and have printed it on a continuous roll of paper, remove the perforated strips from each side of the paper and separate the sheets before you hand in the essay.

2. Write on one side of the paper only. If you submit a handwritten copy, use lined paper and write, in black or dark blue ink, on every other line if the lines are closely spaced. If you typewrite, double-space, typing with a reasonably fresh ribbon. If you write on a word processor, use a letter-quality printer or a dot-matrix printer that closely approaches letter quality.

3. In the upper right-hand corner, one inch from the top, put your name, your instructor's name, the course number, and the date. Double-space between lines. It's a good idea to put your last name before the page number (in the upper right-hand corner) of each subsequent page, so the instructor can easily reassemble your essay if somehow a page gets detached and mixed with other papers. (If you write your paper on a word processor, you can instruct it to print your name before each page number.)

4. *Titles.* Use this form for your title: Double-space after the date and then center the title of your essay. Capitalize the first letter of the first and last words of your title, the first word after a semicolon or colon if you use either one, and the first letter of all the other words except articles, conjunctions, and prepositions, thus:

The Meaning of Truth in the <u>Apology</u>

Notice that your own title is neither underlined nor enclosed in quotation marks. (If, as here, your title includes material that would normally be italicized or in quotation marks, that material continues to be so written.) If the title runs more than one line, double-space between the lines.

5. Begin the essay by double-spacing *twice* below the title. If your instructor prefers a title page, begin the essay on the next page and number it 1. The title page is not numbered.

6. *Margins.* Except for page numbers, leave a one-inch margin at top, bottom, and sides of text.

7. Number the pages consecutively, using arabic numerals in the upper right-hand corner, half an inch from the top. Do not put a period or a hyphen after the numeral, and do not precede the numeral with "page" or "p." (Again, if you give the title on a separate sheet, the page that follows it is page 1. Do not number the title page.)

8. *Paragraphs.* Indent the first word of each paragraph five spaces from the left margin.

9. Make a copy of your essay for yourself and keep it until the original has been returned. It is a good idea to keep notes and drafts too. They may prove helpful if you are asked to revise a page, substantiate a point, or supply a source you omitted.

10. Fasten the pages of your paper with a paper clip in the upper left-hand corner. Stiff binders are unnecessary; indeed, they are a nuisance to the instructor, adding bulk and making it awkward to write annotations.

CORRECTIONS IN THE FINAL COPY

Extensive revisions should have been made in your drafts, but minor last-minute revisions may be made on the finished copy. Proofreading may catch some typographical errors, and you may notice some small weaknesses.

You need not retype the page, or even erase. You can make corrections with the following proofreader's symbols.

1. *Changes* in wording may be made by crossing through words and rewriting just above them, either on the typewriter or by hand in pen:

```
                                      have
The insistent demands for drastic reform has disappeared from

most of the nation's campuses.
```

2. *Additions* should be made above the line, with a caret (∧) below the line at the appropriate place:

```
                                                      from
The insistent demands for drastic reform have disappeared
                                                   ∧
most of the nation's campuses.
```

3. *Transpositions* of letters may be made thus:

```
The insistent demadbs for drastic reform have disappeared
from most of the nation's campuses.
```

4. *Deletions* are indicated by a horizontal line through the word or words to be deleted. Delete a single letter by drawing a vertical or diagonal line through it.

```
The insistent demands for drastic reform ~~reform~~ have disap-
peared from most of the nation's campuse/s
```

5. *Separation* of words accidentally run together is indicated by a vertical line, *closure* by a curved line connecting the things to be closed up.

```
The insistent|demands for drastic reform have disappeared
f͡rom most of the nation's campuses
```

6. *Paragraphing* may be indicated by the symbol ¶ before the word that is to begin the new paragraph.

```
The insistent demands for drastic reform have disappeared
from most of the nation's campuses. ¶ Another sign that the
country's mood has
```

QUOTATIONS AND QUOTATION MARKS

Quotations from the material you are writing about are indispensable. They not only let your readers know what you are talking about; they give your readers the material you are responding to, thus letting them share your responses. But quote sparingly and quote briefly. Use quotations as evidence, not as padding. If the exact wording of the original is crucial, or especially effective, quote it directly, but if it is not, don't bore the reader with material that can be effectively reduced either by summarizing or by cutting. And make sure, by a comment before or after a quotation, that your reader understands why you find the quotation relevant. Don't count on a quotation to make your point for you.

Here are some additional matters to keep in mind.

1. Identify the speaker or writer of the quotation. Usually this identification precedes the quoted material (e.g., "Smith says, . . .") in accordance with the principle of letting readers know where they are going. But occasionally it may follow the quotation, especially if the name will provide a meaningful surprise. For example, in a discussion of a proposed tax reform, you might quote a remark hostile to it and then reveal that the author of the proposal was also the author of the remark.

2. When you introduce a quotation, consider using verbs other than "says." Depending on the context—that is, on the substance of the quotation and its place in your essay—it might be more accurate to say "Smith argues," "adds," "contends," "points out," "admits," or "comments." Or, again with just the right verb, you might introduce the quotation with a transitional phrase: "In another context Smith had observed that . . ." or "To clarify this point Smith refers to . . ." or "In an apparent contradiction Smith suggests . . ." But avoid such inflated words as "opines," "avers," and "is of the opinion that." The point is not to add "elegant variation" (see page 526) to your introduction of someone else's words, but accuracy and grace. A verb often used *in*accurately is "feels." Ralph Linton does not "feel" that "the term *primitive art* has come to be used with at least three distinct meanings." He "points out," "writes," "observes," or "says" so.

3. Distinguish between short and long quotations and treat each appropriately.

Enclose *short quotations,* four (or fewer) lines of typing, within quotation marks:

```
Anne Lindbergh calls the harrowing period of the kidnapping
and murder of her first child the "hour of lead."

"Flying," she wrote, "was freedom and beauty and escape from
crowds."
```

Set off *long quotations* (more than four lines of typing). Do *not* enclose them within quotation marks. To set off a quotation, begin a new line, indent ten spaces from the left margin, and type the quotation double-spaced:

```
The last paragraphs of Five Years of My Life contain Drey-

fus's words when he was finally freed:

    The Government of the Republic gives me back my liberty.

    It is nothing to me without honor.  Beginning with today,

    I shall unremittingly strive for the reparation of the

    frightful judicial error of which I am still the victim.

    I want all France to know by a final judgment that I am

    innocent.

    But he was never to receive that judgment. . . .
```

Note that long quotations are usually introduced by a sentence ending with a colon (as in the above example) or by an introductory phrase, such as "Dreyfus wrote:"

Don't try to introduce a long quotation into the middle of one of your own sentences. It is too difficult for the reader to come out of the quotation and to pick up your thread. Instead, introduce the quotation, as we did above, set the quotation off, and then begin a new sentence of your own.

4. An embedded quotation (that is, a quotation embedded into a sentence of your own) must fit grammatically into the sentence of which it is a part. For example, suppose you want to use Othello's line "I have done the state some service."

Incorrect

```
Near the end of the play Othello says that he "have done the

state some service."
```

Correct

```
Near the end of the play Othello says that he has "done the

state some service."
```

Correct

```
Near the end of the play, Othello says, "I have done the
state some service."
```

5. Quote exactly. Check your quotation for accuracy at least twice. If you need to edit a quotation, for example in order to embed it grammatically, or to inform your reader of a relevant point, observe the following rules:

a) *To add or to substitute* words, enclose the words in *square brackets—not* parentheses.

```
"In the summer of 1816 we [Mary Wollstonecraft and Percy
Bysshe Shelley] visited Switzerland and became the neighbor
of Lord Byron."

Trotsky became aware that "Stalin would not hesitate a moment
to organize an attempt on [his] life."
```

b) *To omit material* indicate the omission (ellipsis) by three periods, with a space before and after each period:

```
The New York Times called it "the most intensive man-hunt
. . . in the country's history" (3 March 1932).
```

If your sentence ends with the omission of the last part of the original sentence, use four periods: one immediately after the last word quoted, and three (spaced) to indicate the omission.

```
The manual says, "If your sentence ends with the omission of
the last part of the original sentence, use four spaced pe-
riods. . . ."
```

Notice that if you begin the quotation with the beginning of a sentence (in the example we have just given "If your" is the beginning of a quoted sentence) you do *not* indicate that material preceded the words you are quoting. Similarly, if you end your quotation with the end of the quoted sentence, you give only a single period, not four periods, although of course the material from which you are quoting may have gone on for many more sentences. But if you begin quoting from the middle of a sentence, or end quoting before you reach the end of a sentence in your source, it is customary to indicate the omissions. But even such omissions need not be indicated when the quoted material is obviously incomplete—when, for instance, it is a a word or phrase.

6. *Use punctuation accurately.* There are three important rules to observe:

a) *Commas and periods go inside the quotation marks.*

```
"The land," Nick Thompson observes, "looks after us."
```

b) *Semicolons and colons go outside quotation marks.*

```
He turned and said, "Learn the names of all these places"; it
sounded like an order.
```

c) *Question marks, exclamation points, and dashes go inside if they are part of the quotation, outside if they are your own.*

```
Amanda ironically says to her daughter, "How old are you,
Laura?"
```

(The question mark is part of the quotation and therefore goes inside the quotation marks.)

In the following example, why is the question mark placed outside of the quotation marks?

```
Is it possible to fail to hear Laura's weariness in her re-
ply, "Mother, you know my age"?
```

7. Use *single quotation marks* for a quotation within a quotation.

```
The student told the interviewer, "I ran back to the dorm and
I called my boyfriend and I said, 'Listen, this is just in-
credible,' and I told him all about it."
```

8. Enclose titles of short works in quotation marks. Short works include: chapters in books, short stories, essays, short poems, songs, lectures, speeches, and unpublished works (even if long).

Do *not* enclose the title of your own essay in quotation marks.

Underline titles of long works. (Underlining indicates *italic* type, used in print but ordinarily unavailable on typewriters.) Underline titles of published book-length works: novels, plays, periodicals, collections of essays, anthologies, pamphlets, textbooks, and long poems (such as <u>Paradise Lost</u>). Underline also titles of films, record albums, tapes, television programs, ballets, operas, works of art, and the names of planes, ships, and trains.

Exception: titles of sacred works (for example, the New Testament, the Hebrew Bible, Genesis, Acts, the Gospels, the Koran) are neither underlined nor enclosed within quotation marks. To cite a book of the Bible with chapter and verse, give the name of the book, then a space, then an arabic numeral for the chapter, a period, and an arabic numeral (*not* preceded by a space) for the verse, thus: Exodus 20.14–15. Standard abbreviations for the books of the Bible (for example, Chron.) are permissible in footnotes and in parenthetic citations within the text.

18

Punctuation

Speakers can raise or lower the volume or pitch of their voices; they can speak a phrase slowly and distinctly and then (making a parenthetical remark, perhaps) quicken the pace. They can wave their arms, pound a table, or pause, meaningfully. But writers, physically isolated from their audience, have only paper and ink to work with. Nevertheless, they can embody some of the tones and gestures of speech—in the patterns of their written sentences, and in the dots, hooks, and dashes of punctuation that clarify those patterns.

Punctuation clarifies, first of all, by removing or reducing ambiguity. Consider this headline from a story in a newspaper:

SQUAD HELPS DOG BITE VICTIM

Of course there is no real ambiguity here—only a laugh—because the stated meaning is so clearly absurd, and on second reading we supply the necessary hyphen in *dog-bite*. But other ill-punctuated sentences may be troublesome rather than entertaining. Take the following sentence:

He arrived late for the rehearsal didn't end until midnight.

Almost surely you stumbled in the middle of the sentence, think-ing that it was about someone arriving tardily at a rehearsal, and then, since what followed made no sense, you probably went back and mentally added the comma (by pausing) at the necessary place:

> He arrived late, for the rehearsal didn't end until midnight.

Punctuation helps to keep the reader on the right path. And the path is your train of thought. If your punctuation is faulty, you unintentionally point the reader off your path and toward dead end streets and quagmires.

Even when punctuation is not the key to meaning, it usually helps you to get your meaning across neatly. Consider the following sentences:

> There are two kinds of feminism—one is the growing struggle of women to understand and change the shape of their lives and the other is a narrow ideology whose adherents are anxious to clear away whatever does not conform to their view.

This is clear enough, but by changing the punctuation it can be sharpened. Because a dash usually indicates an abrupt interruption—it usually precedes a sort of afterthought—a colon would be better. The colon, usually the signal of an amplification of what precedes it, here would suggest that the two classifications are not impromptu thoughts but carefully considered ones. Second, and more important, in the original version the two classifications are run together without any intervening punctuation, but since the point is that the two are utterly different, it is advisable to separate them by inserting a comma or a semicolon, indicating a pause. A comma before "and the other" would do, but probably a semicolon (without the "and") is preferable because it is a heavier pause, thereby making the separation clearer. Here is the sentence, revised:

> There are two kinds of feminism: one is the growing struggle of women to understand and change the shape of their lives; the other is a narrow ideology whose adherents are anxious to clear away whatever does not conform to their view.

The right punctuation enables the reader to move easily through the sentence.

Now, although punctuation helps a reader to move through a sentence, it must be admitted that some of the rules of punctuation do not contribute to meaning or greatly facilitate reading. For example, in American usage a period never comes immediately after quotation marks; it precedes quotation marks, thus:

> She said, "Put the period inside the quotation marks."

If you put the period after the closing quotation mark, the meaning remains the same, but you are also informing your reader that you don't know the relevant convention. Since a misspelled word or a misplaced period often gives the impression of laziness, ignorance, or incompetence, why not generate as little friction as possible by learning the chief conventions?

THREE COMMON ERRORS: FRAGMENTS, COMMA SPLICES, AND RUN-ON SENTENCES

Fragments and How to Correct Them

A fragment is a part of a sentence set off as if it were a complete sentence: *Because I didn't care. Being an accident. Later in the week. For several reasons. My oldest sister.* Fragments are common in speech, but they are used sparingly in writing, for particular effects (see page 542–43). A fragment used carelessly in writing often looks like an afterthought—usually because it *was* an afterthought, that is, an explanation or other addition that really belongs to the previous sentence.

With appropriate punctuation (and sometimes with no punctuation at all) a fragment can usually be connected to the previous sentence.

1. *Incorrect*
Many nineteenth-century horror stories have been made into films. Such as *Dracula* and *Frankenstein.*

Correct
Many nineteenth-century horror stories have been made into films, such as *Dracula* and *Frankenstein.*

2. *Incorrect*
Many schools are putting renewed emphasis on writing. Because SAT scores have declined for ten years.

Correct
Many schools are putting renewed emphasis on writing because SAT scores have declined for ten years.

3. *Incorrect*
He practiced doing card tricks. In order to fool his friends.

Correct
He practiced doing card tricks in order to fool his friends.

4. *Incorrect*
She wore only rope sandals. Being a strict vegetarian.

Correct
Being a strict vegetarian, she wore only rope sandals.
She wore only rope sandals because she was a strict vegetarian.

5. *Incorrect*
A fragment often looks like an afterthought. Perhaps because it *was* an afterthought.

Correct
A fragment often looks like an afterthought—perhaps because it *was* an afterthought.

6. *Incorrect*
He hoped to get credit for two summer school courses. Batik and Hang-Gliding.

Correct
He hoped to get credit for two summer school courses: Batik and Hang-Gliding.

Notice in the examples above that, depending upon the relationship between the two parts, the fragment and the preceding statement can be joined by a comma, a dash, a colon, or by no punctuation at all.

Notice also that unintentional fragments often follow subordinating conjunctions, such as *because* and *although*. Subordinating conjunctions introduce a subordinate (dependent) clause; such a clause cannot stand as a sentence. Here is a list of the commonest subordinating conjunctions.

after	though
although	unless
because	until
before	when
if	where
provided	whereas
since	while

Fragments also commonly occur when the writer, as in the fourth example, mistakenly uses *being* as a main verb.

Comma Splices and Run-on Sentences, and How to Correct Them

An error known as a *comma splice* or *comma fault* results when a comma is mistakenly placed between two independent clauses that are not joined by a coordinating conjunction: *and, or, nor, but, for, yet, so.* If the comma is omitted, the error is called a *run-on sentence.*

Examples of the two errors:

Comma splice (or *comma fault*): In the second picture the man leans on the woman's body, he is obviously in pain.

Run-on sentence: In the second picture the man leans on the woman's body he is obviously in pain.

Run-on sentences and comma splices may be corrected in five principal ways.

1. Use a period. Write two sentences.

In the second picture the man leans on the woman's body. He is obviously in pain.

2. Use a semicolon.

In the second picture the man leans on the woman's body; he is obviously in pain.

3. Use a comma and a coordinating conjunction (and, or, not, but, for, yet, so).

In the second picture the man leans on the woman's body, and he is obviously in pain.

4. Make one of the clauses dependent (subordinate). Use a subordinating conjunction such as *after, although, because, before, if, since, though, unless, until, when, where, while.*

> In the second picture the man leans on the woman's body because he is in pain.

5. Reduce one of the independent clauses to a phrase, or even to a single word.

> In the second picture the man, obviously in pain, leans on the woman's body.

Run-on sentences and comma splices are especially common in sentences containing transitional words or phrases such as the following:

also	however
besides	indeed
consequently	in fact
for example	nevertheless
furthermore	therefore
hence	whereas

When these words join independent clauses, the clauses cannot be linked by a comma.

> *Incorrect:* She argued from faulty premises, however the conclusions happened to be correct.

Here are five correct revisions, following the five rules we have just given. (In the first two revisions we place "however" after, rather than before, "the conclusions" because we prefer the increase in emphasis, but the grammatical point is the same.)

1. She argued from faulty premises. The conclusions, however, happened to be correct. (Two sentences)
2. She argued from faulty premises; the conclusions, however, happened to be correct. (Semicolon)
3. She argued from faulty premises, but the conclusions happened to be correct. (Coordinating conjunction)
4. Although she argued from faulty premises, the conclusions happened to be correct. (Subordinating conjunction)
5. She argued from faulty premises to correct conclusions. (Reduction of an independent clause to a phrase)

The following sentence contains a comma splice:

> The husband is not pleased, in fact, he is embarrassed.

How might it be repaired?

THE PERIOD

1. Periods are used to mark the ends of sentences (or intentional sentence fragments) other than questions and exclamations.

> A sentence normally ends with a period.
> She said, "I'll pass."
> Yes.
> Once more, with feeling.

But a sentence within a sentence is punctuated according to the needs of the longer sentence. Notice, in the following example, that a period is *not* used after "pass." or directly after "said."

> She said, "I'll pass," but she said it without conviction.

If a sentence ends with a quotation, the period goes *inside* the quotation marks unless parenthetic material follows the quotation.

> Brutus says, "Antony is but a limb of Caesar."

> Brutus says, "Antony is but a limb of Caesar" (*Julius Caesar,* II.i.165).

2. Periods are used with abbreviations of titles and terms of reference.

> Dr., Mr., Mrs., Ms.

> p., pp. (for "page" and "pages"), i.e., e.g., etc.

But when the capitalized initial letters of the words naming an organization are used in place of the full name, the periods are commonly omitted:

> CBS, CORE, IBM, NBA, UCLA, UNICEF, USAF

3. Periods are also used to separate chapter from verse in the Bible.

Genesis 3.2, Mark 6.10

For further details on references to the Bible, see page 707.

THE QUESTION MARK

Use a question mark after a direct question:

Did Bacon write Shakespeare's plays?

Do not use a question mark after an indirect question, or after a polite request:

He asked if Bacon wrote Shakespeare's plays.

Would you please explain what the support for Bacon is really all about.

THE COLON

The colon has three chief uses:

to introduce a list or series of examples;

to introduce an amplification or explanation of what precedes the colon; and,

to introduce a quotation (though a quotation can be introduced by other means).

A fourth, less important, use is in the indication of time.

1. The colon may introduce a list or series.

Students are required to take one of the following sciences: biology, chemistry, geology, physics.

Note, however, that a colon is *not* used if the series is introduced by *such as, for example,* or a similar transitional phrase.

2. As a formal introduction to an amplification or explanation, the colon is almost equivalent to *namely,* or *that is.* What is on one side of the colon more or less equals what is on the other

side. The material on either side of the colon can stand as a separate sentence.

> She explained her fondness for wrestling: she did it to shock her parents.

> The forces which in China created a central government were absent in Japan: farming had to be on a small scale, there was no need for extensive canal works, and a standing army was not required to protect the country from foreign invaders.

> Many of the best of the Civil War photographs must be read as the fossils of earlier events: The caissons with their mud-encrusted wheels, the dead on the field, the empty landscapes, all speak of deeds already past.
>
> — John Szarkowski

Notice in this last example that the writer uses a capital letter after the colon; the usage is acceptable when a complete sentence follows the colon, as long as that style is followed consistently throughout a paper. But most students find it easier to use lowercase letters after colons, the prevalent style in writing today.

The use of a colon before an amplication or explanation should not be confused with the use of a *semicolon* before closely related independent clauses that are not joined by coordinating conjunctions. Note the difference between the previous example on Civil War photographs, which required a colon, and the following example, which requires a semicolon:

> Many of the best of the Civil War photographs must be read as the fossils of earlier events; paintings only rarely can be read so.

3. The colon, like the comma, may be used to introduce a quotation; it is more formal than the comma, setting off the quotation to a greater degree.

> The black sculptor Ed Wilson tells his students: "Malcolm X is my brother, Martin Luther King is my brother, Eldridge Cleaver is my brother! But Michelangelo is my grandfather!"
>
> — Albert E. Elsen

4. A colon is used to separate the hour from the minutes when the time is given in figures.

9:15, 12:00

Colons (like semicolons) go outside of closing quotation marks if they are not part of the quotation.

"There is no such thing as a free lunch": the truth of these words is confirmed every day.

THE SEMICOLON

There are four main uses of the semicolon. Sheridan Baker (in *The Practical Stylist*) summed them up in this admirable formula: "Use a semicolon where you could also use a period, unless desperate." Correctly used, the semicolon can add precision to your writing; it can also help you out of some tight corners.

1. You may use a semicolon instead of a period between closely related independent clauses not joined by a coordinating conjunction.

All happy families resemble one another; every unhappy family is unhappy in its own fashion.

— Leo Tolstoy

The demands that men and women make on marriage will never be fully met; they cannot be.

— Jessie Bernard

In our fractured culture, we cannot agree on morals; we cannot even agree that moral matters should come before literary ones when there is a conflict between them.

— Flannery O'Connor

When a cat washes its face it does not move its paw; it moves its face.

In each of the above examples the independent clauses might have been written as sentences separated by periods; the semicolon pulls the statements together, emphasizing their relationship. Alternatively, the statements might have been linked by coordinating conjunctions (and, but, for, or, nor, yet, so). For example:

The demands made upon marriage will never be fully met *for* they cannot be.

When a cat washes its face it does not move its paw *but* it moves its face.

The sentences as originally written, using semicolons, have more bite.

2. You *must* use a semicolon (rather than a comma) if you use a conjunctive adverb to connect independent clauses. (A conjunctive adverb is a transitional word such as *also, consequently, furthermore, however, moreover, nevertheless, therefore.*)

His hair was black and wavy; however, it was false.

We don't like to see our depressed relative cry; nevertheless, tears can provide a healthy emotional outlet.

She said "I do"; moreover, she repeated the words.

Take note of the following three points:

A comma goes after the conjunctive adverb.

Semicolons (like colons) go outside of closing quotation marks if they are not part of the quotation.

A conjunctive adverb requires a semicolon to join independent clauses. A comma produces a comma splice:

```
His hair was black and wavy, however, it was false.
```

3. You may use a semicolon to separate a series of phrases with internal punctuation.

He had a car, which he hadn't paid for; a wife, whom he didn't love; and a father, who was unemployed.

4. Use a semicolon between independent clauses linked by coordinating conjunctions if the sentence would otherwise be difficult to read, because it is long and complex or because it contains internal punctuation.

In the greatest age of painting, the nude inspired the greatest works; and even when it ceased to be a compulsive subject it held its position as an academic exercise and a demonstration of mastery.

(Often it is preferable to break such sentences up, or to recast them.)

THE COMMA

A comma (from a Greek word meaning "to cut") indicates a relatively slight pause within a sentence. If after checking the rules you are still uncertain of whether or not to use a comma in a given sentence read the sentence aloud and see if it sounds better with or without a pause, and then add or omit the comma. A women's shoe store in New York has a sign on the door:

NO MEN PLEASE.

If the proprietors would read the sign aloud, they might want to change it to

NO MEN, PLEASE

In typing, always follow a comma with a space.

We outlined below the correct uses of the comma. For your reference, here is a table of contents for the following pages:

1. Independent clauses (unless short) joined by a coordinating conjunction *(and, or, nor, but, for, yet, so)* take a comma before the conjunction.

Most students see at least a few football games, and many go to every game of the season.

Most students seem to have an intuitive sense of when to use a comma, but in fact the "intuition" is the result of long training.

If the introductory independent clause is short, the comma is usually omitted:

She dieted but she continued to gain weight.

2. An introductory subordinate clause or long phrase is usually followed by a comma.

Having revised his manuscript for the third time, he went to bed.

In order to demonstrate her point, the instructor stood on her head.

If the introductory subordinate clause or phrase is short, say four words or fewer, the comma may be omitted, provided no ambiguity results from the omission.

Having left he soon forgot.

But compare this last example with the following:

Having left, the instructor soon forgot.

If the comma is omitted, the sentence is misread. Where are commas needed in the following sentences?

Instead of discussing the book she wrote a summary.
When Shakespeare wrote comedies were already popular.
While he ate his poodle would sit by the table.
As we age small things become killers.

3. A subordinate clause or long modifying phrase tacked on as an afterthought is usually preceded by a comma.

I have decided not to be nostalgic about the 1950s, despite the hoopla over Elvis.

Buster Keaton fell down a flight of stairs without busting, thereby gaining his nickname from Harry Houdini.

By the time he retired Hank Aaron had 755 home runs, breaking Babe Ruth's record by 41.

With afterthoughts, the comma may be omitted if there is a clear sequence of cause and effect, signaled by such words as *because, for,* and *so.* Compare the two following examples:

> In 1601 Shakespeare wrote *Hamlet,* probably his best-known play.

> In 1601 Shakespeare wrote *Hamlet* because revenge tragedy was in demand.

4. A pair of commas can serve as a pair of unobtrusive parentheses. Be sure not to omit the second comma.

> Doctors, I think, have an insufficient knowledge of acupuncture.

> The earliest known paintings of Christ, dating from the third century, are found in the catacombs outside of Rome.

> Medicare and Medicaid, the chief sources of federal support for patients in nursing homes, are frequently confused.

Under this heading we can include a conjunctive adverb (a transitional adverb such as *also, besides, consequently, however, likewise, nevertheless, therefore*) inserted within a sentence. These transitional words are set off between a pair of commas.

> Her hair, however, was stringy.

If one of these words begins a sentence, the comma after it is optional. Notice, however, that the presence of such a word as "however" is not always a safeguard against a run-on sentence or comma splice; if the word occurs between two independent clauses and it goes with the second clause, you need a semicolon before it and a comma after it.

> His hair was black and wavy; however, it was false.

(See the discussion of comma splice on pages 712–14.)

5. Use a comma to set off a nonrestrictive modifier. A nonrestrictive modifier, as the following examples will make clear, is a sort of parenthetical addition; it gives supplementary information about the subject, but it can be omitted without changing the subject. A restrictive modifier, however, is not supplementary but

essential; if a restrictive modifier is omitted, the subject becomes more general. In Dorothy Parker's celebrated poem.

> Men seldom make passes
> At girls who wear glasses,

"who wear glasses" is a restrictive modifier, narrowing or restricting the subject down from "girls" to a particular group of girls, "girls who wear glasses."

Here is a *non*restrictive modifier:

> For the majority of immigrants, who have no knowledge of English, language is the chief problem.

Now a restrictive modifier:

> For the majority of immigrants who have no knowledge of English, language is the chief problem.

The first version says—in addition to its obvious message that language is the chief problem—that the majority of immigrants have no knowledge of English. The second version makes no such assertion; it talks not about the majority of immigrants but only about a more restricted group—those immigrants who have no knowledge of English.

Other examples:

> Shakespeare's shortest tragedy, *Macbeth*, is one of his greatest plays.

In this sentence, *"Macbeth"* is nonrestrictive because the subject is already as restricted as possible; Shakespeare can have written only one "shortest tragedy." That is, *"Macbeth"* is merely an explanatory equivalent of "Shakespeare's shortest tragedy" and it is therefore enclosed in commas. (A noun or noun phrase serving as an explanatory equivalent to another, and in the same syntactical relation to other elements in the sentence, is said to be in apposition.) But compare

> Shakespeare's tragedy *Macbeth* is one of his greatest plays.

with the misleadingly punctuated sentence,

> Shakespeare's tragedy, *Macbeth*, is one of his greatest plays.

The first of these is restrictive, narrowing or restricting the subject "tragedy" down to one particular tragedy, and so it rightly does not separate the modifier from the subject by a comma. The second, punctuated so that it is nonrestrictive, falsely implies that *Macbeth* is Shakespeare's only tragedy. Here is an example of a nonrestrictive modifier correctly punctuated:

> Women, who constitute 51.3 percent of the population and 53 percent of the electorate, constitute only 2.5 percent of the House of Representatives and 1 percent of the Senate.

In the next two examples, the first illustrates the correct use of commas after a nonrestrictive appositive, and the second illustrates the correct omission of commas after a restrictive appositive.

> Hong Yee Chiu, a Chinese-American physicist, abbreviated the compound adjective *quasi-stellar* to *quasar.*
>
> The Chinese-American physicist Hong Yee Chiu abbreviated the compound adjective *quasi-stellar* to *quasar.*

6. Words, phrases, and clauses in series take a comma after each item except the last. The comma between the last two items may be omitted if there is no ambiguity.

> Photography is a matter of eyes, intuition, and intellect.
> — John Szarkowski
>
> She wrote plays, poems, and stories.
>
> He wrote plays, sang songs, and danced jigs.
>
> She wrote a wise, witty, humane book.

But adjectives in a series may cause difficulty. The next two examples correctly omit the commas.

> a funny silent film
>
> a famous French professor

In each of these last two examples, the adjective immediately before the noun forms with the noun a compound that is modified by the earlier adjective. That is, the adjectives are not a coordinate series (what is funny is not simply a film but a silent film, what is famous is not simply a professor but a French professor) and so commas are not used. Compare:

a famous French professor

a famous, arrogant French professor

In the second example, only "famous" and "arrogant" form a co-ordinate series. If in doubt, see if you can replace the commas with "and"; if you can, the commas are correct. In the example given, you could insert "and" between "famous" and "arrogant," but not between "arrogant" and "French."

Commas are not needed if all the members of the series are connected by conjunctions.

He ate steak for breakfast and lunch and supper.

7. Use a comma to set off direct discourse.

"It's a total failure," she said.

She said, "It's a total failure."

But do not use a comma for indirect discourse.

She said that it is a total failure.

She said it is a total failure.

8. Use a comma to set off "yes" and "no."

Yes, he could take Freshman English at ten o'clock.

9. Use a comma to set off words of address.

Look, Bill, take Freshman English at ten o'clock.

10. Use a comma to separate a geographical location within another geographical location.

She was born in Brooklyn, New York, in 1895.

Another way of putting it is to say that a comma is used after each unit of an address, except that a comma is *not* used between the name of the state and the zip code.

11. Use a comma to set off the year from the month or day.

He was born on June 10, 1965. (No comma is needed if you use the form "10 June 1965.")

A note on the position of the comma when used with other punctuation: If a comma is required with parenthetic material, it follows the second parenthesis.

> Because Japan was secure from invasion (even the Mongols were beaten back), her history is unusually self-contained.

The only time a comma may precede a parenthesis is when parentheses surround a digit or letter used to enumerate a series.

> Questions usually fall into one of three categories: (1) true-false, (2) multiple choice, (3) essay.

A comma always goes inside closing quotation marks unless the quotation is followed by a parenthesis.

> "Sayonara," he said.

> "Sayonara" (Japanese for "goodbye"), he said.

THE DASH

A dash—made by typing two hyphens without hitting the space-bar before, between, or after—indicates an abrupt break or pause.

1. The material within dashes may be something like parenthetic material (material that is not essential), though by setting it within dashes—an emphatic form of punctuation—the writer gives the material more emphasis than it would get within parentheses.

> The bathroom—that private place—has rarely been the subject of scholarly study.

> The Great Wall of China forms a continuous line over 1400 miles long—the distance from New York to Kansas City—running from Peking to the edge of the mountains of Central Asia.

> The old try to survive by cutting corners—eating less, giving up small pleasures like tobacco and movies, doing without warm clothes—and pay the price of ill-health and a shortened life-span.
> — Sharon R. Curtin

Notice that when two dashes are used, if the material within them is deleted the remainder still forms a grammatical sentence.

2. A dash can serve, somewhat like a colon, as a pause before a series. It is more casual than a colon.

> The earliest Shinto holy places were natural objects—trees, boulders, mountains, islands.

> Each of the brothers had his distinct comic style—Groucho's double-talk, Chico's artfully stupid malapropisms, Harpo's horseplay.
>
> — Gerald Mast

A dash is never used next to a comma, and it is used before a period only to indicate that the sentence is interrupted.

Overuse of the dash—even only a little overuse—gives writing an unpleasantly agitated—even explosive—quality.

PARENTHESES

First, a caution: avoid using parentheses to explain pronouns: "In his speech he (Hamlet) says . . ." If "he" needs to be explained by "Hamlet," omit the "he" and just say "Hamlet."

1. Parentheses subordinate material; what is in parentheses is almost a casual aside, less essential than similar material set off in commas, less vigorously spoken than similar material set off in dashes.

> While guest curator for the Whitney (he has since returned to the Denver Art Museum), Feder assembled a magnificent collection of masks, totems, paintings, clothing, and beadwork.

Two cautions: avoid an abundance of these interruptions, and avoid a long parenthesis within a sentence (you are now reading a simple example of this annoying but common habit of writers who have trouble sticking to the point) because the reader will lose track of the main sentence.

2. Use parentheses to enclose digits or letters in a list that is given in running text.

The exhibition included: (1) decorative screens, (2) ceramics, (3) ink paintings, (4) kimonos.

3. Do not confuse parentheses with square brackets, which are used around material you add to a question. See pages 705.

4. For the use of parentheses in documentation, see pages 370–80.

A note on the position of other punctuation with a parenthesis: The example under rule number 2, of commas preceding parentheses enclosing digits or letters in a list given in running text, is the rare exception to the rule that within a sentence, punctuation other than quotation marks never immediately precedes an opening parenthesis. Notice that in the example under rule number 1, the comma *follows* the closing parenthesis:

> While guest curator for the Whitney (he has since returned to the Denver Art Museum), Feder assembled a magnificent collection of masks, totems, paintings, clothing, and beadwork.

If an entire sentence is in parentheses, put the final punctuation (period, question mark, or exclamation mark) inside the closing parenthesis.

QUOTATION MARKS

1. Use quotation marks to attribute words to a speaker or writer. (Long quotations that are set off do not take quotation marks. See pages 703–04.) If your quotation includes a passage that was enclosed in quotation marks, alter these inner quotation marks to single quotation marks.

> According to Professor Hugo, "The male dragon in Chinese art has deep-set eyes, the female has bulging eyes, but as one Chinese scholar put it, 'This is a matter of interest only to dragons.'"

British quotation marks are just the reverse: single for ordinary quotations, double for inner quotations. If you are quoting from a passage that includes such quotation marks, change them to the American form.

2. Use quotation marks to indicate the title of unpublished works, like dissertations, and of short works—for example, a lecture, speech, newspaper article, essay, chapter, short story, or song, as well as a poem of less than, say, twenty pages. (But magazines and pamphlets, like books, are underlined to indicate italics.)

3. Use quotation marks to identify a word or term to which you wish to call special attention. (But italics, indicated by underlining, may be used instead of quotation marks.)

> By "comedy" I mean not only a funny play, but any play that ends happily.

4. Do *not* use quotation marks to enclose slang or a term that you fear is low; use the term or don't use it, but don't apologize by putting it in quotation marks, as in these examples.

Incorrect
"Streaking" was first popularized by Lady Godiva.

Incorrect
Because of "red tape" it took three years.

Incorrect
At last I was able to "put in my two cents."

In all three of these sentences the writers are signaling their uneasiness; in neither the first nor the second is there any cause for uneasiness, but probably the third should be rewritten to get rid of the cliché.

5. Do *not* use quotation marks to convey sarcasm, as in

> These "politicians" are nothing but thieves.

Sarcasm is usually a poor form of argument, best avoided. But of course there are borderline cases when you may want to convey your dissatisfaction with a word used by others.

> African sculpture has a long continuous tradition, but this tradition has been jeopardized by the introduction of "civilization" to Africa.

Perhaps the quotation marks here are acceptable, because the writer's distaste has not yet become a sneer and because she is, in effect, quoting. But why not change "civilization" to "western culture," omitting the quotation marks?

6. Position of quotation marks with other punctuation. Here
are the rules:

(a) Commas and periods go *inside* the quotation marks, except when the quotation marks are followed by parentheses.

"And now, once again," Shelley wrote, "I bid my hideous progeny
go forth and prosper."

"I have an affection for it," she added, "for it was the offspring of
happy days" (*Frankenstein* xii).

(b) Colons and semicolons go *outside* quotation marks.

"I certainly did not owe the suggestion of one incident, nor scarcely
of one train of feeling, to my husband"; there was no good reason
to doubt her word.

(c) Question marks and exclamation points go inside if they
are part of the quotation, outside if they are not.

While Thelma Todd paddles the canoe, Groucho listens to her
chatter, looks at a duck swimming near the canoe, and asks, "Did
that come out of you or the duck?"

What is funny about Groucho saying, "Whatever it is, I'm
against it"?

ITALICS

In typewritten material <u>underlining</u> is the equivalent of *italic*
type.

<u>This sentence is understood to be printed in italic type.</u>

1. Underline the name of a plane, ship, train, movie, radio
or television program, record album, musical work, statue, painting, play, pamphlet, and book. Do not underline names of sacred
works such as the Bible, the Koran, Acts of the Apostles, or polit
ical documents such as the Magna Carta and the Declaration of
Independence. Notice that when you write of *The New York Times,*
you underline *New York* because it is part of the title, but when
you write of the London *Times,* you do not underline "London"
because "London" is not part of the title, only information added

for clarity. Similarly, when you refer to *Time* magazine do not underline "magazine."

2. As suggested on page 535, use italics only sparingly for emphasis. Sometimes, however, this method of indicating your tone of voice is exactly right.

> In 1911 Jacques Henri Lartigue was not merely as unprejudiced as a child; he *was* a child.
>
> — John Szarkowski

3. Use italics for foreign words that have not become a part of the English language.

> Acupuncture aims to affect the *ch'i,* a sort of vital spirit which circulates through the bodily organs.

But:

> He ate a pizza.
>
> She behaved like a prima donna.
>
> Avoid clichés.

4. You may use italics in place of quotation marks to identify a word: *Honolulu* means "safe harbor."

5. You may also use italics to identify a word or term to which you wish to call special attention.

> Claude Lévi-Strauss tells us that one of the great purposes of art is that of *miniaturization.* He points out that most works of art are miniatures, being smaller (and therefore more easily understood) than the objects they represent.

CAPITAL LETTERS

Certain obvious conventions—the use of a capital for the first word in a sentence, for names (of days of the week, holidays, months, people, countries), and for words derived from names (such as pro-French)—need not be discussed here.

1. Titles of works in English are usually given according to the following formula. Use a capital for the first letter of the first word, for the first letter of the last word, and for the first letter of all other words that are not articles, conjunctions, or prepositions.

The Merchant of Venice
A Midsummer Night's Dream
Up and Out
"The Short Happy Life of Francis Macomber"
The Oakland Bee

2. Use a capital for a quoted sentence within a sentence, but not for a quoted phrase (unless it is at the beginning of your sentence) and not for indirect discourse.

He said, "You can even fool some of the people all of the time."
He said you can fool some people "all of the time."
He said that you can even fool some of the people all of the time.

3. Use a capital for a rank or title preceding a proper name or for a title substituting for a proper name.

She said she was Dr. Perez.
He told President Bush that the Vice President was away.

But:

Why would anyone wish to be president?
Washington was the first president.

4. Use a capital when the noun designating a family relationship is used as a substitute for a proper noun.

If Mother is busy, ask Tim.

But:

Because my mother was busy, I asked Tim.

5. Formal geographical locations (but not mere points on the compass) are capitalized.

North America, Southeast Asia, the Far East

In the Southwest, rain sometimes evaporates before touching the ground.

Is Texas part of the South?

The North has its share of racism.

But:

The wind came from the south.
Czechoslovakia is adjoined on the north by East Germany.

Do *not* capitalize the names of the seasons.

spring, summer, winter, fall

THE HYPHEN

The hyphen has five uses, all drawing on the etymology of the word *hyphen,* which comes from the Greek for "in one," "together."

1. Use a hyphen to attach certain prefixes to root words. *All-, pro-, ex-,* and *self-* are the most common of these ("all-powerful," "ex-wife," "pro-labor," "self-made"), but note that even these prefixes are not always followed by a hyphen. If in doubt, check a dictionary. Prefixes before proper names are always followed by a hyphen:

anti-Semite, pro-Kennedy, un-American

Prefixes ending in *i* are hyphenated before a word beginning with *i:*

anti-intellectual, semi-intelligible

A hyphen is normally used to break up a triple consonant resulting from the addition of a prefix:

ill-lit,

2. Use a hyphen to tie compound adjectives into a single visual unit:

out-of-date theory, twenty-three books, long-term loan

eighteenth- and nineteenth-century novels

The sea-tossed raft was a common nineteenth-century symbol of man's tragic condition.

But if a compound modifier follows the modified term, it is usually not hyphenated, thus:

The theory was out of date.

3. Use a hyphen to join some compound nouns:

Scholar-teacher, philosopher-poet

4. Use a hyphen to divide a word at the end of a line. Because words may be divided only as indicated by a dictionary, it is easier to end the line with the last complete word you can type than to keep reaching for a dictionary. But here are some principles governing the division of words at the end of a line:

- a. Never hyphenate words of one syllable, such as *called, doubt, right, through.*
- b. Never hyphenate so that a single letter stands alone: *a-bout, hair-y.*
- c. If a word already has a hyphen, divide it at the hyphen: *anti-intellectual, semi-intelligible.*
- d. Divide prefixes and suffixes from the root: *mis-spell, pro-vide, drunken-ness, walk-ing.*
- c. Divide between syllables. If you aren't sure of the proper syllabification, check a dictionary.

5. Use a hyphen to indicate a span of dates or page numbers: 1957–59, pp. 162–68.

THE APOSTROPHE

Use an apostrophe to indicate the possessive, to indicate a contraction, and for certain unusual plurals.

1. The possessive. The most common way to indicate the possessive of a singular noun is to add an apostrophe and then an *s.*

A dog's life, a week's work
a mouse's tail, Keats's poems, Marx's doctrines

But some authorities suggest that for a proper noun of more than one syllable that ends in *s* or another sibilant *(-cks, -x, -z),* it is better to add only an apostrophe:

Jesus' parables, Sophocles' plays, Chavez' ideas

When in doubt, say the name aloud and notice if you are adding an *s.* If you are adding an *s* when you say it, add an apostrophe and an *s* when you write it. Our own strong preference, however, is to add an apostrophe and an *s* to all proper nouns:

> Jones's book
> Kansas's highways

Pronouns do not take an apostrophe.

> his book, its fur
> The book is hers, not ours.
> The book is theirs.

(Exception: indefinite pronouns take an apostrophe, as in "one's hopes" and "others' opinions.")

For plurals ending in *s,* add only an apostrophe to indicate the possessive:

> the boys' father, the Smiths' house, the Joneses' car

If the plural does not end in *s,* add an apostrophe and an *s.*

> women's clothing, mice's eyes

Don't try to form the possessive of the title of a work (for example, of a play, a book, or a film): Write "the imagery in *The Merchant of Venice*" rather than "*The Merchant of Venice*'s imagery." Using an apostrophe gets you into the problem of whether or not to italicize the *s;* similarly, if you use an apostrophe for a work normally enclosed in quotation marks, you can't put the apostrophe and the *s* after the quotation marks, but you can't put them inside either. And the work really can't possess anything anyway—the imagery, or whatever else, is the author's.

2. Contractions. Use an apostrophe to indicate the omitted letters or numbers in contractions.

> She won't.
> It's time to go.
> the class of '87

3. Unusual plurals. Until recently an apostrophe was used to make plurals of words that do not usually have a plural, and (this is optional) to make the plurals of digits and letters.

Her speech was full of if's and and's and but's.
Ph.D.'s don't know everything.
Mind your p's and q's.
I got two A's and two B's.
He makes his 4's in two ways.
the 1920's

This use of the apostrophe is no longer standard, but it remains acceptable.

ABBREVIATIONS

In general, avoid abbreviatons except in footnotes and except for certain common ones listed below. And don't use an ampersand (&) unless it appears in material you are quoting, or in a title. Abundant use of abbreviations makes an essay sound like a series of newspaper headlines. Usually *United States* is better than *U.S.* and *the Soviet Union* better than *U.S.S.R.*

1. Abbreviatons, with the first letter capitalized, are used before a name.

Dr. Bellini, Ms. Smith, St. Thomas

But:

The doctor took her temperature and fifty dollars.

2. Degrees that follow a name are abbreviated:

B.A., D.D.S., M.D., Ph.D.

3. Other acceptable abbreviations include:

A.D., B.C., A.M., P.M., e.g., i.e.

(By the way, *e.g.* means *for example; i.e.* means *that is.* The two ought not to be confused. See pages 755 and 758)

4. The name of an agency or institution (for instance, the Congress of Racial Equality; International Business Machines; Southern Methodist University) may be abbreviated by using the initial letters, capitalized and usually without periods (e.g., CORE),

but it is advisable to give the name in full when first mentioning it (not everyone knows that AARP means American Association of Retired Persons, for instance), and to use the abbreviation in subsequent references.

NUMBERS

1. Write them out if you can do so in fewer than three words; otherwise, use figures.

> sixteen, seventy-two, ten thousand, one sixth
> 10,200; 10,200,000
> There are 336 dimples on a golf ball

But write out round millions and billions, to avoid a string of zeroes.

> a hundred and ten million

For large round numbers you can also use a combination of figures and words, such as

> The cockroach is about 250 million years old.

Note, however, that because a figure cannot be capitalized, if a number begins a sentence it should always be written out:

> Two hundred and fifty million years ago the cockroach first appeared on earth.

2. Use figures in dates, addresses, decimals, percentages, page numbers, and hours followed by A.M. or P.M.

> February 29, 1900; .06 percent; 6 percent; 8:16 A.M.

But hours unmodified by minutes are usually written out, and followed by *o'clock*.

> Executions in England regularly took place at eight o'clock.

3. Use an apostrophe to indicate omitted figures.

> class of '89
> the '80s (but: the eighties)

4. Use a hyphen to indicate a span.

1975–79

In giving inclusive numbers, give the second number in full for the numbers up through ninety-nine (2–5, 8–11, 28–34). For larger numbers, give only the last two digits of the second number (101–06; 112–14) unless the full number is necessary (198–202).

5. Dates can be given with the month first, followed by numerals, a comma, and the year

February 10, 1986

or they can be given with the day first, then the month and then the year (without a comma after the day or month)

10 February 1986

6. BC (no periods and no space between the letters) follows the year, but AD precedes it.

10 BC
AD 200

7. Roman numerals are less used than formerly. Capital roman numerals were used to indicate a volume number, but volume numbers are now commonly given in arabic numerals. Capital roman numerals still are used, however, for the names of individuals in a series (Elizabeth II) and for the primary divisions of an outline; lowercase roman numerals are used for the pages of a preface. The old custom of citing acts and scenes of a play in roman numerals and lines in arabic numerals (II.iv.17–25) is still preferred by many instructors, but the use of arabic numerals throughout (2.4.17–25) is gaining acceptance.

EXERCISES

1. Correct the following sentence fragments. You may join fragments to independent clauses, or you may recast them as complete sentences.

   a. He left the sentence fragments in the final version of his essay. Instead of trying to fix them.

   b. Her associate left the country. Although their project was unfinished.

   c. Philip Roth argues that closing Newark's libraries will be a costly mistake. That the action will be an insult to Newark's citizens.

   d. He made corrections on the final copy of his essay by hand. Being unwilling to retype the whole paper.

   e. She spent three hours waiting in line in the rain to buy tickets to his concert. Since she was an irrepressibly enthusiastic Springsteen fan.

2. Determine which of the following sentences are run-ons and which contain comma splices. Label them accordingly and correct them appropriately—using any of the five methods shown on pages 710–14.

   a. *CATCH-22* is one of his favorite books, he's reading it now for the fifth time.

   b. Don't write run-on sentences they are not acceptable.

   c. The quarterback was intercepted on fourteen consecutive passes, he was traded the following season.

   d. Ambiguously punctuated sentences are usually confusing often they are humorous.

   e. There are those who warn that computers are dehumanizing students, however such people have produced no verifiable evidence.

3. Correct the following sentences, inserting the necessary colons and semicolons.

   a. I signed up for four courses this semester Spanish, geology, calculus, and composition.

   b. "Every dark cloud has a silver lining" I've found that the cliché doesn't always hold true.

   c. The semicolon is tricky it can be effective, but it is often misused.

   d. I finished my final papers three weeks early consequently, I had nothing to do while everyone else was working.

   e. The case for nuclear power has always rested on two claims that reactors were reasonably safe, and that they were indispensable as a source of energy.

   f. Dinner was a disaster he broiled fish, which he burned he steamed broccoli, which came out soggy and he baked a souffle, which fell.

4. In these sentences insert commas where necessary to set off phrases and clauses.

   a. While she was cooking the cat jumped onto the refrigerator.
   b. Geometry is a prerequisite for trigonometry and calculus is a prerequisite for physics.
   c. He wanted to go to Europe in the summer so he had to take a part-time job.
   d. Although she's aware of the dangers of smoking it seems impossible for her to quit.
   e. Final exams they thought were a waste of time.
   f. Turner's painting *The Slave Ship* probably his greatest work was donated to Boston's Museum of Fine Arts.

5. Insert commas to make the restrictive elements in the following sentences nonrestrictive. Be prepared to explain how changing the punctuation changes each sentence's meaning.

   a. My uncle who owns a farm breeds racehorses.
   b. The circus which returns to New York every winter is attended by thousands.
   c. Teachers who are the ones chiefly entrusted with educating people formally should concentrate more heavily on developing their students' analytical skills.
   d. Athletes who ought to know better sometimes play while injured.

6. Punctuate these sentences using the instructions given in items 6–11 on pages 719–25 as guidelines.

   a. A lone masked silent gunman robbed the only bank in Albuquerque New Mexico on March 10 1885.
   b. Yes it's a sentimental story but I like it.
   c. "You have no taste" he said.
   d. The plot of his detective novel was flimsy weak and unoriginal.
   e. I would prefer not to receive a partridge in a pear tree two French hens three turtle doves and all that other stuff again this Christmas.

7. Place commas correctly in the following sentences.

   a. "Don't write sentence fragments" the instructor said "they are unacceptable."
   b. Arguing with him was useless (he was most stubborn when he was wrong) so she decided to drop the subject.

    c. To revise Mrs. Beeton's famous recipe: you must (1) find your hare (2) catch it (3) cook it.

    d. "A Good Man Is Hard to Find" "Petrified Man" and "A Rose for Emily" are three of his favorite short stories.

8. Correct the following sentences, adding apostrophes where needed. Label each word you correct to indicate whether it is a possessive, a contraction, or an unusual plural.

    a. Its easy to learn to use apostrophes.

    b. The boys books are on their shelves, under their beds, and in their closets.

    c. There are three copies of *Barnet and Stubbs Practical Guide to Writing* in the professors office.

    d. My copys falling apart

    e. In the 1940s ones dollars went farther.

9. In the following sentences, decide what punctuation is needed, and then add it. If the sentence is correctly punctuated, place a check mark to the left of it.

    a. Around his neck is a scarf knotted in front and covering his head is a wide brimmed hat.

    b. Buffalo Bill radiates confidence in his bold stance and looks self assured with his head held high.

    c. The demands that men and women make on marriage will never be fully met they cannot be.

    d. The Polish painter Oskar Kokoschka once said to a man who had posed for a portrait those who know you wont recognize you but those who dont will.

    e. Boys on the whole do not keep diaries.

    f. Children are unwelcome in most New York restaurants that are not Chinese.

    g. Shlomo a giraffe in the Tel Aviv zoo succumbed to the effects of falling down after efforts to raise him with ropes and pulleys were unsuccessful.

    h. Character like a photograph develops in darkness.

    i. In a grief reaction especially when the person has suffered a loss crying comes easily and produces a healthy release from pent up emotion.

    j. There is no God but Allah and Mohammed is His prophet.

10. We reprint below the fourth paragraph of Jeff Greenfield's essay, "Columbo Knows the Butler Didn't Do It," but with-

out punctuation. Go through the paragraph, adding the punctuation you find necessary. Check your work against the original paragraph on page 89. If you find differences between your punctuation and Greenfield's, try to explain why Greenfield made the choices he did.

> *columbos* villains are not simply rich they are privileged they live the lives that are for most of us hopeless daydreams houses on top of mountains with pools servants and sliding doors parties with women in slinky dresses and endless food and drink plush enclosed box seats at professional sports events the envy and admiration of the crowd while we choose between johnny carson and *invasion of the body snatchers* they are at screenings of movies the rest of us wait in line for on third avenue three months later.

11. Here are the first two paragraphs—but without punctuation—of Raymond A. Sokolov's review of a book by Sarah Stage, *Female Complaints: Lydia Pinkham and the Business of Women's Medicine*. Add the necessary punctuation.

> home at the range victorian women in america suffered in shame from all manner of female complaints too intimate to name many of them were the fault of men gonorrhea or men doctors prolapsed uterus and women shrewdly kept shy of the ineffectual and often positively harmful doctors of their day instead they doctored themselves with so called patent medicines the most famous of these was lydia pinkhams vegetable compound mrs pinkham actually existed in lynn mass a center of the progressive spirit hotbed of abolition and feminism
>
> sarah stage who has taught american history at williams college had the acuity to see that lydia pinkham was more than a quaint picture on a label that she was a paradigm of the independent woman of her day building a big business with a home remedy to save her family from bankruptcy caused by a neer do well husband she saw furthermore that many of the important themes and forces of american society before world war I clustered around the medicine itself which was largely alcoholic but respectably bitter

19

Spelling

Life would be easier if a sound were always represented by the same letter. Some modern European languages come close to this principle, but English is not among them. "You" and "ewe" are pronounced identically, but they do not have even a single letter in common. George Bernard Shaw once called attention to some of the oddities of English spelling by saying that *fish* might be spelled *ghoti*. How? *Gh* is *f,* as in *enough; o* is *i,* as in *women; ti* is *sh,* as in *notion.* So, *ghoti* spells *fish.*

This is not the place to explain why English spelling is so erratic, but it may be consoling to know that the trouble goes back at least to the Norman French Conquest of England in 1066; after the Conquest, French scribes spelled English words more or less as though the words were French. Moreover, though pronunciation kept changing, spelling became relatively fixed, so that even in Shakespeare's time spelling often reflected a pronunciation that had long been abandoned. And today the spelling of many words still reflects the long-lost medieval pronunciation. The silent *e* in *life,* and the silent consonants in *knight* and *through,* for example, were pronounced in Chaucer's day.

But medieval pronunciation accounts for only some of our spellings. There are many other reasons for the oddities: the *s* in *island* is there, for example, because scholars mistakenly thought

No, no it's 🥦 *before* 🌸 *except after* 🔥 *!*

Reprinted with permission of Joseph Kohl.

the word came into English through the Latin *insula*. (*Isle* indeed comes from *insula*, but *island* comes from Old English *iland*.) Most rules for spelling, then, must immediately be modified with lists of exceptions. Even the most famous,

> *I* before *e* except after *c*
>
> Or when sounded as *a*
>
> In *neighbor* and *sleigh*,

has more exceptions than cheery handbooks admit. Always *ei* after *c*? What about *ancient*, *efficient*, and *sufficient*? Oh, but in these words the *c* is pronounced *sh*, an easy enough exception to keep in mind. But how can we explain *financier?* And of words where a *c* does not precede the letters in question, does the rule *ie* really govern all those not "sounded as *a* / In *neighbor* and *sleigh*"? How about *counterfeit, deity, either, foreign, forfeit, heifer, height, neither, leisure, protein, seize, their, weird?*

Instead of offering rules with menacing lists of exceptions, we offer a single list of words commonly misspelled in college writing. And here are four suggestions:

1. Read the list, mark any words whose spelling surprises you, and make a conscientious effort to memorize them.

2. Keep a dictionary at hand, and consult it while you are editing your final draft. If you have not formed a habit of consulting the dictionary, you may have to work at it. Begin by noticing what words or groups of words you have trouble with. Then cultivate the habit of doubting your own spellings of these words. When in doubt, don't guess; look the word up.

3. In a notebook, keep a list of words you misspell and try to classify your errors. Most spelling errors occur in characteristic and even predictable patterns. Some errors originate in mispronunciation, or the dropping or slurring of sounds in speech. (Notice, for example, gover*n*ment, Feb*r*uary, prejudic*e*d.) On the other hand, words with a vowel in an unaccented syllable are troublesome because those vowels all sound alike. You'll have to learn to visualize the correct vowel in such words as: dist*a*nt, it*e*m, ed*i*ble, gall*o*p, circ*u*s. Still other errors stem from confusing pairs of words such as: *accept/except, conscience/conscious, past/passed, capital/ capitol.* But you don't have to be aware of all possible errors any more than you need to know all the rules. You need only to classify the errors you *do* make and work at reducing those. The task is really not hopeless.

4. For words that you persistently misspell, invent some device to assist your memory. For example, if you erroneously put an *a* in *cemetery* in place of an *e*, say to yourself "people r*e*st in a cemetery." When you next have to write the word *cemetery* you will remember the associative device *(rest)*, and you will spell *cemetery* with an *e*. Another example: if you repeatedly leave out an *l* from *balloon*, say to yourself—really say it—"a balloon is a ball."

The next time you have to write *balloon* you will remember *ball*. Similarly, tell yourself there's *a rat* in *separate*. A last example, for people who mistakenly put an *n* in *dilemma:* "Emma is in a dilemma." Generally speaking, the sillier the phrase, the more memorable it will be.

Words Commonly Misspelled

abridgment
absence
accessible
accidentally
accommodate
achievement
acknowledgment
acquire
across
actually
address
adjacent
adolescence
adolescent
advice (noun)
advise (verb)
aggravate
aggressive
aging
alcohol
allege
all right (*not* alright)
a lot (*not* alot)
already (*not* all ready)
alter (to change)
altogether
analysis
analyze
apparent
appearance
appreciate
arctic
argument

assassin
assistance
assistant
athlete
attendance
balloon
beggar
beginner
believe
benefit
bourgeois
bourgeoisie
Britain
bureau
bureaucracy
burglar
business
calendar
capital (noun: seat of government, money; adjective: chief)
capitol (building)
category
ceiling
cemetery
changeable
chief
choose (present tense)
chose (past tense)
chosen (participle)
commit
committee
comparative

competent
complement (noun: that which completes; verb: to complete)
compliment (praise)
conferred
congratulate
conscience
conscious
consistent
controlled
controversy
coolly
corollary
counterfeit
criticism
criticize
curiosity
deceive
decision
defendant
definite
deity
dependent
description
desirable
despair
desperate
develop, develops
development
dilemma
disappear
disappoint

disastrous
divide
divine
dormitory
eighth
embarrass
envelop (verb)
envelope (noun)
environment
equipped
equivalent
especially
essence
exaggerate
exceed
excellence
excellent
exhilarate
existence
experience
explanation
familiar
fascinate
fiend
fiery
foreign
foreword (preface)
forty
fourth
friend
gauge
genealogy
goddess
government
grammar
grievance
guarantee
height
heroes
hoping
humorous
hypocrisy

imagery
imagination
immediately
impel
incidentally
incredible
independence
independent
indispensable
insistence
insistent
intelligent
interest
interpretation
interrupt
irrelevant
irresistible
judgment
led (past tense of
    to lead)
leisure
license
loneliness
loose (adjective)
lose (verb)
losing
maneuver
marriage
mathematics
medicine
mischievous
misspell
naive
necessary
necessity
niece
ninety
noncommittal
noticeable
occasion
occasionally
occur

occurred
occurrence
omit
omitted
original
parallel
pastime
peaceable
performance
permanent
persistent
playwright
possession
practically
precede
    predominant
preferred
prejudice
prevalent
principal
    (adjective:
    foremost; noun:
    chief)
principle (noun:
    rule)
privilege
probably
procedure
proceed
prominent
prophecy (noun)
prophesy (verb)
pursue
quantity
realize
really
receipt
receiving
recommend
reference
referring
relevance

relevant	specimen	truly
relieve	sponsor	unforgettable
remembrance	stationary (still)	unnecessary
repentance	stationery (paper)	useful
repetition	strength	usually
resistance	subtlety	various
rhyme	subtly	vengeance
rhythm	succeed	villain
sacrifice	supersede	weird
secretary	surprise	wholly
seize	syllable	who's
sense	temperament	(contraction:
separate	tendency	who is)
shining	theories	whose (possessive
shriek	therefore	pronoun:
siege	thorough	belonging to
significance	tragedy	whom)
similar	transferred	withhold
solely	tried	writing

Finally, a few words about spelling programs designed for use with computers. Programs such as Word Plus or Easy Speller flag any word you use that is not in the program's dictionary. A misspelled word is of course not in the dictionary and thus flagged. But a word flagged is not necessarily misspelled; it may simply not be in the program's dictionary. Proper names, past participles, possessives, and contractions, for example, regularly get flagged. Keep in mind also that most programs cannot distinguish between homophones *(to, too, two; there, their; alter, altar)*, nor can they tell you that you should have written *accept* instead of *except*. Since all of these words appear in the program's dictionary, they arouse no response—even when you may use them incorrectly.

Although the limitations in spelling programs will probably be overcome soon, we nevertheless think it reasonable to suggest that (if you are a poor speller) you learn to spell correctly. After all, even if you regularly use a word processor, you can't assume that you will have one available for every writing task. There are, for instance, quizzes and final examinations. Study our list of words, then, and make yourself independent (*not* independant) of spelling programs.

20
*U*sage

Some things are said or written and some are not. More precisely, anything can be said or written, but only some things are acceptable to the ears and minds of many readers. "I don't know nothing about it" has been said and will be said again, but many readers who encounter this expression might judge the speaker as a person with nothing of interest to say—and immediately tune out.

Although such a double negative today is not acceptable, it used to be: Chaucer's courteous Knight never spoke no baseness, and Shakespeare's courtly Mercutio, in *Romeo and Juliet,* "will not budge for no man." But things have changed; what was acceptable in the Middle Ages and the Renaissance (for example, emptying chamber pots into the gutter) is not always acceptable now. And some of what was once unacceptable has become acceptable. At the beginning of the twentieth century, grammarians suggested that one cannot use *drive* in speaking of a car; one drives (forces into motion) an ox, or even a person ("He drove her to distraction"), but not a machine. Some seventy years of usage, however, have erased all objections.

This chapter presents a list of expressions that, although commonly used, set many teeth on edge. Seventy years from now some of these expressions may be as acceptable as "drive a car";

but we are writing for today, and we might as well try to hold today's readers by following today's taste. If our essays are thoughtful, they will provide enough challenges to the reader; we should not use constructions that will arouse antagonism or that will allow the reader to dismiss our opinions.

You may not be familiar with some of the abuses in the following list; if so, our citing them will not instruct you, but may entertain you.

A Note on Idioms

An idiom (from a Greek word meaning "peculiar") is a fixed group of words, peculiar to a given language. Thus, in English we say, "I took a walk," but Germans "make a walk," Spaniards "give a walk," and Japanese "do a walk." (If we think the German, Spanish, and Japanese expressions are odd, we might well ask ourselves where it is that we take a walk to.) If a visitor from Argentina says, in English, that she "gave a walk," she is using *un*idiomatic English, just as anyone who says he knows a poem "at heart" instead of "by heart" is using unidiomatic English.

Probably most unidiomatic expressions use the wrong preposition. Examples:

Unidiomatic	*Idiomatic*
comply to	comply with
superior with	superior to

Sometimes while we write, or even while we speak, we are unsure of the idiom and we pause to try an alternative—"parallel with?" "parallel to?"—and we don't know which sounds more natural, more idiomatic. At such moments, more often than not, either is acceptable, but if you are in doubt, check a dictionary when you are editing your work. (The *American Heritage Dictionary* has notes on usage following the definitions of hundreds of its words.)

In any case, if you are a native speaker of English, when you read your draft you will probably detect unidiomatic expressions such as *superior with;* that is, you will hear something that sounds odd, and so you will change it to something that sounds familiar, idiomatic—here, *superior to.* If any unidiomatic expressions remain in your essay, the trouble may be that an effort to write impressively has led you to use unfamiliar language. A reader who sees such unidiomatic language may sense that you are straining for an effect. Try rewriting the passage in your own voice.

If you are a non-native speaker of English, plan to spend extra time revising and editing your work. Check prepositional phrases with special care. In addition to using a college edition of an English language dictionary, consult reference works designed with the foreign or bilingual student in mind. One compact book our students find particularly useful is Michael Swan's *Practical English Usage,* published by Oxford University Press. (It is available in a paperback edition for about ten dollars. A bookstore will order a copy for you if it is not in stock. You may also find a copy in your library. If not, the library may be willing to order a copy.) But don't neglect another invaluable resource: students who are native speakers. They will usually be able to tell you whether or not a phrase "sounds right," though they may not know why.

GLOSSARY

a, an Use *a* before words beginning with a consonant ("a book") or with a vowel sounded as a consonant ("a one-way ticket," "a university"). Use *an* before words beginning with a vowel or a vowel sound, including those beginning with a silent *h* ("an egg," "an hour"). If an initial *h* is pronounced but the accent is not on the first syllable, *an* is acceptable, as in "*an* historian" (but "*a* history course").

above Try to avoid writing *for the above reasons, in view of the above,* or *as above.* These expressions sound unpleasantly legalistic. Substitute *for these reasons,* or *therefore,* or some such expression or word.

academics Only two meanings of this noun are widely accepted: (1) "members of an institution of higher learning," and (2) "persons who are academic in background or outlook." Avoid using it to mean "academic subjects," as in "A student should pay attention not only to academics but also to recreation."

accept, except *Accept* means "to receive with consent." *Except* means "to exclude" or "excluding."

affect, effect *Affect* is usually a verb, meaning (1) "to influence, to produce an effect, to impress," or (2) "to pretend, to put on," as in "He affected an English accent." Psychologists use it as a noun for "feeling," e.g., "The patient experienced no affect." *Effect,* as a verb, means "to bring about" ("The workers effected the rescue in less than an hour"). As a noun, *effect* means "result" ("The effect was negligible").

aggravate "To worsen, to increase for the worse," as in "Smoking aggravated the irritation." Although it is widely used to mean "annoy" ("He aggravated me"), many readers are annoyed by such a use.

all ready, already *All ready* means "everything is ready." *Already* means "by this time."

all right, alright The first of these is the preferable spelling; for some readers it is the only acceptable spelling.

all together, altogether *All together* means that members of a group act or are gathered together ("They voted all together"); *altogether* is an adverb meaning "entirely," "wholly" ("This is altogether unnecessary").

allusion, reference, illusion An *allusion* is an implied or indirect reference. "As Lincoln says" is a *reference* to Lincoln, but "As a great man has said," along with a phrase quoted from the Gettysburg Address, constitutes an *allusion* to Lincoln. The student who, in a demonstration at Berkeley, carried a placard saying "I am a human being—please do not fold, spindle, or mutilate" *referred* to himself and *alluded* to a computer card. *Allusion* has nothing to do with *illusion* (a deception). Note the spelling (especially the second *i*) in "disillusioned" (left without illusions, disenchanted).

a lot Two words (not *alot*).

almost See *most*.

among, between See *between*.

amount, number *Amount* refers to bulk or quantity: "A small amount of gas was still in the tank." Use *number,* not *amount,* to refer to separate (countable) units: "A large number of people heard the lecture" (not "a large amount of people"). Similarly, "an amount of money," but "a number of dollars."

analyzation Unacceptable; use *analysis*.

and/or Acceptable, but a legalism and unpleasant-sounding. Often *or* by itself will do, as in "students who know Latin or Italian." When *or* is not enough ("The script was written by Groucho and/or Harpo") it is better to recast ("The script was written by Groucho or Harpo, or both").

and etc. Because *etc.* is an abbreviation for *et cetera* ("and others"), the *and* in *and etc.* is redundant. (See also the entry on *et cetera*.)

ante, anti *Ante* means "before" (*antebellum,* "before the Civil War"); *anti* means "against" (*antivivisectionist*). Hyphenate *anti* before capitals (*anti-Semitism*) and before *i* (*anti-intellectual*).

anthology, collection Because an *anthology* is a collection of writings by several authors, one cannot speak of "an anthology of poems by Robert Frost"; one can speak of a "collection of poems by Robert Frost."

anxious Best reserved for uses that suggest anxiety ("He was anxious before the examination"), though some authorities now accept it in the sense of "eager" ("He was anxious to serve the community").

anybody An indefinite pronoun, written as one word; if two words *(any body),* you mean any corpse ("Several people died in the fire, but the police cannot identify any body").

anyone One word, unless you mean "any one thing," as in "Here are three books; you may take any one."

area of Like *field of* and *topic of* ("the field of literature," "the topic of politics"), *area of* can usually be deleted. "The area of marketing" equals "marketing."

around Avoid using *around* in place of *about:* "He wrote it in about three hours." See also *centers on.*

as, like *As* is a conjunction; use it in forming comparisons, to introduce clauses. (A clause has a subject and a verb.)

> You can learn to write, as you can learn to swim.
> Huck speaks the truth as he sees it.

Like is a preposition; use it to introduce prepositional phrases:

> He looks like me.
> Like Hamlet, Laertes has lost a father.
> She thinks like a lawyer.

A short rule: use *like* when it introduces a noun *not* followed by a verb: "Nothing grabs people like *People*." (A famous ad for Winston cigarettes illustrates the *in*correct use of *like*—that is, the use of *like* as a conjunction before a clause: "Winston tastes good like a cigarette should.")

Writers who are fearful of incorrectly using *like* resort to cumbersome evasions: "He eats in the same manner that a pig eats." But there's nothing wrong with "He eats like a pig."

as of now Best deleted, or replaced by *now.* Not "As of now I don't smoke" but "Now I don't smoke" or "I don't smoke now" or "I don't smoke."

aspect Literally, "a view from a particular point," but it has come to mean *topic,* as in "There are several aspects to be considered." Try to get a sharper word; for example, "There are several problems to be considered," or "There are several consequences to be considered."

as such Often meaningless, as in "Tragedy as such evokes pity."

as to Usually *about* is preferable. Not "I know nothing as to the charges," but "I know nothing about the charges."

bad, badly *Bad* used to be only an adjective ("a bad movie"), and *badly* was an adverb ("she sings badly"). In "I felt bad," *bad* describes the subject, not the verb. (Compare "I felt happy," or "I felt good about getting a raise." After verbs of appearing, such as "feel," "look," "seem," "taste," an adjective, not an adverb is used. If you are in doubt, substitute a word for *bad,* for instance *sad,* and see what you say. Since you would say "I feel sad about his failure," you can say "I feel bad. . . .") But "badly" is acceptable and even preferred by many. Note, however, this distinction: "This meat smells bad" (an adjective describing the meat), and "Because I have a stuffed nose I smell badly" (an adverb describing my ability to smell something).

being Do not use *being* as a main verb, as in "The trouble being that his reflexes were too slow." The result is a sentence fragment. See pages 710–12.

being that, being as A sentence such as "Being that she was a stranger . . ." sounds like an awkward translation from the Latin. Use *because*.

beside, besides *Beside* means "at the side of." Because *besides* can mean either "in addition to" or "other than," it is ambiguous, as in "Something besides TB caused his death." It is best, then, to use *in addition to* or *other than*, depending on what you mean.

between Only English teachers who have had a course in Middle English are likely to know that between comes from *by twain*. And only English teachers and editors are likely to object to its use (and to call for *among*) when more than two are concerned, as in "among the three of us." Note, too, that even conservative usage accepts *between* in reference to more than two when the items are at the moment paired: "Negotiations *between* Israel and Egypt, Syria, and Lebanon seem stalled." *Between*, a preposition, takes an object ("between you and me"): not "between you and I".

biannually, bimonthly, biweekly Every two years, every two months, every two weeks (*not* twice a year, etc.). Twice a year is *semiannually*. Because *biannually, bimonthly,* and *biweekly* are commonly misunderstood, it is best to avoid them and to say "every two . . ."

Black, black Although one sometimes sees the word capitalized when it refers to race, most publishers use a lowercase letter, making it consistent with *white*, which is never capitalized.

can, may When schoolchildren asked "Can I leave the room?" their teachers used to correct them thus: "You *can* leave the room if you have legs, but you *may not* leave the room until you receive permission." In short, *can* indicates physical possibility, *may* indicates permission. But because "you may not" and "why mayn't I?" sound not merely polite but stiff, *can* is usually preferred except in formal contexts.

centers on, centers around Use *centers on*, because *center* refers to a point, not to a movement around.

collection, anthology See *anthology*.

collective nouns A collective noun, singular in form, names a collection of individuals. Examples: *audience, band, committee, crowd, jury, majority, minority, team*. When you are thinking chiefly of the whole as a unit, use a singular verb (and a singular pronoun, if any): "The majority rules"; "The jury is announcing its verdict." But when you are thinking of the individuals, use a plural verb (and pronoun, if any): "The majority are lawyers"; "The jury are divided and they probably cannot agree." If the plural sounds odd, you can usually rewrite: "The jurors are divided and they probably cannot agree."

compare, contrast To *compare* is to note likenesses or differences: "Compare a motorcycle with a bicycle." To *contrast* is to emphasize differences.

complement, compliment *Complement* as a noun means "that which completes"; as a verb, "to fill out, to complete." *Compliment* as a noun is an expression of praise; as a verb it means "to offer praise."

comprise "To include, contain, consist of": "The university comprises two colleges and a medical school" (not "is comprised of"). Conservative authorities hold that "to be comprised of" is always incorrect, and they reject the form one often hears: "Two colleges and a medical school comprise the university." Here the word should be *compose*, not *comprise*.

concept Should often be deleted. For "The concept of the sales tax is regressive" write "The sales tax is regressive."

contact Because it is vague, avoid using *contact* as a verb. *Not* "I contacted him" but "I spoke with him" or "I wrote to him," or whatever.

continual, continuous Conservative authorities hold that *continuous* means "uninterrupted," as in "It rained continuously for six hours"; *continually* means "repeated often, recurring at short intervals," as in "For a year he continually wrote letters to her."

contrast, compare See *compare.*

could have, could of See *of.*

criteria Plural of *criterion,* hence it is always incorrect to speak of "a criteria," or to say "The criteria is . . . ."

data Plural of *datum.* Although some social scientists speak of "this data," "these data" is preferable: "These data are puzzling." Because the singular, *datum,* is rare and sounds odd, it is best to substitute *fact* or *figure* for *datum.*

different from Prefer it to *different than,* unless you are convinced that in a specific sentence *different from* sounds terribly wrong, as in "These two books are more different than I had expected." (In this example, "more," not "different," governs "than." But this sentence, though correct, is awkward and therefore it should be revised: "These two books differ more than I had expected.")

dilemma A situation requiring a choice between equally undesirable alternatives; not every difficulty or plight or predicament is a *dilemma.* Not "Her dilemma was that she had nowhere to go," but "Her dilemma was whether to go out or to stay home: one was frightening, the other was embarrassing." And note the spelling (two *m's,* no *n*).

disinterested Though the word is often used to mean "indifferent," "unconcerned," "uninterested," reserve it to mean "impartial": "A judge should be disinterested."

due to Some people, holding that *due to* cannot modify a verb (as in "He failed due to illness"), tolerate it only when it modifies a noun or pronoun ("His failure was due to illness"). They also insist that it cannot begin a sentence ("Due to illness, he failed"). In fact, however, daily usage accepts both. But because it almost always sounds stiff, try to substitute *because of,* or *through.*

due to the fact that Wordy for *because.*

each Although many authorities hold that *each,* as a subject, is singular, even when followed by "them" ("Each of them is satisfactory"), some authorities accept and even favor the plural ("Each of them are satisfactory"). But it is usually better to avoid the awkwardness by substituting *all* for *each:* "All of them are satisfactory." When *each* refers to a plural subject, the verb must be plural: "They each have a book"; "We each are trying." *Each* cannot be made into a possessive; you cannot say "Each's opinion is acceptable."

effect See *affect.*

e.g. Abbreviation for *exempli gratia,* meaning "for example." It is thus different from *i.e.* (an abbreviation for *id est,* meaning "that is"). E.g. (not italicized) introduces an example; i.e. (also not italicized) introduces a definition. Because these two abbreviations of Latin words are often confused, it may be preferable to avoid them and use their English equivalents.

either . . . or, neither . . . nor If the subjects are singular, use a singular verb: "Either the boy or the girl is lying." If one of the subjects joined by *or* or *nor* is plural, most grammarians say that the verb agrees with the nearer subject, thus: "A tree or two shrubs are enough," or "Two shrubs or a tree is enough." But because the singular verb in the second of these sentences may sound odd, follow the first construction; that is, put the plural subject nearer to the verb and use a plural verb. Another point about *either . . . or.* In this construction, "either" serves as advance notice that two equal possibilities are in the offing. Beware of putting "either" too soon, as in "Either he is a genius or a lunatic." Better: "He is either a genius or a lunatic."

enthuse Objectionable to many readers. For "He enthused," say "He was enthusiastic." Use *enthuse* only in the sense of "to be excessively enthusiastic," "to gush."

et cetera, etc. Latin for "and other things"; if you mean "and other people," you need *et al.,* short for *et alii.* Because *etc.* is vague, its use is usually inadvisable. Not "He studied mathematics, etc." but "He studied mathematics, history, economics, and French." Or, if the list is long, cut it by saying something a little more informative than *etc.*— for example, "He studied mathematics, history, and other liberal arts subjects." Even *and so forth* or *and so on* is preferable to *etc.* Confine etc. (and most other abbreviations, including *et al.*) to footnotes, and even in footnotes try to avoid it.

everybody, everyone These take a singular verb ("Everybody is here"), and a pronoun referring to them is usually singular ("Everybody thinks his problems are suitable topics of conversation"), but use a plural pronoun if the singular would seem unnatural ("Everybody was there, weren't they?"). To avoid the sexism of "Everybody thinks his problems. . ." revise to "All people think their problems . . ."

examples, instances See *instances.*

except See *accept.*

exists Often unnecessary and a sign of wordiness. Not "The problem that *exists* here is" but "The problem here is."

expound Usually pretentious for *explain* or *say.* To *expound* is to give a methodical explanation of theological matters.

facet Literally "little face," especially one of the surfaces of a gem. Don't use it (and don't use *aspect* or *factor* either) to mean "part" or "topic." It is most acceptable when, close to its literal meaning, it suggests a new appearance, as when a gem is turned: "Another *facet* appears when we see this law from the taxpayer's point of view."

the fact that Usually wordy. "Because of the fact that boys played female roles in Elizabethan drama" can be reduced to "Because boys played female roles in Elizabethan drama."

factor Strictly speaking, a *factor* helps to produce a result. Although *factor* is often used in the sense of "point" ("Another factor to be studied is . . .), such use is often wordy. "The possibility of plagiarism is a factor that must be considered" simply adds up to "The possibility of plagiarism must be considered." *Factor* is almost never the precise word: "the factors behind Gatsby's actions" are, more precisely, "Gatsby's motives."

famous, notorious See *notorious.*

farther, further Some purists claim that *farther* always refers to distance and *further* to time ("The gymnasium is farther than the library"; "Let us think further about this").

fatalistic, pessimistic *Fatalistic* means "characterized by the belief that all events are predetermined and therefore inevitable"; *pessimistic,* "characterized by the belief that the world is evil," or, less gloomily, "expecting the worst."

fewer, less See *less.*

field of See *area of.*

firstly, secondly Acceptable, but it is better to use *first, second.*

former, latter These words are acceptable, but they are often annoying because they force the reader to reread earlier material in order to locate what *the former* and *the latter* refer to. The expressions are legitimately used in order to avoid repeating lengthy terms, but if you are talking about an easily repeated subject—say, Lincoln and Grant—don't hesitate to replace *the former* and *the latter* with their names. The repetition will clarify rather than bore.

good, well *Good* is an adjective ("a good book"). *Well* is usually an adverb ("She writes well"). Standard English does not accept "She writes good." But Standard English requires *good* after verbs of appearing, such as "seems," "looks," "sounds," "tastes": "it looks good," "it sounds good." *Well* can also be an adjective meaning "healthy": "I am well."

graduate, graduate from Use *from* if you name the institution or if you use a substitute word as in "She graduated from high school"; if the institution (or substitute) is not named, *from* is omitted: "She graduated in 1983." The use of the passive ("She was graduated from high school") is acceptable but sounds fussy to many.

he or she, his or her These expressions are awkward, but the implicit male chauvinism in the generic use of the male pronoun ("A citizen should exercise his right to vote") may be more offensive than the awkwardness of *he or she* and *his or her*. Moreover, sometimes the male pronoun, when used for males and females, is ludicrous, as in "The more violence a youngster sees on television, regardless of his age or sex, the more aggressive he is likely to be." Do what you can to avoid the dilemma. Sometimes you can use the plural *their*: "Students are expected to hand in their papers on Monday" (instead of "The student is expected to hand in his or her paper on Monday"). Or eliminate the possessive: "The student must hand in a paper on Monday." See also *man, mankind*.

hopefully Commonly used to mean "I hope" or "It is hoped" ("*Hopefully,* the rain will stop soon"), but it is best to avoid what some consider a dangling modifier. After all, the rain itself is not hopeful. If you mean "I hope the rain will stop soon," say exactly that. Notice, too, that *hopefully* is often evasive; if the president of the college says, "Hopefully tuition will not rise next year," don't think that you have heard a promise to fight against an increase; you only have heard someone evade making a promise. In short, confine *hopefully* to its adverbial use, meaning "in a hopeful manner": "Hopefully he uttered a prayer."

however It is preferable not to begin a sentence with *however* unless it is an adverb meaning "to whatever extent or degree," as in "However hard he studied, he couldn't remember irregular verbs." When *however* is a conjunctive adverb, it usually gains emphasis if you put it later in the sentence, between commas: "He failed the examination, however, and didn't graduate." (Compare, "However, he failed the examination and didn't graduate.") Unless *however* is set off in commas it usually sounds insufficiently emphatic. If you want to begin a sentence with a sharp contrast, use *but* or *nevertheless.* Note too that you cannot link independent clauses with a *however* preceded by a comma; you need a semicolon ("He tried; however, he failed"). Even here, however, *but* is usually preferable, without a semicolon.

the idea that Usually dull and wordy. Not "The idea that we grow old is frightening," but "That we grow old is frightening," or (probably better) "Growing old is frightening."

identify When used in the psychological sense, "to associate oneself closely with a person or an institution," it is preferable to include a reflexive pronoun, thus: "He identified himself with Hamlet," *not* "He identified with Hamlet."

i.e. Latin for *id est,* "that is." The English words are preferable to the Latin abbreviation. On the distinction between *i.e.* and *e.g.,* see *e.g.*

immanent, imminent *Immanent,* "remaining within, intrinsic"; *imminent,* "likely to occur soon, impending."

imply, infer The writer or speaker *implies* (suggests); the perceiver *infers* (draws a conclusion): "Karl Marx implied that . . . but his modern disciples infer from his writings that . . ." Although *infer* is widely used for *imply,* preserve the distinction.

incidence, incident The *incidence* is the extent or frequency of an occurrence: "The incidence of violent crime in Tokyo is very low." The plural, *incidences,* is rarely used: "The incidences of crime and of fire in Tokyo. . . ." An *incident* is one occurrence: "The incident happened yesterday." The plural is *incidents:* "The two incidents happened simultaneously."

individual Avoid using the word to mean only "person": "He was a generous individual." But it is precise when it implicitly makes a contrast with a group: "In a money-mad society, he was a generous individual"; "Although the faculty did not take a stand on this issue, faculty members as individuals spoke out."

instances Instead of *in many instances* use *often.* Strictly speaking an *instance* is not an object or incident in itself but one offered as an example. Thus "another instance of his failure to do his duty" (not "In three instances he failed to do his duty").

irregardless Unacceptable; use *regardless.*

it is Usually this expression needlessly delays the subject: "It is unlikely that many students will attend the lecture" could just as well be "Few students are likely to attend the lecture."

its, it's The first is a possessive pronoun ("The flock lost its leader"); the

second is a contraction of *it is* ("It's a wise father that knows his child.")
You'll have no trouble if you remember that the possessive pronoun
its, like other possessive pronouns such as *our, his, their,* does *not* use
an apostrophe.

kind of Singular, as in "That kind of movie bothers me." (*Not:* "Those
kind of movies bother me.") If, however, you are really talking about
more than one kind, use *kinds* and be sure that the demonstrative pronoun and the verb are plural: "Those kinds of movies bother me."
Notice also that the phrase is *kind of,* not *kind of a.* Not "What *kind
of a* car does she drive?" but "What *kind of* car does she drive?"

latter See under *former.*

lay, lie *To lay* means "to put, to set, to cause to rest." It takes an object:
"May I lay the coats on the table?" The past tense and the participle
are *laid:* "I laid the coats on the table"; "I have laid the coats on the
table." *To lie* means "to recline," and it does not take an object: "When
I am tired I lie down." The past tense is *lay,* the participle is *lain:*
"Yesterday I lay down"; "I have lain down hundreds of times without
wishing to get up."

lend, loan The usual verb is *lend:* "Lend me a pen." The past tense and
the participle are both *lent. Loan* is a noun: "This isn't a gift, it's a
loan." But, curiously, *loan* as a verb is acceptable in past forms: "I
loaned him my bicycle." In its present form ("I often loan money") it
is used chiefly by bankers.

less, fewer *Less* (as an adjective) refers to bulk amounts (also called mass
nouns): less milk, less money, less time, *Fewer* refers to separate (countable) items: fewer glasses of milk, fewer dollars, fewer hours.

lifestyle, life-style, life style All three forms are acceptable, but because
many readers regard the expression as imprecise, try to find a substitute
such as *values.*

like, as See under *as.*

literally It means "strictly in accord with the primary meaning; not metaphorically." It is not a mere intensive. "He was literally dead" means
that he was a corpse; if he was merely exhausted, *literally* won't do.
You cannot be "literally stewed" (except by cannibals), "literally tick-
led pink," or "literally head over heels in love."

loose, lose *Loose* is an adjective ("The nail is loose"); *lose* is a verb ("Don't
lose the nail").

the majority of Usually a wordy way of saying *most.* Of course if you
mean "a bare majority," say so; otherwise *most* will usually do. Certainly "The majority of the basement is used for a cafeteria" should be
changed to "Most of the basement is used for a cafeteria."

man, mankind the use of these words in reference to males and females
sometimes is ludicrous, as in "Man, being a mammal, breastfeeds his

young." But even when not ludicrous the practice is sexist, as in "man's brain" and "the greatness of mankind." Consider using such words as *human being, person, humanity, people.* Similarly, for "manmade," *artificial* or *synthetic* may do.

may, can See under *can.*

me The right word in such expressions as "between you and me" and "They gave it to John and me." It is the object of verbs and of prepositions. In fact, *me* rather than *I* is the usual form after any verb, including the verb *to be;* "It is me" is nothing to be ashamed of. See the entry on *myself.*

medium, media *Medium* is singular, *media* is plural: "TV is the medium to which most children are most exposed. Other media include film, radio, and publishing," It follows, then, that *mass media* takes a plural verb: "The mass media exert an enormous influence."

more Avoid writing a false (incomplete) comparison such as: "His essay includes several anecdotes, making it more enjoyable." Delete "more" unless there really is a comparison with another essay. On false comparisons see also the entry on *other.*

most, almost Although it is acceptable in speech to say "most everyone" and "most anybody," it is preferable in writing to use "almost everyone," "almost anybody." But of course: "Most students passed."

myself *Myself* is often mistakenly used for *I* or *me,* as in "They praised Tony and myself," or "Prof. Chen and myself examined the dead rat." In the first example, *me* is the word to use; after all, if Tony hadn't been there the sentence would say, "They praised me." (No one would say, "They praised myself.") Similarly, in the second example if Prof. Chen were not involved, the sentence would run, "I examined the dead rat," so what is needed here is simply "Prof. Chen and I examined. . . ."

In general, use *myself* only when 1) it refers to the subject of the sentence ("I look out for myself"; "I washed myself") or 2) when it is an intensive: ("I myself saw the break-in"; "I myself have not experienced racism").

nature You can usually delete *the nature of,* as in "The nature of my contribution is not political but psychological."

needless to say The reader may well wonder why you go on to say it. Of course this expression is used to let readers know that they are probably familiar with what comes next, but usually *of course* will better serve as this sign.

Negro Capitalized, whether a noun or an adjective, though *white* is not. In recent years *Negro* has been replaced by *black* or African-American.

neither . . . nor See *either . . . or.*

nobody, no one, none *Nobody* and *no one* are singular, requiring a singular verb ("Nobody believes this," "No one knows"); but they can be referred to by a plural pronoun: "Nobody believes this, do they?" "No one knows, do they?" *None,* though it comes from *no one,* almost always requires a plural verb when it refers to people ("Of the ten people present, none are students") and a singular verb when it refers to things ("Of the five assigned books, none is worth reading").

not only . . . but also Keep in mind these two points: 1) many readers object to the omission of "also" in such a sentence as "She not only brought up two children but practiced law," and 2) all readers dislike a faulty parallel, as in "She not only is bringing up two children but practices law." ("Is bringing up" needs to be paralleled with "is also practicing.")

not . . . un- Such an expression as "not unfamiliar" is useful only if it conveys something different from the affirmative. Compare the frostiness of "I am not unfamiliar with your methods" with "I am familiar with your methods." If the negative has no evident advantage, use the affirmative. See pages 487–88.

notorious Widely and unfavorably known; not merely famous, but famous for some discreditable trait or deed.

number, amount See *amount.*

a number of requires a plural verb: "A number of women are presidents of corporations." But when *number* is preceded by *the* it requires a singular verb: "The number of women who are presidents is small." (The plural noun after *number* of course may require a plural verb, as in "women are," but *the number* itself remains singular; hence its verb is singular, as in "is small.")

of Be careful not to use *of* when *have* is required. Not "He might of died in the woods," but "He might have died in the woods." Note that what we often hear as "would've" or "should've" or "must've" or "could've" is "would have" or "should have" or "must have" or "could have," *not* "would of," etc.

off of Use *off* or *from:* "Take it off the table"; "He jumped from the bridge."

often-times Use *often* instead.

old-fashioned, old-fashion Only the first is acceptable.

one British usage accepts the shift from *one* to *he* in "One begins to die the moment he is born," but American usage prefers "One begins to die the moment one is born." A shift from *one* to *you* ("One begins to die the moment you are born") is unacceptable. As a pronoun, *one* can be useful in impersonal statements such as the sentence about dying, at the beginning of this entry, where it means "a person," but don't use it as a disguise for yourself ("One objects to Smith's argument"). Try to avoid *one;* one *one* usually leads to another, resulting in a sentence that, in James Thurber's words, "sounds like a trombone solo" ("If one takes oneself too seriously, one begins to . . ."). See *you,* pages 769.

one of Takes a plural noun, and if this is followed by a clause, the preferred verb is plural: "one of those students who are," "one of those who feel." Thus, in such a sentence as "One of the coaches who have resigned is now seeking reinstatement," notice that "have" is correct; the antecedent of "who" (the subject of the verb) is "coaches," which is plural. Coaches have resigned, though "one . . . is seeking reinstatement." But in such an expression as "one out of a hundred," the following verb may be singular or plural ("One out of a hundred is," "One out of a hundred are").

only Be careful where you put it. The classic textbook example points out that in the sentence "I hit him in the eye," *only* can be inserted in seven places (beginning in front of "I" and ending after "eye") with at least six different meanings. Try to put it just before the expression it qualifies. Thus, not "Presidential aides are only responsible to one man," but "Presidential aides are responsible to only one man" (or "to one man only"). See page 520.

oral, verbal See *verbal.*

other Often necessary in comparisons. "No American president served as many terms as Franklin Roosevelt" falsely implies that Roosevelt was not an American president. The sentence should be revised to "No other American president served as many terms as Franklin Roosevelt."

per Usually it sounds needlessly technical ("twice per hour") or disturbingly impersonal ("as per your request"). Preferable: "twice an hour," "according to your request," or "as you requested."

per cent, percent, percentage The first two of these are interchangeable; both mean "per hundred," "out of a hundred," as in "Ninety per cent (or percent) of the students were white." *Per cent* and *percent* are always accompanied by a number (written out, or in figures). It is usually better to write out *per cent* or *percent* than to use a per cent sign (12%), except in technical or statistical papers. *Percentage* means "a proportion or share in relation to the whole," as in "A very large percentage of the student body is white." Many authorities insist that *percentage* is never preceded by a number. Do not use percentage to mean "a few," as in "Only a percentage of students attended the lecture"; a percentage can be as large as 99.99. It is usually said that with *per cent, percent,* and *percentage,* whether the verb is singular or plural depends on the number of the noun that follows the word, thus: "Ninety percent of his books are paperbacks"; "Fifty percent of his library is worthless"; "A large percentage of his books are worthless." But some readers (including the authors of this book) prefer a singular verb after *percentage* unless the resulting sentence is as grotesque as this one: "A large percentage of the students is unmarried." Still, rather than say a "percentage . . . are," we would recast the sentence: "A large percentage of the student body is unmarried," or "Many (or "Most," or whatever) of the students are unmarried."

per se Latin for "by itself." Usually sounds legalistic or pedantic, as in "Meter per se has an effect."

pessimistic See *fatalistic.*

phenomenon, phenomena The plural is *phenomena;* thus, "these phenomena" but "this phenomenon."

plus Unattractive and imprecise as a noun meaning "asset" or "advantage" ("When he applied for the job, his appearance was a plus"), and equally unattractive as a substitute for *moreover* ("The examination was easy, plus I had studied") or as a substitute for *and* ("I studied the introduction plus the first chapter").

politics Preferably singular ("Ethnic politics has been a strong force for a century") but a plural verb is acceptable.

prejudice, prejudiced *Prejudice* is a noun: "It is impossible to live entirely without prejudice." But use the past participle *prejudiced* as an adjective: "He was prejudiced against me from the start."

preventative, preventive Both are acceptable but the second form is the form now used by writers on medicine ("preventive medicine"); *preventative* therefore has come to seem amateurish.

principal, principle *Principal* is 1) an adjective meaning "main," "chief," "most important" ("The principal arguments against IQ testing are three"), and 2) a noun meaning "the chief person" ("Ms. Murphy was the principal of Jefferson High") or "the chief thing" ("She had so much money she could live on the interest and not touch the principal"). *Principle* is always a noun meaning "rule" or "fundamental truth" ("It was against his principles to eat meat").

prior to Pretentious for *before.*

protagonist Literally, the first actor, and, by extension, the chief actor. It is odd, therefore, to speak of "the protagonists" in a single literary work or occurrence. Note also that the prefix is *proto,* "first," not *pro,* "for"; it does *not* mean one who strives for something.

quite Usually a word to delete, along with *definitely, pretty, rather,* and *very.* See page 481. *Quite* used to mean "completely" ("I quite understand") but it has come also to mean "to a considerable degree," and so it is ambiguous as well as vague.

quotation, quote Quotation is a noun, quote is a verb. "I will quote Churchill" is fine, but not "these quotes from Churchill." And remember, you may *quote* one of Hamlet's speeches, but Hamlet does not *quote* them; he says them.

rather Avoid use with strong adjectives. "Rather intelligent" makes sense, but "rather tremendous" does not. "Rather brilliant" probably means "bright"; "rather terrifying" probably means "frightening," "rather unique" probably means "unusual." Get the right adjective, not *rather* and the wrong adjective.

the reason . . . is because Usually *because* is enough (not "The reason they fail is because they don't study," but simply "They fail because they don't study"). Similarly, *the reason why* can usually be reduced to *why*. Notice, too, that because *reason* is a noun, it cannot neatly govern a *because* clause: not "The reason for his absence is because he was sick," but "The reason for his absence was illness."

rebut, refute To rebut is to argue against, but not necessarily successfully. If you mean "to disprove," use *disprove* or *refute*.

in regard to, with regard to Often wordy for *about, concerning*, or *on*, and sometimes even these words are unnecessary. Compare: "He knew a great deal in regard to jazz"; "He knew a great deal about jazz." Compare: "Hemingway's story is often misunderstood with regard to Robert Wilson's treatment of Margot Macomber"; "In Hemingway's story, Robert Wilson's treatment of Margot Macomber is often misunderstood."

relate to Usually a vague expression, best avoided, as in "I can relate to Hedda Gabler." Does it mean "respond favorably to," "identify myself with," "interact with" (and how can a reader "interact with" a character in a play?). Use *relate to* only in the sense of "have connection with" (as in "How does your answer relate to my question?"); even in such a sentence a more exact expression is preferable.

repel, repulse Both verbs mean "to drive back," but only *repel* can mean "to cause distaste," "to disgust," as in "His obscenities repelled the audience."

sarcasm Heavy, malicious sneering ("Oh, you're really a great friend, aren't you?" addressed to someone who won't lend the speaker ten dollars). If the apparent praise, which really communicates dispraise, is at all clever, conveying, say, a delicate mockery or wryness, it is irony, not sarcasm. The passages by Szarkowski on page 555 are ironic, not sarcastic.

seem Properly it suggests a suspicion that appearances may be deceptive: "He seems honest (but . . .)." Don't say "The book seems to lack focus" if you believe it does lack focus.

semiannually, semimonthly, semiweekly See *biannually*.

shall, will, should, would The old principle held that in the first person *shall* is the future indicative of *to be* and *should* the conditional ("I shall go," "We should like to be asked"); and that *will* and *would* are the forms for the second and third persons. When the forms are reversed ("I will go," "Government of the people . . . shall not perish from the earth"), determination is expressed. But today almost nobody adheres to these principles. Indeed, *shall* (except in questions) sounds stilted to many ears.

simplistic Means "falsely simplified by ignoring complications." Do not confuse it with *simplified*, whose meanings include "reduced to essentials" and "clarified."

since, because Traditional objections to *since*, in the sense of "because," have all but vanished. Note, however, that when *since* is ambiguous and may also refer to time ("Since he joined the navy, she found another boyfriend") it is better to say *because* or *after*, depending on which you mean.

situation Overused, vague, and often unnecessary. "His situation was that he was unemployed" adds up to "He was unemployed." And "an emergency situation" is probably an emergency.

split infinitives The infinitive is the verb form that merely names the action, without indicating when or by whom performed ("walk," rather than "walked" or "I walk"). Grammarians, however, developed the idea that the infinitive was "to walk," and they held that one cannot separate or split the two words: "to quickly walk." But James Thurber says this idea is "of a piece with the sentimental and outworn notion that it is always wrong to strike a lady." Notice, however, that often the inserted word can be deleted ("to really understand" is "to understand"), and that if many words are inserted between *to* and the verb, the reader may get lost ("to quickly and in the remaining few pages before examining the next question conclude").

stanza See under *verse*.

subjunctive For the use of the subjunctive with conditions contrary to fact (for instance, "If I were you"), see the entry on *was/were*. The subjunctive is also used in *that* clauses followed by verbs demanding, requesting, or recommending: "He asked that the students be prepared to take a test." But because this last sort of sentence sounds stiff, it is better to use an alternate construction, such as "He asked the students to prepare for a test."

than, then *Than* is used chiefly in making comparisons ("German is harder than French"), but also after "rather," "other," "different," and "else" ("I'd rather take French than German"; "He thinks of nothing other than sex"). *Then* commonly indicates time ("She took German then, but now she takes French"; "Until then, I'll save you a seat"), but it may also mean "in that case" ("It's agreed, then, that we'll all go") or "on the other hand" ("Then again, she may find German easy"). The simplest guide: use *than* after comparisons and after "rather," "other," "else"; otherwise use *then*.

that, which, who Many pages have been written on these words; opinions differ, but you will offend no one if you observe the following principles. (1) Use *that* in restrictive (that is, limiting) clauses: "The rocking chair that creaks is on the porch." (2) Use *which* in nonrestrictive (in effect, parenthetic) clauses: "The rocking chair, which creaks, is on the porch." (See pages 721–23.) The difference between these two sentences is this: in the first, one rocking chair is singled out from several—the one that creaks; in the second, the fact that the rocking chair creaks is simply tossed in, and is not added for the purpose of identifying the one chair out of several. (3) Use *who* for people, in restrictive and in nonrestrictive clauses: "The men who were playing poker ignored the women"; "The men, who were playing poker, ignored the women." But note that often *that, which,* and *who* can be omitted: "The creaky rocking chair is on the porch"; "The men, playing poker, ignored the women." In general, omit these words if the sentence remains clear. See page 489.

their, there, they're The first is a possessive pronoun: "Chaplin and Keaton made their first films before sound tracks were developed." The second, *there,* sometimes refers to a place ("Go there," "Do you live there?"), and sometimes is what is known in grammar as an introductory expletive ("There are no solutions to this problem"). The third, *they're,* is a contraction of "they are" ("They're going to stay for dinner").

this Often refers vaguely to "what I have been saying." Does it refer to the previous sentence, the previous paragraph, the previous page? Try to modify it by being specific: "This last point"; "This clue gave the police all they needed."

thusly Unacceptable; *thus* is an adverb and needs no adverbial ending.

till, until Both are acceptable, but *until* is preferable because *till*—though common in speech—looks literary in print. The following are *not* acceptable: *til, 'til, 'till.*

to, too, two *To* is toward; *too* is either "also" ("She's a lawyer, too") or "excessively" ("It's too hot"); *two* is one more than one ("Two is company").

topic of See *area of.*

toward, towards Both are standard English; *toward* is more common in the United States, *towards* in Great Britain.

type Often colloquial (and unacceptable in most writing) for *type of,* as in "this type teacher." But *type of* is not especially pleasing either. Better to write "this kind of teacher." And avoid using *type* as a suffix: "essay-type examinations" are essay examinations; "natural-type ice cream" is natural ice cream. Sneaky manufacturers make "Italian-type cheese," implying that their domestic cheese is imported and at the same time protecting themselves against charges of misrepresentation.

unique The only one of its kind. Someone or something cannot be "rather unique" or "very unique" or "somewhat unique," any more than a woman can be somewhat pregnant. Instead of saying "rather unique," then, say *rare*, or *unusual*, or *extraordinary*, or whatever seems to be the best word.

U.S., United States Generally, *United States* is preferable to *U.S.*; similarly, *the Soviet Union* is preferable to *the U.S.S.R.*

usage Don't use *usage* where *use* will do, as in "Here Vonnegut completes his usage of dark images." *Usage* properly implies a customary practice that has created a standard: "Usage has eroded the difference between 'shall' and 'will.' "

use of The use of *use of* is usually unnecessary. "Through the use of setting he conveys a sense of foreboding" may be reduced to "The setting conveys . . ." or "His setting conveys . . ."

utilize, utilization Often inflated for *use* and *using*, as in "The infirmary has noted that it is freshmen who have most utilized the counseling service."

verbal Often used where *oral* would be more exact. *Verbal* simply means "expressed in words," and thus a *verbal agreement* may be either written or spoken. If you mean spoken, call it an *oral agreement*.

verse, stanza A *verse* is a single line of a poem; a *stanza* is a group of lines, commonly bound by a rhyme scheme. But in speaking of writing about songs, usage sanctions *verse* for *stanza*, as in "Second verse, same as the first."

viable A term from physiology, meaning "capable of living" (for example, referring to a fetus at a stage of its development). Now pretentiously used and overused, especially by politicians and journalists, to mean "workable," as in "a viable presidency." Avoid it.

was, were Use the subjunctive form—*were* (rather than *was*)—in expressing a wish ("I wish I were younger") and in "if-clauses" that are contrary to fact ("If I were rich," "If I were you . . .")

we If you mean *I*, say *I*. Not "The first fairy tale we heard" but "the first fairy tale I heard." (But of course *we* is appropriate in some statements: "We have all heard fairy tales"; "If we look closely at the evidence, we can agree that. . . .") The rule: don't use *we* as a disguise for *I*. See pages 515–16.

well See *good.*

well known, widely known Athletes, performers, politicians, and such folk are not really *well known* except perhaps by a few of their friends and their relatives; use *widely known* if you mean they are known (however slightly) to many people.

which Often can be deleted. "Students are required to fill out scholarship applications which are lengthy" can be written "Students are required to fill out lengthy scholarship applications." Another example: "*The Tempest,* which is Shakespeare's last play, was written in 1611"; "*The Tempest,* Shakespeare's last play, was written in 1611," or "Shakespeare wrote his last play, *The Tempest,* in 1611." For the distinction between *which* and *that,* see the entry on *that.*

while Best used in a temporal sense, meaning "during the time": "While I was speaking, I suddenly realized that I didn't know what I was talking about." While it is not wrong to use *while* in a nontemporal sense, meaning "although" (as at the beginning of this sentence), it is better to use *although* in order to avoid any ambiguity. Note the ambiguity in: "While he was fond of movies he chiefly saw westerns." Does it mean "Although he was fond of movies," or does it mean "During the time when he was fond of movies"? Another point: do not use *while* if you mean *and;* "Freshmen take English 1–2, while sophomores take English 10–11" (substitute *and* for *while*).

who, whom Strictly speaking, *who* must be used for subjects, even when they look like objects: "He guessed who would be chosen." (Here *who* is the subject of the clause "who would be chosen." *Whom* must be used for the objects of a verb, verbal (gerund, participle), or preposition: "Whom did he choose?"; "Whom do you want me to choose?"; "To whom did he show it?" We may feel stuffy in writing "Whom did he choose?" or "Whom are you talking about?" but to use *who* is certain to annoy some reader. Often you can avoid the dilemma by rewriting: "Who was chosen?"; "Who is the topic of conversation?" See also the entry on *that.*

whoever, whomever The second of these is the objective form. It is often incorrectly used as the subject of a clause. "Open the class to whomever wants to take it" is incorrect. The object of "to" is not "whomever" but is the entire clause—"whoever wants to take it"—and of course "whoever" is the subject of "wants."

who's, whose The first is a contraction of *who is* ("I'm everybody who's nobody"). The second is a possessive pronoun: "Whose book is it?" "I know whose it is."

will, would See *shall* and also *would.*

would "I would think that" is a wordy version of "I think that." (On the mistaken use of *would of* for *would have,* see *of,* pages 761–62.

you In relatively informal writing, *you* is ordinarily preferable to the somewhat stiff *one:* "If you are addicted to cigarettes, you may find it helpful to join Smokenders." (Compare: "If one is addicted to cigarettes, one may . . .") But because the direct address of *you* may sometimes descend into nagging, it is usually better to write: "Cigarette addicts may find it helpful . . ." Certainly a writer (you?) should not assume that the reader is guilty of vices ("You should not molest children") unless the essay is clearly aimed at an audience that admits to these vices, say a pamphlet directed to child molesters who are seeking help. Thus, it is acceptable to say, "If you are a poor speller," but it is not acceptable to say, to the general reader, "You should improve your spelling"; the reader's spelling may not need improvement. And avoid *you* when the word cannot possibly apply to the reader: "A hundred years ago you were faced with many diseases that now have been eradicated." Something like "A hundred years ago people were faced . . ." is preferable.

your, you're The first is a possessive pronoun ("your book"); the second is a contraction of *you are* ("You're mistaken").

LAST WORDS

A rich patron once gave money to the painter Chu Ta, asking him to paint a picture of a fish. Three years later, when he still had not received the painting, the patron went to Chu Ta's house to ask why the picture was not done. Chu Ta did not answer, but dipped a brush in ink and with a few strokes drew a splendid fish. "If it is so easy," asked the patron, "why didn't you give me picture three years ago?" Again Chu Ta did not answer. Instead, he opened the door of a large cabinet. Thousands of pictures of fish tumbled out.

Acknowledgments

Woody Allen. "The Colorization of Films Insults Artists and Society," *The New York Times,* 26 June 1987. Copyright © 1987 by The New York Times Company. Reprinted by permission.

Maya Angelou. "Graduation" from I KNOW WHY THE CAGED BIRD SINGS. Copyright © 1969 by Maya Angelou. Reprinted by permission of Random House, Inc.

Alexandra Armstrong. "Starting a Business," MS MAGAZINE, March 1988. Reprinted by permission of MS Magazine.

Russell Baker. "Coming to Grips with Death," from GROWING UP. Copyright © 1982 Russell Baker. Reprinted by permission of Don Congdon Associates, Inc.

Russell Baker. "The Flag." Copyright © 1975 by Russell Baker. Reprinted by permission of Don Congdon Associates, Inc.

Mary Field Belenky et al. "Reminiscences of College." From WOMEN'S WAYS OF KNOWING: THE DEVELOPMENT OF SELF, VOICE, AND MIND, by Mary Field Belenky, Blythe McVicker Clinchy, Nancy Rule Goldberger, and Jill Mattuck Tarule. Copyright © 1986 by Basic Books, Inc. Reprinted by permission of Basic Books, Inc., Publishers.

Pat Bellanca. "Jimmy Buffett is Going Coconuts." THE WELLESLEY NEWS, March 13, 1981. Copyright © 1981 Pat Bellanca. Reprinted by permission of the author.

Saul Bellow. From THE VICTIM. Copyright 1947 by Saul Bellow; renewed © 1974. Reprinted by permission of Vanguard Press, Inc., a division of Random House, Inc.

Robert Benchley. "How to Get Things Done" from THE BENCHLEY ROUNDUP. Copyright 1954 by Nathaniel Benchley. Reprinted by permission of Harper & Row, Publishers, Inc.

Barbara R. Bergmann. "Pay Equity: How to Argue Back." MS MAGAZINE, November 1985. Copyright © 1985 Barbara R. Bergmann. Reprinted by permission of the author.

Robert Bly. "Love Poem" from SILENCE IN THE SNOWY FIELDS. Copyright © 1962 by Robert Bly. Reprinted by permission of the author.

David Boaz. "Let's Quit the Drug War," from THE NEW YORK TIMES, March 17, 1988. Copyright © 1988 by The New York Times Company. Reprinted by permission.

Sissela Bok. "To Lie or Not to Lie?—The Doctor's Dilemma," THE NEW YORK TIMES, 18 April, 1978. Copyright © 1978 by The New York Times Company. Reprinted by permission.

Jorge Luis Borges. "The Gaucho and the City: Stories of Horsemen." THE NEW REPUBLIC, May 19, 1982. Published by arrangement with the Estate of Jorge Luis Borges.

David Bruck. "The Death Penalty." From THE NEW REPUBLIC, May 20, 1985. Reprinted by permission of The New Republic.

Anthony Burgess. Excerpt from LANGUAGE MADE PLAIN. Copyright © 1964 by Anthony Burgess. Reprinted by permission.

Leonard Cammer, M.D. "How to Deal with the Crying," from UP FROM DEPRESSION. Copyright © 1969 by Leonard Cammer, M.D. Reprinted by permission of Simon & Schuster, Inc.

Leonard S. Charlap. "Letter to the Editor," THE NEW YORK TIMES, 19 December 1977. Copyright © 1977 by The New York Times Company. Reprinted by permission.

Ruth H. Cohn. "Letter to the Editor," THE NEW YORK TIMES, 20 July 1978. Copyright © 1978 by The New York Times Company. Reprinted by permission.

Malvine Cole. "Beavers and Cattle." THE NEW YORK TIMES, April 16, 1988. Copyright © 1988 by Malvine Cole. Reprinted by permission of the author.

Laura Cunningham. "The Girl's Room." From THE NEW YORK TIMES, September 10, 1981. Copyright © 1981 Laura Cunningham. Reprinted by permission of William Morris Agency, Inc. on behalf of the author.

Sharon R. Curtin. From NOBODY EVER DIED OF OLD AGE. Copyright © 1972 by Sharon R. Curtin. Reprinted by permission of Little, Brown and Company.

Joan Didion. "Los Angeles Notebook" from SLOUCHING TOWARDS BETHLEHEM. Copyright © 1966, 1967, 1968 by Joan Didion. Reprinted by permission of Farrar, Straus and Giroux, Inc.

Joan Didion. "On Keeping a Notebook" from SLOUCHING TOWARDS BETHLEHEM. Copyright © 1966, 1967, 1968 by Joan Didion. Reprinted by permission of Farrar, Straus and Giroux, Inc.

Paul Diederich. From MEASURING GROWTH IN ENGLISH.

Copyright © 1974 by the National Council of Teachers of English. Reprinted by permission.

From "Dodgers Keep Perfect Record in Knocking Out Southpaws," MICHIGAN DAILY, September 29, 1955. Reprinted by permission of The Associated Press.

Jim Doherty, "How Cemeteries Bring Us Back to Earth," THE NEW YORK TIMES, 31 May 1982. Copyright © 1982 by The New York Times Company. Reprinted by permission.

Mamie Duff, "Dedication Doth Not a Good Teacher Make." Reprinted by permission of Mamie Duff, Staff, Lockwood Press.

Nora Ephron. "A Few Words About Breasts: Shaping Up Absurd" from CRAZY SALAD: SOME THINGS ABOUT WOMEN. Copyright © 1972 by Nora Ephron. Reprinted by permission of Alfred A. Knopf, Inc.

Bergen Evans, "Sophistication," THE NEW YORK TIMES BOOK REVIEW, 7 September 1971. Copyright © 1971 by The New York Times Company. Reprinted by permission.

Edward Morgan Forster. "My Wood" from ABINGER HARVEST. Copyright © 1936 and renewed 1964. Reprinted by permission of Harcourt Brace Jovanovich, Inc. and Edward Arnold.

Patricia Freeman. "The Einstein of Happiness," CALIFORNIA LIVING, 23 October 1983. Reprinted by permission.

Eileen Garred. "Ethnobotanists Race Against Time to Save Useful Plants." HARVARD UNIVERSITY GAZETTE, May 24, 1985. Reprinted by permission of the Harvard University Gazette.

Paul Goldberger. "The Statue of Liberty: Transcending the Trivial." THE NEW YORK TIMES, July 17, 1986. Copyright © 1986 by The New York Times Company. Reprinted by permission.

Margaret Gooch. Library exercises (following research paper in Chapter 10) reprinted by permission of Margaret Gooch, Wessell Library, Tufts University.

Paul Goodman. "A Proposal to Abolish Grading" (editors' title). Reprinted from COMPULSORY MIS-EDUCAITON by Paul Goodman, copyright 1964, by permission of the publisher, Horizon Press, New York.

Stephen Jay Gould. "Women's Brains" from THE PANDA'S THUMB: MORE REFLECTIONS IN NATURAL HISTORY. Copyright © 1980 by Stephen Jay Gould. Reprinted by permission of W. W. Norton & Company.

Jeff Greenfield. "Columbo Knows the Butler Didn't Do It," THE NEW YORK TIMES, 22 April 1973. Copyright © 1973 by The New York Times Company. Reprinted by permission.

Dorothy Grunebaum. "Woman Who Hissed." THE NEW YORK

Walter Hooper. Copyright © 1970 by C. S. Lewis Pte Ltd. Reprinted by permission of Curtis Brown, London and William Collins Sons & Co. Ltd.

Peter H. Lewis. "But Can You Say It in 1's & 0's?" THE NEW YORK TIMES, March 1, 1988. Copyright © 1988 by The New York Times. Reprinted by permission.

Alan P. Lightman. "Elapsed Expectations," THE NEW YORK TIMES MAGAZINE, 25 March 1984. Copyright © 1984 by The New York Times Company. Reprinted by permission.

Walter Lippmann. excerpt from column in THE NEW YORK TIMES, 20 February 1942. Copyright © 1942 by The New York Times Company. Reprinted by permission.

K. N. Llewellyn. From "The Bramble Bush: On Law and Its Study." Copyright © 1981 Oceana Publications, Inc. Reprinted by permission.

From "Lord, They've Done It All," TIME, May 6, 1974. Copyright © 1974 Time Inc. All rights reserved. Reprinted by permission from Time.

Lyrics from "Lift Ev'ry Voice and Sing" (James Weldon Johnson, J. Rosamond Jonson) Used by permission of EDWARD B. MARKS MUSIC COMPANY.

Anne Hebald Mandelbaum. "It's the Portly Penguin That Gets the Girl, French Biologist Claims." HARVARD UNIVERSITY GAZETTE, Jan. 30, 1976. Reprinted by permission of the Harvard University Gazette.

Jack S. Margolis. "And All Those Others" from THE POETRY OF RICHARD MILHOUS NIXON. Copyright © 1974 by Jack S. Margolis. Reprinted by permission of the author.

Sister Lydia Martin-Boyle, H.O.O.M., "Adman's Atlanta." Reprinted by permission of the author.

Gerald Mast. From THE COMIC MIND. Copyright © 1973 by Gerald Mast. Reprinted by permission of the Estate of Gerald Mast.

Yona Zeldis McDonough. "Sisters Under the Skin." THE NEW YORK TIMES, April 2, 1988, Op-ed. Copyright © 1988 by The New York Times Company. Reprinted by permission.

John McPhee. From ORANGES. Copyright © 1966, 1967 by John McPhee. Reprinted by permission of Farrar, Straus and Giroux, Inc.

Margaret Mead and Rhoda Metraux. "On Friendship—August 1966." From A WAY OF SEEING. Copyright © 1961, 62, 63, 64, 65, 66, 67, 68, 69, 1970 by Margaret Mead and Rhoda Metraux. Reprinted by permission of William Morrow and Co., Inc.

Jonathan Miller. From THE BODY IN QUESTION. Copyright © 1978 by Jonathan Miller. Reprinted by permission of Random House, Inc. and International Creative Management.

Jovanovich, Inc. and renewed © 1970 by Marjorie T. Parsons. Reprinted by permission of Harcourt Brace Jovanovich, Inc., the Executors of the Virginia Woolf Estate and The Hogarth Press.

William Butler Yeats, "The friends that have it I do wrong." New York: Macmillan, 1908.

From "The Balloon of the Mind" from THE POEMS OF W. B. YEATS: A NEW EDITION edited by Richard J. Finneran. Copyright 1919 by Macmillan Publishing Company, renewed 1947 by Bertha Georgie Yeats. Reprinted by permission of Macmillan Publishing Company and A. P. Watt Ltd.

Art

Page 17. Printed with the permission of The Poetry/Rare Books Collection, University Libraries, SUNY at Buffalo.

Page 52. Graphische Sammlung Albertina, Wien.

Page 62. Courtesy, Museum of Fine Arts, Boston.

Page 63. Courtesy, Museum of Fine Arts, Boston.

Page 79. Courtesy, Notman Photographic Archives, McCord Museum, McGill University.

Page 80. © ARS NY/SPADEM, 1989.

Page 81. © ARS NY/SPADEM, 1989.

Page 82. Courtesy, Museum of Fine Arts, Boston.

Page 83. Courtesy, Museo del Prado, Madrid.

Page 84. (top) Copyright Robert Frank, from *The Americans*, 1958; (bottom) Courtesy, John T. Hill, Executor, Estate of Walker Evans.

Page 99. (top) Fridmar Damm/Leo de Wys, Inc.; (bottom) Richard Laird/Leo de Wys, Inc.

Page 114. Alinari/Art Resource, N.Y.

Page 117. From MAZES II by Vladimir Koziakin. Copyright 1972 by Vladimir Koziakin. Reprinted by permission of the Berkley Publishing Group.

Page 295. Reprinted by permission of the Atlanta Chamber of Commerce.